LONDON
BOMBED, BLITZED AND BLOWN UP
The British Capital Under Attack Since 1867

Ian Jones MBE

Frontline Books

LONDON: BOMBED, BLITZED AND BLOWN UP
The British Capital Under Attack Since 1867

This edition published in 2016 by Frontline Books,
an imprint of Pen & Sword Books Ltd,
47 Church Street, Barnsley, S. Yorkshire, S70 2AS

ISBN: 978-1-47387-899-0

CIP data records for this title are available from the British Library

For more information on our books, please visit
www.frontline-books.com
email info@frontline-books.com
or write to us at the above address.

Printed and bound by CPI Group (UK) Ltd, Croydon, CR0 4YY
Typeset in 10.5/12.5 point Palatino

Contents

Acknowledgments

The idea for this book began when I saw a photograph of the crater caused by a First World War Zeppelin bomb outside the Strand Theatre in Catherine Street just off the Aldwych. I was already aware that a V1 flying bomb had exploded in the Aldwych in the Second World War and, as an Explosives Officer working for the Counter Terrorism Command of the Metropolitan Police, I had dealt with the aftermath of an explosion which killed an IRA bomber in almost exactly the same place. It occurred to me then that it would be interesting to look at the history of the bombing of the capital. For me the research has been fascinating. I have visited hundreds of places where bombs have exploded or been rendered safe and met many people who have provided a wide variety of assistance, ranging from providing documents to personal accounts of bombings. Without their assistance none of the following would be possible.

In no particular order I need to thank the following: At the Tower of London, Dr Jeffery Parnell, Bridget Clifford and Vic Duggan; from Westminster Abbey, the Librarian, Dr Tony Trowels; the Police Forensic Branch for kindly agreeing to let me read early copies of HM Inspector of Explosives Reports; Steve Venus for his knowledge and expertise on German Second World War bomb fuzes, and Chris Ranstead for his help with Second World War Royal Engineer bomb disposal casualties.

Peter and Tim Gurney were immensely helpful providing much information and many useful leads particularly for the early terrorist campaigns. Roger from the City of London Police Museum and Maggie Bird from the Metropolitan Police Museum. Lucy Price from the London Fire Brigade Museum; Reg Journet for all his help and his wife for the tea and biscuits. I spoke to many Police Officers whom I hope will forgive me for not including their ranks or medals. Tony Ashforth, Andrew Ashwood, Pete Bordini, John Bunn, Cliff Cadman, Paul Challis, Mike Chipperfield, Tony Davis, Dennis Gold, Harry Greig, Trevor

ACKNOWLEDGMENTS

Heap, Leslie Horslen, Alan Jackson, Neil Kemp, Liz Kenworthy, Steve Mockett, George Mould, Andy Payne, Steve Roberts, Ralph Shortland, Tony Silvestro, John Sullivan, Fred Titchener and Vic Wilkinson. In particular I would like to thank John Bunn for reading the draft manuscript and making many suggestions to improve it.

The following Explosives Officers also kindly helped: Mick Coldrick, Colin Goodson, Peter Gurney, Graham Lightfoot, Derek Pickford, Paul Myring, Nick Nice, Terry Thompson, Dick Travers, Dave Williams, Ron Wilson and Phil Yeaman. Ron, who has sadly since passed away, kept an outstanding record of events in the first twenty years of the office. I am indebted to Steve Howorth who spoke at length about the death of his father Ken and who provided his note books and pictures for reference. I was fortunate enough to be allowed to visit the Crime Museum in Scotland Yard which still holds exhibits from the first IRA attacks in London. I must also thank Sandy Sanderson from the Explosives Ordnance Disposal Technical Information Centre (EODTIC) for all his help, but in particular for lending me a personal treasure which was a copy of the Manual of Bomb Disposal (Provisional) 1941 which provided a detailed insight into bomb disposal operations early in the War. Martin Hinchcliffe from the National Army Museum. Firefighters Sean Clarke, Ian Munro and Tyrone Robinson, and Andy Brown who spoke about their experiences at Aldgate. All the staff at the National Archives and at the Main MoD Library. I have relied heavily on Norman Longmate's outstanding books *The Doodlebugs* and *Hitler's Rockets* for information on both the V1 and V2 missile attacks on London. I must thank Mr Ford from the Royal Hospital Chelsea and the staff at the Royal Engineers Library and Royal Engineers Museum and last but not least the staff at the New Scotland Yard Library, which has now moved to Hendon and been combined with the Peel Library. Finally, I am indebted to my wife Catherine, not only for her patience and encouragement, but also for her editing skills without which the book would never have been completed.

The views expressed in the book are entirely my own, as are any mistakes that may have been made.

Ian Jones, 2016

Chapter 1

With Flame and Incandescent Terror

'It is bombs not bombers that count.'
Lord Tiverton.

When it comes to being bombed London is unique. Although it cannot claim to be the most bombed capital city in terms of the weight of explosive detonated – that dubious honour belongs to Berlin or Tokyo – it has endured the most varied and unrelenting attack since the discovery of explosives, particularly high explosives. Whilst many other capital cities have been bombed, none have suffered to the same extent from the twin ravages of aerial bombardment in war and terrorism in peace. For example, Berlin escaped air attack in the First World War and, whilst Paris was bombed, it was the people of London that were to be subject to the first strategic bombing campaign in an attempt to crush their morale. In the Second World War, in comparison to London, Paris was hardly touched. Which other capital city came under sustained missile attack on the scale that London did? Madrid has had to contend with both the Basque terrorists and the aerial bombing by the Condor legion in Spain's Civil War, but again not to the extent that London had to suffer from the Luftwaffe and terrorism. When I started researching this book the one method of attack that I could not attribute to London was suicide bombers. Sadly, that changed with the awful atrocity on 7 July 2005, when Islamic extremists detonated three bombs on trains in tunnels on the London Underground system and an hour later another on a No.30 bus in Tavistock Square.

Founded on the great River Thames with its majestic curve, which in later years gave it away to the night bombers, London has always been

1

a leading commercial and economic centre, steeped in history and tradition. As the cradle of democracy, and with an array of unique attractions it is, and always has been, the preferred destination for thousands of tourists each year. Inevitably, as such a focal point, it has over the years attracted the wrath of both foreign governments and others disaffected with their lot. Bombs have often been their chosen instruments of persuasion with the inevitable consequences of death and destruction.

Not surprisingly, it is the people of London who have borne the brunt of their violent assaults. The capital was, and still is, a large and tempting target. This has two implications; firstly, it is not easy to miss, but secondly its size means that it is difficult to completely destroy. For example, originally it was only London that was a suitable target for the V1 flying bombs, the world's first cruise missile, and the V2, the first ballistic missile. These were, by today's standards, hugely inaccurate; a flying bomb aimed at the Tower of London might hit any part of the capital.

During my research I was astonished by the extent of the destruction in places that we all hurry passed and where now there is little or no obvious trace of what went before. From the first Irish Republican bomb in Clerkenwell in 1867, to date, London and its population have been under almost constant attack. Terrorism features in almost every decade from the 1860s to the present and has caused much damage, particularly during the late 1980s and early 1990s. However, by far the greatest destruction was from the air. The Zeppelin and Gotha bomber raids in the First World War being but a foretaste of what would happen in the Second. Then the capital was devastated, firstly by the Luftwaffe who rained down bombs in 1940-41 and maintained a sporadic hit-and-run campaign thereafter. Later, in the closing stages of the conflict when victory was assured, there were the frightful random strikes of the vengeance weapons. In the Second World War London truly was a battleground with its citizens on the front line as much as any serviceman or woman. Unlike the Somme or Normandy, where the immaculate cemeteries with their dead laid out in regimental rows vividly spell out the price to be paid for freedom, there is no specific memorial in the capital which records the high price paid in blood by its citizens.

After the Second World War there was a short period of calm. In some areas important buildings and most of the churches damaged by the bombing were painstakingly restored. In others, where the destruction was complete, new and often cheap and functional replacements appeared. The bombers, however, returned. This time they came not by air, but in buses, cars, vans and trains. They planted their bombs secretly amongst the innocent population and slithered away into the shadows. Sometimes warnings were given, but often not, with the inevitable consequences for those whose fate dictated that they were in the wrong place at the wrong time.

Much has been written about the conventional bombing of London. There are books on the Zeppelins, the Blitz and the VI and V2 missiles. In comparison very little has been written on the terrorist and criminal activities. In this book I have tried to encompass both, but in doing so have had to take a fairly narrow perspective. I am profoundly aware of all that I have left out, particularly during the Blitz. I can only plead that to cover such a span of years some things had to be excluded.

There are three linked strands that run through the text. Firstly, it is my basic premise that 'it is bombs and not bombers that count'. This fact was recognised as early as the First World War when Lord Tiverton, an officer of the Royal Naval Volunteer Reserve, undertook work to study the selection of targets, their vulnerability to attack and the types of bomb required to destroy them. He was the first of the planners of air warfare to base his work on the assumption that the bomb, and not the bomber, was the vital element in air bombardment. He was conscious that very little was known about the different types of bomb and their effects. He posed such questions as, are several small bombs more effective than one big one, did they increase the chance of a hit, and would the use of incendiaries to cause fires be a more effective form of attack? Actually for aerial bombing it transpires that a mix of large high explosive bombs and tens of thousands of incendiaries are needed to overwhelm civil defences and wipe out cities. It was a mix of large bombs and incendiaries during the Blitz that ripped the heart out of the City of London and destroyed some of the most historic parts of the capital.

From this book's perspective, Lord Tiverton's assertion also holds true in the case of criminal and terrorist bombs. In London the bomb has been the primary weapon of the various terrorist groups that have been active in the capital. Those behind the outrages are, unquestionably, directly responsible for the crimes they commit, even though in some of the worst atrocities they may try to deflect the blame. The accountability for the death and destruction caused by tossing a device into a crowded restaurant, or leaving a massive vehicle bomb in the City, is undeniably that of the perpetrators. It could be argued therefore that they, and the organisations behind them, are the ones that count and obviously there is some truth in this. This book's focus though is on bombs and their effects, not the background political, historical or criminal reasons for their use. So in this case Lord Tiverton assertion that 'it is bombs not bombers that count' is still relevant.

Other than the scale of the assaults, I have been surprised by the similarities in terms of objectives, effectiveness and the responses elicited between aerial, terrorist and criminal bombing. Bombing campaigns are the tactical weapon in the terrorist's arsenal for those seeking to bring political change by forcing incumbent governments to the negotiating table. On 7 July 2005, the Islamic extremist bombers used less explosive than was contained in any one of the 50,000 high explosive German bombs dropped during the Blitz, but the political, social and psychological impact was out of all proportion to the size of the devices. Whereas the latter were just a minor factor in the middle of a world war, the full implications of the suicide bombings are still being felt.

Terrorist methods can be split into two groups, sabotage and terror. Those which employ mainly sabotage are intended to disrupt everyday life or economic functions, for example attacks against power stations or the transport system. In these the public are not a specific target, but casualties amongst them are often inevitable and are, for the terrorist, morally acceptable. Terror attacks can be symbolic, striking at groups of people or individuals or against, what they see as, monuments of oppression. As Lenin said 'the purpose of terror is to terrorise' and indiscriminate bombing can do just that. The function of these types of attack is to intimidate the general population and so directly influence those in power. The hope is that an atmosphere of intense terror will be generated which so intimidates the people that the authorities seek negotiations to prevent further attacks. It has been said that this, in established societies, never works, and seems only to generate an entrenching of positions and a clamour for revenge. In his book about the history of the IRA, Dr J. Bower Bell, in relation to the 1930s bombing campaign, said:

> To shatter the normal ties of British life, to transform millions of men in to frightened ciphers, to overawe an entire people was a fantastic undertaking.[1]

Some today would draw different conclusions from the Madrid commuter railway bombings in 2004. It could be argued that in that instance pure terror worked and did influence policy, and was the catalyst for the withdrawal of Spanish troops from Iraq. But it should be understood that that was concerned with external foreign policy and not threats to internal affairs. An extensive bombing campaign did not work for the Basque terrorists. Although it will probably never be officially admitted, there is no doubt that the large vehicle bombs deployed by Provisional Irish Republican Army (PIRA) in London in the 1990s did have a major economic impact which in turn spurred on the requirement to find a political solution to troubles in Northern Ireland.

In principle, at the instant of detonation, there is no difference between a terrorist or criminal device, an aerial dropped bomb or a missile warhead. When they explode they all produce fundamentally the same physical effects. The explosive, whatever it is, undergoes a rapid physical change in which a shock wave disrupts potentially unstable molecules which recombine to form gas and in doing so generate intense heat. The rate of this reaction varies, but for most high explosives, it is in the region of 3,000 to 8,000 metres per second. TNT, for example, detonates at 6,700 metres per second. This rapid reaction generates a supersonic shock wave which radiates out from the point of the explosion decaying exponentially in intensity as the distance increases. It is this shock wave that shatters everything. There is also an intense fireball and this is followed by the blast and fragments from the bomb container. The explosion will generate secondary explosive effects, including fragmentation produced from nearby objects, particularly glass, and from structures near the point of detonation. When the destructive effects of the bomb itself cease there are the hazards left at the scene including the risk of fire or further explosions from escaping gas, fatal shocks from shredded electricity cables, flooding and the danger of collapse of unsafe buildings. It is into this cauldron of chemical and physical mayhem that it is necessary to insert the human being and assess their responses to it. For those intimately involved in an incident, the effect of blast and fragments can have the most devastating impact. Those, who are not killed, suffer the most grievous wounds and are subjected to a wide variety of intense emotional stress. Rescuers are confronted with horrific scenes which they can never forget.

This is probably the appropriate place to advise the reader that the following chapters cannot adequately describe the toll in terms of human suffering, nor the physical damage caused by the bombs that have detonated across London. It is certainly true to say that over the whole period no two bombs have gone off in exactly the same place, no two incidents could be described as identical and it is also true that no single incident looked the same to any two persons who observed it.

In a bombing, when the numbers of dead and injured are small, it is much easier for people, not involved with an incident, to comprehend the tragedy. They can relate to comparatively small numbers of victims, up to a maximum of perhaps twenty to thirty. They do this, maybe subconsciously, by imagining and putting faces to the same numbers of people in terms of close family and friends or a class from school, or the members of a local sporting team. However, there comes a point when, as casualty numbers mount, the individual victim is lost in the overall disaster. Although not a bomb, a good example of this phenomenon would be the suicide attacks on the Twin Towers in New York. It was difficult to comprehend, as the aircraft crashed into the towers, that you were witnessing hundreds of people dying. Later, when the buildings collapsed, another two thousand people lost their lives. The individual was subsumed in the scale of the disaster but, pre-collapse, the ghastly image of individuals jumping to certain death to escape the flames had a much more psychological impact.

There is, and always has been, something abhorrent about the use of bombs. In his book *The Dynamiter*, Robert Louis Stephenson wrote:

> He who was prepared to help the escaping murderer or to embrace the impertinent thief, found, to the overthrow of all his logic that he objected to the use of dynamite.[2]

The bombs, the tools of the bombers and implements of destruction have, in London, quite rightly never succeeded in achieving their aim. But they have caused changes in everyday life ranging from the evacuation of children in the Second World War (an act prompted by the bombing in the First) to the disappearance of military uniforms and pennants on military staff cars in the 1970s. Prior to the last PIRA campaign most of the military staff working at the Ministry of Defence went to work in uniform and service personnel walking around so dressed was a common sight. Today they can once again be seen in uniform as the 2012 Olympics so clearly illustrated. That said the awful killing of Fusilier Lee Rigby in 2013 has led to review of the policy. The bombs are also responsible for the development and deployment of closed circuit television (CCTV), the temporary disappearance of litter bins on main line stations and, more recently, the appearance of ugly concrete blocks and less obvious steel posts to prevent suicide bombers driving explosive-laden vehicles into some of our most vulnerable buildings.

For completeness I have also covered the worst of the accidental explosions in the capital. These have produced exactly the same physical effects as the bombs and the most significant are worthy of description. Many of these involve domestic gas which has been a regular and persistent killer. The biggest explosions though, and most destructive, have involved gunpowder and bulk TNT and these are described in detail.

The second thread that runs through the book is that of bomb disposal. Bombs that explode present the authorities with a comparatively straightforward problem which, essentially, boils down to rescue, recovery and repair. In addition, in terrorist bombings, there is the vital task of retrieving forensic evidence. This does not mean that dealing with the aftermath of an explosion is not a dangerous, disturbing, difficult or complex operation – it is. Bombs that fail to explode present different challenges.

Like many bombs that followed, the first attempt to blow up Parliament was a failure and the main perpetrator, Guy Fawkes, was captured before he could light the fuse leading to the hidden barrels of gunpowder. As the fuse was not lit the disposal of the bomb was a simple matter of removing the gunpowder from the cellars. From the terrorist bombing in the 1870s, through both World Wars and the subsequent terrorist campaigns, bombs were fitted with a variety of different fuzes. For clarity it should be pointed out that a burning fuse with a flame at its core is spelt with an 's' whereas a mechanical or electrical fuze for a bomb is spelt with a 'z'.

These man-made initiators have all proved unreliable to a greater or lesser extent and the bombs they were fitted to have frequently failed to explode and at some point have to be rendered safe. Other bombs have been deliberately left with long delay timers and booby-traps to deter or complicate the Bomb Disposal Officer's work. Bombs that do not explode lose none of their potential to cause death and destruction, and they have to be rendered safe, removed or destroyed in situ. Whenever they are found, their condition has to be assessed and if they still pose a serious danger they need to be appropriately dealt with. This may necessitate the cordoning of large areas and the evacuation of people from their work or homes with the resultant disruption to daily life. In time of war this results in the loss of vital production or suspension of essential transport services. Populations will put up with casualties from bombs during air raids or from terrorist devices when no warnings are given, but they will not readily tolerate needless casualties after the event.

This book is not intended to be a full and detailed technical account of the techniques used in rendering bombs safe. For those that wish for that sort of technical detail there are excellent books – *Unexploded Bomb* by Major A.B. Hartley MBE, RE, for example – which provide the full story of bomb disposal in the Second World War and which describe the constant technical battle between the bomb fuze designers and those trying to make them safe.

Equally, it would be irresponsible to explain in detail how terrorist devices are rendered safe today. The significant developments and major turning points, however, will be described where they are relevant to London.

No single organisation has been responsible for bomb disposal in London. Initially, it was HM Inspector of Explosives. In the First World War, artillery, ordnance and engineer officers undertook the role (although this usually amounted to little more than recovering bombs from scenes or police stations); between the wars some police officers rendered bombs safe; in the Second World War, after much argument, the task fell squarely on the shoulders of the Royal Engineers and to a lesser extent the RAF and Royal Navy. In addition, there were air-dropped parachute mines which were responsibility of the Royal Navy. Many of the men employed on bomb disposal operations in London during the war died doing their duty. In the post-war era the Metropolitan Police have employed Explosive Officers to carry out the role assisted when necessary by the military. The book will explore how these various organisations came about and look at some of the outstanding work that they have undertaken.

In life, the greatest acclaim is allotted to moments of high drama. It is the moments of outstanding success or the worst tragedies that people remember. In all the bombing campaigns against London, both conventional and terrorist, behind each success or tragedy there were countless hours of training, preparation and waiting to deal with that single moment. Be they fighter pilots or anti-aircraft gunners, emergency service or Civil Defence volunteers, specialist surveillance teams or local 'Bobbies on their beat', without their courage, patience and fortitude London would not have survived to be the place it is today. It is the last group of people that I want to concentrate on next.

The final thread, which is constant throughout the bombing, is the work of the all the police forces in London. This is not to say that other organisations, for example the Fire Service, the Ambulance Service, civil defenders and other volunteers have not performed a vital role in some or all the bombing campaigns. They did, and some of their valiant work will be described. But police officers have played a crucial and active part in every aspect of the defence of London from bombing. It was police officers that removed a bomb from the Palace of Westminster in the first Irish Republican Campaign. They responded to the attacks in the First World War, guiding civilians to safety, stopping bolting horses and even seizing unexploded bombs intent on keeping them as evidence to prosecute the Kaiser after the war. During the Second World War, police officers, including the auxiliaries and war reserve constables, were a vital element in all manner of activities concerned with Civil Defence and the preservation of the capital. Winston Churchill said of them when talking about their contribution to civil defence:

> If I mention only one of them to-night – namely the police – it is because many tributes have already been paid to the others. But the police have been in it everywhere, all the time. And as a working-woman wrote to me in a letter, 'What gentlemen they are'.[3]

The police then lived amongst the communities they served much more than they do today and, consequently, they suffered the same as their neighbours. In fact, most of them saw much worse because they responded to and assisted with all the incidents in their division. Since then they have been centre stage in the post-war terrorist and criminal bombings. During this time there have been hundreds of bombs and countless thousands of false alarms. Every one of them is investigated by a police officer who responds to a bomb threat, a call from a worried member of the public or an explosion. At the scene they make a difficult but crucial initial assessment of what action is required. It is, in my opinion, one of the most difficult and dangerous jobs they undertake.

That said, it is generally accepted that those who are engaged in some form of useful activity in the face of danger tend to be less fearful or aware of the consequences of it. Police officers responding to bomb threats or explosions are often so preoccupied with their duty that there is no time to be afraid. Many have paid the ultimate price for their dedication to duty. This book focuses on the work of these officers. It is those who are first on scene and have to deal with the confused, chaotic and disorganised situations they find, often working against the clock, that have the hardest job. This may involve evacuating people from the area around a suspect bomb, or giving immediate lifesaving first aid to badly injured victims.

Once order has been established and casualties cleared, other vital work is undertaken. Recently, with major advances in forensic science, the scenes of even the most horrendous terrorist bombings can still yield vital evidence. After an explosion, skilled exhibits officers sift through the debris searching to recover tiny fragments which provide indications as to the nature of the device, or which furnish evidence or intelligence enabling investigators to link suspects to the scene or to other atrocities. It is an absorbing and fascinating subject, which is sometimes undertaken in the most difficult and distressing circumstances.

The public should not underestimate the dedication and skill of police officers at all levels who have toiled tirelessly over the years to prevent atrocities and catch the bombers. For example, those police officers who worked to recover the bodies and evidence from the scenes of the suicide bombings on 7 July had the most unenviable task. In particular, those who worked deep underground had to cope with a whole range of problems, including; working in confined spaces, wearing protective clothing, dealing with heat exhaustion (the temperatures soared after the emergency lighting had been put in place), vermin, asbestos dust and the filth from the explosion, not to mention the physical dangers from the sharp and jagged wreckage and, finally, the mental stress of coping with all of the above. The wretchedness of operating in such an environment can never be understood by those who have not witnessed it.

At the other end of the scale, the various Commanders of the Counter Terrorism Command and their Senior Investigating Officers have had to work long hours managing massive enquiries requiring the control and coordination of a wide range of resources all under constant and, at times, intense pressure, to catch the bombers. The result of this sustained effort has been the arrest and conviction of hundreds of criminals and terrorists and their subsequent imprisonment. Equally important, and often not publicly acknowledged, many atrocities have been prevented in covert pre-emptive operations.

In this account neither the criminal enquiries, into the bombings, nor the work of the present day specialist officers, are described, as clearly I have no expertise in either discipline. It would benefit future generations, if someone suitably qualified, undertook to record all this good work. I say this because when I was researching the 1939-40 IRA campaign there was a compete dearth of records or information about how the police dealt with the problem then.

No matter what the origin of the bombs, there is one recurring theme throughout the book. It is the capacity for fear before the event, the courage and resilience of those directly involved in it, the ability to recovery afterwards, and history's ability to heal the wounds. A good example of the latter is the bombing on 7 July. Not the most recent one, in which pictures of the shattered bus in Tavistock Square are engrained on the current generation of Londoners, but the second German daylight raid exactly eighty-eight years earlier in the First World War which caused more casualties than the recent attack, but which few will be aware of today.

It is of course impossible to ignore the people of London who have suffered and endured at times the most horrendous ordeals. That they survived is, first and foremost, down to their dogged determination and fortitude. In the worst of the bombing during the Second World War there was another vital factor, and that was censorship. What Londoners were allowed to know was very heavily censored. Pictures of damage were all subject to severe scrutiny and, almost without exception, photographs showing the bodies of the dead were banned. There was very restricted footage of incidents showing seriously maimed or injured people being rescued from their homes and places of work. What was publicised was plucky victims being rescued from totally devastated buildings and the smiling 'Cockneys' drinking tea and giving cheery V signs. If there had been coverage of incidents as we have today, for example, pictures of the scene outside the Admiral Duncan pub in Soho in April 1999 after it had been bombed, then we may have lost the battle for the morale of the people as the real extent of the carnage was unveiled.

Next it is necessary to limit the scope of the book in terms of the area to be covered. London is defined in many ways geographically and none of these meet my requirements. To help me I intend to revert to my first basic premise that it is bombs not bombers that count. No matter what the politicians publicly state in relation to bombing, it is death, destruction and misery that drive public opinion. When the bombs start to detonate the politicians inevitably become driven by events. It follows that the closer the bombs explode to the heart of the capital, with its government buildings and commercial and financial centres, pound for pound of explosive, the more influential they are. In his book *Most Secret War*, R.V. Jones clearly makes the point when referring to the Baby Blitz:

> But in one of these early attacks a few bombs fell fairly near Whitehall, which caused more interest at the top level than may have been the case, and once again I found myself summoned to the Cabinet Room.[4]

Another good example of this trend would be to compare two similar terrorist bomb attacks. Most people will remember the terrible assassination of Airey Neave when an under-car booby-trap bomb detonated as he drove his vehicle out of the underground House of Commons car park. How many readers, however, remember the murder of Sergeant James Chapman who was killed by a similar bomb outside a recruiting office in Wembley in May 1990? It is not contended in any way that in terms of human suffering the people in these central areas are more important than anywhere else, clearly they are not. Neither are the central areas any more important than the rows of terraced houses that surround them. It is a sad fact, though, that in terms of influence, the bombs in these central areas have more sway.

It is equally true that, for most people, it is more interesting examining the bombing and defence of London's celebrated buildings and well-known places at its core rather than the destruction of a family house in the outskirts. Although, as the occupants of the houses in Warrington Crescent, Maida Vale, and some other residential streets will discover, I have not totally ignored this aspect of the bombing. For that reason, I intend to concentrate on Central London, although reference will be made to any of the significant events that happened in Greater London. For simplicity, Greater London I now take to be everything inside the M25, and Central London to cover the City of Westminster and the City of London itself.

During my research I visited many establishments in London often to examine specimens of bombs or devices. During this I found one live bomb and four others still containing significant residues of explosive or incendiary mixtures. Some of these had been on public display for years. In truth none of them have presented a serious hazard and all have subsequently been rendered inert. I have no doubts that that somewhere in London there are still more live bombs waiting to be discovered.

There are still a few clues to London's brutal past. In some places fragment damage is clearly visible and in others, memorials or lonely plaques mark the spot where some tragic event or atrocity occurred. I will also highlight some of these. When you pass one of the sites, and there are plenty of them, stop and pause for a while to think of the events that went before. Close your eyes and imagine that horrendous moment twenty, sixty or even one hundred and thirty years ago when a bomb exploded. Picture the blinding, incandescent flash of flame which invokes an automatic primeval response as the victims try to duck out the way. Then being engulfed by an invisible, but devastatingly destructive, shock wave, which hits you before the sound of the explosion. At peak strength it smashes shatters and pulps all in its path. Then imagine the searing heat and the ear splitting thunderclap a split second after the detonation, and in the same instant, for many people, time for some obscure unprompted thought, for example, being thankful that one's loved ones are not with you, or worse still knowing that they are.

Then there is the tinkling of falling glass and the rumble of collapsing masonry. For those who survive the initial explosion, there used to be a short period of comparative calm as they regained their senses, these days that moment may no longer exist as hundreds of alarms are triggered and add their ear-piercing screams to an already shambolic situation. Next, the stunned and shocked survivors use their senses, or their remaining senses, to absorb and assess their predicament in some devastating new reality. Perhaps stumbling from the wreckage of a building, picking oneself up off the street, or worse lying pinned in some pitch-black isolated pocket under tons of rubble. And then the real horror as they discover the still and grotesque figures of the dead, often torn and mutilated – or even worse the lonely isolated fragments of others. Deeply shocked, other survivors make their way from the scene often unable to react to the moans and groans of other victims. Although shocked the images of the scene are burned into their memories often to return to haunt them time and time again. Soon the sound of sirens fills the air as the emergency services race to the scene. And then shouts and calls from the rescuers and strong hands which guide and soothing voices which reassure, and finally the realisation that the first and worst part of the ordeal is over.

Like my colleagues in the Explosives Office, the police and other members of the emergency services, I have witnessed such scenes, although in my case mercifully few, and when all is done that can be done, I always stop and say a prayer for the victims, good or bad.

I also ponder why it must happen. I have concluded there can be no real explanation for the death, destruction and the misery the bombs invariably bring. But Pilot Officer T.R. Hodgson, who was killed in action in the skies over Germany in 1941, came close when he wrote:

'And he is rising mad who searches here for meaning.'

NOTES:
1. Bower Bell, J., *The Secret Army - The History of the IRA 1916-1970*, Anthony Blond Ltd, London, 1970.
2. Stephenson, Robert Louise, *The Dynamiter*.
3. Winston Churchill broadcast, 9 February 1942.
4. Jones, R. V., *Most Secret War*, Hamish Hamilton, London, 1978.

Chapter 2

First Innocent Victims

'There is no such thing as an innocent bystander since almost everyone is a collaborator with the oppressors.'
The Science of Revolutionary Warfare, Johann Most.

Friday, 13 December 1867, lived up to its ill-omened reputation for the working class residents of the Victorian terraced houses in Corporation Lane, Clerkenwell. Unfortunately for them their homes were immediately opposite the wall of the exercise yard of the local House of Detention. At approximately 15.45 hours a white ball was thrown over the prison wall into an unusually empty exercise yard. The ball was meant to herald a jailbreak, but for reasons that will become apparent, the escape attempt was already doomed to failure. After throwing the ball into the yard, a member of the Irish Republican Brotherhood (IRB) lit a short length of fuse leading to a barrel containing a charge of at least 100 pounds of gunpowder. A claim published in an Irish Newspaper some seventy years later suggested that there was significantly more and actually 548 pounds of explosive were used. Whatever the actual size, the charge had been placed up against the prison wall and hidden under a tarpaulin. The fuse on being touched by a match, had spluttered into life and smoking and hissing the flame at its core snaked its way towards the gunpowder in the barrel. As the perpetrators took cover there was a blinding flash and an enormous explosion. No thought had been given to the effects of such a large quantity of gunpowder exploding in such a confined area. As the clouds of grey-white smoke drifted away and the dust cleared, a sixty-foot gash could be seen in the prison wall, but no escapees emerged from the hole as the exercise yard was deserted. Across the narrow road, the nearest of the row of terraced houses were completely shattered. Those immediately opposite the centre of the blast had their front walls blown in. Further away windows and doors were blown out of their frames and the tiles stripped from the roofs. Glass windows all around were smashed into thousands of vicious shards. As bewildered neighbours rushed to the appalling scene to help with the casualties, it became clear there would be many dead and badly injured people. Chief Inspector Williamson who attended the incident described it as so many dolls' houses all with their fronts blown out exposing the contents to view.

The prisoner that was supposed to escape in the chaotic aftermath of the explosion was Colonel Richard O'Sullivan Burke. He was an IRB arms dealer of some repute and had been arrested earlier in the year. He was one of a group of some 150 Irish Americans who had committed themselves to the Republican cause. Born in County Cork he had emigrated to America and fought in the Civil War with the 15th New York Engineers where he learnt how to use explosives. He had risen to the rank of colonel and at the end of the campaign returned to Ireland where he joined the Fenian Brotherhood taking on the task of procuring weapons and explosives. He had been arrested in conjunction with this and was imprisoned in the Middlesex House of Detention in Clerkenwell. Such a key figure in the movement could not be left to rot in prison so a plan for his escape was hatched.

A group of IRB supporters, working on Burke's instructions, had purchased a quantity of gunpowder from the reputable firm of Curtis and Harvey, and transferred it into an old barrel for disguise. The plan of escape was quite simple; during Burke's normal exercise period the barrel would be placed up against the prison yard wall and when the charge exploded a substantial hole would be created. To prevent injury to Burke a white ball was to be thrown over the wall as a warning that an explosion was imminent. He would then, under the pretext of having got a small stone in his shoe, move to a corner of the yard and take cover. The date for the escape was set for Thursday, 12 December in mid-afternoon. Initially all went to plan and the ball was thrown over into the prison yard but then, demonstrating the fickle nature of explosives, it all went wrong.

On that day there was a very lucky, but unidentified, man in Corporation Lane who witnessed the failed escape attempt. After the explosion he wrote to the Metropolitan Police Commissioner recounting his story.[1] He said that on the Thursday he saw two men near a covered barrel, but as he approached they ran off. He walked past the barrel, at the time believing that the men were ordinary workers, but on looking back he saw smoke coming from under the cover. Though he could not see it, the smoke was the coming from the burning fuse. He returned to the spot and as he did so the smoking stopped, for whatever reason, the

15

fuse had gone out before it reached the gunpowder. He thought the whole episode a little strange and stayed by the covered cask for a while waiting for the men to return. When they did not he left the scene and carried on with his business. In the light of subsequent events, he was deeply troubled that he had not reported the matter but said that at the time he had not considered the activity suspicious. He was concerned that if he had known more about the situation he could have prevented many poor people from dying in the explosion the following day. Sadly, the signature on the document is illegible and the man will remain anonymous.

He should not have felt guilty, however, because the authorities had already got wind of the plan. Information, from a reliable source, was received that the rescue of Richard Burke was being contemplated. The detail even included the time, the method and the signal with the white ball. The informant was not identified, but a letter was received with the information at the Home Office on the morning of 12 December. It was signed by Superintendent Daniel Ryan, part of G Division of the Dublin Metropolitan Police, and had been despatched the previous day.

Immediately the prison officers were issued with arms and all exercise in the yard was prohibited. Yet despite this new level of alert no routine patrols were established around the prison perimeter and no warning was given to the local people about the plot. The upshot was that when a re-run of the previous day's failed attack took place on Friday, 13 December no one noticed the barrel hidden under a tarpaulin. This time the fuse functioned correctly and, as already recounted, a large charge of Curtis and Harvey's best powder devastated the area at about 15.50 hours. Of course this was of no use to Burke who was secured well within the jail. The eventual toll of the casualties is unclear with sources quoting different numbers. It seems most likely that it was fifteen dead and a further 120 injured, some fifteen of whom suffered permanent disability. This information, cast in stone, comes from a large memorial, which can still be seen today. It was erected in memory of the victims in St James's Church nearby. This states that three persons were killed at the moment of the explosion; three others died in hospital within a few days and a further nine later succumbed to their wounds. The youngest to die was a seven-year-old girl, Minnie Julia Abbott, an innocent victim of the plot. (It will be seen that one of the recurring themes in the book is the killing of children.) One of the injured was the brother of the little girl, a lad called Arthur Abbot, who lost the sight in one of his eyes; the damage to the other was such that by 1890 he became totally blind. He was apparently a familiar sight in the Gray's Inn Road in Holburn, where his wife used to take him to beg every day.

He could still be seen at his pitch in 1938 just before he died. A fund set for the victims eventually raised over £10,000, a significant sum in those days, and set a precedent sadly oft-repeated over the next 130 years. The incident is also one of the very first to be photographed as the scene of a crime.

The effects of such an unprecedented outrage were immediate. It was initially thought that it heralded the start of a major bombing campaign and the Army and police were stood by to deal with any further outrages. Over the next few days thousands of citizens were sworn in as special constables whose duties were to protect the capital's infrastructure. The Commissioner of the Metropolitan Police, Richard Mayne, was severely criticised for ignoring the warning of the escape attempt and offered his resignation, but this was refused. The feeble reason given for ignoring the warning was apparently that it had specified that the prison would be 'blown up' and not 'down' or 'across'. The search for explosives therefore was restricted to areas underneath the prison.

The political impact was significant; the 'Irish question', which had hovered in the wings of British political thinking, was forced into centre stage. Fenian violence, as Gladstone noted, had persuaded the British public:

> To embrace in a manner foreign to their habits in other times the vast importance of the Irish controversy.[2]

The impact of the explosion and consequent publicity, was not lost on the Fenians either, and in subsequent IRA campaigns they would look back to the effects of this in some small way to justify their actions. The explosion also disturbed Karl Marx and Friedrich Engels who naturally, in principle, supported the Fenians and their struggle. They recognised that this outrageous attack, which had only killed and maimed working class people, merely served to alienate the others from the cause. Marx wrote to Engels after the explosion and said:

> The last exploit of the Fenians in Clerkenwell was a very stupid thing. The London masses, who have shown great sympathy for Ireland, will be made wild by it and driven into the arms of the government party. One cannot expect the London proletariat to allow themselves to be blown up in honour of Fenian emissaries.[3]

In the subsequent inquiry six people were arrested; three close to the scene and three others later. Only one doubtful guilty verdict was gained and this was that of Michael Barrett. Many people, including establishment figures, were concerned about this conviction and thought that it was unsafe, as Barrett had several eyewitnesses who swore that he was in Glasgow at the time of the escape attempt, but it did no good and he was condemned to death. After being sentenced he made an impassioned speech from the dock, he said:

> I have never willfully maliciously, or intentionally injured a human being, that I am aware of, no, not even in character, I love my country and if my life was ten times dearer that it is, and if I could by every means redress the wrongs of those that persecute my land by the sacrifice of my life, I would willingly and gladly do so – I will meet my death without a murmur.[4]

The notoriety of the case did not end there. Barrett had the dubious distinction of being the last man to be publicly executed in England. Worse still, his executioner was the odious William Calcraft. He was one of the longest serving hangmen and worked as such between 1829 and 1874, during which time he was reported to have been responsible for 400-450 deaths. Despite his indisputable experience, he had gained a reputation for botching the job. Gallows had by then been built with a hidden trap door designed to despatch their victims quickly, but Calcraft persisted in using a traditional short drop of just a couple of feet. This often condemned his victim to a cruel, slow and harrowing death by strangulation. On some occasions, if it took too long, even for the loathsome Calcraft, he would take to climbing on the back of the hanging body or pulling at their feet to speed the process. Worse still, he seemed to enjoy his job and his manner and appearance were far from solemn offering no comfort to the condemned.

It was Calcraft who despatched Barrett. On the morning of 26 May 1868, the convicted man was escorted from Newgate Prison to the gallows outside. A vast crowd had gathered to witness the event. Many had queued for hours for a last chance to see this grim but compelling public spectacle. Calcraft had developed a special executioner's belt. Made of leather it fitted round the victim's waist and had two restraining wrist straps. Using this, Barrett's hands were pinioned to his sides and he was led to the scaffold. A cap was drawn down over his eyes and the rope placed and adjusted round his neck. In front of the baying crowd Barrett went, as promised, silently to his death. The atrocity at Clerkenwell, was the first on the UK mainland, it was also the worst in terms of the number of people killed from a single Irish Nationalist bomb. (On the mainland the highest number of casualties in a single attack was in the Birmingham pub bombings in 1974 where in two separate incidents bombs detonated killing a total of twenty-one people).

In 1868 the IRB hatched another plan, this time to blow up the Horseferry Road and Curtain Road gas works. Informers again got wind of the plot and the buildings were searched. A barrel of gunpowder was found at the Curtain Road gas holder and safely removed. In light of this the Gas Light and Coke Company promptly instructed all of its Irish workers to sign an 'Address of Loyalty to the Queen', and all duly did so.

Gas is still and has always been the cause of hundreds of accidental explosions. As early as 1822, a mishap was recorded which resulted in the destruction of the Prince of Wales' Pagoda, when a wine servant set off to investigate a gas leak with a lighted candle, an oft-repeated mistake. For example, in 1824 a similar accident happened when an inexperienced person sent to investigate the smell of gas also approached the scene with a lighted candle - the resultant explosion confirmed the leak and left a large hole in Westminster Bridge Road.

Gas works themselves were vulnerable, and the largest accidental gas explosion recorded in London occurred on 31 October 1865, when Nine Elms Gas Works on Battersea Road blew up. An estimated million cubic feet of gas exploded and killed eleven workmen. The incident was reported in the *London Illustrated News*:

> Those who saw the explosion describe it as one vast upheaving of flame shooting high in the air, with a burst that shook everything around. People nearly a mile off were thrown violently down, and persons in houses in streets adjacent to the works received some severe burns from the heat of the flames. The flames indeed were so high that even though it was the middle of the day they guided firemen to the scene from long distances.[5]

Gas explosions are a regular occurrence, cause many deaths and injuries, and continue to this day, but it is only intended to cover one more of these in this book.

The Clerkenwell bomb was not the only cause of casualties from explosives. As the industrial revolution gathered pace so did the requirement for greater quantities of gunpowder. These were needed to satisfy the demands of the mining, quarrying and construction industries. Gunpowder, the standard explosive of the mid-eighteenth century, had always been a hazardous and unreliable substance. The danger comes from its sensitivity to flame and spark and it was frequently involved in inadvertent explosions. The unreliability came from the fact it is hygroscopic and, if not protected by a waterproof barrier, rapidly absorbs moisture and becomes impossible to initiate and therefore useless. Cromwell's comment 'Put your trust in God, my boys, and keep your powder dry' was a testament to its susceptibility to the damp.

In the mid-nineteenth century there was a total lack of control over who manufactured, stored and sold explosives. Not surprisingly this culminated in a number of disasters, the worst being a massive explosion at Messrs Ludlows in Birmingham in December 1870, in which fifty-three people were killed. Strangely October seems to be a fated month for such accidents; on 6 October 1854 there was a huge explosion in Erith and ten years later on 1 October, another at Gateshead. Other disasters in the same month included an explosion in Woolwich in 1866 and another in the same location in 1867, when some explosive cartridges caught fire; in 1868 there was the Great Barnsley firework explosion; followed a year later by the Notting Hill explosion and in the same month another detonation in Cornwall.

As a result, the first Explosives Act was eventually passed in 1875 to regulate the manufacture, storage and use of all such material. It was enforced by Her Majesty's Inspector of Explosives and came under the control of the Home Office. It was led by the flamboyant Colonel Sir Vivian Derring Majendie. He was an officer in the Royal Artillery who had specialised in explosives, and munitions design. He and his team were empowered to enter any establishment to check on their working practices and investigated every accident involving explosives.

Prior to the 1875 Act, London's growing population was blissfully unaware of the threat posed to them by the unscrupulous, improper and negligent manufacture and carriage of explosives. This changed dramatically on 2 October 1874, when a tragic accident occurred on the Regent's Canal when the 'fly boat' *Tilbury* blew up killing her crew and causing significant damage.

Although it resulted in the total destruction of Macclesfield Bridge in Regent's Park, and damage to houses close by, there was an element of good luck. It will be seen that it was fortuitous that the explosion occurred exactly where it did because, had it happened a little earlier or later in its journey along the canal, the consequences could have been catastrophic.

On 1 October 1874, *Tilbury* had been loaded with cargo at City Road Basin along with five other 'fly boats'. These were long, narrow, flat-bottomed barges some seventy feet long and seven feet abeam. At the stern was a small cabin which doubles as a wheel house and living quarters for the crew. In this cabin there was a small stove, and lamps for light. The remainder of the boat was further divided into four portions each of which could take cargo, although there were no fixed bulkheads as such. The total capacity of the hold was some twenty-three tons. Later examination of the manifest for *Tilbury* showed that amongst the cargo that day were five tons of gunpowder in barrels, one cask of petroleum and four barrels of Benzoline. This hazardous mixture and other assorted cargo had been loaded in the evening and the hold covered and sealed by tarpaulins.

At 02.00 hours on the morning of 2 October the 'fly boats', in the order *Jane, Dee, Tilbury, Limehouse* and *Hawkesbury*, set off, being towed by the steamboat *Ready*. All bar *Limehouse* had cargos of gunpowder. The boats were linked by ropes some ten to twenty yards in length. At about 05.00 hours, just as the boats were passing through the deep cut to the north of Regent's Park, there was a small explosion. Witnesses described this as a 'blue bursticle [*sic*]'. The nearest survivor of the subsequent explosion, William White, the helmsman of *Dee*, described this as 'a burst of flame which seemed to come from out of the hatches'.

According to White, he hailed *Tilbury* and reminded the crew that they had powder aboard. The helmsman on *Tilbury* retorted that he had been almost blown out of the boat. White then shouted to the helmsman of *Jane* the lead barge to tell the steamboat 'Ready' to stop. This order was complied with and the engines stopped, but moments later a voice from *Tilbury* was heard to say 'Go on'.

Seconds later there was a blinding flash and terrific explosion. *Tilbury* was torn asunder and her crew, Charles Beeson, William Taylor and Jonathon Holloway killed instantly. *Limehouse*, immediately behind, was holed and sank, and *Dee*, immediately in front, was seriously damaged. The Macclesfield Bridge, constructed of cast iron and brick arches took the full force of the blast and disintegrated. Significant damage was also done to the closest houses in Prince Albert Road. In one of them, William Edwards, who was dressed, but resting on his bed, was blown to the floor. He clambered out of a broken window and went to find his father. Whilst doing so he noticed that the bridge was missing and that the area was illuminated by the flickering glow of burning gas from a fractured gas main which used to run across the bridge. It was an eerie sight in the pre-dawn blackness.

Colonel Majendie was summoned by messenger on the morning of the explosion to investigate the incident. His first task was to examine the scene and assess the effects of the explosion. He immediately noted that at the time of the blast *Tilbury* was in the middle of a cutting some twenty-one feet deep. The explosion therefore took place in a location that was extremely favourable to the occupants of the nearby houses. To start with, the gunpowder was stored below the waterline in the barge and this would have offered some considerable lateral resistance to the blast. Secondly it was deflected upwards by the high banks of the cutting; finally, the bridge itself, which was totally destroyed, absorbed much of the energy from the explosion. As a consequence, the damage to the surrounding property was not as bad as would have been expected. On the ground there were scorching effects from the flash out to fifty yards, indicating the size of the fireball. Serious structural damage was limited to 200 yards, although the North Lodge, just thirty yards from the centre of the blast, was totally destroyed. Structural damage of a less serious nature went out to 400 yards and glass damage was recorded out to two and a half miles, the greatest distance at which the explosion was heard was at Orpington some seventeen miles away.

At Regent's Park Zoo, no building escaped undamaged. Indeed, to some extent the blast was channeled down the cutting towards the buildings which were set either side of the canal and they suffered accordingly. The Parrot House had several impacts from flying debris including parts of *Tilbury* and sections of the bridge. Fortunately, the injuries to the animals were trifling. The director of the zoo and some of his staff went to all the houses immediately after the explosion and by calling and speaking to the various animals managed to stop them jumping and running about. As daylight gradually appeared several more keepers arrived and helped calm the remaining animals that were still in a state of nervous excitement.

A considerable number of birds escaped their enclosures and for many days after the explosion the zoo received letters from persons reporting sightings of new and exotic birds, many of which were eventually recovered.

Colonel Majendie was tasked to discover the cause of the explosion. The key facts recorded were that:

1. The main explosion on the 'Tilbury' was preceded at a brief interval by a muffled explosion and a burst of vivid blue flame, without smoke, from the area of the barge's cabin and hold.
2. This burst of flame was sufficiently alarming to cause strong comments from both the helmsman of *Tilbury* and *Dee*, which in turn led to the tug being ordered to stop because *Tilbury* was believed to be on fire.
3. The concern caused by this initial flash was immediately allayed because afterwards there was nothing but stillness, during which the steamer went ahead again.

4. Almost immediately the streamer went ahead the five tons of
   gunpowder aboard *Tilbury* blew up.

The enquiry centred on the possible causes of the blue flash. It was soon
discovered by examination of other similar barrels of Benzoline and
petrol that they were rarely in perfect condition. They were subject to
rough handling which damaged the seals and therefore there was a
certain amount of leakage. Experiments demonstrated that a small
amount of benzoline left on a sponge in a closed bottle would evaporate
and produce an explosive atmosphere. When initiated with a flame this
caused a small explosion with a characteristic blue flame and no smoke.

It was concluded that this phenomenon was a significant factor in the
cause of the accident. After loading the cargo and sealing the hold with
tarpaulins, there was leakage and evaporation of the fuels, which slowly
built up an explosive atmosphere. Eventually, after several hours, this
fuel-air mixture reached the cabin bulkhead and seeped through. One
of the many ignition sources there then set off the vapour, which in a
classic fuel-air explosion, flashed through the hold of the vessel, but did
not appear to cause serious damage. The crew of *Tilbury* witnessed this
but after the initial flash detected no other effects. However, something
near to the gunpowder barrels must have caught fire which, moments
later, caused one to explode and this in turn instantly set off the others.

The report concluded that the haulage of gunpowder on the vessels
was carried out with a degree of carelessness and neglect of even the
most elementary precautions. Furthermore, it concluded, that if even
the most basic safety rules had been taken, the accident would never
have happened. Concern was expressed that London and other large
towns had been exposed for years to the risk of catastrophe. It noted
from manifests that between July and September 1874 the Grand Union
Canal Company had shipped over 274 tons of gunpowder and many
gallons of volatile spirits. It finally noted that the proposed 1875
Explosive Act would afford the public much more safety by more
closely regulating the movement of explosives.

The rebuilding of the bridge commenced not long after the explosion.
Following an inspection of the damage it was decided that some of the
massive cast iron pillars that supported the old cast iron superstructure
could be re-used. They are still there today, holding up new brick built
arches. A close inspection of the pillar on the tow path on the north-east
corner of the bridge reveals unusual proof of the incident. The outer
pillar, after inspection, was re-used but was rotated through one
hundred and eighty degrees before being bolted down. Evidence to
support this comes from the fact that the pillar clearly shows the effects

of wear caused by the tow ropes from the horses that trudged up and down the path. These ropes had, over time, worn smooth grooves in the metal at the base of the pillar. You would expect these to be on the side of the bridge closest to the canal and indeed on inspection there are some there caused by wear after the bridge was rebuilt. But if you look on the side of the pillar facing away from the canal you can see the grooves that were worn in the metal before the explosion.

NOTES:
1. The National Archives (TNA), MEPO 3/1788: Clerkenwell Explosion - Attempt to rescue Richard Burke from the Middlesex House of Detention.
2. Bishop, Patrick and Mallie Eamonn, *The Provisional IRA*, William Heinemann Ltd, London,1987.
3. Quoted on http/www/marxist.com.
4. Quoted on http//archives.tcm.ie/thekingdom/202/05/30/story4340.asp.
5. *Illustrated London News*, 4 November 1865.

Chapter 3

The Dynamite War and Infernal Machines

'The Metropolis of those days lived in a state of nerves, never knowing from one moment to the another what might happen in any public place in the way of an explosion.'
Edwin Woodhall, Special Branch, 1883.

As well as gunpowder the 1875 Explosives Act also took into account the new and more powerful high explosives that were being developed towards the end of the nineteenth century. In particular, it covered the guncotton and nitroglycerine based explosives which were being produced in ever-increasing quantities. It must be understood that after centuries of using gunpowder they represented a major step forward in the technological development of explosives. Unlike gunpowder, which essentially burnt rapidly, the new compounds detonated. When subjected to a sufficiently large shock, the unstable molecules would instantly break their bonds and recombine to form gas and heat. The process of decomposition released vast amounts of energy which in those days was considered instantaneous.

Nitroglycerine's origins went back to 1847 in Paris when an Italian chemist, Ascanio Sobrero, discovered a new and powerful oily substance that he called pyro-glycerine. This dangerous and unstable explosive was so sensitive that it was not until 1863 that Alfred Nobel claimed to have tamed the oil and had the courage to start producing it in quantity for commercial use. For its day it was the most advanced and destructive compound known to man and was initially thought to be the ideal portable force. Unfortunately, the liquid had not been subdued, it deteriorated rapidly after manufacture and a number of frightful accidents occurred when storing, transporting or using the new 'Nobel's patent blasting oil'. This included a tragic incident in which Nobel's brother was killed in an accidental explosion. The lethal liquid, quite rightly, gained a fearful reputation and in some countries its manufacture and use was banned.

Nobel, a single-minded man and eminent chemist, did not give up on the liquid and after much experimentation managed to finally curb the most dangerous properties of the oil by absorbing it in kieselguhr earth, and so dynamite was born. Nobel hoped that it would bring peace to the world and he wrote:

> My dynamite will sooner lead to peace than a thousand world conventions. As soon as men will find that in one instant, whole armies can be utterly destroyed, they surely will abide by golden peace.[1]

History has proved how sadly misguided he was. The explosive still retained its fearful reputation and conjured up all kinds of appalling nightmares, some of which found their way into the literature of the time. Robert Louis Stephenson's *The Dynamiters* written in the early 1880s projected the fall of the England and the massacre of thousands at the hands of the 'Dynamitards'. Stephenson, ahead of his time, also considered biological attacks, and wrote of plans to break up the drainage and sewage system and in doing so cause death by outbreaks of devastating typhoid pestilence. Another novelist Donald Mackay wrote *The Dynamite Ship* which had Irish Nationalists bombarding the Palace of Westminster with dynamite shells fired from a gun some twenty feet long and with a range of eighty miles.

As always, the reality was somewhat different, but it was with dynamite that the Fenians intended to force the British out of Ireland. They planned to destroy the country's vital infrastructure using the power of the new and supremely violent explosive.

Between 1881 and 1887 a campaign was launched against three of Britain's major cities by teams of bombers whose goal was an independent Ireland. Two main groups of American Irishmen were responsible for the violence; O'Donovan Rossa's Skirmishers and Clan na Gael. Although Liverpool and Glasgow were targeted early on in the campaign, the focal point for the attacks was Central London. The targets in the main were limited to public buildings, the Tower of London and the railway transport system including the new underground.

It is a story of intrigue, treachery and betrayal, and was the catalyst for the reorganisation of the police Criminal Investigation Department

(CID). Like subsequent campaigns it was indiscriminate, unpredictable and the devices used were prone to both lethal premature explosion and total failure. The attacks, one at the very centre of Government, shocked and stunned the authorities into action and led to the creation of the Special Irish Branch. The bombs, although not totally unexpected, caught the Metropolitan Police unprepared and came at a time when the CID was recovering from a shocking scandal. The department was still in its infancy and had grown from a total of fifteen detectives in 1869 to some 250 in the late 1870s. At the time a major racket had been uncovered and three of the four Chief Inspectors had been arrested for running a betting fraud syndicate from France. The repercussions were still rebounding from the trial of these men when the Fenian bombs started exploding across the United Kingdom which, of course, included Southern Ireland at the time. It was the CID which had to deal with the Irish bombing campaign in London. To say that Scotland Yard did not have the confidence of the public at the time was an understatement. Consequently, the Home Secretary requested help from the Royal Irish Constabulary to deal with Irish Nationalism and a detachment of these green-uniformed armed militia were despatched to the capital to guard the seat of Government.

In the aftermath of the betting scandal an ambitious barrister, Howard Vincent, had taken over and rebuilt the CID into a force of some six hundred officers. In the early 1880s he recommended that a specialist squad be formed to track down the Fenian bombers and shortly after his retirement the new Special Irish Branch was formed. The Branch was, and generally still is, connected with political crime, assassinations, terrorism, revolution and sabotage. Their brief is surveillance, infiltration and intelligence gathering, but unlike the early activities of the security services, they are accountable for their actions in law.

The first Fenian attack was on 14 January 1881, when a simple bomb placed in a ventilation grid in Salford Barracks, Manchester, exploded without warning in the early evening. The only victim was an innocent young boy of seven who was killed and another who was injured. It was reminiscent of the later tragedy, not far away, in the centre of Warrington on 20 March 1993 when the Provisional IRA detonated two bombs, whose victims were again children. Aged just three, Jonathan Ball, who was out buying a mother's day card with a baby-sitter, was killed instantly and Tim Parry, aged twelve, was badly injured and died of his wounds in hospital five days later. Both bombings, over 100 years apart, produced widespread condemnation of Irish Nationalists.

In fact the Fenian movement had already been penetrated by informers, and the Home Secretary of the time had received plenty of

27

warnings of further outrages. Crucially though, there was a lack of specific detail in terms of when and where the attacks would occur. He wrote to Howard Vincent on 23 January 1881:

> The reports that come in to me as to the possibility of explosions under the auspices of the 'Skirmishing Committee' become more and more alarming. I am much disturbed at the absolute want of information in which we seem to be with regard to the Fenian organisation in London. All other objects should be postponed to our efforts to get some light into these dark places. If anything occurs there will be a terrible outcry.[2]

There was also considerable concern about the possible assassination of the Prime Minister and senior members of the Cabinet. Threats were received at Scotland Yard that Gladstone was about to be shot. When Gladstone was warned of the threat by Vincent he agreed to notify the police of his movements. At that time, he normally walked alone between the House of Commons and Downing Street. He was persuaded to accept the protection of a plain-clothes police inspector armed with a revolver. Unfortunately, this arrangement regularly failed because Gladstone would often step out from the garden of Downing Street and not pass the officer waiting for him inside the front door. So began the role of the protection officers, for both royalty and politicians, which has grown over the years into a significant and no less easy task today.

The first attack in London against the establishment was by men from the Rossa Skirmishers, probably Patrick Coleman and Edward O'Donnell. Their target was the Mansion House in the heart of the City, opposite the Bank of England and the Royal Exchange. The building had long been a target for frustrated, riotous Londoners and it had specially hired watchmen to protect it. Under the cover of the foggy night of 16 March 1881, the two men slipped into the city and headed for the Mansion House. The bomb was to be planted outside the 'Egyptian Hall' designed by the Earl of Burlington and so called because of its similarity to the hall of the same name described by Vitruvious in his book *De architectura*.

Their bomb was built into a packing case and was two-feet square and five inches wide. It was filled with fifteen pounds of coarse blasting powder and strongly bound with iron hoops. It was pierced in the middle and a length of burning fuse was in position ready for lighting. The whole was wrapped in newspapers with a final outer layer of brown paper designed to make it look like an innocuous heavy parcel.

When they arrived at the target, the two men were disappointed to discover that the Mansion House was empty. There should have been a Lord Mayor's banquet with many important guests, but this had been cancelled because of the assassination, by a bomb, of Czar Alexander II three days before.

Nevertheless, the bomb was placed in a recess below the east window of the Egyptian Hall and the fuse lit. The two men then scurried away from the scene because they knew the beat of the local constable took him passed the spot every fifteen minutes. At 23.30 hours Constable Samuel Cowell of the City Police discovered the parcel, the paper wrapping of which had caught fire. He quickly extinguished this and pulled out the burning fuse, which had but moments left before it reached the main charge. He then took the unexploded device to the nearest police station. It was immediately apparent from the examination of the bomb that it was most likely connected to the issue of Irish independence because around the explosive charge, were four newspapers; two American, one from Glasgow and an Irish one with a recent date.

The attempted bombing, by all accounts, had the effect of making Queen Victoria very nervous and concerned with the possibility of Buckingham Palace being blown up. It also generated a new sense of internal threat which was troubling and unsettling to the Victorians. They lived in a country approaching the very peak of its international power and an attack on its capital was, to say the least, disconcerting.

It has already been recorded that there were many accidents at the time involving explosives and that it was the responsibility of Inspectors of Her Majesty's Inspectorate of Explosives to investigate them all. This was done in a thorough and detailed way and in the process the Inspectorate's officers learnt a lot about the causes and effects of explosions. This was fortuitous because, with the start of the campaign by the Irish Nationalists, the police naturally turned to them to investigate and deal with the new threat posed by unexploded infernal machines and terrorist explosions.

Shortly after the Mansion House attack, Customs officials, probably acting on information received, intercepted a number of infernal machines being smuggled into the country from America via Liverpool.[3] The devices, ten of which were recovered, were concealed in cement barrels. They were examined by Professor J. Campbell Brown. His report showed them to be viable and well-constructed. They were made of zinc canisters which were filled with a booster of homemade nitroglycerine, similar to dynamite, and a main charge of gun cotton. They were to be initiated by a pistol device triggered by clockwork.

Devices similar to these were to be used later in attacks on the London transport system.

On 12 May 1882, another attempt was made to bomb the Mansion House and yet again it was a failure. This time the device consisted of a white lead canister which contained a charge of blasting powder. This was to be initiated by a length of rag which was placed into the centre of the powder. This rag had been lit but had gone out before reaching the main charge. Once again it was recovered and examined by members of HM Inspector of Explosives.

The next attacks were on 20 and 21 January 1883, when O'Donovan Rossa's Skirmishers struck Glasgow setting off three bombs. The first destroyed a gasholder containing some 350,000 cubic feet of coal gas. The second bomb was discovered by passers-by on the Possil Road Canal Bridge. One of the group, Adam Barr, was a young soldier on leave, he apparently approached the bomb which was in a box and put his hand into what looked like fine, brown sand. When he touched this there was a fizzing sound, followed by a small explosion and he was quite severely burned, the others in the party being slightly injured. Luckily, once again, the main charge failed to detonate and much of the device was recovered intact. The final bomb went off in a shed belonging to the Caledonian Railway Company in the early hours of Sunday morning. Colonel Vivian D. Majendie investigated these explosions and later linked the attacks to those that were to follow in London.[4]

On 15 March there were two detonations in the capital. One against *The Times* offices was another partial explosion, but the second produced a fearful blast which reverberated around the seat of government in Whitehall. The bombers' first objective was to strike at and silence, at least for a day or two, *The Thunderer* the voice of the nation. The bombers crept into Play House Yard off Queen Victoria Street and planted a bomb, in a hat box, on the ground near a basement window. The bombers then inserted a new type of timing device and, after twisting a stopcock to start the system working, left the scene.

The method of initiation of these bombs is of interest because they used the first recorded improvised acid delay systems. It is well known that acids will react with some chemicals to produce instant fire. The homemade delay in the device outside *The Times* consisted of a tube into which a large percussion cap was placed and sealed at one end. On top of this cap was a mixture of sugar chlorate. A further tube was placed into this mixture that had a number of holes in the bottom and this was stuffed tightly with tissue paper. If a strong acid was added it would slowly eat its way through the paper. The acid was contained in yet another tube, which was fitted with a stopcock that could be opened to allow the acid to flow on to the paper. After a delay, normally of some twenty to forty-five minutes, the acid came into contact with the sugar chlorate and the mixture would burst into flames and initiate the strong percussion cap. This in its turn was capable of detonating the early sensitive nitroglycerine-based explosives.

That night, outside The *Times* buildings, for almost thirty minutes, the acid ate through the tissue paper stuffed in its tube. Then at about 19.50 hours there were reports of a small explosion variously described as a rifle shot, a muffled gun, and the firing of distant cannon. Some workmen and a timekeeper rushed out to the scene and stated that the yard was all lit up by a fire coming from a box under the window of the publishing office. A young lad who was filling a pail of water at the moment of the explosion promptly handed it to a Mr Alfred Evans, who in turn threw the water on the burning box extinguishing the fire. He then stamped on some of the box contents, which had been scattered and were burning on the ground. Police who arrived at the scene recovered the box, and some of the material from the ground, and took this evidence to the local police station. Here it was examined by Colonel Majendie and his assistant Dr Dupré.

The bomb consisted of an oval-shaped japanned tin bonnet box filled with ten pounds of lignine dynamite. This particular form of the dynamite simply used sawdust to absorb the nitroglycerine oil. In the light of further evidence, it is most likely that this was a homemade explosive. To make it the bombers first made nitroglycerine, a very dangerous process in itself, and then to reduce its sensitivity to shock it was poured onto an absorbent sawdust base, the final product being known as lignine dynamite. In the remains of the device recovered at *The Times* it was found that the sawdust contained a concentration of thirty percent nitroglycerine. For some unknown reason the device failed to detonate as planned and had merely caught fire.

The second target that night was a new set of government buildings in Parliament Street. The MP for Sunderland, Mr E.T. Gourley, was speaking in the House of Commons when, shortly after Big Ben had struck 21.00 hours, there was the unmistakable sound of a significant explosion. In those days, of course, the capital would have been much quieter at night with no motor traffic, aircraft or other noises, so the sound of the explosion would have seemed much louder. The seat of the blast was quickly found and discovered to be at the rooms of the Local Government Board. It was located in a block of buildings situated between Whitehall and St James's Park. The device was placed on the window sill of No.8. (Today the location can be seen at the end of King

Charles Street on the left-hand side when facing Whitehall.) Majendie was summoned to the scene and quickly satisfied himself that it could not be a coal gas explosion and was the work of a nitro compound. He examined the damage noting that the blast had destroyed thirteen yards of wooden hoarding and had shattered about eight feet of the stone balustrade in front of one of the windows. Other windows were broken out to some 100 feet. He estimated the size of the blast at around twenty-eight pounds of poor quality lignine dynamite, which was equivalent to twenty pounds of ordinary dynamite. This, he noted, was the weight of the charge found in the infernal machines discovered in Liverpool. He therefore confidently deduced that it was the work of the Fenians. It was also noted that the explosion had occurred on the day of the University Boat Race and many police officers had been diverted from their normal duties. It was considered that this had made the bombers' task much easier.

These outrages stirred the imagination of a concerned public and the authorities were notified of all sorts of potential dangers. For example, the Home Office received a letter from a Mr F. Wiginton of the River Thames Watermen and Lightermen. In it he requested an urgent appointment with the Home Secretary, Lord Harcourt, to discuss a most pressing matter. The request for a meeting was turned down, but Mr Wiginton was asked to write again outlining his concerns. In his letter he warned of the dangers to the Houses of Parliament and the major bridges over the Thames from barges laden with gunpowder. He explained that these, fully laden, routinely passed down the Thames from the gunpowder mills of Messer's Curtis and Harvey to magazines, arsenals and trading ships in the docks in London. If one of these was to explode, then it would blow up half of the capital. The barges he thought needed to be securely guarded. He also warned of the possibility of 'combustibles' being thrown from the bridges over the Thames to set fire to the barges as they passed underneath. This could produce the most catastrophic result, perhaps reminiscent of the *Tilbury* explosion a decade earlier. There is no indication if any investigations were carried out into this threat, but in a reply to Mr Wiginton it was stated that the carriage of explosives was governed the 1875 Explosives Act and enforced by Thames Conservancy. It also stated that it would be very difficult to set barges alight by dropping something from bridges.

Another enterprising individual, Joseph H. Jones, capitalised on the situation by selling his patent fire extinguishers. These combined a bucket of water and special chemicals which apparently produced significant quantities of foam. An advertisement claimed they would extinguish fires of cotton, wool and Greek Fire and would keep for ten years. Another worried citizen wrote to the Home Secretary and warned that the new electric wires could be used to make explosions, although quite how was never satisfactorily explained.

Those with expert knowledge of the new nitroglycerine explosives tried to allay the fears of the public over substances they felt partially responsible for creating. In a letter to *The Times* Mr George M. Roberts, the technical manager for Nobel's Explosive Company Limited, stated:

> I have often by way of experiment, exploded a pound of dynamite suspended from the end of a fishing rod by a string about six-foot long, holding the rod in my hand the while. As there was no solid matter to project I received no injury, and the end of the fishing rod was not even scratched. About three foot of the end of the string at the end of the rod was always left uninjured.[5]

It is not clear what the purpose of this dangerous experiment was. Nor is the length of the fishing rod known or how often the experiment was repeated. However, if it is true, Mr Roberts's very robust approach to the use of explosives was matched only by the medical profession's lack of awareness of tinnitus or high tone deafness in later life. Not that this type of experiment would necessarily be conducive with a long and healthy life.

Later, on 27 March 1883, another group of eight dynamiters arrived in Liverpool aboard the Cunard liner *Parthia* led by a Dr Gallagher and his brother Bernard. They established a bomb factory in Birmingham where they manufactured nitroglycerine. Auspiciously, an unknown informer alerted Inspector John Littlechild of the Special Irish Branch about their activities and they were arrested. But this was not done before they had made and moved considerable quantities of this highly unstable explosive. It was intended that the nitroglycerine was to be conveyed to London in rubber bladders, however, apparently these were not available and so fisherman's waders were bought and used instead. These held some forty pounds of the explosive and were packed in portmanteau and taken via train to London where they were hidden in a flat in Blackfriars Road. The men were shadowed by the Special Irish Branch officers and arrested in the capital. When the explosive was examined by the appointed Home Office experts, they decided it was so dangerous that it was immediately destroyed.

The arrests, however, did not stop the attacks. The next in London was on the transport system in the evening of 30 October 1883, when two infernal machines were used to target the recently opened underground railway. The first of these explosions occurred at about 19.25 hours in a tunnel near Praed Street Station of the Metropolitan Line. Shortly afterwards at 20.00 hours another explosion rocked the tunnel between Westminster and Charing Cross on the District Line. Luckily there was no loss of life, but in the first blast sixty-two people were injured to varying degrees. The investigation into both incidents was an excellent example of early post-blast analysis and the results showed how blessed both the passengers and bombers had been.

In the first attack the 'up' train on the Metropolitan Line had just left Praed Street Station and was moving into a short length of tunnel when there was an explosion under the third class carriage at the rear of the train. The blast shattered the glass in the station and blew out all the gaslights, including those used for signalling. The two rear third class coaches suffered considerable damage and the gaslights on the whole of the train were extinguished. Fortunately, the running gear survived and the train driver, despite the lack of signals, continued on steadily until the train reached the next station at Edgware Road, a principle that holds good to this day. Here the injured were able to leave the train. Five were admitted to St Mary's Hospital, but most appear to have gone home suffering from minor injuries and shock. The conduct of the driver in not stopping was praised because, had he halted in the dark, it was thought that the injured passengers would have got out onto the down line track. There they would have been hit by a train coming in the opposite direction which passed the spot just moments after the blast.

The second explosion was in the tunnel between Westminster Station and Charing Cross. Fortunately, this time no train was involved and there were no casualties and the damage was limited some broken glass, ruptured telegraph and signalling lines and the extinction of a number of gas lights. The explosion left a small crater in the ballast on the side of the track.

Colonel Majendie and another Inspector of Explosives, Captain J.P. Cundill, carried out a detailed investigation of both scenes. They were quickly able to rule out gas and gunpowder as the cause. The former because there was no significant damage to any of the gas systems and all the gas reservoirs were intact. Gunpowder was ruled out because explosions of this material always leave a solid residue and a peculiar smell. Furthermore, the concentrated effects of the blast indicated that a nitro compound had been used. The final proof was the discovery of many copper fragments at Praed Street Station. These, it was ascertained, came from a detonator that was needed to initiate the new dynamite explosives. In both cases it was considered that the bombs had contained the equivalent of approximately two pounds of dynamite. The bomb on the District Line seems to have functioned exactly as designed; it was thought to consist of a charge of dynamite, probably homemade, a length of burning fuse and a detonator.

However, the circumstances around the explosion at Praed Street indicated that the bombing went seriously wrong and that the bomber (or more likely bombers) was very lucky to escape. A search of the tunnel revealed a piece of safety fuse approximately seven inches long. This would provide a delay of approximately thirteen seconds, from lighting the fuse, to the detonation of the explosive. When examined it was discovered that this fuse had not been lit, and therefore could not have played any part in the detonation of the bomb. The fuse was in good condition and as there had been no blasting in the tunnels for years it was considered most unlikely that it was from this source. Furthermore, it was considered too much of a coincidence that a new section of fuse could have been dropped by another innocent party near the scene of the explosion. It therefore was most likely linked with the bomb in some way – but how? When the witnesses to the event were questioned many of them recalled seeing a very bright light underneath the train just before the explosion. When the underside of the front carriages was examined it was discovered that there was evidence of burning under this portion of the train. Close examination of these burnt areas revealed that they contained particles of zinc. Zinc was also discovered at the site of the explosion. Experiments revealed that when a pound of dynamite was wrapped in a light zinc sheet and set on fire, the explosive burned, without exploding, but in doing so the metal produced a strong bright light.

It seems likely, therefore, that the bombers were travelling in one of the front first class carriages which, it was established by enquiries, were often empty. The bomb which contained some form of nitro explosive was to be initiated via the length of safety fuse and dropped onto the track, where it would have exploded some thirteen seconds or so later by which time the train would have been well clear of the area. What appears to have happened is that somehow, in the process of trying to light the fuse, the explosive in the bomb itself caught fire and began to burn furiously. The perpetrators in, no doubt, some considerable panic, dropped the bomb out of the carriage, still burning furiously, hence the light reported by the witnesses. At some point the safety fuse, which had not been properly crimped into the detonator fell out and was subsequently found on the track. When the flames reached the detonator it functioned and set off the residual explosive under the rear carriage of the train. The bombers must have remained on the train, counting their blessings at the close shave, and made off in the confusion when the train reached Edgware Road Station.

Majendie concluded his report by stating that these outrages were distinct from the other attacks that had been carried out. He, however, linked them with the following statement:

> But if anything were needed to establish the connection, the link, as it seems to us, would be supplied by the savage disregard for life, and indifference as to the consequences to wholly innocent persons.[6]

In early February 1884 a thirty-year-old Irish-American cabinet maker called Harry Bruton arrived in Britain on the German steamer *Donau*. He purchased two large leather suitcases on his way to London where he took up lodgings and employment as a cabinet maker. It was later established that he, and at least one other person, had smuggled in almost 100 pounds of commercial explosive of a type known as Atlas Powder A. They assembled four bombs intended for use against mainline railway stations.

In the evening of 25 February 1884, the men launched the first coordinated assault against London's rail network by leaving a number of time bombs in the cloakrooms of four stations. The first indication of the attack was in the early hours of the following morning when an explosion devastated the cloakroom of the London Brighton and South Coast Railway terminus, now Victoria Station.

Several persons in and about the station described the explosion as being formidable in character, resembling the firing of a cannon, sharp and well defined. It was immediately succeeded by a flash of flame from coal gas which escaped from a fractured main and started a small fire in the debris. Fortunately, some night-watchmen were working on the platform adjusting a hose and this was promptly turned on the fire. With the help of the Metropolitan Fire Brigade, who arrived shortly afterwards, the flames were quickly extinguished.

At the time of the blast the station was closed for the night and this contributed to the fact that only two persons were hurt. Both were injured by falling debris. Mr Fitzroy Bagot, late Royal Artillery, remained at the scene to recount his views on the events that night. He stated that after the explosion there was a very strong smell of exploded nitro compound. He added that he had sufficient experience of such in the Army to enable him to speak authoritatively on the matter. Some people reported two explosions, it seems probable that either those persons were deceived or that an echo or reverberation must have been mistaken for the second.

The damage to the cloakroom was severe but outside it was limited to broken glass. This was smashed out to eighty-nine yards which was recorded at the Windsor Castle public house. Colonel Majendie investigated the explosion in detail and concluded that it was the work of an explosive of great force, the equivalent of about twenty pounds of nitroglycerine and under no circumstances could it have been a gas explosion.

The following morning Queen Victoria cabled Harcourt, the Home Secretary, saying 'Shocked to see the account of fresh explosion. Trust it was an accident and no lives lost?' She was quickly told that it was certainly not an accident, but that fortunately no lives had been lost. She was later told by Harcourt that the origin of these devilish schemes was certain. They were planned, subsidised and executed by assassination societies of American Feinians, who announced their intention and openly advertised them in the newspapers published without restraint in the United States.

As a result of the explosion at Victoria, searches were initiated at all the mainline stations to look for other suspicious bags. The first was found on 27 February, when a suspect case was discovered by a member of the staff at Charing Cross Station. It was fastened with two straps, but was not locked. On being opened by the searcher, a Mr Chamberlin, he discovered some packages or slabs of strange description, and the matter was reported to the police. They concluded that the slabs were probably dynamite and arranged the transfer of the portmanteau to the Royal Arsenal at Woolwich, and at the same time sent a telegram to notify Majendie of the occurrence. There is no information on how the bomb was conveyed to Woolwich, presumably some poor police constable was given charge of the device and told to take it by horse and carriage to the Arsenal.

On his arrival at Woolwich, Majendie examined the case. After removing some clothing, he found a metal box and forty-five slabs of explosive. These slabs were identified as 'Atlas Powder A' a type of dynamite used commercially in the United States and not licensed for use or importation into this country. The explosive was carefully removed and then the investigation into the metal box began. It was made of a tinned iron, measuring 6 x 5 x 5 inches, with a yellow lacquer on the outside. The box had a hinged lid and the junction of the lid and box was roughly luted with a material like cobblers' wax.

The box was removed and opened under suitable precautions which are not recorded. Inside was an American 'Peep of Day' alarm clock made by the Ansonai Clock Company of New York. When the clock was removed and turned over it was discovered that the back had been removed, and that a small nickel-plated vest pocket pistol, with the wooden grips detached, had been fastened to the movement by copper wire. It was so arranged that the alarm winder handle was in such a position that when, at the time set for the alarm, it began to turn it would impinge in the last part of its movement on the trigger of the pistol. This had, in fact, actually happened, the trigger had been pulled and the hammer of the pistol gone forward. Close examination revealed that it had struck the rim of a copper cartridge but that this had misfired. At the muzzle of the pistol was the greater part of a block of 'Atlas Powder A' into which, were embedded seven plain detonators. To ensure the detonators functioned, some short strips of quick match had been placed in several of these. This whole system was to act as a timer designed to detonate the bomb. In total there was over twenty pounds of explosive, making it an infernal machine of some considerable power and destructive effect. Subsequent trials with the pistol and some new ammunition showed that out of twenty attempts, only three cartridges misfired.

Having just finished their work, Majendie's men received information that yet another device had been located at Paddington Station. It was again in a portmanteau and had been deposited at 17.30 hours on 25 February. They rushed to the scene, opened the portmanteau and partly dismantled the device. It was found to be, to all intents and purposes, exactly the same as the one from Charing Cross. This one had failed because the winder had jammed, although this was not immediately appreciated. The reason for this was, as Majendie said at the time, due to: 'A circumstance of a most extraordinary and we might perhaps say sensational character.'[7]

It seems that whoever had built this infernal machine had fastened down the winder handle (by which the trigger was pulled) in such a manner that there was a chance of it being fouled by a click stud (part of the clock) and so prevented the handle from turning and reaching the trigger on the pistol. So small was this impediment to the action that it went unnoticed when it was removed from the portmanteau. It being late in the day, an unnamed member of Majendie's team took the firing apparatus home without separating the pistol from the clock, not something that would be advised today! Somehow, either during its removal from the case or during the journey home and unnoticed by the officer, the clock had been jolted and had restarted. In the early hours, when the clock reached its assigned alarm time the winder turned, this time it was not fouled by the click stud, and the officer was woken in his bed with some considerable shock when the pistol discharged next to him in his room.

It was evident that in the case of the Paddington Station bomb, the clock had reached the set firing time and the alarm had begun rotating when the winding key fouled on the click stud. The firing system was therefore in a parlous state in which the slightest touch or jolt could restart it at the any time. Clearly this had important implications for the normal procedure of moving complete devices to the Royal Arsenal at Woolwich. Had it been done in this case there was a good chance that the device might have functioned en route, or after it had been delivered. It may seem odd to the reader that live devices were not rendered safe before they were moved. In some countries this was (and still is) common practice and is the preferred method of dealing with small devices. These are placed in bomb proof containers before being removed to an isolated site for subsequent demolition or disruption.

On 1 March Majendie was summoned to the City Police Station in Old Jewry to examine yet another device which had been discovered that morning in Ludgate Hill Station. Like the others it had been deposited in the left luggage area on 25 February but this time at 20.00 hours. The reason for the failure of this device was a yet another misfire of the cartridge in the chamber of the gun.

Majendie now set about linking the recovered devices with the explosion at Victoria. It may seem obvious that these were connected, but to stand up in a court of law it had to be proved. Items that had been recovered and examined after the explosion at Victoria Station included a clock main spring and a winding wheel, both of which had exhibited signs of damage consistent with being in close proximity to an explosion. Inspection of these, in conjunction with the London manager of the Ansonai Clock Company, confirmed that they were from a clock of similar make to those in the failed devices. There could be no doubt therefore that the explosion at Victoria was accomplished by means of an infernal machine and that it was the work of the Fenians. Many police officers investigating explosions over the last forty years would recognise the importance of establishing this vital evidential link.

Majendie, finally concluded, that it was indeed fortuitous that, of the four devices that had been placed, only one had functioned. Two of the failures being due to the misfire of the cartridges in the pistol and the other, in the case of the bomb in Paddington Station, due to the stoppage of the alarm winder which prevented the pistol firing. He had no doubt that the perpetrators were cruel and cowardly men and that, had all the bombs functioned, there could well have been many deaths or serious injuries.

In April 1884 some bombs, apparently intended to blow up the Government, were found in the possession of a Mr John Daly, arrested in Birkenhead on Good Friday. In a much-copied technique since then, it was decided that a trial would be carried out using one of these bombs to establish the effects of a successful attack. A mock-up of the Cabinet Office was constructed and the bomb placed in it surrounded by twelve wooden dummies. The resultant explosion peppered the dummies which were all hit with between seventeen and forty-nine fragments. In another trial it was also discovered that the explosive was very sensitive and that the bombs detonated if dropped more than two feet.[8]

The arrests did not stop the bombings or the flow of intelligence about them. In late 1883 Scotland Yard had received an anonymous letter threatening to 'blow Superintendent Williamson off his stool' and dynamite all the public buildings in the capital.

Initially nothing happened, but as predicted in the anonymous letter, on the night 30 May 1884, there were indeed a series of attacks, with three bombs functioning and a further device being recovered from Trafalgar Square. Two bombs exploded almost simultaneously in St James's Square. The first, at 21.18 hours was outside the Junior Carlton Club. It shattered windows but did little structural damage other than leaving a small crater. Twelve people were injured at the club, most suffering from cuts by flying glass with others suffering from shock. It was recorded, with some dismay, that several bottles of the finest wine were broken by the blast.

The second explosion occurred at the residence of Sir Watkin William Wynn, some fifteen seconds after the first. The bomb had been left on the stone window sill of the morning room on the ground floor of 18, St James's Square. The explosion shattered the sill and damaged the surrounding stone work as well as breaking windows all around the area. There was a party assembled in the morning room at the time of the explosion, but miraculously most escaped injury. This was due to the fact that they were not seated directly in front of the window when the bomb functioned, but were off to one side. Two servants who were standing near the front doorstep of the house were injured, one seriously.

Two minutes later a third bomb detonated. This had been left in a public urinal which was located on the ground floor immediately under the CID offices of the Metropolitan Police Force building in Scotland Yard. The explosion wrecked the urinal and did considerable other damage to the building. It severely wounded a policeman as well as injuring a number of people in an adjacent public house.

Shortly afterwards, at 21.35 hours, a boy passing Trafalgar Square found a small black bag placed by one of the Lions at the foot of

Nelson's Column. The bag was recovered to Scotland Yard where, being locked, it was cut open. It was found to contain eighteen slabs of 'Atlas Powder A'. One of the slabs was fitted with a detonator and a length of safety fuse which was ready for lighting, but this did not appear to have been attempted. The total weight of explosive was some eight and a half pounds.

On further detailed inspection it was discovered that one of the blocks of 'Atlas Powder A' had a number of empty holes in it where it appeared that detonators had been fixed into the block and then withdrawn. This indicated that at some point the block had been prepared for firing using a pistol in a method similar to that on the bombs in the left luggage rooms at the mainline railway stations. Clearly the high failure rate of the devices convinced the bombers to return to the simple and more reliable method of detonating the bombs using a burning fuse. The disadvantage being that only short fuses could be used and therefore the bombers were going to be in the vicinity when the devices went off.

One consequence of the bombing was that further restrictions were proposed which would place constraints on the manufacture, importation or use of explosives. This included the requirement for suppliers to keep detailed records of all persons who were purchasing explosives.

Surprisingly Majendie argued against this. He pointed out that firstly the attacks had all used illegally imported or manufactured explosives. He also recognised the importance of the use of explosives in industry, particularly mining and quarrying, and considered that further restrictions would incur financial penalties and inhibit building and development work. Furthermore, additional restrictions would in no way diminish the prospect of further outrages.

On 12 December 1884, an attempt was made to blow up London Bridge and the reports spoke of a significant explosion. During the investigation at the scene a diver was used and found some fragments of granite which were evidently broken from the blocks which were part of the pier of the bridge. Several large baulks of timber, which had been firmly bolted to the masonry of the bridge, had also broken away. Their examination confirmed that the explosion must have been of significant size. The bed of the river was apparently very much disturbed for a considerable space about the pier.

After the explosion an emergency meeting of the City of London Council agreed a reward of £5,000 for information leading to the arrest of the perpetrators. Furthermore, it was suggested that a pardon be offered for information leading to the arrest of the perpetrators or to persons actually involved in the bombing. The Home Office objected to such offers of financial reward and made the point that they were, in the case of Irish terrorism, generally ineffective. What was needed, for terrorist crimes, it noted, was more secret intelligence and discreet activity in procuring it, rather than public proclamations which were more illusory than effectual.

In this particular case they need not have worried, the investigation into the incident revealed that the three conspirators John Flemming, Mackay Lomasney, a former Captain in the US Army, and his brother, apparently died when the bomb they were trying to place on the south-west buttress of the bridge exploded prematurely. The combined effects of the explosion and the strong tides in the Thames removed all trace of the three men and their boat. Fortunately, very little damage was done to the bridge.[9]

In the New Year, on 2 January 1885, an explosion, involving a couple of pounds of nitro compound, occurred in the Gower Street tunnel of the Metropolitan Railway. The railway then ran the whole length of Euston Road, underneath the street. The seat of the explosion was close to a signal box which was damaged. By chance it also happened as two trains were passing, both of which were fairly crowded at the time. The third class carriages suffered most from the explosion, but the locomotives of the two trains were not damaged. The signalman in the wrecked signal box stated that the floor of the box heaved up in the explosion and he was half-stunned. However, he speedily ascertained that the signal apparatus was safe, and he re-lit the gas and telegraphed warnings up and down the line. Fortunately, there were no serious casualties, although one lady had her nose cut by flying glass, and two other gentlemen had cuts to their faces and wrists. Above ground a crowd speedily collected at a vent shaft at the head of Ossulton Street, from which, at the time of the explosion, a quantity of smoke issued. In keeping with the 'stiff upper lip attitude' of the times, it was later reported that 'passengers were greatly alarmed and many ladies fainted'.

Superintendent Williamson, of Scotland Yard, and the superintendents and inspectors of various districts, arrived at the Gower Street Station half an hour after the explosion, and immediately proceeded down the line. They discovered the signal box eastward of St. Pancras Church partially wrecked, the signal wire separated, with the clock having stopped at 09.14 hours. Close inspection showed that the explosive material could not have been gunpowder, as the surrounding brickwork was not blackened. It therefore had to be either dynamite or guncotton. It was concluded that the method of attack was similar to those that had previously occurred on the Underground, and that the bombers had been traveling on a previous train and had thrown the bomb with its fuse burning from one of the carriages.

The last attack in London in the 1880's campaign was another multiple outrage, and occurred on 24 January 1885 when bombs exploded at the Tower of London, in Westminster Hall and in the House of Commons itself.

The outrage in the Tower of London was due to the detonation of between five to eight pounds of nitro explosive in the armoury, and it injured four people. There was a fire immediately afterwards, but the troops on duty, under command of the adjutant, managed rapidly to extinguish it, in the process earning praise for their efforts from the chief of the London Fire Brigade. There was much sensationalist press coverage and reports of the Tower being completely blown up, but actually the heavy stone construction prevented serious damage. The guards on hearing the explosion quickly shut the gates of the Tower preventing anyone leaving, and a number of people were detained for questioning. One of them, James Cunningham, aged twenty-two, was clearly very nervous and, after failing to satisfactorily answer simple questions on his address and background, he was arrested. Later he and an accomplice Burton were tried, convicted and imprisoned for causing the explosion.

For Police Constable William Cole, a veteran of twenty-five years' service, Saturday, 24 January 1885, should have been a normal and uneventful day. The Palace of Westminster, where he was on duty, was open to the public but it was quiet and peaceful. Amongst the visitors were a Mr Green and his wife. As they descended into the crypt, a few minutes before 14.00 hours, they noticed that there was what they thought was a mat, with clothes on top, which was smoldering. They reported this to Police Constable Cole who was posted near the crypt. Cole knew that there was no mat there and immediately went to the place to investigate. There he found a square package on the centre of the lower tier of steps, leading from the crypt to Westminster Hall. Cole turned the package over and saw that it was burning; a hissing sound coming from the centre. The package appeared to be made of fine sacking with strings of webbing at the top and on the side which was uppermost. It was quilted with pockets, each of which contained a square cake of a yellowish substance. Without hesitation Cole picked it up and found that it was of considerable weight and immediately suspected it was a bomb. Shouting 'dynamite' he at once ran up the stairs with the intention of taking the bomb into New Palace Yard.

When he reached Westminster Hall he met Police Constable Cox and said to him:

'Tom it is dynamite!'

To which Cox replied, 'There is no mistake it is.'

The pair then proceeded to the door when a hot and adhesive substance ran from the parcel burning the fingers of Cole and causing him to drop it. Almost instantly the package erupted in a ball of flame and the two officers were blown over by the blast. A considerable amount of damage was done including a hole caused by the collapse of the floor into which both of the constables fell badly hurt.

On hearing the explosion, the duty officer, Inspector Ebenezer Denning, rushed to the Hall. The scene that greeted him was one of utter confusion. Of the two officers, Cole was unconscious whilst Cox was rolling about talking incoherently and hitting out with both fists, despite being held down by two other officers. The wall at the end of the Hall had been completely shattered and the dust of ages blown off all the roof timbers. In the contemporary Sergeant's journal, both the injured police officers were recorded as being 'black as niggers' – something that today would be completely unacceptable.

Whilst all was still confusion, another blast rocked the Chamber of the House of Commons. The second bomb had been left under the seats, known as 'Under the Gallery', where the broadcasting box is today. Mercifully all those in the chamber had left before the detonation, many to investigate the first blast. The device was of significant size and almost totally destroyed the Peers' Gallery. The Speaker's Chair and the Government front benches were also badly affected. Some idea of the power can be gathered from the fact that the damage extended as far as the Member's Lobby and the Post Office.

Back in Westminster Hall, Lady Horatia, the wife of the Deputy Sergeant at Arms, was bathing the wounds to Police Constable Cox's brow and neck. Inspector Denning made arrangements for the removal of the still-unconscious Cole to hospital. Mr Green and his wife, and some other ladies who had been quite close by, had recovered sufficiently from the shock and were able to return home shortly afterwards, although it was noted that the ladies were 'bereft of their upper garments'. Pending the arrival of police reinforcements, the assistance of Lady Horatia was again requested. It should be explained that at the time the Deputy Sergeant's residence was above St Stephen's entrance which are now the member's rooms known as St Stephen's Tower. Inspector Denning asked Lady Horatia to ensure that, as her front door opened on to the Hall, no one was allowed to pass through it on any account. In this duty she proved an equal to any police officer for she reported that a man with a foreign accent insisted on entering despite her informing him that this was not possible. A brief disagreement followed, but she stood her ground and eventually had the footman throw him out. This, it turned out, was unfortunate because it later transpired that the man was Dr Dupré, assistant to Colonel Majendie.

There were several persons in the crypt at the time of the explosion and they undoubtedly owed their lives to the brave actions of the two policemen. The incident was naturally brought to the attention of Queen Victoria who conveyed a message to the two injured policemen through the Home Secretary Harcourt and the Commissioner of Police. Both officers were praised for their bravery and devotion to duty and wished a speedy recovery from their considerable injuries. In the case of Cole, it said:

> The gallant conduct of PC Cole, who knowing full well the terrible risk he incurred, endeavoured at the peril of his own life to remove the burning explosive from the building, demands a special recognition. That by this daring act of self-sacrifice he averted a greater disaster cannot be doubted; and I have the pleasure to inform him, that in addition to the professional award he will receive, it is Her Majesty's intention to confer on him the distinction of the Albert Medal.[10]

On Thursday, 2 March 1885, at the exact spot of the explosion, by which time the damage had been repaired, Cole received his medal from the Home Secretary in Westminster Hall. To add to this the Commissioner of Police promoted both men to sergeant, without examination. The tale does not end there. Cole, due to his injuries, was unable to work for long and was pensioned off. He died five years later in November 1900, leaving his widow without any means of support. A case was put forward by Scotland Yard for his widow, who was of excellent character, to be awarded a small pension. In July 1901 in a letter from 10 Downing Street it stated: 'The King has approved the award to Mrs Cole, widow of the dynamite explosion hero, of a civil list pension of £30 a year.'[11]

The day's outrages resulted in a complete review of the security arrangements in public buildings, and in particular for the protection of the Crown Jewels after the attack on the Tower of London. This included the question of whether the public should, in future, be admitted at all. The committee raised to review the procedures requested that Colonel Majendie be asked to visit the Tower with the remit of advising on precautions to be taken to prevent further bombing attacks. Majendie's report highlighted many areas of concern, in particular the safety of the

Crown Jewels which he considered were very vulnerable to damage or destruction. He wrote:

> The arrangements for the protection of the Crown Jewels, plate and insignia appear very inadequate. They are enclosed in a large glass case, and outside this, at little distance is a very open railing, forming a sort of outer cage, the bars of which are 5 ¼ inches in the clear.
>
> It would be quite easy for a person to introduce a small charge through the railing close to the case, and the explosion of a very small charge indeed would suffice to produce injury to the enormously valuable contents of the case.
>
> A charge so introduced, discovered in time, could be drawn back through the railings only with very great difficulty, if at all, even if a person of sufficient courage were at hand to attempt it.[12]

He recommended that the Jewels were further protected by a substantial glass case, that the lighting was improved, that certain dark areas were protected by gratings, and finally additional Warders should be placed on guard. Many of his recommendations would be recognised as sound and sensible precautions today. It was also considered vital that anyone entering the Tower with a parcel be forced to open it by an attendant and disclose its contents. Majendie also recommended that the ends of the cannons be blocked to prevent bombs being slipped into them, a practice still in force today.

The man allegedly responsible for the House of Commons bomb, the Carlton Club bombing and possibly several others, was Luke Dillon. His parents had moved from Ireland to Leeds and then emigrated to America when he was six-years-old. He was said to be a stern, scrupulously honest man who deeply loathed England. After his trip to England to participate in the Dynamite War he returned to America. He was later caught trying to blow up the locks of the Welland Ship canal in Canada; this would have prevented Canadian troops sailing to help the British with the Boer War. He endured a long and arduous prison sentence before being released.

Although his bombs were the last to explode, it did not mark the end of the Fenian campaign. In June 1887, two Irishmen, Thomas Callan and Michael Harkins, arrived in London. They allegedly intended to disrupt Queen Victoria's Golden Jubilee celebrations by planting bombs in Westminster Abbey and elsewhere during the thanksgiving service on 21 June. Once established in the capital they contacted another Fenian cell. However, unbeknown to the two newcomers, this cell was already

46

under surveillance by the Special Irish Branch. In the event, no attempt was made to disrupt the Jubilee celebrations which passed off peacefully, and since then some doubt has been expressed over the authenticity of the threat.

No moves were made against the men until September when two of the original members of the group disappeared. It was decided that Harkins should be arrested and he was apprehended and questioned. During a search of his room a revolver, and an empty case which smelled of dynamite, was discovered. Harkins was coerced into taking the detectives to Callan's residence, but when they arrived the second man had moved on to a boarding house in Baxter Street and was busy trying to get rid of his explosive. At first he tried flushing it down the toilet, but this blocked the drains and the landlady made him pay the workmen who cleared it. They recovered the offending explosive, but not knowing what it was simply put it in a dustbin for disposal.

This was not the end of the matter. A nosy neighbour decided that the damp clay-like material would be just right to line his pigeon loft. He recovered it all and decided to dry it out in his oven, luckily for him he started with a small sample. Unaccountably the resulting explosion escaped the attention of the police. However, Callan was arrested shortly afterwards and gave police his last address. When they visited the boarding house, the landlady recounted the story of the blocked drain, and the neighbour explained how his oven had exploded. A further search resulted in almost twenty pounds of dynamite being recovered and this was despatched to Majendie for disposal. In February 1888 both Harkin and Callan were convicted and sentenced to fifteen years' imprisonment.[13] It brought the first Irish Nationalist campaign on the mainland to a close.

It was not only in Britain that there were bombings and in the HM Inspector of Explosives Report of 1892, Majendie wrote with insight about the problems facing the world. The use of English has changed, but the sentiment holds good today and has stood the test of time. He wrote:

> The past year has been remarkable for the number and grave character of the outrages which have been accomplished or attempted abroad, in the furtherance of political, social, industrial, or personal objects. At no former period in our experience have there been so many desperate attempts – some of them only too fatally successful – to destroy life and property by means of dynamite and similar explosives. There is only one gratifying consideration in connection with the long and dreary list of these outrages, and that is that the

frequency and cosmopolitan character of crime of this sort probably bring us much nearer to a time when an international agreement will be arrived at whereby criminals of this class will, like pirates, be treated as enemies of the human race and pursued from country to country and debarred from shelter or sympathy in any part of the civilised world, and this without reference to whether the actuating motive was political, industrial or other. Indeed it is difficult to understand how any motive can be deemed to sanctify or palliate so horrid and dastardly form of offence, one of the most deplorable features of which, as we have remarked before, is the callous indifference to whether the consequences fall on persons wholly innocent of any participation in, and connected with, the particular matter or cause against which the crime is directed.[14]

Throughout the period, not surprisingly, there were a great many incidents which were recorded as scares, hoaxes and false alarms, some of which were investigated by the Majendie and his men. Sensational reporting in the London newspapers in November 1893, spoke of bomb under Westminster Bridge, about fifty yards from the terracing of the House of Commons. The investigation into the incident revealed that a waterman was looking for some tools which had been dropped by men working on the Bridge. Whilst searching he found an artillery shell on the concrete of the third arch of the bridge from the Middlesex side. The shell, which was live, had been thrown from the bridge by some unknown person, presumably simply to get rid of it into the water. Unfortunately, not enough force had been used and the shell had, like many fired in wartime, dropped short of the intended target, and become lodged on the bridge.

The end of the Fenian mainland bombing campaign did not result in the disbandment of the Special Irish Branch. Instead the word 'Irish' was dropped from the title and Special Branch, or SB as it is now sometimes known, was formed. It would become involved in many other bombing campaigns in London. Neither did the end of the Fenian campaign result in the fear of bombs diminishing.

NOTES:
1. Quoted on http:/www.absoluteastronlmy/topics/Afred Nobel.
2. Jeyes, S.H. and How, F.D., *The Life of Howard Vincent*, George Allan and Company, London, 1912.
3. TNA, CUST33\390: Importation of Infernal Machines.
4. HM Inspector of Explosives Report No.L - The Circumstances attending three Explosions which occurred in Glasgow on the night of Saturday the 20 January and the morning of

Sunday 21 January, 1883 by Colonel V.D. Majendie, CB.

5. TNA, HO 144/84/a25908.
6. HM Inspector of Explosives Report No LV - Circumstances attending two Explosions which occurred on the Underground Railway, London on the 30 October 1883, by Colonel V.D. Majendie, CB and Captain J.P. Cundhill RA.
7. Report on the Circumstances attending an explosion at the Victoria Railway Station, Pimlico, on the 26 February 1884, and attempted explosions at Charing Cross, Paddington and Ludgate Hill Railway Stations, by Colonel V.D. Majendie CB and Colonel A. Ford.
8. Lewis Harcourt Diary, 27 April 1884, Box 735, folio 45, Bodleian Library Oxford.
9. TNA, 144/145/A33008: The London Bridge Explosion.
10. TNA, 144/148/A38413: Award to PC Cole.
11. TNA, 144/148/A38413: Award to PC Cole.
12. TNA, WO 32/6004: Tower of London.
13. Allason, Rupert, *The Branch, A History of the Metropolitan Police Special Branch 1883-1983*, Secker and Warburg, London 1983.
14. Annual Report by HM Inspector of Explosives, 1892.

Chapter 4

Anarchists and Suffragettes

'We are trusting, if I may say so, very largely to 'luck' to relieve us of any sudden call for the disposal of a dangerous infernal machine – and it must be admitted here to that 'luck' has favoured us in a most remarkable degree.'
Colonel Vivian Majendie HM Inspector of Explosives, 1 March 1894.

The Fenians were not the only group in the late nineteenth century using bombs to further their political aims. Across the Channel, in mainland Europe, the anarchists were in the midst of a major bombing and assassination campaign, and a series of deplorable terrorist attacks had rocked many countries. One of the earliest attacks, however, which fortunately failed, was in Britain. Whilst Grand Duke Constantine of Russia was visiting London on 13 September 1880, an attempt was believed to have been made to kill him. A bundle of explosives was placed on the railway line between Bushey and Watford with the intention of blowing up the train on which the Duke was travelling. Chief Superintendent Copping of the Metropolitan Railway Police and Scotland Yard investigated the case but nothing was conclusively proved.

This failure was followed by a dramatic success abroad with the spectacular assassination of the Russian Czar Alexander II using bombs in 1881. This inspired other anarchists all over Europe to attack their rulers and the aristocracy. Some of these radicals escaped or had been expelled from the continent and took refuge in London, considered by many to be a safe haven. Much plotting allegedly took place, but in the main the anger of these revolutionaries was directed at the lands they left.

In England there was an alleged incident in 1892 when a bomb-making factory was discovered in Walsall. It aroused much public interest and controversy. Four men were arrested and accused of conspiracy to cause unlawful explosions. When arrested they were found to be in possession of anarchist literature, including the early stages of a plot to use time bombs to blow up an opera house and incinerate alive the bourgeoisie inside. Also uncovered were other implements for supposedly making bombs, but no actual explosive devices themselves. To gain a successful prosecution the case had to be proved that the accused were intent on not only making, but also using lethal bombs. Allegations were made during the trial that Chief Inspector Melville of Scotland Yard and members of Special Branch used paid informers, and also an 'agent provocateur' to set up the case from beginning to end in order to gain a conviction. Eventually the four accused were found guilty and imprisoned for terms of five and ten years. A recent study of the case concluded that whether or not the accused were victims of a police trap, the convicted men were guilty of planning to make bombs, but were too incompetent to present a real danger.[1]

In Europe it was France, and in particular Paris, that was subject to a sustained campaign with many bombings. One of the worst was on 12 February 1894, when a bomb was thrown into the Café Terminus killing one man and injuring many others.

Three days later it was London's turn. William Smith, the conductor on a horse-drawn tram on Car No.379, which ran between Westminster and Greenwich, issued a ticket to a young, diminutive man with a foreign accent. He seemed to be nervous and kept looking at a brick-sized parcel that was on the seat next to him. At the Greenwich terminus he jumped off the tram in a hurry and gave the impression that he had gone further than intended. He called out to a passer-by and asked the way to Greenwich Park. This was pointed out and he hurried off in that direction. The time was noted by John Bone, the Timekeeper for the London Tramways Company as 16.16 hours; he knew this because he had recorded that the No.379 Tram was about a minute and a half late.

In the Greenwich Observatory two of the staff were working late. They were in the computing room when at about 16.45 hours they heard a sound that was described as a sharp and clear detonation. They looked out of their door and saw a number of men running towards the zigzag path that led up to the Observatory. Near it a man was staggering drunkenly and then collapsed to the ground. The two staff ran over to the scene and it was initially thought that the victim had shot himself. But when they got closer they could see he was terribly injured. Simultaneously, Sullivan the park keeper, and a police constable, arrived. At first it seemed that the man might still have a revolver hidden in his hand, which he cradled to his chest and which was wrapped in a blood-soaked handkerchief. The constable reached down and pulled this away only to discover to his horror that there was no gun and that the man's hand had been completely blown off. The victim, though in shock, was automatically trying to stem the bleeding from the shattered stump. It later transpired that one of his fingers was blown as far as the Observatory wall, and in keeping with the times, Sir Melville Macnaghten, the Assistant Commissioner of the Metropolitan Police, remarked: 'So have I seen a bail fly off at cricket in the direction of long leg.'[2]

The gathering crowd also saw the man had a gaping hole in his stomach. Sullivan held him up and heard him weakly whimper 'Take me home, take me home' before collapsing. A local doctor, William Willes, arrived shortly afterwards, but there was little he could do. A stretcher was fetched and the casualty conveyed to the nearby Seaman's Hospital. Here he was seen by the house surgeon who noted that he was mortally wounded and beyond help. He lived for about twenty-five minutes after his admission and died shortly after saying 'I'm cold'.[3]

Scotland Yard soon established that the young man was Martial Bourdin, a twenty-six-year-old Frenchman. Despite a detailed investigation, it proved impossible to establish a clear picture of the man and his character. Some painted him as a trusting simpleton, but other evidence would suggest that this was not the case. He had come to London in 1888 and had helped his brother who already had anarchist tendencies. Whilst in the capital he joined the Autonomie Club based in Windmill Street off Tottenham Court Road, where English and foreign anarchists were known to gather to plot and plan atrocities. He was sent to America in the early 1890s on behalf of the anarchist movement and during his stay he may have gained knowledge of explosives. There were unconfirmed reports of him giving lectures on bomb-making to members of the Autonomie Club on his return.

The investigation into the affair also failed to establish a satisfactory explanation for the selection of the Greenwich Observatory as the target for the attempted bombing. It has been suggested that Bourdin was intending to symbolically blow up time itself, but there is little evidence to support this and the bomb he was carrying was clearly not powerful enough to do any significant damage to the Observatory. Other sources suggested that there was a link with the Paris bombing three days earlier. It was believed by the French police that the materials for the bomb at the Café Terminus had come from England. There was some conjecture that Bourdin had decided to bomb the Observatory and then flee to his home country. On his body was found: £13.00 pounds in gold (a considerable sum in those days); a membership card for the Autonomie Club; a ticket for a 'ball' in aid of revolutionary purposes and a piece of paper with explosives formulae written on it in Latin. The members of the Autonomie Club certainly seemed to be expecting a strong reaction to the bombing, and no evidence was found in the subsequent raid by the police on club the premises.

Whatever the explanation, like many bombers to follow, he died at his own hand when the device he was carrying exploded prematurely whilst it was being prepared for use. The bombing caused something of a sensation in the press and caused much excitement at Greenwich. Sullivan, the park keeper, revelled in the attention and explained that, during the days following the explosion, he had in all his experience never seen so many people in the park.

The Home Office took steps to ensure that Bourdin's funeral was not a rallying point for extremists. In the event though, only a few people turned up and it was they who had to be protected by the police from a hostile crowd. As the entry in the Burial Register confirms, Martial Bourdin's final resting place is in St Pancras Cemetery, Finchley, row nine, plot twenty-nine. No minister was present at his funeral.

The story of his death became the inspiration for the book, *The Secret Agent*, by Joseph Conrad, which was published in 1907. In this, the evil mastermind, 'The Professor' plans an attack on the Greenwich Observatory which ends with the bomber being blown to pieces when he trips and falls in the park. Of the event Conrad wrote graphically that it was:

> A blood-stained inanity of so fatuous a kind that it is impossible to fathom its origin by any reasonable or unreasonable process of thought, for perverse unreason has its own logical processes. But that the outrage could not be laid hold of mentally in any sort of way, so that one remained faced by the fact of a man blown to pieces for nothing even most remotely resembling an idea, anarchistic or other. As to the outer wall of the Observatory, it did not show so much as the faintest crack.[4]

The story was revived again in the film *Sabotage* by Alfred Hitchcock, in which a dupe carries a bomb onto a bus and dies as it explodes accidentally whilst travelling along the Strand. Bizarrely a PIRA bomber, Eddie O'Brien, died in 1996 when a bomb he was carrying exploded as he was getting off a bus in the Aldwych just off the Strand.

The final peculiar link with the incident is that in America, the United Airlines (UNA) bomber, Theodore Kaczynski, was allegedly inspired by Conrad's book. It seems that it was part of the motivation for his eighteen-year bombing campaign against American scientific institutions, and he apparently used Conrad as one of his aliases.

The anarchist movement was believed to be responsible for one other attempted attack. This involved two Italians, Francesco Polti and Giuseppe Farnara. The former was arrested in a London street with explosives in his possession. It was thought that he intended to bomb the Royal Exchange although some consider the target was the Stock Exchange, which was full of the bourgeois. The Provisional IRA made a similar error when they bombed the Baltic Exchange instead of the Stock Exchange over a century later. The motive for the Polti's bomb was equally odd, for this attempted atrocity was in retaliation for the annual invasion of Italy by British tourists. Both men were tried, convicted and imprisoned.

At the time, seldom a week went by in London without a suspect bomb being reported and, though it nearly always transpired there was nothing in it, it was a constant worry for the police and the Home Office. Sir Melville Macnaghten serving in London at the time, recalled an incident in which a suspect infernal machine was found under the seat of an omnibus on its arrival at the Victoria terminus. It had been taken from there to Gerald Row Police Station by the conductor whose story, given in perfectly good faith, was as follows. For the previous few days a gentleman speaking with an Irish-American accent had always been seen on his bus carrying a parcel wrapped in brown paper. That evening he had offered the conductor a shilling to take it to the waiting room in Victoria Station and bring back with him the receipt. The conductor remembering the explosion of 1883 declined, but went on to state that after the man had got off the omnibus he discovered the parcel under one of the seats. It was heavy when he picked it up and he was convinced it was a bomb and took it to the police station. The duty inspector immediately immersed the package in water and apparently it 'hissed at him'. The practice of putting bombs in water was sound in the days when gunpowder was sometimes used as the main filling, as has already been stated, it readily absorbs water becoming inert when wet.

The parcel was left immersed until the following day and then conveyed to the Home Office to be examined by un-named Explosives Officers. First though it was left isolated in an apartment for a further twenty-four hours, and it was recorded that 'nobody much liked the look of it'. Eventually the sodden parcel was unwrapped by a group of experts and the cylinder inside prised open. A dark sticky substance was found and a small quantity removed and tested with a flame. None of the Explosive Officers present recognised it as an 'old friend'. Some more of the substance was extracted and this time sniffed and tasted. These new tests solved the mystery – it was a tin of syrup of figs.

Majendie, still serving as Chief Inspector of Explosives, was responsible for the investigation of all incidents involving suspect bombs including that above. Afterwards he wrote to the Home Office highlighting his concerns about the lack of suitable arrangements to deal with infernal machines should they be discovered in London, it was, in his view, unacceptable that they were dealt with in an ordinary office inside the Home Office. Majendie further noted that there were many amongst the population who were ready and willing to avail themselves to the use of explosives to enforce their political agenda or further their anarchical designs. There were, he said, no adequate measures in place in London to deal with these threats. To illustrate the point Majendie described what would happen if at some crowded railway station or in, or about, some public building there was grounds for believing that some formidable infernal machine had been found. There were, he warned, no means for dealing with such a device. It was probable that persons would be found who, as on previous occasions, would undertake the removal of the machine at terrible personal risk; but it was quite conceivable that this would result in a terrible tragedy, as had happened recently in Paris in the Rue des Bon Enfants when five French Policemen were killed when a bomb they were moving exploded.

At the time, as a result of the numerous attacks in Paris, and their experience of dealing with failed munitions after the Franco-Prussian War, the French were considered to have the best and most advanced methods of bomb disposal. They had designed a special vehicle with which to remove infernal machines and other ordnance. There was even reported to be a smothering device to localise the effects of an inadvertent explosion. In London there was a feeling in the establishment that there was a danger of being left behind in the development of equipment and methods needed to deal with infernal machines and that this, for the leading world power, was quite unacceptable.

Majendie was granted authority to visit Paris to view their arrangements, and arrived in the city on 28 March 1894. He was impressed by the systems they had adopted to deal with infernal machines. When a suspect device was discovered a police officer was ordered to guard it and at the same time information was conveyed to the office of the Principal Chemist that a bomb had been found. From here one of four principals, or in some cases, where the threat was not deemed too high, one of their assistants, proceeded to the scene and examined the suspect article without opening or handling it unnecessarily. If it was decided the machine was of no serious consequences the item was transported to the nearest of four bastions which had been designed for the purpose of opening and examining exploding devices.

If an assistant, and not one the Principal Chemists, was summoned to the device, and he was unwilling to move it, then one of the Principal Chemists, whom was always on duty, was contacted for further advice. This gentleman then attended the incident and decided on the necessary action that needed to be taken.

If the decision was made to move the device to one of the bastions it was transported in a simple one-horse phaeton that had good springs and was fitted with special India-rubber tyres. The bomb was put on a bed of wood shavings and the driver, with the Principle Chemist or his assistant aboard, set off for the nearest bastion. There had been some discussion about producing a bomb-proof cart in which iron shields would prevent the lateral dispersion of fragments, but this was abandoned because some of the devices had very large charges – for example, the one at Rue de Clichy was thought to contain sixty pounds of explosive. This amount would simply overwhelm any proposed armoured structure and in the event of a detonation the iron itself would fragment producing lethal shrapnel adding to the effects of the explosion. Today moving bombs by such methods seems quite bizarre and even downright dangerous, but then there was a greater sense of duty and tolerance of personal danger.

On arrival at the bastion, the device was moved into a small shed, which was surrounded by stout earth walls. Inside were powerful hydraulic rams, which could be operated remotely to break open a bomb. Alternatively, small charges of dynamite could be placed alongside the device and fired remotely, in an attempt to blow it apart without setting it off. The use of remote opening systems and explosive disruption methods using a donor charge was very advanced for its time and was the forerunner of many of the techniques used today. If the bomb had soldered joints, then there was a mercury bath into which one of the sides of the container could be placed to dissolve the soldered seam.

In particular, the French had had great success with the hydraulic rams. The movement of these was slow and easily regulated and enabled even the stoutest metal machines to be broken into remotely, without setting off the explosives contained therein.

Finally, the French had concluded that if it was considered too dangerous to move a device without appreciable risk then it was to be blown up in situ. However, before this could be done, it was necessary to gain approval from the Minister of the Interior, and of course evacuate the people from the danger area. Majendie disagreed with this idea, stating that firstly a bomb could always be moved to another less important location. Secondly, he argued that by destroying the machine in situ the work of the anarchist was being achieved by the authorities. He considered that it would be unacceptable in London to explode a powerful bomb in places like the House of Commons, the Home Office, the National Gallery or St Paul's Cathedral. He concluded that, giving weight to all the arguments, exploding a machine in situ was one which could only be resorted to in cases which were so rare or extreme, and under circumstances which were so exceptional, that it scarcely called for serious consideration. Inevitably this meant that an Officer from HM Inspector of Explosives who was required to deal with such a device was committed to moving it and undertaking significant personal risk.

At the end of the visit Majendie concluded that in the matter of dealing with the disposal of infernal machines, bombs and suspect packages, the arrangements in Paris were much more complete and elaborate than our own. What London required was firstly an efficient form of communication so that if an infernal machine or bomb was discovered then there would be no delay in the information being relayed to the offices of HM Inspector of Explosives. In silent hours the information needed to be relayed to the Whitehall home of Majendie, or to one of his subordinates. It was recommended that Scotland Yard and the Home office should be linked using the new telephonic system which would enable the quick passage of information and enable any suspect device to be examined at the earliest opportunity. Next, suitable arrangements needed to be made for the removal of suspect items to a place where they could be examined safely. Finally, there was a need for such a place (or places) to be constructed which were closer to Central London than Woolwich Arsenal.

As regards to the location of places needed to deal with exploding devices, a number of problems arose. The enormous area London covered when compared with Paris meant that, in theory, more sites would be required. It was also stated that it was much harder to find suitable locations, which were sufficiently remote from thickly populated areas where bombs could be deposited, examined and if necessary destroyed. Bearing in mind the large number of parks in London it is not clear why this was considered such a problem. Finally, there was the problem that the nature of the devices that might be encountered was uncertain. They could have large or small explosive charges, a wide variety of initiation systems and many different types of container. This made it impossible to prescribe anything like a standard or uniform method of rendering devices safe which would be suitable for each occasion a bomb was found.

After much deliberation it was decided on the following: there needed to be a location which was readily accessible for the examination and if necessary destruction of small parcels or bombs, without public risk or observation. Next, there needed to be a place which was less accessible but in which larger bombs could be examined and again destroyed in situ if circumstances demanded. Finally, there needed to be a location where bombs of a very formidable nature could be taken without exposing the public to too much risk. Within London two key security areas were considered. The first area was around the Home Office and New Scotland Yard, which essentially covered the most important areas of government and secondly the City district which included St Paul's Cathedral, the Bank of England, the Mint, the Guildhall, the Mansion House and the Tower of London.

It was recognized that it was important that any suspect infernal machine should not be moved too far through the crowded streets and therefore, there should be a place for disposal in each of the two main districts. These would be capable of dealing with small devices. For larger devices an area was required, which was remote from houses and from which the public could be excluded. This would contain a sunken bombproof cell. For the case of formidable bombs, it was considered that they should be conveyed well away from London before being exploded.

For small devices, two sites were recommended. One was on Duck Island, situated just behind Downing Street in St James Park. The other, to take care of the City, was, with the War Department's permission, to be located in Tower Ditch at the Tower of London. For medium size devices it was thought a suitable bombproof chamber could be built in Hyde Park in the area known as the gravel pit. Lastly, for the infernal machines of very formidable nature, it was recommended that they were moved to Woolwich Arsenal to an area known as the 'Thunderer Cell'. This had been constructed for a trial, which involved bursting one of the battleship HMS *Thunderer*'s immense 12.5-inch muzzle loading guns. This was to investigate the circumstances of an accident on her sister ship, HMS *Devastation*, when a shell exploded in a forward turret killing eleven and injuring thirty-five other sailors.

Like many sound plans it was stopped in its tracks by the financial constraints imposed by the Treasury and in the end only one site was built and this was on Duck Island in St James's Park. Approval was given for the construction in May 1894, with the work being undertaken by the Royal Engineers under the supervision of the Fortification Department. It was decided at a site meeting that the size of the building would need to be at least ten by ten feet and that the base would need to be sunk by at least four feet. The base was to be constructed of concrete and the actual building itself was to be of unspecified light materials. The hydraulic presses and a special iron protective shield were to be supplied and fitted by the Fortification Branch but all other tools and equipment were to be provided by the Royal Arsenal at Woolwich.

To get infernal machines, explosives or other ordnance found in public places to the site, a special cart was constructed. It was agreed that a handcart should be used but that its purpose should remain secret so that the general public would not become alarmed if they saw a policeman moving it through the streets. Because of the secrecy of the project, the Home Office decided not to use private contractors to make it and again turned to the Fortification Branch of the War Office to seek advice on the construction. The eventual design consisted of a four-wheel cart with special India-rubber tyres. It carried a wicker basket, which was lined with three thicknesses of metal springs and a rope net hammock, to actually place the device in. At least one cart was built, but there is no record that can be traced of it ever being used.

The same lack of records applies to the site on Duck Island. It was constructed and commissioned but there are no details of the work undertaken there. During the First World War it was noted that the site was in use for dismantling shells and bombs (presumably those dropped in air raids). This, however, is only mentioned in passing, in a note which requests that the Island be re-supplied with tools because most of those on the original scaling were missing. The site was also used for storage of explosives and ammunition in the Second World War. After this it fell into disuse. There are some records of gelignite being stored there in the 1950s for breaking salt heaps during the winter months. By the early 1990s it was in a complete state of disrepair and a decision was made to demolish the rotting timbers, fill in the hole and remove the machinery. The equipment was moved to the Royal Engineer museum at Chatham where, apparently. it still resides today.

Returning to the misuse of explosives, HM Inspector of Explosives Reports from the late 1880s reveals other intriguing incidents involving the use of explosive devices by 'cranks' and criminals. One malicious and wicked case involved the discovery of bombs in a flat in

Westminster in November 1883. Two men, both Germans, were arrested. The investigation into the incident indicated that the owner of the flat, a man named Woolf and an accomplice named as Edward Bondurand, intended to blow up the German Embassy. There was no political motive behind this. It was, it seems, a plan intended to implicate some innocent persons in the explosion and in so doing collect a reward which it was assumed would be offered after the event. The men were committed for trial but acquitted due to lack of evidence.[5]

In 1887 a bomb exploded in a carriage of an Inner Circle underground train in Aldergate Station. One man was killed instantly, with another succumbing to his wounds later, a further fifteen people received minor wounds. The investigation showed that the bomb used high explosive which had been hidden under an empty seat in a third class carriage. The delay to it functioning was a simple burning fuse and this had probably been lit at the previous station Farringdon, where the perpetrator left the train. Several witnesses at this station reported seeing smoke coming from the carriage as it departed. There was no prosecution in the case. However, the police investigation indicated that an ex-employee with a grievance probably was responsible.

In another odd criminal case, on 25 October 1902, the Reverend George Martin, an unattached clergyman of the Church of England, was arrested for having in his pocket a one pound tin of gunpowder which he said he was going to use to blow up the stand at St George's Church as a protest about its erection on consecrated ground.

Also recorded in HM Inspector of Explosives Reports was the first criminal use of nitroglycerine to blow open safes. In Fulham, on 28 February 1903, a safe belonging to the Anglo American Oil Company at Crabtree Wharf was blown open by a quantity of high explosive placed in the lock. This blew the door open and an undisclosed amount of money was stolen. It set a trend that would continue for the next eighty years.

Disturbingly, explosives were also used on occasions to commit suicide. There were five such cases in 1892 involving explosives. In London, in a particularly grisly case, a woman aged thirty-eight from St Luke's Street purchased a ha'pennyworth of gunpowder, which she then poured into her mouth and lit. The gunpowder did not explode but burnt terribly fiercely like a blow torch. She suffered appalling burns and succumbed to her injuries the following day.

A tremendous scare was caused in 1894 when a company from Tamworth sent twenty-four copies of a new magazine stuffed inside empty shell bodies to government offices. Their aim was to win a prize for the best and most original way of advertising a pub. They certainly did that!

Another feature of the HM Inspector of Explosives Reports, around the turn of the century, was the danger people were placed in because of the development of early plastics which were highly flammable and were used in everyday items. For example, one of the earliest patented plastics was celluloid, which was only just deemed unsuitable by the military for use as a propellant because it burnt too slowly, nevertheless, it was still highly combustible. It was employed in all manner of ways, probably one of the best known being its use as film for the early movies. In 1910 there was a serious fire in an unnamed theatre on the Strand when a film caught alight. It was clearly a common occurrence as the report noted that:

> The fire appears to have originated in the usual manner, viz the film became broken below the gate aperture, and the end remaining in the gate became ignited. The machine (projector) continued to run long enough to pay out another foot or two of film from the top spool, and this length seems to have been ignited by the flame in the gate.
>
> Efficient spool boxes were in use on the machine, and the fire would have been confined to the short lengths between these, but two spare rolls of film were lying unprotected on the ironwork stand beneath the machine. The short lengths of burning film fell from the machine on to this and ignited it.[6]

It was with some difficulty that the fire was extinguished by which time much smoke had found its way into the auditorium. Other accidents included a woman who was killed when a celluloid comb she was wearing in her hair caught fire whilst she was making toast. At Lambeth an enquiry was held into the death of a young woman who was killed whilst wearing flannelette clothing and a number of celluloid combs. These caught fire whilst she was standing near a grate and she was so badly burned that she eventually succumbed to her injuries. In another case a boy threw a lighted match at a companion who was wearing a collar made of celluloid. It caught fire and he was very seriously burned.

There was also a danger, particularly in flourmills, from dust explosions, the mechanics of which at the time were not understood. Any combustible material in sufficiently finely divided particles can form a suspension in air, or a dust cloud. If the correct proportions of dust and air are present, the cloud will be potentially explosive and can be set off by any spark or flame. Industrialisation had led to the construction of massive multi-storey warehouses along the Thames waterfront and, in these, as bags of flour were being loaded and unloaded, the necessary conditions for an explosive fuel-air mixture occurred. In St Saviour's Flourmill in Tooley Street on 13 January 1892, a massive fuel-air explosion resulted in a very serious fire which destroyed all the machinery in the eight-storey building and resulted in the destruction of some 280,000 bags of flour. Several firemen were injured in their attempts to control the blaze.

Another problem, that continues to this day, was the tendency for explosives and ammunition to be dropped into the rubbish for disposal. In June 1904 the refuse barge 'Nile' was loading at the Council's Wharf, Ebury Bridge, when an explosion occurred. The result was that the two men who were loading the barge were blown up. One man being seriously injured and losing the sight in one eye, and the other escaping with minor injuries. When the barge was examined after the incident a significant haul of explosives was recovered, including a large number of Lydite (an early high explosive) charges, a seven-pound tin of gunpowder, numerous small arms cartridges and a number of regimental cap badges. An investigation by both Scotland Yard and the Board of Trade failed to trace the origin of the explosives to any organisation but it was clear that these were most likely discarded government stocks. No other persons dealt in such an unusual collection of munitions and explosives; anarchists made infernal machines, miners used blasting explosives and fuses. No sane person would have such an assorted collection of explosives apart from the military, not to mention the clue of the cap badges.

As a consequence of the incident the Secretary for State issued a by-law prohibiting the disposal of explosives in the refuse. It also banned the carriage of such explosives in any boat or barge appropriated for the removal of refuse. The penalty for contravention of the law was laid down as a maximum of £10 for a first offence, which was doubled for subsequent convictions.

As HM Chief Inspector of Explosives, Majendie without doubt, made a significant contribution to the safety of the public, particularly in his involvement and enforcement of the 1875 and subsequent Explosives Acts. As the first occupant of the post, he set a very high standard, which has been maintained ever since to the benefit of all concerned. He died in 1898 and was laid to rest in St Paul's Cathedral.

After the turn of the century another bombing campaign of which little is known or publicised began. British women had long been arguing for both universal and women's suffrage since the 1860s. The momentum for women's votes accelerated when Emmeline Pankhurst and her daughters Christabel and Sylvia founded the Women's Social and Political Union (WSPU) in 1903. This was a more radical movement than some of the earlier organisations and it adopted the slogan 'Deeds not words'. The lack of political progress led to the party becoming more radical and much more confrontational with the establishment. On 18 November 1910, a protest in Parliament Square became shockingly violent both in terms of the protest and the police response. This further hardened the women's attitude and they began to adopt more extreme actions. They waged a campaign of guerrilla warfare, orchestrating many forms of attack including arson and vandalism on a large scale. This included: smashing windows in Oxford Street; burning down sports pavilions; searing golf courses with acid; severing telephone lines; slashing cushions on the seats of trains; breaking street lamps and many other similar acts.

One of the most militant campaigners was Canadian born Mary 'Slasher' Richardson. In just two years she was arrested nine times for a variety of offences. She smashed windows in the Home Office and Holloway Prison and set fire to a country house. She was also thought to be one of the main protagonists in the women's bombing campaign.

In February 1913 a bomb was used to blow up the house of David Lloyd George, the Attorney General, in Walton-on-the-Hill, causing significant damage. It was estimated that this device had contained at least five pounds of gunpowder. Shortly afterwards in another attack there was an attempt to blow up a reservoir but fortunately it failed.

On 14 April a small, oval-shaped, cream tin, containing a charge of gunpowder with an electrical firing system, was discovered by the police at the Bank of England and, after removal to a police station, it was rendered safe. Most of the explosive was removed and the remains of the device now reside in the City of London Police Museum.

A month later another device was found near the Bishop's Throne in the chancel of St Paul's Cathedral on 8 May 1913. It was wrapped in both brown paper and in pages from the militant newspaper *The Suffragette*. Mr Harrison, who was cleaning in the choir and chancel, discovered the device in situ. He explained that this area of the Cathedral was quiet at the time and whilst dusting he bent down and his attention was attracted by a very slight ticking sound. Looking around for the source of the sound he found the brown paper parcel. He picked this up and took it straight to the Dean's Verger, Mr Skinner, who placed it in a bucket of water and then took it to one of the police officers on duty outside the south door of the Cathedral. A service was just starting at the time and the clergy were informed of the possible presence of an infernal machine, but it was decided to continue as normal. The bomb was taken to Bridewell Police Station where it was examined in the afternoon by Major Cooper-Key, RE, one of the new experts working for HM Inspectorate of Explosives.

The main charge, of which there was about three-quarters of a pound, was in a metal holder. The means of initiation was considered at the time to be ingenious, but today would be recognised as a standard mechanical time delay. There was a movement from a watch, which was affixed to a metal holder, connected to it was a small battery and the detonator. The watch mechanism had been adapted so that there was an electrical contact working with the hour hand. According to Major Cooper-Key's report the bomb was apparently set to fire at midnight the previous day. It had probably failed because of a poor contact. He explained that had the device functioned it would have done extensive damage, destroying the Bishop's Throne and part of the choir, and may well have caused a significant fire.

The carcass of this bomb has survived and is in the City of London Police Museum. It was built into a Keen's Genuine Imperial Mustard tin. The tin was divided into two compartments by the insertion of another tin, this one originally designed to hold BSA Lubricants. This contained the explosive filling. Recent analysis of traces of the explosive left, indicates that potassium nitrate was the key constituent. In the other half of the tin was a battery, wires and cotton wool, which would presumably have been soaked in some sort of accelerant. On top of the tin was a simple rotary on-off switch, which probably acted as an arming system. It is likely that this is the remains of the bomb, which was described by Major Cooper-Key but that the watch firing mechanism is missing. For its time it was a sophisticated device and if hidden in an everyday object, such as a bag, would not arouse suspicion and would pass anything but the closest inspection.

Another Suffragette bomb containing gunpowder, which used nuts and bolts as shrapnel, was found in early May 1913 in the waiting room at Liverpool Street Station. With it was a note which read 'votes for women'. Later, on 16 May, a further bomb was discovered at Westbourne Park Station. The movement then attacked the fashionable church of St George's, Hanover Square, where a famous stained glass window from the Malines was damaged when a small bomb exploded. In December, two small bombs detonated outside Holloway Women's Prison but did little damage.

The bombing campaign continued in 1914, with churches proving the most popular targets. On Sunday 1 March, an explosion occurred at about 20.55 hours at the Church of St John the Evangelist, in Smiths Square, Westminster. The actual site of the explosion was in the North Gallery, under the seat of the second pew from the front, close to the pulpit. The damage was confined to the displacement of a couple of planks and the bulging and slight cracking of the glass in two or three places of the large stained glass window over the altar at the East end of the Church. An inspection of the site suggested that the damage was caused by about half a pound of gunpowder. There were small explosions in St. Martins-in-the-Fields and Spurgeon's Tabernacle on 5 April and 10 May respectively. Then on Sunday, 12 May, another attempt was made to bomb the Church in Smiths Square, but this time the device was found and rendered safe.

Westminster Abbey was targeted on 12 June 1914, this time the bomb was built into two bicycle bells, with nuts and bolts again acting as shrapnel. It was hidden inside a 'Dorothy' bag[7], and this was hung over the back of one of the pinnacles of the Coronation Chair in the Chapel of Edward the Confessor. Beneath the chair was the Stone of Destiny, (now returned to Scotland) the emblem of power of the Scottish Kings, which was brought from Scone to London by King Edward I. At about 17.40 hours, whilst many worshipers and visitors were in the Abbey, there was a terrific explosion. Fortunately, there were no injuries and the material damage was slight. The pinnacle of the chair on which the bomb was left was blown off, and flying fragments damaged some stonework nearby.

There were about eighty to 100 people in the Abbey at the time of the blast. An eyewitness reported that he was about twenty yards from the Coronation Chair when the bomb exploded. The noise was said to be deafening, and a huge column of white smoke shot right up to the roof. Clouds of dust and fragments of plaster rained down from the ceiling adding to the confusion. The people quickly rushed for the exits and made their way into the street. At the same time Abbey officials and police from the House of Parliament rushed to the scene to find out what had happened. The Abbey was immediately sealed off and an investigation began.

It was perhaps no coincidence that at the time of the explosion, no more than 100 yards away, the House of Commons was debating the best way of dealing with the violent methods of the most extreme suffragettes.

Three days later, on 14 June, another explosion occurred at St George's Church, Hanover Square, after the evening service. The device had again been left under one of the pews. The front book rest was thrown down and the side of the pew wrenched off, the boards at the back torn off and the woodwork smashed. In addition, some of the individual stained glass panes in a large window were smashed. It was the last suffragette bomb in London although there were a few more elsewhere in the country.

The suffragette bombing campaign ended abruptly when Britain and Europe were plunged into the First World War in August 1914. Emmeline Pankhurst instructed the Suffragettes to stop their actions and support the Government in the conflict against Germany. Women from all walks of life did vital work during the Great War and at its end they were given limited rights. Finally, in 1928, they achieved suffrage on the same terms as men.

NOTES:
1 Harper, John, *The Walsall Bombs*, West Sussex, March 2005.
2 MacNaughten, Sir Melville CB, *Days of my Years*, Edward Arnold, London, 1915.
3 TNA, HO144/257/A55660: Extract from *The Times*, 27 February 1894.
4 Quoted on www.nmm.ac.uk/explore/astronomy-and-time/astronomyfacts/history/propaganda-by-deed-the-greenwich-observatory-bomb-of-1894
5 TNA, Supp 6/614: HM Inspectors of Explosives Annual Reports.
6 TNA, LAB 59/7: HM Inspector of Explosive Annual Report 1910.
7 Wasby, Percival-Prescott, *The Coronation Chair*, Ministry of Works, London, 1957.

Chapter 5

Monsters of the Purple Twilight – The Zeppelin Raids

'You must not suppose that we set out to kill women and children, we have higher military aims.'
The first Zeppelin commander to fall into British hands alive.

L ike most pioneering activities, the first Zeppelin raid on London on 31 May 1915, was a feat of skill, endurance and courage which pushed both the primitive mechanical, aeronautical and technical capabilities of the airship *LZ 38*, and the physical and mental capabilities of the crew, to the limit. Like air raids ever since, the outcome of this enterprising, but hazardous, operation culminated in indiscriminate death and destruction, including the murder of a three-and-a-half-year-old child Elsie Leggatt.

Commanded by Hauptmann Erich Linnartz of the Army Air Service, *LZ 38* was one of a new breed of million-cubic-foot, four-engine Zeppelins. It was a fine clear May night with a rising full moon and light winds when the airship slipped over the British coast, overhead Margate at about 7,500 feet, at 21.42 hours. The Zeppelin was met by a brief burst of ineffective ground-based machine-gun fire. She moved north towards Shoeburyness, being fired on again at 22.10 hours.

It was a frightening and unnerving experience for the crew. No doubt the minds of some of them dwelt heavily on the prospect of being burnt alive. And they were right to worry. The Zeppelins not only dropped devilish devices – they were large, lumbering incendiaries themselves. Encased inside their outer canvas skins, and attached to the lattice of duralumin girders in specially lined bags, were bubbles of highly flammable hydrogen. Slung beneath the vast streamlined skin were four Maybach engines, which consumed hundreds of gallons of highly volatile fuel per flight and which also needed several tens of gallons of lubricating oil to keep them turning. And then there was the payload itself, a mixture of lethal high explosive and incendiary bombs, initiated by simple, primitive and unreliable fuzes, which were strung out below the massive frame. All these components were vulnerable to attack from either anti-aircraft fire from the ground or from machine guns mounted on the flimsy British fighters sent up to challenge them. Despite being cloaked in darkness they were, if found, slow and vulnerable to attack. Being slowly engulfed in fire and crashing to the ground was the most likely consequence of any successful engagement.

In that event, the terrible dilemma for the crew was what to do; they could stay with the burning Zeppelin and hope, against the odds, that it hit the ground sufficiently slowly and in such a way that there was a chance, just a slim chance, of escaping before being swallowed up and incinerated by a ball of fire from the burning hydrogen and petrol. The grim alternative of course was to jump; plummeting to earth fully conscious for half a minute or more knowing the outcome was certain death. It was 'Hobson's choice' and none of the crew relished either option. Many of the later Zeppelin crews would be forced to make such a decision.

At 22.52 hours, *LZ 38* seemed to hesitate as she passed over Brentwood, her commander trying to fix her position prior to the final run in for the first assault on London.

The city was not totally unprepared and had the beginnings of an air defence system, thanks to the efforts of Winston Churchill who had taken on the responsibly as part of his duties as First Lord of the Admiralty. He had personally drafted instructions for the use of aircraft, searchlights and guns, and given guidance to the police, fire brigade and, to a lesser degree the civil population, when under bombardment. Unfortunately, insufficient progress had been made and although telephone and telegraph alerts had gone to police stations, there was no proper way of warning the people.

Previously, a few night flights by friendly aircraft had been made over the capital. These had established that, to the air observer, the parks would appear very dark, but the glow from the limited lighting even then made observation of long straight streets like the Mile End Road and Victoria Embankment plainly visible. It was planned to try and reduce the overall light levels and add lights to the parks to break up their dark outlines. So began the drastic dimming of London, the first palpable sign of the growing threat from the Zeppelins, but nothing could disguise the River Thames as it flowed through the capital. As one German captain said later when the searchlights were trained on them: 'Let the English blind us all they will, in order to lead us astray, the old Thames with its capricious bends and turns provides us with quite an excellent means of finding how the land lies.'[1]

There was also concern for the fate of the civil population from this novel form of attack. The then Home Secretary, Mr Reginald McKenna, noted that although the attacks would probably be militarily insignificant, the loss of life caused by Zeppelin raids should be regarded as of vital importance to the civilian population. As such they could not be ignored.

Linnartz and *LZ 38* were now on track to pass directly over the unsuspecting occupants of 33 Cowpers Road, Stoke Newington. Four families lived there each taking a different level of the house. On the first floor, Samuel Leggatt and his young family slept soundly in their beds, blissfully unaware of the perilous and imminent menace that was steadily advancing on them in the darkness. The Zeppelin's bomb racks were laden with a mixture of four high explosive bombs, about twenty grenades and ninety incendiaries. The four larger bombs were spherical in shape and weighed some sixty-two kilograms with complex and unreliable mechanical delay fuzes. The grenades, each some two kilograms in weight, were not of sufficient size to cause more than superficial damage to property. They were anti-personnel devices, their casings being serrated like the British 'Mills' bomb so that on bursting high velocity fragments would be thrown in all directions. They would of course be lethal in a crowded room or thoroughfare. The incendiaries bombs were conical in shape and charged with thermite and benzol surrounded by a layer of tow and finally dipped in molten pitch. The thermite served to start the fire, which was spread by the benzol while the tow kept the fire burning for some fifteen minutes.[2]

Linnartz commenced his attack at 23.20 hours. The first bomb dropped was an incendiary, which crashed through the ceiling and first floors of 16 Alkham Road, Stoke Newington, it penetrated through two bedrooms and destroyed the contents by fire. Charitably the official report stated that this was some 300 yards south-east of Stoke Newington Railway Station and that possibly this was the target. If it was, it demonstrated the inaccuracy of aerial bombardment which would plague all bombing campaigns up until the recent use of precision guided weapons (and even these still fail or are incorrectly targeted).

Next the Zeppelin turned south and dropped another series of high explosive grenades and incendiaries, one of the latter struck 33 Cowper Road. It smashed through the roof, fortunately missing the family that were asleep there, and continued down splintering the wood on the second floor and coming to rest on the first floor. Here it functioned.

Woken by the crash as it smashed through the roof, Samuel Leggatt instinctively set about rescuing his children. He managed to get four out from the flames; May, aged eleven, George, aged ten, Nellie, aged seven, and Dorothy, five. All had been burnt or injured by falling debris. Samuel was in a terrible state of shock himself and was suffering the effects of smoke inhalation as well as being badly burned about the hands and face. In the chaos and the confusion outside the house he was escorted to Kingsland Hospital by a neighbour who had to carry May, who was the most seriously burnt, and was unable to walk. At 23.30 hours the Fire Brigade arrived and extinguished the fire in the house. In the dark and bewildering circumstances, no one noticed, that three-and-a-half-year-old Elsie Leggatt was missing. About half an hour later Police Constable Churchill discovered the terribly burnt body of little Elsie, she had tried intuitively to escape the flames by crawling under the bed in the back room of the first floor. A local doctor, Dr Matheson, was called and pronounced life extinct, stating that poor little Elsie had been burnt to death. Subsequently Police Constable Churchill recovered the gutted carcass of the bomb to Stoke Newington Police Station where it was kept for some time as evidence of the murder of poor little Elsie.[3] Sadly, May Leggatt subsequently died of her wounds and both the children were buried together. It was reported that many thousands of people lined the route of their funeral. At the subsequent inquest on Elsie, the verdict was that: 'Death was due to suffocation and burns caused by an incendiary bomb from a hostile airship.'[4]

Not all the deaths could be directly attributed to the Zeppelin's bombs. The *Hackney and Kingsland Gazette* reported that, at the inquest into the death of twins born prematurely on the morning after the raid, the Coroner had stated that he did not think that the loss of the infants could be laid at the door of the German Emperor. A little later though, in a different case, one British jury returned the verdict of wilful murder against the Kaiser and the Crown Prince of Germany. This was reached despite the advice of the Coroner who objected because it was a useless verdict against persons that could not be brought to justice in this country.

Back on the night of the raid, Linnartz continued southeastwards dispensing more bombs and causing further fires and casualties. The Shoreditch Empire Hall was struck by three incendiaries, which did slight damage, and a grenade which detonated outside, fortunately caused no casualties. The audience was in the building at the time and any tendency to panic was prevented by the manager who addressed and calmed the crowd. The police report noted that: 'The band played lively airs while the audience left the house in an orderly manner.'[5]

The Zeppelin continued until it reached Whitechapel and the Commercial Road, dropping more bombs but causing only minor damage. She then turned northeast and dropped seven grenades in quick succession. These landed in a yard at 13a Berners Street, killing a horse, and in Christian Street with more serious consequences. Here two bombs fell in the carriageway killing ten-year-old Samuel Reuben, who according to the records, was disemboweled and otherwise badly mutilated. Eleven other persons who were in the street were also injured to varying degrees. One of them, Leah Leahman aged about thirty, sustained a compound fracture at the base of the skull and lacerations of the right breast. She was detained in the London hospital where her condition was later described as 'hopeless'.

Linnartz made no attempt to bomb the docks, a target with undoubted military significance, which was only one mile from his position at the end of his first run. Indeed, he had by then dropped some eighty-five of his missiles during the passage from Stoke Newington to Commercial Road. The Zeppelin ceased bombing and continued northeast for approximately three miles. Then, between West Ham and Leytonstone, the remaining bombs were released. The last fell on the Fillebrook Road at about 23.35 hours.

In total thirty grenades and eighty-nine incendiaries were dropped in the Metropolitan Police area. The total casualties of this first raid were seven killed and thirty-five wounded. One of the four larger bombs landed on the Nevill Arms Public House, Stoke Newington and failed to explode. It was recovered by Police Constable Edmond Forbes and taken to local police station where it was apparently registered in the property book. He later posed for a photograph with the bomb sat between his legs and now adorned with its weight in pounds; a copy still hangs on the wall in Hackney Police Station. In this novel form of warfare, no consideration was given to the chance of failed bombs subsequently detonating and, as happened above, they were simply recovered to police stations.

The attack was the fulfilment of the prophecy made by H.G. Wells in his novel *The War in the Air* written in 1908. In it, massive German Zeppelins destroyed the buildings and bridges in New York. It would, though, be almost a century before the terrorists of 9 September 2001 achieved such destruction.

In fact, the people of London were not the first to suffer; in the first few weeks of the war Liege and Antwerp were both struck by aerial bombs from Zeppelins. The reporting of these events rekindled the words of Wells and struck fear into the hearts of many citizens, but in fact the Zeppelins of the day were still primitive craft with limited performance and were incapable of such raids.

London was to be the first capital city whose people were to be tested by strategic bombing, the aim of the raids being to break their spirits by unrelenting bombardment from the air. Life was to be made unbearable by destroying homes and disrupting supplies. The City of London, the financial and commercial heart of the nation and empire, was to be obliterated. After the first raid, a German newspaper, the *Neuste Nachrichten* of Leipzig, said:

> The City of London, the heart that pumps the vital life blood of the brutal huckster nation, has been sown with the bombs by the German Airships whose brave pilots had the satisfaction of seeing the dislocated fragments rise up to the dark skies in lurid tongues of flame.

While the spirit of the people of London was never even close to breaking as a result of the Zeppelin raids, they did suffer grievous casualties and a great deal of distress. Over the preceding century, Londoners had become conditioned to thinking of war as something that happened in distant lands and they would remain protected from harm, safe in their island fortress, well away from the horrors of the battlefield. The first Zeppelin raid destroyed this concept and for the first time since the Civil War, civilians were directly in the firing line and their morale under threat. Many, however, considered the bombing had the reverse effect. True, but exaggerated, stories of atrocities carried out by the Germans had appeared in the press early in the war. In Belgium the 'Uhlan' baby killers and Prussian 'Rapists' ran amok. The Zeppelin raids were used to further vilify the Germans as ruthless, pitiless murderers and baby killers.

In war it is easy to find reasons to break the constraints thought to apply to civilised nations. This was the case with the bombing of London. Initially the Kaiser had resisted moves to bomb the city, but the French bombing of Karlsruhe, allegedly itself in retaliation for other raids, was used as the final justification for the unrestricted bombing of London. With it for the first time civilians far behind the front line became legitimate targets.

The next significant attack on London was on the night of 8/9 September 1915. This time the centre of the capital was bombed from the air, but it was not by an army Zeppelin, it was the German Navy that carried out the raid. It was also the first time a bomb of significant size, capable of doing serious structural damage, was dropped.

The custom of naming weapons has been around for centuries – for example, the massive six ton cannon made in 1457 which stands proud in Edinburgh Castle is called 'Mons Meg'. The same practice applies to munitions which are often adorned with names, characters or messages, most of them derogatory and often the product of a warped sense of humour, motivated by a thirst for revenge. Interestingly, these slogans or pictures are often applied by non-operational ground crew or others not immediately at risk. The enormous (for its time) 300 kilogram (660 pound) bomb slung under Lieutenant-Commander Mathy's Zeppelin L 13 was called *Leibesgabe* or love gift. It came with this name from the German workers who were already beginning to tighten their belts as a result of the Royal Navy's blockade. The bomb was designed by the German APK – *Artillerie Prufungs Kommission* (Artillery Test Commission) – and contained a significant charge of high explosive and an impact fuze. It was intended to obliterate the Bank of England or Tower Bridge.

To make sure the *Leibesgabe* hit the proposed target Mathy's *LZ 13* was equipped with a state-of-the-art, telescopic bombsight mounted upside down and directed towards the ground. It hung pendulum-like on four bearings and the line of sight was projected fifteen degrees forward. There were a number of settings for height, which were mechanically fed into the system. The sight itself had sets of crosshairs and by placing the first on a target and then using a watch and noting when a second crosshair passed the aiming point, *LZ 13's* ground speed could be established. Using this information, it was possible to predict where a bomb would fall by dropping it as the first crosshair passed the target. The calculations took no account of the aerodynamics of the bomb and it was assumed they were dropped in a vacuum. The time of flights had been established and was twenty-three seconds from 3,000 metres, and thirty seconds from 4,000 metres. Ironically, training in bomb aiming was carried out near Dresden, a city that would feel the full force of strategic bombing in the Second World War. Mathy approached London from the north slowing down as he passed over Potters Bar and headed towards High Barnet. The first smaller bombs were released over Golders Green. These may have been aimed at the airfield at Hendon, and might have been used to confirm the calibration and settings of the bombsight.

The Zeppelin pursued her course over north-west London at slow speed passing over the corner of Regent's Park going towards Euston

Station where she resumed dropping bombs with serious results. At 22.39 hours three incendiaries fell between Woburn Place and Upper Bedford Street and another in Russell Square. A hotel in Bedford place was damaged by fire. The next bomb dropped landed in the centre of Queens Square, breaking all the surrounding windows, but did no serious damage to the buildings, which included several hospitals. Five incendiary bombs then fell on Osmonds Yard, followed by others in East Street, Emerald Street, Theobald's Road and Lamb's Conduit Passage. A great deal of damage was done by the incendiary bombs before the fire brigade bought them under control. At 22.41 hours another high explosive bomb fell and wrecked a public house, *The Dolphin*, in Red Lion Street, and the premises of the now defunct National Penny Bank. When it detonated it sent a lethal shower of fragments scything down Lamb's Conduit Passage. A number of people who had gathered there were cut down, one was killed and a further sixteen were injured. The clock in *The Dolphin* was stopped at the moment it detonated and can still be seen in the pub today. After the raid the German press claimed it had destroyed the Bank of England, and used a picture of the wrecked premises of the National Penny Bank, in which the word 'bank' could be seen to (erroneously) substantiate the claim.

The next bomb, an incendiary, followed by a high explosive one, landed between Bedford Row and Jockey's Fields. The damage was limited to broken windows, but four women were injured.

At 22.51 hours, a further seven incendiary bombs crashed into the area around the Grays Inn Road and the Clerkenwell Road. This was followed by a high explosive bomb, which smashed into Laney's Buildings, Portpool Lane, where it killed four children and injured six adults besides severely damaging the building. More incendiaries and a high explosive bomb fell on Hatton Garden. Then another high explosive bomb detonated in Farringdon Road doing major damage to the buildings there. Today, outside No.61, there is a plaque which records the event and the building was renamed 'Zeppelin House'.

There was then a short break before three incendiaries fell in the road south of Smithfield Market. The delay may be due to the preparations to drop the 300 kilogram *Leibesgabe* which was released overhead St Bartholomew's Hospital. It landed in Bartholomew Close and detonated with a massive flash. The supersonic shock wave it produced devastated the four sides of the enclosure, smashing walls and doors and shattering glass into millions of potentially lethal shards. Mathy overhead was clearly impressed and wrote afterwards: 'The explosive effect of a 300 kg must be very great, since a whole cluster of lights vanished in its crater.'[6]

The Zeppelin stayed on track and more bombs fell along a line south of London Wall. At Moorgate Street two high explosive bombs fell, one of which failed to explode. The others detonated, damaging offices and injuring six women. Had he continued his course Mathy would have had the real Bank of England, then the Tower and Tower Bridge in his sights. However, after Moorgate *LZ 13* turned northeast and made for Liverpool Street Station dropping more bombs on her way. One high explosive bomb landed on an omnibus at the corner of Bloomfield Street and Liverpool Street killing three men and injuring many others. A soldier, Hector Poole, of the London Regiment was on leave and having supper in a restaurant in Aldersgate when the lights went out. He rushed to the sound of the explosion and saw the devastated bus. The driver of the vehicle was standing in the centre of the road; he was gazing at his bleeding hand from which several fingers were missing. He was clearly in deep shock and had no idea what had happened. He told Poole that he thought that he had run over someone and asked for help to get him out. Looking under the bus Poole saw the head and shoulders of a man, but the rest of his body had been blown to pieces. It appeared that the bomb had entered the bus over the driver's head and then travelled at an angle right through the structure before bursting on the road under the conductor's platform. He had been killed and the other passengers blown by the blast towards the front of the bus. The sole exception was a young girl aged about nine who was seated on the remains of the floor of the vehicle with the lower part of both of her legs missing. The next bombs just missed the Liverpool Street mainline station but tore up the track just to the north. Tragically yet another omnibus was struck by the last high explosive bomb, which fell in Norton Folgate. It killed nine persons including the driver who had his legs blown off and died on the way to hospital. A further ten people were injured.

Down below, the area was defended by a 1-pounder 'Pom Pom' gun of dubious serviceability. It had been captured from the Boers in 1899 and was located in the grounds of Gresham College in Barnard's Inn. It was manned by a crew of city gentlemen led by the Master of the Tower Armouries, Sub Lieutenant Charles Ffoulkes. He was desperately keen that the Gresham gun should make history and be the first to engage an enemy craft over the City of London. There was, however, a dilemma in that the old gun only had ammunition fitted with percussion fuzes which functioned on impact. If they missed the Zeppelin then they would inevitably rain down on London exploding where they landed. It had already been informally agreed by the gun crew that the chances of hitting an airship would be in the region of 100-1, so the odds for

London were not good. Nevertheless, as *LZ 13* drifted over towards the river it was illuminated by a searchlight on the Wakefield Tower and Ffoulkes gave the order to open fire. The gun stuttered into life and eleven shells hurtled up towards the Zeppelin. This being done before the official order was given to engage the enemy. Almost immediately afterwards all the other guns, including another in Cannon Street station and one mounted on the top of Tower Bridge, opened up on Mathy's craft as it escaped across the river. No hits were observed and no details are recorded to indicate which unlucky Londoners were on the receiving end of the plummeting shell fired by Ffoulke's gun. (It will become apparent later that, although great for morale, our own anti-aircraft fire contributed to the numbers of civilian casualties in both world wars.) After the action Ffoulkes was asked to justify why his gun opened fire early. On explaining that it was mostly for historical reasons, he was given a mild reprimand. He also arranged to keep the first two cartridge cases from the gun, one of which still resides in the Tower of London.[7] The weapon itself was also preserved, and can now be seen in the Imperial War Museum. Shortly afterwards, Sir Percy Scott was put in charge of the defence of London, and he recognised that all the 1-pounder 'Pom Pom' guns were useless and they were withdrawn from service.

Mathy then took his ship north and it was seen over Old Street moving towards Tottenham and Edmonton. Here the gun on Parliament Hill may have got a round close to the airship because she suddenly ditched a load of ballast, omitting a greenish grey cloud of water, and climbed away to 10,000 feet. To round off the night's events a crew member in *LZ 13* dropped, by parachute, a scraped ham bone in a bag. It was found in Wrotham Park Barnet. Round the shank was painted a German tricolour and below on one side was a picture of a Zeppelin dropping a bomb on the head of an elderly civilian in a very stiff collar and black tie. He was labelled 'Edward Grey' and seems to be saying 'what shall I poor devil do'. On the other side of the bone was inscribed 'a memento from starved-out Germany'.[8]

Michael MacDonagh, a reporter for *The Times*, witnessed the assault and saw the Zeppelin overhead, describing it as a long narrow object of silvery hue. Like many people, he was more fascinated than frightened and he wrote: 'I felt like what a watcher of the skies must feel like when a new planet swims into his ken. For it was my first sight of an enemy airship!'[9]

The following morning, MacDonagh went out to see the effects of the bombardment; he walked the course of destruction left by the Zeppelins bombs, noting that there were crowds of visitors who seemed more curious than angry that the capital had been attacked. There was heavy censorship of the raids and no independent reports were allowed. The Press Bureau only made reference to a Zeppelin visiting a London district and dropping some incendiary and explosive bombs. The official report into the raid noted that:

> As seen from the below the airship gave an impression of absolute calm and absence of hurry. After she had bombed Liverpool Street, she apparently passed quite slowly northward as if her crew were contemplating their work at leisure and without the slightest fear of being hit.

The total casualties for the raid were 109. There were thirteen men, three women, and six children killed, with a further forty-eight men, twenty-nine women and ten children injured, some severely. The recriminations began immediately after the attack, as the propaganda machines swung into action. The British press, for its part, expressed outrage that a Zeppelin could bomb Central London with such ease.

Mathy and his crew, on the other hand, received a hero's welcome. On 18 September he was summoned to see the Kaiser himself, and was later interviewed by Karl von Weigand, of the *New York World*. Mathy boasted of his exploits. He gave the impression that he was so low that he skillfully avoided the dome of St Paul's. He also took credit for not dropping bombs on the Cathedral, despite claiming that the English had established a battery of guns beneath it. Mathy, when questioned further by von Weigand about his height, stated that he had no desire to help give the English his range, as they were already quite good enough. He also justified his attack claiming only to have bombed legitimate military targets. He emphasised that London was one vast military centre, and a well-defended city in every sense, as far as the laws of war were considered. He claimed to have no wish to kill or maim women or children or other non-combatants. It is astonishing how a well-educated and apparently civilised man justified his actions by ignoring the real consequences on the ground, believing that he had only struck military targets and turning a blind eye to the reality of what he did. It is a common trait repeated by nearly all bombers whether they are aviators or terrorists.

Back in London, one of the early questions raised was that of warnings. It had been decided by the authorities not to issue warnings for two reasons. Firstly, it was not always possible to detect the Zeppelins and even if it was, there was no guarantee they would attack London. Secondly, it was thought that warnings such as the sounding of horns, blowing hooters or the ringing of bells would simply serve to bring people out onto the streets where it was now clear that they were most vulnerable. Instead public notices were issued advising that the best thing to do in an air raid was to keep in doors and if possible get into the nearest cellar or basement.

The only other precaution taken was the introduction of a stricter blackout, but it was still nothing like that which would be enforced in the next war. When Zeppelins were thought to be approaching the capital all the trains were stopped and their lights put out. The reason for this was that all the major rail lines in the south-east converge on London and it was important that they did not act as guides for the raiders. The upshot was that crowds of people gathered on dark platforms, unable to get home, until the trains started again.

Further raids were undertaken during this period both on London and other parts of the country. These were carried out by single Zeppelins but were mostly ineffective. The next significant attack on the capital was to be by five airships which were readied and despatched on the night of 13-14 October 1915. It was to be the bloodiest Zeppelin raid of the war. Mathy took part, but avoided Central London, although he did manage to drop bombs on Woolwich Arsenal where one man was killed and another eight inured. Another Zeppelin, the *LZ 14*, approached London from the south-east but dropped most of its bombs on Tunbidge Wells and Croydon killing nine and injuring fifteen. Zeppelin *LZ 16* lost its bearings and bombed Hertford killing and injuring exactly the same number of people as *LZ 14*.

Kapitänleutnant Joachim Breithaupt a young, bold and brave officer with piercing blue eyes, commanded the last airship in the attack, *LZ 15*. It was his first raid on London and he was determined to attack the very heart of the city. He brought his airship in according to plan from the north, initially crossing the coast at Bacton at 18.35 hours. He then proceeded down past Thetford, and shortly afterwards picked up the glow of London's lights in the distance. On her run in to the capital at Broxbourne, *LZ 15* flew over a mobile 13-pounder anti-aircraft gun which opened up on her, getting off eight rounds. She was estimated to be almost immediately above the gun and quite low at about 5-6,000 feet. Breithaupt immediately retaliated dropping four high explosive bombs. Three landed within 100 yards of the gun detachment blowing the men off their feet but fortunately not causing any serious casualties. Close by, a 30-cwt lorry and a car were destroyed. The shock of being brought under fire caused the Zeppelin to turn a half circle and jettison some ballast and fuel to enable her to gain height. Then, regaining his composure, Breihaupt continued southwest heading for Central London. He seems to have been uncertain of his position because for some time he went west towards Wembley before turning back and heading for the Edgware Road and Regent's Park. By all accounts here the engines were cut so as to make no noise and *LZ 15* drifted with the northwest wind towards Charing Cross. At 21.25 hours the carnage began with a salvo of high explosive bombs.

In the dimly-lit streets below Londoners and soldiers and sailors, either injured or on leave, were enjoying themselves, as much as they could, in the circumstances prevailing during the second year of the war. The theatres all around the Strand were full and the pubs were still selling beer. Those inside were completely unaware of the approaching Zeppelin until the first bomb struck. It detonated outside 15 Exeter Street, killing one and injuring two people and damaging other houses. Several other missiles followed in quick succession. The second, in Wellington Street, took a heavy toll; it landed between the Lyceum Theatre and the *Morning Post* offices where it detonated amongst a crowd of people who had gathered outside and were watching the searchlights scanning the night sky trying to locate the Zeppelin. Seventeen were killed, twelve seriously injured and a further nine slightly injured. This included some of the customers who were inside *The Bell* public house.

At the side of the Lyceum, a Mr Hanson, who had been in the theatre and had left by a side door after the explosions, went over to help an old beggar woman who was sitting with her back to the road on some steps. He called to her, 'come on granny don't just sit there – let us help you' but she was dead with the most awful wounds to the front of her face. It seems she had been blown back into a sitting position where she died. Back inside the Lyceum theatre there was some panic but an officer who was present, restored order. The bomb had dropped during an intermission and there were only a few people in their seats. Most were spread out in the bars, corridors and vestibule. There were no casualties inside the theatre as the people were protected from the lethal fragments by solid walls. The audience returned to their seats and then were advised to wait until the situation became clearer. Outside there was a devilish scene as in the flickering light of a fire from a broken gas main the wounded were tended to by stretcher parties and carried away.

The third bomb in Catherine Street exploded in the road and seriously injured one person and wounded eight others. The fourth and fifth straddled the Aldwych, one landing outside the Strand Theatre where another four were killed and five seriously injured and the theatre itself damaged. Number six and seven detonated between the Aldwych and

New Inn. At the Gaiety Theatre which was playing *Tonight's the Night* the manager asked James Wickham, aged fourteen, one of the call boys, to post a letter just before the bombs began falling. He took it and with another call boy Billy, set off for the post box in Catherine Street. They were in the open crossing the Aldwych in front of the Strand Theatre when the bomb struck. Billy was killed instantly and young James was badly injured with fourteen pieces of shrapnel being removed from his body in hospital. However, staying at the Gaiety might not have saved the two boys as another young lad called 'Nelson', the official messenger who was blind in one eye, died there alongside an electrician. Several other members of the public were injured. In accordance with the tradition, the show went on, but Leslie Henson an actor at the theatre recalled, 'I never worked so hard as to raise a laugh as on that night'. Around the corner another man, Mr Hutchinson, recalled seeing a vile old woman robbing the dead in Kingsway.

In the House of Commons a debate on the second reading of the Finance Bill was in progress when the noise of the explosions rumbled through the gallery. A low cry of 'Zeppelins' passed round and immediately the members rushed out into New Palace Yard where they were joined by several Peers from the House of Lords. Only the Chancellor and the Speaker remained behind to carry on the debate. In New Palace Yard the watchers were all gazing skywards. There was little light except the slight glimmer from shaded lamp posts. The face of Big Ben was in darkness as was the Clock Tower which usually had a lamp glowing to tell Londoners the house was sitting. In consequence, it was dark apart from the stars which twinkled in the distance. Suddenly the Zeppelin was spotted as it flew parallel to the Thames. The beams from two search lights locked on to the airship, and in their radiance, she looked like a thing of beauty sailing through the night, but she was still dispensing death.

Two incendiaries fell on the Royal Courts of Justice which caused a small fire. These were followed by the eighth and ninth high explosives bombs which fell in Carey Street, without causing significant damage or casualties. The tenth bomb landed on two old houses in New Square, Lincoln's Inn, wrecking the upper storeys but failing to penetrate the lower levels, thanks to their old and solid construction, which dated from 1697. The eleventh bomb functioned in Old Square and sent fragments smashing into the surrounding buildings and seriously damaged the old sixteenth century stained-glass windows in the Lincoln's Inn Chapel. Today, a plaque on the side of the chapel points to the spot where a round stone used to mark the point of impact. The stone is now gone although it is possible that a small square chrome metal stud now indicates the spot. However, the fragment strike marks on the side of the chapel are still clearly visible.

The Reverend Phillip Sydney had just returned to his rooms in Gray's Inn Square and was seated in an armchair removing his boots when he heard the explosion of the twelfth bomb that landed in Chancery Lane, ripping up the surface of the roadway and smashing the water and gas mains below the road. Thinking it was the 'Zepps' again, he decided it would be safer to go downstairs. With just one boot on he got as far as the landing when the thirteenth bomb detonated in the gardens just below his room. The blast ripped a great oak door off its hinges and hurled it past the Reverend, missing his head by inches. At the same moment he was blown off his feet getting knocked out in the process. The next thing he remembered was a light being shone in his eyes and two people standing over him. One said, 'He's dead I'm afraid. Let's get him out of this.' Startled by such an announcement, he explained that a bomb had blown him up, but not killed him, a fact which was plainly obvious. Actually, he had been blown down two flights of stairs by the explosion and was lying in the doorway to the street, almost completely covered in rubble. His clothes had been torn off but by some miracle he was unhurt other than a deep cut to his left hand and some minor bruises.

Three more incendiaries were then dropped, causing fires in South Square and Gray's Inn. Four more landed in Hatton Garden and another in Farringdon Road.

The onslaught now halted for a moment as the Zeppelin turned east and headed for the City. The next two high explosive bombs fell at Finsbury Pavement, damaging several buildings. One soldier and three other persons were killed and ten injured. The Zeppelin now struck a southeasterly course towards the Tower of London, but if that was the aiming point the bombs fell wide of the mark. The next partly demolished a small hotel in the Minories, killing another person and injuring a further eight people, shards from the bomb casing also killed a horse. The next two bombs fell either side of the railway leading from Fenchurch Street Station between Great Prescot and Royal Mint Street. The track was damaged as was Leman Street Station, and another six people were injured. The last bomb on London landed between Well Close and Princess Square wrecking a tarpaulin factory and killing another horse. Breithaupt now took a course towards Limehouse, but when the airship came under fire from the guns at Woolwich, he turned abruptly north and disappeared into the darkness.

To add insult to injury there were casualties from our own anti-aircraft fire. *L 15* had been vigorously engaged by the guns defending

London, although none managed to hit her. Unlike the impact fused shells used by the Gresham Gun, the bigger guns had time combustion fuzes designed to detonate the shells in the vicinity of the Zeppelins. Most of these functioned but much damage was done in and around Poplar and Limehouse by falling fragments. Some of the shells failed to explode in the air but did so when they fell back to earth. William Clayton, aged thirty, was killed when one detonated in Farringdon Road, and others landed, doing damage in Oxford Street and in the Public Library in Great Smith Street in Westminster.

On 23 September 1915, another squadron raid was planned with twelve airships taking part. Eight were to attack the Midlands, and four newly-designed super Zeppelins were to attack London. By now, London was galvanised to resist and measures had been put in place to take offensive action against the night intruders. Key amongst these was the deployment of night fighters from airfields scattered around the capital. For the pilots flying alone at night it was a new and most dangerous occupation. To start with they had no illuminated instruments or gun sights, no navigation aids and no method of ground control other than chasing the Zeppelins by observing bursting flak or when they became coned in searchlights. Despite these shortcomings, the brave young men still clambered into their flimsy aircraft and persevered with their task of hunting down the Zeppelins.

A major technical innovation was the ability to charge their Lewis guns drum magazines with a lethal mix of new tracer, incendiary and explosive bullets. These took advantage of the Zeppelins Achilles' heel – the reliance on the highly inflammable hydrogen gas to keep the craft aloft. Once alight a Zeppelin was doomed. With guns loaded with a mix of Brock or Buckingham incendiaries, along with tracers and Pomeroy explosive bullets, the days of the Zeppelins bombing London were numbered.

Almost a year later, on 2 October 1916, Mathy's Zeppelin *LZ 31* was shot down near Potters Bar. The credit goes to Second Lieutenant W.J. Tempest after he attacked the airship some 12,000 feet above the earth. He recorded: 'As I was firing, I noticed her begin to go red inside like an enormous Chinese lantern, then a flame shot out of the front part of her and I realized she was on fire.'[10]

Many in Central London saw the doomed Zeppelin in her death throws. High in the sky they could see a red glow from her innards, which rapidly spread along the length of the cigar shaped body, gaining in intensity all the time. Rapidly losing buoyancy the airship tipped forwards, the glare from the fire illuminating the sky for miles around.

The spectacle lit the darkened streets and even the Thames was flooded in a ruddy glow. The display seemed to last two or three minutes, and people stood around fascinated, not knowing whether to laugh or cry. When, as the stricken vessel disappeared from sight, a muffled cry could be heard all over the capital.

As the Zeppelin began her fiery death plunge, Mathy and his crew must have faced that terrible decision, 'jump or burn'. The captain chose the former, as local villagers discovered when they raced to the crash site. Close to the scene lit by the flickering flames from the burning hydrogen and fuel of the *LZ 31*'s twisted remains, they found Mathy. He was lying on his back half embedded in the damp soil. Some say for the first few minutes he showed signs of life but then expired. All eighteen of the remaining members of the crew perished with him. The loss of Mathy, probably the best of the Zeppelin commanders, was a major blow to the naval Zeppelin fleet and with him perished the hopes of subjugating Britain from the air. There was no doubt that these slow and lumbering raiders had had their day.

Although the Zeppelins continued to prowl the night skies, they no longer dared venture over the capital. Mostly they stayed over East Anglia, often dropping their bombs harmlessly in the countryside. A new generation of bigger and higher flying machines had been developed, but two factors counted against them. At the greater heights the crews were exposed to a combination of freezing temperatures and, more importantly, a lack of oxygen in the thin air. This caused tremendous physical hardships and reduced operational effectiveness; it resulted in an increase in the number of accidents and morale suffered. The other factor was the effects of the winds at higher altitudes, about which little was understood at the time. These seriously affected the ability of the Zeppelins to hold their planned courses.

In London the question of issuing public warnings was one which still caused some considerable controversy. The purpose of the warnings was obvious to all, it would allow the lights to be dimmed, and would give people the opportunity to take shelter in good time. It sounds simple but there were problems. It assumed that firstly people would seek shelter and that the authorities could issue prompt and reliable warnings of attacks. Neither of these assumptions could be guaranteed. In the early raids people actually flocked out on to the streets in large numbers to witness the events unfolding in the sky above them, almost as if it was 5 November and firework night. This made them vulnerable to the biggest killer fragments from the bombs which scythed through the streets. It also put them at risk from falling shrapnel and unexploded shell which fell back to earth. Casualties soon persuaded most people of the dangers of such a practice.

There was also the issue of unexploded bombs, and instructions were issued in July 1916 dealing with their disposal. The problem was addressed in a paper which looked at the disposal of wreckage, bombs or fragments of bombs which had fallen from hostile aircraft. The first imperative was considered to be the collection of intelligence about all enemy dropped munitions which would be of use to the Navy or the Army. The Defence of the Realm Regulation, 35 B was issued, which made it obligatory for every person to assist the authorities in the collection of these items. All bombs or fragments of bombs were to be taken to the nearest military or police authority. Bombs handed to the police were to be held and the military immediately notified. Large or bulky unexploded bombs were to be guarded until they could be properly disposed of by experts. It was falsely assumed that if they had failed to explode they were unlikely to do so.

The experts were military officers with some experience of explosives, mostly being from the Royal Engineers, the Royal Artillery, or qualified Inspecting Ordnance Officers from the Ordnance Corps. New or unusual bombs were to be dealt with by specialists from the War Office, but there was no indication of who these men were. It is possible that civilian HM Inspector of Explosives Officers were also employed on these duties, perhaps making use of the specialist facilities on Duck Island to disassemble bombs remotely.

It was soon established that it was possible to distinguish between Zeppelins of naval or army origin by the examination of unexploded high explosive bombs after raids. The naval airships carried pear shaped bombs, whereas the army Zeppelins were equipped with spherical bombs. It was found that some of the early spherical Zeppelin bombs were particularly dangerous as they had clockwork time delay fuzes. It was noted that: 'This bomb is most dangerous to touch or move when unexploded, owing to the possibility of the clockwork fuze being set in motion. No one but an expert should be allowed to touch a bomb of this type if found unexploded.'[11]

To support the experts in their work, technical descriptions of most of the bombs were provided, importantly including information on the method of operation of their fuzes. This included diagrams showing the various states in which the fuzes might be found.

The instructions issued for the disposal of incendiaries provide a revealing illustration of the novelty which surrounded the disposal of failed air-dropped munitions. Unexploded bombs of this type, it explained, should be laid horizontally until ready for destruction. Then they could be either dropped from a height of thirty feet after removing the safety pin or, if the pin was already removed, they could be placed in a heap and set on fire with the aid of a little petrol. In both these operations a distance of not less than thirty yards was to be maintained between spectators and the spot chosen for their destruction. This type of bomb, it noted, had been found attached to an aluminium petrol tank which burst on striking the ground. These, if still attached, had to be torn away from the bomb, and the bomb removed elsewhere for destruction.

Even with incendiaries, it is difficult to imagine undertaking bomb disposal operations today with crowds of spectators only thirty yards away, particularly if the method of disposal was to deliberately set the bomb off.

Other organisations within the capital also began to take the consequences of the raids more seriously. The London Electric Railway Company, for example, expressed concern about the breaching of the Bakerloo railway tunnel under the Thames and recommended the provision of steel doors. There was enormous concern about the possibility of a major disaster resulting in the flooding of sixty-five miles of the tube system. The proposed scheme called for 136 tons of mild steel and thirty-four tons of cast steel to build the substantial doors needed to safeguard the tunnels, but this would not be released by the Ministry of Munitions. After a great flurry of correspondence, the Ministry agreed the use of discarded shell steel. The gates were to be designed to withstand a pressure of 210 tons of water.

It is difficult to assess the overall impact of the raids on London by the Zeppelins. There was quite often a period of temporary paralysis during and just after a raid. This, in turn, had a knock-on effect on war production. The rail transport system was also affected with many of the lines being shutdown altogether during raids. On some occasions an official, not public, warning would lead to the total shutdown of the rail network in the southeastern region of the country. The consequences of which again impinged on wartime production. Finally, many of the defending guns and aircraft were diverted from the Western Front where shortages of men and materials impacted on operations there. There never was, however, a point at which the morale of the people was seriously threatened.

Although they did not know it, for the moment the people of London were free of the airship menace, although another threat would emerge in the coming months.

The Zeppelins did, however, initially take the blame for the worst explosion ever witnessed in London. At 18.48 hours on Friday, 19 January 1917, on a cold, grey, overcast night, people living in Silvertown area saw the bright burning orange glow of a substantial fire coming from the Brunner-Mond and Co explosives factory on Crescent Wharf. Four or five minutes later there was what many described as a gigantic white flash, which was the result of an estimated fifty-three tons of TNT detonating. The effects are hard to imagine. Looked at theoretically, the explosion of such a large quantity of high explosive can be quite accurately described. The detonation wave would have passed through the explosive at some 6,500-7,000 metres a second. A white hot fireball would have erupted some fifty metres across and the products of detonation would have generated a supersonic shock wave that would advance out, shattering everything in its path. Burning debris and flying rubble would be projected over a wide area causing damage and secondary fires everywhere. This theory, however, fails to portray the truly horrifying effects of such a blast.

For the people in the immediate area it was a truly terrifying experience. Those closest to the centre of the explosion were simply vaporised. Those far enough away to survive the blast were tossed through the air like rag dolls suffering multiple injuries, whilst others were buried as buildings collapsed. Further out people in the open were struck by fragments of glass, mortar and steel. Sixty-nine people were killed outright and several hundred others injured.

In the comparative calm in the immediate aftermath of the detonation, the people in Silvertown were so shocked and stunned that they could do little more than claw their way out of the ruins of their homes and do their best to tend to the injured. Hundreds of ordinary people from the surrounding area flocked to the scene and searched and dug through the rubble of factories and homes to rescue survivors. Firemen and appliances from outlying stations deployed to the scene to fight the secondary fires. Within hours a massive response was organised. Troops and other emergency services were ordered to the location to assist with rescue operations and first aid stations were set up. Later, emergency centres in churches, town halls, boys' clubs and Seaman's Missions were established and, by the day after the explosion, were catering for some 600 people. An Emergency Explosion Committee was created to help organise clearing up, reuniting and re-housing families and providing immediate financial and medical assistance to the injured and bereaved. The King and Queen and the Prime Minister, David Lloyd George, went to the scene the following day to see the devastation for themselves.

A survey by the Ministry of Munitions after the event showed that there was total devastation of buildings out to approximately 250 yards with most of the fatalities occurring in this area. Up to 500 yards most of the brick buildings were partially demolished. Beyond 650 yards the destruction was limited to structural damage with doors and window frames being dislodged. Claims for broken to glass and fallen plaster were numerous out to two and three-quarter miles to the north and east and three-and-a-quarter miles to the south and west. Further out claims were received for damage from Knightsbridge, (eight miles) and South Norwood (nine miles). The most distant claim was from Watford. In total over 60,000 properties were affected by the blast. The sound reverberated over a huge area and was reported in Southampton almost 100 miles away.

The nearest gas works to the explosion was at East Greenwich on the opposite side of the Thames. One of the gas holders was completely crushed by the shock wave and totally wrecked, releasing some eight million cubic feet of gas which caught fire and flared up for a brief moment. As eyes all over London turned to the sound of the explosion it was this eerie short-lived flame that shot into the air lighting up the surrounding area and reflecting off the low cloud that most saw and reported. It was another cloud, that of the Official Secrets Act, which descended after the blast. It was to be responsible for the myriad of rumours, including word that Woolwich Arsenal had been blown up, that followed the explosion. The only official acknowledgement of the incident was a brief statement, released on the Friday night, and published the following day it read:

> The Ministry of Munitions regret to announce that an explosion occurred this evening at a munitions factory in the neighbourhood of London. It is feared that the explosion was attended by considerable loss of life and damage to property.[12]

The inquiry into the incident was carried out under the auspices of the Assistant Under-Secretary of State, Sir Ernley Blackwell, with assistance from officers of HM Inspector of Explosives. They pieced together the background and events leading up to the explosion.

In 1915 there was a desperate shortage of TNT for munitions. The Royal Artillery had started the war favouring the shrapnel shell which, like a flying shotgun, sprayed hundreds of lethal balls at the enemy. Experience, however, rapidly demonstrated that in most circumstances, and in particular for breaking wire and demolishing trenches, the most effective projectile was the high explosive shell. The problem was that the main filling of these shells, TNT, was in short supply. Indeed, in May 1915, Sir John French the commander of the British Forces blamed the failure of the battle of Festubert on a shortage of high explosive munitions. His views, apparently leaked to *The Times*, led to the munitions scandal, indirectly to the collapse of the government, and the formation of the Ministry of Munitions. It was soon established that the existing capacity for the production of TNT was insufficient and that the plans for new Government factories would take too long to construct, leaving a shortfall in capacity between supply and demand. As a consequence, there was a search for emergency facilities which could be used to fill the gap until the more modern, specially-built factories came on line. One of these was the derelict Brunner-Mond factory at Silvertown which had been used to produce soda up until 1912 when it became unprofitable and was closed down. It was quickly established that this plant, with minimal modification, could be used to purify crude TNT into that which was required for shell fillings.

At the time TNT was considered to be a very safe explosive, so much so that in 1910 it was exempted from the provisions of the 1875 Explosives Act. In truth, it is very insensitive to shock and burns steadily in small quantities without detonating. Under the prevailing circumstances therefore it was deemed acceptable to use this plant, despite the proximity of rows of terraced houses, factories, docks, and a branch line of the Great Eastern Railway. At the Brunner-Mond site, the machinery in place was adapted and, with the addition of a large melting pot, the factory began the process of purifying TNT in the summer of 1915. On 29 December 1916, the factory was inspected by officials from the Safety of Factories Branch of the Ministry of Supply and they observed in the first line of their report: 'The situation and the surroundings of this factory, dealing as it does with large amounts of explosive must be regarded as unsuitable: but as they cannot be changed it is most necessary that every care be taken to minimise the risks of explosion.'[13]

Prophetic words indeed. It was just three weeks before the destruction of the plant.

The process for purifying the explosive was straightforward. About five tons of the crude TNT at a time would be melted in a large metal pot. The liquid was then dissolved in warm alcohol, a partial vacuum applied, cooling the solution and causing the TNT to crystallise. This was then run into a centrifuge which removed the alcohol and most of the impurities. The whole process was repeated and the final product, TNT flake, was packed into fifty-pound cotton bags for despatch to the filling factories. All this work took place in a building known as the

Danger Building. The plant was run on a twenty-four-hour basis using three shifts. The total workforce being some 268 people most of them employed in, or close to, the Danger Building.

On that fateful day in January there were just twenty people working in the Danger Building, ten women and ten men. All the survivors were interviewed by the Committee investigating the accident. One was a lad of seventeen named James Arnell. His task was to work under the melt pot sweeping up spilt TNT and alcohol. Whilst doing this he noticed what he described as molten lumps of glass dripping on to the floor. Another worker saw the drops at the same instant and shouted for those working up at the melt pot to come down. Arnell recalled shouting fire and dashing out of the building and running out of the works scaling a fence and heading for the North Woolwich Road. He had been there a few minutes thinking he was safe when the explosion occurred. He was hurled down by the blast, knocked unconscious and temporarily blinded.

The shift foreman, Edgar Wenborn, became aware of the fire at about the same time, as Arnell recalled him shouting from the ground floor for the building to be evacuated. He then ran off to inform the plant manager, Dr Angel. Another man, Frederick Blevins, the assistant chemist, heard the alarm, shouted a warning to his friend and as he left the nearby laboratory saw the melt pot room burning fiercely. Strangely, he went back into the room to recover his hat and coat and then set off for the main gate warning people to run as he went. On reaching the 'clocking on' office he turned back for a second time to try and find Dr Angel. He met him near his office apparently on his way to the plant and begged him to run, but Angel seemed intent on going back to the office perhaps to make an emergency telephone call. Blevins then went back through the main gate and met firemen coming in. He warned them that an explosion was imminent and before he had got far down the road he heard a terrific rumble and then was blown over by the blast.

Two of the female employees, Hetty Sands and Ada Randall, were working in the area in the early evening and described all as apparently normal. At around 18.45 hours they decided to take a tea break and visit the toilets on the way. This toilet was about a 120 yards from the Danger Building. Whilst they were in the toilet Hetty recalled hearing two faint noises 'like an iron door being banged'. She shouted to Ada to run out and see what was happening. Ada went into the yard and came back in shouting 'Good God! It's all afire!' Both rushed out of the lavatory and recalled seeing that the top of the melt pot room was ablaze. They instinctively ran away from the fire, meeting another girl, Alice Davies on the way. She joined them and they bolted to the factory's perimeter fence. They were considering how to get over this when the TNT detonated. Alice was the last of the nine women staff to get out of the plant and survive the explosion.

It was believed that Dr Angel had, after telephoning for assistance, gone back into the Danger Building to help fight the fire with the foreman, Edgar Wenborn, and the men on the shift. They must have known there was little chance of containing the blaze. Dr Angel, Wenborn and thirteen other men died instantly at the moment of detonation. All could have fled the scene and may have survived, but chose to stay and fight the fire. For their bravery both Dr Angel and Wenborn were awarded the Edward Medal. All the women, bar Catherine Hodge who was most likely in the melt pot room when the fire started, escaped.

The local fire station was only about a hundred and eighty metres from the plant perimeter. It was run by Station Officer Betts, and the crew included his son Tom and his brother J.J. Betts. They had been made aware of the fire just after it had started. There were a number of small explosions which alerted Tom Betts, whose attention was also drawn to the blaze by a small boy. He saw a huge red glow coming from the factory and raced into the station and sounded the alarm bell. The on-duty crew manned their one motor pump and within two minutes were heading for the main gates of the factory. There they met assistant chemist Blevins who shouted a warning that they should run. At that instant the explosion occurred. One of the firemen J.J. Betts recalled that the next thing he knew was that he was lying on his back some 200 feet away. He came round in a pile of rubble and noted that the factory had simply vanished. All around him he could hear the cries of the wounded, many of them women and children. The scene was lit by many fires started by flaming debris from the plant.

Taking all the evidence into account the investigating committee concluded that the origin of the catastrophe was the fire and that this had broken out in the melt pot room or the melt pot itself. The fire quickly gained great violence indicating that the TNT itself was alight and that there was an interval of five or six minutes before the massive explosion.

It was estimated that there were a total of eighty-three tons of TNT at the plant before the explosion. This was made up of twenty-eight tons of crude TNT, twenty-seven tons being processed and twenty-eight tons of completed TNT flake. In addition, there was nine tons of TNT oil in steel drums. Amazingly, five tons of this was recovered intact after the blast. By examining the site, and paying particular attention to the craters, it was estimated that about thirty tons of TNT had burnt away after the blast, and that so had four tons of the oil. This left approximately fifty-three tons which detonated simultaneously.

Rumours about the cause of the explosion and the number of casualties were rife, some talked of 5,000 dead. The committee therefore took great care in calculating the number of dead and injured. They concluded that there were sixty-nine immediate fatalities and ninety-eight persons seriously injured of whom four subsequently died. There were 328 less serious injuries. A further 500-600 people were estimated to have been treated in local clinics for cuts and bruises. As always though, stark simple numbers of casualties do not convey the awful impact of the accident, this can only be gained by looking at a few personal tragedies and lucky escapes.

A local beat bobby, Edward Greenoff, remained at his post warning others when he could have fled, and was killed instantly in the blast. He was posthumously awarded the King's Police Medal. An engine driver, George Galloway, was passing the factory in his train at the same time, his train was wrecked and he was killed. Equally unlucky was lorry driver John Ellis, who was blown from the cab and killed. A young clerk from the Tate Sugar Refinery saw the fire and ran to his manager's house to tell him. He had just knocked on the door when the plant blew and the house collapsed; he was killed by falling masonry. In Mill Road, a large piece of iron plate smashed through the roof of a house killing one child and seriously injuring another. Two houses away, the Hart family, a mother, two children and two grandparents, all escaped, but her husband, Mr Hart, who had left the house seconds earlier, was hit by flying debris and later died in hospital from head wounds. One man dragged four badly injured children from a house, and then collapsed. It was only then that those around him realised that his right foot had been almost severed by flying glass. Others had lucky escapes. For example, a large section of boiler plate from the Danger Building was blown into Lyle Park where it narrowly missed a courting couple.

It was important that the cause of the fire was established, firstly to prevent a reoccurrence elsewhere, but also to stop the wild stories that were in circulation. There was talk of an invisible black Zeppelin which had drifted over Silvertown with its engines off before dropping a massive new bomb on the plant. There was, surprisingly, a grain of truth in the darkened Zeppelin story. It was known that the Germans were trying to develop a black paint for the airships skins which would make them almost impossible to find at night. Other stories talked of saboteurs and spies, and suspicion even fell on the owners of the plant who had German ancestry.

The Committee looked into all possible causes of the fire, and it was confident, after a major enquiry by the police, that there was no serious evidence to support the sabotage theory, although it was impossible to completely rule out malicious causes.

It was concluded that the evidence obtained was insufficient to determine absolutely the cause of the fire, but it seemed most likely that there were two possible explanations. The first was that it was a spark caused by friction or impact. The second was the spontaneous ignition of the TNT in or about the melt pot. The magnitude of the disaster was due to the unnecessary quantities of explosive accumulating in the Danger Building.

The main conclusion of the report was that the Order of Council Act of 1910, which excluded TNT from the main provisions of the Explosives Act, should be repealed. Until then much stricter control of the purification process was advised, as was the need for better independent inspection methods.

The full report into the incident, which provides greater detail of the events, can be read at the National Archives. Under the forty-year rule this was not released to the public until 1957, although it appears that it was not fully declassified until 1974.

A memorial to the dead was erected and is located at the entrance to the old site. This can now be seen underneath the extension to the Docklands Light Railway just to the west of the fire station which was rebuilt, yet again, in the 1960s.

There is also a plaque dedicated to the firemen and their families who lost their lives on the station wall. Sadly, for Silvertown, the district was to be devastated again, this time by German bombers which unloaded tons of bombs right across the area during the Blitz in the Second World War

NOTES:
1. Robinson, Douglas, *The Zeppelin in Combat*, Foulis & Co, Londn, 1966.
2. TNA, WO 95/5454: AA Defence against Zeppelins – General HQ, Horse Guards, Intelligence Circular No.8, dated July 1916.
3. TNA, MEPO 2/1650: Metropolitan Police Reports on the Raid of 31 May 1915.
4. Hook, John, *The Air raids on London during the 1914-18 War, Booklet 4 The Raids on the City of London*, privately published, 1987.
5. TNA, MEPO 2/1650: H Division Metropolitan Police Report on the Raid of 31st May 1915.
6. Robinson, *op.cit.*
7. Ffoulkes, Charles, *Arms and the Tower*, John Murray, London 1939.
8. Jones, H.A., *The War in the Air, Being The Story Of The Part Played In The Great War By The Royal Air Force*, Clarendon Press, Oxford, 1922.
9. MacDonagh, Michael, *In London During the Great War*, Eyre and Spottiswoode, London 1935.

10. Robinson, *op.cit.*
11. TNA, Air 1717/27/19/34: Miscellaneous Reports on German Bombs.
12. Paris, Michael, *Silvertown 1917*, Ian Henry Publications Ltd, Essex, 1986.
13. TNA: Report of the Committee into the Cause of the Explosion which Occurred on Friday 19 January at Chemical Works of Messrs Brunner Mond and Company Limited, Crescent Wharf, Silvertown in the County of Essex 1917.

Chapter 6

Frightfulness – The First World War Bomber Raids on London

'If I were asked what event of the last year has been of the most significance to the future of humanity, I should reply that it is not the Russian Revolution, nor even the stern intervention of the United States in a sacred cause, but the appearance of a single German aeroplane flying at high noon over London last November.'
Lord Lovat Fraser, July 1917.

Like many actions in warfare, the first aeroplane raid on London, on 28 November 1916, was a bold, daring and solo act, the audacity of which took the defenders completely by surprise. In the capital, its passing was overshadowed by the triumphant news of the destruction of two Zeppelins which had taken part in an abortive overnight raid on the Midlands.

Far from London, as midnight approached, Second Lieutenant, Ian Pyott dispatched *LZ 34* north of Hartlepool. A stream of explosive, incendiary and tracer bullets from his Lewis gun ignited the hydrogen inside the Zeppelin and, like a massive fiery torch which lit up the night for miles around, she plunged into the sea. A few hours later the same fate befell *LZ 21* when she was attacked off Yarmouth. No crewmen survived from either ship, but the after-action report on the destruction of *LZ 21*, noted that the gunners were still valiantly firing as the dirigible, in her death throes, began her dive into the sea. It was apparent to the jubilant staff in the War Office that bright and hazy morning that, in the face of such losses, the Germans could not continue the Zeppelin raids in their current form for long. Less than six hours after the sea extinguished the flames from *LZ 21*, no one in London was aware that, above them, the noise from a single German aeroplane heralded the arrival of a new and much more dangerous threat. With what, at the time, was considered the most impetuous impudence, a solitary German single-engine biplane, known as an L.V.G., swept unseen over Central London. By all accounts what prompted this bold venture has never been clearly established. What is certain is that Leutnant Walther Ilges, the plane's captain and observer, and his pilot, Deck Officer Paul Brandt, flew undetected in broad daylight to the heart of the British Empire. At 11.50 hours six, 12-kilogram bombs, aimed at the Admiralty and Whitehall, were thrown by hand from the aircraft.

The bombs missed their mark by the proverbial mile and a series of small unexplained explosions rang out between Brompton Road and Victoria Station. For those on the ground the detonations were the first indication of the presence of a hostile aircraft. At 106 Brompton Road, then a baker's shop, a chimney was destroyed. At 13 Lowndes Square, a bomb landed on a wooden roof and detonated, sending fragments two floors down into the basement kitchen. Next, at 15 Pavillion Road, an office was wrecked, and then in Eccleston Mews, Belgravia, a roof was damaged and some windows broken. In Belgravia Mews East, opposite No.23, a bomb detonated on the cobbles breaking windows and riddling two garages with splinters. Here two men were slightly injured. Finally, the last bomb struck the Victoria Palace Music Hall, opposite the station. It destroyed some five feet of a dressing room roof and injured one woman who, although not seriously physically hurt, suffered considerable distress and shock. In all, four men and five women were slightly wounded. It wasn't until 12.34 hours that the Admiralty Air Department was notified of the raid. By then Ilges and Brandt were well on their way home, unfortunately their luck deserted them over the English Channel when the single engine on the L.G.V. failed. Brandt managed to stretch the glide of his aircraft to the far shore of the Channel, where both men were captured after making a forced landing on the coast near Boulogne. So ended the first aeroplane raid on the capital. Like many others to follow, though, the bombs missed their target and the crew failed to get home.

The incident was unparalleled in British history. London had been bombed from the air at midday, when the people in the streets were at their busiest. Initially, few in authority grasped the significance of the solo effort; particularly as little damage was done. Others, however, were less sanguine. Some had already realised the proud integrity of the British Isles, which for centuries had relied on sea power, was lost when Bleriot landed in Dover in 1909. The first unopposed bombing of the capital reinforced this belief. *The Times*' editorial the following day pointed out that the Zeppelins were large, costly, very vulnerable and could only operate at night, but aeroplanes were, by comparison, quick, cheap and much more elusive. Even more vociferous was Charles Grey, an outspoken aviation enthusiast and founder of *The Aeroplane*. He foresaw the day when massed bombers would attack the capital, breach the inadequate defences and rain bombs down on its citizens. He said: 'When aeroplane raids start, and prove more damaging than the airship raids, the authorities cannot say that have not had a fair warning of what to expect.'[1]

How right he was. The Germans had concluded in the autumn of 1916 that the Zeppelin conquest of London was no longer feasible. They decided that the assault must continue, but that it would be the most modern aeroplanes (then under development) that would carry the fight to the enemy capital. It was estimated that just six of the planned new machines could carry the same bomb load as a Zeppelin. In complete secrecy they set about establishing a new squadron for the task of subduing England from the air. The unit, which was officially named Kagol 3, became known as the *England Geschwader* and was commanded by Hauptman Ernst Brandenberg. He was an experienced observer, a natural leader and a capable organizer. Only thirty-four-years-old he had been severely wounded in the infantry in 1914 and had been considered unfit for further front line service. Undeterred, he had joined the German air service. His task with the new squadron was to strike at British morale and crush their will to resist, and at the same time dislocate vital communications and the war industry. This was to be achieved principally by attacking London and the coastal ports, targeting the vast depots and supply dumps that surrounded them. To all intents and purposes it was the true start of strategic bombing, the Zeppelins having failed to make much of an impression, but it was a tall order for just one man and a squadron of bombers.

The tool, which was to be the instrument of this new strategy, was the Gotha G IV Bomber. Deliveries of the new aircraft were due to start in February 1917, with the aircraft being despatched to new bomber bases near Ghent just 170 miles from London. This large twin-engine biplane required a crew of three and was capable of carrying a bomb load of 300 kilograms to the British capital. The German plans for the bombing of Britain were built around the delivery of the new Gotha bombers but it was not until March 1917, after manufacturing delays, that the aircraft arrived and the squadron began training in earnest for the assault on London.

The paramount requirements for secrecy meant that only those in the high command and in the *England Geschwader* knew of the proposed plans. Because of this veil of secrecy there was no official reason for other enterprising German pilots not to have another crack at London. Consequently, the first night raid by an aircraft on the capital was yet another unauthorised solo effort. It was a surprise not only for London, but also for those in Belgian confidentially plotting the destruction of the city from the air. On 6-7 May a lone Albatros C VII, piloted by Offizierstellvertreter Rudolf Klimke and his observer Oberleutnant Walther Leon, obtained local authority from their squadron commander to bomb the capital. Aided by a full moon and favourable winds, they reached the target at about 01.00 hours and dropped five small 12-kilogram bombs along a line from Holloway to Hackney. Casualties were light with one fatality, two injuries and minimal damage. The Albatros and its crew returned safely, but the jubilant reception was short lived. Both men and the squadron commander were severely reprimanded for the attack when higher authorities became aware of it. London had not been bombed for some six months and it was intended that the first attack by the Gothas would be both a strategic and tactical surprise. Unauthorised raids by single aircraft dropping ineffectual quantities of bombs had no part in this plan.

Brandenburgh's plans for a surprise strategic attack on London were eventually scuppered by one of this country's traditional allies, the weather, albeit aided and abetted by pressure from the German High Command to begin the offensive. He was forced to commit his Gotha's to raids on Folkestone and later Sheerness, and these incursions were, quite rightly, interpreted as a prelude to an assault on the capital.

It was not until 13 June 1917, that the intent to bomb London, turned into deadly reality. In terms of casualties it was the worst raid of the war, killing 160 people and injuring a further 414. In addition, one person was killed and a further nineteen injured by anti-aircraft fire. Physiologically it had the most profound impact on the confidence of the British public.

The morning of the raid was fine, and the area between Belgium and the Thames Estuary, lay between two anticyclones in which, critically, the wind velocity was almost zero and the visibility reasonable. Just after breakfast a formation of eighteen Gotha bombers lumbered into the air and climbed steadily to 12-14,000 feet and headed straight for London. The raider's numbers were reduced by unreliability and only fourteen reached their target, flying in a loose diamond formation. Most observers recorded hearing the sinister, undulating hum of the twin Mercedes engines of the Gothas as they approached their target. The unsynchronised throbbing of these engines produced their own distinctive sound long before the aircraft were seen and the loud volume was thought to be because of the number of aircraft flying tightly together. Although bombs were dropped over a wide area, the central objective appeared to be the City of London itself, with St Paul's Cathedral and Tower Bridge providing the necessary landmarks.

The Gothas dropped several groups of bombs, the first between East Ham and Royal Albert Docks, the second seemed to be aimed at the City itself, with Liverpool Station as the target. The third and fourth clusters landed on Southwark and Dalston, and the final batch at Saffron Hill. No official warning of their approach was made, and to many, the aircraft looked like harmless silver insects, glinting in the sun. Some witnesses said they looked quite beautiful and no one on the ground was aware of perilous situation they were in. For most people it was only at around 11.40 hours, when the first bombs began to fall and the sound of explosions echoed around the city, that it dawned on them that a raid was in progress. Around Liverpool Street Station some seventy-two bombs landed in a radius of less than a mile. They struck the ground in a concentrated pattern when compared to the previous experience of the Zeppelins, three of the bombs actually hitting the terminus.

Despite the sound of the explosions, some workers, particularly those employed in noisy factories, still had no idea a raid was in progress. Mrs R. Tripp, who worked in a government factory in Central Street, recalled the following:

> The machinery was going, and I and all the girls were happily working when, all of a sudden, we felt the building shake. Someone came rushing in and said 'An air raid, quick'. I was one of the first down the stairs and into the street, when a constable PC Alfred Smith of the Metropolitan Force, rushed up and pushed me and all the others back again; he had just shut the door when a bomb dropped and he was killed along with some passers-by. I was buried in the debris for hours, but suffered only shock.[2]

Sadly, Police Constable Smith has the dubious record of being the first of many policemen to be killed whilst on duty in air raids on London. After the attack, at a public meeting addressed by the Home Secretary, Sir George Cave, and the Commissioner of the Metropolitan Police, Edward Henry, details were provided of a public fund for Smith's widow and child, and a citation was read out which said:

> Indifferent to the danger he ran over to force 153 girls back into their munitions factory on Central Street when they tried to leave during

a Taube [actually a Gotha] bomber raid. He managed to push them back off the street to safety but lost his own life in the process.[3]

Smith was right to push the women back into the building; the biggest killer of these bombs was the lethal shards of metal which sliced through flesh and bone. It was, generally speaking, much safer to be inside a building rather than in the street. There was, as will be seen, the risk of a direct hit but this was lower than being caught out in the open and struck by fragments. Police Constable Smith's courageous act is not forgotten and there is an inscribed tablet in his memory in Postman's Park, Aldersgate Street. He was buried in the cemetery in Stoke Newington where his grave can still be seen today, but like many First World War headstones, the details are beginning to fade.

Liverpool Street Station, as we have heard, was hit by three, 50-kilogram, bombs and of these one failed to explode. The two that detonated fell close together; one on the edge of Platform No.9 blew the third coach of the Hunstanton train to pieces and set the train on fire. This killed four people and injured a further seventeen. The second bomb exploded on the opposite side of the same platform and set fire to two coaches. These were serving as medical assessment coaches in which military doctors were examining members of the Great Eastern Railway staff. The bomb set fire to some gas cylinders in the coaches and three people were burned to death on the train including a Royal Army Medical Corps Sergeant. In total, sixteen persons were killed and fifteen injured in and around the station. The fire took an hour or so to bring under control. A good deal of glass was broken, but traffic was not interrupted and little significant damage was caused to the station.

Another 50-kilogram bomb landed on 65 Fenchurch Street which was an ordinary four-storey building. The bomb burst through the first two floors before detonating. Ten people in the upper part of the building, which was completely demolished, were killed. The nose of the bomb, not surprisingly, came through to the ground floor, as did a few fragments, but otherwise there was little damage at this level. The basement was practically intact. There was a clear message here for the protection of the public, but it would take time and bitter experience before the lesson was properly learned.

Further along, at 109 Fenchurch Street, a much smaller 12-kilogram bomb detonated by the chimney on the roof. The housekeeper's wife, who was on the top storey, had her head severed from her body.

Bombs that failed to explode could also kill buy their sheer weight and momentum. At 11 Billiter Street, a 50-kilogram bomb passed through the roof of the building and smashed through four floors to finish up in the basement where it lay on the stone paving. Two people were killed by it on the upper floors as it tore its way through the building.

At Shoreditch several bombs were dropped killing and injuring many people and causing total confusion. They were running in all directions in panic. A number of horses also took fright at the sound of the explosions and bolted. In Tabernacle Square, Police Constable Charles Penn was at his post when he saw a pair of frightened horses attached to a cart racing towards him in sheer terror. Bravely he caught hold of the reins and after being dragged for seventy yards he managed to bring them under control. Having tethered them he returned to his post where he gave first aid to an injured woman. Bombs were still dropping and another horse with a heavily laden van bolted down the road towards him. He dashed forward and succeeded in bringing this frightened animal to a halt as well. Constable Penn paying no heed to his own safety warned more people to take cover and stopped a further two runaway horses, before assisting with the removal of injured people to hospital. For his outstanding conduct he was awarded the King's Police Medal, a financial reward from the Bow Street Fund and a silver medal from the Royal Society for the Prevention of Cruelty to Animals.[4]

One their way home the Gotha bombers released the last of their bombs over Poplar, causing the most awful tragedy. It has already been explained that, in general, the safest place during a raid was inside a building unless it was subject to a direct hit; that is exactly what happened at one small infants' school. A 50-kilogram bomb crashed into the Upper North Street School. It passed through the roof and first floor before bursting in a ground-level classroom. By then the bomb had had its tail ripped off, but the main charge in the forward portion exploded, creating utter carnage. It killed eighteen children and injured over thirty others; two of the dead were killed by the bomb striking them as it passed through the upper floors.

Pupils at the school later recorded their horror at what had happened. Mrs T. Myers, then a young pupil, was in the terrible position of knowing her younger sister was close to the point of the blast:

> I was a child of 11 attending North Street School, Poplar, when the deafening explosion came, thinking only of my little sister aged 5, I rushed down the stairs with another pupil. I forced my way along a corridor which was filled with men and women frantically searching for their children and all were screaming and shouting. I could not find my sister anywhere and it was two hours later when my father found her dead in the mortuary.[5]

Only two of the dead were over five years old. A week later the young victims were buried, three privately, but the remaining fifteen were laid to rest in a common grave in the East London Cemetery. A sixteenth coffin containing unidentified remains was also buried with them. The tomb can still be seen today. There is also a memorial to the children, paid for by public subscription, in Poplar Recreation Ground off Woodstock Road.

The German propaganda war was lost along with the children's lives in the instant of the explosion. At the funeral memorial cards were handed out to the relatives. Part of it read:

> The Germans don't kill women and little children from the sky for the mere fun of the thing. It is part of their scheme of frightfulness. They believe that the murder of the little ones will cause the parents to revolt and overthrow authority, and by that means peace will come. Of course they are wrong again.[6]

Retaliation and revenge were the understandable cries of the bereaved on the streets. For those responsible for the defence of the capital the ramifications of this deadly raid were immediate, and all aspects of its defence were subject to critical review. No one then, or later in the Second World War, grasped the key lesson that terror alone would not succeed; it would stiffen not stifle resistance. This appalling incident, more than any other, was to have a major impact on the plans and preparation for evacuation of children in the Second World War. The need to protect the young, the elderly and the infirm was clearly established that day.

Much of the outcry reinforced the view that the Germans were evil, ruthless and uncivilised killers whose bombing of defenceless women and children was unjustifiable. Not all saw it that way though, Lord Montagu of Beaulieu told the House of Commons in late June 1917:

> The Germans have the perfect right to bomb London. It is defended by guns and aeroplanes, and it is the chief centre for the production of munitions. We are, therefore, but deluding ourselves in talking about London being an undefended city and about the Germans in attacking it being guilty of an act unworthy of a civilised nation.[7]

Characteristically, the bomb droppers also saw their actions as entirely justifiable. Brandenburg was acclaimed a hero overnight and the papers announced triumphantly that 'Fortress London' had been bombed. The Gotha commander was summoned to the Supreme Headquarters to be congratulated and to recount the details of the raid in person. The Kaiser and his staff were thrilled at the success, particularly as according to Brandenburg most of the bombs landed in the docks, amongst the city warehouses, on a station and probably Tower Bridge as well. To put icing on the cake, the new Gotha aircraft had flown well and all had landed safely back at their aerodrome. After enjoying a short weekend leave fate intervened, and Brandenburg was severely burned when the aircraft taking him back to Ghent crashed on take-off and caught fire.

Back in London the repercussions of the raid were still being felt. The effect of the Gothas was much more shocking to the public than the Zeppelins. The latter had snuck in stealthily and relied on dark moonless nights to reach their targets. The public implicitly understood the difficulty in finding and shooting them down. The Gothas were different as, bold as brass, they had struck at the heart of the nation, for the most part unopposed, and had suffered no casualties. There was an element of disbelief that this could be allowed to happen to a nation whose empire was at its zenith and who ruled much of the world. Three key questions asked were, why was there no system of public warnings, what could be done to reduce the casualties and why had the defences proved so inadequate?

It seems obvious now that setting up an air raid warning system to alert the public was an absolute imperative, but incredibly it was not the case then. To the politicians and generals there was more at stake. The howls from the press and others after the first major raid forced them to address the issue but finally, after much deliberation on 26 June they decided, once again, against issuing alerts.

There were conflicting theories about the effects of such public warnings. It had already been established that it was not the explosions, but the bomb splinters, which caused most casualties. The concern was that, in future raids, if warnings were given, people would flood out into the streets to view the proceedings instead of taking cover. In doing so they would become more vulnerable to the bombing. Many people were actually quite excited about the raid and, like modern day 'rubber neckers' at accidents, ghoulishly wished they had been there to see the spectacle. Another theory was that warnings would serve to spread panic amongst the population. These factors though concealed the real reason for not giving public warnings. The major concern was that alarms, either false or positive, would cause stoppages in critical war industries. Later there was some evidence to support this view, as after an air raid warning some workers would automatically take the rest of the day off.

The active defence was also found lacking and, to add insult to injury, neither the guns nor the defending fighters managed to shoot down any of the enemy aircraft. Finally, as already noted, in addition to the casualties caused by the enemy, one man was killed by an anti-aircraft shell which failed to explode as designed but did so when it fell back to earth. A further nineteen people were injured by falling fragments from shells which had exploded over the city. The danger from anti-aircraft shell which failed to detonate at the right time was to kill many people, and the number of casualties increased in proportion to the size of the barrages. There was a clear need to re-design the fuzes so that if they failed to detonate at the required time then there was another separate, self-destruct system which would detonate them before they fell back to earth. Then the danger would be reduced to the risk of being struck by falling metal fragments. But, like everything else, all this would take time.

During the raid, an unexploded bomb had fallen into the corner of the now dry moat around the Tower of London. The curator asked to keep the bomb after it had been rendered safe. It would, he said, be an interesting exhibit for future generations. On 19 June the General HQ Home Forces in Whitehall wrote to say the bomb had a damaged fuze which could not be removed and therefore it had had to be destroyed.

After the raid, studies were undertaken into the types and effectiveness of the new bombs being dropped by the Germans. The 50-kilogram bombs were found to be quite unreliable in operation. Of the total of sixty-nine dropped, five seem to have burst in the air and a further twenty-three failed to explode on impact. Ignoring the airbursts this gives a failure rate of thirty-three per cent. An examination of the recovered bomb fuzes revealed that they were of a percussion impact type and no explanation could be given for the bombs that airburst. It was found that the 50-kilogram bombs would easily penetrate the roof of a building and, in all but the most exceptional cases, explode in the attic space. However, the large high explosive charge of some sixteen kilograms meant that it would cause significant damage at least two further floors below.

It was discovered the 12-kilogram bombs, as well as containing a main charge of TNT, also had a small tin filled with a mixture of TNT and red phosphorous to act as a spotting charge at the base of the bomb. This would produce a white cloud of smoke at the point of impact when the bomb burst. The official British reports at the time, perhaps reflecting the mood of the nation, noted that:

It will doubtless be stated by the Germans that the phosphorous is to give a white cloud on detonating to show the spot at which the bomb burst. But though this is partially true, the chief object of the phosphorous is evidently to poison wounds as a smoke cloud could be produced equally well by several non-poisonous chemicals.[8]

The 12-kilogram bombs had a fuze which could be set to operate on impact or after a one-fiftieth of a second delay. The latter would let the bomb penetrate the roof of a building before exploding. When set without the delay, it was established that the small 12-kilogram bombs burst on impact even when they struck a thin slate roof. In this instance the room immediately below was subject to lethal splinters, but below this there was comparative safety. The failure rate of the smaller bombs was much lower at only 7.7 per cent.

At the Tower of London, the attack raised the question of the admission of the public during raids. On the day of the raid, visitors in the White Tower were asked to go down into the dungeons, an obvious place of safety. There was concern that if it became known that it was bomb proof, it may lead to a rush of people to the Tower to obtain shelter at small cost, or nothing on a free day. It was also suggested that if a bomb landed on the Tower when a large number of the public were inside, it might lead to serious consequences. The real reason for the concern, however, which was only alluded to, was that, if as a safe haven the dungeons were full of the public, they might not be available for the privileged residents living in the Tower. The eventual consensus was that it was best to stop admission when air raid warning was received, but not to force out people who were in the Tower. It should be noted that at this stage of the war an air raid warning system for the general public was still not in operation although warnings would be passed directly to the Military in the Tower.

On the morning of 7 July 1917, another large anticyclone extended from Iceland to the North Sea. The wind was light and there was little cloud. By 10.00 hours over London the sky was covered with a layer of high stratus cloud and there was a hazy atmosphere. These were, once again, ideal raiding conditions, and by then the Germans were already well on their way. The badly injured Brandenburg had been replaced by a new commander, Rudolf Kleine, and he was eager to emulate his predecessor's success. He led twenty-two Gothas in a loose formation across the North Sea where they were sighted at some 12-14,000 feet crossing the coast south of Clacton. By pre-arranged plan they headed northwest so as to come round and attack London from the north, they then turned east and flew straight for the coast and home. They were engaged by a number of anti-aircraft guns along the route which caused the bombers to spread out quite widely. As the formation turned south for its final approach to the capital, the Gothas seemed to split into three groups, consisting of two flights of nine and another four in a tail. They started releasing their bombs at about 10.20 hours.

The first missiles released landed in the Stoke Newington, Edmonton and Tottenham areas. Shortly afterwards the City and the banks of the Thames were hit. The City police recorded the attack only lasted three minutes starting at 10.32 hours. Within the City a total of twenty-six bombs were dropped (twenty-one x 50kilogram and five x 12kilogram) of which seven failed to explode. Severe damage was caused to several office buildings and warehouses, and in Cox's Court, Little Britain, four houses were set on fire and gutted. There were seven fatalities, all of which were men, and a further nineteen men were injured along with six women and one child.

After this another salvo of bombs fell near the banks of the Thames as well as on vessels in the river. Three bombs were dropped in Bishopsgate Goods Station; one fell in Bethnal Green, which, although it failed to explode, injured two men, two women and six children. One 50-kilogram bomb was dropped in Buxton Street Spitalfields, but did little damage.

Conversely a small 12-kilogram bomb proved that in the right circumstances it could be just as lethal as the larger bombs, with one falling on Tower Hill with devastating results. It landed on the premises of W.J. Murray, killing seven men and a child, and injuring further fifteen persons. The blast also destroyed three vans and killed the same number of horses.

For all the gunners' efforts no aircraft were hit or downed over London. However, the guns fired a much larger number of rounds and, predictably, the level of casualties from anti-aircraft fire was greater. The toll on London's civilians was ten killed and fifty-five injured by falling shells which detonated when they struck the ground. In the worst incident in Albion Street Rotherhithe, a woman and two men were killed and a further four women and five children injured. It was of considerable concern to those in authority that twenty per cent of the fatalities and nearly thirty per cent of the wounded were attributable to friendly fire.

The newly issued anti-aircraft guns that ringed the capital were themselves proving less than reliable. At the Finchley gun site, Lieutenant H. Wilkinson RNVR reported that his crew only fired a total of eight rounds from their 3-inch 20-hundredweight piece. On loading the sixth round, the breach failed to close sufficiently to fire but, after recocking, the round was kicked home. It got worse, with the seventh and eighth rounds a lead hammer had to be used to thump the breach closed. The ninth round jammed completely and was only moved after a quarter of an hour with the aid of a wrench, a sledge hammer and a baulk of timber. Investigations later discovered that cause of the jamming was a stamping on the breach of the gun which very slightly distorted the face. When the metal warmed up during rapid fire, it expanded, and this was sufficient to prevent the breach mechanism being closed after firing a few rounds.

One bomb struck the Central Telegraph Office in Newgate Street, detonating on the roof. Such was the force of the explosion that it shattered extensive wooden hutments which had been erected on the roof in support of the War Office. It then caught fire. Casualties were fortunately light as much of the building had been evacuated. However, a portion of the parapet of the roof was blown down and an old soldier doing sentry duty in the street below was killed by the falling rubble. The direct hit on the building was one of the very few that could be claimed by the Germans as being a legitimate target. It was of course struck more by luck than judgement.

In all, seventy-one high explosive bombs were dropped in the City and in the Metropolitan Police District before the Gothas departed for home. The total casualties from both the bombs and friendly fire were fifty-four killed and 190 injured.

The fires that resulted from the raid so strained the fire brigade and such was the fear of the threat of future raids that representations were made to the War Cabinet. As a result, instructions were given for the return from the armed forces of all those uniformed firemen that had joined the colours. The brigade was also forced to introduce a system of co-ordination for all the different fire brigades that operated in the London area.

This second daylight raid on London aroused even more intense indignation amongst the population. How could these lumbering bombers be allowed to disgorge their loads over the capital unopposed? To the man in the street it seemed that the politicians and the military, who had both promised much after the June raid, were still powerless to prevent the Germans bombing at will.

There was also much disquiet in the Commons and many MPs felt that the second success of the raiders was a serious blow to national pride. Londoners in general felt that the defenders had done little to confront the Gothas and that much more needed to be done to protect the capital's population. Several other issues were also raised.

The first was, once more, the thorny question of public warnings. People wanted to know why the Government was so perverse in its refusal to give notice of incoming raids, especially as private warnings had been issued to the military, police and the some other official organisations. Despite the strength of feeling about the lack of warnings, nothing seemed to change the Government view that general alerts would have an unacceptably adverse effect on production. Prior to this raid several private warnings had caused factories to briefly close down, but in the event no raids took place. The worry was that if these warnings were broadcast more widely there would be long stoppages at the munitions factories which could in turn result at shortages at the front. Consequently, there would be greater loss of life in the trenches and it was recognised that the price paid by the fighting men was high enough already.

Although a procedure was officially in place to deal with unexploded bombs, it seems this had not percolated down to those on the ground. More often than not, they were still recovered by the police and taken to the local station. This is precisely what happened to one of the unexploded bombs in the 7 July raid. Police Constable G. Asquith was on duty in Tooley Street, Southwark, when he was summoned to deal with a bomb which had penetrated all five floors of Messrs Barns, Jam and Pickle factory, in Battle Bridge Lane. The bomb was covered in grease, so he wrapped it in a sack and carried it off to Tower Bridge Police Station, where he laid it on the table in the charge room. Bombing was still a novelty and that probably explains why many other police officers wanted to see and touch the recovered exhibit, one constable apparently even brought his children into Station to see it. It would seem that, at that point, the potential dangers were pointed out and the bomb was taken to the cells. A couple of hours later the officer who had brought his children to see the bomb had the impudence to complain that it was dangerous and that it should not have been touched.

A similar incident apparently occurred with an unexploded shell. To highlight the dangers of the number of blind munitions falling back to earth, one MP produced a blind shell which, he said, had crashed through two floors of his city office. It was passed down the bench for inspection, but the curiosity to handle it died when another Member pointed out that it had not exploded 'up to this moment'.

The new attacks also raised some potentially interesting legal problems. The Law Journal commented on the legitimacy of diverting bombs by using special roofs or sandbags on to other premises. It noted that it was technically illegal to construct something on your land which diverted a nuisance onto your neighbour's land. For example, in 1911, in a test case in South Africa, a farmer had escaped a plague of locusts by lighting fires on the perimeter of his land and diverting the insects onto his neighbour's. The judgement reached in this case was, that when a nuisance was on his land, measures could be taken to abate it at his own peril, but not at the expense of his neighbours. However, before the nuisance reached his land he could deflect it at the expense of others.

At first sight therefore, it appeared that owners could protect their premises and divert bombs onto others. Unfortunately, however, it was noted in common law, that the owner of land also owns all of that vertically above and below that land. It seems, consequently, that as bombs were dropping almost vertically, in the eyes of the law, it was already on his land before impact and consequently it could not be diverted. So a person who built a deflector which pushed a bomb onto someone else's property was essentially breaking the law. This was, of course, all hypothetical, constructing such deflectors was impractical, and even if they had been built the bombs would have detonated on impact, so the obscure point of law was never put to the test.

General Smuts, who had witnessed the July raid, was put in charge of the defences, a job he carried out with great energy. He quickly recognised the weakness of a dispersed command and advocated a single authority to control and co-ordinate all the defences. The result was that the London Air Defence Area (LADA) was formed to control all the observer corps personnel, anti-aircraft guns, fighter aircraft and warning systems. The guns in particular were redeployed to try and form a barrier to the north and east of the capital. This transformed the protection of London and its environs from an almost defenceless city to much more of a fortified stronghold. The task also convinced Smuts of the immense potential of strategic air warfare. He had the intellect and foresight to realize that, in a time in the not so distant future, aerial operations would devastate enemy lands by the destruction of industrial and populous centres. This would be on a vast scale and would become the principal operation of war in future years.

The Gothas never attacked London again in daylight but carried out several other raids against coastal towns. It was during these they realised that all the defences had been considerably stiffened and that further daylight attacks, particularly on London, would lead to unsustainable losses. As a result, they were forced to reconsider their tactics. The obvious answer was night bombing, and although this had its own difficulties, for example navigation and night flying were still in their infancy, it was preferable to facing the growing strength of the guns and Royal Flying Corps. The problem, or at least the problem the Germans perceived they had, was that they could not now attack pinpoint targets. In reality, despite reports to the contrary, they had not achieved the accuracy they claimed in daylight anyway. For the night missions the crews were given the freedom of action to strike military targets of opportunity, in essence, a licence for totally indiscriminate bombing.

For the population of London, the switch to night bombing was a reversion to the days of the Zeppelins, but there was a subtle change. The massive bulk of the dirigibles and their silver skins meant that they were easy to see on moonlit nights. Londoners had soon learnt that against them a bright full moon was their protector, keeping the dirigibles at home. In contrast, the Gothas needed the moonlight to enable the crews to fly at night.

For the defenders, who at least had some experience of night flying and hunting Zeppelins, the task of finding the Gothas at night was practically impossible. They were smaller, quicker, harder to hit and less vulnerable to machine-gun fire when struck. It was thought that guns and searchlights would be more effective than aircraft, and they were re-deployed in a rough semi-circle twenty-five miles east of Charing Cross. Another proposal was the deployment of a balloon and apron barrage. These consisted of three balloons each 500 yards apart and linked by horizontal cables. From these at twenty-five yard intervals vertical steel wires were hung. These steel curtains were intended to be placed so as to guard key points. The first trial in Richmond Park on 21 September 1917, got off to the most appalling start. As preparations were being made to release the balloons, a violent gust of wind caught them. In an almost instinctive attempt to control the contraption two of the handlers, Air Mechanics H.E. James and W.J. Pegge clung on to their handling lines trying to hold the balloons down. Both were swept aloft and fell to their deaths. James managed cling on until the balloon was about 1,000 feet and then fell. Pegge managed to climb up into the balloons rigging but later fell from an unknown height over Croydon. Despite this setback several balloon aprons were to become operational by 1918.

The first Gotha night raid was on the night of 4-5 September 1917, and the casualties were nineteen killed and a further seventy-one people injured. Only five enemy aircraft reached London which was bombed from 23.20 hours through to 00.10 hours. Bombs landed all over the metropolis. One aircraft, released four 50-kilogram bombs evidently aiming at Charing Cross Station. The first fell in Agar Street, on the Strand outside the main entrance to Charing Cross Hospital, it killed two Canadian soldiers, a woman, and injured several others. Many of the windows in the hospital were shattered showering some patients in glass. The next landed on the Little Theatre in Durham Street, doing considerable damage to the building but not causing any casualties. The third bomb fell in Victoria Embankment Gardens, and the fourth, and most-deadly, detonated on Victoria Embankment close to Cleopatra's Needle. A tramcar which was passing at the time was peppered with fragments and wrecked. Of those on board, two men including the driver and a woman were killed and a further eight injured. According to Mr A.E. Green, a conductor on another tram, his vehicle was about to swing off Westminster Bridge Road when the condemned single-decker appeared. The driver of this shouted 'Hi mate I am two minutes late. Will you let me pull out in front of you?' Green's driver agreed and let the tram through; they were then slightly delayed before they set off along the Embankment. The late tram ahead of them was just opposite Cleopatra's Needle when the bomb detonated. Apparently the driver was still pulling at his controls to stop the tram as his life ebbed away. The damage to Cleopatra's Needle was never repaired and today stands testament to the incident; a plaque details the night's events. Fragment damage to the base of the obelisk and pedestal of the right hand sphinx are plainly visible as are penetration marks on the bronze flanks and paw of the sphinx itself.

This single attack was followed by what was to become known in London as the 'Harvest Moon' offensive. It was to be the first taste of a sustained bombing campaign. It was a mini Blitz, and like the Blitz that would follow, the raiders carried a higher proportion of incendiaries than seen hitherto. The first raid on the night of 24-25 September began with sixteen Gothas, but of those only three managed to reach and bomb the capital. One 50-kilogram bomb landed in front of the old Bedford Hotel where it detonated, killing thirteen and injuring twenty-two. A plaque on the rebuilt Hotel now marks the spot.

The following night another fifteen aircraft set off for London, but again only three crews braved the defences to actually bomb the city, most of the other aircraft attacking Dover and targets in Kent. After a brief respite the next attack, on 28-29 September, was planned to be the heaviest so far, in which a force of twenty-five Gothas and two new machines would aim to bomb Central London. The new aircraft, which were recalled from the Eastern front, to take part in the operation, were known as Riesenflugzeug or Giant aircraft. A number of designs were made, but the one used against London was the Mark VI. The use of the Giant was significant. They were, as the name suggests, massive aircraft, technologically advanced for their time, well defended and capable of carrying a much larger payload of some 1,000 kilograms of bombs to London. To keep them in the air they had four engines in two nacelles driving two pusher and two tractor propellers. Their wingspan was about thirty-six feet, bigger than that of a Second World War Lancaster. Like many aircraft of the time they needed constant care and, in the case of the Giants, mechanics had stations alongside the engines to perform vital maintenance operations whilst the aircraft was in flight. The official British wartime analysis of the aircraft was somewhat scathing it noted that: 'The 'Giant' is a heavy lumbering machine, and its occupants are not usually of the first rank amongst German airmen.'[9]

This was propaganda at its best; the truth was that the aircraft was a fine flying machine. It paid the ultimate compliment to the crews, in a total of twenty-eight sorties against England, not one of the Giants fell to the defenders.

In the event the weather once again saved the capital, of the few aircraft that crossed the coast most scattered their bombs over a wide area, with none landing on London. They tried again on the following night, 29-30 September. This time some of the aircraft did manage to penetrate the defences and bombed the hapless people below.

By now, at last, there was a system of public warnings in place. After experiments with whistles and car horns, the London officials decided to try the bugler system as used in Paris to warn of approaching enemy aircraft. Several hundred boy scouts responded to an appeal for buglers. The Home Office promptly disowned the scheme, because of the fear that the boy scouts might be injured whilst on air raid duty. A businessman then offered to pay for a Lloyd's insurance policy to cover 350 of the lads. This would provide for £50 if any were killed on duty or, in case of injury, half the sum was available for medical expenses. Eventually it was agreed that Police Officers mounted on bicycles would ride through the streets with whistles and white placards with the simple words, 'POLICE WARNING TAKE COVER' in bold red paint.

There had been enough casualties by now for people to get over their inquisitiveness. When warnings were sounded, pedestrians could be seen running to take cover and omnibuses and cars seemed to speed up to get out of the centre of London. Many people started taking cover in the underground and there were some signs of panic. One report from the Oval Station suggested that people were in danger of being forced on to the line because of the numbers trying to get out of danger. Some tube travellers had difficulty in getting out of a train as the platform was so packed.

The bombers returned for a third successive night and this time it was estimated that six Gothas managed to penetrate to the heart of

London bombing between 19.40 and 20.45 hours. The 'Harvest Moon' offensive ended with a raid on the night of 1-2 October, and was the sixth attack in eight nights. But like the previous day only six of the attacking force pressed on to London.

Over the whole period, sixty-nine people were killed and 260 wounded, mostly in the capital. There were some signs that the bombers were having the desired effect. It was not the physical effects of the bombs themselves, but the fact that there was serious disruption of people's lives. In the raids, the bombers took off singly and then proceeded over the capital in a steady stream, this meant that the disruption often lasted for many hours. The transportation systems shut down, the capital was darkened and people were stranded for hours at stations, bus and tram stops. More seriously, as feared, there was a clear impact on war production. A study ordered by the Minister of Munitions, Churchill, revealed that, at the key Woolwich Arsenal facility, after the first raid on 25 September, only one third of the night shift at the filling factory had turned up for work. Production that evening was twenty percent less than normal, in later raids production dropped to an alarming sixty percent. Although only a small sample, Churchill concluded that the disruption at Woolwich was typical of what was happening over a wide area of London.

The situation was not aided by the press who had given the attacks much coverage. Alarmist headlines, rumours and, in many cases an honest lack of sleep, made nerves begin to jangle. Two newspapers hinted that the Prime Minister, Lloyd George, had abandoned his official duties for fear of air raids and had retreated to his country home. He angrily challenged this assertion and was publicly awarded both damages and an unreserved apology.

In the raids, the destruction caused by the anti-aircraft barrage was reported to be considerable and covered a wide area. Damage was distributed more or less evenly from Kingston-on-Thames in the southwest to Leytonstone in the northeast and from Hampstead in the northwest to Bromley in the southeast. The scale of the barrage was quite significant. For example, on the raids on 28 and 29 September and 1 October, 7,162; 8,961 and 9,353 rounds were fired respectively. With a failure rate probably running at around ten percent it meant that approximately 2,500 live shells fell back on to London. Fortunately, casualties attributed to the guns were quite light with four killed and fifty injured on the three nights.

The casualties were serious enough, however, to prompt an investigation to analyse the effects on the ground of the different types of shell fired. Three types of shell were used, high explosive, shrapnel and a new incendiary design. The high explosive shell was designed to burst near the enemy with the fragments doing the damage. These shell had a Number 44/80 Fuze, operating on time only and not impact. Generally, if the time element failed and the projectile fell back to earth, they would not explode on impact with a structure like a roof, which fractured when hit. They would, however, detonate if they struck a very hard surface like a road or pavement. When they detonated in the air the shell would often produce quite large fragments and some of these did significant damage to slate roofs. However, provided people stayed at least one floor below the roof they were reasonably safe other than from a direct hit from an unexploded shell.

The shrapnel shells that were used posed a problem, in that the design was such, that when the shell functioned correctly the complete empty body would naturally fall back to earth. In the 'Harvest Moon' offensive, these empty bodies did considerable damage around Charing Cross and Greenwich. Owing to their weight and size they had quite significant penetrating power and could go straight through a three-storey house from roof to the ground floor. The brass fuze bodies, being small and compact, also penetrated a long way through houses. Finally, the shrapnel balls themselves were recovered in large numbers, but in general they only broke slates and tiles on roofs.

The last type of shell, the AZ (Anti-Zeppelin) was fortunately only fired in small numbers, but it did cause a serious fire risk. As the name suggests, they were intended for use against Zeppelins, and their vulnerable hydrogen cells, and it is not clear why they were used against the Gothas and Giants. When fired the shells would ascend to a set height at which the fuze would function. When this happened a special incendiary composition (Dr Whiteley's No.28) inside the shell would light and the pressure would blow off the base of the shell. It would then trail a ball of fire until the composition burnt out. Clearly, if it hit an airship, the results would be fatal. If it missed, it would fall back to earth. One such example fell through the roof of the Mansion House with the remnants of its incendiary composition still burning and caused a minor fire. The danger of these shells, which weighed ten pounds, coming down still burning, or if not almost red hot, was significant. They would penetrate right through a three-storey house and were highly likely to set it on fire in the process.

A close study of the areas affected showed that it was not possible to connect the damage done in any particular area with any specific batteries of guns. So redeploying the guns to try and prevent damage was not a serious proposition. Wherever they were sighted, if the crews tracked and fired at enemy aircraft as they passed through the guns' complete range template, some fragments and shell were bound to fall somewhere on the capital.

It was not until the last day in October that the Gothas were directed against London again. This time a force of twenty-two aircraft were despatched, and in a new attempt at greater destruction, half of the total bomb load of 12,800 pounds were incendiaries. London was to be set ablaze. The idea had been considered in November 1914 by Grand Admiral Tirpitz. He had argued for such measures. Referring to the aircraft and Zeppelins as everything that 'flys and creeps' he said:

> I am not in favour of frightfulness, single bombs from flying machines are wrong; they are odious when they hit and kill an old woman, and one gets used to them. If one could set fire to London in thirty places, then what in a small way is odious would retire behind something that is fine and powerful.[10]

In the autumn of 1917, hopes of setting London ablaze were revived with the development of a new 10-pound incendiary bomb. The new bombs were streamlined in shape and carried a small explosive charge in the tail. This burst the bomb open on impact, causing it to scatter the incendiary composition inside. The new filling was semi-solid paraffin which was partially dissolved in benzol which also contained either potassium chlorate or barium nitrate which provided an additional supply of oxygen. The bomb, because of its shape and construction, possessed considerable penetrative power; in one case a bomb passed clean through a two-storey house and buried itself five feet in the ground. The Germans had great hopes of them and calculated that if fires broke out everywhere panic and confusion would reign in the enemy heartland. Should there be a strong wind then the fires were expected to join up forming conflagrations, and raze parts of the capital to the ground. Recollections of a disastrous fire in 1897 in the Cripplegate area of the City, which destroyed 100 buildings and caused £1,000,000 worth of damage, inspired such hopes.

Fortunately, the great expectations of the German commander, Kleine, were dashed. Only ten of his bombers got through to the capital and the results of the bombing were derisory. The failure rate of the new incendiary was similar to the 50-kilogram high explosive bombs and ran at about thirty per cent. Of some 100 or more incendiaries dropped when the bombers departed, only two or three persistent fires were visible.

The winter weather now began to seriously affect the ability of the German bombers to continue their operations. All had to be suspended until the night of 5-6 December when conditions were once again suitable. This time sixteen Gothas and two Giants attacked, and they carried loads made up of seventy-five per cent of incendiaries. Only six bombers reached London crossing at intervals between 04.30 hours and 05.40 hours. A total of 267 incendiaries, two 100-kilogram high explosive bombs and seven 50-kilogram high explosive bombs were dropped. Once more the eagerly anticipated mass conflagrations failed to materialise, but according to the fire brigade it was quite a close run thing. Fifty-two fires were started, the most serious of these being in Shoreditch, Whitechapel Road, South Lambeth Road and Gray's Inn road. The fire brigade was pleased to report that their co-ordinated efforts had worked well and motorised fire engines from as far as Twickenham and Wembley had been called in to help with the most serious blaze in Shoreditch. Although there was significant damage, from the German perspective, the results of the fire raids were sorely disappointing. Clearly who ever had designed and carried out the trials with the new incendiary bombs had seriously overestimated their fire-raising ability. This in turn, had raised unattainable expectations amongst the bomber crews who, after doing their best in the winter conditions to get the incendiaries on target, were demoralized by their poor performance. The First World War raiders never again carried significant loads of fire bombs and reverted to high explosives.

Despite the undoubted failure of the incendiaries, the Germans did not abandon the idea raising great fires. They turned their attention to the development of a new and more effective incendiary. The result was the *Elektronbrandbomben* which was made out of pure magnesium with a thermite booster in the centre. The thermite was needed to get the magnesium casing burning but, when it did so, it burnt with great violence at some 2,000-3,000 degrees Fahrenheit. A simple, reliable fuze ensured that most would light on impact. It weighed just one kilogram, and trials proved that the Giant aircraft could carry thousands. Had they done so, they might have achieved the desired fire storms beyond the scope of the primitive fire appliances of the day. Operations were planned for the summer of 1918, using masses of incendiaries, but by then the writing was on the wall and it was clear the Germans could not win the war. The General Staff, perhaps influenced by the Kaiser, realized this, and with an eye to the future forbade their use on London.

The vision of devastating fire raids of course did not die. The *Elektronbrandbomben* was further developed in the 1920s and later with minimal modification became the standard Luftwaffe incendiary. During the Second World War when fire raids were resurrected, these types of incendiaries were dropped in huge numbers, first by the Germans, but later their employment was perfected by the British, with horrendous results for people of Hamburg and Dresden.

The last raid of 1917, on the night of 18-19 December, was significant for the defenders because it saw the first loss of a Gotha to a night fighter. The raid itself caused significant damage and British intelligence estimated 11,000 pounds of bombs and a few incendiaries were dropped. Fourteen people were killed with a further eighty injured.

The first raid of the New Year was carried out on the night of 28-29 January 1918. It was to be another bad day for Londoners. Most by now were taking shelter when the raids were in progress and this day was no exception. One of the Giant aircraft, *R39*, had, amongst others, two 300-kilogram bombs in its payload. It arrived over London at 00.15 hours and dropped one of its larger bombs. The intended target was the Admiralty but it actually landed outside 93 Long Acre, the home of Oldham Printing works which published *John Bull* magazine. The three-storey building was steel-framed with thick concrete floors, which trials on equivalent structures had shown would detonate the 50-kilogram bombs on the top two floors and that fragments would not penetrate down to the cellar. It was therefore designated as a public shelter. Its basement that night was crowded with some 500 people. The large bomb missed the building by inches, penetrated a drain and exploded underground with terrific force, severely shaking the foundations of the outer walls and setting fire to some rolls of paper stored in the cellar. Finding one exit blocked, the occupants in the cellar began to panic. However, the police arrived and were able to organise a more orderly evacuation of the building. A young lad, Mr J. Sullivan, recalled regaining consciousness only to discover his leg was trapped under a piece of machinery. He remembered women and other children lying near him some bleeding and burning. Somehow, despite his injuries, he extracted his leg and, covered in printer's ink, he fought his way to an exit where a fireman picked him up and carried him to safety. Many others escaped, but before all of the people could be got out, the front wall of the building collapsed. In turn the floor above gave way and tons of printing presses came crashing down crushing many people. High above them the captain of the *R39*, now on his homeward journey, reported that he could see the red glow of a large fire burning in the heart of London.

At close quarters it was a nightmarish scene, many people were trapped, and the flames which had still not been extinguished, were licking around the remaining survivors. Firemen directed their hoses onto the fires to douse them, but in doing so the cellar rapidly began to flood, threatening to drown the very people they were trying to save. When the flames were finally out, the rescue workers cut through the rolls of paper and tangled wreckage to aid those still alive. It was a grim, unenviable task and went on long into the morning. A crowd of people gathered to watch the process. One of them, Michael MacDonagh, wrote:

> The wrecked printing-works is a frightful spectacle, it has been so inhumanly mangled – if I may use the expression – by the bomb. A German explosive bomb is not content with killing human beings and demolishing buildings; it also hacks and gashes, making everything it destroys a horror to look at. When I got to the place, the ruins were still being searched for bodies, I saw some brought out. They were maimed and distorted almost beyond identification.'[11]

This single bomb caused the greatest number of casualties in any one incident in London in the First World War. Eighty-five badly wounded people, some with severe injuries including burns, were recovered from the cellar. Thirty-eight of London's citizens died at the scene. One of them was the Vicar of St Paul's, Covent Garden, Reverend E.H. Mosse, who had been looking after his parishioners at the time.

News of the disaster spread like wildfire and created much anxiety within the population. The following night just three Giant aircraft attacked London. They caused some damage, but casualties were also caused that night by people stampeding at shelters. In London, two men, six women and six children were killed with a further fourteen people injured.

The next incursion by the Germans was on the night of 16-17 February. It was carried out by a small number of the Giant aircraft but was significant because R39 was laden with what was to be the biggest bomb dropped on London during the war. It weighed 1,000 kilograms, and had a main charge of almost 500 kilograms of explosive. The crew claimed to have dropped it on Victoria Station. In fact, it landed more than half a mile away in the grounds of the Royal Chelsea Hospital. It exploded at 22.32 hours by the North Pavilion in which a Household Company officer's family was living. It killed him, his wife, her sister and three of his children. The building was one of those erected by Sir Christopher Wren at the end of the seventeenth century; it was razed to the ground. The concussion from the bomb was reported as being particularly heavy. The impact points for these bombs was of course random, in that they rarely landed anywhere near their intended aiming points. Twenty-seven years later another indiscriminate weapon, a V2 rocket, would land in almost exactly the same place causing more death and destruction.

Another of the Giants, *R12*, whilst flying up the Thames near Woolwich, flew into one of the new balloon aprons. The impact caused the aircraft to lurch to one side and it dropped a wing and began a violent sideslip dropping 1,000 feet before the pilot, Leutnant Lötte, managed to regain control. One of the mechanics riding on the nacelle of his engine was thrown against the red hot exhaust stacks and had his hands severely burnt. *R12* almost immediately dropped its two 300 kilogram bombs which landed in Woolwich Garrison, hitting the church and the barracks with the loss of seven dead.

In the biggest effort made by the Giants, six of the aircraft were dispatched to attack London on the night of 7-8 March, leaving their base at ten-minute intervals. Only three managed to reach London. Disconcertingly for Londoners there was no moon, normally a sign that they could sleep safe and sound in their beds. The weather en-route was not good, with cloud and very little ambient light, nevertheless, the grey band of the River Thames was just visible and provided the much-needed navigational fix. In Giant *R 39* was another 1,000-kilogram bomb. The captain of the aircraft released the monster intending to hit Paddington Station. By now it will be no surprise to the reader to discover it landed half a mile away where it hit 67 Warrington Crescent. The bomb burst through two floors before detonating. The house, a four-storey Victorian terrace, was completely destroyed. A choking dust rising from the disemboweled building filled the surrounding streets. Twenty other buildings close by were severely damaged by the force of the blast. In one of them, the occupant was on the top floor playing the piano, when the walls were blown in by the force of the explosion. The floors gave way and he was found dead in the cellar. A further 400 people suffered minor injuries mainly from broken glass. The final toll was twelve killed and twenty-three injured. This demonstration of the immense destructive power of a single bomb made a deep and lasting impression on the occupants living nearby. Once more, the morbid curiosity came out in some people, and the crescent became a tourist attraction as people from all over the country went to the scene to view the damage. Even the King and Queen and other high dignitaries attended, escorted by Lord French. Today at Warrington Crescent you can see clearly see where the bomb exploded. The neat row of identical houses is broken at the point of impact and a completely new building was erected in its place.

The last attack on London on the night of 19-20 May, was carried out by the largest number of machines that ever raided England in the First

World War. According to the German semi-official account, the capital was to be attacked by thirty-eight Gothas and three Giants. Most did not make it and the best estimate is that thirteen of the former type and one of the latter reached London. Of the machines that made it, only one managed to bomb the centre. This aircraft dropped a series of 50-kilogram bombs which detonated at 26a Kings Street, St James's, the outer circle at Regent's Park, Park Crescent in Marylebone and Bolsover Street. The remaining aircraft dropped their bombs all over greater London and the southeast. This last raid was greeted by the most impressive anti-aircraft barrage in which over 30,337 shells were fired. More importantly, the night fighter force had their most successful night, shooting down three of the Gothas with a fourth crashing for unknown reasons. The final death toll was forty-nine killed and 177 injured. For the population of London their ordeal was, for the moment, over; the Germans would not return to the capital for another twenty-two years.

One legacy of the war was that strategic bombing had come of age and had found a quick and ready place in the mind of the German military. The bombing of cities was clearly in keeping with the Teutonic idea of *Schrecklichkeit*, which held that acts of frightfulness were in keeping with the idea of paralysing the enemy's will to resist. In 1927 the Germans carried out their own detailed review of the bombing of Britain in which London was the key target. It examined three main aspects of the campaign; the effect on the morale of the population, the military implications and the economic cost. They considered that morale was the most important of the three and noted the curve of moral intimidation rose steadily after the commencement of the daylight raids by aircraft. Initially, according to the Germans, there was a minor sense of irritation, particularly when the raiders could be seen. The report made an interesting analogy with Britain as a sporting nation. If the planes could be seen, they could be shot and attacked by fighters in the air. This, it was thought, was a fair game and a spectacle not to be missed. This attitude, however, was rapidly replaced by fear when the night raids began. Then there was a perception of being defenceless as the public had no idea when or where the bombs would land. This fear reached its peak during the 'Harvest Moon' period and then remained at that level for the remainder of the war. According to informants, at the time, the bombing induced alarm and panic in the communities being bombed and this resulted in local riots. There was also traffic dislocation, an increased cost of living and a feeling of insecurity. Clearly, the Germans concluded, the raids had caused a significant effect on the mental health of the nation. At one point the report recalled an

American engineer stating that the raids had led to great inconvenience which included domestic servants leaving their employers. It is hard to believe now that this was considered sufficiently important to be included in such a report. Others interviewed for the study included a Swiss neutral who talked of panic, people leaving for the country, women screaming in terror, pandemonium at tube stations when air raid sirens went, and later riots for food which was running short. An even more severe result of this 'Gothagitis' was an increase in people suffering from nerves, hysteria, madness and suicide.

On morale, the report then made a key statement, which intimated that there was definitely a sense of depression which weakened the nation's will to fight, but that the weight of bombs was insufficient to cause a total collapse of morale.

In terms of the military achievements the raids were also considered a major success. Much damage was done to the military machine, although it noted that the news of the damage was suppressed by the authorities so it could not be accurately assessed. This was not true, but to it has to be conceded that the withdrawal of a significant numbers of guns and aircraft from the western front lessened the fighting power there. The economic effects of the air raids were also concluded as being severe, with both the transportation system and many factories being sorely affected. Once again this was probably overstated.

The report concluded that this was the first serious attempt to carry out war far behind the armies in the field. It reflected that the German bomber strength was insufficient for the task. If there had been sufficient resources available at the critical period in October 1917, then continuing the offensive would almost certainly have had an impact on the outcome of the war. After this, as the interval between raids increased, then the ability to strike terror into the hearts of the population decreased. Furthermore, in addition to the stubborn character of the British, the government kept such tight control of the press that the morale effect was reduced.

Everything in the main body of the report seemed to indicate that mass bombing could be decisive in future wars. In the final paragraph, however, it noted that:

> The fantastic ideas of finishing a war in a few days by raids of powerful bombing squadrons and the destruction of the capital and industrial centres by bombs and poison gas are utopian. At present there are practically no means of carrying such a plan into effect. It should, moreover, always be borne in mind that the means of defence will always keep pace with those of attack and that science will serve

both. Great Britain however received her first blow to her external vulnerability which has lasted for hundreds of years and it is plain that the British policy of the future will be largely influenced thereby.[12]

It seems odd that having subscribed to the effectiveness of the German raids on Britain, this final paragraph casts serious doubt on its future war-winning potential. As far as the British experience was concerned, there can be no doubt that, at the end of the war, the bomber had emerged in the popular mind as the most dangerous weapon the conflict had spawned. As the German report suggested, in countering it, the country had developed a very effective daylight anti-aircraft defence system. This was based on observers, fighter aircraft, guns, and balloons. At night, even with the addition of searchlights, the task of defending the capital was recognised as being much harder. It was then down to people to demonstrate the will to resist and many harsh lessons had been learnt in this respect. The importance of local organisations to put in place measures to protect the public was eventually grasped, as was the need during raids for the police to maintain control of the area attacked. This enabled relief work to start as soon as possible after a raid, and it included the use of voluntary bodies such as the YMCA and Salvation Army which went to assist the victims once they had been rescued. Fortunately, overall, the damage to dwellings was light and it was shown that most people whose houses had been damaged could be accommodated with friends or neighbours. Nevertheless, there was a need for some lodgings provided by Local Government and also food and financial assistance for bombed out families. The bomb in North Street School also highlighted the imperative to evacuate, children, the elderly and the infirm.

The basis of a system of military and civil defence of the key British target, London, had therefore been established at the end of the war. It will be seen that, when resurrected in the late 1930s, and with the addition of radar, all the blocks were in place to withstand the assault in the next conflict. In daylight the RAF would win the battle for the supremacy of the skies, but at night it was the civil defenders that would have to take up the challenge.

NOTES:
1. Fredette, Raymond, *The First Battle of Britain 1917-18*, Cassell, London, 1966.
2. Hook, John, *The Air raids on London during the 1914-18 War, Booklet 4, The Raids on the City of London*, privately published, 1987.
3. ibid.
4. Farmery, Peter, *Police Gallantry 1909-1978*, Periter and Associates Pty Ltd, New South Wales, Australia, 1995.

5. Hook, *op.cit.*
6. Hyde, Andrew P., *The First Blitz*, Pen and Sword Limited, Yorkshire, 2002.
7. Fredette, *op.cit.*
8. TNA, Air 1/2123/207/73/14: The Aeroplane raids of the 25 May -13 June 1917.
9. TNA, Air/1/2123: Air Raids 1918, dated April 1918.
10. Fredette, Fredette, *op.cit.*
11. MacDonagh, Michael, *In London During the Great War*, Eyre and Spottiswoode, London 1935.
12. TNA, Air 1/27/13/2214: German Report on the Bombing Campaign Against Great Britain dated 1927.

Chapter 7

War Trophies and
The Second IRA Campaign

**'An army which limits itself to violent speeches and
passive parades was far too tranquil for many of the new
generation and not a few of the elders either!'**
The Secret Army - The Story of the IRA 1916-1970.

A fter the failure of the first Fenian campaign on the mainland, the
principal focus of the action to force Irish independence was in the
land of Ireland itself. The promise of Home Rule in 1914 was suspended
after the outbreak of the First World War and was followed by the Easter
Uprising in Dublin in 1916. An increasingly bitter struggle followed in
Ireland which resulted in partition in 1921. The Irish Free State was
formed in the South whilst in the North the six counties remained part
of the United Kingdom. This unsatisfactory division caused a bitter civil
war in Ireland which ended in 1923. Over this period there was a very
limited campaign on the mainland. Active IRA units were formed in
1919 and 1920 from the large Irish communities working and living in
Britain. All told, about 1,000 volunteers enrolled in these units, although
how many were actually prepared to carry out acts of sabotage was
another matter.

It has been a hallmark of all the IRA campaigns that it adopt
traditional military terms, particularly battalions and companies in
order to give the impression of much greater strength than actually
exists. In the capital, in the 'West London Company', it was estimated
that there were only two dozen men who could be counted on to
support violent operations. The initial actions of the London units were
limited to small demonstrations outside Wormwood Scrubs Prison in
support of the Irish prisoners on hunger strike there. Whenever they

gathered, the IRA sympathisers came to the same conclusion; they must do something more violent to take revenge for British actions in Ireland. This resulted in some of the volunteers carrying out attempted assassinations, sabotage and many arson attacks. For example, on 14 June 1921, a group of men armed with revolvers forced their way into 3 Fairholm Road, West Kensington, looking for, and intending to kill, Captain Wood of the 2nd East Lancashire Regiment. When they discovered he was not at home they poured petrol over the floor of the house, set fire to it, and decamped. Fortunately, the fire was quickly extinguished with limited damage. Other volunteers carried out a wide range of disruptive activities. There were arson attacks on the farms on the outskirts of the capital, in Croydon and in West Molesley. In mid-June 1921, attacks on both the telegraph system around London and the rail network's signal boxes caused considerable damage. These acts of sabotage were carried out by physically cutting down telegraph poles or setting fire to signal boxes. Sometimes they included violent and frightening assaults. On 16 June 1921 at Barking, a group of six armed men broke in to a signal box. They threatened and beat the Signalman with revolvers, tied him to a post nearby, then poured petrol or paraffin into the signal box and set it alight.

They had other, much grander ideas, which included major acts of destruction, but fortunately lacked the resources to carry out the attacks. Planning and preparations were made for a truck bomb to be driven to and parked outside the Houses of Parliament and similar plans for the destruction of a bridge over the Thames. There was even a scheme for poisoning horses in Buckingham Palace. Luckily none of these operations came to fruition. There was one attempted bombing; this was on 1 July 1921 when a device, which failed to explode, was left outside the Ministry of Pensions' buildings in Regent's Park. Like the fuse on the failed bomb the campaign fizzled out shortly after this when a truce was established with the Republican leadership in Dublin. It held for eighteen years in London.

It wasn't only the IRA who were using bombs in London at this time. The criminal, as opposed to the politically motivated, use of explosives can be basically broken down in to three distinct categories. The first is the use of bombs for revenge; the second is for extortion and the third the use of explosives for safe-blowing or gaining access to properties. There were examples of the first and the third during the 1920s and 1930s. In this account, the use of explosives to blow open safes, is covered in more detail in Chapter 17, as the offence was a much more common occurrence then.

Revenge was the motive for an attack in February 1923, when improvised devices were sent through the post to three different people. These contained pistols, which were so arranged that anyone obeying the opening instructions would inadvertently pull the trigger and fire a cartridge. The position of the pistol was such that the bullet would be directed at the midriff of the person opening the parcel and would cause grave injuries. In this case, interviews with the three recipients produced a common motive, leading to an obvious suspect who was detained. After his arrest the parcels were examined and forensically linked to the offender. An officer from HM Inspectors of Explosives helped investigate the incident and gave evidence at the Old Bailey. The perpetrator was found guilty and was sentenced to seven years' imprisonment.[1]

After the First World War the country was awash with surplus munitions held in explosives stores and munitions dumps. The formal disposal of these was undertaken in workshops all over the country under the auspices of the Disposal and Liquidation Committee. This often involved the breakdown of ammunition to recover the explosive filling and expensive metals, particularly copper and brass. One such facility was the Slade Green Filling Factory, situated midway between Erith and Dartford on Crayford Marshes. It was originally a munitions works under government control but had been taken over by Messrs W. Villa Gilbert Limited. The factory consisted of a number of ammunition process buildings, all separate from each other, with access from Slade Green by a narrow winding road over the marshes.

On 19 February 1924, a number of women were at work breaking down Very pistol cartridges, extracting the powder and separating the different stars. Just before 09.00 hours, there was a sudden flash which started a small fire, and moments later this reached a number of broken-down illuminating stars which exploded en-masse, producing a dazzling white flash which blinded many of the women working there. Vast amounts of smoke from the burning ammunition filled the room and the building was engulfed in flames and multiple small secondary explosions. Miss Charlotte Coshall, the forewoman, and seven of the women managed to get out of the building, some with their clothes alight. Tragically, eleven others were trapped by the fire.

Bravely some of those who escaped turned back at once but, found it impossible to reach the unfortunate victims trapped in the building due to the intense heat of the fire. Others rushed towards the gates of the works screaming for help. One eye-witness said another foreman ran to the scene and had tried to lift a girl through a window but the heat and smoke were too great and he fell back and subsequently died of his burns. The awful suddenness of the catastrophe combined with the heat, smoke and fumes prevented any further immediate rescue attempts. When help eventually arrived only one woman, Edna Allen, was found alive, but she was terribly burned. She was taken to Erith Cottage Hospital but died during the night. The final toll was thirteen dead, twelve of them women.

Another major source of surplus munitions turning up where they were not wanted was that of souvenirs. Despite regulations prohibiting it, souvenirs of all types were avidly collected by all 'Tommies' to take home as war trophies. These trophies covered a wide range of military items, including munitions and particularly grenades, which were, (and still are) most popular, presumably because they fit easily into a pocket and as a souvenir 'look the part'. Other ordnance included cartridges cases, shells, and aircraft and mortar bombs. In fact, during the war itself, so many items of live ordnance were being sent back from the front that the Post Office employed an ex-military officer to examine such items and he was eventually injured in an explosion.

Many servicemen, after a time, decided to get rid of their ordnance souvenirs, particularly if the items were live and illegal. There were three basic methods of disposal. A common practice was to throw the offending item out with the rubbish. This, on 19 January 1919, led to a Lewis grenade exploding in Bermondsey Council's incinerator. Fortunately, this happened late in the day and no one was injured.[2] These types of incident became known as 'War Trophy' accidents and there was a steady flow of killed and injured as a result of them.

The second method of disposal was simply to hide the offending munitions. Many were either buried in gardens, parks or waste land, or hidden in an attic or cellar, working on the basis that if you can't see it can't hurt you. This of course is fine until, inevitably, the item is eventually found. Not long after the war during the renovation of a pub, some workmen found an old Mills grenade which had been hidden in an obscure dark corner under the bar counter. They took it out and thinking nothing of it placed it on the top of the bar. From here the grenade somehow found its way onto a small fire in the landlords' living room which was immediately behind the public bar. Shortly after it was placed on the coals, the landlord's wife brought in one of her young children to bathe in a tub in the warmth of the hearth. Without warning the grenade exploded, killing the child and seriously injuring the mother. It is thought that another of her children, aged four, found the grenade on the counter and took it through to the living room and, unseen by anyone, innocently popped it on the fire. The delay in the grenade exploding, was thought to be that because the fire was so small it took some time before the explosive in it cooked off.[3]

Clearly the safest method of disposing of unwanted ordnance was to hand the offending items over to the police or the military and for them to arrange for their safe disposal. The initial response by the police in the 1920s, although practical, was slightly worrying. In one document detailing the disposal of such unexploded ordnance it noted:

> This would include all, or nearly all, war trophies, fuzes, grenades and small shells which may safely be thrown into any deep water which never dries up, but before doing this it would be well to report the nature of the article to headquarters. In the meantime, the article should be carefully removed to an isolated shed or open place where its explosion would not cause serious damage, care being taken not to turn it over or shake it more than necessary.[4]

The same document noted the dangers of handling bulk blasting explosives, many of which were nitroglycerine based and could become highly unstable if not stored correctly. As well as the risk of detonation, these nitroglycerine explosives also caused the most appalling headaches if handled without protective gloves. There was also a stern warning about dealing with plain detonators; it noted that they could be handled with ordinary care, but that no attempt should be made to extract the explosive from the exposed end by scratching or scraping. This would inevitably cause it to explode and in doing so would blow a couple of fingers off the hand holding the detonator.

Fortunately, the official procedure for dumping unexploded ordnance into deep water does not seem to have lasted long, and later arrangements were made for the police collect to all such items. Those considered to be in a safe condition were stored at police stations and collected for disposal on a routine basis. Those items considered to be in a dangerous condition were immediately transported to government magazines in Plumstead, which were in a part of the Woolwich Arsenal site. The transport in those days of course could well be a bicycle. Once at Woolwich they were disposed of, normally by demolition. In an exceptional emergency, however, it was still possible to throw the items singly into deep water which never dried up. One can imagine that many 'emergency situations' must have arisen on cold, wet, winter's nights when a Police Officer was faced with the choice of cycling to Woolwich or dropping the item in the Thames or a nearby pond.

Despite the obvious concern of local ponds filling up with munitions, the procedures seemed to work quite well. However, problems arose a little later when, in 1922, Major Cunningham from the HM Inspectorate of Explosives at the Home Office, received a letter from a Mr Webb of Crouch End, who asked for a number of 'Pom Pom' shell to be collected for disposal. These, he was quite clear, were live, because he personally brought them back from the Boer War. Major Cunningham advised Mr Webb that this was a matter for the local police. They, not surprisingly, were not keen to undertake this task and eventually an experienced officer from the military was contacted and collected the shells for disposal.

This subsequently caused quite an inter-departmental storm over who was responsible for such items. The police view was that experts from the Home Office should deal with these matters, but Major Cooper-Key and Colonel Thomas, representing HM Inspector of Explosives, disagreed. Before the war it was noted that the Home Office was only responsible for dealing with explosives and infernal machines. If the latter were found, the procedure was the police would attend the incident and carry out, what today we would call, cordon and evacuation, to safeguard the public. It then required Special Branch to notify the duty Explosives Officer and he would attend the scene and deal with the device. During the First World War this responsibility was handed to the military authorities. After the war it was agreed that the Home Office would take back the task of dealing with explosives and infernal machines. Further investigations revealed that the disposal facility on Duck Island, although sadly neglected could, with minimal repair, still be used. However, the bomb cart was located and discovered to be totally beyond repair. Some thought was given to procuring a new one or a similar system using a motor vehicle, but these plans never came to fruition.

The Home Office, however, did not intend to send Explosives Officers to deal with unexploded shells found buried in the ground or other munitions that were discovered or surrendered to the police. The main reason being that, as already explained, post war, the numbers of munitions being discovered and recovered was huge. It was suggested by Major Cooper-Key that the military should take on this liability under guidance from the Master General of Ordnance, who they argued, in the case of British ammunition, were technically still the owners of such items. The War Office flatly refused to undertake responsibility for such work. The matter of anti-aircraft shells buried or embedded in buildings was specifically mentioned and remained unresolved. The police were instructed not to move or touch such items. There was now an impasse and although the police saw it as unsatisfactory, the issue was left in limbo until such time as a critical case arose. For the police it was 'Hobson's choice' and they had no option other than to deal with all ordnance that was found or handed in, although there was agreement that in exceptional cases advice could be sought from HM Inspector of Explosives. The police instructions stated that, in general, most ammunition found, if handled with care, would not pose any danger. This was true, munitions are designed to be safe to handle and use. Furthermore, it must be remembered that many of the police officers had served during the Great War and were familiar with a wide variety of munitions.

An idea of the scale of the problem of War Trophies can be seen in the 1934 HM Inspectors of Explosives Report which records that in the Metropolitan Police area alone, in the sixteen years since the end of the war, over six tons of shells, bombs and other explosives were deposited in the magazine at Plumbstead. There is no record of what was thrown into the Thames, other rivers or deep ponds.

As far as munitions were concerned these unsatisfactory procedures continued to work until, in 1934, Police Constable Withall, who was conveying a Mills grenade to Plumbstead on his bicycle, was involved in a minor accident with a lorry. Fortunately, he was not seriously injured but his cycle was damaged and he put in a claim for compensation. In the investigation into the accident it was recorded that grenades, which were once considered safe to handle, could become dangerous with age. It noted that in Constable Withall's case the safety pin on the grenade was very nearly rusted through and, worryingly, when he was knocked off his bike, if the pin had failed, the grenade might have functioned. This once again raised the question of how unexploded ordnance should be dealt with and the whole subject was reviewed again. The enquiry revealed that the transport of ordnance to Plumbstead, when it was too heavy to take on a cycle, was often by train, tram or bus. It was quickly established that the transfer of such explosive items in this manner contravened the Railway's Act and, furthermore, it was considered irregular to transfer such items in other Public Service Vehicles. It was therefore agreed that in future police vans would be used to move all such dangerous items.

The review also noted that there were now many young police officers who had no knowledge of munitions. It was further made clear that it was unfair to the public and the police to move such items until it was confirmed that they were safe to move, but the question remained who would do this? It seems that an impasse was again reached and the view which prevailed was that ninety-nine percent of the explosives or munitions deposited with the police since the end of the Great War had lain dormant for many years and were not 'dangerous' in the strict sense of the word. All that was needed was careful handling and packing so that they would not fall or roll about during the journey to Plumstead.

For infernal machines or dangerous explosives, the importance of safeguarding the public was reiterated. Once a device was safely isolated, then an Explosives Officer from the Home Office would come to deal with it. If it was necessary to move the bomb before inspection by an Explosives Officer the report stated that: 'The greatest care should be taken to do so as gently as possible and without shaking or turning it over; and it should be placed in an as isolated place as possible – a yard or garden or other open place. If a burning fuse is attached this should be pulled out or quenched with water.'[5]

It would be a few more years before importance of these instructions became clear.

After the Great War explosives, such as gunpowder, were still freely available in shops and had some surprising uses, apparently including chimney cleaning. In the 1920s, in many cases, the method of doing the family washing consisted of using a ten gallon cast iron bowl which, for some unfathomable reason, was referred to as a copper. The bowl was enclosed in a cement-rendered brick-like structure constructed over a fire grate with a door, and the whole built into a corner of a house, normally the scullery. Obviously it was necessary to keep the copper chimney swept as it seemed to 'soot up' more than other flues which made the fire beneath inefficient. It was common practice to buy a packet of gunpowder, about the size of a dozen boxes of matches, from the local oil shop. The pack was thrown on to the burning fire and the fire door immediately slammed shut, and held closed using a broom head. Seconds later there would be a satisfactory 'WOOF' which would rattle the copper, but more importantly the explosion blew out all the soot which formed a black mushroom cloud at the top of the chimney. Afterwards the fire would burn much more brightly.

In 1939, with the ominous shadow of another European war hanging over the country, the people in London had to face a second bombing campaign by the IRA. In the late 1930s the old IRA leadership was seen as increasingly out of touch and ineffective and a new man, Seán Russell, was elected to the Army Council. Russell and his supporters advocated a more active role in attacking the forces of the Crown, both in Northern Ireland and on the mainland. However, despite this growing conviction, and a desire to bomb London to the negotiating table, the reality was that they had almost no explosives or suitably trained volunteers available to take on the job. Faced with the need to meet the demands of an overseas campaign, Russel turned to an old friend, Seamus O'Donovan. He was a skilled explosive expert and, more importantly, had a greater understanding of the difficulties of mounting an extended operation on the mainland.

O'Donovan drafted a document, which was later to become known as the 'S Plan', which Russell accepted without amendment. Its objectives were well beyond the IRA's technical and operational capabilities at the time, but in great secrecy between the spring and summer of 1938, extensive technical and tactical preparations for a mainland campaign were undertaken. Key amongst these was the training of a new generation of bombers and bomb makers. Classes were held both in Ireland and on the mainland, one of these allegedly on the grass in Hyde Park. However, teaching men how to make and assemble improvised devices is not a simple task, particularly if the training is purely theoretical. The gulf between being told how to make a bomb on paper and the reality of actually making one is immense, particularly as a simple mistake can, and has on many occasions, lead to a fatal explosion.

To be effective, the IRA realized that they would need a sustained effort and to support this there was frenzied activity. New personnel were recruited and vetted, more bomb classes were organised, supplies of bomb making chemicals were acquired, gelignite and detonators were stolen, and a system of safe houses and couriers organised. The first real indication of a serious campaign was on 19 October 1938, when two men were arrested in Ilford in a stolen van. They were discovered to be in possession of illegal explosives and were later convicted and imprisoned.

The first operation in Northern Ireland in November 1938, was an attack on the customs posts in Strabane and Clady. It was a disaster, and three of the bombers died, when their improvised device exploded prematurely. Nevertheless, by 12 January 1939, with preparations for the attacks on the mainland complete, an ultimatum was delivered to the Foreign Secretary, Lord Halifax, demanding the withdrawal of all British armed forces and other civilians from every part of Ireland. A time limit of 15 January was given for the British Government to acknowledge receipt of the demand and signal their intent to comply with its content. Despite the arrests in October, there had been little other supporting intelligence about the IRA preparations for a bombing campaign and, understandably, the British government was more concerned with events in Central Europe and treated the communications with contempt. The IRA also miscalculated; they appeared to have reckoned that the United Kingdom was in such a state of jitters in the face of the Nazi menace that she would belie her past and yield to any action that threatened her war preparations. The fact was that the country was more united at that time than it had been for many years, and unlikely to bow to such threats.

The day after the expiry of the deadline, Monday 16 January 1939, there were seven major explosions at power stations and electrical lines, two of these being in London, followed by more explosions the following day. At hastily convened meetings Special Branch and the intelligence services planned their response and detectives descended on the Irish populations in the major cities. Elsewhere security was stepped up with police patrols around the most of the vulnerable points. The press printed stories of the outrages and the public demanded protection, but the bombings continued.

The seriousness of the threat was underlined on 29 January 1939, when over a ton of explosives was recovered along with a stock of firearms and a large quantity of modified alarm clocks from the Edgehill district of Liverpool. The latter all had holes drilled in the face of the glass designed to take a wire which would act as a contact with one of the hands on the clock face, thus making an electrical firing circuit.

The task of dealing with suspect items and the examination of scenes of explosions clearly fell to HM Inspector of Explosives. Instructions were issued, under Home Office Circular 3456, that their support could be called upon by dialling Whitehall 8100, extension 47.[6] A little later, instructions were issued by the Home Office on how police officers should deal with suspect devices. Firstly, it covered bombs in places where the public might meet. In this case, where the bombs were built with electrical circuits and alarm clocks police officers were told to cut one of the wires, but that they should not put any strain on them or cut them if they were close together, as this might complete an electrical circuit. In doing this they were told not to touch the clock. After this the bomb should be guarded at a safe distance until expert assistance arrived. If the bomb was in an isolated area and the clock was ticking, then the bomb was to be left in place for twelve hours and guarded at a safe distance. If it failed to detonate then and experts from HM Inspectors of Explosive should be summoned to deal with it. If the clock was not ticking, then the expert was to be summoned immediately.

The instructions also covered dealing with suspect items like cases which might be found and be thought to contain a bomb, the advice was that:

No complicated or 'infernal' machine has been used up to the present, but if a package, bag or case is found in such a place or in such circumstances as to give rise to suspicion that it may contain an explosive charge, it should be removed to the nearest open place of safety. This removal should be carried out in such a way as to expose the infernal machine to as little shaking, or spilling of any liquid contents as possible. It should be placed in a tub of water or preferably a pond or stream from which it could be recovered.[7]

It seems bizarre today that police officers with no formal training were, as a matter of routine, expected to deal with such infernal machines. It also seems incongruous to expect a police officer to carry a suspect bomb without shaking, but clearly in those days they were made of sterner stuff and, as will be seen later, some officers bravely complied fully with these instructions.

On 3 February 1939, bombs detonated in the left luggage offices of the Tottenham Court Road and Leicester Square Underground Stations, and a short while later an 'alarm clock bomb' was found at Acton Lane Station. These attacks were very similar in principle to those in the 1880s. Bombs in suitcases were deposited in the left luggage compartments and, using alarm clocks with the minute hand removed, were set to detonate in the early morning. At Tottenham Court Road, the bomb exploded at 05.55 hours and severely injured one of the staff who had a fractured fibula and tibia, a broken arm and several cuts and abrasions. The police managed to identify the type of suitcase by questioning the staff and examining the fragments after the explosion, and quickly put out an appeal for information from anyone who had recently sold such cases.

In the early hours of 2 March 1939, William Morgan was driving his car around the North Circular. He was approaching the aqueduct at Stonebridge where the Grand Union Canal passes over the road. He was about thirty yards short of it when there was a bright flash and the sound of an explosion. He applied his brakes and saw bits of masonry falling onto the road. He went to the nearest telephone box and informed the police. A number of officers, including an Inspector Curry, rushed to the scene. Arriving at about 02.28 hours they found obvious signs of an explosion on the footpath on the southeast side of the bridge which conveys the Grand Union Canal over the North Circular Road. Water was slowly escaping into the roadway through the cracked basin of the aqueduct immediately below the point of damage.

The bomb was estimated to be of considerable size, as seven feet of the granite kerbing at the water's edge had been blown away, and several feet of the footpath were damaged and cracked above and below the water's surface. The basin of the aqueduct was split, and damage to the parapet ran for about thirty feet with a ten-foot section being blown into the road. In addition, windows in many of the surrounding factories were broken.

The immediate scene was searched and a number of items found, including metal and porcelain fragments, and part of a solid rubber ball. These were handed to experts from the Home Office, Dr Watts and Major Crawford, who attended the scene. Their examination of these proved negative and nothing was ever concluded about the construction of the bomb. The following day a dam was erected around the damaged area to enable that part of the canal to be emptied so that the aqueduct could be properly inspected for damage, repaired and a further search for components of the bomb made. This was done, but nothing of consequence found.

In view of the Irish terrorist acts prevailing at the time, and the large Irish population in the area, there was what was described as, intense police activity in the surrounding neighbourhood. With the assistance of Special Branch, 163 addresses in the Harlesden and Willesden areas alone were visited and searched by the police, and the Irish occupants subject to lengthy interrogations. In addition, all Irish persons who had been arrested for minor offences were picked up and questioned. Finally, all the local Irish pubs and popular dance halls were visited, but no useful leads to the perpetrators were obtained.

A few days later the same IRA team struck again, this time leaving a bomb near the electricity sub-station at Harlesden. The bomb, which was wrapped in brown paper, failed to detonate and was eventually found by a workman, Thomas Pope, on the afternoon of 8 March. He was tasked to investigate some broken asbestos sheeting which covered some high tension cables. Whilst investigating the damage he discovered a parcel which he took out and partially unwrapped. He saw it contained a greasy substance and wires and he left it there and went to report the matter. Another labourer, Albert Harris, went to have a look at it. In his statement he then described what happened:

> I saw it contained an alarm clock, and a small electric battery, also an oblong parcel wrapped in brown paper. I went back to the sub-station and told the operator to inform the police. I then went back to the parcel and with a pair of wire cutters I cut the wires from the battery to the parcel and one of the wires from the alarm clock to the parcel. I noticed the alarm was set to go off at 2.30 pm, but that the clock had stopped at 6.42. The clock was not ticking when I first saw it.[8]

The bomb, having been rendered ineffective according to the duty officer, was seized and eventually handed to Major Crawford of the

Home Office. He removed the contents of the parcel and took out the detonator from the main charge, which appeared to him to be a mixture of gelignite and potassium chlorate. The wrappers in the parcel were for 'Polar Ammon Gelignite' and these were sent off for fingerprinting. The explosives were later taken to Woolwich and examined by a Mr Dupré (the son of Doctor Dupré already mentioned in the earlier IRA campaign who had followed in the footsteps of his father) he decided they were in a very dangerous state and, other than a tiny sample, ordered the rest to be immediately destroyed. The cable that had been targeted by the IRA supplied high voltage power at 132,000 volts and, had it been destroyed, would have caused widespread disruption to the local electricity supply.

Central London was also attacked and a bomb, left in a flower bed outside the Grosvenor House Hotel in Park Lane, detonated in the early morning of 18 March 1939.[9] The explosion was heard by War Reserve Constable George Boniface and Police Constable Shepherd who raced to the scene. One officer kept watch on the area whilst the other telephoned the Police Information Room. The bomb shattered the flower bed and smashed windows all around. It was still some months before the Second World War, but even then the windows had been covered in tape to prevent injuries from flying glass.

Later that month an attempt was made to destroy Hammersmith Bridge. A group of four men hired a car and told the driver they wanted to go to Ewell. En-route they overpowered him and hijacked the vehicle. They prepared two large bombs in suitcases and then drove to the bridge. Once there they placed one bomb at each end of the span and sped off. A minute or so later a pedestrian walking across the bridge saw one of the suitcases and opened it. Inside he described seeing a mass of burning rags and heard a hissing noise. He immediately picked up the case and flung it over the railings into the river. Moments later there was an explosion and a column of water, allegedly some sixty feet high, was thrown into the air. Not long afterwards the second bomb on the bridge detonated causing significant damage, which cost over £1,000 to repair. It was the first of three attempts by the IRA to destroy the bridge.

In March and April public toilets were attacked with explosions in Kilburn and Elephant and Castle. At one toilet in Boswell House, WC1, an attendant, Mr Harold Stanton, was interviewed after the explosion. He explained that to prevent too many cubicles having to be cleaned, the furthest few away from the entrance had their doors locked and were only opened on customer request. In this case a man wanted to use the far toilet. Mr Stanton stated that he opened the door and dusted down the seat and left the gentleman to his business. He was surprised, however, when the man came almost straight out of the lavatory. He thought at the time that the visit was a bit quick. Mr Stanton watched the customer leave and climb up the stairs; moments later there was an explosion which wrecked the toilets.

In April, seven bombs were planted during the night in, or near, shop premises of which five exploded. Police officers on the beat were warned to look out for suspicious packages. In the early hours of 4 May 1939, Police Constable Ernest Hayward was on duty in Tottenham Court Road when he discovered a parcel in the window of a shop, and correctly guessed that it was a bomb. He bravely moved the parcel from the window to the edge of the pavement, where he unwrapped it, finding a rubber balloon containing liquid. Beside the balloon was a round paper package from which a fuse was protruding. He immediately separated the balloon from the package and, keeping them apart, put them in a bucket of water. He then carried the contents of the bucket to the nearest police station. Further examination revealed that the packet contained a charge of gelignite with a time fuse and a detonator attached to a double rubber balloon containing an acid-based initiator. For his gallantry Constable Hayward was awarded the King's Police Medal. Three other similar bombs exploded the same night causing considerable damage.

As well as high explosive bombs based on stolen gelignite, the IRA made use of a home-made explosives and wide variety of other devices. Some notebooks captured around this time provided detailed instructions on how to make a home-made explosive called 'Paxo' and incendiary compositions. 'Paxo' it noted could be manufactured by purchasing a number of common chemicals which in themselves would not arouse suspicion. Detailed formulae were also supplied giving guidance on the amount of explosive required to demolish walls and bridges. Investigations revealed that much of the information had been lifted from an American treaty on explosives and incendiary compositions. Failed devices which were investigated by Explosives officers were found to be almost identical in construction and clearly followed the details provided in the captured notebooks.

The IRA also used chemical weapons, the first of which functioned in cinemas in Liverpool. These consisted of American tear gas canisters which had had their initiation mechanisms removed and replaced by an improvised acid delay system. Some may consider the use of tear gas a minor offence but, for the victims in the audiences, it was a menacing and frightening experience. When the devices functioned the area immediately around the bomb would be swamped in a cloud of choking irritant gas. People would start coughing and their eyes start streaming and initially, before the staff realized what was happening and put the lights on, they would be stumbling and falling in narrow aisles in the darkness trying to escape the effects of the gas.

In London more cinemas were attacked but these operations did not always go according to plan. At about 21.00 hours on 31 May, Joseph Malone went into the 'gents' toilets in the Victoria cinema on the Vauxhall Bridge Road with the intention of starting an improvised delay on a magnesium incendiary bomb which was combined with some unknown irritant powder. However, whilst trying to do this the device functioned prematurely and the magnesium was initiated. Malone was shocked, burnt and mildly gassed. He was found by another man and quickly explained that he had felt faint and had sat down when he saw a bomb and it exploded. A St John's Ambulance man on duty in the cinema dressed Malone's wounds and he was taken to hospital. In the meantime, the police had been informed and arrived on the scene. After a brief explanation they went straight to the hospital where they confronted the injured Malone who, almost right away, confessed to the bombing and added immediately that he was working alone. His statement makes interesting reading. He said:

> This afternoon on the 31st May, 1939, I was in Hyde Park and put together the gas bomb. I had had for two weeks a balloon, slightly thicker than a toy balloon. A fellow gave it to me. I will not give you his name. I bought some wax but I don't wish to say where I bought it. I also bought a magnesium flare and some powder which is harmless but smells terrible. This is the stuff I put together in Hyde Park this afternoon.

Malone then went to the cinema and into the toilet where he said:

> I squeezed the bulb which is wax, and it [the bomb} should have gone off a quarter of an hour later. But I squeezed too hard and it went off in my hand. It knocked me out; I was not exactly unconscious, but dazed.[10]

Back at the scene, other officers who went in to recover the evidence of the attack were forced to hang back because of the gas. They waited until gas masks arrived from the police station before recovering the evidence. The fact that the masks were available was another indication of the preparations being made for the Second World War. In custody, the following day, Malone asked if there had been any other 'excitement' the previous evening. When being told there was none, he commented: 'Another half a dozen should have gone up, I suppose the bloody yellow rats funked it.'

This information indicated that many other incendiary/gas bombs were to have been planted. There was concern that devices may have been left but had failed to function and the police embarked on a massive search of all the cinemas and theatres but nothing was found.

On Friday 9 June a campaign was launched against the Post Office with incendiary devices setting light to post boxes and later a device exploding in a sorting office in London.[11] Between 20.15 and 21.22 hours, balloon incendiaries were placed in a total of two district post offices boxes and six pillar boxes, in some cases more than one device was slid into each box.

In Russell Square, Police Constable Albert Overall was on duty when a lorry driver told him that a pillar box was on fire in Tavistock Square. He proceeded to the scene and could see smoke coming from both apertures of the letterbox. Just then the fire brigade arrived who quickly pumped water into the box. Soon a postman arrived and opened up both the 'London', and 'Country' sides of the box. A fireman put his hand into the 'Country' side and began pulling out the mail when a package burst into flame in his hand. The rest of the letters were pulled out and another suspicious buff-coloured envelope found. Inexplicably a fireman struck this with an axe, and not surprisingly, this also exploded.

At Bedford Place there was another fire in a letterbox, but this seemed to quickly go out and a postman opened up the box and began to remove the letters. Two burnt envelopes fell to the ground. Detective Sergeant Frank McGinn was watching this process when he saw another envelope similar to those that had already functioned in the postman's hand. He pointed to it and said, 'You had better give that one to me'. It had just been passed over when it burst into flames and the detective received minor burns to his hands, chin eyebrows and upper lip. At another scene a postman was also burnt when removing mail from the letterboxes.

The way this, and other incidents were dealt with, illustrates a failure to appreciate of the dangers of dealing with incendiary devices. Police officers were expected to cope with whatever was found with no formal training at all. Although HM Inspectors of Explosives Officers were supposed to deal with infernal machines it seems that they were not on immediate call and did not attend every incident. Altogether over sixteen incendiary devices, or parts of devices, were recovered and sent to Woolwich for forensic investigation.

Even though in real terms the damage was insignificant, there was universal outrage against the attacks and the response was draconian. All leave in most of the Metropolitan Police districts was cancelled. Boarding houses all over the country were raided and special guards were posted on the Houses of Parliament, St Paul's Cathedral and Westminster Abbey. Despite this, bombing continued countrywide with devices going off in London, Birmingham and Manchester, where one device caused a fatality and many injuries.

On Saturday evening 24 June 1939, a team of IRA bombers attacked Central London again. A whole series of high explosive bombs detonated causing much alarm and confusion. Devices exploded around Piccadilly, the main targets being the Midland, Westminster and Lloyd's Banks. The whole front of the Midland bank collapsed after the explosion there and the crowds of people, who had gathered for a night out at the cinemas and theatres, began to panic.

One of the bombs laid was placed in a cubicle in an underground gent's toilet at Oxford Circus. From his cabin the attendant, Thomas Hackett, noticed several men come in and out and one in particular went into cubicle seven and left almost immediately in an obvious hurry. Hackett instantly went to inspect the toilet and discovered a brown paper parcel. He straight away suspected it was a bomb and placed it in a bucket of water and hosed it down as well. He then started to undo the parcel and a blue black substance fell out as well as a black piece of burning fuse. He went upstairs and called to two police officers on duty nearby, who after a brief inspection confirmed it was a bomb. They poured more water onto it and this time a white substance came out and floated on top of the water. Police Constable Butler decided to take the bomb in the bucket to Phoenix Yard which was close by. So as not to draw attention to himself the constable wore one of Hackett's brown coats having discarded his tunic top and helmet. He then carried the bomb in the bucket to Phoenix Yard where he opened the parcel fully, and eight sticks of gelignite fell out. He then arranged for the details of the incident to be passed to the Information Room at Marylebone Police Station where the duty officer was informed of the bomb.

Not far away, on the same night, another police officer working for the Vice Squad in the West End, was about to become renowned for his intervention in another incident. Detective Inspector Robert Fabian was at his desk in Vine Street Police Station at around 22.00 hours when he heard the ominous sound of an explosion which rattled the windows and shook the doors of his office. Without hesitation Fabian grabbed his hat and gas mask and set off in the direction of the blast in Piccadilly. Arriving at the scene, a number of uniformed officers were keeping back crowds of inquisitive sightseers gathered at the corner of Glasshouse Street, where the seat of the explosion was evident. Fabian forced his way through the crowd and surveyed the wreckage. It was clear to him this was the work of an IRA bomb. Whilst looking at the scene he noticed a brown wrapped parcel, close by, which was poorly hidden behind a traffic signpost.

Suspicious, he walked bravely over to examine the suspect parcel. It was carefully wrapped and the ends of the paper were sealed with adhesive tape. It was not the sort of wrapping he would have expected from a purchase in a West End Shop. He touched the parcel with his fingers and immediately noted that it seemed hot. He turned to the uniformed officers and told them to move the crowd further back as he had found another bomb. He gingerly picked up the parcel, as his first thought was to dump it in a bucket of water, but there was not one handy. At this point he noted that the parcel seemed to be getting hotter and feared that the bomb would explode any minute. He began to feel very alone, noting that if the bomb was of a similar size to the one that had just gone off he was in mortal danger. He placed the bomb back on the ground and considered his options.

He knew absolutely nothing about explosives, particularly gelignite, but clearly something must be done. By now a crowd of several hundred had gathered and their eyes were all trained on him waiting to see what he would do next. His prayers were answered by the arrival of the fire brigade and he shouted for a bucket of water. The response was not what he expected and he was informed that they had no bucket. The senior fire officer adding unhelpfully: 'What do you think we represent? Southend 1.'

At that point Fabian decided that he had to dismantle the device. He knelt down next to it on the pavement pulled out his old and blunt pocket knife, cut the adhesive tape and unfolded the paper at one end. He gently placed his hand inside and could feel a small a stick of explosive wrapped in a grease proof wrapping. With great care he pulled it, and from the label, could see that he was dealing with four-ounce sticks of Polar Ammon Gelignite. He pulled out a further six sticks before finding the one he was after. This contained the fuse and the detonator. He sliced the explosive in half, separated the fuse and then placed this in his pocket. He then pulled out two further sticks making a total of two and a half pounds of explosive. Crouching down and looking inside the parcel he could see a small pile of grey powder with a green liquid filled balloon in the centre. As he pulled this out he knew that the device was safe. His final action was to cut all the sticks of Gelignite into small pieces, place them into cigarette and cigar boxes, which he recovered from the scene of the first explosion, and then he carried the lot into Vine Street Police Station, where he dumped everything in a neat red line of fire buckets. That same night a number of other devices exploded throughout the capital injuring half a dozen people but not causing any deaths.

Examination of the device Fabian dismantled showed that the terrorists used a wax capsule of sulphuric acid inside the balloon. When ready for use the wax capsule would be crushed releasing the acid which steadily ate through the thin balloon skin, mixing with the grey powder and bursting into flame, this being sufficient to light the fuse leading to the detonator. For his outstanding bravery Fabian was awarded the Police Medal for gallantry which was presented to him on 6 February 1940 by King George VI.

At the Aldwych, at 23.10 hours, another bomb detonated inside the letterbox of Lloyds Bank at Inversek House, opposite the Gaiety Theatre. Extensive damage was done to the fittings on the ground floor. The bomb was actually dropped into a metal letterbox which was built in to the wall of the bank. This had the effect of directing most of the blast into the building and not out on to the street. Even so, nine of the large plate glass windows were shattered, with the glass being blown out of the frames and across the street.

The outside flap of the letterbox box was blown through the side of an omnibus which was stationary at a bus stop opposite the bank. A number of people standing there were injured, mainly by flying glass. It was fortunate that more people were not injured, or even killed, because the bomb was set to go off around the time the performances finished at two nearby theatres. Fortunately, the Theatre Royal in Drury Lane did not close until 23.15 hours, and the Dutchess three minutes later at 23.18 hours. Had the performances finished a little earlier many more people would have been out on the streets queuing for busses or walking to tube stations.

Jeremiah Lougheed, walking with a friend at the time of the explosion, made a statement about the incident in which he said:

> As we were passing the bank there was a terrific bang and glass showered all around us. I saw another man walking in front of me fall to the ground. I could see he was hurt. I went to pick him up. As I did so I was carried away by a sudden rush of air which came from the Bank and I was blown against a tree. There was an iron rail around the tree. I fell against it and struck my head on it. As I was lying there I was struck by flying glass. I did not see or remember any more. I was taken to hospital where three stitches were inserted in my head.[12]

Major Crawford from HM Inspector of Explosives, who went to the scene, estimated that he damage was caused by three pounds of explosive. In an attempt to prevent further attacks of this sort, the Bank agreed to look at the possibility of all letter boxes being emptied after the last post on a Saturday and then being sealed.

The attacks in the heart of the capital caused a further public outcry and difficult questions were being asked in the House of Commons. On 24 July 1939, the British Home secretary conceded that, since the beginning of January, there had been 127 terrorist outrages, killing one person and seriously injuring a further thirty-five. As a result, the Prevention of Violence Bill was introduced which required the registration of all Irish people living on the mainland. The Bill also tightened immigration procedures and it allowed the deportation of suspects without trial. Before it could be passed there were two further outrages, this time at mainline stations in London on 26 July. At Victoria station a bomb exploded in the cloakroom injuring five people. At King's Cross a similar device tore the legs off Alistair Campbell a brilliant young doctor from Aberdeen who subsequently died in hospital. His wife was also seriously injured along with two luggage counter attendants.

In August, a plot to blow up the Bank of England and a number of government offices was thwarted and possibly, because of this, subsequent attacks were mounted outside the capital. The worst incident occurred in Coventry where a bomber, who had been handed a bomb, which was 'up and running' panicked and abandoned it. When it was given to him he placed it in his bicycle basket and set off for the intended target. He was delayed en-route and when time began to run short he simply abandoned the cycle and bomb in the Broadway. It detonated a few minutes later, killing five people, injuring sixty more and causing considerable damage. Britain was horrified. Retribution was swift with raids on every known Irish home in the Coventry area and many people were arrested. The incident shook the IRA leadership; they were, they claimed, still trying to avoid fatalities amongst the civilian population. There was now a lull in the campaign partly as a result of the Coventry bomb, but also because the security forces were beginning to catch up with the bombers. Many of the IRA active service men were constantly on the move from house to house and had little time to take part in further attacks.

There is some tentative evidence to suggest that there were links between the Abwehr (the German intelligence service) and the IRA at this time and certainly M15 and Special Branch devoted much time and effort investigating such claims. For example, under interrogation one agent, codenamed *Zig Zag*, named another man, Herman Vosch, who was allegedly trained in sabotage. He claimed Vosch had been involved with the IRA, including preparing bombs and actually participating in the attack on Hammersmith Bridge. Further work indicated that this man was actually Karl Barton who had worked in London around this time. Nothing seems to have been conclusively proven though and it is probable that this was more talk than truth.[13]

O'Donovan, the architect of the S Plan, later undoubtedly established links with the Abwehr, and visited them three times, the last trip in August 1939 just before the outbreak of the Second World War. He hoped to secure further funding and material assistance for the campaign. There are some stories that the Abwehr did actually supply some equipment to the IRA but there is no substantial evidence to support this.

When the Germans invaded Poland and war was declared by Britain on 3 September 1939 the stakes were raised considerably. The Irish government, wishing to remain neutral, was aware of O'Donovan's activities and there was concern that, in the new circumstances of another European war, if strong links were established between the IRA and the Abwehr and both civilian and military casualties mounted, Britain might just consider invading the South. Avoiding provocation was vital, and the Irish Government realised that to maintain their neutrality they would have to draw the IRA's teeth and they set about disrupting the support organisation based in Southern Ireland.

Despite this, in the first year of the Second World War, the campaign in London continued unabated and in early November sixteen pillar boxes were attacked in Central London all of which caught fire. Similar devices actually got into the mail system which resulted in the mail sacks on some trains catching fire. On the night of 18 November, four bombs detonated in shop windows in Piccadilly and Regent's Street. Two devices failed and were recovered in Piccadilly and Park Lane. The recovered bombs consisted of three sticks of gelignite and a detonator and short length of safety fuse. The fuse was attached to an acid-filled wax-lined rubber balloon which was contained in a 'Gold Flake' cigarette packet. A few days later, on the 24 November, similar bombs were used to blow up two police boxes and two telephone kiosks. There was apparently some intelligence to suggest that these bombs were being constructed in Dublin and that the mixture being used to initiate them was being made from a formula provided by a German chemist.

On the 21 December 1939, the IRA attempted to set fire to the Kingsway Post Office using an incendiary device posted through one of the boxes on the outside of the building. A witness, Mr Frank Rendell, was waiting outside the post office when the attack happened.

According to him, at about 17.05 hours, a man walked up to the post office and tried to push a package into the aperture. As he did so there was sudden flash and a loud bang. The man quickly put both hands in his pocket and walked briskly away from the scene. Mr Rendell walked up to him and said: 'You had better stop here a moment.' But almost immediately another voice rang out saying: 'That's the bloke that did it.' At which point the perpetrator took off through the crowds. Rendell gave chase but in the darkness (the blackout was in place) lost the suspect after a couple of corners.

A postman, Albert Clarkson, working inside the post office, also witnessed the event. He first noticed smoke coming from one of the side doors of the posting boxes. At that moment two young lads opened the side door of the post office building and said someone was trying to blow up the building. Clarkson then immediately opened the rear of the letter box and noticed a considerable amount of smoke. He pulled out the internal basket but no letters appeared to be on fire. He went outside and saw the remains of a balloon lying on the floor and covered this with sand.

Two other witnesses reported that, at about 17.15 hours, they were approaching the office when they saw a brightly coloured object fall from the mouth of the letter box to the ground, where it burst into flame. At the same moment a man was seen to be running from the post office followed by another with many people shouting 'stop him'.

A little later that evening, another incendiary functioned at Mount Pleasant Post Office. The mail had just been collected from the sub-post office in Grays Inn Road and was being unloaded when a device functioned. The letters caught fire, but this was immediately extinguished by staff at the post office with sand. An examination of the charred remains revealed the remnants of a balloon and an envelope. Whilst this investigation was on going, yet another incendiary exploded at 19.15 hours when mail was being loaded on to a van ready for transport to Euston Railway Station.

The same day, between 18.25 hours and 19.35 hours, a further five devices exploded at the sorting office in Eversholt Street. Mr Arthur Drake, a temporary sorter, was injured when one of these exploded and he received treatment for burns to his hands and face. In each case it was reported that there was a bright flash followed by a sizzling sound. The investigation revealed traces of a sticky black substance and bits of red balloons. Whilst the office was being searched another device exploded.

During 1939, there had been a total of 242 outrages or attempted outrages throughout the country, the majority in London. These included the use of high explosive bombs, incendiaries and tear gas devices. In total they caused seven deaths and injured ninety-eight people. In London sixty-two people were arrested. Explosives Officers from HM Inspector of Explosives visited the scenes of most of the incidents. The bombing continued in 1940 and the Annual HM Inspectors of Explosives Report for that year noted there were fifty-three IRA outrages. Unfortunately, secrecy and wartime restrictions were imposed and they did not publish details of the attacks, and it has proved impossible to establish exactly where and when all these incidents took place. However, they included a failed device on a bus at Victoria station on 7 February 1940, and then two weeks later there was an explosion in a gent's toilet in Marble Arch which did significant damage and injured two people. This was followed by another explosion in a litter bin by a bus stop outside the Cumberland Hotel. This explosion broke several windows and injured thirteen people. In early March a bomb detonated outside the Westminster Bank in Park Lane, causing considerable damage, but no casualties. Later in the month another bomb outside the Paddington Town hall damaged an Air Raid Precautions control centre. On 18 March another failed bomb was discovered in a litter bin in Grosvenor Place and later that day a bomb exploded in the Westminster Refuse Dump in Gatcliff Road. It was thought that this was a device left in a litter bin in Covent Garden which was then collected by the council workmen and detonated much later than intended. This was the last bomb to explode in London in the 1939-40 IRA campaign.

By now, many of the IRA men had been arrested in both Southern Ireland and the United Kingdom and this, in conjunction with total censorship and a lack of funding, brought the campaign to a spluttering conclusion. As usual, throughout the period, certain malicious members of the public evidently considered that the opportunity to display a warped sense of humour was too good to miss and concocted a number of hoaxes in the shape of dummy bombs. A good deal of time was wasted dealing with them.

In terms of generating sheer terror in this campaign it is probably true to say that the IRA lacked the will to go for the jugular. Indeed, the architect of the plan, Sean Russell, said in an interview with the *Los Angeles Examiner* in May 1939 that: 'Up to this time, under my specific orders bombs have been placed and exploded so that no one gets hurt.'[14]

Nevertheless, in those two years far more bombs and incendiaries were deployed than in many of the years of the subsequent IRA campaigns from 1973 onwards, although it must be acknowledged that some of the bombs in the latter campaign were huge in comparison.

From a police perspective they were ruthless in the way in which they pursued the IRA and in this they were aided by being given sweeping powers, particularly after war was declared. For the people of London, the campaign by the IRA was quickly forgotten as there was another and much more serious threat looming. War had been declared and it would not be long before the Luftwaffe unleashed the deadliest and most destructive attacks in the history of the bombing of London

NOTES:
1. TNA, LAB 59/16: HM Inspectors of Explosives Report 1923.
2. TNA, MEPO, 2/1761: Explosives: Depositing in dustbins.
3. TNA, LAB, 59/23: HM Inspectors of Explosives Report 1930.
4. TNA, MEPO 2/4345: Collection of explosives for conveyance to War Department Magazines.
5. TNA, MEPO 2/4345: Collection of explosives for conveyance to War Department Magazines.
6. TNA, HO 144/21356: Explosions in London, Manchester and Warwick 16 January 1939.
7. TNA, KV 4/232: Notes for the guidance to police as to how to deal with an explosive charge.
8. TNA, MEPO, 3/1278: Statement of Albert Arthur Harris, Northolt, 8 March 1939.
9. TNA, MEPO, 3/1304: Explosion at the Grosvenor House Hotel, 16 March 1939.
10. TNA, MEPO, 3/1284: Report on the Explosion at Victoria Cinema, June 1939.
11. TNA, MEPO, 3/1286: Various Reports on Explosions in Letterboxes, 9 June 1939.
12. TNA, MEPO, 3/1289: Statement of Jeremiah Lougheed, Ilford, June 1939.
13. TNA, KV 2/2461: Details of Barton Karl.
14. TNA, HO 144/21358: Sean Russell, IRA leader arrest in Detroit.

Chapter 8

Fear

'I think it is as well for the man in the street to realise that there is no power on earth that can prevent him from being bombed. Whatever people tell him the bomber will always get through.'
Stanley Baldwin in the House of Commons, 10 November 1932.

Although, retrospectively, the First World War air raids on Great Britain were not large in scale or duration, they did have a significant psychological impact, particularly on the citizens of London who bore the brunt of the attacks. In terms of physical destruction, the damage was, in the overall context of the war, insignificant. Even so, the effect on production was, at times, out of all proportion to the scale of the raids and this would later provide the 'Bomber' theorists with evidence to support some of their more outlandish claims. In purely economic terms, considering all the effort the Germans put in to the bombing, particularly the cost of the raw materials for the construction and maintenance of the Zeppelins, it is doubtful if they gained much serious advantage from the raids. It is clear though that, in the long run, what they did do was force the British military into laying sound foundations for the establishment of an effective air defence system that would later play an absolutely crucial role in the Second World War. Although the creation of this system of defence was by no means a foregone conclusion, and required significant effort, the lessons learned during the bombing in the First World War were vital to its formation. What was not obvious to anyone in the lead up to the Second World War was that the system, and all its components, was in place. It would not prevent deadly and devastating raids, but a combination of all its elements both defensive and offensive did stop the total collapse of morale that many had predicted.

The lead up to the Second World War was a difficult and perplexing time. Predicting what might happen was inevitably an inexact science. For every theory put forward there was always a contrary opinion. Many people believed that the politicians simply would not allow another European war to break out, and therefore plans to defend the capital were irrelevant. Others argued that mass panic and hysteria were inevitable once the bombing started. In the event the casualties proved far less than envisaged, although in human terms they were still horrendous, and the greatly feared gas attacks never materialised. Contingency planning for ill-defined threats was, and still is, one of the hardest tasks. For those in positions of authority the tendency to err towards the worst-case scenario when formulating strategy is understandable.

In the lead up to the war the fear of bombing prayed on the minds of the citizens in the capital, and there were good reasons for this. Between the wars much theoretical work was done on the concept of strategic bombing based on the analysis of the effectiveness of the First World War raids. This was later supported by the newsreels showing the bombing of Guernica and other towns and cities by Franco's forces during the Spanish civil war. The main conclusions seemed to vindicate the people's fears. In the early 1930s the idea of aerial bombardment was almost as haunting as the spectre of nuclear war was at the height of the Cold War. At the time it was intellectually fashionable to believe that advanced industrial civilisations were at the mercy of the bomber and that major cities were nothing more than strategic liabilities.

It was an era of constant escalation, as the performance of modern military aircraft rapidly improved. As they flew higher, faster and with greater bomb loads, so the estimates of casualties spiraled. There was a whole raft of secret War Office studies into the subject. In 1925 the Air Staff estimated that air raids on London would kill 1,700 people and injure 3,300 in the first twenty-four hours. By 1937 it was thought that for each ton of bombs dropped fifty people would be killed or injured and that the Germans could deliver 600 tons per day, resulting in 30,000 casualties daily. In the spring of 1939 the British Air Staff, in a further worst-case estimate, calculated that the Luftwaffe, using its long range bombers, could deliver a maximum of approximately 700 tons of bombs on London per day and that they could sustain this level for two weeks, after which the capacity would tail off. It maintained that each ton of bombs would kill or wound fifty people when dropped in a built-up area. Therefore, in the first two weeks of any offensive there could potentially be 500,000 casualties. The estimates continued to escalate and, by 1940, the Luftwaffe was thought to be capable of dropping 950 tons of bombs per day. As late as June 1940 when the Battle of Britain had started, the Prime Minister's office was comforting itself that there might only be 18,000 deaths a day once the bombing of the cities started in earnest.

These secret apocalyptic visions of the bombing offensive were reinforced by popular fiction. In *The War in the Air* by Major Hilders, an alias for a Lufthansa pilot called Dr Robert Knauss, the story was told of a short intense war between France and Britain. The key battles were fought in the air, and the central episode was the destruction of Paris by a British air fleet, which dropped a combination of high explosive, incendiary and gas bombs toppling the Eiffel Tower, and turning the centre of the city into a ruined and desolate desert. The population that survived the onslaught went mad with fear and resorted to rioting and looting. The communists raised the red flag over the city and, in the face of a second devastating raid and revolution in the streets, the French government sued for peace.

The thriving film industry also reinforced the feelings of vulnerability to air attack. One of the biggest British films released in 1936, was *Things to Come*, by H.G. Wells, which opened with the complete collapse of civilisation in a war, which started with heavy air attacks on major cities. In a clever psychological twist, the first bomb dropped was shown exploding in a cinema full of people, a point not lost on the audiences of the day.

This sensationalism was not restricted to the popular press; there were many serious writers on air power who believed that a knockout blow could be achieved by a sudden and overwhelming assault from the skies. As early as 1921, the father of air power doctrine, an Italian General, Giulio Douhet, foresaw the attack of cites with high explosive, gas and incendiaries. These, he concluded, would produce results similar to the great barrages of the First World War and would affect civilians more than trained soldiers. The stress, shock and horror of these would quickly break the morale of the people. The psychological yield of such attacks would be tremendous; people would flee the cities for the countryside and persistent, poisonous gas would ensure they never returned. Production would collapse and, ultimately, the war-fighting capability of the country would follow. In England influential writers such as J.F.C. Fuller and Liddell Hart echoed Douhet's assertion that the civilian population could not withstand serious aerial bombardment.

A measure of the fear generated, at the time of the invasion of Czechoslovakia, can be gained from early Mass Observation reports. Voluntary 'observers' from all over the country and from many walks of life produced these. Some revealed that a surprising number of Britons contemplated killing their families if war broke out. 'I'd sooner see kids dead than see them bombed like they are in some places,' said one woman, thinking of the scenes from Abyssinia and Spain.[1]

Even in official circles, the level of apprehension can be gauged from the instructions that were issued to troops who would provide assistance to the civil authorities in the London area in time of war. It stated that troops would be required to deal, for the most part, with a friendly, though perhaps panic-stricken population. It recognised that air attack might temporarily disrupt the planned central control of the capital. A Regional Commissioner's office was set up in London which would act as the central government's representative if the normal administrative systems broke down. To assist the Commissioner, should the need arise, he would have resource to call upon troops to be used in formed bodies of men. Their priority task would be to assist the police in maintaining law and order and ensure the free movement of traffic. The troops were only to be used if the civil authorities' resources were exhausted. It was considered that the deployment of troops was likely to be a major factor in preventing panic both prior to air raids and when hostile actions ceased. For this reason, it was seen as desirable that crowds of frightened people should perceive troops as helpers and not suppressors. However, some of the examples given where troops might be deployed indicate the level of concern in high office, for example:

> Crowds of people gathering to get into a railway station from which few trains are running and a grave danger exists of people being trampled to death or pushed on to live rails.
>
> The police reserves are insufficient, so the local inspector calls on the nearest body of troops to assist in the marshalling of the evacuees and the organising of queues.
>
> A street has been bombed and crowds are preventing the movement of fire engines, ambulances and rescue services.
>
> A wealthy shopping quarter has been bombed and looting is going on in jewellers and other shops. Troops are called to clear the area.
>
> Crowds without food have taken refuge in open land in the suburbs. The civilian authorities have organised soup kitchens, which have been rushed by hungry people. Troops are required to restore order and organise queues.[2]

Whilst it was clear that the use of troops was aimed at the restoration of law and order with the minimum use of force, it was accepted that, on occasions, lethal weapons might have to be used. Officers were reminded that the action they took was their responsibility particularly when opening fire and, it noted some form of warning had to be given by megaphone or bugle before the order to shoot was given. It was thought that it would be rarely justifiable to open fire except in the event of sabotage by enemy agents or in the case of looting by disorderly crowds. When dispersing crowds by less lethal means it was pointed out that this should be done by troops with fixed bayonets. It was explained that, 'The threat of cold steel will often have the desired effect without further action.' Troops were reminded that when pushing crowds before them, those in the rear dictated the pace at which the people at the front could move and that time for an orderly dispersal should be given. In some circumstances it was envisaged that armoured vehicles could be used, an example given being of the escort of food convoys through the East End, which were being looted by a starving and disorderly population. These stringent measures reflect the unease in government and military circles of the threat posed by mass bombing.

The dread of being drenched from the air by poison gas indisputably generated the greatest fear, and today, with the current terrorist threat, still does evoke feelings of acute anguish. There is something insidious about the use of gas which poisons and kills by the simple acts of breathing or touching. Between the wars there were still soldiers suffering and dying from the long-term effects of mustard, chlorine and phosgene gas and their vivid memories, and those of other survivors, did nothing to dispel the horrors of this type of warfare. The fear of chemical weapons was further revived when, in 1936, the Italian air force dropped mustard gas on the totally defenceless and uncomprehending Abyssinians with, not surprisingly, devastating results.

Within this framework of the fear of bombing must be added the fact that there were tremendous social tensions within the country when these theories of Armageddon abounded. These were well summed up by Constantine Fitzgibbon who wrote:

> The working class, massacred in 1914-18, cheated, as it thought, out of the promised fruits of victory, lied to by the popular press and later plunged into the hopeless quagmire of mass unemployment, not unnaturally regarded the governing class with deep suspicion and dislike.[3]

There was genuine concern in some government circles that the bombing would simply be the catalyst, which would result in the overthrow of the establishment. Therefore, at all levels throughout the population, the prospect of being bombed had generated a level of trepidation which in some quarters was verging on hysteria.

There were of course contrary views, but these did not fit in with the expectations of the time and were generally overlooked. There was some hard evidence to suggest that the chemical weapon threat was overrated. On the outskirts of Hamburg in 1928 a chemical factory exploded releasing some eleven tons of phosgene, one of the deadliest gases of the First World War. The cloud drifted through the outskirts of the city and out into the countryside where it dissipated. For such a large and concentrated release of gas, the casualties were remarkably light with only eleven dead and two hundred hospitalised.

Equally, the bombing in the Spanish civil war, although horrific, did not produce the expected numbers of fatalities and injuries in terms of casualties per ton of bombs dropped. This evidence indicated that terror bombing might not be the decisive weapon that everyone thought, but it would not stop all sides trying to prove that it was.

What all this fear and uncertainty did was to create an atmosphere in which there was the will to spend money on planning and preparing for the defence of the country. Memories of the First World War and the hatred of the 'Hun' were still fresh in the minds of thousands of men who had first-hand experience of the Germans on the field of battle. Over a decade later, many of these former servicemen now held positions of power and influence in government and industry, and they used their authority to put in place measures which were vital for the future survival of the country. In 1932, the cornerstone of British Defence Policy, the Ten Year Rule, was abandoned. In simple terms this stated that the country would not be involved in a major conflict in the ten subsequent years. As the war clouds gathered defence spending rapidly escalated. For example, the armed forces budget rose from, £113m in 1929 to £292m in 1939.[4] Whereas the Army and Navy budgets were almost doubled during the period, the expenditure on the RAF increased six fold.

The military task of preventing the enemy bombers reaching the capital and dispensing their loads, clearly fell to the fighters of the RAF and the anti-aircraft guns and barrage balloons of the Army. Once the bombs had been released, the responsibility for dealing with the aftermath fell to the police, fire and medical services, the Air Raid Precautions (ARP) organisation and some voluntary services. The first serious plans for Civil Defence were drawn up in 1935 under the auspices of the Home Office. The main areas of responsibility were: the expansion of the fire services; evacuation planning; measures for the protection against gas and bombing and the establishment of various elements of a broad organisation to deal with the after effects of bombing and gas attacks.

152

Above: A view of the damage to Macclesfield Bridge after the explosion on the barge *Tilbury*. Some of the cast iron pillars which were not too badly damaged were reused in the reconstruction of the new bridge, but rotated through 180 degrees. Today, if you look closely, you can see the grooves worn on the pillars by the tow lines prior to the explosion on the side furthest from the water. (Author)

Left: Sir Vivian Derring Majendie posing with the initiation mechanism for the Paddington Infernal Machine. He was instrumental in setting up the systems necessary to deal with the bombs used by the IRA in their campaign during the 1870s. (Author)

Above: The damage after the explosion of a bomb in the urinal underneath Scotland Yard in May 1884. (Author)

Left: A sketch of the scene after the explosion on the hill outside the Greenwich Observatory which killed the anarchist Martial Bourdin. The explosion occurred roughly at the spot marked (a), whilst (b) indicates where Bourdin's body lay. (Author)

Above left: The remains of the device constructed inside a Keen's Mustard Tin which can be seen in the City Police Museum. It may be the device which was found at St Paul's Cathedral. (Author)

Above right: Police Constable Edmund Forbes poses with the bomb he recovered from the Nevill Arms Public House in Stoke Newington after the first Zeppelin raid on London on 31 May 1915. (Author)

Below: A general view of the devastation at Silvertown following the accidental explosion of some fifty tons of TNT. It shows the complete destruction of the factory. (Author)

P·C·EDWARD GEORGE ·
BROWN GREENOFF
METROPOLITAN POLICE
MANY LIVES WERE SAVED BY HIS
DEVOTION TO DUTY AT THE
TERRIBLE EXPLOSION AT
SILVERTOWN · 19·JAN·1917·

Above: Hidden away in Postman's Park, a public space in central London, a short distance north of St Paul's Cathedral and the site of the former head office of the General Post Office (from which the park derives its name), is the Memorial to Heroic Self Sacrifice. First proposed by painter and sculptor George Frederic Watts in 1887, the memorial was unveiled, in an uncompleted state, in 1900. It commemorates ordinary people who died saving the lives of others and who might otherwise have been forgotten. One of the names on the memorial is that of Police Constable Edward George Greenoff, who helped to evacuate the Brunner Mond factory. Then, aware of the danger he was facing, Greenoff remained outside to warn passers-by of the risk of an explosion. When that explosion did take place, the head injuries he suffered proved fatal; he died nine days later, aged 30. He was posthumously awarded the King's Police Medal. (Historic Military Press)

Above: A German postcard depicting members of ground crew bombing-up a Gotha in preparation for an attack on the UK during the so-called First Blitz. The Gothas carried out twenty-two raids on Britain in the First World War, dropping 84,740kg of bombs for the loss of sixty-one aircraft. (Historic Military Press)

Above: During the First World War there were fifty-two Zeppelin and airship raids on England that, between them, led to the deaths of 556 people; a further 1,357 were injured. On 13 October 1915, a single airship inflicted damage across the centre of the City of London, including at Lincoln's Inn where scars from the bombs can still be seen in the stonework. The bomb itself fell in the roadway in the foreground – the spot is actually marked by a small bronze disc. (Courtesy of Robert Mitchell)

Below: The damage that can still be seen on this Sphinx on London's Victoria Embankment. It was caused by fragments from a bomb which exploded in the roadway nearby during the first air raid on London by German aeroplanes a few minutes before midnight on 4 September 1917. (Courtesy of Robert Mitchell)

Left: The monument erected in memory of the eighteen children killed in the bombing of Upper North Street School. (Author)

Below: The IRA detonated a bomb inside the letterbox of Lloyds Bank at Inversek House, opposite the Gaiety Theatre in Aldwych, at around 23.00 hours on 24 June 1939. The explosion blew the windows out and sent shards of glass flying across the street, injuring several people. It was fortunate that there was not a greater number of casualties, or even fatalities, as the bomb was set to detonate around the time the performances finished at two nearby theatres. (Author)

Above: Eight people were injured and widespread damage was caused when bombs planted by the IRA exploded at two London Underground stations, more specifically those at Tottenham Court Road and Leicester Square, on 3 February 1939. This image depicts some of the wreckage caused by the explosion at the latter. (Historic Military Press)

Below: A series of bomb explosions in different parts of London took place in the early hours of 1 April 1939. This photograph shows broken glass and shattered windows, the result of the IRA's device, at the premises of Heal & Sons in Tottenham Court Road. (Historic Military Press)

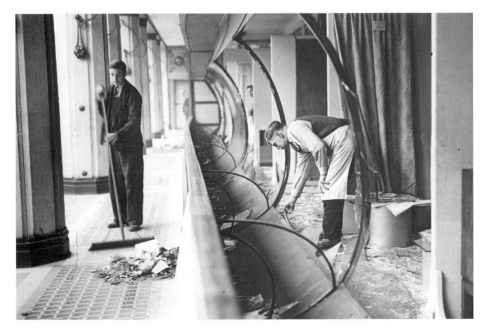

Above: Only a day after the announcement of the discovery of the Irish Republican Army's 'S Plan', outlining details for a new terrorist campaign, a huge explosion occurred in the Parcels Office at King's Cross Station on 3 August 1939, causing the damage seen here. It was reported that fourteen persons were injured, including one man whose leg was blown off. (Historic Military Press)

Although it got off to a slow to start, a vast amount of work was done in preparing the country for an assault from the air. Spurred on by the Italian's use of chemical weapons, courses for ARP training were introduced. Initially police officers and fire officers from London attended these, followed by the first volunteer wardens. The threat from incendiary bombs was one of the topics covered, and the Home Office Fire Advisor laid on a demonstration at Barnes in 1937 in which a number of fires were dealt with by 'teams of girls with only a short period of training'. Doctors were instructed in recognising and treating the symptoms of gas poisoning and a new pattern of civilian gas mask was produced. By the end of 1937 some 21,000,000 of these civilian masks were stored in regional depots. Despite the series of international crises, which came and went, these were not issued to the public. The major factor behind this decision was that the development of a suitable system to protect small children and babies had not been completed. Understandably it was considered politically unacceptable to provide protection for adults and not for their offspring. Even mundane items like steel helmets and sandbags were being manufactured in huge quantities and being stored ready for use.

The country was divided into regions with London, the smallest but most densely populated, becoming No.5. There was a Regional Headquarters and beneath it several Group Headquarters. Each Group contained a number of Boroughs. The primary task of the Group was to move resources within its boundaries to reinforce Boroughs should they become overwhelmed by an attack. The Borough was effectively the tactical unit of Civil Defence and had its own Report and Control Centre, most often in the town hall. The Borough was then subdivided into Districts often with upwards of a 1,000 persons acting as wardens. The basic unit of defence was the warden's post which was manned by three to six wardens and was given a small area of responsibility, the size of which varied, but normally would contain some 500 people. The wardens themselves were supposed to be responsible members of the public, chosen to be leaders and advisors to their neighbours in an area where they were well known, liked and respected. The majority met these requirements. Like beat bobbies, they got to know their areas in intimate detail, knew most of the inhabitants by sight if not by name and provided expert local knowledge to police, firemen, ambulance and the rescue services at incidents.

The wardens were the capital's foot soldiers. Before the war and just after it was declared, they attended training courses, issued gas masks, checked the blackout and generally supported the public. They did much good work, but the prevailing attitude at the time meant that talk of war, and preparations for it, were not readily or enthusiastically received in some quarters. Many wardens, as depicted by Hodges in *Dad's Army*, were regarded as 'Little Hitlers', draft dodgers, wasters of precious petrol and a hindrance in general to the war effort. When the first bombs dropped this attitude drastically changed and the wardens came into their own. They reported incidents in their area, and were generally amongst the first on the scene of an explosion. They provided the initial assessment of casualties and damage and submitted requests for additional help and assistance as required.

It was obvious from the start that the Metropolitan, City and other smaller police forces in London would be required to play a critical part in the defence of the capital. Police War Instructions, circulated just before the beginning of the conflict, made it clear that every police officer should be properly trained in all manner of air raid precautions. They were able to bring to the task a well tried and tested organisation which was, in the nature of police work, decentralised and therefore had built-in redundancy and hence survivability. If, under air raid conditions, a breakdown of normal communications occurred it was agreed by the Commissioner of the Metropolitan Police that a decentralised control system would be established. This went down to the Inspectors' level within the eighty-five subdivisions of the Metropolitan Police area. The Inspectors would have the necessary powers to maintain law and order in their divisions and, as already discussed, could call on troops to assist if their resources became exhausted.

Largely due to their good communications and redundancy in the system, the police were given full responsibility for installing and operating the dreaded sirens used for air raid warnings. These wailing alarms were electrically operated or hand-cranked and over 500 were installed on the roofs of police stations and police boxes throughout the capital.

By 1938 it was clear that, in the defence of the capital, more police would be needed and three types of auxiliaries augmented the regulars. They were re-engaged pensioners who volunteered to return, Special Constables accepting service on a full time paid basis, and by far the largest contingent, men recruited for war service only.

Importantly, police officers had qualifications of a kind which no other body of men could offer. The very nature of their training and operational work meant that they were, in comparison to others, cool and clear-headed in emergencies, and were able to deal with distressed individuals or panicky crowds. They had the public's confidence and people looked to them for leadership in frightening or perplexing situations, ones that bombing was likely to generate. Some of the duties police officers were required to undertake were an extension of their peacetime roles; for example, traffic control, keeping roads clear for essential vehicles and setting up diversions. In addition, the police were, more often than not, first on the scene at major peacetime incidents, including fires and gas explosions so they were used to taking control, rescuing people, searching debris for survivors and evacuating occupants from damaged houses. Another advantage they had over the other Civil Defence organisations was that most police officers were accustomed to dealing with injury and death. They had been to suicides, murders or accidents and seen and dealt with dead bodies of both sexes and all ages. Their duties meant that they had also had to administer first aid to persons with a range of injuries at many of the varied calls they attended. Certainly vehicle accidents, in those pre-seat belt days, seemed to generate the most appalling injuries.

Some of their duties, however, would be entirely new and little consideration was given to the stressful effects of these, combined with long hours of work. Initially police officers were required to report for duty at their station every time an air raid warning sounded, meaning they had to get up whatever the hour and, in most cases, cycle to their place of work. When the Blitz started the disruption and exhaustion this caused quickly became unacceptable and the order was soon rescinded.

HM Inspector of Constabulary, Colonel G.H.R. Holland, expressed some misgivings about the high level of reliance on the police in a report written at the time. This concerned the growing tendency to dump all the extra duties on the police, which was the outcome of the confidence placed on the reliability and efficiency of their organisation. It noted, however, that there was a desire to avoid the expense of setting up a completely new organisation to undertake the tasks.

One of the new duties was learning to deal with all aspects of chemical warfare, and the police underwent extensive training to cope with this terrifying and feared weapon. A gas warfare school was set up at Winterbourne Gunner in Wiltshire where police officers were instructed on the measures to be taken to protect the populace in the event of this type of weapon being unleashed. In fact, in the early stages of the war, it was probably the efficiency and openness of the British anti-gas arrangements that played a major role in convincing the Germans not to even consider using the weapon, particularly as at the time their defences were almost non-existent. It will come as no surprise for the reader to discover that some seventy years later; with new terrorist threats emerging, police officers are once again attending such courses at the same old location, Winterbourne Gunner.

Later in the war police officers attended other specialist courses. The Incident Officers course was designed to teach them how to deal with the aftermath of an explosion, and to supervise rescue operations more effectively. After the Blitz, some police officers also attended Bomb Reconnaissance Courses and became qualified Bomb Reconnaissance Officers. One Inspector who attended the course, illustrated the point that a little knowledge can be a bad thing. He commented that although he was worried about bombs before the course, by the time he had completed it he was absolutely 'shit-scared'.

The entries in Station Inspector Langdon's Occurrence Book from Deptford and Rotherhithe provide a clear indication of the detailed preparations for war undertaken by the police at a local level. As will be seen later, it also documents the abrupt and brutal change from the planning phase to the deadly reality of events on the ground when the air raids started in earnest. Prior to the bombing, the book recorded a mine of useful information. It listed: all the vulnerable points and who was to guard them; beat details for officers after air raids; air raid warden posts, and contact numbers for each; an extensive telephone list covering every conceivable type of crisis even listing different numbers for emergency sewage repair works during, or after raids; the detention of aliens and their movement to specialist reporting centres; lighting restrictions and regulations, including the size of the slits in lamps and their maximum output; gas decontamination duties; shelters and their capacity; trenches in parks and their capacity, for example, those dug in Bermondsey Park were capable of sheltering 975 people, and finally details of all the defence regulations and new police powers.

As far as bomb disposal was concerned, the instructions were a bit vague and retrospectively a little naive, although this was no fault of the police. It recorded that a police officer finding an unexploded bomb would immediately inform the Report Centre of the Local Authority, giving details of its approximate size and location. There the staff would call out a party of Royal Engineers from 502 Field Company who were based at Richmond Road, New Barnet. In addition, a rescue squad with sand bags would be sent to the scene, the Borough Engineer would be informed and arrangements made with the Public Utilities to be ready to disconnect any services which might be damaged. It was naively assumed that that was all that needed to be done. Practical experience would soon change this.

Despite the understandable lack of awareness about dealing with unexploded bombs, the document shows that the police at least had a clear idea of their roles and responsibilities, although no amount of planning would fully prepare the officers for the onslaught when it started. No one knew how they would cope with the bombing when it came, but at least they were better prepared than some other organisations and the civilian population.

Clearly the Fire Service also had a vital role in the defence of the capital and required a massive expansion if it was to be in a position to cope with the predicted numbers of fires. To this end in 1938, an appeal was made for volunteers to join the Auxiliary Fire Service (AFS). Initially only a handful of people came forward, but a vigorous campaign calling for volunteers was initiated and thousands of men and women responded. The aim was to achieve a fifteen-fold increase in the strength of the regular fire brigade.

The AFS personnel needed both training and equipment to be effective. To start with there was a good deal of resentment on the part of the professional firemen, many of them considered that the recruits of the AFS, a motley crew to say the least, were wholly unsuitable for the role they were being asked to undertake. The 5,000 women volunteers in particular were scorned and many were permitted only to undertake menial tasks such as cooking, washing up and scrubbing floors. Fortunately, the intervention and leadership of both the fire brigade and the General Secretary of the union ensured that the men and women of the AFS were tolerated and given some much needed training and equipment. In the so-called 'Phoney War' these men and women would gather round peace-time blazes in much higher numbers than were actually required to try and gain practical experience in fighting fires. In January 1940 the AFS was amalgamated with the London Fire Brigade proper to improve the command, control and co-ordination of the expanded service. Despite this when the bombing started in earnest, very few of the AFS personnel had ever faced a real fire. For their part the regular firemen had no concept of the sheer size, scale and ferocity of the fires that they were about to confront.

The question of fires caused by small incendiary bombs was not exclusively the domain of the fire services. For some years the Home Office had been examining the question of how ordinary householders, staff at factories and members of the ARP services might be trained to defeat the novel and formidable threat posed by small, scattered incendiary bombs. The Chief Inspector of Explosives formed the Incendiary Bomb Committee to acquire knowledge of the bombs' performance and how they could best be extinguished. How the people faired will be discussed in a later chapter.

Because of the horrendous casualty estimates, extensive provision was made to deal with the wounded. Initially a three-tier system was envisaged. Firstly, a multitude of First Aid Posts were to be established and it was intended that these would shield the hospitals from the walking wounded. Next there would be central casualty clearing stations where initial treatment would be given to the seriously injured before they were shipped to the third-tier, base hospitals situated beyond a fifteen-mile radius of Central London. To support the hospitals and move the wounded, the Ambulance Service recruited many additional staff, and although there was nowhere near enough ambulances to meet the projected requirements, arrangements were made for other vehicles to be requisitioned and adapted to carry stretchers.

This proposal, based in principle on a military system, did not work in reality. Many First Aid Posts were actually situated in hospitals and teams worked from there to deal with those with minor injuries. Later, as experience was gained, teams of Mobile Aid Posts were established. These included doctors, nurses and equipment which could be transported to an incident to provide immediate first aid. The hospitals themselves were prepared for mass casualties. Operating theatres were moved to basements, preparations made to evacuate the upper floors of buildings and additional beds procured. Plans were also made to blast-proof some of the critical areas within hospitals, mainly using sandbags.

Rescue teams, which were eventually divided into light and heavy units, were also formed. Their job, quite simply, was to attend the scene of bombings and extricate those people trapped in the ruins of buildings. It was discovered very early on in the bombing that, even under what appeared to be the complete and total collapse of a building, people could still survive trapped in tiny spaces under tons of rubble. They were entombed under stairwells, by being close to a wall or even sheltering under furniture such as robust tables. It was clearly vital for the maintenance of morale that these stricken people were rescued at the earliest opportunity. The rescue parties quickly developed specialist skills such as tunnelling through tons of dangerous rubble, often using timbers found in the debris to construct supports, to rescue trapped people.

The Women's Voluntary Service (WVS) made a major contribution towards defeating the bombers. Set up by Lady Reading and started with five names from her address book, the organisation was to grow to peak strength of 1,300,000 in January 1941. It gave women without an immediate role in the defence of the country the opportunity to get involved. As its name implies, it was strictly 'volunteer' and made up from women from all walks of life. The organisers were, however, often women with a certain status in the local community, the doctor's or the vicar's wife, a member of the parish council, a school governor or a retired headmistress, and sometimes single women of independent means, all of whom displayed leadership skills and a willingness to get 'stuck in'. Under their direction the members, mainly working class women, prepared for war. Their motto was 'The WVS never says no', but none of the women at the start of the war realized how much their services would be in demand or how their responsibilities would escalate. Amongst their duties was the provision of all manner of support at bomb incidents. The Salvation Army also provided much needed assistance. The distinctive uniforms of both these bodies could be seen at all crisis points. They helped out in air raid shelters, at bomb scenes, in rest centres with evacuees, and often aided the police with the preparation of casualty lists. They would be seen wherever people needed help, providing tea and sympathy in equal measure.

One other establishment deserves mention and that is the Ministry of Information, or as it became known to many, the 'Ministry of Disinformation'. It was charged with several functions including boosting and monitoring morale, producing propaganda and acting as a censor. The Mass Observation organisation, which has already been mentioned, was set up in 1937 and was a key contributor to the Ministry's ability to monitor morale. It consisted of a wide range of people, many of them professionals, who were tasked to submit reports into what the people really thought. It was seen by many as a home intelligence gathering organisation and in some quarters it was regarded as being communist dominated and actually likely to be more subversive than supportive of the war. Certainly, many MPs regarded themselves as being much better able to judge the morale of the people. Nevertheless, the organisation was commissioned to provide information on various aspects of morale, particularly in those areas subjected to heavy bombing raids.

As well as generating information and encouraging people, the Ministry was charged with protecting national security by controlling the news released to the public from all sources. This, it was initially thought, would only cover military matters, but total war demanded more than that and although it was a voluntary system, almost complete control on what could or should be published in the press was established. This ensured that when the 'Battle of London' commenced only those views, which supported the cause, prevailed.

As far as censorship was concerned steps were taken to allow the authorities to snoop on all of its citizens. Mail was censored and as many as 200,000 letters a week were opened and the contents scrutinized, telephone calls were monitored and telegrams read.

The bomb that devastated North Street School in Poplar in the First World War highlighted the need to evacuate young children. Detailed planning went into making arrangements to move them, along with the infirm and the elderly, into the safety of the countryside at the commencement of hostilities. Furthermore, steps were planned to prevent people gathering at churches, cinemas and football grounds to reduce the risk of mass casualties. As always there were of course those who disagreed with this view. They argued that in the First World War there were few raids and that concentrating people in one area made sense, but in the coming conflict if people were dispersed throughout the city then they would just provide a larger target for the bombers.

Much effort went into looking at the best method of protecting those that stayed behind and had to endure the bombing. The understandable failure to accurately predict how raids would unfold, and the population react, had many unknown implications. One of these was the fear of the deep shelter mentality. It was expected that at the commencement of hostilities mass raids would begin almost immediately. The approaching bombers would be undetectable (the development of radar being top secret, still in its infancy, and its capabilities known to only a few) until they crossed the coast and then it would only be seven minutes flying time to the centre of the capital. If there were deep shelters, then they would have to be evenly spaced throughout the city. It was considered that the seven minutes available, from the moment of the first warning to the bombers being overhead, was simply not be enough time for people to leave their homes and offices, walk to the nearest shelter, enter it and move down to the safe levels. There was a fear of panic as crowds gathered at the entrances and were unable to gain access as the bombs began falling. The result would be that they would be caught in the streets, and the First World War raids had taught people that it was here that they were most vulnerable. The other fear was that, after one or two massive raids, the people would simply disappear into the shelters and not come out. This in turn would cause problems with sanitation; spread of disease and, most importantly from the government perspective, would paralyse the output from London's crucial industrial base. Deep shelters for the ordinary people were therefore not constructed and restrictions put on the use of the underground system. Instead Anderson shelters, brick-built shelters and later Morrison shelters were introduced. These provided a considerable degree of protection against anything other than a direct hit. Their construction and various merits will be described later.

By mid-1939 a huge amount of effort had gone into planning for the defence of the United Kingdom with London at its heart. An idea of the scale of the undertaking can perhaps be gained by looking at the arrangements being made for the purchase and distribution of defence stores. It included the provision of: 2,500,000 Anderson shelters; 50,000,000 respirators; 475,000,000 sandbags; 1,800,000 civilian steel helmets; 1,850,000 anti-gas suits; 20,000 tons of bleach; 50 tons of gas detector paint; 50,000 stirrup pumps and many other items.[5]

The preparations had not all gone smoothly, were not carried out uniformly and much more would need to be done. But the basic building blocks were in place and the people geared up for the anticipated onslaught within hours of war being declared.

NOTES:
1. Charles Madge and Tom Harrison, *Britain by Mass Observation*, Penguin Special, London, 1939.
2. Assistance by troops to the Civil Authorities in Civil Defence – London Area, Security Document No.L.D / 10 May 1939.
3. FitzGibbon, Constantine, *The Blitz*, Macdonald, London, 1970.
4. Smith, Malcolm, *British Air Strategy Between the Wars*, Table IX.
5. O'Brian, Terrence, *Civil Defence*, HMSO, London, 1955.

Chapter 9

Anti-Climax

'Everywhere houses were being closed, furniture stored, children transported, servants dismissed, lawns ploughed, dower houses and shooting lodges crammed to capacity; mothers-in-law, and nannies were everywhere gaining control.'
Evelyn Waugh.

The declaration of hostilities, in September 1939, brought about one of the first surprises of the war. In the weeks that followed neither the country in general nor London in particular, were subjected to an all-out air assault by the Luftwaffe. Although the air raid sirens erupted within minutes of Chamberlain's declaration of war speech at 11.38 hours, and police officers were seen riding their bicycles blowing whistles and warning people to take cover, no enemy aircraft appeared over the capital. One Metropolitan Police Sergeant from the Isle of Dogs remembers meeting one of his men coming towards him after the first alarm had sounded. He was fully kitted out with his steel helmet, eye shield, gas proof jacket and trousers and had his gas mask at the ready. It was of course a warm day and the officer was already sweating profusely. The sergeant escorted him back into the police station where the Duty Officer remarked: 'For goodness sake, Constable, you frighten me; god knows what you would do to the public!'[1] The alert was in fact caused by an unidentified aircraft which turned out to be French.

After the collapse of Poland there was a standoff along the French border, whilst the Germans assimilated the newly conquered territories and repositioned their forces. Well into the New Year the war continued to make very little impression on the people of London. When the knockout blow failed to arrive, the people's mood changed from one of calm resignation to one of complacency and skepticism.

162

For most, the principal change, and by far the biggest irritant, was the blackout. Initially, for some city dwellers, it had been a fascinating and revealing time as many had never seen the night sky so clearly without the reflections and glow of street lighting. For others the almost total darkness of some nights was unfamiliar, intimidating and often unnerving. For some, naturally nervous people, night brought the unrelieved gloom of darkened streets and a brooding sense of danger. There was a primeval fear that the darkness invoked and it drained the vitality from peoples' lives. Those with an introvert nature often found themselves unable or unwilling to go out after dark; their world shrank to the confines of their immediate surroundings. It wasn't universal though and a few, for example some criminals and lovers, relished the new opportunities the darkness provided. That said, it did work both ways for the criminals, and as one policeman said, 'If a copper couldn't see a crook, then the crook couldn't see the copper' and with the addition of the war reserve constables there were an awful lot more of them about.

In fact the blackout was much more than just a nuisance and the number of road traffic accidents rocketed. Despite about half a million cars being taken off the road, the casualty rate soared. In the three months up to November there were 2,975 deaths, over a 1,000 more than over an equivalent period in 1938. The surgeon to the King observed in the *British Medical Journal*, that by frightening the nation into blackout regulations, the Luftwaffe was able to kill hundreds of people a month without even dropping a bomb. In an attempt to remedy this, white lines were painted down the middle of many roads which, up until then, were the exception rather than the rule, something we have the blackout to thank for today. Another annoying, but less serious problem, was commuting; the buses and trains were all blacked out which meant that reading was impossible, so vast numbers of workers sat, sullenly in the dark, on their way to and from work. Many considered it unnecessary. In trials it had been established that the sparks from both the electric tramcars and from Underground trains on the surface could be seen for many miles from the air. Despite the clamour from the public, the Government firmly maintained the need for the precautions, but announced experiments were being conducted to try and resolve the issue. However, as already noted in the First World War, the reality was that nothing, except the darkest night, could hide the clear reflection of the Thames and its estuary which would guide a bomber to the heart of the capital.

Enforcing the blackout was mainly a police responsibility. Although wardens could request that persons observed the blackout they could not enforce the new regulations and this was left to police officers. Early on the task was taken very seriously and whilst enforcing it the first Metropolitan Police fatality occurred which was directly attributable to the war. Police Constable George Southworth was on duty in Harley Street when he saw a light glowing on top of a building. Having failed to get any response from the occupants by knocking on the door, he decided to take action himself to turn it off. He tried to gain access to the house by smashing a lower balcony window, but his progress through the building was blocked by an internal door. Undeterred he went back out and began to scale the outside wall of the house, heading towards the fourth floor, where the offending light was shining. He had nearly reached the window when he slipped and fell to his death.

The Blitzkrieg which overwhelmed France, and saw the British evacuated from Dunkirk, refocused the nation on its national defence. The Battle of Britain followed and the prospect of an all-out assault on the country steadily grew. If London was going to be cowed into submission by the Luftwaffe, the actual instruments of destruction were the bombs and incendiaries they would drop. The initial categorisation of German bombs was by type: there were General Purpose bombs; Semi-Armoured Piercing bombs and Armoured Piercing bombs. As approximately eighty percent of the bombs dropped on the UK were of the first type, only these will be described. General Purpose bombs, known to the Germans as *Sprengbombe-Cylindrish* (SC), were thin-walled, high-capacity bombs primarily designed to destroy their targets by the effects of blast, although fragments from the casing also presented a serious danger.

The smallest of the most commonly dropped bombs, the 50kg, contained between twenty-one and twenty-five kilograms of TNT. They then stepped up in size; the larger ones being given nicknames by the British bomb disposal teams. There were 250, 500, 1,000 (called 'Hermann' - because it was short and fat), 1,200, 1,800, ('Satan') 2,000 and 2,500 ('Max') kilogram bombs. The largest, 'Max', was filled with an impressive and immensely destructive 1,700 kilograms of high explosive.

Of course no bomb is of any use (if that is not, in itself, a contradiction in terms) unless it is detonated at the right time and place, and it is the job of the fuze to do this. For their bombs the Germans developed a whole series of electrical fuzes that were unique to the Luftwaffe. Traditionally most fuzes were fitted in either the nose or the tail of the bomb body, however, in the German designs they were fitted into fuze pockets, in the sides of the bomb. The top of the fuze was connected to the aircraft bomb release system by an umbilical cord and, at the moment of release, they were armed by an electrical charge. It is not necessary to describe how they operated in detail and enough to know that there were three basic types. The first and the most common were electrical impact and very short-delay fuzes. These would explode at the moment of impact, or after a few milliseconds delay, allowing the bomb to penetrate its target before functioning. The second type was the long-delay fuze which, after impact and when the bomb had come to rest, set a mechanical clock running. This would explode the bomb at a preset time, up to eighty hours after it had landed. The final type was the anti-disturbance fuze designed with various switches which would arm after the bomb came to rest and cause it to function if it was subsequently moved. The small 50kg bombs only had a single fuze pocket, but some of the larger bombs had provision to take two fuzes. Normally one of these would be a delayed action type, which would be complemented by an anti-disturbance fuze, to prevent the bomb being easily disarmed.

Because of a shortage of the larger capacity high explosive bombs during the Blitz, the Germans also dropped a number of anti-ship magnetic mines on the capital. They came in either 500 kilogram or 1,000 kilogram varieties. They were thin-walled, cylindrically in shape with a hemispherical nose and cone shaped tail. Because of their light construction they needed a parachute to slow their rate of descent otherwise they would have broken up on the impact with the water, or in London's case, when they hit the ground. If the mine fell into at least eight feet of water, hydrostatic pressure and the dissolution of a soluble plug activated the magnetic firing system. If it fell on dry land, or in less than eight feet of water, then a clockwork fuze ran for seventeen seconds before the mine detonated. This delay later proved crucial in saving the lives of some bomb disposal officers. Last, but not least, were the incendiary bombs, these will be examined later.

So, London faced a formidable array of different munitions. They all of course had one weakness; no matter how well designed and manufactured, some were going to fail. This should have come as no surprise to those in authority, as evidence from the First World War, of both aerial bombardment and artillery fire on the Western Front, would have shown them that failure rates could reach up to thirty percent. The question of who was going to deal with all the unexploded bombs was reminiscent of the 'war trophy munitions' problem after the First World War and no one seemed to want to take responsibility for it. The issue was being batted about between the Army Council, the Air Ministry and the Home Office, and as late as 1939 was still unresolved.

Prior to 5 November 1938, the proposed and accepted method of dealing with unexploded aircraft bombs was that the police would report all such objects to the nearest military authority who would arrange their disposal. Post that date, it was accepted that this was unsatisfactory and the proposal was put forward that the ARP should take responsibility for all unexploded bombs under the auspices of the Home Office. HM Inspectors of Explosive at the Home Office, under whose detailed control it would fall, argued against this, explaining that the ARP did not have the necessary technical training at even the most basic level of the safe handling of explosives. The proposed disposal procedure also displayed a complete lack of understanding of the nature and the size of the problem. It was envisaged that after raids the ARP Wardens would go out, recover unexploded bombs, and take them to dumps where the military would blow them up. Even the most basic evaluation of this plan would have revealed it as unworkable. Who would dig for bombs that were deeply buried, what equipment would be needed to lift and carry them, and what about the danger from the different fuzes? Even though practically nothing was known about the German fuze designs at the time, a look at the equivalent types used by the RAF, which although they differed in their method of operation, would have highlighted the problems.

Perhaps influenced by previous plans to deal with infernal machines, no serious thought was given to defusing the bombs where they fell, the policy of destroying them in situ or moving them with the fuze in place, being favoured. Despite its obvious flaws this proposal was accepted, but with the additional provision that initially the work would be undertaken by the Royal Engineers whilst the ARP organisation was being properly trained. It was planned that small teams of Royal Engineers would be based at key locations where they would teach ARP volunteers the skills of bomb demolition, digging and revetting, and the construction of sandbag walls.

It was a completely unsatisfactory state of affairs and Sir John Anderson, on whom the overall responsibility had fallen, wrote, 'I do not see how I could discharge this responsibility, in any immediate urgency.' Not surprisingly the scheme collapsed shortly after war was declared in October 1939 due to the lack of volunteers from the ARP and the War Office was forced to accept that it would have to take on the responsibility for bomb disposal. Having been coerced into the role, the staff began provisionally planning for the task.

By November bomb disposal parties from Royal Engineer units were being formed and they would bear the brunt of the work at the beginning of the Blitz. The main requirements at this stage were an understanding of demolition techniques and the ability to construct sound sandbag emplacements for blowing bombs up in situ. The first formal order called for just twenty-five bomb disposal sections which consisted of an officer and fifteen men. In February 1940, the responsibility for bomb disposal was unequivocally accepted by the War Office and further plans drawn up. In addition to the Royal Engineers, the Royal Navy took responsibility for mine disposal and all bombs finishing up below the high water mark. The RAF took responsibility for bombs on RAF stations and those in crashed aircraft. Some inspecting ordnance officers from the Royal Army Ordnance Corps also participated in bomb disposal duties. All were ill-prepared for the task they had been asked to undertake; they had little or no formal training, very limited intelligence on German bombs and no specialist equipment. Fortunately, though, they had buckets of courage.

The lack of technical intelligence was a serious worry. At that time the only modern German bomb in this country was one of the small 50kg examples which had been brought back from Spain by a journalist. (The record does not indicate if it was live or inert.)[2] With great foresight in this vital area, a key and timely decision was now taken to form a technical committee to investigate all matters relating to bombs and their fuzing arrangements. The result was the Unexploded Bomb Committee which held its inaugural meeting in May 1940. It was to be staffed by some of the best brains in the country who would combine their considerable intellect, with cold-blooded courage, to provide novel technical means of dealing with the new menace.

In June, as the Luftwaffe regrouped in new bases in France, a further 109 bomb disposal sections were formed. Although some officers and men volunteered for bomb disposal work, most finished up in the role through routine postings. There were no specific requirements or qualities regulating their selection and, from an Army perspective, it was simply another military task. There was, however, one group of officers, who became involved in bomb disposal that need special mention; those who entered the Royal Engineers and were given an automatic Commission because of the technical and professional qualifications they held in civilian life. Many of them finished up in bomb disposal sections. According to Major A.B. Hartley MBE, RE there was a good reason for this. He noted when one of these specially commissioned officers asked why so many of his comrades were posted to bomb disposal units, a staff officer explained that:

> The training of an officer in regimental duties is a long and expensive process and that junior engineer officers, regimentally trained, were in short supply. To employ considerable numbers of such officers on duties where life expectancy was ten weeks, and which could very

well be performed by the immediately commissioned, would be nothing less than spendthrift.[3]

At the time the only method of dealing with unexploded bombs, which for whatever reason could not be destroyed in situ or moved, was to uncover them by careful excavation and then remove the fuze which was secured in position by a locking ring. This normally involved using a cold chisel and a hammer to tap the locking ring round, and once removed, simply lift out the fuze. Losses were inevitable and the need for a more scientific approach to the problem was desperately needed. Fortunately, the Unexploded Bomb Committee was already designing such equipment. One of the first items developed and issued was a universal key. It consisted of a long bar with adjustable lugs and could be used to remove the locking rings. Though simple in design and method of operation, it was a much better proposition than using a hammer and chisel on an unexploded bomb.

The Crabtree Discharger was the next important piece of equipment issued to the Bomb Disposal sections. This was used to render safe bombs fitted with one of the most common impact fuzes, the Number 15. It fitted over the boss of the fuze and had two prongs which, when pushed down, depressed the plungers in the fuze and in doing so drained the capacitors in the firing circuit and effectively rendered the fuze inoperative. Later the Germans countered this technique with the introduction of the Number 25 impact fuze which would detonate if the plungers were depressed.

By the end of August 1940, before the major assault on London began, there were already 2,500 unexploded bombs waiting to be dealt with elsewhere in the country. Roads were closed, factories deserted and undamaged homes left empty while their occupants joined the flow of refugees and added to the strain imposed on the relief organisations and essential services. It was quickly learnt that in many cases unexploded bombs were causing more disruption, delay and public inconvenience than those which detonated. The Prime Minister, Winston Churchill, took a personal interest in the activities of the bomb disposal units and accorded them the highest priority for research into new methods of disposal.

As the problem of unexploded bombs escalated, more bomb disposal sections were formed and more men were pitched into the battle, but still with almost no training or equipment. It is a credit to them that they overcame all the obstacles put in their path. They used their initiative and energy and developed a spirit typical of small units under intense pressure. It was the heroic age of bomb disposal and to quote Hartley again, it was: 'A period of individual prowess when urgency and a lack of knowledge and equipment led to the taking of fantastic risks, fantastic escapes, and many many deaths.'[4]

The Germans, in planning their bombing campaign, made deliberate use of long-delay time fuzes. When used, there was the real danger of unexploded bombs detonating long after the 'all-clear' had been sounded. This factor was central to the overall German bombing strategy, the aim of which was to stifle industrial output, halt vital transport, disrupt communications and intimidate the population by forcing them to stay away from areas where there were known to be unexploded bombs. The more serious consequences for the fledgling bomb disposal teams was that, in high priority cases, they had to dig for and recover delayed action bombs in the full knowledge that the longer they dug, the more likely it was that the bomb would detonate.

The first long-delay time fuze, the Number 17, was recovered on 13 August 1940. Trials with this, and others recovered soon afterwards, revealed that the delay could be anything from two-and-a-half to eighty hours. However, the bomb disposal teams were to learn by bitter experience that, when set for a long delay, they had a nasty habit of stopping just short of the intended firing time. Any movement of such a bomb was likely to restart the clockwork mechanism with the consequent risk of an imminent explosion. The recovery of this first Number 17 fuze had immediate repercussions. It was decided initially that, except in the most pressing of circumstances, a buried bomb could be left in position with the area around it cordoned and evacuated for at least ninety-six hours, the additional sixteen hours being a safety margin.

About this time, in an attempt to reduce casualties, orders were also issued that, after digging down for a bomb and when its position permitted, a rope should be attached to it and that it should be given a good shaking and jolting from a safe distance. It was then to be left for half an hour before being removed, in the hope that, if a Number 17 time fuze was fitted and that it had stopped near the end of its run, it would be restarted and the bomb would detonate before teams returned to work on it.

Another deadly booby-trap device, designed to prevent bombs being easily disarmed by the removal of the fuze, was introduced early on in the bombing. The first intact one was recovered in Swansea by Lieutenant Lawrence Archer RE who was awarded a George Cross for his actions. The booby-trap, called a Zus 40, was fitted beneath a Number 17 time fuze. Any attempt to remove the latter by unscrewing the locking ring and lifting it from its pocket would result in the Zus 40 functioning and setting off the bomb. The addition of the Zus 40 meant that any bomb fitted with a Number 17 fuze, which could not be detonated in place, would have to be rendered safe by another method. The cat and mouse game between the British bomb disposal men and the German fuze designers had started in deadly earnest.

There is considerable leeway when defining the first raid on London as the London Civil Defence Area included parts of Hertfordshire, Essex, Kent and Surrey. However, the first bombs in the Greater London area fell on 8 June 1940 in Addington. The first casualties were a month later in Loughton on 26 July. Edward Chumley, an ARP warden, was on duty when the alarm sounded. He and three other men, including auxiliary fireman Jim Varley, were on call ready and equipped with a Buick saloon car and trailer pump for fighting fires. As the weather was fine they were standing outside their shelter when they heard the sound of guns followed by the roar of an enemy aircraft flying low overhead. They dived for cover and a moment later there was a tremendous explosion. All Chumley remembered was trying to get up amidst a cloud of choking dust and rubble. He was helped to his feet and then gave a hand to pull out Jim Varley who had been hit by a fragment from the bomb which had penetrated his helmet from back to front killing him instantly. The Buick was completely wrecked and, as they stood there regaining their senses, they heard someone calling for help across the road. A house had been hit and the whole front ripped away. They managed to get in and rescue, what they afterwards politely described as, a rather well-built lady. Unfortunately, it was discovered a little later that, Mrs Jane Page, aged seventy-six, who lived at 14, The Drive, on the opposite side of the street, had been killed.

On 15 August the airfield at Croydon was attacked and the following day Wimbledon was struck in a raid which killed fourteen and wounded fifty-nine. The first night raid was on 22-23 August in which Harrow was hit by several high explosive bombs. One was a delayed-action type which blew up the following morning. The Barclays Bank at 112 High Street, Wealdstone, was also hit. The manger and his family who lived upstairs had a lucky escape when the bomb half-demolished the building.

In the same month a remarkable man, Squadron Leader Moxey, was killed trying to defuse a bomb which had fallen on the airfield at Biggin Hill. He had joined the infantry in the First World War and took part in the Somme offensive, before transferring to the Royal Flying Corps. After the Armistice he remained in the service for a while and developed some expertise in aerial bombs and fuzes. He re-joined RAF in 1940 on the Special Duty list and, due to his previous experience, became an RAF bomb disposal expert. In May of that year he travelled to France to collect intelligence on unexploded bombs to try and discover more information about their methods of operation and fuzing arrangements. During the retreat to Dunkirk he was almost captured by the Germans, and only escaped by buying and fleeing on a French motorbike. He was involved in bomb disposal early on in the Battle of Britain and also examined bombs in crashed German aircraft. At about 17.20 hours on 27 August, he was summoned to Biggin Hill to deal with an unexploded 250kg bomb. This had two fuze pockets with one of the fuzes being a Number 17 clockwork type. He managed to remove one fuze but when at 22.10 hours, he tried to extract the second; the bomb detonated, killing him instantly. He was posthumously awarded the George Cross for his bravery. Tragically for his family his son, who joined the air force as a pilot, was shot down and killed on 27 August 1942, exactly two years to the day after the death of his father.[5]

In early September just after Moxey's death, an organised study of the bombing began. A system was established for examining all aspects of air raids with the scientific aim of deducing the enemy's tactics and methods of operation. This enterprise became known as the 'bomb census'. To start with, for practical reasons, it could only be applied in London and Birmingham but, as its value became apparent, the study was extended countrywide, although this was after the worst of the bombing on London. Many important lessons were learned about the effectiveness of the various defences and the different types bombs dropped. When the tables were turned later in the war this information was exploited and applied to make the bombing of Germany more effective.

It was around this time, just before the start of the Blitz proper, that the term 'incident' was adopted. Until then, particularly in the police parlance there were only 'occurrences'. It was the civil defenders that embraced the term 'incident' and its use gradually spread. Mr John Strachey, a London Warden, said of it: 'The word is wonderfully colourless, dry and remote; it touches nothing which it does not minimise.'[6] It covered absolutely everything ranging from the death in a bombing of two foxes, to the worst single bombing incident of the war in which 178 people were killed and sixty-two injured. It is still the word of choice today when the police need to describe an event, without giving away any clue as to what has actually happened.

The first bombs to hit Central London were a stick that fell on Fore Street, in the City on the night of 24-25 August 1940. Today a commemorative stone built into a wall in Fore Street marks the spot. It states that the first bomb fell at 00.15 hours. This does not agree with the Home Security and Air Ministry records which give the estimated time as a few minutes later between twenty and twenty-five minutes past midnight.

These bombs were the catalyst for a change in the course of the Battle of Britain. The following night Bomber Command despatched a force of eighty-one bombers to attack Berlin in retaliation and the same medicine was administered for the following few nights. Despite claims of only attacking military targets, it is clear now that bombs fell indiscriminately all over Berlin and the surrounding countryside. Hitler was furious, and Göring's claim that enemy bombers would never reach Berlin was in tatters.

With intelligence incorrectly reporting that the RAF were on their knees, the German High command hurled the full force of the Luftwaffe against London in the hope of finishing them off. This would compel the dwindling numbers of RAF fighters and their pilots into the air to defend the capital. Revenge would be swift and sweet, and if the capital could be reduced to rubble and the people's will crushed, then so much the better; the invading armies would have a much simpler task.

Hitler on 4 September 1940, at the peak of his power, delivered a fanatical speech proclaiming to the world:

> When the British throw two or three thousand kilograms of bombs, we will unload 150,000, 180,000 or 200,000 kilograms. If they attack our cities we will simply erase theirs.[7]

At the Luftwaffe headquarters, the staff set about planning for the new phase of operations but it was not totally unexpected. Two months previously on 30 June 1940, Colonel General Jodl, Chief of the Armed Forces Combined Staff, prepared a paper entitled 'The Continuation of the War Against England'. It was, to all intents and purposes, to be a re-run of 'Frightfulness' in the First World War. The memorandum outlined the methods by which the people of Britain would be subdued. This specifically included terror attacks against the English centres of population.

It was time for terror to be given its turn and the scene was set for the bloodiest and most brutal chapter in the history of the bombing of London.

NOTES:
1. Ingleton, Roy, *The Gentlemen at War, Policing Britain 1939 -1945*, Cranborne Publications, Kent, 1994.

2. Hogben, Arthur, *Designed to Kill*, Patrick Stephens, Northamptonshire, 1987.
3. Hartley MBE, A.B., *Unexploded Bomb - A Short History of Bomb Disposal*, Cassell, London, 1958.
4. ibid.
5. Roberts, Steve, *A Brief History of Squadron Leader E. L. Moxey GC*, researched and produced by the Great War Research Services, 2000.
6. O'Brian, Terrence, *op. cit.*
7. Keesing's Contemporary Archives, Volume 1940-1943.

Chapter 10

The Blitz – The Storm Breaks

'A light step is essential when walking near an unexploded parachute mine.'
Supplementary Police Order 241-1940.

Over the last 140 years, with the exception of one period, the chances of a Londoner being directly caught up in an incident involving a bomb were, and still are, incredibly small. That exception was the Second World War where the opposite applied. It is estimated that everyone that lived in the capital for the duration of the war, and stayed within a fifteen-mile radius of Charing Cross, was subjected to a hit or a near miss. Today, I find it hard to grasp the scale, intensity and sheer ferocity of the assault on London during the course of the conflict. During my research, with a couple of notable exceptions, I have been forced to rely on second-hand memories and written accounts. In most cases, the horror of what happened has been taken out, watered down or glossed over, and this is reminiscent of what happened in reports at the time. Those who actually dealt with the aftermath of the bombing, and saw first-hand the effects of high explosives on the frail human body, mostly kept the images and memories to themselves. At a higher level, pictures of casualties and damage were ruthlessly censored and official reports of raids were, necessarily, bland and uncommunicative. At the end of the first great raid on London the official communiqué said:

> Fires were caused amongst industrial targets. Damage was done to lighting and other public services, and some dislocation to communications was caused. Attacks have also been directed against the docks. Information on casualties is not yet available.[1]

174

Clearly this was essential propaganda, but it was a complete understatement of what took place.

London's real ordeal started on 7 September 1940, a day which became known in the East End as 'Black Saturday'. Dawn brought another bright, clear late summer's day and ideal flying conditions. For the weary Battle of Britain pilots, waiting anxiously by their aircraft, there was immense relief that most of the telephones which would dispatch them into the air remained silent. The staff in the 11 Group Control Room and the Sector Headquarters were also puzzled by the lack of activity; clearly something was brewing, but what? With the constant attacks on the RAF's airfields, there was concern that the Germans were beginning to get the upper hand in the struggle for air superiority in the southeast of the country. It was not until late afternoon that the first ominous blips on the radar screens gave an indication that a concentrated force of aircraft was being assembled for a raid.

It must have been just before 17.00 hours that it became clear that this was no ordinary raid. Such a concentrated and mighty force could only have one target and that was London. The head of Fighter Command, Dowding and his Group Commander, Keith Park, quickly realized this. But for the population of London, despite the air raid sirens, which some people now ignored, there was no such appreciation. Away to the east, the Luftwaffe aircraft massed in a huge, phalanx-shaped formation, which was stepped from 14,000 to 23,000 feet. It advanced on a twenty-mile front towards the Thames Estuary. Like a relentless juggernaut the bombers bore down on the capital. Though harried by more and more Spitfires and Hurricanes, the protective screen of Messerschmitts mostly held them at bay and the British fighters were unable to seriously blunt or deflect the bomber force.

Below and ahead of them the people of London, and those in the East End in particular, had no idea of what was about to befall them. After a year at war the apocalyptic air attacks prophesised by the pre-war planners had not materialised and many mistakenly believed that the threat was overrated. There was the sound of guns, but this was nothing new, although as time progressed the barrage grew louder and louder. Those people that had not taken shelter and bothered to look up saw the sky filling with the bombers' tiny flecks and above them were the milky contrails spilling out from behind the higher-flying fighters. And then it began. The Luftwaffe crews in their Dornier Do 17s, Heinkel He 111s and Junkers Ju 88s began to crank open their bomb doors. Sticks of bombs began to tumble from the racks in the aircraft plunging down towards the people below. The sounds of explosions rippled right across the east of London. At Rotherhithe, Limehouse and Millwall, bombs detonated in a crescendo of noise. They kept on falling, striking Surrey Docks, Woolwich Arsenal, and creeping closer to Tower Bridge. The moment was recorded in the Rotherhithe area in an entry in the Station Officer's Incident Log. It noted at 17.15 hours that, in the tunnel area, eighteen high explosive bombs exploded, 500 incendiaries fell, and that there were an unspecified number of delayed-action bombs. The casualties recorded were two dead, eleven seriously injured and twenty-two slight injuries. The toll would swiftly grow.

It was the docks that took the full force of the raid that late summer afternoon. Close to them the Londoners in their terraced houses suffered terribly. Deafened, bewildered and suffering from shock from the seemingly relentless and concentrated bombing some people, in panic, took to the streets to flee, not aware, in their stunned state, that being in the open was the worst place to be in an air raid. Those that remained in their shelters huddled down as the detonation waves from exploding bombs reverberated around them. Above them ballooned clouds of smoke and dust from the numerous fires. In a matter of minutes, hundreds of terraced houses, shops, factories and dockside warehouses were struck. Many received direct hits and were blown to pieces whilst incendiaries set fire to the ruins and other damaged premises. Fires quickly kindled and took hold right across the area. Fire stations from the whole of the East End dispatched crews to fight the blazes that were soon burning out of control. At the docks, crews were playing powerful jets of water into the flames but making little impression and more reinforcements were needed. Trying to get suction pumps into the deep water in the docks was something crews had practiced, but not with bombs detonating all around them. Within half an hour of the raid starting the fire control centre at West Ham was requesting an additional 500 pumps from London Regional Control at Lambeth.

Up until this point four-fifths of London's auxiliary firemen had not been to a serious incident and it was a true baptism of fire. Even for the regulars, the task was immense. The all-clear sounded around forty-five minutes later, at 18.00 hours, as the final wave of bombers swept on over the City, Westminster and Kensington before wheeling away on their return journey to France. By then, great spiraling clouds of smoke obscured the sky from the inferno raging below. Back at Lambeth, at the fire brigade's regional headquarters, the control room map displayed the true state of affairs. In the sector that displayed the overall situation it showed that there were nine conflagrations, a fire service term for fires totally out of control and rapidly spreading. These included the fires at Surrey and London docks. In addition, the board showed nineteen thirty-pump fires, forty ten-pump fires and over one thousand smaller blazes.

Like the fire crews, the police, ARP wardens and rescue services were also quickly overwhelmed. Communications failed, streets became blocked and the area descended into dirty, dusty and smoke-laden chaos. Cohesive central control of events collapsed. But the previous years of planning and training now paid dividends, and small groups and individuals, without regard for their own safety set about their appointed tasks. Vital information was eventually passed, reinforcements poured in, and people were rescued and evacuated. Many hundreds of brave deeds were performed, most going unnoticed in the confusion. Some were recorded; for example, one of the incident commanders, Mr J. Blake, heard that a fireman was lying injured in the heart of the fire in the docks area. He set off by car to rescue him but his vehicle was wrecked by a bomb, and so he continued on foot through the inferno to try to locate the wounded man. He finished up rescuing six firemen. For his bravery he was awarded a George Medal.

In Rotherhithe many dazed, shell-shocked and bewildered refugees were moved to Bermondsey to one of the pre-planned evacuation centres at Keeton's Road School. Later that night it would prove to be a fatal, but not incorrect decision, for those escaping the horror down by the river. They may well have been helped by Miss Grace Rattenbury of the Invalid Children's Aid Association, who was also a member of the WVS. She assisted with the evacuation of people in the area driving a WVS van into the midst of the inferno to pick up survivors and continued doing this until late in the evening, when all the people that needed moving had been rescued. During this time, she displayed immense courage and determination particularly as she was subjected to further bombing and the real danger of being cut off by fire. The roads themselves were extremely dangerous with craters and piles of rubble and there was the ever-present risk of further explosions from delayed-action bombs. On more than one occasion that evening she was forced to throw herself down to escape the blast from one exploding close by. Throughout she remained calm and confident and her actions steadied everyone. When her van was inspected the following morning it was discovered that the paint was badly blistered by the encroaching flames, for her actions she too was awarded a George Medal.

Many others also learned abrupt and harsh lessons of modern warfare. Dr Morton recalled that in her training, and in the training of the first aid parties, the importance of cleanliness and scrubbing up before treating patients had been drilled into them. On that first evening and night, what struck her was the amount of dirt and dust that surrounded every explosion; this drifted in the wind and caked everything. Rescued casualties emerged stunned and absolutely filthy, covered from head to foot in centuries of ingrained dust and dirt. Many patients came into hospital with their mouths, ears and eyes full of muck and grit and they were always grateful for clean water to clear away the grime.

As Grace Rattenbury had discovered, many of the bombs dropped by the Luftwaffe were fitted with time fuzes which had been set with two different delay periods. Some were set to go off two-to-four hours after landing and began exploding randomly and without warning after 19.00 hours. The remainder had longer delays of ten-to-fourteen hours. These bombs had no purpose other than to disrupt the rescue efforts, by killing or maiming those responding to the hundreds of calls for help and who went to fight fires and free survivors. Like everyone else, the bomb disposal teams in London, who were required to deal with this new menace, were totally overwhelmed by the task that now faced them.

As daylight faded the bombers returned, and overnight, another 247 aircraft dropped more loads of high explosive bombs and incendiaries, mostly in and around the docks. This time they came over in a steady stream with the last aircraft departing just before the dawn. They had no difficulty finding their target as vast swathes of docklands were still ablaze.

In the late evening, Sergeant Peters of the Metropolitan Police had a grim introduction to the Blitz. He was ordered, with several other policemen, to attend an incident at Keeton's Road School. This rest centre was the one where, earlier on in the evening, many of the evacuees and refugees from Rotherhithe had been sent. At around 22.00 hours a bomb of considerable size hit the school and calls for help were sent out. On reaching the building Sergeant Peters and his men went through the playground and could see many of the classrooms were on fire. In one room they saw a fireman lying on a make-shift bedstead and his face looked as if it had been skinned. A little further along Peters and another officer were searching, by the glow of the flames, through the debris when his companion bent down and picked up what he thought was a piece of bread. To their horror it turned out to be the remains of the limbs of a small child. Both were so disturbed by what they had found that they left the school and went back out into another part of the street. Here they discovered even more bodies lying in the footway and the road. Unable to come to terms with what had

178

happened they stood and watched motionless for a few moments. To their relief some of the bodies showed signs of life and it became clear that not everyone was dead. They did what they could to aid the injured, the work helping distract them from what they had just seen.

This was the reality of mass bombing. For those that have not witnessed an explosion close by and felt its awesome power, nor seen its effects, they can never really know what it is like. These policemen and hundreds of other civil defenders and ordinary civilians confronted this uncompromising truth that day. Many of the victims, men, women and children, had been appallingly disfigured. The rescuers saw mutilated bodies and parts of bodies, teeth and broken jaws, shredded lungs in slashed-open chests, skulls burst apart, blood trickling from grotesquely distorted or crushed limbs and shattered pelvises. People with their life-blood drained away lying, grey and motionless under slabs of rubble and coated in dust. Similar scenes were recorded across the docks and the East End that day and night, and would continue to be re-enacted in hundreds of towns and cities for the remainder of the war.

In Central London most people were not really aware of the disaster in the East End; somehow it seemed a remote and distant place. As they looked east with the setting sun at their backs the glow from the fires in the docklands could be clearly seen. It was only those in the report centres who were sending reinforcements to the scene as fast as they became available that could begin to understand the savage pounding that the East End had suffered.

The Luftwaffe, when it had returned that night, disgorged most of their bombs into the inferno below, but some crews waited that extra minute which meant their loads struck Central London. A stick of five bombs detonated around Victoria Station and Victoria Street. It was, compared to the events in the East End, nothing but a scratch, but people were killed and injured all the same, and the destruction was real enough. It was a bad time as the pubs had just closed and people were about on the streets waiting in the darkness for buses. Hard lessons about being vulnerable in the open were learned yet again, but too late for some. The iron replica of Big Ben, later a meeting point for Special Forces, witnessed the event. To the scene sped the police, civil defenders, rescue parties and ambulances with their stretchers. For many of them it was their first encounter with violent death or injury and they reacted in different ways, but all coped, although some suffered from delayed shock later that night.

To try and put the first major raid on the capital into perspective more tonnes of bombs and incendiaries were dropped on London on that day than in all the First World War attacks put together. There are various estimates of the tonnage of bombs dropped in the Great War; they range from a minimum of 290 tonnes[2] to a maximum of 368 tonnes of bombs.[3] In just forty-five minutes on 7 September 1940, some 348 bombers dropped more than that on the East End. In twelve hours the figure had almost doubled when, under the cover of darkness, a further 330 tonnes of bombs and nearly 16,000 incendiaries were delivered into the carnage below. A more up to date comparison would be with the suicide bombers on 7 July 2005. Each detonated approximately 3-5 kilograms of high explosive. The smallest of the German high explosive bombs dropped on 7 September contained five times that amount.

As dawn came up on 8 September, the remaining population of the East End of London, although it did not know it, had survived the most devastating bombing attack of the war to date. The previous day's tea-time raid, more than any other on the capital, delivered a higher concentration of bombs into a comparatively small target area, in a very short time. Although on many occasions the Germans dropped more bombs and caused more casualties, they never again achieved the same local intensity. By the end of the night 436 men, women and children lay dead and 1,600 were severely wounded.

The task of compiling these essential, but disheartening, figures fell to the police. During the war the Civilian War Death Form was introduced, which had to be completed by the person who found a body or parts of a body. This showed the precise place the deceased was found and, where possible, the date and time of death. Unfortunately, the people who often completed these forms (the rescue units, ARP wardens, stretcher bearers and others) were not always of an administrative bent, and their priority, naturally, was the extrication and treatment of the living. Consequently, the information recorded was quite often limited to a few sketchy details, and often no name was provided. The completed, or partially completed, forms were then delivered to the casualty centre at the local police station. In the Metropolitan Police area, the local station was also responsible for gathering information from the mortuaries and hospitals in its locality and compiling a combined list of casualties. These were then forwarded to Scotland Yard where they were collated to make one final list. These consolidated figures were then sent back out to the police divisions and back to the stations. An essential component of the system was speed and, inevitably, inconsistencies crept in. Another problem was that many bodies, especially those that were severely mutilated or had been involved in fire, could not be identified. There was a requirement to try and match up the dead with the missing, but for a myriad of reasons this was not always possible. Eventually it was decided to set up a Central Casualty Bureau at Scotland Yard, which would maintain a complete record of casualties. This would be in the form of alphabetical lists with indexes to facilitate searches. By the end of the war this bureau had details of over 30,000 dead and 50,000 seriously wounded in London. The bureau still exists today and is activated after any serious terrorist incidents, major accidents and events like the devastating Boxing Day Tsunami in the Far East in 2004.

Of course the final unenviable job for the police on the ground was notifying close relatives of casualties. This, difficult task, was always carried out with a heavy heart. There is no easy way of knocking on a door and telling someone of the death of a loved family member.

During the day on Sunday, 8 September 1940, the Luftwaffe returned again and although they concentrated on the riverside districts, bombing was more widespread and covered every Metropolitan Borough. In the early part of the night they mostly dropped incendiaries to start fires and then later heavier bombs began to fall. Amongst the more well-known buildings hit were the stables of the Household Cavalry at Knightsbridge Barracks and the Royal Courts of Justice.

During the first three night raids on London there had been little anti-aircraft fire because the technology did not exist to aim the guns effectively. On 10 September this changed as it had been decided that the anti-aircraft guns would fire regardless of the limited chances of success. It was a tremendous boost to the morale of the Londoners who felt that at least something was being done to counter the bombers. In fact, although almost guns fired blind, the barrage forced the German bombers higher and higher, with the result that all pretence of serious military targeting was lost and the loads of bombs that were dropped fell indiscriminately right across the capital. The initial concentration on the docks and the East End soon ended and the bombing shifted to greater London.

The greater dispersion of the bombs meant that the civil defenders were at work all over the capital. In Neal Street, near Covent Garden, a bomb detonated in a fruit wholesaler. The building collapsed into a heap of wreckage in the narrow street completely blocking it; worse still a fire developed in the building next door. It was known that there were people in the upper floors of the collapsed building and heavy rescue parties arrived on scene to search for survivors. In addition to having to contend with dangerous overhanging debris they were soon drenched from the hoses of the firemen fighting the fire next door. In the light of the flickering flames the rescue crews scrambled through the rubble of the collapsed building and extricated the dead and the wounded.

War has a way of springing nasty surprises and the Germans' use of delayed action bombs, on a large scale, now began to have a serious impact on London. Two bombs fell in Holborn in Shelton Street and Sussex Street, neither of which exploded immediately. The police and ARP wardens had to carry out an evacuation on a massive scale and no one was really sure what distances needed to be applied in these circumstances. In Sussex Street some two hundred people gathered a few possessions and headed for the Rest Centres.

Initially it was impossible to differentiate between unexploded (failed) or delayed action bombs, and both were proving to be much more of a menace than had been anticipated. At this time the numbers of unexploded bombs had reached the point where, it is probably true to say that, they posed one of the principal threats to civil activities and wartime production. They immobilised railway junctions and long stretches of line, blocked main roads, and approaches to vital factories and airfields. Churchill wrote of them: 'There is no doubt that it is a most effective agent in warfare on account of the prolonged uncertainty which it creates.'

Initially huge evacuation areas were stipulated, and this closed down vast swathes of the most badly bombed areas and thousands of people had to leave their homes. It rapidly became obvious that these cordon distances were unworkable and, as experience was gained, more practical areas were designated. Not all activities ceased inside the danger areas and, courageously, the rescue and fire-fighting teams continued with their work despite the threat from delayed action bombs, some paying a heavy price for their bravery. Back in Sussex Street the bomb there exploded without warning at 06.00 hours the following morning.

The Royal Engineer bomb disposal sections in London were at full stretch trying to deal with the new problem. Despite the information about clockwork long-delay fuzes and anti-removal devices many brave teams of sappers were still digging down, locating bombs and rendering them safe. On the outskirts of London, on the Caterham-Purley Branch of the Southern Railway, four sappers from No.97 Bomb Disposal Section were killed whilst trying to render safe an unexploded bomb. They were Sergeant Smith, Corporal Lindsey, and Sappers Brady and Bush.

On 12 September a Royal Engineer bomb disposal team used a new piece of equipment, the steam sterilizer, for the first time. The prototype, designed and built in a matter of weeks, was intended to overcome the problem of not being able to remove time fuzes because they might have a Zus 40 booby-trap fitted beneath them. German bombs at the time

182

were filled with TNT or a mixture of TNT and other explosives. It is, on balance, a very stable explosive which melts at 80° C. It will, therefore, become a liquid if dropped into boiling water. (It will be recalled that TNT, prior to the Silvertown explosion, was considered so safe that it was not subject to the provisions of the 1870 Explosives Act.) The stream sterilizer took advantage of this low melting temperature. It consisted of a trepanner, which cut a hole in the side of a bomb and then a system for injecting steam into the hole that caused the TNT filling to emulsify and drain out. It sounds simple, but in fact designing a piece of equipment that could be attached to any size of bomb, which would trepan a hole, stop automatically when it had cut through the metal and reached the explosive and then switch to steam, was not easy.

On that morning, reports were received that a 250kg unexploded bomb was lying on the surface of Regent's Street. It had struck a building, which had arrested and deflected its fall, and then had skidded out into the street where it had come to rest. The initial examination of the bomb was carried out by Captain Kennedy RE and showed that it was fitted with two of the Number 17 long delay fuzes, one of which was definitely ticking. Aware of the likelihood that these might also be fitted with the Zus 40 booby-trap, he decided to try to defuse the bomb using the newly developed steam sterilzer. He ordered it to be sent to the site and at the same time requested assistance from the designers who agreed to send out a technician to help. In the meantime, Dr Merriman of the Unexploded Bomb Committee learned about the project and asked for permission to attend the scene. Shortly afterwards, he arrived accompanied by the chairman of the Committee, Dr H.J. Gough.

Just after 15.00 hours they set about positioning the steam sterilizer and started it working. Once fitted to a bomb, it was designed to be operated, semi-remotely, from a position of comparative safety, behind a sandbag wall built a reasonable distance from the bomb. After a while, it was thought that the bomb's outer casing had been penetrated, and it was switched to steam and, in theory, the emulsified explosive should have started leaking out of the hole. After an hour of steaming, nothing seemed to be happening and Captain Kennedy went forward to inspect the bomb. All the time it was ticking away its existence, and of course, none of the men knew the length of time which had been set on the fuzes by some distant unknown Luftwaffe armourer earlier that day. Kennedy discovered that the drill had failed to penetrate the body of the bomb, and all that the steam had succeeded in doing was heating up the steel casing. The drill was repositioned and they tried again but with the same result. By now all of them were acutely aware that time was running out. Kennedy next rolled the bomb over to try and cut though the other side as it was known that the thickness of the bomb casing was not always uniform. He repositioned the cutter and tried again and this time the body of the bomb was successfully penetrated, but now the automatic switch to start the steam failed. Kennedy approached it yet again succeeded in forcing the system to work using a hammer and a pinch bar. At 17.55 hours the steam was applied and soon, to everyone's relief and satisfaction, liquid TNT could be seen streaming from the bomb. Five minutes later, with most of its charge still intact it blew up taking with it the prototype steriliser.

Fortunately, at the time, all the members of the team were behind cover and no one was seriously injured. Despite the failure, a huge amount had been learned about the practical use of the new equipment and the defects with it that needed to be rectified. These were addressed and steam sterilizers in modified form went on to become one of the most effective pieces of equipment in the bomb disposal team's armoury.

Not far away, at St Paul's Cathedral, another bomb was being dealt with which was probably the most famous in London during the Second World War. The bomb, a 1,000kg 'Hermann', had been dropped in the early hours of Thursday, 12 September. It had plummeted into the pavement at the southwest corner of the Cathedral at Dean's Yard, and continued down through the earth coming to rest under the clock tower. For three days, men under the command of Lieutenant Robert Davies, RE, from both 16 and 17 Bomb Disposal Companies, toiled to locate and recover the bomb. It was no easy task and early on in the operation it was discovered that the bomb had fractured a gas main and three men suffered from its effects. The bomb was finally located some twenty-seven feet down in the sub-soil. Unusually, for this size of bomb at that time of the war, it was reported to be fitted with a long-delay time fuze. Because of this, and the possibility of an anti-withdrawal device, the fuze was left in place and the bomb hauled out of its hole using a substantial block and tackle and two small lorries. Once out of the ground the bomb was loaded onto another truck and, with police officers clearing a way through the East End, it was allegedly driven by Lieutenant Davies to Hackney Marshes where it was destroyed by demolition. Had it exploded where it was, the bomb would have undoubtedly done significant damage to the Cathedral. The story got into the press, and Davies became an overnight sensation. For his work, he was awarded a George Cross which he received much later in February 1942. Another was awarded to Sapper George Wylie, who had assisted Davies throughout the operation. Wylie put his medal up for auction in 1977 and it was purchased by the city Merchant Bankers, Charterhouse Japhet, whose offices at Paternoster Row look out onto St Paul's. It was presented to the Cathedral, where it is now on permanent display in the Treasury in the Crypt.

This interesting story does not end there. Three months after being presented with his medal by the King, Davies was arrested. It was a matter of acute embarrassment for the Army as, for some months they had had evidence of misconduct going back to the very early days of the Blitz. He was subsequently court-martialled with thirty charges of fraud and dishonesty being made against him. He was found guilty, cashiered from the Army and sentenced to eighteen months in prison. It also seems probable that the bomb removed from St Paul's did not have a ticking time fuze, nor did Davies drive it to Hackney Marshes. It was a Lance Corporal Bert Leigh that did this. After his release from prison Davies dropped out of sight and later emigrated to Australia. It was a sad conclusion to what at the time was a great morale-boosting story. Despite the flaws in his character it should not be forgotten that Davies worked through the worst of the Blitz and rendered safe many bombs.

Although by now the dangers of removing fuzes was fully understood by all those involved in disposal operations, in exceptional circumstances, bombs might still be rendered safe by withdrawing the fuze from its pocket. In mid-September, Lieutenant James RE, was tasked to Westminster where, after a night raid, the fire brigade had discovered, in daylight, a 50kg bomb perched on the top of a surviving stonewall of a gutted building. This presented an immediate danger to the nearby firemen and needed to be dealt with at once. When James arrived on scene he found that the wall was anything but stable and was hissing as the water being played on to it evaporated. On the other side of it was a mass of red-hot bricks and debris from the collapsed structure. He borrowed a fireman's ladder and ascended to the top of the wall and tackled the bomb in its precarious position. He unscrewed the locking ring on the bomb fuze, a difficult task because the bomb was still very hot and required the use of a hammer and chisel. Once done, he extracted the fuze, removed the gaine (booster charge) and the booster pellets, put all of those in his pocket, and finally kicked the de-fuzed bomb off the wall. Descending with scorched and blistered hands he helped load the bomb on his truck and drove away.

On Friday, 13 September, Buckingham Palace was struck by a stick of bombs; two fell on the red gravel of the internal quadrangle, one through the roof of the Royal Palace into the Chapel, and one, which later proved to be a delayed-action bomb, bored into the road in front of the forecourt. The bombs in the quadrangle did little significant structural damage but they shattered the windows and shrapnel shredded some of the pictures hanging in the Ambassadors Hall. At the time their Majesties were sitting about eighty yards away; the King later recalled seeing the flashes followed by the sound of the detonation of the bombs. The Royal Chapel was less fortunate; the bomb there penetrated the roof and floor and exploded above the basement. Four men sheltering there were injured, one of whom subsequently died. The Chapel interior was wrecked although the structure itself held firm. The bomb that landed in the roadway penetrated a short distance, but being a delayed-action type did not detonate. It was decided that there was an immediate need to build a sandbag wall around the bomb to protect the Palace façade. An unnamed rescue service man volunteered to build the wall, but first there was a need for sandbags. It was quickly established that there was a stack of these in the Royal Stables and a warden set off to get them. On arrival, however, he was met by one of the officials from the stables, a real 'jobs worth' who questioned the need to use these particular sandbags, as the bomb was outside the Palace grounds and they were for use inside the perimeter. An argument ensued which was won by the warden, but only after he agreed to personally sign for 534 sandbags. Soon a chain was formed delivering sandbags to the rescue service man and within a short time a wall of five feet thick and six feet tall had been built. The bomb eventually exploded at 08.40 hours the following morning, the Palace suffered little damage and the rescue service man, quite rightly, received a George Medal.

On 15 September, the Germans mounted two major daylight raids on the capital. As the first enemy formation approached London at midday, it was pounced on by several squadrons of Spitfires and Hurricanes. Some attacked head on and a short while later a further five squadrons under the leadership of Douglas Bader smashed into the flank of the formation. It was a devastating blow and those bombers that reached London scattered their loads over Battersea, Lambeth, Clapham, Victoria, Camberwell, Kensington, Chelsea, Crystal Palace, Lewisham, Wandsworth and Westminster. Although there was much destruction and many casualties, the wide dispersion of the bombs meant that the Civil Defence services were able to deal with the incidents much more effectively.

In the afternoon a second raid approached, but this was also met by a storm of refuelled and rearmed RAF fighters and the tight German formations were once again scattered. The bombs were dropped indiscriminately all over the whole of Greater London, with no tight concentration in any one area. It was probably around this time that the significance of the fighting dawned on the airmen of both sides. The RAF hounded the Germans and watched them turn and stream south for home. As for the Luftwaffe many of the aircrew were overawed by the numbers of RAF fighters still opposing them. They had been told too many times that they were facing the 'last fifty Spitfires'. It would not wash anymore. Never again would the Luftwaffe bombers challenge the RAF fighter's en masse in daylight over London. There were still some daylight raids, but these were mainly by small numbers of bombers or fighter bombers and although they harassed the population, little of military significance was actually achieved.

After the first raid on 7 September, the Luftwaffe had maintained relentless pressure on the capital bombing it day and night. In those eight days, the people had been projected into the front line of a modern, round-the-clock, war. They had had to face a deluge of thousands of high explosive bombs and countless incendiaries. They were not a disciplined body of men like soldiers, sailors and airmen in the services, but even so most came through the ordeal well.

With the end of the daylight campaign the German bombers were able to step up their night-time activities with London still the primary target. From mid-September onwards the coming of darkness was a prelude to repeated night raids, and the lack of light complicated everyone's task. The ack-ack guns had to resort to almost un-aimed barrage fire, the RAF's night-fighting capability proved to be almost non-existent, and the tasks of the civil defenders became much harder.

With vast numbers of bombs falling on the capital, the unexploded bomb problem continued to grow exponentially, as did the need for new men to deal with the threat. The requirement for bomb disposal sections had been drastically increased from the original twenty-five in late 1939, to a proposed establishment of 440 sections by 12 September. There was still practically no training and only limited equipment, and many of these sections only existed on paper. To fulfil the requirement some General Construction Companies of the Royal Engineers were converted to the role although they would not become operational until mid-October. By then the strength of the Royal Engineer Bomb Disposal organization had risen to 10,000 all ranks. The men were desperately needed as, by 20 September 1940, the number of reported unexploded bombs had peaked at 3,759. At the same time, statistical controls began to be enforced which would record as much detail about the bombs as possible, including types, fuzing arrangements and, for those fitted with delay action fuzes, the time between impact and functioning if it was known. This information would pay dividends later on.

It is often assumed that the responsibility for actually dealing with bombs fell to the officers and senior NCOs of the Royal Engineers and that the junior ranks just did the digging, but in the early chaotic days, this was not always the case. On 12 September, a bomb in the Great West Road was being investigated by Corporal George Mundy and Sappers from No.32 Bomb Disposal Section based at Hounslow. The exact circumstances will never be known, but it seems that having found the bomb, Mundy phoned for advice from his section commander, Lieutenant Glover, but neither he nor his deputy Sergeant Buckley were immediately available to help. Using his initiative, the Corporal borrowed a rope and a crowbar from a nearby garage and set to work on the bomb. Whilst trying to render it safe and with several of his men standing around it, the bomb detonated. They had no chance, and the only saving grace was that they were all killed instantly. The records show that along with Corporal Mundy, Sappers Vincent Mulrooney, Leonard Saunders, William Slater, Eric Walker, Leonard Watts and one other, unidentified, individual died.

In the same month, in an intensification of the deadly cat and mouse game, the Germans introduced another new and dangerous fuze. This was the Number 50 and it was fitted with a very sensitive anti-disturbance trembler switch. It was designed to arm shortly after bomb had come to rest, normally a matter of just a few minutes, after which time even the slightest movement would cause it to function. It was reported later in the war, after some trials in the Middle East, that the fuze was so sensitive that in some cases it would function if the casing of the bomb was struck with a pencil.

The need to recover and learn more about these deadly fuzes was probably a contributory factor in the death of some more sappers. They were dispatched, on 24 September, to deal with a 250kg bomb which had been dropped ten days earlier on 34 Hazeldene Road, Bexley. Once they found it they discovered that it had a Number 17 clockwork delay fuze, and one of the new Number 50 anti-handling types. Because of the danger it was initially decided to build a massive sandbag wall, and blow up the bomb in situ. However, after building the wall, the decision was taken to try and recover the new fuze for examination by the Unexploded Bomb Committee. It was thought that, as the bomb had lain dormant for a considerable time, the capacitors in the Number 50 fuze would have lost their charge, and it would be possible to steam out the main filling of TNT. On 2 October, work began. A hole was drilled in the side of the bomb casing between the two fuze pockets and steam applied. After some difficulties the TNT was seen to be pouring out of the bomb and forming a pool beneath it. That night, the section commander, Lieutenant Jinks, reported that he was sure that the bomb was almost empty, but on checking, discovered there was still plenty of TNT in it. Operations were suspended and resumed in the morning. After a few more hours steaming Jinks went back to the bomb, declared that it was empty and the steam sterilizer was shut off. The bomb and the equipment were then left to cool off. After a while Jinks asked for two volunteers to help him move the bomb which was now set in a mass of re-solidifying TNT. Accompanied by Sappers Williams and Lewis he went into the house. Moments later there was a huge explosion. No trace was ever found of the three men and those outside were only saved by the massive sandbag wall which had been built earlier. An investigation and search of the crater revealed nothing, as was often the case with large bombs. A later report concluded that the most likely cause of the explosion was that the Number 17 fuze had restarted when the bomb was moved and that not all the filling had been steamed out of the casing. When that detonated, so did the remainder of the TNT, which was had solidified under the bomb.

With such large numbers of unexploded bombs, it became necessary to introduce a priority system for their disposal, which allowed for those most seriously disruptive to the war effort to be dealt with first. By now all incidents involving suspected unexploded ordnance were reported as they occurred by the ARP organisation through various controllers to, in London's case, the Regional Commissioner. It was his responsibility to classify these bombs according to their priority for disposal as laid down by the Cabinet. Four basic categories were introduced, although the first was split into two sub-categories:

A1. - Immediate disposal essential to the war effort, but deliberate demolition of the bomb cannot be accepted.

A11. - Immediate disposal essential to the war effort, demolition of the bomb can be accepted.

B.- Disposal of the bomb important to the war effort and public morale, but not at the risk of bomb disposal personnel which immediate action would entail.

C.- Disposal necessary, but not urgent.

D.- To be dealt with when convenient.

In London there were so many unexploded bombs that normally the Regional Commissioner delegated this responsibility to the Borough Controllers and they set a daily list of priorities. This was then handed over to the officer commanding the local bomb disposal unit who would allocate the work to his sections accordingly. The Regional Commissioner, however, maintained the right to overrule the Borough Controller if an overriding priority task came in.

The importance of prompt and accurate reports about the fall of bombs and other missiles which did not explode was vital for the defence of London. Slowness or the failure to report their presence might result in unnecessary loss of life or avoidable damage to property. Equally important was the danger from false reports due to a lack of knowledge or excessive caution. In these cases, bomb disposal teams could spend hours digging for non-existent bombs, with the result that other, genuine ones, were left unattended. There was, therefore, a need for experienced officers to carryout reconnaissance on sites with suspected unexploded bombs to either verify or eliminate their presence. This in itself could be a dangerous task.

According to Captain Hunt RE, he investigated some 862 unexploded bombs in his area of East London. Of these forty-seven exploded after he had done his reconnaissance or whilst they were being worked on. In one case he was ordered to investigate a suspect bomb at Westbourne Road Station. He made arrangements to attend the scene at 10.00 hours but was delayed because the previous raid had caused havoc on the roads. He arrived fifteen minutes late only to be told that the bomb had detonated at 10.05 hours. Had he arrived on time he would almost certainly been standing right on top of it when it exploded.

On the night of 16-17 September 1940, there were reports of new weapons being dropped by parachute on London. Investigations quickly established two important facts; firstly, that these were parachute mines and secondly they were not very reliable as, out of twenty-five dropped, seventeen had failed to explode. These mines were used because at that time the Luftwaffe was running low on stocks of large conventional bombs and they were the only high capacity explosive munitions available. The mines were much more expensive to manufacture, technically complex and obviously, originally designed for use against shipping.

The use of the mines removed any last vestiges of claims the Germans had to bombing only military targets. Once released from the carrying aircraft, a parachute deployed to slow the weapon's descent; so in terms of accuracy it could only be dropped in the general area of a target, the chances of hitting it were small and its final impact point was at the mercy of the wind.

A feature of the mines was their terrific blast effect. Ordinary bombs would often penetrate buildings or the ground before they exploded and this would attenuate or deflect some of the blast. This was not the case with the parachute mines. As already noted, the design of their fuzing system was such that they did not function on impact but after a short delay, which was normally seventeen seconds. Thus after descending comparatively slowly under the parachute they would come to rest on roofs or on the ground, before detonating. In some cases, when they hit a tall building, the parachute would snag leaving the mine suspended in the air. The largest mines contained 700 kilograms of high explosive and this produced a massive blast wave which flattened buildings and caused damage over a large area. The accepted safety distance for a mine was 350 yards. If you draw a circle 350 yards radius almost anywhere in London, it is immediately apparent that it requires the evacuation of vast numbers of people. Then replicate it seventeen times (the number of mines that failed in the first night) and the consequent disruption to both lives and business becomes apparent, not to mention the detrimental effect on war production.

The disposal of unexploded parachute mines was a Royal Navy responsibility; fortunately they already had gained much experience on them from work outside London. It had been another cat and mouse game, with the Germans fitting a number of 'prevention of stripping' systems, as the Navy preferred to call them. These systems meant that any attempt to dismantle a mine and discover the secrets of its workings would result in a booby-trap charge firing. This danger had already tragically been demonstrated when a mine which had been thought to be safe was taken to the mine warfare school at HMS *Vernon* near Portsmouth for exploitation. Whilst being further disassembled, a secondary booby-trap charge functioned, killing five men and badly injuring several others.[4]

As soon as the news of the mines in London reached HMS *Vernon*, ad hoc teams of officers, petty officers and junior ranks were hurriedly dispatched to deal with the new threat. At the same time the Royal Engineer bomb disposal teams were warned of the dangers of approaching the mines with any metallic objects which might cause them to explode. The first team to arrive was led by Commander G. Thistleton-Smith RN who set out from HMS *Vernon* at about 08.00 hours. On his arrival in London he discovered that over 2,000 people had been evacuated from the Edmonton and Walthamstow area because of the presence of three, unexploded, magnetic mines. One had landed on a tennis court and the other two amongst the crowded terraced houses in the area. The people were keen to get back to work and into their homes and by 17.00 hours the mines had all been rendered safe. The following day the teams were reinforced by a number of other

191

Naval parties. Like their Army colleagues, these early pioneers had little formal training, and a paucity of equipment but, of course, limitless courage. Many were not even regular naval officers, but belonged to the Royal Naval Volunteer Reserve (RNVR) or the Royal Navy Reserve (RNR).

There were many miraculous escapes, often brought about by the fuze with its seventeen second clockwork delay. Unlike the bomb fuzes, the clockwork systems in mines were large and loud. Anyone working on a mine would clearly hear the escapement mechanism 'tick-tocking' if the clock started running whilst it was being rendered safe. Mines which failed would often come to rest in precarious positions with the clocks in a highly sensitive state where even the vibration of passing traffic could cause them to start. If this happened the team working on the mine had two options; run for it, or try to remove the locking ring, extract the fuze and throw it away before the small initiating charge in it exploded; Hobson's choice indeed.

In one example in London, Lieutenant Armitage RNVR and Sub Lieutenant Wadsley RNVR were tasked to deal with a Type D mine. Lieutenant Armitage was actually at the mine when ominously he heard the clock start to tick. He fled as fast as his legs would carry him, and according to the reports at the time, just got round a corner of a building, some thirty yards when the mine detonated. This sheltered him from the worst of the blast but even so he was hurled through the air and badly shaken and bruised. Nevertheless, he reported for duty the following day. His bravery at this, and many other incidents, was recognised and he was one of the original recipients of the George Cross which was presented to him by the King at the first investiture for the medal on 24 May 1941.

Another mine that failed to detonate was found on a railway bridge over the Metropolitan Line in Clifton Avenue, southwest London. Lieutenant Hodges RNVR and Lieutenant Spiers RNR, who were sent to deal with it, approached the mine and wrapped its parachute around part of it to stop it rolling about. They then set about the locking ring which kept the fuze in place. Using a hammer and punch they began tapping this round, when Hodges heard the clockwork mechanism start ticking. They both ran for it; Spiers managed to get about twice as far from the mine as Hodges when it detonated. Spiers escaped suffering shock and bruising, but Hodges was admitted to Richmond Hospital where he remained for several weeks recovering from serious injuries.

Two other sailors, Sub Lieutenant Easton RNVR and Ordinary Seaman Bennet Southwell, dealt with a number of mines in London. One had lodged at the top of a block of flats from which there was no escape if the fuze in it started running. Having successfully rendered this one safe they were tasked to another mine in Clifton Street, Shoreditch. Whilst working on it they heard the menacing noise of the hydrostatic valve close and the clock started ticking. They both ran for it. Unfortunately, they failed to put sufficient distance between them and the mine when it detonated. Easton suffered a fractured skull, a broken pelvis, severe bruising and shock as the blast caught him. The less fortunate Southwell, who had not got as far, was blown to pieces.

When circumstances permitted, and to give themselves a better chance of survival, other mine disposal men built low wall sandbag refuges. Where possible these were positioned just out of line of sight of the mines. The refuges were placed at the maximum distance the sailors could run and throw themselves into, within the seventeen seconds running time of the fuze.

Sadly, some did not get the chance to run. Lieutenant Commander Dick Ryan RN and Chief Petty Officer Reginald Ellingworth went to Hornchurch where they rendered safe a mine threatening the airfield there. They then attended another, which was close by, in Dagenham. It is not clear exactly where this was, as reports of its location vary, some suggesting it was in a warehouse and others that it had crashed through the roof of a house nearby. Recent investigations indicate that it was probably hanging from the eaves of a house in Oval Road. Both men walked over to examine it and were killed instantly when it detonated a short while later. They were both posthumously awarded the George Cross.

The early naval mine pioneers in London were relieved after a short but intense period of duty and others moved in to continue the work. One of them, Lieutenant Ernst Gidden RNVR, was tasked to a mine, which had landed on Hungerford Bridge coming to rest on the live rail where it welded itself to the track. This complicated Gidden's job considerably and it took him over six hours to disarm the mine. His first and most dangerous task was to release it from the live rail so that he could turn it over and gain access to the fuze which, Sod's Law, had dictated had come to rest underneath the main body. This could only be done by brute force, but eventually Gidden managed to rotate it. Then there was the delicate matter of removing the fuze which, because the fuze pocket was badly distorted had to be done with a hammer and chisel. For his bravery he was awarded the George Medal, to add to the George Cross he had already received earlier in the war.

In West End Central Police Station in Saville Row there is an interesting reminder of the bombing during the Blitz. There is a letter written on 1 October 1940 by J.W.D. Blenkin, the Station Inspector, to his wife in Surrey which, amongst other news, records the effects of a parachute mine (which he calls a landmine) which detonated on 21 September 1940. It killed three people, injured a further twenty-two and damaged the police station, he wrote:

I am so sorry you have had such a lot of bombs as I know well how unpleasant they are, but as nearly all of them have fallen in fields not much harm has been done fortunately; it does seem to indicate however that the Jerries are getting a bit shy of the London barrage and are either dropping their bombs before they reach it and turning straight back or else being chased away by our night fighters and jettisoning their bombs as they go. We had a visit from the Duke of Kent today. Apparently he wanted to see a Police Station working under difficulties and was recommended to us. He went first to Saville Row and inspected the damage there and then came on here (to Trenchard House). He was attended by the Commissioner, I was introduced to him and shook hands with Royalty for the first time. He asked me 'How long had I been a Policeman etc.,' 'was I hurt in the explosion,' 'was there a lot of glass whizzing about'. I said 'yes plenty, but fortunately it whizzed past me'. The Commissioner chipped in to say, 'he is not only worried about the Police Station but also because they have dropped three bombs in Mid-Surrey golf course!' Actually that was the first time I had heard about the Mid-Surrey bombs. Perhaps we shall have some new large size bunkers there after the war.

St George's Hospital have just rung up to say that another of our men has died from wounds received last week. [Authors note: believed to be Police Constable Reginald Stanbridge] He was a most charming fellow and was the husband of the girl who runs the boarding house at Mortehoe where he was thinking of going. His wife came up to see him last Friday, but as he was apparently going on alright and as she had a lot of guests and evacuees to look after, she went back again and he collapsed so suddenly that it was impossible to get her up here again in time. In fact the hospital told us at 7.30 p.m. that he was dangerously ill and asked us to send for her which we did, and then they rang up again at 10.00 to say that he had died, so we had to send another message. All very sad and unpleasant. I went to see him on Sunday, he looked terribly ill then and was really a ghastly sight, but he was able to talk and seemed quite cheerful though obviously in great pain.

All this blasted glass, in his case a large electric light bowl fell on his head and after seeing the shocking effect of glass of all sorts and the queer way glass travels, I want you to move everything breakable from the billiard room, all the ornaments from all over the room including the fireplace alcove, all the pictures and all the electric light fittings except one bulb.

Also if possible I should put the babe (H.N.L BLENKIN) under the billiard table or at any rate right up against it away from the window. The billiard table at Saville Row didn't budge and only got a few small cuts on the cloth although the wall of the room was blown down and the windows blown out and several of the frames. Admittedly we had a land mine at Saville Row and the blast was extra terrific but several of our men had pieces of glass which went clean through their arms and out the other side and one man had a bit right through his leg above the knee, so even a much smaller explosion would make glass fly about enough to hurt considerably.

The more I think about last Tuesday's explosion the more I realise how lucky I was. I have examined the room where I was carefully since and found that the door was blown off its hinges as I was going towards it and about two yards away. It had a round glass panel in it about 18" in diameter and that was of course blown clean out so there must have been quite a lot of glass flying about in the room, even if the windows were fortunately blown outwards. It's now 11.15 p.m. and the all clear is just going. I wonder how long it will last for.

This interesting letter not only illustrates the courage of those living and working in London, but also indicates the fact that the bombing was by now becoming a routine event.

Casualties continued to mount in the Royal Engineer Bomb Disposal Sections and on 5 October, at 27 Connor Road, Dagenham, a bomb detonated as a team was trying to render it safe. It had been uncovered in the front garden of the house and it had two fuzes. It was decided to move the bomb, and as this was being done, it detonated. It killed Lieutenant William Ash RE and Lieutenant Leslie Foster RE, along with Sapper Leslie Hitchcock, Sapper Robert Lewis and Driver Ernest Websdale. Seven other men who were some distance away were wounded and had to be taken to hospital for treatment.

During September, all of the Civil Defence services in London, particularly those in the East End which were initially overwhelmed on 'Black Saturday', rapidly adapted to the threat. Amidst the fires, wreckage and rubble they learnt from their experiences and, at every level, steps were taken to improve all aspects of Civil Defence. It could not, and did not, stop other disasters, but after each successive raid more lessons were learnt and better procedures devised and adopted.

Manpower, equipment and other resources were quickly dispatched to incidents and rapidly, and with ever increasing efficiency, they dealt with the scenes of devastation caused by the German bombs.

As well as the immediate rescue and treatment of the bomb victims, there were the longer term healthcare problems caused by the need to look after so many badly maimed or injured people. To deal with the sudden influx of casualties the government had to create a unified Emergency Hospital Service providing free treatment for all. This service was gradually extended so that, by the end of the war, it provided a solid basis on which the National Health Service was later founded.

The September offensive against London that started on 'Black Saturday' continued unabated for four weeks. It was intended to be a knife to the heart of the nation, a knockout blow which would vanquish the capital and leave the political leaders with no choice but to sue for peace. It failed decisively. People went about their business day and night; aware that after the sirens sounded and the noise of aircraft was overhead, they might be blown to bits at any moment. Regardless they carried on, maintaining as much of a routine as they could, in such difficult circumstances. It had, though, been a dreadful month; over 10,000 high explosive bombs had been dropped, 5,730 people had been killed and over 10,000 seriously injured. It is hard to imagine people enduring such losses and hardship today.

NOTES:
1. Constantine FitzGibbon, *The Blitz*, Macdonald, London, 1957.
2. Morris, Captain Joseph, *The German Air Raids on Britain 1914-1918*, H Pordes, London, 1969.
3. Cole, Christopher and Cheesman E.F., *The Air Defence of Great Britain*, Putnam, London, 1984.
4. Poland, E.N., Rear Admiral CB CBE, *The Torpedo Men – HMS Vernon's Story 1872-1986*, Privately Published, 1993.

Chapter 11

The People - Under Cover and Under Fire

'But the bomb has its limitations – it can only destroy buildings and kill people. It cannot kill the unconquerable spirit and courage of the people of London.'
Commentary from the film *London Can Take It*.

The Blitz on London, which started in September 1940, and continued through the winter until the spring of 1941, subjected the people of the capital to the world's first heavy and sustained aerial bombing campaign. The intensity can be judged from Luftwaffe records which noted that, for the period London was the target, seventy-one major raids took place, in each of which at least 100 tons of bombs were dropped. In many of these well over 500 tons of ordnance were delivered. On 18-19 April 1941, for the first time, over 1,000 tons of bombs were scattered over the capital along with 153,000 incendiaries. The continuous nature of the bombing can be gauged from the fact that, in addition to these major raids, there were scores of other harassing attacks. After 7 September 1940, bombs fell on London for fifty-six consecutive nights. This remorseless attack, against the heart of the empire, was the enemy's most concentrated effort of the war against any single British target.

To achieve their aim of subduing the population of London, the Germans would have to kill and maim people in vast numbers and completely reduce whole swathes of the capital to rubble. In this respect Hitler, and his henchmen, had entirely overrated the capabilities of the Luftwaffe and were completely deceived by the geography of London because, at the start of the war, it was one of the least densely populated capitals in the world.

It has been calculated that, in 1940, only twenty-two percent of Central London was built up, and if Greater London was taken into account then this figure dropped to ten percent. Furthermore, only a small percentage of this was residential property although this was concentrated in specific areas. The unpopulated areas consisted of woods, farmland, parks, playing fields, golf courses, cemeteries, gardens and waste land. In addition to these there were thousands of roads, railways, surface tube lines, canals, lakes, docks, and of course the River Thames itself. Inevitably during a raid many bombs, particularly the small 50k types, would fall in these areas, detonate, and do relatively little damage. For example, how many bombs must have plunged into the River Thames, other rivers or the docks themselves during the first attack on 'Black Saturday' and did little more than kill some fish? An example of such a bomb might be the 1,000kg 'Hermann' which was found on 2 June 2008 during dredging operations on the River Lee. Not only did it land in the water, but it failed to explode. Another good illustration from the very centre of London would be the bombing of Buckingham Palace on 13 September 1940, which has already been described. The crew that dropped the bombs no doubt gleefully reported that they had delivered their lethal cargo right into the heart of the capital. This was true, but in fact only one bomb hit the target, the rest missed the Palace landing in the road, quadrangle and gardens doing little lasting damage. In some areas, like the East End, where there were repeated and more concentrated attacks, some areas were completely wrecked, but in succeeding raids many bombs exploded on these derelict areas simply re-arranging the rubble of previous hits.

The population was also lower than normal because of the evacuation of the children, the sick and the elderly. It is true that some returned during the Phoney War, but most left again when the serious bombing started. Many other people, particularly the wealthy, who had the necessary means and no overriding need to stay in the capital, also packed up and left for the duration of the conflict.

Clearly, the above assertions do not hold good for every individual borough; some were more densely populated than others, and the bombs were not evenly distributed. But, overall, it was a fact that London was not a tightly packed or heavily populated target. Some Londoners seemed to be aware of this inbuilt capacity to survive the bombing. Richard Hillary, a Battle of Britain fighter pilot, who wrote *The Last Enemy*, spent some time in London during the Blitz. He was speaking to a taxi driver who remarked, 'Jerry's wasting 'is time trying to break our morale, when 'e might be doing real damage on some small town'. This was true as the later raids on places like Coventry, Hull and Plymouth illustrated.

The German planners also failed to take into account the unparalleled Civil Defence measures that had been put in place, including the construction of shelters which were, naturally, the safest place to be during a raid. It was only in the immediate lead up to the war that serious consideration was given to providing proper protection for the public. There was a key difference between a bomb-proof shelter and a blast, or splinter-proof one. The former would protect the occupants from a direct hit from the largest bomb; they were normally deeply buried, were labour intensive and time consuming to construct, and consequently were very expensive. The latter were cheaper and provided a good level of protection against everything except a very near miss or a direct hit.

The debate about what provided the best level of protection was influenced by many factors, and arguments about what should be built and where, went to and fro. If large numbers of small shelters were provided, then the chances of some being hit were high. If large shelters were used, the chances of a direct hit from a bomb were much reduced, but if one was struck, there would be mass casualties. There was no definitive answer to these theoretical questions which only practical experience could resolve. In the end, as always, the lack of funding by the Treasury was the limiting factor on what was built. The outcome was a mix of different types of protection which ranged from trenches dug in London's parks, to deep bombproof designs for key government staff and officials.

At home, many had to rely on Anderson shelters. These were simple to manufacture erect and were, most importantly, cheap. They were initially designed to go inside a house, but this was impractical unless it was very large. Most went into gardens, but in the poorer areas of terraced houses, many Londoners simply did not have a garden either. The shelters consisted of two sections of curved corrugated steel bolted together at the top and sunk into the ground. They were then covered with at least eighteen inches of earth. Despite their primitive construction and many defects, such as flooding and having an open end, they did prove remarkably effective, particularly those that were concreted in position. Only when subject to a very near miss would a partial collapse be caused. The main effect of blast on this type of shelter was the cracking of the concrete where the front and back sheets projected through the casing. Only in a few cases were the occupants of the shelters injured and mostly this was due to debris being blown through the entrance. They would withstand the blast from a 50kg bomb falling six feet away (I think two large paces gives a better feel for the distance) and a 250kg bomb at twenty feet.[1]

In May 1940 a pamphlet, 'Your Home as an Air Raid Shelter' was issued which gave advice to those who did not have space for a shelter, on how to prepare a safe refuge in the strongest part of a house. Previously much emphasis had been placed on gas-proof refuges, but now, as all the population had gas masks, this was of lesser importance, and resistance to blast took a higher priority. Obviously cellars provided a high degree of protection, but there were very few of them, particularly in the cheaper rows of terraced houses around London. In some areas brick coal bunkers were modified to provide a safe haven, but these were small, cramped and the thought of using them had little appeal.

A later innovation, not introduced until the autumn of 1941, but used throughout the remainder of the war, was the Morrison shelter, named after the leader of London County Council. These metal cages were designed to provide a safe location inside properties and took account of the fact that many people chose not to leave their houses during raids. Morrison shelters properly constructed and sited inside houses proved, like Andersons, to be remarkably effective. They would take the weight of a collapsed three storey house and still protect the people sheltering inside. A study on the fate of occupants in houses totally demolished in explosions produced the following results; of 115 people inside the shelters, only eight were killed, twelve seriously injured and sixteen slightly injured. In the cases examined, forty percent of the occupants escaped unaided, and in the remainder they had to be dug out. In houses damaged beyond repair, in a survey of twenty-two people and eight houses, there were no fatalities and only one serious injury.[2]

In one incident, a 250kg bomb detonated when it hit a 1930s two-storey house which was totally destroyed in the blast. The occupants were inside a Morrison shelter on the first floor about fifteen feet from where the bomb detonated. The shelter was blown through the ground floor ceiling and came to rest in the rubble below. The occupants were dug out by a rescue party after about ten minutes and, other than understandable shock, only suffered minor injuries, some of these occurring whilst they were being cut out.

For the wealthy there was the option of a purpose built, specially designed, concrete shelter dug in to a garden and these featured in the more affluent areas. One was discovered in Chelsea during the refurbishment of a large house in 2005. Hidden near a group of old and well-established trees and looking like a sixties rockery, workmen discovered the shelter whilst clearing the land. Soundly built, spacious, with internal lights, a heater, a telephone and benches, this would have not only protected the occupants against everything except a direct hit or a near miss from a very large bomb, but also provided a degree of comfort not afforded by the Andersons.

It has been made clear that being caught out in the open during a raid and being cut down by flying shrapnel or secondary fragments was a serious problem and produced many casualties. The public needed shelters which they could occupy rapidly if they were caught out away from home when a raid began. The result was the appearance of hundreds of brick built shelters. Initially there was a considerable scandal over the design criteria for these, and in addition many were constructed with sub-standard cement. Those built in such a manner were considered to be death traps which were liable to collapse under minimal external loading. They became known as 'Morrison Sandwich' shelters. A grim joke derived from the fact that the negative pressure wave, generated after a large bomb exploded, could suck out the walls and drop the nine-inch concrete roof slab straight on top of the occupants. However, once the design and build standards were improved, they provided essential protection for the public and hundreds sprung up all over London. They were, though, dark and dingy affairs and initially had no provision for seating or public utilities. Many rapidly degenerated into the proverbial Black Hole of Calcutta and it took some time before improvements were made which enabled people to remain in them, in some measure of comfort, for the duration of a lengthy raid.

In addition to these purpose-built shelters all the local government authorities carried out inspections of both commercial and private properties with a view to reinforcing cellars and basements to make them into public shelters. This included the necessary work to provide suitable entrances and exits. There are, in parts of London, still signs that point to these shelters today, for example Lord North Street in Westminster.

Finally, there was the Underground system which has already been mentioned. The government had tried to discourage its use, to keep it clear for the speedy movement of troops in the event of an invasion, and for moving the injured and evacuees. They feared that the once people went into the tubes they would turn troglodyte and not come out. But the populace saw the safe refuge of the Underground, which was bomb proof at the deeper levels, and nothing could stop the movement of thousands of people into the system when the sirens sounded. In the face of official dithering the people's takeover of the Underground was a sign of their self-reliance and basic instinct for survival. Thus when the serious bombing started, most people had some form of shelter in which they could take cover.

During the war, the Germans mainly relied on twin-engine medium bombers. They never had large numbers of heavy four-engine aircraft like the Lancaster or Flying Fortress which were capable of carrying substantial bomb loads. When the daylight raids ceased and the Germans resorted to less concentrated and inaccurate night bombing, the comparatively small loads of bombs they carried were spread over a much wider area. Taking this into account, the size of London and the distribution of the population, it can be surmised that apart from localized areas, for example the East End where the population may have been overwhelmed, taken as a whole, the raids on London were light. This does not in any way diminish the fact that the raids were horrendous in terms of casualties and damage, and that for those people actually being bombed it was, at times, a traumatic and almost unbearable experience. The premise that the bombing was relatively 'light' is certainly true, in terms of scale, if comparisons are made with places like Hamburg, Dresden or Tokyo, later in the war. This should be borne in mind when reading about the reactions of people in the following paragraphs.

The population's underlying resilience and resistance in the face of the bombing was not understood by anyone at the time, and least of all by the German leaders who had marveled that, till then, the Luftwaffe had crushed all resistance before it. From their perspective the raids were going to deliver a devastating blow to morale. It was hoped to make the people stampede out of the capital and reduce the infrastructure to ruins. However, other than this vague aim, there was no real strategic planning by the Germans; it was assumed that, by dropping more and more explosives and incendiaries, they would eventually succeed. In fact, one commentator suggested that the bombing was: 'A confused arrangement looking much more like the aimless destructive outbursts of a child with conflicting impulses than the results of clear decisive planning often regarded as the prerogative of totalitarian leadership.'[3]

So how did the Londoners cope with these deadly childish outbursts, and adapt to conditions that had, hitherto, never been known by a modern society?

During the early raids naturally robust or high spirited people tended to be excited and elated about the experience of being bombed. In escaping from mortal danger without injury, the mere act of survival had a curiously moving and even exhilarating effect on them. They were very communicative about their experiences and escapes and laughed and joked with some excitement about 'still being alive'. But in later, heavier raids, the strain wore even these people down and they talked much less about their bombing experiences. They were more subdued and were preoccupied instead with maintaining normality and dealing with the consequences of the bombing.

By contrast people who were of a more nervous disposition in the earlier Blitz and who had found it hard to cope from the start of the raids, showed many more signs of anxiety and edginess in later attacks, even though by that time, the conditions and the chances of survival were generally much improved. At first these people might have been able to control themselves with an effort, later they were inclined to start to cry and shake when the sirens sounded.[4]

The heavy destruction of civilian property, the evacuation made necessary by unexploded bombs and continuous night attacks created problems of quite an unexpected character. Although post-raid services to support the population rapidly expanded, this took time, and initially the homeless and dispossessed were often left to their own devices. Many returning to their bomb damaged or destroyed homes felt a desperate sense of helplessness as they viewed the ruins of their property. Bombs were no respecters of class, and could in an instant, sweep away years of hard work, and destroy irreplaceable and cherished possessions. The owners had the miserable task of recovering any salvageable belongings from bombed-out buildings, arranging alternative accommodation or making good damage to their houses. Often, with the essential utilities disrupted, even basic things like cooking and washing required a special effort. When more support became available, the owners of bombed-out or damaged properties had to make various claims. Just completing the forms and then finding out where to send them was a strain. For those in such a position, their continued survival depended on their ability to cope with the business of their material loss.

Populations who have been exposed to air attacks on a significant scale undergo a wide variety of emotional stresses. During a raid every person in the danger area is tormented by the possibility of death and injury, not only to themselves but, more often than not, to those people that are near and dear to them. Under these conditions there is a marked incidence of emotional shock even amongst persons who are mentally stable. After the first serious raid, which directly affects an individual, there is the added fear of waiting for the next. The population know it is coming, but the uncertainty of when, where, and the scale of the attack leave many with feelings of dread and anticipation which disrupt normal functions.

So it was for the Londoners during the Blitz. When the sirens wailed, there was the move to the shelters and then the waiting. This was followed by the drone of the engines of the enemy bombers and the sharp reports of the anti-aircraft guns as they opened up. Finally, there are the thunderous detonations, as the bombs exploded. Those in deep shelters were protected from the worst of the noise which, in some cases, was reduced to a distant rumble. But those in the brick-built surface shelters, Andersons or simply sheltering in their homes had little protection from the noise and the concussion waves from bombs sweeping round them. Although these did not directly physically affect the individual, as bombs and incendiaries burst closer and closer, causing fires and destruction, the emotional stress built like steam in a pressure cooker. The threat of imminent death or serious injury coupled with a feeling of utter helplessness became seriously unnerving. Other than praying, individuals could do nothing about their predicament to increase their chances of survival, and simply had to sit and wait for the danger to pass.

However, provided they only suffered remote misses with no injury, most emotionally stable people rapidly adapted to these situations and recovered reasonably quickly when the all-clear sounded. A little later there was immense relief and the feeling, common amongst survivors of all kinds that they had got away with it.

For those unfortunates subjected to very near misses, things were different. When a bomb detonated and destroyed a house or a shelter and the walls came crashing down round an individual, or a powerful explosion hurled them to the ground, then the most acute and persistent feelings of fear were aroused. This may have involved the narrowest escape from death, being wounded, entombed in a collapsed building or seeing a loved one killed or mutilated. The emotional shock in these cases was profound and ranged from a dazed helpless stupor to jumpiness and a morbid preoccupation with the horrors of what had occurred.

On 7 September 1940, Mrs Nancy Spencer, an assistant on an ambulance, recalled a terrible journey to collect casualties from the Oriental Road area of Silvertown. On arrival at the scene she went to a shelter and asked the forty or so people, who were cowering there, which amongst them, were injured. There was no response so she called again, but the people seemed not to hear, or if they could, not to care. Eventually she tapped a woman on her shoulder and repeated the question again, at which point she was told there was an injured woman, baby and boy, all of whom had been dug out of collapsed buildings. She decided to load these casualties on to her ambulance and asked if there was an ARP warden who could help her. Someone told her he was dead, but no one offered to lend a hand. In the end she cajoled a couple of men to help her and loaded a total of fifteen injured people on to the ambulance for transfer to a hospital. These people, shocked, bewildered and helpless were all typical examples of very near miss victims.

One study into bombing by MacCurdy examined groups of people after raids to assess their reactions and it drew some interesting conclusions. The heavier the raid, the higher the proportion of the population in the community who would suffer very near misses. Not surprisingly, in these raids, the incidence of emotional shock and other severe reactions increased. However, MacCurdy explained that the frequent rise in the morale of the community under constant fire as follows; in a large city like London there would inevitably be many more remote misses than very near misses. If a remote miss person has more courage after a raid than before it, and if courage, like fear is contagious, and if the numbers of very near miss victims in a population is small overall, it follows that after a raid there must be, by and large, an improvement in the morale of the community.

Night raids are naturally much more unsettling than daytime ones. The fact is that terror is much more frequently experienced by people in darkness than in the light. At night the flashes from exploding bombs can be seen from a greater distance compared to daylight, and that coupled with the sounds of them detonating created the perception of a much more threatening environment.

The most logical reason for the increased fear at night is the reduced effectiveness of sight, one of the key senses. Darkness alters the balance of the senses and the loss of vision in particular, impedes an individual's ability to work out what is safe or dangerous in their immediate environment. More than any other, sight is the sense needed to help people escape from dangerous situations. In an air raid this might be finding a shelter or, if caught up in an incident, fleeing a fire or clambering out of a damaged building.

To make matters worse, hearing and smell can work against people in the dark. Loud noises and acrid smells alert the individual to some form of danger and instinctively trigger the use of sight to evaluate it. Make a sudden and loud noise in a group of people and heads automatically turn to face the apparent danger. But when it is very dark, this complementary use of the senses does not work. The individual is alerted to some danger, but does not necessarily know what it is. It is easy to imagine being trapped, at night, in the ruins of a partially collapsed building, and then getting a whiff of smoke which must mean fire. In daylight it might be possible to escape; in the dark, clambering over debris and searching for an exit, would be much harder.

Another casualty of the dark, unless you are physically holding somebody, is the loss of personal contact. In daylight, amongst groups of people sheltering, there is always the reassuring glance, or wink, from some stout-hearted relative or friend. Such a simple act would often reassure, and help calm the nerves of the more vulnerable. In the dark, alone with their fears, these people suffered from a much greater feeling of isolation and helplessness.

Finally, the body's natural rhythms are much easier to dislocate at night, and the disruption of sleep, particularly over a prolonged period, makes people tired, tetchy and much more susceptible to nervous breakdowns and illness. To help the people of London overcome the problem of a lack of sleep the government issued free earplugs and a picture of Churchill was circulated which purported to show him asleep with plugs in position, but it didn't work. Strangely the reason is related to night and noise again. If you could hear the sound of the guns and bombs exploding, then at least you knew roughly what was going on. With earplugs in nothing could be heard and it was left to the imagination to guess what was happening. Most people seemed to prefer the noise.

In some circumstances lights at night could cause intense worry. Observers noted that the population would become peculiarly sensitive to any chink of light showing during a night-time raid. The perception was that the unseen enemy above could see this, and would be drawn to it like moths round a lamp, homing in on it as their single aiming point.

In general, during the Blitz, those that were required to work through the bombing suffered less mental anguish than those who sat at home or in shelters with nothing to occupy them. This was particularly true for workers in close knit teams, or those who had responsibility for others. An auxiliary fireman said that: 'Most of us had the wind up to start with, especially with no barrage. It was all new, but we were unwilling to show fear, however much we might feel it. You looked around and saw others doing their job. You could not let them down. You just had to get on with it.'[5]

Age also had a bearing on the adult population's attitude to the bombing, and this was especially apparent when comparing the young and the old. London at the time was flooded with young men, and to lesser extent women, who had been mobilized into the armed forces from many counties. Many of them, particularly aircrew, recognised the very real possibility of being killed or badly wounded in action.

Londoners too were well aware of the risks to life and limb especially with the constant reminders all-around of what bombs could do. It generated a 'live for today for tomorrow we die' philosophy and gave rise to a profound change in moral attitudes, particularly amongst the young, possibly arising from the perceived uncertainty of any long-term future. For some the thought of dying a virgin, and not experiencing one of the basic pleasures of life was, in itself, a cause of anguish.

The result was a noticeable difference in the behaviour of the younger members of the public. Fights or brawls in public became more common place; there was a perceptible change in people's respect for other people's property; a loosening of sexual morals and a willingness to transgress and commit crimes, which were justified by the needs of the time. The black market flourished and a majority (and not a minority) of people were prepared to engage in transactions which they ultimately knew were the result of some criminal activity. For example, an investigation into garage owners over the sale of petrol outside the rationing system, discovered amongst the illicit customers, a knight, a former mayor, a distinguished soldier, a hotel proprietor and several police officers.[6] All these changes in behaviour were brought about in part by the bombing and the threat of an uncertain future.

At the other end of the scale a lot of elderly people took a very fatalistic approach to the bombing. They resigned themselves to the fact that if a bomb had their name on it there was nothing they could do about it. Many of them, particularly in the less heavily bombed suburbs and especially as the cold winter nights approached, simply ignored the warning sirens altogether, preferring their own homes and the comfort of their own beds to the air raid shelters. They regarded the danger with a degree of detachment and accepted it as we all accept the potential hazard of crossing the road today.

Another powerful influence on people was the effects of the bombing on animals. Within days of the war being declared, it was estimated that almost 400,000 pets, most of them cats, were put down. Despite this there were still thousands of pets in London when the air raids proper started. Those that had escaped the cull were not allowed into shelters. In Hyde Park, for example, the ARP wardens provided white posts to which pets could be tied to whilst their masters took cover during raids. It caused their owners much distress to leave their pets, who truly were innocent victims, to the mercy of the bombs, whilst they sheltered.

As well as domestic pets there were many working animals who contributed to the war effort. Large numbers of horses were still in use delivering coal, milk and other services and they were a key resource for the capital's smooth running. It is said that animal panic is almost as infectious as that of human beings; equally it is true that people sometimes care more for animals than humans. There were many occasions when police officers and others went into stables to rescue horses from fires, or tried to calm and reassure them in the worst of the bombing. One man recalled during the Blitz that he went into a smouldering stable to try to rescue some horses. He found what he described as a row of massive roast meat joints and, as often happens when confronted by an unpleasant truth, it took him several seconds before he realized that it was row of dead horses that been tethered and had been unable to escape the flames. It was the only time he cried during the war.

The response to raids gradually changed as the Blitz progressed. Once the serious attacks on the capital started there was increased fear of successive raids. But many of the people of resolute character, and who fell into the remote miss category, grew bolder as time progressed and would ignore air raid warnings until the last minute when aircraft could be heard overhead or the guns opened up their barrage. After the raids many citizens would ignore notices about unexploded bombs and return to their homes despite the risks. Being bombing was becoming part of their routine.

It became apparent towards the end of September that the Luftwaffe's assault was going to be a prolonged affair and, as the nights lengthened more time was spent in shelters. Warnings often lasted from just after dark until just before dawn. It meant that, for those that took cover, it would not simply be a case of ducking into shelters to dodge a short raid; they would stay there all night. No provision had been made for the long hours that people would be wedged together; eating, sleeping and doing everything else necessary for survival. This had implications for health, hygiene and availability of space.

The continued ability of a community to survive the chaotic and fearful effects of a raid was largely dependent on the capability of the Civil Defence organisation to rescue, treat, re-house and provide for the welfare needs of the people once the all-clear had sounded. This was lacking initially, and the pre-planned rest centres proved inadequate in terms of protection, sanitation and amenities provided. No provision had been made for a stay of more than a few hours, and blankets and spare clothing and other essentials necessary to replace things destroyed by the bombing were very scarce. By the end of September, a rest centre population of some 25,000 had piled up in the London region of which over 14,000 were in desperately overcrowded venues. The local government response to these new challenges varied; some boroughs were very good but others were awful. Some of the worst hit boroughs failed to cope effectively at all. Stepney, for example, was considered by government inspectors to still be in a total state of chaos weeks after the heaviest bombing had ceased.

The continuance of normal activities helped relieve the strain. The people were, in spite of everything, able to move around and enjoy relative freedom, working and crucially talking to others about their experiences. The fact that the milkman still appeared, postmen tried to deliver mail and telegrams, the busses and trains ran (even if there were delays and diversions), and the pubs were open, albeit often with little beer, all served to reinforce the feeling that no matter what happened, the individual person could and would survive. Black humour also helped relieve the strain. On one damaged East End police station some wag had written, 'Please be good we are still open'. Towards the end of October, the phrase 'London can take it' became commonplace. The origin is unclear but the Ministry of Information through the mass observation reports, noted that, although Londoners were feeling the strain of the relentless assault, their morale was unlikely to be broken.

A factor in maintaining this morale was the swift and efficient manner in which casualties were dealt with both in terms of being rescued and treated. Of equal importance was another crucial, but disagreeable task which was carried out by the mortuary attendants whose unenviable duty was to recover the dead. The point has already been made that censorship was total and that pictures of bodies were rarely publicized, equally the people shown being rescued, were the ones without severe injuries, or if they were, at least outwardly, these were not obvious. There are thousands of sanitized images showing wrecked buildings, and other damage, sometimes with cheerful Cockneys giving 'V' signs and drinking tea. These were normally taken long after the casualties had been rescued, bodies removed and the scene generally cleared. It is easy to forget that many of those pictures show the location of the untimely deaths of so many innocent civilians.

After a raid, the need to clear away all trace of these unfortunate victims, as quickly and efficiently as possible, was vital for the maintenance of morale. In some respects, dead bodies acquire an almost child-like quality of their own. They must be protected, covered up, and treated tenderly with care and respect. During the war this crucial activity was rarely touched on or written about outside official circles.

Alan Seymour was employed as a mortuary attendant and had the wretched job of recovering the bodies, or body parts, from the scenes of explosions. His very first task was on the night of 2 October 1940 during a particularly heavy raid. On arrival he was directed by the incident commander to attend to a body lying in the street covered by a blanket. Now came the moment of truth that he had long dreaded and he had to force himself to walk down the road to the body and turn back the blanket that covered it. He said:

> I don't know what horror I expected to see, but all that was revealed was the calm, rather beautiful face of a young girl of about seventeen, unmarked as far as I could see but lying on her side as if asleep.
> We were not allowed to presume death, and always had to get the doctor's permission to remove a body, even when it was obvious that life was extinct.
> I took the shoulders to turn her on her back, and then realised she was beyond all aid as when the torso turned the legs remained in the same position as before. One of her hands touched mine, and it was still quite warm. We decided the only way to lift the body was to roll it in a blanket; this we did after a struggle, the lumbar region had a great hole in it, and there was a rush of blood when we moved it.[7]

It was not the worst that Seymour would have to deal with as the war progressed. On one occasion he and his crew were tasked to an Anderson shelter which had received a direct hit. They did not expect to find any significant remains, but the local Doctor explained that it was important to try and confirm that two people had been killed in the explosion. This required them to dig and sift the soil for pieces of body and although many remains were discovered they were so pulped and so small that they could not be used to identify the persons involved. Eventually around dawn, after many hours digging, they recovered close together, part of a suspender belt and a pair of men's braces. This satisfied the local doctor that there were two casualties and the gruesome work was halted.

There were lots of Alan Seymours who carried out this essential task. It was done in a quiet, calm and professional manner with due deference to the dead. As far as I can establish there was no counselling then. Occasionally, black humour helped the men and women through the most difficult situations, but most of the time they just got on with the job.

The sizes of bombs being dropped by the Luftwaffe steadily increased as the Blitz progressed, a fact which was noted by Ministry of Home Security Research and Experiments Department which did much good work establishing the effectiveness of the various types of bomb.[8] Although the results were not published until well after the end of the

Blitz they are relevant to what happened on the ground. Initially the payloads of the German aircraft mainly consisted of 50kg and 250kg bombs, although, as previously recorded at St Paul's, a few 1,000kg bombs were dropped. The Germans realized that in terms of physical destruction the larger bombs were more effective and used more of them, but ran out of stock rapidly. As a stop-gap they used comparatively expensive parachute mines of either 500 or 1,000 kilograms which also contained a high proportion of explosive. As the German production of bigger bombs caught up with demand, more of the larger types were carried. A common philosophy of all bombing campaigns, both terrorist and conventional, seems to be that if small bombs do not get results, use more and bigger ones until they do.

In general, a 1,000kg bomb was likely to do significantly more damage than say four 250kg bombs. There were straightforward reasons for this, firstly in terms of explosive the total content of four 250 kilogram bombs would be around 500kg, whereas a single 1,000kg bomb would contain 600kg, twenty percent more explosive. Secondly, in terms of their destructive effects, a single charge of 600kg would demolish a much larger area than the combined effects of the smaller bombs. Surprisingly, further analysis, showed that ton for ton similar amounts of damage was done for all bombs up to 500kg.

In terms of producing fatalities it was another matter, and the analysis had to take into account where the casualties occurred. Generally, the results of the study for all bombs showed that people in houses were three to four times safer than those in the open and people in Anderson shelters were five times safer than those in houses. They also indicated that, ton for ton, 50kg bombs produced twice the casualty rate as 250kg and 500kg bombs and about the same as parachute mines.

The explanation for the different casualty rates for bombs up to 500kg appears to be that, in the case of people in houses that suffered a direct hit, they had little or no chance of surviving, unless they were inside some form of internal shelter. However, the act of the destruction of the house that was hit accorded significant protection to those in neighbouring houses. It follows that when a greater number of smaller bombs were dropped there were more direct hits which meant that they were bound to cause more casualties. Parachute mines of course often came to rest in the open before detonating and there was no attenuation of the blast at all.

We have seen that, generally, those that had to work through raids were either so busy, or worried about letting their colleagues down that they continued with their tasks despite the risks. All were extremely brave. Another group of men displayed a different kind of courage.

These were the bomb and mine disposal teams. Being small, tight-knit, communities' news of casualties naturally spread quickly. Amongst the officers and men there could be little doubt about the dangers of the job they were undertaking and that the odds were stacked against them. It took cold-blooded courage to go into an area where there was a known unexploded bomb, dig down to it (not in itself an easy or risk-free task), uncover the fuze(s) and render it safe. All the time knowing that a clockwork fuze might re-start or a new type of booby-trap fuze might function killing those nearby instantly. The men would not dwell on such matters except perhaps in the dark hours. One man wondered whether or not he would see the flash before he died. Writing of them Churchill set them apart from other men. He remarked: 'Somehow or other their faces seemed different from those of ordinary men, they were gaunt, they were haggard, their faces had a bluish look, with bright gleaming eyes and exceptional compression of the lips all with a perfect demeanour.'

There was always danger when working with bombs, sometimes catching out experienced men who thought they were safe. On 10 October 1940, a 250kg bomb had been recovered with a badly damaged fuze. The bomb had passed through a cast iron drain and was so deformed by the process, it was decided that it was no longer capable of functioning. It was loaded onto a truck and driven to the Duke of York's Barracks in Chelsea, where the men stopped to eat their evening meal. Lieutenant Lionel Carter saw the bomb with the fuze in position and decided that it should have been taken directly to the bomb cemetery which had been established in Regent's Park. For one man now, luck intervened; he was the driver of vehicle and asked permission to have the rest of the evening off as he had a date. Lieutenant Carter agreed to this as he was prepared to drive the lorry himself. A number of other men volunteered to come along, not only to help move the bomb, but also so that they could be dropped off at a pub on the way back. As they were driving up the Marylebone Road, near Madam Toussauds, the bomb exploded without warning. Lieutenant Carter, Corporal Laurence Sharp and Sappers William Archer, John Cookson, William Cubitt and William Pass all died in the blast.

On the night of 3-4 November, thanks to bad weather, there was the first break in the bombing. After nearly two months of consecutive raids the sirens did not sound. Three days later, however, during a comparatively light raid, the police suffered their highest number of fatalities in one night when a bomb hit the old police station at Kilburn. No one in the building survived the explosion, but fate played a number of strange tricks resulting in some members of the shift being out of the station when it was hit. Police Constable Don Milburn, who recalled the events, was one of the few officers of the shift to survive. He had been given leave from 3 to 5 November to get engaged and but for this he would almost certainly have been in the building when it was hit. When he returned from his leave on the morning of 6 November he heard of the catastrophe and immediately went to the station to help with the rescue operations.

The previous night, the duty shift had arrived and booked on just before 22.00 hours. They were, Sergeant McGee, Police Constables John Brown, Charles McInnes, Clifford Howell Davies, Charles Summers and Donald Light. In addition, there were War Reserve Policemen Bert Borham, Gerard Harvey, Llewellyn Davies, George Wallis, Len Bowes, George Smith, Thomas Coe and Tom Craven and last Special Constable Acton.

As already intimated, chance played a hand in deciding who would live or die that night. The only two members of the relief that should have definitely remained in the station for the entire shift were Sergeant McGee and Police Constable Donald Light, who was the switchboard operator. The others should have split between doing four hours out on the beat and four hours on standby in the station. Around midnight there was a report that there was an incendiary fire in a building next to the Masons Arms. At the time, the men were in the station, some playing cards. Charlie Summers should have attended the incident but because of the card game Donald Light and Special Constable Acton volunteered to go. Around the same time, Sergeant McGee realized that he had left his food behind. As it was a comparatively quiet night, and he lived close by, he decided to go home and grab a meal.

The bomb struck as the three men were making their way back to the station. Donald and Acton were almost there and McGee pedalling his bike a little further away. To them the raid suddenly seemed to be intensifying when without warning they heard the rush of air which announced a stick of bombs landing very close by. The two men nearest the police station threw themselves down and were engulfed by the enormous shock wave from a large bomb which squarely struck the station building. As they lay there, large quantities of debris crashed around them – but nothing major hit them. When the dust settled they looked up and could see, even in the dark, that the police station was completely demolished. Sergeant McGee was blown off his bike by the blast and hurled against a nearby wall. All three men, on regaining their senses, rushed to the scene to look for survivors. Donald always claimed that he could hear the voice of Charlie Summers calling for help beneath the rubble. But as they scrambled over the wreckage it became apparent that there was little hope of finding anyone alive. As the word of the disaster spread, additional police officers from further afield arrived along with the ARP and rescue parties. Their efforts were in vain, however, and it took two full days to recover the twelve dead officers. In addition, the body of Bob Boast, the section house cleaner, was recovered making the total death toll thirteen. It was the worst number of casualties suffered by the Metropolitan Police in any single incident during its history.

The losses amongst the bomb disposal teams also continued to mount. On 19 November 1940, 5 Bomb Disposal Company Royal Engineers suffered more casualties. At Dellwood Gardens in Ilford a bomb was uncovered and it was discovered it was fitted with a long-delay fuze. A stethoscope was used to check the state of the fuze which confirmed that it was not ticking. Digging continued, to find out if a second fuze was fitted. As this was being done the bomb exploded killing Lance Corporal Thorpe and Sapper Douglas Hurley. Three other sappers who were further away when the bomb detonated were injured and taken to hospital.

On 8 December 1940, a bomb was reported outside 590, Romford Road, Manor Park, close to the main London to Chelmsford road which had to be closed. This caused serious traffic dislocation and on 13 December, men from 5 Bomb Disposal Company Royal Engineers under Captain Michael Blaney RE was tasked to deal with it. The bomb which had penetrated to a considerable depth was one of the most dangerous sorts, a 250kg fitted with two fuzes. One of these was clearly a clockwork time fuze and the other an anti-disturbance Number 50. It was decided that the best method of dealing with the bomb would be to fit the steam sterilizer and steam out the bomb's filling. Tragically, as subsequent events would show, the lorry carrying the equipment broke down and so this option was ruled out. At the site they had other equipment and this included a magnetic clock stopper. This was a powerful electro-magnet which when fitted and switched on, produced a magnetic field which was sufficient to stop the clockwork mechanism running. It was known that fitting one of these to a bomb with a Number 50 fuze, without the condensers being discharged, could set it off. It was thought that after four days, it was unlikely that the condensers would have retained sufficient charge to work. The cumbersome electro-magnet was dropped into the shaft and put on the bomb and the current switched on remotely from a safe distance. At the same time, an electronic stethoscope was positioned close to the time fuze, with a cable which ran to a listening post some distance away. Here a soldier would maintain a listening watch to ensure that the fuze remained stopped. Should it start, he would shout a warning to the men working on the bomb, and with luck they would have time to escape before it detonated.

Captain Blaney decided to hoist the bomb out and take it to Wanstead flats where it could be destroyed by demolition without doing any damage. Unfortunately, it proved impossible to haul the bomb straight out because the lifting strop fouled the heavy clock stopper. As a consequence, it was necessary to remove the stopper for the short period, whilst the bomb was being removed from the hole, and then to immediately re-fit it once it was clear.

A rope was threaded through a pulley and connected to a joist from the house and members of the team began to pull the bomb out of its hole. As the bomb came in to view it was swinging and Captain Blaney stepped forward to steady it. It was at this moment, when it was a couple of feet above ground, in the most dangerous position it could be, that it detonated. The sapper team had no chance and were scythed down.

One man had a lucky escape, but it was paid for by another. The lucky man was Staff Sergeant Fox. He had been helping to pull up the bomb, but Staff Sergeant Roberts who was listening to the electronic stethoscope had become cold and cramped and had asked Fox to swap places with him. They did so a few moments before the bomb exploded. Along with Blaney, Lieutenant James, Staff Sergeant Roberts, Lance Corporal Mills, Sappers MacLaren and Maycock and Drivers Lauchlan and Pickering were killed instantly. In addition, Inspector Henry Lane of the Metropolitan Police who was standing across the road lost his life. Fox confirmed during the subsequent investigation that he had not heard the clockwork fuze ticking before the clock stopper was removed. It was assumed that the capacitors in the anti-disturbance fuze had retained sufficient charge which initiated the bomb.

Blaney was subsequently awarded the George Cross for his outstanding work at the forefront of the bomb disposal effort in London. A road, Blaney Crescent, was named after him and a memorial built at the scene. Sadly, the latter has long since disappeared.

As the war progressed questions of manpower became more urgent and, in November 1940, the Director of Bomb Disposal agreed to take men from the Non-Combatant Corps (NCC). These men, although conscientious objectors who refused to fight, agreed to assist with bomb disposal operations. In the following months several hundreds of them joined bomb disposal teams across the country. At first they were received with mixed feelings by their regular Army counterparts who made their hostility plain. However, after a short settling in period, most of the conscientious objectors were found to be punctilious about their duties and did an excellent job.

One of them was Lewis Goodwin, a twenty-seven-year-old serving with 216 Section NCC but seconded to 22 Bomb Disposal Company Royal Engineers. He worked in and around London and was involved with the disposal of many bombs. One example was a parachute mine which was destroyed by demolition in a twelve-foot pit at Thames Haven in early 1941. Goodwin survived the war and brought up a family. One of his children, Liz, who joined the Metropolitan Police, would have her own confrontation with the effects of a bomb as she was caught up in the suicide attacks in 2005.

NOTES:
1   TNA, HO 197/29: Report by Bexleyheath Council on domestic shelters, 15 September 1945.
2   TNA, HO 191/51: Morrison Shelters, Table 1a and b.
3   Richard M. Titmuss, *Problems of Social Policy*, HM Stationary Office, London, 1950.
4   International Journal of Psychoanalysis, Vol 23 (1942), page 28.
5   FitzGibbon, Constantine, *op. cit.*
6   Ingleton, Roy, *The Gentlemen at War, Policing Britain 1939 -1945*, Cranborne Publications, Kent, 1994.
7   Ramsey Winston G., *The Blitz Then and Now*, Volume 2, Battle of Britain Prints International Limited, London, 1987.
8   TNA, HO 196/13: Ministry of Home Security Reports.

Chapter 12

Fire Bombs and Firefighters

'The fact that a largely inexperienced force of amateur firefighters faced and mastered the fires in the early weeks of the Blitz with considerable success was little short of a miracle.'
Neil Wallington.

From the very first raid on London, the Luftwaffe used incendiary bombs. Indeeed, the destruction of the city by fire had always been central to the Germans plan. Hitler had said: 'Have you ever seen a map of London, it is so densely built that one fire alone would be enough to destroy the whole city. Göring will start fires all over London, fires everywhere, with countless incendiary bombs of an entirely new type. Thousands of fires. Göring has the right idea: high explosives don't work but we can do it with incendiaries; we can destroy London completely. What will the firemen be able to do about it once it is really burning?'[1]

The fact that London, overall, was not a particularly densely packed target has already been discussed. There was, however, a grain of truth in what Hitler had said, and some areas like the East End, Elephant and Castle and the City were vulnerable to attack by fire. After every bombing raid on London there were fires of different sizes and intensity and the battles against them were as real as any fought by the personnel in the armed forces. The fire brigade bore the brunt of the action, but the people played their part and, without them stopping some of the smaller fires from developing into major blazes, there would have been many more, large, all-consuming conflagrations.

The Luftwaffe had in service two distinct types of bomb for starting fires. Firstly, there were conventionally shaped bombs of 50, 110 or 250 kilograms filled with various flammable mixtures or sub-munitions.

They used standard impact fuzes and most had additional high explosive bursting charges to scatter the contents over a wide area. These types functioned on impact and produced fires which were beyond the capabilities of anyone other than the fire brigade.

The second type, and by far the most common, was small 1kg incendiaries, which became known as IBs (Incendiary Bombs). These could be tackled by the public. The basic bomb consisted of a magnesium body filled with a thermite incendiary mixture and was fitted with a simple impact fuze. When the bomb struck a hard surface, such as a tiled roof, the impact triggered the fuze which initiated the thermite filling in the core of the bomb. This burnt at an extremely high temperature which ignited the magnesium shell, or casing, which also burnt fiercely with intense heat. There was considerable spluttering for a minute or two as the magnesium burnt, during which time white-hot metal could be thrown up to ten metres. After this the remainder of the bomb collapsed into a pool of molten metal which continued to burn for up to ten minutes, but without the spluttering.

They could be delivered in one of two ways. Firstly, there were non-expendable containers carried by an aircraft which on activation would rapidly dispense the bombs in a pre-set pattern. The biggest of these carried 700 incendiaries and an aircraft delivering bombs from one of these would leave behind a trail of fire in its wake. Later in the war the incendiaries were carried in releasable containers which would open during their descent and, like modern day cluster bombs, produce a shower of bombs in a concentrated pattern.

The question of how to deal with these bombs had been considered as far back as 1937 with the formation of the Incendiary Bomb Committee by HM Inspector of Explosives. Even then it was recognised that the people would have to play their part in defeating the threat posed by these devices. The Committee had acquired a number of different fire-raising bombs and looked at how the 'amateur' could fight them. They initially concluded with the light magnesium types that nothing could be done to actually extinguish the burning bomb once the outer body caught fire, but that they could be moved using a long handled scoop or hoe and a sand container. Later work established that even if the bomb itself could not be extinguished, ordinary people could control the subsequent fire with minimal equipment, this of course being with the ubiquitous stirrup pump and bucket which was approved for use in August 1937.

From a historical perspective, the lowly stirrup pump must rank, along with the civilian gas mask, as one of the most important protective instruments developed to safeguard people during the

Second World War. The Incendiary Bomb Committee undertook a series of experiments with the pump during its development and discovered that the key to success was an adjustable nozzle. Using a spray rather than a jet was the best way to tackle the burning magnesium body. It would not extinguish the bomb but the spray could be used to minimise the incendiary effect of the burning metal and significantly reduce the incidence of secondary fires. When the body of the bomb had burnt out the more powerful jet could be used to tackle any surrounding fires it had caused.

These small IBs would penetrate any ordinary roof material, such as slate or tile, and lodge in the upper storey of the building, where fires would develop. Unless the bomb entered through a window, the chances were that it would be arrested by the first boarded floor below the roof. In many cases this was the roof or attic space, which was difficult to access and presented major problems for all fire-fighters. Accordingly, advice was given that all inflammable materials were to be removed from this space and the floor protected against fire. It was recommended that a two-inch layer of dry slag or sand was laid on the floor or, if this was too heavy, then a layer of corrugated iron sheeting. In addition, the woodwork in the roof was to be protected by rock-anhydride plaster or fire resistant paint. Even lime wash would provide a delay in the setting alight of the roof timbers. An even better solution, which sadly was rarely practicable, was to prevent the penetration of the roof space. This could be achieved by either a quarter-inch of mild steel plate, one layer of sandbags or five inches of concrete. Bombs that crashed through thin roofs and landed on non-combustible surfaces inside buildings, for example concrete floors in factories, could be dealt with by using sand mats which were placed over the bomb. Although this would not extinguish the fire, it would contain the shower of molten metal while the thermite burned. This made the bomb less efficient and helped prevent the fire spreading.

When an incendiary bomb penetrated a roof, it was necessary to subdue and localise the fire it caused as soon as possible to prevent it burning a hole through the floor and establishing secondary blazes. For the average man or woman, the main weapon against the incendiaries was the aforementioned stirrup pump and bucket. Normally manned by a crew of three people, the pump could deliver one and a half gallons of water a minute. When used as a spray the system had an effective range of twelve-fifteen feet but the jet could throw water out to double that distance. The apparatus came with a twenty-five feet length of hose which enabled the pump and the lead firefighter to be separated. This meant that with a fire in an attic it was possible to have one person fighting the fire, one below pumping and the other replacing and refilling buckets of water. It was estimated that six to eight gallons of water were sufficient to tackle an IB and any secondary fires it caused provided it was tackled soon after it had landed. Alternatively, if it was feasible the bombs could be scooped up with specialist rakes or even a shovel and carried outside to burn themselves out harmlessly on the ground.

The incendiaries were, in the early days, fair game for everyone. Every citizen from shop girls to city gents could be seen scooping up the bombs, putting out small fires and helping rescue people from lightly burning buildings. The sight of people in their nightclothes shovelling away burning incendiary bombs was commonplace and many a building was saved by their valiant efforts.

The Germans were clearly aware from open sources that the bombs were being dealt with by the public and they decided to make their task much more dangerous. They quickly developed and introduced new and deadly variants of the IB. The first of these looked outwardly similar to the original model, but had a secondary warhead. These bombs were first reported being dropped in mid-October 1940 and started causing casualties immediately. The Explosive Incendiary Bomb (ExpIB) had a high explosive charge in the tail which was detonated when the burning thermite reached it, normally a minute or so after it landed. Although the charge was quite small, the effect was substantially similar to a hand grenade going off in a room. The fragments were deadly at close quarters and could cause severe injuries out to thirty feet or more. It was more than enough to kill or injure anyone close by who was trying to move or extinguish the bomb. The initial advice to those approaching these bombs was that: 'Protection for persons dealing with the bombs with either stirrup hand pump or long handled shovel is with a wet blanked, folded double hanging over the left arm (i.e. four thicknesses) and held so that when the bomb is approached the blanket hangs down from the arm and shields the face, body and legs.'[2]

It is doubtful if the blanket would have provided effective protection against high velocity fragments, but it would have offered some defence from the shower of molten magnesium produced when the explosive charge functioned. The wet blanket folded in such a manner would also have been very heavy and difficult to use in confined spaces. Quite often people simply ignore the added risk when fighting these bombs particularly if they were trying to save their own home.

Colonel G. Symonds, a well-known technical advisor to the government, made the comment that the proportion of explosive bombs to ordinary ones was so small that 'anyone tackling them had a sporting chance that they would not be exploders'.[3] The main thing, he said, was to get to and fight the bombs quickly. He advised that people should get a sandbag, and covering their face and chest, get as near the bomb as they could, lay the sandbag on it and then retreat as quickly as possible. Once the bomb had burnt out the fire could be fought with a stirrup pump and the water jet. It did not always work.

An incident involving an explosive incendiary of this sort occurred in Gloucester Terrace on 13 January 1941. The ARP Warden, Mr A. Winter, was at his post when he saw what he thought were ordinary incendiaries drop and catch fire. One was in the open in Craven Road and the other landed on the stone porch just outside 129 Gloucester Terrace. He grabbed a stirrup pump and bucket and rushed over to the scene. As he arrived he saw another man come out of the front door. Winter shouted that he had a pump, but the man replied that he was going to drop a sandbag on the burning bomb. Just as he did this it exploded with a sharp crack and parts of the burning magnesium body were scattered all over the porch. The man with the sandbag collapsed to the ground calling for help. Just then another figure appeared at the front door and started to drag the injured man back into the flat and was assisted by a uniformed serviceman who appeared on the scene. The warden, realising the injured man was being cared for, turned round just as another shower of incendiaries landed and he set about dealing with them despite the obvious risks of an explosion. Some of the citizen firefighters had the unpleasant thought that if they were fighting one of these nasty little fire bombs inside a confined space, such as an attic, and the secondary charge functioned, they might be too severely injured to move, and subsequently be burnt to death.

The next development was the Incendiary Bomb Explosive Nose (IBEN). This was a 1kg incendiary to which an explosive nose had been fitted giving a total weight of 2.2kg. On impact the incendiary functioned as normal but, at the same time, a burning fuse in the nose was initiated. This burnt for up to seven minutes and then detonated the charge in the nose. This presented a hazard even after the main incendiary had burnt out and was intended to prevent firefighters getting to grips with secondary fires before they took hold.

The final variant, the Incendiary Bomb Separating Explosive Nose (IBSEN), worked in a similar manner but on impact, as the bomb smashed through a roof, the fuze set off a small charge of gunpowder which blew the incendiary portion of the bomb and the explosive nose apart. The incendiary portion would burn as normal, but the explosive section had a small length of safety fuse which provided a delay before setting off a high explosive charge. Both sections of the bomb would invariably land up in the same room, or roof space, but in different places. Anyone fighting a fire caused by one of these bombs could, unknowingly, finish up standing, kneeling or lying very close to the separate explosive nose which, when it detonated, was likely to cause serious injury or death. A further effect of these heavier incendiaries was that they would penetrate further into buildings before coming to rest.

The problem for all firefighters, both professional and amateur, was that whilst the explosive incendiaries were burning they could not be distinguished from the standard IB. Consequently, every single bomb had to be treated with the utmost caution. Any bomb which was not tackled immediately had to be dealt with from behind some sort of cover. The wet blanket seems to have been rapidly discounted and items, such as, a heavy desk top or other suitable substantial hand-held shields were advised. Dustbin lids were popular as shields but provided limited protection against high-velocity fragment attack. Illustrations from the time normally show an upturned table top, from behind which the firefighter only exposed his forearm and hand.

The inclusion of a small percentage of these new explosive incendiaries had the desired effect and, after the initial casualties, word of the dangers spread rapidly. Although the additional risk did not totally stop people from tackling the bombs, the public were more reluctant to fight them than previously. A lot of course depended on where they landed. Homeowners in particular would abandon the safety of their shelters, and go into the rooms or attics to fight the fires to try and save their property and belongings from destruction. Once there they would be exposed to the potentially lethal effects if a secondary warhead was fitted and it detonated. Analysis of casualty figures from later in the Blitz showed that these fiendish incendiaries caused more casualties per tonne dropped than any other type of bomb. This tactic, of mixing a small number of high explosives bombs with incendiaries, to stop shop owners carrying out the latter, was copied by the IRA many years later.

Thousands of people attended courses and demonstrations on how to fight the fires caused by the incendiaries. Unfortunately, with the introduction of the new explosive types of bomb, there were avoidable accidents. At a firefighting demonstration run by an ARP warden, the un-burnt tail portion of a 1kg incendiary was used to augment a quantity of magnesium mixture. Unknown to the warden, the tail was part of a failed explosive incendiary bomb. Having lit the charge and given the magnesium a few moments to get going he prepared to show the assembled crowd how to fight the fire. At this point the explosive in the tail detonated and, of the thirty adults and twenty children present, thirteen were wounded. Sadly, one young boy of eight subsequently died of his injuries. In another similar accident in which an explosive incendiary was inadvertently used for training, another three persons were injured.[4]

Of course the main burden of firefighting, particularly when a blaze took hold, fell on the fire brigade. Throughout the Blitz the firefighters of both sexes, from the regulars and the auxiliaries, displayed outstanding bravery. As well as being subject to the traditional dangers associated with fighting fires they had to be out in the open during raids, which by now should be clear, was the most dangerous place to be.

Typical of the firefighter's bravery, when it came to ignoring risks, and an example of extraordinary luck, occurred in Great Portland Street in mid-September 1940, whilst a fire was being fought during a raid. A turntable ladder was being used as a water tower to project a jet onto nearby roofs. The ladder was fully extended to 100 feet and a fireman was about to secure himself to the top of it with a safety belt. Without warning a second bomb whistled by and detonated in the street below. There another fireman operating the ladder controls and a fire officer standing nearby were both cut down and severely injured, the latter dying later in hospital.

The fireman at the top of the ladder, who one would have thought had no chance, had the most remarkable escape. When the bomb detonated, the chassis of the turntable ladder was blown into the building and the rear axle and ladder base station, collectively weighing some four tons, was blown right over a nearby roof top with various sections of the ladder. However, the uppermost section, with the fireman on it, caught on a projection, turned through 180 degrees and finished hanging down over the front of the burning building. The unfortunate man was, at this point, thrown off and fell a small distance to the pavement to be covered in debris from the building. When the dust settled a search was made of the area and he was found very badly injured. After months of treatment he eventually recovered and at the end of the war was able to run a pub not far from King's Cross.

In another gruesome incident a shower of incendiaries dropped around a group of firemen attending a blaze. One man was struck by one of these nasty little bombs which passed straight through his back, killing him instantly.

The firemen weren't always safe in their stations either. There was an incident in Rathbone Street sub-station, just off Oxford Street, where a direct hit from a bomb killed seven firemen outright. Three others were injured, one of them being Auxiliary Fireman, Harry Errington. A fire broke out in the debris beneath two of the injured firemen and it looked as if they would be burnt to death. Despite his own injuries Errington was able to extract himself and then in a Herculean effort, managed rescue the other two men at great personal risk. He was badly burned in the process, but did survive the war.

With the onset of winter of 1940, any realistic prospect of invasion was deferred due to the weather. This saw a change in the Luftwaffe's bombing strategy and the failed 'knockout blow' was replaced by one of more widespread attacks on ports and commercial centres intended to inflict more substantial damage to the war effort. London suffered what might be called 'lighter bombing' throughout this phase of the Blitz although there were still several big raids on the capital.

One of those was on 29 December 1941. This raid targeted the square mile of the City and for about three hours it was showered with incendiaries and high explosives. The area was tightly-packed with warehouses, workshops, offices and churches and was known to the fire brigade as 'the danger zone'. There were many narrow streets and alleyways, some with passageways over the top linking the buildings. Unlike the wider streets elsewhere, they did not provide natural firebreaks. Many of the warehouses were stuffed full of inflammable materials and the buildings themselves were often made of wood. The tragedy of that night was that much of the subsequent damage was avoidable but, as often happens in major disasters, a series of independent factors combined to create an incident much worse than the sum of its parts. The result that night was a fire which came within a hair's breadth of becoming an all-consuming and unstoppable firestorm.

Had the occupiers of the buildings provided some basic provision for firewatchers, many of the incendiaries could have been dealt with before they had a chance to take hold and develop into serious fires. This was already being done elsewhere in London by ARP Wardens, Police Officers and many ordinary men and women who were trying to protect their neighbourhoods. Despite the threat from the explosive incendiaries many people were still confidently dealing with them and either physically removing them from buildings, smothering them where they lay or extinguishing the subsequent fires. Where this could not be done, or they were beaten by the ferocity of the flames, they would remain at the scene, call for fire brigade and ensure they had access to the fires.

The City was, and still is, mainly a commercial area with very few residents. On 29 December 1940, because of the Christmas break, it was largely deserted, with only a few firewatchers on duty. Worse still, all the premises were, understandably, secured for the holiday period, some with thick chains and heavy padlocks. These security measures would later prevent the firefighters getting immediate access to buildings and hence the source of the fires. The Luftwaffe began dropping their loads of incendiaries just after 18.00 hours and within a short time fires were burning in roofs in Cheapside, Queen Victoria Street and near to the Guildhall in Gresham Street. The sprinkling of high explosive bombs dropped with them compounded the problems on the ground. The Luftwaffe was by now using more of the larger, higher capacity, bombs and these not only caused casualties amongst the firefighters, they disrupted many of the smaller water mains and devastated the twelve large ones that crisscrossed the City. An emergency supply of water being drawn from the Thames and fed north towards the area was also hit by bombs and knocked out.

The firemen deployed to the scene watched in horror as, one by one, their pumps lost pressure and the flow of water steadily decayed to nothing more than a trickle. Crews fighting the blazes were left powerless as their hoses dried up and they gradually lost control of the fires. These rapidly linked up generating a fearsome heat and the hapless firemen were forced to retreat.

Serious fires were reported in Southwark and the Minories with others beginning to take hold elsewhere. Amazingly, St Paul's almost in the centre of several growing fires was safe. It was one of the few buildings which had an effective fire watching scheme and although not all of the men were on duty when the raid started, those that lived close by rushed in to help.

The first hits on the Cathedral were sometime after 20.00 hours when a shower of incendiary bombs bracketed the building and dozens others landed in the surrounding area. Firewatchers on the roof of the *Daily Telegraph* building in Fleet Street, who could see the west end of the Cathedral, reported a veritable cascade of the bombs most of which hit and ricocheted off the dome. Others fell into the long stretches of the Nave and Choir roofs and some into what are known as the pocket roofs which were lower down over the aisles. Other bombs fell in the Cathedral Gardens producing an eyrie, fairy light, effect. In all over twenty-eight incendiaries had hit St Paul's and its precincts.

The most treacherous of these incendiaries lodged in some of the roof timbers and started fires. The first bomb, which had landed in the Library aisle, was attacked by the firewatchers and extinguished using water from the mains, but thereafter, as a result of high explosive bombs detonating nearby, the water pressure fell. From then on, all the pre-laid fire hoses proved useless. To fight the fires, they had to rely on stirrup pumps and sandbags. Fortunately, with great foresight, the Cathedral had been prepared for such an assault and tanks, baths and pails of water, along with other firefighting equipment, had been placed at strategic points throughout the building. These had been so arranged that anyone going up to fight fires would have immediate access to these vital resources. And so the men set about the fires, and many individual battles were fought and won which prevented them running out of control.

There was one bomb which nearly brought about a catastrophe. A telephone call from the Cannon Street fire station reported that the dome itself was on fire. A squad of men was immediately dispatched to deal with this. They found that one incendiary had not bounced off the dome but had partially penetrated the outer shell and functioned. Though the dome itself was not on fire, the lead of the shell was beginning to melt and it seemed that it would not be long before the roof timbers would catch light. It was realised that, if the fire took hold, the Dome itself it would act like a chimney, and air would be sucked up through the hole which would rapidly create a furnace. The volunteers who fought the fires up in the dome, not only had to have a head for heights, but also a leaning towards acrobatics. However, as they went up and set about the fire it seemed that God lent a hand as the bomb burned a hole sufficiently large for it to dislodge itself and it dropped outwards onto the Stone Gallery where it was much more easily extinguished.

About this time, with flames licking all around the Cathedral, a message that St Paul's must be saved at all costs, was received via the Guildhall from the Prime Minister. Although much appreciated it was not needed as the men were already working to the limit of their endurance to save the building.

As the fires around the Cathedral grew in intensity another factor which contributed to the maelstrom began to take effect. There was a strong wind which fed the fires their essential oxygen and, as they grew in intensity, they began to generate their own fearsome supply drawing air into the fire from all directions. These winds lifted huge burning fragments up in to the sky and whisked them off to new locations where some started fires in other areas. For the senior firemen on the ground the situation was getting further and further out of control. Reinforcements had been called in from a wide area and told to bring what water they could, but it was rapidly exhausted and was totally inadequate to tackle such a massive conflagration.

The final factor which was to hamper the firefighters was that at the height of the raid the Thames was at a very low ebb and to get at the water the men had to wade out, waist deep, into freezing mud to try and get their connecting hoses to the waiting fireboats which were far out in the tideway. Trailer pumps were manhandled down stone steps to the edge of the mud to try and get access to water with which to fight the fires. By now, some 1,700 fire appliances were deployed to try and save the City.

Whilst the front line firefighters were still exclusively men it must not be forgotten that many auxiliary firewomen were performing vital support tasks by driving logistic vehicles and delivering crucial fuel and stores. It must not be forgotten also that all the time the Luftwaffe was still cascading fresh bombs amongst them.

The Guildhall, whose own fire defences had initially proved effective, eventually succumbed to the constant flow of embers which landed on the roof from the fire in the neighbouring Church of St Lawrence Jewry. Sadly, it was destroyed. It also looked for a while that St Paul's might succumb to the fires which, by now, were blazing all around it. Thanks to Herculean efforts of the firemen down by the Thames, the first good news came through, that the water supplies were being restored. These provided, at best, an intermittent flow, but it was enough to give the thousands of waiting firemen the means they needed to take on the conflagration.

The Wren churches suffered. St Bride's and St Jame's, with their tinder-dry roof beams, quickly succumbed to the effects of the small incendiaries and once alight were almost impossible to put out. The roofs timbers burnt through and then crashed to the ground inside the walls. One Cockney fireman was apparently heard to say, 'Bleeding lot o' wood that Wren bloke used didn't 'e?' Many crews had narrow escapes from collapsing buildings or from the risk of being encircled by fire, some having to abandon their equipment and escape through burning streets to safety. Not all succeeded and one man recalled later passing a trailer pump crew working hard on a fire: 'I thought when I passed them that they were all too near. Just at that moment a wall which looked as if it was bulging dangerously crashed down on them. As we looked around all we could see was a heap of debris with a hose leading towards it.'[5]

As the night progressed the tidal waters of the Thames flowed back into the centre of the capital and, thanks to miles and miles of hoses, the flow of water to the pumps increased sufficiently to enable serious firefighting action to be taken. By 03.00 hours, with the river in full flood, the battle began to sway the firemen's way. The flames were contained and the heart of the fire began to burn itself out. Of the 1,500 fires logged in the London Region that night only twenty-eight were outside the square mile of the city. During the battle fourteen firefighters were killed, and over 250 other men and women injured. In recognition of the bravery displayed by the fire brigade that night seventeen awards were given for gallantry including four to the auxiliary firewomen. The firefighters that were killed or injured died became another statistic in the fire brigade's roll of honour. In total 404 firemen were killed and over 3,000 injured during the war in London.

The post-raid investigation into the causes of the fire highlighted the need for fire-watchers in all buildings who could immediately tackle the small fires started when the incendiaries landed. It was well known that a team of three men, or women, with six buckets of water and a stirrup pump could often extinguish a fire in a few minutes before it took hold properly. The government acted to ensure that these measures were put in place and strictly enforced. Fire watching schemes and firefighting parties were made compulsory. Furthermore, after the Blitz, on 18 August 1941 the National Fire Service was formed to improve co-ordination.

NOTES:
1. Quoted in Elias Canetti, *Die Gespaltene Zukunft*, Munich 1972.
2. Harrow Urban District Council, ARP/T Circular No.67 dated 18 October 1940.
3. Article in the *Police Review* February 1941.
4. TNA, LAB 59/34: 66 Annual Report of His Majesties Inspectors of Explosives.
5. *Front Line 1940 – 41 The Official Story of the Civil Defence of Britain*, Ministry of Information, His Majesty's Stationary Office, 1942.

Chapter 13

Bombs, Builders and Business as Usual

'The story of the use of explosives in war is a long and fascinating one that reflects singularly little credit on the human race.'
Major A.B. Hartley MBE, RE.

In the lead up to the Blitz much work was done to protect vital parts of the capital's infrastructure from bomb damage. Initially key installations and historic buildings were protected by massive sandbag walls. For instance, 60,000 sandbags were piled around parts of Westminster Abbey. Later purpose-built blast walls were designed and constructed to shield the occupants in the lower levels of buildings which were considered essential to the war effort. It will be seen in a later chapter that, at the Aldwych, they could prove remarkably effective at saving lives.

Once the bombing started, there was a tremendous political and economic imperative to keep London working by ensuring the infrastructure remained intact or, if that failed, rapidly repairing damage. The railway network was a key part of this and it was crucial that it was kept open so that essential freight could be moved and commuters got to and from work. Most of the London terminal stations suffered direct hits, and there was considerable damage at Paddington, St Pancras, Waterloo and King's Cross. Equally there were hundreds of hits or near misses on the permanent way. The easiest damage to repair was the straightforward crater made by a near miss from a high explosive bomb. It was a simple matter of clearing the rubble and then checking the level and the alignment of the tracks. Where bombs fell on the track then the rails would need to be replaced and any damage to signalling equipment repaired.

More complicated to repair or replace were bridges, viaducts and tunnels. To start with the engineers called to plan the repair of such structures had no previous experience to guide them and they displayed the most astonishing ingenuity and improvisation. Moreover, it was often done in the shortest possible times. For example, on 8 September 1940, a heavy bomb exploded on a viaduct 100-feet wide between Waterloo and Vauxhall which supported the eight running lines that carried heavy suburban traffic and mainline trains. The bomb struck the ground between the tracks at one side of the bridge, penetrated the brick arch immediately below then blew up with great force and violence. At the point of detonation several of the arches were completely destroyed and the bridge piers shattered. Buildings both sides of the arches were also badly damaged by the blast. Three railway lines were left hanging in the air but were, surprisingly, otherwise undamaged. All traffic in and out of Waterloo had to be stopped and the damage assessed. Any interruption to the working of Waterloo was of the utmost seriousness and a high priority was placed on the repairs.

Engineers decided that, by shoring up the arches furthest away from the explosion, traffic could be resumed on two of the eight tracks. This was achieved within ten hours, but the limited repair still severely restricted the work of the mainline station. In the meantime, it was determined that the quickest way to restore full services would be to build retaining walls either side of the most badly damaged areas, demolish any unstable masonry and then simply fill the area in between with ballast. This was possible because at the point of detonation the arches used to support the railway did not provide any form of access. The filling material was brought to the spot by hopper wagons containing quarry refuse. This consisted of small stone chippings, which were quickly and solidly packed into the area between the walls. Thus within eight days of the incident another two tracks were opened. The permanent way was finally restored to full working order on 1 October.

The biggest cause of delay to the railways though was not the damage from bombs that functioned, as this could be repaired, but the threat of explosions from unexploded bombs. When these were on, or near the tracks, or close to stations, it led to large parts of the network being closed and cordoned off.

As experience of dealing with unexploded bombs, and in particular a better understanding of the different fuzes and how they worked was gained, it allowed the threats they posed to be re-evaluated. There was considerable political pressure to do this and, understandably, levels of risk were accepted that would not be tolerated today.

One remarkably robust paper on the subject carried out an interesting but approximate analysis of the risks. It established that of 1,009 unexploded bombs examined by bomb disposal teams, only ninety-three had long-delay fuzes. The others had failed impact fuzes which were unlikely to detonate if they were not moved or disturbed. From these figures it was immediately apparent that the chances of an unexploded bomb subsequently detonating were about one in ten. Of the 1,009 bombs recovered 422 had struck the ground and penetrated beyond what was termed the danger distance. It was assumed that at these depths, if the bomb functioned, most of the blast and all of the fragments would be arrested by the earth on top of the bomb. The distances they had to penetrate were; ten feet for 50kg bombs, fifteen feet for 250kg bombs and twenty feet for 500kg bombs. This further reduced the risk from explosions to 1 in twenty-five. Furthermore, if four trains an hour each 200 feet long passed over the track at a speed of 5 mph then the chance of an explosion dangerous to rail traffic was 1 in 250.

From observations made by bomb disposal personnel it was further established that of 154, 250kg bombs dropped with delay-action fuzes, 52.8% detonated within eight hours, 65% within twelve hours and 75% within fifteen hours. From this it was concluded that the danger to rail traffic from these bombs was 1 in 500 after eight hours and 1 in 1,000 after fifteen hours. By examining the different sizes of failed bombs that landed within twenty feet of a railway and the dangers they presented if they exploded, it was considered that the risk to a train from an unexploded bomb twenty feet away was 1 in 7. Quite how this was established is not clear.

The upshot was that the risk of ignoring all unexploded bombs was approximately 1 in 250. The risk of ignoring all unexploded bombs after fifteen hours was 1 in 1,000 and the risk of ignoring all unexploded bombs over twenty feet from the track after fifteen hours was 1 in 7,000. It was estimated that there were only between 200 and 300 unexploded bombs close to the railways. If all these bombs were ignored it was concluded that the chances of a train being involved in an explosion were minimal and even then the risk of staff being injured was even lower, although presumably this was only true for freight trains where there were only the driver and fireman on the engine, and the guard at the end of the train. For some reason passenger trains seem to have been discounted.

The report concluded that the greatest dislocation to the railways was caused by the closures due to delayed-action bombs. It also noted that any delays in moving vital stores away from the ports, particularly

London docks, might result in them being destroyed by bombing. There could be nothing worse than ships surviving the dangerous sea passage to this country and then having their essential cargos destroyed before they could be unloaded and moved from the docks because of a paralysed railway system. Therefore, it was decided that steps should be taken to persuade the railways, all private companies back then, to ignore the risks from all unexploded bombs.

These sort of pragmatic decisions were extended to other areas. For example, the maintenance of safety precautions for unexploded bombs for longer than necessary, caused avoidable hardship to persons evacuated from their houses as well as the overcrowding of rest and feeding centres. Government officials urged that the public be allowed (and if necessary persuaded) to return to their homes as soon as possible after safety periods had elapsed.

In the case of buried unexploded bombs of 50kg or 1,000kg or over, (but not 250 and 500 kilogram bombs) experience had shown that the risk of detonation owing to delayed action was very small. In these cases, the restrictions on cordon and evacuation could be relaxed as soon as the bombs had been certified as such by a qualified Royal Engineer Bomb Reconnaissance Officer from a bomb disposal unit. The measure of relaxation clearly varied depending on the specific details of an incident but, in general, it was determined that it should be possible to allow the reoccupation of houses except those within thirty feet of a 50kg bomb and sixty feet of a 1,000kg bomb. Similarly, traffic was able to pass unless the bomb actually fell in the road.

Full restrictions, however, had to be maintained for 250 and 500 kilogram bombs because they were likely to be fitted with long-delay fuzes and secondary anti-handling systems. This ruling also applied where it was impossible to diagnose the size of the bomb until it was uncovered.

Where bombs fell in open spaces or parks where their disposal was a low priority, it was not always necessary to maintain the full restrictions until the bomb was finally removed. In these cases, it could be weeks before bomb disposal teams became available to deal with them. The Regional Headquarters reviewed such cases after ninety-six hours and, in consultation with Bomb Reconnaissance Officers, minimal safety distances were applied. In all such cases the public were warned by suitable notices not to approach too close to the area. These sorts of no-nonsense decisions kept the capital working.

Other schemes sought to protect critical points from serious damage which would cripple London's ability to contribute to the war effort. London Transport gave the most serious consideration to the security of the Underground system against flooding. The main concern was the breaching of the tunnels near or underneath the Thames which would result in the immediate and catastrophic flooding of the whole of the central Underground network.

Studies indicated that this could be prevented, with limited consequences to the operation of the system, by sealing off some areas with concrete bulkheads and, in others, providing six-ton steel sliding doors with rubber seals which could be closed during air raids. In practice these massive doors could be closed in one minute using electrical power and in four minutes if the doors had to be shut by hand. Control of the doors included arrangements to ensure that trains under the Thames would be allowed to exit the danger sections of the tunnels before they were sealed.[1]

Once again, it was the threat from delayed-action bombs which presented the principal problem for the Underground network where it passed near or under the Thames. During air raids the floodgates were closed to prevent the entire system flooding in the event of a bomb exploding and breaching a tunnel. The problem with delayed-action bombs falling in the river was that they could explode after the all-clear, when the gates had been re-opened. To prevent this special detection apparatus was designed and fitted where the tunnels passed under the river at Charing Cross, London Bridge and Wapping.

Hydrophones were placed in the river bed and connected by cable to an amplifier at the shore which in turn used existing telephone lines to send all the signals received to recording apparatus in Kensington. The hydrophones recorded all the sounds conveyed through the water and thus there was a permanent record of all the activity below the surface. It had been established that a bomb plunging into the river, which did not explode, produced a distinctive spike at the hydrophones which was clearly visible on the trace at the recording station. It was also discovered that this could be replicated by firing rifle bullets into the river from boats or bridges and that the recorders would spike at the instant the bullet hit the water. Other recorders were then used and the time the signal took to travel through the water and reach other hydrophones, was measured. These had special filters which would discriminate between the constant noises produced by river traffic and the sudden impact of a bomb or rifle bullet. By a fairly simple process of triangulation it was possible to locate the position where the bullet or bomb had entered the water. Unfortunately, no record of the systems operational use seems to exist. Neither are there any directives on how an unexploded bomb would have been rendered safe, had it been detected entering the water within the danger area near the

Underground tunnels. Presumably the task would have fallen to Royal Navy divers.

Although not as important as the railways, the roads too had to be kept open, particularly those arterial routes which led into the heart of the capital. When cratered and blocked it was, of course, much easier to set up temporary diversions for roads, but these often caused long delays, and repairs still had to be carried out promptly. A good example of such a high-priority clearance task occurred at the beginning of 1941. The New Year brought no respite for the people of London and there was a minor raid over the capital on the night of 1-2 January and this sporadic activity continued until the first major attack of 1941 ten days later. During this, in the late evening of 11 January, a large bomb burst through the road in front of the Bank of England and detonated in the circular underground booking hall for Bank Station. The explosion, in a confined space, was devastating and killed everyone sheltering there. The blast was then channeled down the escalators into the underground itself blowing several people off the platform and on to the tracks. This could not have happened at a worse moment as a train was entering the station. The driver's hands were blown from the controls and, despite automatic braking, the train continued for some distance and ran over some of the wounded people who were lying on the track. Rescuers that arrived could not get down to the train from Bank Station and they had to make their way to the scene underground from Liverpool Street. They recovered the injured, taking them back out along the track the way they had come. Having been down to the scene of the suicide bombing at Warren Street in July 2005, I am acutely aware that the simple sentence I have just written does not do due justice to the difficult and traumatic time that the rescuers must have faced that night at Bank Station.

With the wounded rescued and the dead recovered, the next critical task was the repair of the damage to the area which, then, was at the hub of one of the busiest traffic centres in the City. The morning after the incident at 10.30 hours the Officer Commanding 691 General Construction Company, Royal Engineers was given the job. The flexibility of military resources was then well demonstrated. One and a half hours later forty sappers and 260 pioneers were at the scene. With the aid of five cranes, twenty-five lorries, one bulldozer, twenty-five compressors and six oxyacetylene sets, they set about breaking up the wreckage and clearing away the rubble.

During the following thirteen days, 2,713 tons of concrete and 356 tons of steel were removed from the site an average of 236 tons per day.

It was immediately apparent that a permanent repair would be a long and difficult task and a decision was made to erect a temporary bridge for the most important east-west traffic. Later the area around the edge of the crater was filled in and a roundabout made for the use of other traffic. The bridge was opened on 3 February 1941 by the Mayor of London who walked across it followed by the men of the Construction Company. The station was back in action by 17 March and the whole area fully restored and the temporary bridge removed by the beginning of May. This process of reconstruction was repeated thousands of times all over London as the authorities and the people repaired or patched up damaged infrastructure and property.

On Thursday, 13 February 1941, in the early evening, the first 2,500kg bomb nicknamed 'Max', which contained 1,700kg of explosive, was released by a single aircraft over the outskirts of London. There was a devastating explosion as it detonated in the gardens between two rows of houses running down Ravenstone Road and Borthwick Road in Hendon. In the blink of an eye, it totally destroyed eighty-four houses, severely damaged another seventy-eight and made another eighty-four temporarily uninhabitable. It killed seventy-five people, injured 445 and left 600 homeless. Rescue work continued until the Sunday, when all hope of finding further survivors was abandoned, and a church service was held on the site to commemorate the dead. Repair and reconstruction work then began in earnest. The member of the Federation of British Industry who had said earlier 'Bombs have made builders of all of us' could not have spoken truer words.

The battle between the bomb disposal teams and the German fuze designers continued unabated. The Germans developed and introduced new fuzes including anti-handling types and as soon as one was recovered intact, the scientists, working for the Unexploded Bomb Committee, set about trying to find new methods of rendering them safe.

The story so far was that the early impact fuzes were immunised by using the simple two-prong Crabtree Discharger set. To prevent this, the Luftwaffe introduced new fuzes which would detonate if any attempt was made to discharge them by this means. The solution was ironically a solution. A fluid known as BD (Bomb Disposal) liquid was introduced into the fuze using a vacuum technique which would drain the capacitors and make it safe.

When the long-delay time fuzes were introduced, a remote fuze extractor was designed, but the Germans countered this by fitting the anti-withdrawal Zus 40 underneath it. The loud ticking of the early time fuzes was clearly audible through an electronic stethoscope, and was used to monitor the state of a bomb. The Germans must have learned about this because they subsequently developed an almost silent mechanism. The steam sterilizer and trepanners had been introduced to cut holes in bomb walls and steam out the filling and a magnetic clock stopper had been designed to stop the fuze ticking during this operation. To prevent this, the Germans had fitted a secondary Number 50 anti-handling fuze which would detonate the bomb if it was moved. It was also likely to detonate if the clock stopper was fitted and switched on before the capacitors were drained. Experiments to jam the clockwork mechanism of the fuzes by filling them with thick or fast setting liquids were countered by the Germans sealing the fuze to prevent the liquid being injected. And so it went on and would continue right up until the end of the war.

Before any action could be taken to render safe a bomb, the key requirement was to find it and then identify the fuze or fuzes. It should not be imagined that this was always an easy task. Unexploded bombs were found in the most unusual, inaccessible or unlikely places. There was, for example, the grisly matter of dealing with unexploded bombs in graveyards. It was recommended that where the removal of such a bomb would involve disinterring the dead then the bomb should be abandoned. However, if the cemetery was near an important road or railway vital to the war effort then the bomb would have to be dealt with as soon as possible. In such cases the local authorities had to obtain a licence under the Burial Act from the Home Office before such work could begin, although in urgent cases the licence could the applied for retrospectively.

Bombs which failed to explode would also often penetrate the earth and finish up in the sewers beneath the city streets. Lieutenant G.R. Owens, Royal Engineers, was tasked to such a scene and had no choice but to clamber down into the sewer to inspect the bomb. He said:

> The stench was pretty terrific and I recall the NCO in charge saying that the air was so foul that you had to 'fart' to get some fresh air! The bomb was in an awkward position. I had to lay prone to get at the fuze. After a few minutes I had to go up top for some fresh air.[2]

Another danger was from camouflets which many of the military and civil defenders were not aware of, particularly in early days of the bombing. These were formed when a bomb penetrated soft earth and exploded underground, but the force of the explosion was insufficient to produce a crater. Instead the force of the explosion formed a cavity underground with a thin crust of earth at its edges caused by the compression of the soil. The result was a subterranean void which was filled with the gases from the products of detonation, one of the main ones being the deadly gas, carbon monoxide. The camouflets could last for several weeks or even months if not disturbed. In some cases, the crust would withstand the weight of a man, but in others would collapse immediately. In one reported incident about three weeks after a stick of bombs had caused much damage, a little girl, aged eight, fell through the crust into a camouflet. A brave boy aged twelve was lowered into the cavity to try and rescue her but he too was overcome by the carbon monoxide. Finally, two ARP wardens arrived, descended into the hole and were also overcome by fumes. All four died.

Camouflets or suspected camouflets were roped off and local residents warned of the dangers. It was impressed on all that the issued gas masks provided absolutely no protection against carbon monoxide poisoning and that the only way to work in a camouflet was with breathing apparatus. When they were found, bomb disposal teams used explosives to collapse them, but were not responsible for the subsequent filling of the resulting crater.

Bombs that failed to explode, especially large ones, could also do significant damage if they hit and passed through a building. In some cases, the damage was such that it could be confused with the effects of a small bomb going off. It was the Bomb Reconnaissance Officer's job to go to and assess all reports of unexploded ordnance. If an incident proved to be a false alarm, then they had the authority to discredit it and so prevent unnecessary disruption to civilian life. Up until the end of the Blitz all the Bomb Reconnaissance Officers were Royal Engineer officers, but later, as already noted, police officers and ARP wardens attended courses to reduce the burden on the military officers and free them for other tasks. The enthusiasm of these new Bomb Reconnaissance Officers was generally speaking tremendous. These men very quickly built close affiliations with their local bomb disposal units and gained much mutual respect and trust. In return they often considered themselves to be an integral part of the disposal unit.

The diameter of the hole where a bomb entered the ground usually gave a good indication of the size of the bomb. For example, anything between eight to twelve inches normally indicated a 50kg bomb. At the other end of the scale, holes over twenty-six inches would indicate a 1,000kg bomb or larger. Large bombs which failed to explode could, in some soils, produce large splash craters where the physical impact of the bomb was enough to produce craters ten-feet wide and four-feet deep. It was important that Bomb Reconnaissance Officers were aware of this because it was possible to conclude that a 1,000kg bomb splash crater was, in fact, the detonation of a 50kg bomb. A mistake like this could have potentially fatal consequences.

Every now and then, at scenes of explosions, innocent items, such as, old boilers and gas cylinders were prone to cause alarm and despondency amongst rescuers. When partially uncovered in the rubble of a demolished house or factory their cylindrical shape could take on the sinister appearance of an unexploded bomb. Sometimes areas would be cordoned and evacuated before Bomb Reconnaissance Offices came along and identified the items for what they really were.

There were also untrained people who became 'self-proclaimed' experts and, as always, in these situations, familiarity bred contempt and accidents happened. This danger was shown on 9 December 1940 when an unidentified ARP warden brought a piece of battered tubing into the local ARP Headquarters. It did not appear to be dangerous and it was left on a desk for further examination. Most likely it was a Number 17 time fuze still in its central tubing which, for some reason, had been thrown out of a bomb. This sometimes happened when bombs struck buildings at unusual angles, failed to detonate, and broke open. The Chief ARP warden, W. Coyne and two other staff were sitting in the Headquarters near the desk, when there was blinding flash and a terrific explosion which caused a fire. This was promptly dealt with and, luckily, no serious injuries occurred, but the danger of such ill-informed procedures was illustrated. All were reminded of the need to leave such items outside, sandbag them, put out danger notices and wait for properly qualified bomb disposal officers to deal with them.

Like the First World War there was also the danger from unexploded anti-aircraft shells. Even though most had self-destruct systems fitted, many failed to detonate and fell back to earth where they had to be dealt with. Although it was realized that they were potentially dangerous it was decided that the local authorities would be justified in removing them if it was clear that bomb disposal units were unable to do so immediately because of higher priority work. London Regional Circular No 287 stated that, in general, anti-aircraft shells should not be touched, but where they were interfering with public life, production or near a public highway or gardens they could be removed. It stated: 'Could the following members of the Civil Defence Services be instructed to carry out this work and in the event of them refusing to do so could disciplinary action be taken against them.'[3]

It then went on to specify that Rescue Parties, Wardens, Stretcher Parties and other similar services could move unexploded shells. Not surprisingly, many of the men and women in these organisations rejected such instructions, but there always seemed to be someone on hand who would move the offending items.

It must be understood that the majority of the thousands of bombs dropped, whether they detonated or not, caused some degree of disruption, chaos and confusion. Everywhere people's lives were lost or dislocated and major or minor dramas played out. Immense efforts were made, at every level, to cope with the death and, destruction that the bombs were causing, but it did not always run smoothly and despite people's best efforts, mistakes were made often causing friction amongst the various emergency services. For example, in early March, a bomb fell in the precincts of Liverpool Street Station and a Bomb Reconnaissance Officer was tasked to do an initial reconnaissance of the site. He gave what he thought were clear instructions on the size of the area that needed to be cordoned and evacuated and then left the scene to deal with another higher priority incident. For some reason, which will never be known, his instructions were either not clear, not followed, not correctly enforced, or never passed on to the men that worked in the area. The upshot was that, when a delayed action bomb detonated some time later, three workmen were killed. All were inside the area that was supposed to have been cleared. Correspondence on the matter flew between several agencies with each blaming the other for the loss of life. The reality was that, with this level of bombing, decisions were being made by tired men under considerable pressure with conflicting priorities. Sadly, despite everyone's best efforts, there were bound to be mistakes, some with tragic results.

During this intense and incredibly busy period, much thought was given to how the casualties in bomb disposal units could be reduced. One concern was the process by which the Regional Commissioners graded bombs with the A1 classification. This meant that immediate disposal action was required despite the risk to the lives of bomb disposal teams and this sometimes led to unnecessary deaths. For example, during a raid on the night of 8-9 March 1941, a bomb fell in King Edward Street in the City. It was classified as Category A1 because it threatened to destroy a GPO exchange and tube message system. A bomb disposal team was dispatched without delay to deal with the bomb which the entry hole indicated was one of the very dangerous 250kg types. Whilst work was underway, at the most dangerous time before the first ninety-six hours had elapsed, the bomb detonated killing sappers, Taylor and Garner and badly injuring an officer and senior NCO. The real tragedy was that when the bomb detonated it did not do any damage at all to the GPO facilities. Afterwards it was clearly established that the initial classification of the bomb as A1 was unnecessary and had resulted in the death and injury of very brave and skilled men which was totally avoidable.

During the same raid, there was another catastrophe at the Café de Paris located beneath the Rialto Cinema in Coventry Street, near Leicester Square. Being underground the Café was considered to be a comparatively safe location and people would go on drinking and dancing despite the German bombers being overhead.

At 21.50 hours two 50kg bombs penetrated the roof of the Café, one of which detonated in the crowded ballroom, the other failed to explode. The explosion killed the band leader, 'Snake Hips Johnson', another member of his band plus many of the customers on and around the dance floor. It was a particularly black night and the incident highlighted the difficulties faced by all of those responding to explosions where there were high numbers of killed and injured. With such a level of casualties there should have been a major response by the Civil Defence services, but as often happens in the fog of war there were many failings that night. After the incident there was an enquiry with all sides blaming each other for what went wrong.

The first report to highlight the failures was by the commander of 71 R.S.D. (Rescue Service Detachment) who reported that 'at 21.45 hours [sic]' they had arrived at the Café to deal with the aftermath of an explosion. This time conflicted with the time the bomb was reported to have hit the building, but suffice to say the rescue men were on scene very shortly after the bomb exploded. The commander reported that:

> The place was in a hopeless muddle. Dead and dying were lying all around. With no stretchers or even first-aid dressings and the lack of experienced workers led to allowing any Tom, Dick or Harry to enter the building, many of whom were worse for drink, and a few who had entered the place for looting.
>
> There was no organised system of dealing with the job and the entire absence of stretchers or first-aid equipment resulted in absolute chaos.
>
> On entering the building the thing that struck me was a few police, who tried to be officious, but allowed anyone to enter without challenge except the Rescue Service. On obtaining access I saw dead bodies lying in the entrance to the main hall. These bodies were being trod on by drunks. The limited number of stretchers, camp beds, doors and ladders, etc, which the rescue service could obtain had to be used for live casualties, most of whom were placed roughly on the improvised stretchers without even having their injuries examined

and in a number of cases they were taken from the lighted hall with arterial bleeding, and were left to bleed to death on the dark pavement.[4]

The report, dated the day after the incident, also stated that there was no proper medical attention for at least forty minutes and a complete lack of first aid men with stretchers. One woman who had had most of her clothes blown off and was badly injured was carried out into the street and left lying on the pavement. A passing lorry driver who had stopped to help took off his coat to cover her as no blankets were available. The lobby of the Rialto Cinema was used as a shelter for some of the casualties, but the first of these was placed immediately inside the door. As more injured were being carried into the lobby by the rescue squads they finished up standing on casualties lying unattended in the darkness. The rescue men who had very limited first aid training were forced to use tablecloths and the field dressings from dead servicemen to patch up the wounded as best they could. The walking wounded were taken across the road to another building, but had to wait half an hour before they were treated.

Finally, after all of the wounded had been removed the stretcher parties arrived. They avoided handling the most mutilated bodies and removed the 'clean dead', the rest of the work being left for the rescue men and volunteers. During this time apparently some people including two ARP medical officers stood around doing nothing. All in all, it was a damming indictment on the handling of the incident from the perspective of Rescue Service Detachment.

The initial post incident report by the Ambulance Service reinforces how chaotic the situation was. At the very start of the incident, due to a problem with communications, the first, first aid parties to arrive who could have saved lives were sent away. A full response was not on scene until approximately forty-five minutes after the explosion. On arrival at the scene the senior ambulance man noted that:

> The approach and entrance to this incident were hopelessly blocked by civilians, and no attempt was being made by the police to relieve this. Most of this service (the Police) were inside the Café, purely sightseeing; in fact, a number of soldiers fortunately took it upon themselves to form two cordons across the pavement, making a passage for the ambulance to work from.
>
> One of the worst sights of the evening was two police officers kicking and dragging an officer (a major I think) up the stairs in the full view of the general public saying he was drunk. They were, in

my opinion, not competent to discriminate between drunkenness and shock – and, anyway it was a disgraceful sight.[5]

The report went on to slate the Incident Officer who was inside the building, was not efficiently controlling events outside and could not be recognized because he was not wearing the necessary identification.

The two reports, written almost immediately after the event, give a clear insight into the distressing work that all responders to such incidents were required to undertake. They also highlight the chaos and confusion that surround such a rescue and give an indication of the stress that all parties were under. It is interesting to note that no one, at least in the reports that have survived, had the slightest concern about the unexploded bomb on the premises.

In this disturbing case clearly a formal enquiry was required to establish why the response had been so poor, and how the situation could be improved in future incidents. At the outset it was recognized that nothing is easier, after the event, to deal with an incident differently. Equally, desk-bound and with no real pressure, it is easy to answer the 'what if' questions, or retreat to the land of 'what might have been'. The inquiry was tasked to look at four key areas, they were:

Why no ambulances arrived until approximately forty minutes after the incident was first reported?

The failure of police officers to cordon and control the incident, and the apparent lack of a competent Incident Officer.

A general view that the wardens had collectively performed poorly that night.

A dispute about the time that the bomb had actually landed.

The easiest question to deal with was the last. Some women had stated that they were being treated for injuries received by the bomb at around 21.20 hours. It was soon established that another thirteen bombs had landed in the Westminster area earlier in the evening and that their injuries were as a result of these. The first information about the bomb in Café de Paris was sent to the local Report Centre by West End Central Police Station at 21.50 hours. This stated that 100 people were trapped and asked for a mobile casualty unit to attend. The Report Centre immediately requested the attendance of rescue parties, as at this time the priority appeared to be rescue rather than first aid, but an ambulance and two stretcher parties and a mobile casualty unit were ordered to the scene. At 22.19 hours the police asked for more ambulances and first aid parties, but for some reason this request was ignored. A warden near the scene at this point stated that just one ambulance was needed. At 22.22 hours there was yet another request for more ambulances from the police; they reported at that time that there were '120 dead and no ambulances'. After this further calls for ambulances from different people were received and more units were dispatched to the area.

The Incident Officer, Mr Parker-Morris, arrived on the scene at about 22.15 hours and after a quick inspection of the Café de Paris immediately requested more ambulances. He established that ambulances had initially reported to the warden's post near the scene at 22.00 hours and had treated a few lightly wounded people who had walked there. Then, due to poor communications and thinking no others needed treatment, they left the area. The result at the Café de Paris was that survivors of the explosion and friends of the injured along with some people passers-by, set about recovering casualties and getting them dispatched to hospital in taxis or other cars in a disorganized manner. When the ambulances finally returned, they set up a shuttle service and conveyed forty-seven injured persons to hospital. Once established this seemed to work quite well.

Mr Parker-Morris made no criticism of the police for not establishing a cordon. This he considered was not necessary initially and, when it was needed to get casualties away, the police and a number of soldiers were organised to set up the necessary cordons.

After the removal of the live casualties, arrangements were made for the removal of the dead. He acknowledged that in the early stages of the operation a few bodies had been placed where they would be trodden on, but remarked that this was only done so that the quickest access to the wounded could be achieved. Once the wounded were rescued, most of the corpses were shrouded and moved to the nearby Honey Dew restaurant where they were to be left overnight.

The report then states that: 'On opening the Honey Dew Restaurant Mr Parker-Morris sent the O/C Mobile Unit to the temporary mortuaries and he discovered two of the supposed corpses, with signs of life, and he sent them to hospital.' Finally, noting that drinks were still being served at the bars, Mr Parker-Morris sent the stretcher and rescue parties back to their units.

The questions raised over the police actions at the scene were looked into in detail. One area of concern was over who should control such an incident. It was established that, in general, the police should try to establish cordons around any scene, move all those not involved with the incident out of the way, divert traffic and send all the emergency vehicles to the location given by the Incident Officer. The police normally should not try to take over and control the inner workings of the bomb scene because they had not attended the specialised courses to enable them to run the rescue operations in detail. It was noted that police officers who had attended the specialist incident offices courses, often remarked that they had no idea that there was so much to learn about running an incident. It was also accepted that in the early stages of any incident involving rescue and multiple casualties there would inevitably be a period of chaos and confusion and people would instinctively go to the aid of the injured.

The report noted that the incident officers from the ARP organisation had no official authority over the other Civil Defence services and their actions were often dependent upon their strength of character and not the automatic acceptance of orders which could be expected in the police force or the military.

The report also noted that there had always been a certain amount of mutual criticism between the police and the ARP services over the work at incidents. Though, on the whole, co-operation was good, there were many occasions when the police took the view that the ARP services did not rescue people in an efficient and energetic manner. Conversely the ARP services alleged that the police, rather than carrying out their external control function, tended to try and become amateur rescue parties for which they were not trained. Cases were reported where the police monopolised rescue work and trained rescue parties had to set up cordons. In another case an inspector and his men spent an hour trying to rescue a trapped woman without success during which time they refused a doctor and rescue parties access, and so caused considerable and unnecessary distress to the casualty. Eventually they gave up and the trained rescue services quickly released her.

These situations arose because the police often got to incidents first. Even if wardens were quickly on scene their main duty was to carry out an initial reconnaissance and send off their reports detailing the additional resources needed to deal with the incident. This meant that there was some delay before the rescue of casualties actually started. The police had no such duties and naturally did what they could to rescue people immediately. Once they had started on the task it was obviously quite difficult for them to relinquish it when the trained rescue parties arrived.

The major failure at the Café de Paris on the night it was bombed was a breakdown in communications. Had the initial ambulance crews on scene not returned to their posts after treating the walking wounded then casualties could have been given first aid and moved to hospital much more quickly. Overall, the enquiry concluded the incident was well run after the arrival of Mr Parker- Morris. It was noted that during the initial response at the majority of bomb scenes there was always a period of considerable confusion. The test of a well-run incident, was not that it appeared to run smoothly and efficiently to the outsider, but that order was rapidly evolved when the various Civil Defence services arrived. At first glance the report seems a bit of a whitewash but it must be re-stated that this activity was carried out in the cold and dark, under blackout conditions which complicated everyone's task. Furthermore, bombs were still falling and, by then, everyone was tired after months of continuous attack. Ultimately, of course, the Germans were to blame for the tragedy and not the rescuers.

The Luftwaffe continued to attack London and on the night of 19-20 March 1941, a force of almost 500 bombers headed for the capital. They carried 470 tons of high explosive bombs and 122,292 incendiaries. The docks were the main focus of the attack, but all the eastern and southeastern boroughs were hard hit, with a smattering of bombs falling all over the rest of the capital. It later transpired, from information in a captured diary, that one aircraft carried another massive 2,500kg 'Max'. According to the German airman who wrote the diary, it landed squarely in the docks, destroying a tanker and a warship. He said that the flash of it detonating lit up the whole of London, reminiscent of the comment from the Zeppelin commander Mathy when he dropped the 300 kilogram 'Leibesgabe' in the First World War. Like Mathy's bomb, it fell over a mile away from the intended target and demolished a large institute in Poplar.

Not surprisingly, with the numbers of incendiaries dropped, fires once again developed over a wide area and 1,881 were reported. Of these, three were classified as conflagrations, ten as major and fifty-three as serious. Casualties too reached record levels with 631 people being killed. To the people it became known simply as the 'The Wednesday Raid'.

A month later, on 16-17 April, there was another major raid lasting from 20.50 hours until 05.18 hours. A force of an estimated 685 bombers, some of which flew two sorties, dropped 890 tons of high explosive bombs and 152,000 incendiaries. All fell indiscriminately over the south and centre of the capital. Eighteen hospitals and thirteen churches were damaged and over sixty public building affected, including the House of Commons. Initial casualty reports indicated that 1,179 people were killed and twice as many injured.

Two days later, Goering's birthday present to Hitler was to mount yet another massive raid against London in which, for the first and only time, 1,000 tons of bombs were dropped. Not surprisingly, the capital and its people suffered as a result. The raid lasted from 21.15 hours to 04.15 hours, during which time some 700 bombers crossed the city. A mix of incendiaries and high explosive bombs caused over 1,460 fires, killed over 1,200 people and injured a further 1,000. The East End bore the brunt of the Luftwaffe's hostility and the people remained shocked and dazed at its ferocity for many days afterwards.

On 10-11 May 1941, the Luftwaffe launched its final major assault before most of its units were transferred eastwards for the great attack on the Soviet Union. Over a period of five hours, bombers droned overhead releasing mostly loads of high-capacity, high explosive bombs and incendiaries. The combination did great damage and caused serious fires and the centre of the capital was seriously damaged. The House of Commons' Chamber was destroyed. Westminster Abbey was hit, as were the British Museum, the Law Courts, the War Office, the Mint, the Mansion House and the Tower of London. Five of the Halls of the City Companies were destroyed and many famous churches damaged. The Elephant and Castle junction was the centre of one conflagration which ripped the heart out of the area.

By the time the raid was over 1,473 men, women and children lay dead and 1,792 were injured. The dead included the mayors of Westminster and Bermondsey. In all these raids there were countless acts of great bravery by members of the public as well as the emergency services and the Civil Defence teams.

This final flurry of attacks left hundreds of unexploded bombs and failed anti-aircraft shells requiring disposal. One bomb, probably dropped in the final major raid, smashed into a house on the now non-existent Gurney Street off the New Kent Road and failed to detonate. The impact so severely damaged the house it hit that it had to be pulled down and cleared. In the chaos of the time the bomb, which had buried itself in the ground, went unnoticed, but as will be shown later, as it lay cocooned in the earth it lost none of its potential to kill and maim.

By now the Royal Engineer bomb disposal teams were much better organised to deal with the threat. They were aided by the analysis of various statistics that had been compiled since mid-September 1940. These showed that between October and May 1941, 10% of bombs dropped in the United Kingdom failed to detonate on impact or very shortly afterwards. On average, about 8.5% of these unexploded bombs were fitted with long-delay fuzes and blew up without warning up to eighty hours after they had been dropped. The remaining 91.5% were considered to be 'duds'. Of these duds 85% percent were fitted with impact or very-short-delay fuzes and 6.5% were fitted with long-delay time fuzes, the clocks of which had failed to run properly.

In general, it was only a percentage of the 250 and 500 kilogram bombs that were fitted with long-delay action fuzes and examinations showed that 25% percent of the former and 10% of the latter were fitted with these. In both types of device, it was found that in 25% of the cases the bombs were fitted with a second anti-handling fuze designed to prevent the time fuze being removed. In addition, a high proportion of the long-delay-time fuzes were discovered to be fitted with the anti-withdrawal Zus 40 device, but these were never fitted behind other fuzes. Only ten out of 5,459 of the smaller 50kg bombs were fitted with a delay action fuze, although there was no room behind it for a Zus 40 anti-withdrawal device. Only three in 235 of the 1,000 kilogram 'Hermanns' had time delay fuzes and none of the larger bombs were fitted with these.

From the foregoing statistics, and with a good understanding of the methods of operation of the German fuzes, it was then possible to establish fairly rigid rules regarding the disposal of the various types of bomb. For disposal purposes it was assumed that all could be potentially fitted with a delay action fuze and/or anti-handling or anti-withdrawal devices. In every case, therefore, the key objective of the bomb disposal teams was to uncover the fuze pockets and establish the type(s) of fuzes fitted. It was accordingly stipulated that work on digging for an unexploded bomb would not start for at least ninety-six hours of its falling, unless its immediate disposal was essential to the war effort. This allowed for a sixteen-hour safety margin before digging started for bombs fitted with time fuzes. When digging did start great care had to be taken to ensure the bomb was not struck or moved which might cause an anti-handling fuze to function or a stopped timer to restart. Bombs were never to be moved, no matter how long ago they had fallen, before the type of fuze fitted was exposed and recognised. 'Sod's Law' seemed to rule in these circumstances and bombs that were uncovered invariably (according to the men in the disposal units) seemed to have come to rest with the fuze pockets hidden underneath the bomb.

Clearly, all anti-handling fuzes had to be immunized before a bomb could be moved. This often meant leaving it until the charge in the capacitors had leaked away and hoping that a long-delay fuze was not fitted, or that if it was, it had failed. If anti-handling fuzes were not fitted every effort was made to hold clockwork mechanisms by using the magnetic clock stopper. Sometimes this was not possible and the instructions of the day noted that: 'It may not always be possible to achieve this, in which case there is a very definite risk.'[6]

Direct-acting, short-delay fuzes had to be immunized before the bombs were moved, no matter how long they had been in the ground. It was permissible to remove short-delay, direct-acting or anti-handling fuzes once they were immunised, however, because of the Zus 40 anti-withdrawal booby-trap sometimes fitted beneath long-delay time fuzes, these were never to be extracted.

All bomb disposal personnel were warned that the enemy would change his tactics without warning and introduce new and dangerous fuzes designed to kill them. Finally, in principle, it was established that as much work as possible should be done remotely, particularly extracting fuzes.

Sadly, despite these procedures and principles being established, there were still casualties. On 12 May 1941, the day after the worst of the Blitz was over, there was a tragic accident involving bomb disposal personnel at Erith Marshes. It involved Lord Suffolk who had become one of the bomb disposals organisations' most engaging and colourful characters. He was a retired Guards officer with a sound scientific background who, at the outbreak of war, had volunteered to work for the Department of Scientific Research, part of Ministry of Supply. He soon became involved in all matters relating to bomb disposal operations, particularly where it was thought delayed action bombs or those with anti-handling systems were involved. A remote section of Richmond Park had been set aside for experimental work on bombs and there Lord Suffolk, with his driver, Mr Fred Harts, and his secretary, Miss Morden, were often seen working on unexploded ones. In addition, they regularly attended bomb sites to observe and assist with bomb disposal operations. The extraordinary way in which Lord Suffolk avoided disaster in the most menacing situations resulted in him and his two loyal staff becoming known as 'The Holy Trinity'.[7]

Lord Suffolk pioneered and extensively tested many disposal techniques himself before others were allowed to do the same. In particular, he was closely involved in attempts to stop delayed action clockwork fuzes by firing bullets into the mechanisms.

The exact circumstances leading up to the death of Lord Suffolk and others will never be clear. The seeds of the disaster were sown in mid-April when it was decided that the bomb dump at Erith Marshes needed to be closed so that the land could be ploughed and used for crops. There were a number of bombs on the site, some of which had had their fuzes removed and some which had not. The decision was made to move the former to Richmond Park and deal with the latter in situ. There was one particularly dangerous bomb, a 250kg, which was fitted with both a Number 50 anti-handling fuze and a Number 17 clockwork time fuze, and instructions were issued that this should not be touched until it had been finally rendered safe. Plans to dispose of this by demolition had been postponed because the nearby demolition pit was full of water. Steaming it out did not seem to have been an option either because of a lack of clean water.

When the first un-fuzed bombs were moved to the Bomb Disposal Experimental Section at Richmond Park, the problem of the 250kg bomb was discussed with Lord Suffolk and, helpful as always, he decided to go to Erith and render it safe. Around midday on 12 May 1941, he, along with his driver, secretary and a number of men from the Experimental Section, went to deal with the bomb. Shortly after arriving and inspecting the bomb he reported that it was ticking and that he needed to be sent a magnetic clock stopper and an electronic stethoscope as soon as possible.

Staff Sergeant Atkins and Lance Corporal Browning of 25 Bomb Disposal Company Royal Engineers were despatched to Erith with the necessary equipment. They met Lord Suffolk about 400 metres from the scene and it was decided that the clock stopper should be fitted to the errant bomb as soon as possible. Lord Suffolk and his assistants drove over to the bomb followed by Staff Sergeant Atkins and a Guy truck (which held the bank of batteries to run the clock stopper) driven by Driver Sharrat. A number of other soldiers from the experimental unit also went across to the bomb.

The clock stopper was fitted to the bomb and its base plate removed. Shortly afterwards Sapper Liposta and another man were sent to get some water for the steam generator. Whilst they were doing this the bomb exploded. Lance Corporal Browning, who had not gone over to the bomb, recalled:

> I saw the flash and then heard the report, I then saw Lord Suffolk's van upright but on fire. The Guy truck had part of the front blown away and the other lorry had just started to catch fire. I immediately went over with Sjt. [sic] Cole and did all I could to help the casualties. Two ambulances then arrived. I helped to put the casualties into them. I then proceeded to put the flames out in the second lorry.
>
> I went to the hospital in one of the ambulances. During the journey Lord Suffolk's lady secretary, who was in my ambulance died.[8]

No trace was ever found of Lord Suffolk, Fred Harts, Staff Sergeant Atkins, Driver Sharrat or Sapper Hardy. In addition, Sapper Dutton and Sapper Gillet died of their injuries. Miss Morden has the sad distinction of being the only woman killed on British bomb disposal operations during the Second World War.

Looking back over the period, as far as the Royal Engineer bomb disposal teams were concerned, it is true that, as often happens under conditions of extreme danger, the men at the forefront of the battle had rapidly gelled into close-knit communities. They accepted, without question, the dangers they faced daily, courageously and conscientiously continuing with their work. With all such groups of people a sense of humour, often of the black variety, helped the men deal with the daily pressures of life and death. The poem below gives an idea of the spirit of such men[9]:

Bomb Disposal not Self Disposal

This is the tale of Lieutenant Toms
Who used to play about with bombs.
He was not the least afraid
To vivisect a hand grenade
Bombs he habitually unloaded
To find out why they had not exploded.
He'd come in to the mess at night
With little sticks of gelignite
And hand around the wet canteen
Samples of Nitro Glycerine.
When people saw him off they ran –
He was a very lonely man,
And when he went on leave, his wife
Went off to an aunt who lived in Fife
And took the children too, a rather
Unkind reflection on their father.
Toms, though deserted in this fashion
Could not forget his ruling passion
And took his cousin's youngster Tom
To see a lovely new time bomb.
And then sat down to pull and jerk it
Thinking he knew how to work it
No matter what Toms had thought
The cousins are a small Tom short
And bits of Lieutenant Toms were seen
Falling like rain in Bethnal Green.
I cannot tell you more of Toms
But please don't play about with bombs.
Anon

250

This amusing ditty should not, however, deceive the reader into thinking that bomb disposal during the period was an amusing occupation; it was a dangerous and deadly business. The strength return for the Commander Royal Engineers London indicates that for the period from September 1940 to 31 January 1941, nine officers and forty-three other ranks were killed, and two officers and twenty-two other ranks injured. The high mortality rate compared to the wounded would indicate that the men were working next to or very close by the bombs when they detonated.[10]

The officers and men in their sections invariably established close working relationships with their local Civil Defence staff. They were much respected and after the death of Captain Crump and Sergeant Bumstead, on 16 January 1941, the Regional Commissioners penned a note to the men's Officer Commanding, Major Yates, expressing their sympathy and admiration for the work they had done.

As for London, after the attack of 10-11 May there were only a few minor raids and these stopped after 27 July 1941. The capital and her people had survived an eleven-month bombing campaign the like of which, at the time, no others had endured. It is estimated that some 50,000 bombs and countless thousands of incendiaries had been on dropped on the London region. Much has been made of the spirit and fortitude of the people during this time, particularly immediately after the war. The popular opinion was that there was a strong bond of national unity, the mixing of social classes and the notion of good humour and stoicism throughout the worst of the bombing. The newsreels portrayed the plucky Londoners, emerging from the ruins of their homes, spirit intact, and ready to go on in the face of insuperable odds.

More recently, critical revisionist histories suggest that it was a much closer run thing and that there were times, and areas, where the bombs overwhelmed the Civil Defences and left people close to physical exhaustion and on the edge of a complete collapse in morale. The truth lies somewhere between the two. For many who were the subject of very near misses or who lost loved ones, the cataclysmic experience left them numb and disbelieving. Later, those same people chose to remember what they wanted to about the experience which was not necessarily the truth. So horrific were some of the experiences that there was a natural tendency to suppress the memory of these.

There were also constant reminders of the sacrifices being made by others, particularly the soldiers, sailors and airmen of the armed forces and the need to ensure they were not let down, although at the height of the Blitz more civilians were being killed than servicemen. The people did carry on, they tried not to worry their loved ones and made the best of the circumstances they found themselves in. For Londoners the very worst was over but, tip and run raids, a mini Blitz and the V weapons would plague them right up until the end of the war.

NOTES:
1. Nock, O.S., *Railways at War 1939-45*, BCA, 1999.
2. Wakeling, Eric, *The Danger of UXBs*, BD Publishing, Bourne End, 1996.
3. TNA, HO 207/25: Bromley ARP letter dated 29 January 1941.
4. TNA, HO 186/2432: Incidents in Westminster.
5. TNA, HO 186/2432: Incidents in Westminster.
6. Manual of Bomb Disposal (Provisional) 1941, The War Office, 30 October 1941.
7. Hartley MBE, A.B., *Unexploded Bomb A Short History of Bomb Disposal*, Cassell, London, 1958.
8. Statement by 2127394 L/Cpl Browning, 25 Bomb Disposal Company RE, May 1943.
9. In Bomb Disposal Papers held at the Royal Engineers' Library.
10. TNA, Commander Royal Engineers (Bomb Disposal) London Strength Return, 31 January 1941.

Chapter 14

Respite, Raiders and Rockets

**'There are air raid alarms almost every night but
hardly any bombs.'**
George Orwell, 1943.

The morning of 6 June 1942 dawned a fine day at Gurney Street, Elephant and Castle, one of the worst-bombed areas of the capital, and many housewives and others were sitting on their doorsteps in the pleasant, early-morning sunshine. There had been no German bombing in the area for months and much of the district had been cleaned up within the limitations of what could be achieved in wartime.

Then, without warning, the street was shaken by a huge explosion. The peaceful summer scene was shattered, houses collapsed and torn and bloody shapes lay about everywhere. The dormant bomb referred to in the previous chapter, which had lain buried beneath the rubble in the demolished house in Gurney Street, had inexplicably detonated. When and exactly where it had fallen was never finally established beyond doubt, but local people who survived seemed sure it was one of the last bombs dropped during the Blitz on 10-11 May 1941. It had hit a house, without exploding but the damage had been such that the building itself was demolished and the site cleared. This would indicate a bomb of considerable size had hit the premises. Clearly, in these circumstances it was the job of the Bomb Reconnaissance Officer to determine that the damage was from an unexploded large bomb and not a small 50kg that had detonated. It was never determined if the building had been actually surveyed after the raid, and it may be that it was just missed in the confusion of the aftermath of the bombing. What was clear was that the bomb had been below ground for at least a year. From the damage it was estimated that it must have been 500kg in size, and may have been fitted with a vibration-sensitive fuze or a

253

time fuze which had stopped but had somehow restarted. One theory was that the vibrations running through the ground from the near-by tube trains as they rumbled in and out of Elephant and Castle station could have restarted the clock, but this seems unlikely. Just what caused the bomb to explode on that sunny, peaceful morning was never explained.

Within minutes of the explosion dozens of rescuers were on scene and set about tearing at the rubble to try and rescue survivors. They had with them a crude and newly deployed electronic listening device, which used microphones placed in the rubble, to try to help locate buried victims. Every so often the cry would go out 'Silence please, silence,' and the ARP men, firemen, police, rescue parties, and all the other volunteers stopped work and stood motionless. A loud-speaker at the site then broadcast to any survivors in the wreckage to knock a brick or make some other noise if they could. Unfortunately, there were no answering cries or knocks and an eerie silence was the only response. Work continued throughout the night but no one was found alive. The final death toll was eighteen killed, half of them children, with many others badly injured.

Following the news of this disaster, people took a much more serious approach to the possibility of other unexploded bombs and in the next three weeks over 170 reports of forgotten munitions were investigated. Most were false alarms, but a total of twenty-two further bombs were discovered and rendered safe. A major review of unexploded bombs was undertaken and the report into them was the forerunner of another document which examined all abandoned or allegedly abandoned bombs post war.

In July 1942 the Luftwaffe began tip-and-run raids using small groups of aircraft. These were normally made by fast, low flying fighters-bombers carrying a minimal bomb load; they were often made in bad weather which hindered the efforts of the RAF to shoot them down. In the early days most of these were not directed at London. Later there were some proper raids. For example, on 17-18 January 1943, the capital was attacked by over 100 long-range bombers dropping some forty-seven tons of bombs. It was during this raid that another deadly fuze was first used with the sole purpose of killing bomb disposal officers.

Bravery, professionalism and, with the development of new complex equipment, technical proficiency, were undoubtedly the key attributes employed by the London bomb disposal teams. However, luck was also a necessary ingredient, and it was certainly in evidence in the recovery of the first of the new booby-trap fuzes. The bomb that contained it crashed into Lord's Cricket Ground and penetrated the Bakerloo tube line underneath the pitch. This closed the Underground and the bomb was graded as A1, meaning that it required immediate disposal. The Officer Commanding the local bomb disposal company summoned Sergeant L.C. Waite and told him to take a working party to the scene, adding that Captain Frank Carlile RE would join them there later. On arrival, Sergeant Waite inspected the entry hole which was the biggest he had ever seen and was at least seven feet across. The brickwork on the roof of the tunnel had collapsed and, along with a pile of earth, was lying on the floor of the track. Peering into the hole Waite could see the faint gleam of railway lines either side of the collapse, but little else. He requisitioned the groundsman's ladder and descended into the tunnel. Waite then summoned help from Lance Corporal Mumby and, with the aid of two shovels, they set about uncovering the bomb. Mumby was the first to find part of it and, in accordance with the minimum risk procedures, Waite sent him to safety, along with the other men who had crowded round the top of the hole.

Waite cleared the rubble away from the rest of the bomb which he established as a 500kg fitted with a well-known impact fuze, the Number 25 B. As always there were a number of subsidiary markings on the fuze body which, in this case, included a small Y stamped in the factory batch number. About this time Carlile arrived and asked Waite to prepare the normal discharger equipment for dealing with a Number 25 B fuze.

With this prepared, the two men then set about neutralizing the fuze which involved filling it with a BD liquid designed to short and drain the internal condensers. A Number 25 B fuze should have absorbed twenty cubic centimetres of liquid, but despite their best efforts only five cubic centimetres could be forced in to the fuze. This was not considered all that unusual, and in view of the need to get the Underground open as soon as possible, it was decided to drag the bomb back out through the hole it had made on impact. Sergeant Waite removed the bomb filler cap and took it to the local workshops where it was drilled and fitted with a large lifting bolt. A crane was borrowed and, with the filler cap refitted, a steel hawser was attached and the bomb was dragged back up to the surface of the cricket ground, where it was loaded on to a lorry. As this part of the task was almost complete Carlile left the scene, but asked to be collected later from the Company Headquarters to supervise the final disposal of the bomb at Hampstead Heath.

Having packed away all the equipment the men, plus the bomb, set off for the Headquarters where Carlile was waiting. According to Waite the Captain was pleased that the worst was over. Waite, however, said that he had a hunch that this bomb was different and that since no significant bombing of London had taken place the Germans designers had had plenty of time to develop a new fuze. Carlile apparently just grinned.

At the Hampstead Heath bomb cemetery, the offending item was unloaded and the two men fitted a remote fuze extractor. They walked off to a safe distance and pulled the cord which would finally lift the fuze out of its pocket and make the bomb safe. This was a simple and well-established process which should have extracted the fuze from the bomb body, but inexplicably it failed. When they walked back to the bomb they discovered that the fuze was about half way out but that it had jammed. At this stage Carlile decided on more brutal methods and asked Waite to go to his driver and find a screwdriver and hammer from his tool kit. This may seem a cavalier act but on many occasions fuzes would become stuck in their pockets because of the distortion caused by the violent impact of the bombs. On hearing what the pair intended to do the driver apparently remarked, 'You silly bastards!' In fact, only the screwdriver was needed and with this the fuze was prised out of its pocket.

Straight away they noticed that it was different from normal Number 25 B fuzes and that it was fitted with a steel wire which was designed to prevent extraction. Realizing the importance of this discovery it was immediately taken back to the Company Headquarters from where it was subsequently dispatched to the Directorate of Bomb Disposal and on again to the Department of Scientific Research. At the same time a signal was sent to all bomb disposal units warning them not to attempt to immunize any fuze with unusual supplementary markings.

When it was dismantled scientists discovered the secrets of the new design. It was fitted with a battery and three mercury tilt switches set up in different planes. After the bomb, in which one of these fuzes was fitted came to rest, the tilt switches were set so that they would close the firing circuit if the bomb was moved in any plane. Unlike the previous anti-handling fuzes where the capacitors had a limited life, the battery in this fuze meant the bomb could remain live for weeks and possibly months. During the examination it was established that the reason the bomb failed to function when it was moved, was that one of the arming wires had come adrift. For Carlile, Waite and all the men, luck had intervened to keep them safe. More importantly, the secret workings of the new fuze had been revealed. Had the arming wire not come adrift and the bomb detonated and killed Waite and his men there may have been many more deaths of bomb disposal personnel before the significance of the simple Y was discovered. Sadly, having survived his time in London dealing with hundreds of different bombs, Captain Carlile was killed on 14

August 1943. He had been posted to Horsham in West Sussex where, whilst handling a mine fuze, it exploded and killed him.

Shortly after instructions had been issued about the dangers of the new Y fuze, another unexploded bomb was located at a warehouse in Battersea. On inspection it was also discovered to have the subsidiary Y marking stamped into the aluminium fuze body. The bomb was graded as A1 because of its location; furthermore, the Directorate of Bomb Disposal wanted confirmation that the Y was a definite indicator that it was booby-trapped. A team was assembled and using new radiographic apparatus it established that the bomb fuze had three tiny mercury tilt switches.

The officer in charge of the disposal operation, Major C.A.J. Martin MC, RE, now had the problem of how to render the bomb safe. He elected to remove the base plate of the bomb without disturbing it and then try to steam out the filling. This was possible because the bomb had come to rest nose uppermost and was wedged and partially embedded in a steel bed plate under a lathe. Access was not easy, but despite this the base plate was successfully removed and the TNT filling exposed. It was considered that letting the bomb heat up too much during the steaming process was inadvisable. Therefore, at the same time as a jet of steam was played on to the explosive by hand, another hose had to be used on the outer casing to keep the body and fuze cool. Unable to carry out this action on his own, Martin was assisted throughout by Lieutenant R.W. Green RE. The pair lay in a narrow depression under the bomb playing both steam on the filling and water on the casing and collecting the liquid TNT as it dribbled out of the rear of the bomb.

After several hours the officers managed to steam out sufficient explosive to expose the fuze internally and were able to remove the gaine and make it safe. This fuze was immediately taken for examination, at which point the presence of the mercury tilt switches confirmed it was indeed a deadly booby-trap. Clearly, removing the base plate from the bomb and steaming it out would not always be possible. It was considered that the risks of moving a bomb fitted with a Y fuze during this operation and setting it off were unacceptably high. Equally, even the slightest distortion of the bomb body might make the process of removing the base plate impossible. After some laboratory trials it was established that if a bomb fitted with a Y fuze was chilled to -27°C then the battery would become temporarily powerless and in such a condition the fuze could be safely removed from a bomb. The proposed method initially required the use of liquid oxygen but the procedure needed to be operationally tested.

Obligingly, the Germans dropped another bomb fitted with the Y fuze near the Albert Bridge on the River Thames. This time Major J.P. Hudson RE of the Bomb Disposal Directorate had the unenviable job of working on it. When it had been delicately uncovered there was some good news; the fuze was uppermost. This simplified Hudson's task and gingerly he built a clay dam around the fuze head. He then filled this dam with liquid oxygen keeping it replenished for two to three hours until there was a frost ring twelve inches in radius right around the locking ring of the fuze. Hudson reckoned that the frost must by now have reached the batteries and made them inoperative. He then had a few minutes to extract the fuze before the batteries warmed up. Using a jemmy he managed to extract it, remove the gaine and so rendered safe the bomb. In doing so another procedure for rendering safe Y fused bombs was established. There was a problem though in that the use of liquid oxygen which boiled off during use was particularly dangerous. Most unexploded bombs were in confined locations and the risk of a fire as the oxygen levels increased was unacceptable. Later dry ice or liquid nitrogen was used. These gave the same result but without the risk of fire. The bomb disposal men had won yet another small victory against the enemy's fuze designers.

On 20 January 1943, a group of German fighter-bombers, each carrying a single 500kg bomb, participated in the most audacious daylight raid on London since the end of the daylight bombing in 1941. Around midday the single-engine Focke-Wulf Fw 190s flew in at low-level dropping bombs and strafing with cannon and machine-guns. By this stage of the war the air raid warning systems had become lax and that day, by chance, most of the barrage balloons used to discourage this type of low flying had been hauled down to allow the gunners to calibrate their radars. (This could not be done with the balloons in position as it produced hundreds of false echoes.) As a result, no air raid warning was sounded to herald the arrival of the fighter bombers.

The German aircrafts' height as they skimmed across the capital was estimated at between 200 and 1,000 feet. They dropped a number of bombs in Greenwich, Bermondsey, Deptford and Lewisham. By far the most serious incident was at Sandhurst Road School in Catford. A bomb hit the three-storey building and lodged in the second floor before exploding some fifty seconds or so after impact. When bombing at low level this delay was necessary to give the fighter-bombers time to be well clear of the area before the bomb exploded. It also gave time for twenty-seven children to be evacuated out of the ground floor windows. Then there was a tremendous explosion as the bomb detonated inside the building causing three storeys to collapse into a heap of smoking rubble. Those children who had escaped from the building were running around screaming as civilians and rescue workers flocked to the scene to help the injured. Altogether thirty-eight children and six teachers were killed and a further sixty seriously injured.

Bombs, like the 500kg described in the incident above, are always directly responsible for death and destruction, but on 3 March 1943, it was the threat of bombs which caused one of the worst single disasters in London during the war. Like the great fire in December 1940, it was a combination of unrelated circumstances which led to the catastrophe.

It happened at Bethnal Green, then a working class neighbourhood in which the majority of houses offered little protection from air raids. During the Blitz the area had suffered a heavy pounding, and the remaining population in the district had learnt the importance of taking shelter underground during raids. One of the shelters adapted for use in the area was a tube station which had been under construction, together with sections of the adjoining tunnels, at the beginning of the war. The single entrance consisted of a stairway which was L-shaped with nineteen steps down to a landing and then a further six to the underground booking hall. From this hall two escalators led down to the deep shelter. In total it provided sanctuary for 5,000 people in bunks with space for another 5,000. The shelter had been in regular use since its conversion, but the numbers using it had dwindled from several thousand at the end of the Blitz to just a few hundred regulars in 1943. The population, however, was very aware of press reports of the raids being carried out by the RAF on Berlin and the consequent risk of retaliatory attacks by the Germans. On the night of the disaster there seemed to have been the general expectation of a raid in the area.

That night the alert sounded at 20.17 hours, by which time only a few hundred regulars were in the shelter. As a result of the sirens, people began to gather at the single entrance and walk down the steps in an orderly manner to safety below. At about the same time, two cinemas disgorged their customers and several buses stopped to let people off to take shelter. Ten minutes or so later, people were arriving faster than the capacity of the stairs could cope with, and the entrance became packed with people queuing to get to safety. Many above ground were still orderly, but those some distance from the entrance were growing nervous and anxious to get out of harm's way.

There was a little gunfire at this time but no bombs had dropped for miles around. Regrettably, those queuing were not aware that a new anti-aircraft rocket system had been installed in the nearby Victoria

Park, Hackney. This secret weapon consisted of large numbers of rockets which, although fairly inaccurate were, when fired en-masse, capable of producing a massive box barrage. The launchers fired salvos of 100 rockets at a time and they accelerated to 1,000 mph in one and a half seconds, time fuzes in the warheads detonating simultaneously at the desired height in a single tremendous roar. The rockets were given the codename 'un-rotating' projectiles and the groups of launchers were known as 'Z rocket batteries'.

At precisely 20.27 hours the battery at Victoria Park discharged a salvo of rockets and moments later the warheads exploded in the air in a terrifying crescendo of noise. This new and unfamiliar barrage caused the people waiting to get into the shelter, or making their way to it, a great deal of alarm. Some threw themselves to the ground, and others were apparently heard to say words like 'they are starting dropping them', or 'it was a landmine' and other similar alarming observations. The crowd surged forward towards the entrance to the shelter sweeping those in front of them forward. This placed an immediate pressure on those on the top of the stairway who were descending into a darkened tunnel.

A woman near the bottom of the first set of stairs, who was said to be leading or holding a child, tripped over and fell. She finished up on the landing where the L-shaped stairway turned right and then led down a further six steps into the booking hall. As a result, or simultaneously, a man fell on her left leg pinning her. The momentum for the crowd behind was unstoppable and in a matter of seconds a falling and interlaced mass of bodies had formed an immovable mass on the flat platform. Behind them the people on the stairs were unable to stop and piled on top of those already crushed and dying in front of them.

Outside there were still 100-150 people trying to get into the shelter. They were becoming more and more anxious and it seemed to them that, for some reason, they were being deliberately stopped from gaining the sanctuary they sought. In front, on the stairs, all movement had come to a stop and there was much confusion and shouting. There were loud and distressing cries, and slowly those behind began to realize something had gone terribly wrong. But with the firing of another salvo of rockets and gunfire those outside were becoming more desperate to get into the shelter.

Inside, at the shelter end of the stairs, the position was different but equally tragic. There were four wardens whose job it was to stop people loitering in the booking hall and to control the flow of people on to the escalators. It was one of these that noticed that the stream of people had stopped and went to investigate. Almost simultaneously the muted screams of those people being crushed rang out. By the time they got to the top of the first set of six stairs there was already a wall of tangled bodies and their efforts to extricate anyone were futile because of the weight pressing down on them from above.

The senior warden, realizing what was happening, telephoned the police immediately at 20.40 hours and followed this with a second, more urgent, call on the need for rescue parties and ambulances. At about 20.45 hours the first police officers arrived and tried to restore some sort of order outside the shelter. As yet no one was aware of the terrible scenes down below. As those people at the top of the stairs who were able to move, climbed back out, efforts were started to rescue those trapped and injured. From then on a well-co-ordinated rescue effort began but it was too late for the people in the stairwell.

By the time the last body had been removed the casualty list was 173 dead and sixty-two injured. The deceased included eighty-four women and sixty-two children. Like many accidents the incident, was over in seconds.

In his official report into the event Laurence Dunne MC stated that: 'The stairway was, in my opinion, converted from a corridor to a charnel house in from 10 to 15 seconds.'[1]

The report concluded that there was a need to install a crush barrier at the top entrance to prevent a reoccurrence of the accident, that the entrance should be screened so that decent lighting could be applied in the stairway, and that the stairs should have handrails. The accident itself was considered to have been caused by a number of people losing their self-control at a particular place and time, and that this was compounded by the poor structural design and lack of police control at the entrance.

By the end of 1943, with Bomber Command's offensive seriously beginning to bite, the Germans made the decision that there would be reprisal attacks against the United Kingdom which become known as the 'Little Blitz'. In contrast to the attacks of 1940 and 1941, when a stream of bombers would be over the capital for an extended period, the Luftwaffe adopted the tactics of Bomber Command in which the attacks would be concentrated in the shortest possible time. They also emulated the RAF in resorting to the use of all types of incendiaries mixed with large, high explosive bombs. Cluster type bombs containing hundreds of incendiaries, many fitted with explosive charges, were released which were timed to open near the ground where they would form a concentrated pattern. At the same time, 2,500kg 'Max' bombs would be dropped in an attempt to kill or maim those who had not taken shelter and were fighting the fires. This gave the new National Fire Service and the fire guards their first real test. The latter were, on a few occasions, driven to the shelters by the high explosives and were overwhelmed by the largest fires. Even so it was estimated that the fire guards, braving both the high explosive bombs and the risk from the small explosive incendiaries, extinguished about 75% of the fires before they took hold. The shortness of the raids meant that the Fire Service could rapidly concentrate resources and set about containing and extinguishing the bigger blazes. By adding additional observation posts, fires could be spotted early on, and the firemen quickly tasked to the incidents. The aim was to get operations underway at the incipient stages of the fires and so prevent serious conflagrations. The bombing concentrations in some areas were such, however, that it did not always work.

On 21-22 January 1944, the largest force of bombers to attack London on any night since July 1942 was detected on the radar screens. The raiders dropped some 268 tons of bombs including the highest number of the largest bombs ever dropped on London during the whole of the war. These large bombs were capable of producing massive damage amongst residential housing areas, which rendered people homeless in the depths of winter. The shock waves as they detonated were also heard for considerable distances. They rapidly changed the habits of many Londoners who were now accustomed to ignoring the minor raids and sleeping in their own beds. After four years of the dreary wartime existence the thought of going back to the old nightly routine of sleeping in the Underground or in garden shelters had a very negative impact on morale. There was a heavy demand for the Morrison shelters in which people could remain in their homes, with a high degree of protection, during raids.

For the remainder of January and all of February there were a whole series of raids during which significant damage was caused. At Battersea about 3,000 homes in an area of some twenty acres were destroyed or made uninhabitable. In Chelsea a block of flats collapsed under a direct hit and casualties were heavy. In Fulham, 1,200 people were made homeless and there was a major forty-pump fire. In these attacks a further 1,000 people were killed and double that number injured. They continued up until late March when the Germans effort was switched to the south coast to try and disrupt preparations for D-Day. For Londoners there was once more a short respite.

NOTE:
1. Dunne, Lawrence MC, *Report on an Inquiry into the Accident at Bethnal Green Tube Station Shelter on the 3 March 1943*, HM Stationary Office, London 1945.

Chapter 15

The V1s – Target 42

**'My teeth had been practically blown out in the explosion
and the inside of my mouth was full of pieces of skin.'**
Joe Carter, victim of a V1 explosion at Battersea.

At the peak of the Blitz the detonations of exploding bombs of
various sizes merged into and overlapped each other so that at the
end of a heavy raid there was no really accurate tally of the number
actually dropped. This was not the case when the V1 flying bomb
offensive was launched against London in June 1944. The need for
intelligence about the system meant that from the first to the very last
missile, almost every flight and point of impact was recorded in detail.

It was at about 04.24 hours on 13 June 1944 when the air log propeller
on the front of the third V1 flying bomb launched against England (the
first two crashed) reached its pre-set value. The propeller was linked to
a gearing system which counted the miles flown since the missile's
launch. At that moment, two igniters were fired which locked the
rudder and elevators of the V1 into position and additionally drove two
sets of spoilers down from the tail. The deployment of the spoilers
disrupted the smooth airflow over the elevators and immediately
pitched the missile forward into a steep dive. This sudden change of
direction caused a negative G force, which starved the pulse jet of fuel,
and the throbbing of the engine suddenly stopped. Seconds later the
bomb slammed into the bridge over Grove Road, Bethnal Green, which
carried the four tracks of the main line between Liverpool Street Station
and Chelmsford. The warhead, containing some 850 kilograms of high
explosive, detonated in a blinding flash.

After years of pioneering engineering, technical development and
testing, the familiar consequence of all the effort was, not surprisingly,
the death of innocents. Six people died in the explosion, including Mrs

263

Ellen Woodcraft and her eight-month-old baby Tom, thirty others were seriously injured and a further 200 made homeless.

The military authorities, but not the people, had been expecting the assault by a new weapon of war. There had been ample intelligence from various sources including 'Enigma' and this was complimented by RAF photo-reconnaissance aircraft which had identified many unusual launching ramps in western France all pointing at the heart of London. The secret codename *Diver* had been given to the new menace although this did not refer to the missile's final plummet to earth. A number of secret contingency plans had been prepared to deal with the new threat, but the information was highly classified and distributed on a strictly need-to-know basis. At Grove Road, a Royal Engineer Bomb Disposal Officer arrived at the scene to survey the wreckage and institute a search for fragments. As the day progressed his arrival was followed by more, and more, senior officials from various organisations.

By mid-day, in official circles, there was a feeling of relief. The fact was the Germans had launched a total of ten flying bombs that morning with the Tower of London as the central aiming point. Of these half had crashed on take-off, one simply disappeared, probably into the Channel and three exploded in southern England. Only one had reached its intended target. Officials at the site over-estimated the size of the warhead at between 1,200 and 2,000 kilograms of high explosive; but even then this was significantly less than the ten tons some had feared. In his book *Ack Ack*, General Sir Fredrick Pile noted that, amongst the wreckage at the point of impact, a fuze from a heavy anti-aircraft shell was found. This raised the possibility that his command may have, in fact, shot down the first V1. The fuze could of course have been a relic from a previous raid and the truth will never be known. If the missile was shot down, however, it highlighted the folly of using the anti-aircraft guns over populated areas; left alone the V1 might just have flown on past the main target.

It had previously been arranged with the Ministry of Information that no details of the attack would be published and there would be no public statement on the new enemy missile. The reason was not so much to deny information to the population of London, but to prevent the Germans gaining knowledge of where the missiles were landing and so enable them adjust their aim. The result was that the press was informed that a raider had been shot down and crashed in east London. Unfortunately, *The Times*, the following day, reported that the plane had fallen on a railway line in the East End. The Germans had only lost one aircraft over the United Kingdom that night, but this was not operating over London and crashed in Essex, so despite the secrecy, it was obvious that at least one of their missiles had struck close to the intended target.

Nevertheless, at the end of the first day, there was considerable optimism amongst some of the senior military and scientific community that the long awaited assault by pilotless aircraft was nowhere near as devastating as had been predicted. At the Cabinet Office Lord Cherwell commented to Professor R.V. Jones on the feeble German effort: 'The mountain hath groaned and given forth a mouse.'[1]

Jones replied that they knew the Germans could launch at least twenty V1s a day and that this optimism was unwarranted. He was later proved correct and, for a multitude of reasons, the V1 would have a much greater effect on morale than had been predicted.

In contrast to the British feeling of relief, the Germans were bitterly disappointed that their grandiose scheme for the unleashing of a devastating night attack on London had failed. A second salvo of missiles scheduled to be fired at 08.00 hours was abandoned and an investigation launched into the failures. In the subsequent inquiry, the commander of the unit narrowly escaped court martial for the dismal failure. Nevertheless, after tremendous efforts, another wave of missiles was ready for launch on the evening of 15 June. The message ordering the attack stated simply that the aim point would be 'Target 42', the code for London. It would start with a salvo of missiles at 23.18 hours with an impact time in London of 23.40. It would then continue for a further five hours with missiles being launched in quick succession. In total, 244 V1s were launched and although many crashed and some fell short, seventy-three got through to Greater London, of which eleven were shot down over the capital but still exploded when they hit the ground. Imagine the impact today if seventy-three one-ton vehicle bombs were detonated at random overnight in London.

People on the flight path witnessed the new and ominous throbbing of the missiles as they passed low and fast overhead, the flame extending out of the back of the pulse jet lighting up the night sky. Every few minutes another, then another, would race across the sky heading for London.

Initially, in London, the diving missiles confused the on-duty civil defenders who were not privy to the secret intelligence on the missiles. A warden in Thornton Heath recalled his firefighting squad becoming more and more excited as subsequent V1s arrived and then dived into the ground. 'Look', one man exclaimed, 'they are shooting the bastards down like flies'. It wasn't long, however, before it became apparent that no defences were that good, and that these were not enemy aircraft, but some new machine of war.

It was clear that in the face of such an unexplained onslaught a public denial would be counterproductive and since rumours were already spreading like wildfire it was decided the policy of silence was unsustainable. On the morning of 16 June, in the House of Commons, Herbert Morrison announced that: 'It has been known for some time that the enemy was making preparations for the use of pilotless aircraft against this country and he has now started to use this much-vaunted weapon.'[2]

He went on to explain the importance of denying the enemy information about the accuracy of the V1s by allowing reports of where they had landed to be disclosed in the press. Therefore, other than indicating the whole of the South of England had been subject to attack, no further details were to be given. Later, as will be seen, this policy was to have serious repercussions on the morale of the people of London because it gave the impression to the rest of the country that the whole of the south of England was being bombed not just the capital.

The new missiles were at first called 'flying bombs', 'pilotless aircraft', or 'buzz bombs' from the noise of the harsh sounding pulse jet. Within a few days, however, the name that seemed to stick was the 'doodlebug'. Unlike the insect, though, the V1s were neither slow, nor bumbling. The comedians amongst the population had their day and suggested they be called 'Bob Hopes' (bob down and hope for the best) or, more crudely, 'Hitler's Virgins' because they had never had a man inside them.

In fact, the V1 was a small pulse jet propelled, mid-wing monoplane, with a single fin and rudder. When viewed from below in silhouette it had a sinister appearance described as having 'the deathly crudity of a black cross; angular, simple, narrow and entirely without beauty'. It flew straight and level at between 2,000 and 3,000 feet remorselessly heading for its target on a one-way trip of destruction. The pulse jet on its back making a hideous noise perhaps best described as an old two-stroke motorcycle without a silencer. At night the pulse jet left a flaming trail easily seen by observers on the ground. Unlike manned aircraft they could be flown in all weathers and at any time.

Five days after the first missile had been launched the deadly potential of the V1 and its ability to cause mass casualties came to the fore. On the morning of Sunday, 18 June 1944, three missiles were heading for the heart of London. Up until then no V1s had landed in the Westminster area. But, on that morning the region's first bomb landed on Hungerford Bridge in the early hours; the next landed on Carey

Mansions in Rutherford Street, demolishing the building. Mercifully, though, the casualties from these two bombs were light with ten killed and a further fifty-two people injured.

The third bomb to hit Westminster was launched just after 11.00 hours. It tipped forward in its terminal dive some twenty minutes later. Sat back from Birdcage Walk at the end of the Parade Square outside Wellington Barracks was the Guards Chapel. The congregation who attended that morning had come to listen to the Reverend R.H. Whitrow, Chaplin to the Brigade of Guards. They included Colonel Lord Edward Hay, commanding the Grenadier Guards, and many others.

Just down the road that Sunday morning, Professor R.V. Jones, who was responsible for much of the analysis of the intelligence on the V1 (and later the V2), was working in his office in Whitehall. He was in conversation with a colleague by telephone when he heard the unforgettable noise of an approaching V1. Then, when the engine cut out, he remarked that, 'This is going to be a pretty close call'. He took cover under his desk and, moments later, the blast shattered most of the windows in the building. He went out of his office and saw that the Guards Chapel, just 150 yards away, had been struck. Civil Defence teams and Guards from the Barracks were on scene almost immediately, recovering the dead and seriously wounded. There was nothing Jones could do to help, but the sight of the stretchers, coupled with a sea of fresh green leaves torn from the trees in Birdcage Walk, brought home to him the difference between one ton of explosive in actuality and the one ton they had predicted in the abstract six months previously.

Examination of the scene of the explosion established that the V1 had exploded on the roof of the chapel which then completely collapsed landing on the congregation below. When the final casualty list was complete it was established that 119 people were killed in the Chapel, and a further 102 seriously injured, some of whom died later, thirty-nine others escaped with minor wounds.

The Germans had called the V1 the *Vergeltungswaffen*, literally meaning vengeance or retaliatory weapons, the '1' being added for propaganda purposes to indicate that it was the first of a new series of secret weapons to be deployed.

Once officially acknowledged, and as the intensity of the bombardment grew, the flying bomb offensive came as a tremendous psychological blow to the people of London. Five years of war, with blackouts, rationing, hard labour and long hours had sapped the strength of even

267

the most resolute. The successful invasion of Normandy, with Allied troops firmly established in Western Europe, had lifted spirits and boosted morale and there was an understandable air of optimism about the future. In some quarters there was the unfounded assumption that the war would be over by Christmas. The attack on 15 June, when V1s detonated all over London, crushed this rise in morale and sowed the seeds of doubt for the immediate future. The fear was that if the almost exponential rise in the numbers of missiles getting through to London continued, it might make living in the capital unbearable.

In many respects the new onslaught was different from traditional bombing. The speed of the flying bombs meant that the warning times were reduced, and the launching of successive missiles over protracted periods resulted in extended periods of alert. Although initially launched at night to maintain surprise, the missiles were now being dispatched round the clock. German aircraft, other than a few hit and run raids by fighter-bombers, had long been banished from the skies over Britain in daylight, and during this time the population were generally free from the fear of raids. The arrival of the V1s abruptly changed that. This in turn had a knock-on effect on the civil defenders, especially the ARP Wardens, many of whom were exhausted having been at their posts or actively involved in rescue work since the first wave of bombs were fired.

Goebbels, the German propaganda minister, summed up the omnipresent nature of the V1 in the following vein:

> The effect of the German bombardment lies in its persistency ... I can imagine how, quite apart from the damage it might cause, it would gradually build up on your nerves. It's like toothache. The pain is of itself is not so bad. But when your tooth aches and throbs all day and all night, then you can't think clearly, in fact all you can do is think about this accursed pain.[3]

Although there was little initial demand for evacuation, people again started to make use of shelters, particularly at night. But this did not solve the problem caused by the almost constant high-alert state. By 21 June, an average of fifty V1s a day were falling on Greater London. A day later one fell near the top of Constitution Hill and demolished the wall around the garden of Buckingham Palace. The area of repaired wall can still be clearly seen today and one of the streetlamps still has its light at an odd angle where it was bent by the blast. A second flying bomb landed in the Palace Gardens five days later, but the King and Queen continued to live in London and experience the ordeal.

As always, the individual response to the new threat depended on a multitude of factors. This included people's natural outlook on life, their degree of responsibility and their experiences of previous bombing raids. The timid and nervous people, particularly those who had suffered near misses, reacted badly, whereas those made of sterner stuff seemed able to ignore the risks, and carried on as normal a life as was possible under the circumstances. For the population as a whole though there were three phases of response. Initially there was much bravado about the attacks, but as casualties mounted, people became anxious and fearful and finally, as the weeks dragged on a weary numbness seemed to overwhelm everyone. To survive the population developed new patterns of living to circumvent the worst of the dangers of the new missile.

It is a basic fact of life, particularly in face of the imminent threat of death or serious injury that the human brain rapidly responds to deal with a new menace. In no time at all, Londoners' ears were tuned into the novel throaty roar of the doodlebugs, which fortunately was distinctly different from the noise of normal aero engines. More importantly, in most cases, it was the cessation of the sound, followed by the silence, which indicated the missile had tipped into its terminal dive. This characteristic understandably elicited a high degree of tense expectation in the handful of seconds between the motor cutting out and the explosion. And for those below a wave of fear, anticipation and anxiety spread out in the probable impact area. There was time to take cover if it was close by or to drop to the ground, but not enough to dodge the point of impact.

Despite there being a clear difference between the sound of the V1 and other aero engines, an instruction was issued by Whitehall to the RAF and USAAF that their pilots should, if possible, avoid flying over London and, if they had to, they should not under any circumstances suddenly throttle back as this sudden change in noise level was enough to send people scuttling for cover. There was also a request that the use of motorcycles be banned in London, especially at night, as their engines could easily be confused with the sound of a V1 by half-asleep Londoners. However, as most of these motorcycles were military dispatch riders on vital war work, the request was denied.

That fact that V1 was a 'robot' missile had its own peculiar influence. With a manned bomber there was the feeling that at least the crew could be got at and killed, even if it was after they had dropped their bombs and done their damage. There was no such prospect with the V1s as they relentlessly appeared over the capital. A fireman made the point succinctly when comparing the manned bomber and the V1: 'There was a time when he'd skulk off when it was getting near daylight, but it doesn't matter now. All the Spitfires in the world can't put the breeze up a blinking plane without a pilot.'[4]

Anderson and Morrison shelters, many of which had fallen into a state of disrepair, were rapidly renovated. Provision of more the latter, which allowed people to stay in their homes, was made a top priority. People without these returned to the Underground and other public shelters as the numbers of flying bombs increased.

The decision to head for a shelter was another cause for concern. The point has already been made that unlike conventional air raids which had a limited time span, the V1s were launched almost continuously. People who ducked into a shelter on the first warning would come out after the all-clear sounded, and then almost immediately duck in again as the sirens heralded the approach of yet another missile. This, particularly in wartime factories, resulted in an alarming drop in production which threatened the manufacture of a wide range of vital supplies for the forces at the front. The dilemma was whether or not people should be warned. It was finally decided that warnings would be given, but that there would be a danger warning of two-second blasts followed by two second intervals. This, it was hoped, would give approximately one and a half minutes warning of the imminent arrival of a V1 over London. The all clear would be a long, six-second blast. Area schemes were also introduced where the warning would only be given when a V1 was detected approaching some fifteen-miles out on a direct line of flight. Eventually, many such localised schemes were adopted where spotters, on roofs, would watch for the approach of a V1 and, only if it were heading for the establishment concerned, would a local warning be given, just in time for everyone to rush to the nearest shelter to take immediate cover. It must have been a nerve-wracking existence.

At official level a number critical decisions were taken. Firstly, the obvious conclusion was drawn that there was no benefit in the anti-aircraft guns shooting down the V1s over London. Experience had shown that very few exploded in the air when hit and the effect was to simply guarantee the missiles would plunge down onto the capital. Secondly, the need to avoid mass casualties, as had happened at the Guards Chapel, resulted in a decision to discourage large numbers of people from gathering in one place. The Underground was again discussed and the dangers of the system being breached by a missile impacting in the river near Charing Cross were evaluated. The expert advice was that the V1s fuzing system was very efficient and almost always functioned immediately on impact and therefore would explode on hitting the water. Consequently, the tunnels under the Thames were not considered to be at grave risk.

As the V1s continued to rain down on them, the people of London became more and more anxious and morale was unquestionably shaken. The detonation of a ton of explosive in London could be heard reverberating for several miles. The effect of the weather which, during the early period of the offensive was close, wet and cloudy, meant that the sound of the explosion would reflect off the clouds and roll around like distant thunder. The cloud of course also shielded the V1s from the attentions of fighter command, from those guns whose fire was not radar controlled, and from the eyes of the victims below. In a nation already obsessed with the weather, it was as if the elements were conspiring against the people as well. Even the strict censorship, although necessary, had its impact; the bland statements emanating from the censors and reiterated by the press stuck to the official line. It was southern England that was being bombed, the attacks were of little significance and the people, as always, were coping magnificently. Londoners knew differently, particularly those who had been the victims of a near miss, and there were many of these.

Perversely, there was little sympathy from the rest of the country. It was observed that this indifference, from outside the flying bomb impact area, was due to the fact that the war had taught all the people in the country to become a great deal more callous than they used to be. After years of conflict and its hardships, they were content with dealing with their own troubles without worrying about other people. Home Intelligence reports confirmed that, in the Midlands in particular, the population were apathetic to the Londoner's experience of flying bomb attacks. The blanket ban on reporting damage and casualties made people elsewhere think the flying bombs were not actually much of a problem. Londoners felt that the rest of the country did not understand what they were going through. To remedy this lack of understanding it was suggested that London should be designated as the principle target of the flying bombs, but this did not happen.

Many of those wealthy enough or lucky enough to have relatives outside London once again took the decision to self-evacuate, a visible sign of fear which was, of course, no comfort to those who had to stay behind. London had been tidied up since the end of the Blitz, the streets had long since been cleared, dangerous buildings had been demolished, damaged buildings repaired, glass replaced and all the normal services restored. It seemed such a regressive step to have to go through all the pain and hardship again. As Lord Alanbrooke said, speaking on behalf of all Londoners: 'Flying bombs have again put us in the front line.'

As June progressed the casualty figures grew disturbingly. In the worst month of the Blitz in September 1940, 5,546 people were killed and just over 7,000 injured in the London region; in the fourteen days and nights of flying bomb attacks up to the morning of 29 June 1944, 1,679 people had been killed and about 5,000 injured. The damage, too, was significantly worse. In the Blitz many of the bombs dropped were the small 50kg type. Groups of these were, overall, less destructive in terms of blast than the single bigger bombs. Furthermore, other than the parachute mines, even the larger German bombs penetrated the ground or buildings before detonating, which reduced the blast effect. This was not the case with V1 which detonated instantly on impact and therefore the blast was directed outwards at its most destructively efficient level. This high level of destruction took everyone by surprise. By 27 June over 200,000 houses had been damaged to a greater or lesser extent. It was estimated that 22,000 homes were being damaged or destroyed every twenty-four hours, and that in the worst case, a single V1 landing in the middle of a residential area could damage, to varying degrees, 1,000 homes. These figures climbed remorselessly as the days passed. By 30 July it was reported that 17,540 homes were completely demolished with a further 800,000 damaged, of which three quarters had been rendered habitable by emergency repairs.

It rapidly became clear to those in authority that this damage was, potentially, the most serious threat posed by the V1. People displaced from their homes had to move in with relatives and friends or into temporary relief centres. It was an awful process repeated thousands of times all over London. In the worst case, the occupants of houses would be dragged out of the wreckage of their homes by the rescue services. If they were not too badly injured or shocked, then the miserable task of trying to salvage a few precious possessions would begin. For those at work when their house was struck they would return in the evening, expecting to find all their creature comforts, only to discover that they were gone or seriously damaged. As one woman simply recalled: 'A policeman took me to where my home had been.'

For many this was a massive psychological shock, and not something that was easily overcome, particularly for the more elderly victims who saw all their worldly goods reduced to rubble. It was a heart breaking and soul destroying experience and was far removed from the official accounts of cheerful resignation displayed in the heavily censored press.

To redress the problem the highest priority was accorded to the task of repairing damaged homes to at least make them habitable and restore the basic services of water, light and gas. Initially most of the work was left to private building companies organised by the local authorities. It rapidly became apparent, that this was not enough and rapid-repair squads were established which could rapidly patch up slightly damaged houses in which tiles had been blown off roofs and windows shattered, the aim being to make them quickly weatherproof and therefore habitable. To supply the workforce at its peak, two million tiles and the same number of roof slates were being supplied to London each week. It was estimated that, in total, 150 million would be needed along with 400,000 doors and millions of square feet of glass.

Before June was out there was to be another dreadful incident. Two bombs landed in the West End; the first, just after midday, hit the roof of the annexe to the Regent's Park Hotel in Brewer Street. It killed a chambermaid and injured many people, but the general consensus of the rescue teams was that it could have been worse. The next bomb, an hour later, detonated in the Aldwych. Sweeping in a wide crescent and linking the Strand, Fleet Street and Kingsway, the area was home to a number of important buildings. They included the lofty and massive BBC building at Bush House, the Air Ministry in Adastral House and Australia House an imposing building in Doric classical style. It was also home to the Waldorf Hotel and the Aldwych and Strand Theatres as well as a selection of smaller shops and businesses.

It was the end of lunch time and lots of people in the crescent were in the open returning to their offices or visiting the local banks and post offices. The V1 plummeted into the roadway almost midway between Bush House and the Air Ministry HQ in Adastral House. It may have struck a vehicle and detonated because in the pictures of the scene there is not even a small crater which you would expect from a bomb of this size. Across the road, a ten-foot-high blast wall, designed to shield the lower levels of Adastral House, did its work protecting that part of the building, but was shattered in the process. The mass construction of the surrounding buildings was fortunately strong enough to stand up to the forces unleashed by the explosion, and thankfully none of them collapsed catastrophically. Even so the shock wave ripped through the windows shattering furniture, fixtures and fittings. Several buses which outwardly look like solid affairs, showed their weakness, and had their thin red metal bodies totally stripped away leaving only the bent and twisted chassis.

For those members of the public walking through the area, some of whom had ducked into doorways when they heard the V1's motor quit, there was no escape. They were killed by a combination of blast and fragments. Their bodies lay crumpled in the street up against the walls of buildings where they had been blown by the blast. As the dust cleared, dazed, shocked and stunned people began to stumble out of the surrounding buildings.

A BBC employee recalled: 'It was as if a foggy November evening had materialised at the throw of a switch, through the dust and smoke the casement of the bomb lay burning in a corner of Kingsway: three victims lay unmoving at the top of the steps only thirty yards from where we had crouched and huddled figures were scattered all over the road.' One of them was War Department Police Constable George Pitman who had been on duty outside Adastral House.

The Westminster Civil Defence control had a flying column of rescue and ambulance vehicles on the way to the incident moments after the impact. They arrived at a scene of utter carnage. The whole area was strewn with debris, rubble from the buildings, twisted bits of metal from the buses, the remains of the V1 itself, and splintered bits of wood from the tree-lined crescent. Amongst this detritus lay the dead and severely wounded, with the less seriously injured stumbling around still shocked and dazed and waiting for assistance.

First aid centres were opened up in nearby buildings to give initial treatment to the lightly wounded. Fortunately, a convoy of military trucks were nearby and they were requisitioned and redirected to the scene to take the lightly wounded to nearby hospitals. The fire service arrived and doused several areas with water to prevent fires becoming established. Meanwhile, some of the wardens and the first aid men went to each body to verify they were dead, a ghastly and distasteful task. Many other individuals, including off duty military personnel, attended the incident and offered assistance where they could. One man, lying confused and shocked, was gently lifted up and a lighted cigarette placed into his lips. Others stood and stared, not sure what to do.

In stark contrast to this scene of death and destruction, there is a photograph taken of a bus in Fleet Street, less than a mile from the Aldwych which shows the rest of the population continuing with their daily lives oblivious of the slaughter. The bus which the people are alighting from, had almost certainly just come from the Aldwych. A delay of a couple of minutes in departing could have had them at the impact point. Alternatively, a slightly different setting on the missile could have resulted in it impacting in Fleet Street instead. What the picture demonstrates, so forcefully, is the fact that despite the omnipresent danger people had no choice but to carry on with their lives as best they could in the prevailing circumstances.

Back at the Aldwych, the scene was rapidly being returned to some semblance of normality. The wounded were gone, the dead and remains of the dead recovered into the grey mortuary vans, and the fire brigade had washed away the blood with their hoses. Teams of salvage men arrived to clear the rubble from the streets and begin rudimentary repairs to the buildings. The WVS set up an incident inquiry point and began to collate the casualty list, not an easy task because so many of the victims were passers-by who just happened to be in the area when the V1 exploded. Nevertheless, the women volunteers quickly and efficiently handled the hundreds of enquiries about the casualties. Most of the people working in the area commuted into the Central London and, for many relatives, it was not until they failed to turn up at home that evening that they got the first inkling that all was not well. The lucky amongst them found their loved ones in hospitals.

At a time when the Allies were clearly winning the war, the official need to evacuate large number of Londoners from their homes at the start of the V1 campaign seemed to be a regressive and unnecessary course of action. It was an acknowledgement that the Germans were not defeated and that they could still inflict serious casualties and significant damage on the capital. The government had made provisional plans for the evacuation of four priority classes of people. These were: women with children under five; children of school age; expectant mothers; and the old and infirm. Even so, by 27 June, no formal decision had been taken to execute this plan, but as the casualties mounted it became clear that this was an unacceptable state of affairs and on 1 July orders went out for the evacuation to start. The first parties departed on 3 July and an announcement was made in the House of Commons on 6 July confirming the process had started. Once again the question must be asked, was it the detonation of the Aldwych V1, so close to Whitehall where all those in power worked, which contributed to the decision to finally give the order to evacuate the most vulnerable?

Another unfortunate set of people who had to be added to the four groups above, and who had to be assisted with evacuation, were those who had already been bombed out of their homes. What, though, if you did not fit into one of the special categories? The official line was that those engaged in essential war work should remain and Churchill made it clear in this respect that Parliament and the major government departments would stay put. However, citizens who were not engaged in vital war work were encouraged to leave, although absolutely no help to do so was provided by the government. After the beginning of the official evacuation, it is estimated that almost 1,500,000 Londoners left the capital, and in addition to this must be added those who had gone of their own accord in the proceeding weeks since the arrival of the first V1.

There was, of course, a danger inherent in mass evacuation and that was the concentration of large numbers of evacuees at mainline stations. The movement of such vast numbers of people was never going to be a slick and smooth process; there were insufficient trains, overcrowding and the inevitable long queues. Those being evacuated would all have already been subjected to the effects of the V1, some physically and all mentally. There was a widespread fear of being killed while patiently waiting for a place on a train that would remove them from the danger. Paddington Station, in particular, was overwhelmed and the situation became serious despite the best efforts of the staff. There were unruly stampedes for trains and, as always in these cases, the fittest and strongest won. One observer noted that a young mother went over to join an older lady with three small children, her face a picture of fatigue, desperation and fear. She remarked, 'It's no use. We can't get away,' and with that she burst into tears.

On 2 July 1944, the Germans reached their peak efficiency when 161 flying bombs crossed the coast. In that same week ending on 8 July, a total of 820 bombs were plotted. More than fifty percent of these bombs reached their London target.

On 3 July another serious V1 incident occurred, but this time many of the casualties were American soldiers. At 07.45 hours a bomb struck Turks Row in Chelsea, which had been used as a 'casual centre' to base an odd variety of American units. Most of the men involved had been on their way to help civilians who had been hurt in an attack earlier that morning near Lambeth. Some of the men were loaded on trucks waiting to move and the remainder were sitting in the street waiting for more transport. The bomb was heard approaching by one of the men's officers, Captain Smith, who ordered them to scatter, but it was too late. One of the five storey blocks of flats collapsed under the effects of the explosion and falling masonry caused many of the casualties. In total, sixty-four American servicemen were killed along with ten civilians.

The worst day for the number of V1s actually reaching the capital was 2 August 1944. The Germans launched salvos of missiles, most of them during the night, and a total of ninety-seven exploded inside Greater London. For the citizens who Alanbrooke had described as 'being in the front line once again', particularly those in the south of the capital, it meant that one ton bombs were exploding, at random every few minutes. Of the urban districts, Penge was the worst afflicted. In eighty days every single one of its 6,000 homes was destroyed or damaged, two thirds of them being hit more than once. One in twenty of its population (after the evacuation of women and children) had been killed or injured.

As well as the casualties, which were serious enough, one historic building a day was being destroyed or severely damaged. Some of those which had survived the Blitz now succumbed to high explosives. In Holborn, the lovely Staple Inn was flattened; in Westminster, St Georges Church was hit; in the City, Customs House and five Churches were wrecked; in Greenwich, Charlton House was demolished; in Camberwell, Dulwich College was struck and in Southwark; the Cathedral was badly damaged. Some buildings had lucky escapes, including Tower Bridge which was the Germans' central aiming point. Two V1s actually arrived precisely on this target. On 12 July 1944, a bomb hit 100 yards west of the Tower, just missing the tug *Naga* which was damaged and sunk. The bridge itself suffered slight damage from blast. Then on 3 August another bomb in its final plunge struck the ornamental cast iron work on the crest of the bridge on the North Tower, detonating moments afterwards when it hit the water. The roofing on both Towers was damaged and the bridge which was in the 'up' position had to be closed until a further assessment of the damage could be made.[5]

For one group of men, the V1 was not posing quite so much of a problem as expected and that was London's bomb disposal units. The Germans had solved many of their reliability problems and by using two or three different fuzes in each warhead only a very small percentage of V1s failed to explode after impact, including those that were shot down.

The reliability of the fuzing system was, however, by no means duplicated in the rest of the V1's systems. As well as a high percentage of missiles crashing on take-off, many others developed strange and curious habits, not all of which might be laid at the door of non-lethal damage by fragments or bullets from the defenders' guns. The results proved both interesting if not unnerving for the people of London.

There were 'circlers', 'twisters' and routine 'divers', the last-named not linked to the codeword for their use, but for those bombs that plunged earthward with their engines still running. Worse still were the 'floaters' or the 'gliders'. These were missiles in which the fuel ran out, or the fuel system failed, and the bomb glided on, silently, to their impact point sometimes covering many miles. An official American report based on 205 incidents showed that rogue V1s were not uncommon and that four percent of them power-dived to impact. In other cases, there were glides of ten seconds or more. The longest being 202 seconds, in which time a missile, decelerating from some 400 miles an hour, could have travelled an extra ten miles.

Although hit many times, Central London did not suffer as much as the southern boroughs. The majority of the early missiles landed south of the River Thames, in slightly less populated areas. One of the key pieces of information needed to get the V1s close to their aiming point was detailed weather information which, of course, was denied to the Germans. If the speed of the wind, which is generally westerly over the British Isle, was under estimated then the outcome would be that the missiles would inevitably drop short. Incorrectly predicting the wind speed would affect the German's range calculations and the settings needed to place the mean point of impact of the V1s on the Tower of London.

Because of the Germans' inability to fly aerial photographic reconnaissance missions, the outcome was that they were effectively firing blind. Senior officials were aware of this, and the Ministry of Information's insistence on using the phrase that the attacks were on southern England denied the Germans any assistance on plotting their fall of shot. This, however, did provide scope for deception, by allowing details of missiles impacting in northwest London to be reported. This was possible and could be done by feeding false information to captured and turned German agents who were thought to be operating freely in Britain. The result of such deception could lead the Germans to shorten the range even further and hence move the mean point of impact further back into south London. Politically it was not that easy a decision to make.

It was argued that this would cause some of the missiles that fell short anyway to fall in open country before reaching the outskirts of London, and although more people would be killed or injured in the south, overall the casualty rate would be reduced. This plan caused an agonised debate in the Cabinet Office. Herbert Morrison, the MP for Lambeth, argued that, 'We must not play God' in deciding where the bombs might fall. He considered that any attempt to divert bombs from the Westminster, Mayfair and Belgravia area on to the proletariat in the south was simply unacceptable. In the back of their minds the Cabinet must also have been concerned that if the plan went ahead and news of it leaked out then there would have been uproar in south London. Despite the official line, and the policy adopted by the Cabinet office that it would be wrong to intervene with where the V1s fell, there is some evidence to suggest that the plan, unapproved, went ahead.

When the V1 launching sites were overrun in Europe, a map was discovered which detailed where the Germans thought the flying bombs were landing. This showed their agents' reports of impacts, recorded as black dots, in the central and northwest areas of London. In some V1s the Germans fitted radio transmitters which enabled them to roughly plot the real impacts points. These were also plotted on the map and showed dots mainly to the southeast of London. Had the Germans trusted these and not the agents' reports then the missiles mean point of impact would almost certainly have been adjusted north. The final proof comes from an analysis of actual V1 explosions plotted by Civil Defence regions. It shows clearly that the numbers south of the river were significantly higher than those in the north, Croydon having the highest total of 141 hits.

A major review of the defences was undertaken in early July 1944. It was decided that the system in place, consisting of fighters, guns and balloon defences, was badly coordinated and needed revision. The guns were sited around the North Downs in a five-mile belt and the fighters operated freely all over the southeast. As always, much was dependent on the weather. On good days, the fighters had priority and the guns were silent, on medium days the guns could fire but not if a fighter was pursuing a V1. On bad days the guns had priority. This did not work well and several fighters were shot down.

It was therefore decided to move the guns to the coastline and give them free reign over the narrow costal belt. Either side of this the fighters had priority, and as a final line of defence, there was a balloon barrage on the edge of Greater London. This plan was adopted late on 13 July and after a massive logistical effort most of the guns were in place four days later. Although the fighter success rate declined, the guns, many using new proximity-fuzed ammunition, began to take their toll on the flying bombs and the overall kill-rate increased. This grew from a poor twenty-four percent in the first week of the campaign to an outstanding seventy-four percent in the last week of August.

The members of the Civil Defence organisation, once again, made an enormous contribution to the eventual defeat of the flying bomb. Observation officers on posts on high buildings all over London plotted the course and the fall of the missiles. This information was relayed to the National Fire Service and the rescue services and teams were immediately dispatched to the devastated areas. The response was such that, after an explosion, the flying columns of rescuers and firefighters were almost immediately on scene and many lives were saved by their timely interventions. Flying bombs landing on or close to a building brought down tons of rubble, but also left voids where people in Morrison shelters, hiding under stairs or even stout tables might survive.

Extracting them was a difficult and dangerous task. More often than not it would prove impossible to move heavy debris without the risk of further collapse so the firemen and rescue squads would tunnel into the areas containing the trapped and often wounded and frightened people. It was a hazardous business at the best of times. It called for a mixture of delicately removing debris combined with the acceptance of a high degree of personal risk by the rescuers if they were to get people out. A false move could leave both victims and helpers dead.

As always, the police made their contribution. In Chelsea during August 1944 a flying bomb hit an accommodation block being used by the Women's Auxiliary Air Force. Police Sergeant Fred Harding lived nearby and was in his bed when he was woken by the blast. He dressed quickly and was one of the first on scene. With some other local residents, he made his way to the top floor where he knew the women's dormitory was situated. Once there he was horrified by what he saw:

> The sight that met us is hard to describe. There seemed to be dozens
> of hospital type cast iron beds, all displaced, upside down or on their
> sides. Bed linen and female clothing where everywhere ... The
> background was dominated by the pitiful sight of the women. Some
> were trapped and dead, some were trapped and screaming. A few
> were moving about like zombies. The irony of that incident is that all
> those women were supposed to be sleeping in the undamaged brick
> air raid shelters across the street. They had ignored the order and,
> regretfully, had suffered accordingly.[6]

The threat posed by the ground-launched V1s was finally ended when the Allies overran the launching sites in France in early September 1944. This brought some relief, but by then the Germans were air-launching the missiles from aircraft over the North Sea; in fact, the first had been launched this way in July. Fortunately, they were never deployed in large numbers or posed the same threat as the waves of ground-launched missiles.

In the overall context of the battle against the V1s they were to prove a nuisance rather than a serious menace, but those that did get through still maimed and killed. The final fling for the V1 came in 1945 when, in March that year, a series of modified missiles with smaller warheads and longer range were launched from Holland. These will be examined in the next chapter.

Between 13 June and 1 September 1944, some 2,419 V1 missiles had detonated across London causing much death and destruction, but the loss of the launching sites, and better defences, gave good reasons to think the worst was over. The Home Security Intelligence summary for the twelve hours ending on 5 September 1944, recorded that there was no reported activity with flying bombs or aircraft.

Two days later Mr Duncan Sandys, (later Lord) announced that 'except possibly for a few last shots, the Battle of London is over'. It is dangerous to predict things in war with such certainty and less than twenty-four hours later he would be proved decisively wrong.

NOTES:
1. Jones, R.V., *op. cit.*
2. Keesing's contemporary archives, 10-17 June, Page 6505.
3. Brooks, Geoffrey, *Hitler's Nuclear Weapons*, Leo Cooper, London, 1992.
4. Wallington, Neil, *Firemen at War, David and Charles*, Newton Abbot, 1990.
5. TNA, PRO 192/602: Air Raid Damage No.5 Region Tower Bridge.
6. Ingleton, Roy, *op. cit.*

Chapter 16

The V2s – City of Silent Death

'What an awe inspiring murder weapon.'
Goebbels, 23 September 1943.

Reminiscent of the first Zeppelin bombing of London on 31 May 1915, and the first V1 in June 1944, the first V2 rocket which exploded in the capital was a formidable technical achievement. It was the result of years of dedicated work by the scientists and engineers of the Third Reich. Other similarities included: poor accuracy which made it totally indiscriminate, the lack of warning, and the underlying aim, which was to spread terror in its wake. The most poignant comparison, however, must be that, like little Elsie Leggatt in the First War and baby Tom Woodcraft killed by the V1 at Grove Road, the first V2 killed an innocent toddler, three-year-old Rosemary Clarke who died in her cot. She was killed by the first rocket fired at London which was launched at precisely 18.38 hours on 8 September 1944, and which hurtled back to earth and detonated five minutes later in Staveley Road, Chiswick.

Rosemary was in the front upstairs bedroom of the house; her six-year-old brother John was lucky to be in the bathroom at the rear of the building. He was shocked and dazed by the effect of the blast but survived although a piece of the rocket casing hit the back of his hand leaving a scar. He later recalled that there was not a mark on his sister but that the blast had collapsed her lungs and killed her.

Exactly sixty years later a small memorial was erected near the spot where the missile fell. A few months later, on 8 May 2005, representatives from Chiswick planted a cherry tree as a symbol of peace and reconciliation at Peenemünde, the birthplace of the rocket where there is now a museum. The choice of a cherry tree was particularly symbolic because Staveley Road had been laid out with the new and fashionable oriental cherry (Prunus Kazan) in the 1920s. Today the difference in the thickness of the old trees and those planted in the late 1940s show the extent of the damaged caused by the V2 rocket's warhead.

Back in 1944 there were no thoughts of reconciliation. The people in west London and many in other areas had heard the detonation of the warhead, followed almost immediately by the sonic boom it left in its wake. Most were not too perturbed, unexplained explosions in London were not, at that time, rare and therefore they were unaware that they had witnessed the start of a new era in the history of warfare.

London cannot claim to be the first city hit by a ballistic missile. The Paris suburbs had been struck by a rocket some ten hours earlier. No one there though realized the explosion had been caused by a new weapon of war or its significance, so the information was not passed back to London. The successful strikes on both capitals were the culmination of fourteen years' work. Back in the 1930s, the German Army had selected thirty-five-year-old Captain Walter Dorenberger to run its rocket research program. Although rockets had been around in various forms for centuries, the use of solid propellants with very short burning times meant that it was only possible to launch small rockets over limited ranges. Dorenberger's vision was to prolong the thrust of the rocket motor by using high-energy liquid propellants which were fed into a combustion chamber and which could burn for prolonged periods. This would provide the necessary power to accelerate a missile smoothly into the stratosphere where it would decelerate, and then under the effects of gravity tip over for its descent back to earth. Such a system would achieve ranges never before reached by any gun or existing rocket. To support him, Dornberger recruited a number of scientists who together had the necessary basic understanding of physics, had the right technical and engineering skills and, most importantly, had the imagination and vision to drive the project forward. Amongst them was a young man named Werner von Braun who much later would be pivotal in supporting the Americans in their quest to put man on the moon.

The development of a rocket designed to carry a military payload continued throughout the 1930s. Despite constant failures and other setbacks, Dorenberger's team solved one problem then another until they had successfully designed and launched a number of prototypes. Immersed in their work, most of them took no notice of the changing political situation and the rise of the Nazis, other than to be relieved that the new regime was willing to continue to pump money and resources into the project. In March 1939, Hitler visited the development site at Peenemünde, but apparently was unimpressed and failed to grasp the potential of the weapon. However, two days after the outbreak of the Second World War the Commander in Chief of the German Army, General Von Brauchitsch, gave his formal support to the project. In doing so he sealed the fate of many of London's citizens some five years later. The task facing the German scientists should not be underrated; not only did they have to develop a wide range of new technologies, they also had to arrange for the mass production of the V2. This required the construction of new factories with specialist production lines manned, initially at least, by the cream of Germany's technicians. By mid-1943, with the war turning against him, Hitler was persuaded to listen to another brief on the rocket programme. This time with the aid of models and a film of successful firings, the Führer was convinced of the rockets' potential.

The final product was known simply as the A4 rocket. Overall it was forty-six feet in length and five feet in diameter at its widest point. It was made in three sections. The nose contained the warhead, fuzes and the control compartment; the mid-section held the alcohol and liquid oxygen fuel tanks; and the rear section, the turbine pump system, the motor chamber and venturi, the exhaust control vanes and the four large stabilising fins. Fully loaded with nine tons of fuel, the rocket weighed thirteen and a half tons. The business end, the warhead, contained almost a ton or, to be precise, 738 kilograms of high explosive. The missile was able to attain hitherto unheard of speeds of up to 3,600 miles an hour; its maximum range was estimated at 225 miles and during its flight it reached an altitude of between 50-60 miles.

The British intelligence services had been aware for some time that the Germans were trying to develop long-range rockets and R.V. Jones was again in the forefront of evaluating the sketchy information received. Evidence from various sources had been analysed and although, there were many who remained sceptical, there was no doubt that some form of rocket was being developed. The worst case scenario hinted that the rocket could weigh seventy tons and carry a ten-ton warhead. This was more than sufficient to cause alarm in government circles. Duncan Sandys, the minister responsible, warned that heavy attacks of this kind against London might seriously affect the Allies' capacity to wage war, particularly if gas was used. Further investigations, and especially the results of photo reconnaissance, convinced the war planners that the facilities at Peenemünde needed the attention of Bomber Command. This was authorised in Churchill's rocket meeting in June 1943. In August a force of heavy bombers struck Peenemünde in three waves, totalling some 586 aircraft. They dropped

1,600 tons of high explosives and 250 tons of incendiary bombs. From an Allied point of view the results looked outstandingly successful and much of the site seemed to have been destroyed. In fact, although there was some serious damage and a few key personnel were killed, the destruction was far less severe than had been thought. Dorenberger later estimated that the rocket program had only been delayed by a month or two.

By October 1943, an order had been placed for the mass production of 12,000 rockets. To escape Allied bombing, component production was dispersed, and the final assembly of the missiles was switched to a new and secret facility in underground caves near Nordhausen in the Hartz Mountains. The workforce there consisted mainly of thousands of slave labourers who were to suffer grievously at the hands of their SS guards. There was inadequate food, brutal treatment and constant hard work for over twelve hours a day. The morality rate was, not surprisingly, very high. Fortunately for London the production of such a complicated and technically advanced project was much more difficult than expected and the Germans were never able to produce the numbers of rockets they planned, or achieve the quality of build that was required for high reliability.

Through the spring and summer of 1944 more and more intelligence confirming the existence of the rocket, and which also more accurately predicted its capabilities, reached the Allies. One of the conclusions drawn from the study of the information was that other than offensive air attacks on the launching grounds and production facilities, there was no defence against a V2 rocket once it had been launched. There was genuine concern that if the rockets started landing on London whilst the V1 campaign was still in full swing then the complimentary effects on morale could be overwhelming.

It was realized that the only practical thing that could be done was to deny the Germans any information about the accuracy and success rate of the rockets by a total news blackout. The Home Secretary's right-hand man, Sir Findlater Stewart, was given the task. Draconian measures were put in place to implement this strategy which, in many ways, was more stringent than those that had been employed for D-Day. They included the suspension of all diplomatic mail; a total ban on overseas travel except for members of the armed forces; the virtual cessation of postal and telegraph services; and close monitoring of, or cutting off, telephone calls, particularly those to Ireland. It was considered that these activities could be maintained for a week to ten days after the first missile impact. In addition, the American and Russian embassies, who had their own secure wireless communications with their mother countries, were approached by the Foreign Secretary and asked not to relay details of the rockets, as it was known that the Germans monitored their frequencies and it was not clear how secure their codes were. Passive defensive measures were also reviewed and plans were put in place for further evacuation of the capital's population.

One question which continued to plague the intelligence community was the cost-effectiveness of such a rocket system and why the Germans were pursuing it. Lord Cherwell was particularly sceptical, claiming that in terms of economic resources the construction of the V2 for the bombardment of London logically made absolutely no sense. It was left for R.V. Jones to answer this difficult question. He argued that a rational approach to the problem could not be applied to the rocket and that the policy decisions driving its development had more to do with fantasy and romance than cold and clear analysis of its true potential. He argued that no other weapon yet produced had such romantic appeal. Here was a thirteen-ton missile, which, on launch, traced a flaming trail to heights never yet reached by man, and then hurled itself 200 miles across the stratosphere at unparalleled speed to descend on a defenceless target. He concluded by saying:

> One of the greatest realizations of human power is the ability to destroy at a distance, and the Nazeus would call down his thunderbolts on all who displeased him. Perhaps we may be permitted to express a slight envy of his ability, if not to destroy his victims, at least to raise one of the biggest scares in history by virtue of the inverted romance with which those victims regard the rocket.[1]

By early September 1944, Jones concluded that a heavy rocket attack could not be mounted before the middle of the month mainly due to the rapid advance of the Allied armies across Europe. However, he did concede that this might cause the Germans to launch a smaller effort sooner than this. On 6 September the Vice-Chiefs of Staff advised that the threat was over and the following day Duncan Sandys made his premature announcement at a press conference that the battle for London was won. The next morning the papers came out with suitable headlines and a picture of Sandys proclaiming the end of the battle. The relief felt by Londoners reading the morning papers was immense, but regrettably would be short-lived. That evening, as R.V. Jones was working, there was an ominous double bang. He looked up at a colleague and said simply: 'That's the first one!' The importance of underestimating the enemy could not have been more clearly demonstrated.

At Chiswick, outside 5 Staveley Road, there was a scene of total devastation. A crater some seven metres deep and fifteen metres across had appeared in the road. On either side, the closest of the neat suburban semi-detached houses had been totally destroyed by the blast. The one small blessing was that, when compared to the V1, the effect of the blast was slightly reduced because the speed of the missile was such that, even with a quick acting fuze, the warhead partially buried itself before it functioned.

The sound of the sonic boom which followed moments after the explosion of the warhead had rumbled right across London. Less than a minute after the first missile hit, a second plummeted into open country at Parndon Wood in Epping. It left another large crater and damaged much of the wood, but fortunately did not cause any casualties. Within the hour, Herbert Morrison, the Home Secretary, Duncan Sandys and many others were at the scene in Chiswick to see first-hand the effects of the new missile. The rescue operation was in full swing with three heavy and five light rescue teams working to release the trapped and recover the dead. By 20.15 hours, just ninety minutes after the impact, the site was cleared of all known casualties.

As well as little Rosemary Clarke, a soldier on leave, Frank Browning, who was walking down the street, was killed instantly by the blast. The third victim, Mrs Ada Harrison, managed to crawl out of her demolished house but sadly died a few moments later in the arms of a local caretaker who had rushed to help. There was significant damage to houses slightly further away from the centre of the blast, with cracked walls, broken windows and stripped roofs in a circle well over a hundred yards in diameter. There were ten serious injuries in these houses and a further ten slightly wounded. That the casualty figures were so low was largely down to the fact that, as a result of the V1 attacks, three of the closest houses to the centre of the explosion were empty. Additionally, many of the local residents were still at work when the missile exploded. At the final count, eleven houses were beyond repair and their remains were demolished; fifteen more had to be evacuated whilst extensive repairs were carried out. A further twelve required significant structural work, but were just habitable. Another 556 suffered slight damage of various kinds.

Sir Findlater Stewart's plans for a total news blackout were immediately implemented. At Staveley Road onlookers and reporters had gathered at the edge of the cordons. Some seem to have been told that a gas main had exploded, although a few, particularly the reporters, were not convinced and soon stories were being filed with the editors of their newspapers about a new missile. They immediately submitted them to the censor, most of them knowing what the outcome would be before the stories reached the government offices. Nothing was to be reported, but everyone knew this news blackout could not be sustained for long. Over the next few days a succession of missiles with their familiar trademark double bang hit the capital. There then followed a slightly ridiculous period when rumours spread like wild fire by word of mouth and almost everyone knew or guessed that some new rocket weapon had arrived, but nobody admitted it publicly. There was much gossip about the mysterious explosions that were echoing across the capital. Loyal citizens, not wishing to adopt a defeatist attitude, talked of ammunition dumps, delayed-action bombs, long-range shelling by German ships, gasometers and even large boilers exploding. Of all the explanations, the exploding gasometer was the one that was tacitly encouraged by the authorities.

On 14 September the daily report on the opinion of Londoners highlighted some of the concerns about the new rocket attack. There was a general feeling of anxiety and defencelessness. Those people questioned felt a government statement was at least necessary to stop refugees returning after the announcement by Duncan Sandys on 7 September and to alleviate the feeling of helplessness and mystery which surrounded the new rockets. Like the V1 attacks, there was concern that those in the rest of the country would have little sympathy for the Londoners in the face of the new assault, particularly in the absence of an official statement on the subject. Action needed to be taken to ensure that the provinces were able to play their part in the defeat of the new threat within the confines of the overall security situation. This included the suggestion that those responsible for allocating billets to refugees should be taken to south London to see first-hand the devastating effects of the new forms of warfare.

The Germans stepped up the V2 launch rate and by the end of September thirty-six rockets had fallen on targets in England, most of them on London. It had been hoped that it might be possible to provide some brief warning of a missile's approach, but it was soon acknowledged that this was simply out of the question. Within the general public there was considerable ill-feeling and a lack of understanding concerning what the authorities were doing about the rockets. Of course, as they had not been officially acknowledged there was little that could be publicly said or done. But it was becoming obvious that the secrecy surrounding the V2s was beginning to be counterproductive and making people cynical about the reasons for the total news blackout. In one case, at an explosion in Walthamstow, when the Regional Commissioner enquired about the time of the incident, he was contemptuously told by a Civil Defence worker, 'The delayed action bomb fell at 04.45 hours sir'.

The only good news was that the scale of the attack was much less than that of the flying bombs and the Civil Defence services were, by now, well-able to cope with the aftermath of a rocket explosion. The maximum number of rockets that had fallen in a day was five and this had occurred only on two occasions, on 16 and 17 September.

Part of the reason for delaying an announcement about the V2 rockets was that it had been hoped that Operation *Market Garden*, which included the attempt to seize the bridge over the Rhine at Arnhem, would result in the liberation of most of Holland. This would have brought the majority of the V2 launching sites under the control of the Allies and halted the attacks. In fact, after the initial airborne landings there had been a temporary halt in the firings, but with failure of the operation the Germans resumed their V2 offensive.

Fortunately for Londoners, the missiles' reliability was still a major problem and in the first three weeks of October only six of the sixty-three missiles fired by the Germans reached the London Civil Defence Region. This made it easier for the policy of silence to be maintained, but it could not last. In the last week of the month twenty-six missiles fell on the capital. On 30 October, V2s hit the Becton Gas works, Victoria docks and Hermitage Wharf in Wapping and the following day five more hit as far apart as Hendon and Croydon.

Some of the rockets fired suffered from an unknown problem which resulted in them air-bursting high over London. This happened at Hendon where fragments of various sizes were scattered over a mile in area. The beginning of November was no better and the list of strikes grew daily as well as the casualty lists and the destruction and damage to property.

In the week ending 8 November 1944, twelve more missiles struck; worryingly the grouping seemed to be improving and more were impacting close to what was considered to be the mean point of impact which was, once again, Tower Bridge. Two of the missiles landed within a mile of this aiming point.

With the onset of winter the people faced another miserable period of what the *North London Press* recorded as 'rheumatism, colds and all kinds of ailments due to dampness and draughts as a result of bomb damaged homes'. Thousands of properties required work to make them weatherproof. It is estimated that during the V1 and V2 offensive 30,000 homes were totally destroyed and a further 1,250,000 damaged. It was a burden shouldered almost exclusively by Londoners, as the majority of other major cities escaped attack.

Officially, of course, nothing was happening and it was hard for those Londoners who had to live through it. Missiles were now falling at the rate of three to five a day, with one in ten air-bursting high in the sky. Of course, within the general target area of London, the actual point of impact was completely random. Some missiles landed in parks, woods and even the Thames, where the one-ton warheads expended their energy to little effect. Others landed in close-packed residential areas – with the inevitable casualties. At 17.13 hours on Sunday, 5 November, for example, there were 249 casualties, eighty-four of them serious, and thirty-one fatalities at Grovedale Road in Islington.

Behind the scenes the newspaper owners and some politicians were seriously questioning the continued policy of total denial. They argued that it would not be necessary to acknowledge where the rockets were landing and that the continuous rumours were now having a detrimental effect on the war effort. Another factor was that the Germans had long since disclosed the existence of the V2. They announced in September that the V1 bombardment had now been supplemented by the V2. Much to Goebbels' annoyance, the claims were reported in the British press without comment.

On 10 November, Churchill revealed to the House of Commons the existence of the V2 rocket, but did his best to play down the casualties and damage it was causing. He explained its basic capabilities and why, because of its speed, no warnings could be given. He also explained that, as the Allied armies advanced further, the launching sites would fall into their hands and it would be harder for the offensive to be maintained. He did warn, however, that this might not stop the attacks as it might be possible for the Germans to extend the range by various means. He concluded by stressing the importance of denying the enemy information on the accuracy of the missiles and asked the House, press and public for their continued support.

In the battle of the airwaves, the Germans responded by putting out a broadcast warning of the dire consequences for the British population from the rockets. In it they concluded that, 'There was no defence', and 'A period of horrible and silent death has begun for Great Britain'. In addition to the V2s, the Germans stepped up launching V1s by aircraft at night. By mid-November they were coordinating attacks, with missiles and flying bombs arriving steadily throughout the hours of darkness. Even though the numbers of both weapons getting through to London was small compared to previous assaults, it was still an unnerving and worrying time for the people.

Now, at least, Londoners could openly discuss the rockets without being branded defeatist and there was much talk. A lot of it centred on the difference between the V1 and the V2. For the man in the street the size and effects of the warheads were comparable, so the discussions were concentrated on which method of delivery generated the most dread. The V2 was feared because there was no warning and people were faced with the knowledge that they might suddenly be simply obliterated. Some of the population found this profoundly disturbing. They were, as Goebbels had said, totally defenceless, and their life or death was held firmly in the hands of the enemy some 200 miles away. Others took the view that it was better to die suddenly and without warning and pointed out that if you heard the double bang then at least you were alive, no matter what damage had been done. Conversely, the comparatively long duration of a V1 flying bomb attack aroused more fear in some people. First, there would be an air raid warning, and then the awful noise of the pulse jet as the V1 appeared overhead, and, worst still, the silence as the motor cut and the missile dived to the ground. For those in or around the impact area these were, without doubt, moments of sheer terror. (If you ran for those few seconds you could be running in to danger). In the discussions about which was worst some people argued that it was much better to have those few seconds in which to at least take some cover than the total impotence against the V2.

On 25 November 1944, the Germans managed to place a missile right in the heart of London at High Holburn. On the same day there was an awful tragedy at the Woolworths store on Goodwood Road, New Cross, where, once again, chance and fate interacted to make a fatal combination. In a time of desperate shortages of everything, the word had gone round the local community that a supply of saucepans had arrived at Woolworths and, as always, if you wanted one you had to be there early and queue. So fate dictated that a line of women, some with young children, was patiently waiting outside the shop for the arrival of the pans.

It was at this moment that a V2 struck. It hit the corner of the Woolworths building and exploded. In a blinding flash the store disintegrated as the high explosive turned bricks and mortar into dust. A cloud of black smoke drifted into the air above the demolished shop. In the street there was utter carnage. A passing Army lorry had been turned over by the blast and a bus close by spun round with some of its passengers sitting dead in blood-covered seats. The queue for the pans had ceased to exist and bits of dismembered bodies had been flung in all directions and were lying in the street. Further away there was the usual damage and casualties, some serious, some light. For a moment there was an eerie silence as the survivors, injured or otherwise, and who were simply shocked and stunned, began to grasp that something awful had happened. Then came the cries and groans of the victims as the pain of their wounds began to bite. Those who could move stumbled away from the scene or began to look for near or dear ones who had been with them, or close by, at the moment of the explosion. One Romford woman wrote:

> When I came to seconds later I found myself over the road pinned to the wall. After a second or two I was released and slid to the ground. I turned to continue my journey and a horse and cart with its driver's legs waving in the air, came wildly rushing round from Lewisham way. I was laughing hysterically. I gradually quietened down and then looked at my child and then myself. Our clothing was undone. Buttons, ribbons etc., all loose and clothing twisted and untidy. My baby's bonnet was twisted grotesquely and hung round her neck. Her hair was blown back tightly as if she had none. She was staring into space, not comprehending. Neither of us was hurt so we continued up the hill, and round the corner a rescuer stopped me and asked me where I was going. I said 'Woolworths, for a saucepan.' He gently turned me round and said, 'not today, my love. Go home and try tomorrow.

The Civil Defence services responded immediately and it was evident that they had a major incident on their hands. Police, light and heavy rescue teams, first aid parties and ambulances soon began to converge on the scene. The task of rescuing and tending the wounded and recovering the dead began. The mobile mortuary vans arrived ready to play their grisly part in the terrible tragedy. It was clear to the incident commander that such was the scale of the devastation that additional outside resources would be needed and the necessary calls were made. Soon four mobile cranes, sixteen heavy and eight light rescue squads were at work assisted by at least 100 firemen and police officers. Seven first aid posts were set up, all working hard to save the lives as casualties were recovered. When darkness fell there was still much work to be done and, ignoring the blackout, floodlights and a searchlight from a local anti-aircraft unit were positioned to provide the necessary illumination. As the temperatures dropped that cold winter evening, the rescue work went on right though until dawn. Even then, however, there were still reports of people trapped.

When the final toll of dead and injured had been tallied it made grim reading. There were 160 fatalities, seventy-even seriously injured and a further 122 with minor injuries. It is probable that this figure was higher but that many of the people with minor injuries knowing the strain the hospitals would be under simply treated themselves.

November was the worst month for casualties in London since the height of the flying bomb menace in August. In all, 716 men, women and children had been killed with a further 1,511 seriously injured. Most of the casualties were due to the V2s with just a few being caused by V1s which were still being air-launched over the North Sea. There was no lull in December with missiles arriving at the rate of some forty a week. One landed in Duke Street in the West End which did have a significant impact on morale, although it did not cause heavy casualties. People were beginning to think about Christmas and the major stores were putting out on display the meagre stocks that they had available. The missile landed at 23.00 hours by the Red Lion pub on the corner of Duke Street and Barrett Street, just off Oxford Street. Beyond the scene of immediate devastation, it shattered windows all along the country's premier shopping thoroughfare. It made many people think twice before heading into the centre of capital to do their shopping. The missile killed a number of American servicemen who had been using the Selfridge's Annexe as a canteen. It also killed some soldiers in a taxi at the centre of the blast; their remains were never found. All told, eight US servicemen were killed and a further thirty-two injured. Ten British civilians also died in the blast.

Morale in the city took a further tumble on 16 December 1944, when it was announced on the radio that the Germans had launched a major offensive through the Ardennes. Two days later the official news spokesman indicated that this was the Nazis last fling, a bit like the failed assault in March 1918, but people were getting cynical about official announcements, and for a brief period there was a nagging doubt that there might be another 'Dunkirk' in the offing. Hitler, it seemed, despite the bombing and relentless pressure on all fronts, was still able to produce nasty surprises from up his sleeve. Relentlessly the V2s kept coming right up to 24 December, but on the Christmas Day itself there was a lull.

Boxing Day saw four missiles land in the UK. The second came down in Islington at 21.26 hours. It was a freezing night and patchy fog had descended over the entire area. Dozens of people had packed the local pub, the Prince of Wales in Mackenzie Road, and were enjoying the Christmas festivities as much as they could. There were more customers than usual this night because the pub down the road had run out of beer and the patrons had headed up to the Prince of Wales were there were still some pints to be had. Some customers had gone down to the cellar, normally the safest place to drink their Christmas cheer. The V2's warhead detonated in the road outside, leaving a crater some thirteen metres across and four metres deep. It caused immense destruction locally and also shattered a major water main. In the Prince of Wales, the floor of the pub collapsed dropping on the customers in the cellar below. Then the remainder of the building fell in on top of the customers who had been in the ground floor bar. As the first fire appliance stumbled on to the eerie scene through the thickening fog they could see a number of small fires had broken out. One of the trailer pumps set its suction hoses into a water dam to get water – but nothing happened. The operator, unsure of what was happening, ran to the dam and shone his torch in through the door and saw that the water was at a normal level but was frozen solid and that the suction strainer on the end of the hose was lying on the ice. Grabbing his axe, he smashed the ice and plunged the suction hose into the water below. Meanwhile, the crater at the scene was rapidly filling up with water from the broken main.

Responders from all of the Civil Defence services were now arriving. In the black and foggy night, central command and control was almost impossible and it was difficult to grasp what had happened and what needed doing as a matter of priority. The fire service soon had the fires under control and the rescue parties, each working in isolation, were doing their best to respond to the cries of the injured. They tunnelled their way into the wreckage towards the pitiful sounds of the survivors in the cellar. It was going to be a long and arduous job which was fraught with danger. The initial estimates of casualties proved inaccurate and as time went by more and more of the dead and injured were recovered. One young lad was trapped for nineteen hours in the freezing rubble before he was freed and taken to hospital. Because of the lack of heating fuels in those cold and bleak days, people were always warmly dressed with several layers of clothing and thick coats. There is no doubt that this helped some of those trapped survive without dying of hypothermia. It would be different in today's centrally-heated world where people wear a minimum of clothing inside buildings. Even so, the final toll was nearly seventy dead and 260 injured.

The New Year brought little cheer for the beleaguered people of London with two out of six missiles launched hitting the capital. On 3 January 1945, a V2 smashed into the grounds of the Royal Hospital at Chelsea. It brought back painful memories of the attack on the night of 16-17 February 1918 when a 300kg bomb had destroyed part of the building and killed five people. This time the V2 landed in almost exactly the same spot. The blast destroyed the North East Wing in Light Horse Court. Again five people were killed. They included Major William Napier, a surgeon at the hospital, and his daughter, Deirdre, Geoffrey Bailey, the Captain of Invalids, Margery May and a pensioner, Edward Gummer.

Attitudes to the V2 were now steadily changing. With the decline in the numbers of V1s the population became more obsessed with the unstoppable rocket. It generated, for all but the most steadfast and unimaginative people, a low level of permanent fear from which there was no relief. The sound of the explosion of the warheads was not new to Londoners, but the sonic booms which followed them could be heard rumbling over a wide area of the capital. It meant that even those out of earshot of the former still knew that some unlucky people had 'got it'. As one man recalled, you would do your best to forget about the missiles and having got them out of your mind there would be a sudden and unexpected wallop as a missile landed close by followed by the sonic boom. And you would think that at least that one had missed you, but subconsciously you would be thinking about the next. Constantly living with the prospect of being alive one moment and then being wiped off the face of the earth the next, with no warning, was terribly disconcerting.

Once the cloak of secrecy had been lifted, the government did all it could to inform the people about the design and capabilities of the new secret weapon. This had been a successful policy as far as the V1 was concerned, but was less so with the V2. The information and diagrams provided seemed to reinforce the feelings of vulnerability and utter helplessness. Once launched, other than a technical failure, there was no defence – nothing could be done. Some V2s could even be seen on clear days or bright moonlit nights. On occasions, it was possible to see either a smoky trail or a pinpoint of light similar to a shooting star as the rocket climbed out of the earth's atmosphere. The Royal Observer Corps plotted many such sightings and consideration was once again given to using them to sound air raid warnings, but practically it would have been of no value. Even if it had been possible to get the sirens sounding all over London, people would barely have had time to get from their place of work during the day, or beds during the night, and into the shelters. Indeed, it may well have made them more vulnerable because, as we have seen, those in the open are generally less well protected from the blast and fragments of a bomb than those inside buildings.

To try and add to the misery, the Germans stepped up the scale of V1 attacks in early January with many more air-launched doodlebugs being aimed at London. The defences now, however, had the measure of these. On the night of 3-4 January 1945, fifty-two V1s were launched, of which only eighteen reached the mainland, and of these only one got through to London. The following night twelve V1s were launched – this time four breached the defences to fall in Woodford, Beckenham, Wanstead and

Lambeth. Although Londoners did not know it, the final attack using air-launched V1s was on 13-14 January when the last three detonated at Southwark, Orpington and Hornsey. But, even then, the Germans were completing more launching ramps in occupied Holland, all pointing at London and ready for a new, longer range version of the flying bomb.

Throughout January and February 1945, the V2s continued to hit Greater London. It was a bitterly cold winter, with little fuel for fires, and of course no central heating. The effects of blast damage meant that thousands of houses had seen their doors and windows blown out and tiles stripped from their roofs. The people still lived in them and, although a huge effort went into the immediate weather-proofing of the more lightly damaged properties, their occupants were often forced to sleep in the numbing cold which chilled them to the bone. An illustration of the devastation that a V2 could cause is provided by the events of 8 January 1945. On that date one of the missiles detonated on the raised embankment at the junction between the LMS and Metropolitan railway lines at the back of 114 Iverson Road, Hampstead. The casualties were light; two people were killed and sixty-four detained in hospital. But the effect of the missile bursting high up on the embankment resulted in fourteen houses being totally destroyed, 152 badly damaged and a further 1,600 needing some sort of repair. For the citizens living in these damaged houses it was truly a miserable time.

Central London escaped the worst of the rocket attacks and the Westminster area, housing the key military and government institutions, got off lightly with only a few missiles landing inside its boundaries. One, on 8 February, exploded in Tavistock Place in the heart of the capital's medical quarter and killed thirty-one people and injured a further fifty-four. This also badly damaged the Central London Ophthalmic Hospital and the Medical School of the Royal Free Hospital.

The worst week for V2 attacks was between the 14 and 21 February 1945, when seventy-one missiles fell. Ironically, for free speech, in March one of them landed squarely on Speakers' Corner on the edge of Hyde Park. It left a massive crater but did little damage. Fortunately, no one was speaking at the time.

Remarkably, for the technology available at the time, General Pile's anti-aircraft gunners looked at placing a curtain of fire in the missiles' path to destroy them in the air, but the task was daunting. Radar sets had to be altered to track missiles out to 300,000 feet at a range of 140,000 yards.[2] There were about two seconds to make a prediction of where the rocket would fall and then fire the guns to make a curtain of flak which would detonate the warhead as the missile flew into the barrage. The guns would actually have to be fired with the missile still thirty miles from the capital. It was estimated that between three and ten per cent of missiles fired at in this manner might be hit. Despite the acknowledged limitations of the system, operational trials went ahead but were abandoned before the last V2 fell.

As the intelligence officers had predicted before the start of the campaign, the only offensive measures that could be taken against the V2 were air strikes against the launching sites, including the logistical system that supported them, and the liberation of Holland, which would put London outside the missiles' maximum range. A rocket could be launched from a suitable piece of hard standing no more than twenty-three feet square in size – and there were thousands of such sites in the Netherlands. With mobile V2 launchers being moved around and most of the missiles being fired at night they were almost impossible targets to find and hit. There were calls for Bomber Command to carpet-bomb areas, but this was initially firmly rejected as being a waste of effort and potentially causing thousands of civilian casualties amongst the Dutch population.

At home, dissatisfaction amongst the population was growing daily. During February, Winston Churchill's private secretary warned that the dissent centred around three subjects. Firstly, there was a perception that if the main weight of the attack had been falling around Whitehall and Buckingham Palace, and not in the south east and the East End, then the measures taken against the launching sites would have been far more vigorous. (Historically it is hard to disagree with this view). Secondly, there was a feeling that the rocket sites were being spared heavy bombing to save Dutch life and property and the complainants felt that if any lives should be lost they should be Dutch and not Londoners. Finally, there was a feeling, once again, that the plight of Londoners was being ignored by the rest of the country and that they were simply being asked to shoulder the burden without sufficient resources being used to stop the attacks.

The dissent amongst Londoners continued to swell as casualty figures climbed and more rockets fell. Infuriatingly, at the same time, news reports continued to stream in about the rapid advance of Allied troops into Germany. Why, Londoners wondered, was the rapid advance into the heart of the Reich so vital, but the occupation of northern Holland, which would stop the attacks, being ignored. Herbert Morrison recorded that both the police and the Regional Commissioner for London were becoming more concerned about the mood of the population.

The pressure for action soon reached such a pitch that calls for heavy bombers to be used against the launching sites in Holland looked a distinct possibility. In the event, a raid by medium bombers from the Second Tactical Air Force on 3 March 1945 vindicated the Air Staff's reluctance to use the heavies. The raid, by fifty-seven Mitchell and Boston bombers, went terribly wrong and almost seventy tons of bombs missed the wood they were aimed at and landed in a heavily built up area causing massive damage and several major fires. These went unchecked as the Germans refused to let the local fire brigade enter the area. As a result, it was reported that some 800 Dutch civilians were killed and thousands of homes destroyed. Of course, ordinary Londoners knew nothing of the futile sacrifice of the Dutch people who had suffered such a terrible fate in an abortive attempt to stop the missiles, but through the Resistance those in authority soon did. It put paid to further mass bombing raids in Holland.

At this point the extended-range V1s got in the act again. After a lull since mid-January 1944, when the air-launched missiles were last deployed, the Germans fired a last-gasp wave of attacks using the latest variants of the flying bomb. This started on 3 March 1945, and the most serious incident that day was at Wood Green where a bomb killed seven people and seriously injured eighteen. Compared to the previous assaults it was a limited campaign, but it was taken most seriously by the defenders, with guns and fighters being instantly put in place to take on the flying bombs. A total of 275 V1s were launched, of which only 125 got through to the coastal defences. Of these, most were shot down and only thirty-four reached Greater London. The last flying bombs to fall exploded at 19.54 hours and 07.55 hours on 28 March at Chislehurst and Waltham Holy Cross, the penultimate missile demolishing Scadury House and injuring four people.

By now the final outcome of the war was beyond doubt, with the Russians almost at the gates of Berlin and the Allied armies advancing on all fronts in North West Europe. But the Germans were grimly clinging on to a corner of Holland from which they continued to launch V2s. For Londoners it was one of the most disturbing aspects of the whole war; the enemy was on its knees, but still the missiles continued to strike unabated. After almost six years of fighting, no one wanted to figure in those last casualty lists. It all seemed so utterly futile and spiteful of the Germans, who, for no logical reason, were determined to keep going until the bitter end.

As if to underline this feeling of unfairness, the final few rockets that struck London also produced some of the worst incidents. The morning of Thursday, 8 March was bright and clear. At Smithfield Market, off the Farringdon Road, it was business as usual. It was at 11.10 hours that a V2 hurtled out of the sky, penetrated the building and detonated in the Underground network beneath it. The buildings collapsed into the crater and those with a frontage on Farringdon Road were completely levelled. Many victims fell into the crater as the floor of the market gave way; others were buried in the rubble from the collapsed buildings. Rescue operations got underway immediately, but from the scale of the devastation it was immediately apparent that this was a very serious incident. The final toll was 110 dead, 123 seriously injured and 243 suffering from lesser injuries. It was the worst incident of the rocket campaign in terms of overall casualties.

The last V2 to inflict major industrial damage landed not in the East End but in West London, just off the Great West Road. It struck at 09.39 hours on Wednesday, 21 March 1945, scoring a direct hit on the Packard factory. The building was completely wrecked and damage caused to several other factories close by, including Pyrene's. One of the workers in this factory described the event in a pamphlet sold to raise money as part of the firm's distress fund:

> The earth is opening up on us, a blinding flash accompanied by a terrifying explosion … 'Get down!' Stunned, staggered, but still semi-conscious, we fall to our knees, a bloody mess. A girl's scream echoes through the office above the falling debris. We rise to our knees, stricken and dazed, bloody and bleeding, wondered what had happened. Stunned we endeavour to tread over the wreckage that was once the Planning Department. I look at young Margie B.. her face is covered in rich red blood. It must be a horrible dream. As we go further and out into the passage I see a bloody trail and realize this tale is now a terrible reality. We make our way to the First Aid Station and come face to face, unrecognisable … with many more casualties.[3]

Even as the noise of the explosion was fading, the Civil Defence services were springing in to action. Rescue parties, ambulances, mobile first aid units and wardens were ordered to the area. A fire had broken out but the fire brigade was on scene very quickly, fighting the blaze. The first warden to arrive had set up an incident control point and undertook a first reconnaissance of the devastated factories. At the same time, a mobile control van was ordered to attend to help coordinate rescue activities. A WVS team also appeared and set up an information point to gather and collate information on casualties.

Hundreds of people, including workers from other nearby factories, were soon all toiling hard to extricate the wounded. As usual it was a grim and difficult task for the rescuers who burrowed into the wreckage looking for survivors, only to be confronted instead by scraps of flesh and other human debris. All told, thirty-two people lost their lives and over 500 were injured, 100 of them severely. Amongst the victims was a Gallipoli veteran who had suffered from severe frost bite and lost his toes during the campaign in the Dardanelles. When a body was found two days after the explosion it was thought that it was him, but confirmation of this was difficult because the body was terribly burned. But when his shoes were removed, cotton wool was discovered in his socks and it was this that enabled him to be finally identified.

The last day that V2 missiles fell on London was 27 March, just over a month before the war in Europe ended. Six exploded: at 00.22 hours in Edmonton, 03.02 hours in Chesunt, 03.30 hours in Ilford, 04.04 hours in Sutton Park, 07.21 hours in Stepney and, the very last, at 16.54 hours in Orpington.

Cruelly, the penultimate one of these was also one of the worst. It was early morning when it scored a direct hit in the centre of a three-block estate in Valance Road, Stepney. The three buildings nearest the impact point, known as Hughes Mansions, were five-storey blocks of flats constructed of bricks and mortar. These mass construction buildings were particularly vulnerable to high-blast loadings. Their design was such that they would withstand a certain level of overpressure, but beyond these limits, they would fail and tumble like a pack of cards. This is what happened to the block of flats nearest the point of impact; it was completely overwhelmed by the blast overpressure and collapsed catastrophically. Even so, inside the rubble there were a myriad of voids in which potential survivors could be trapped. The second building to the east was also almost completely destroyed and the third very badly damaged.

Although some people had left for work, most were still in their homes having breakfast or were preparing to leave. In one of the flats was a fifteen-year-old boy, Ben Glaiziner. He had just said goodbye to his father and was about to get out of his nice warm bed and put on his ice-cold clothing, he recalled:

> As I continued to stare at the bedroom light it suddenly went out and simultaneously there was a flash of blue light. Then nothing.
>
> When I woke up I saw that I was in compete darkness. Then I began to realise that I was completely covered in rubble. I was trapped. I couldn't move. I became terrified and began to scream. When you have a strong urge to scream loudly you must first take a deep breath, just as you do when you want to shout loudly. As I tried to breathe in I experienced a sharp pain in my chest because the rough

surfaces of the rubble began to stick into me, like so many pins. But I could not control myself and I screamed repeatedly. Then the pain became so unbearable that I was forced to stop.

Eventually I began to calm down, I have no idea how long this took. I tried moving my head, I couldn't. I tried moving each of my limbs, I couldn't move them. I lay still for a while and then became angry. I was going to move something because I wanted to; because I had to! I wriggled first one arm then the other and then my legs. It hurt but eventually I compressed the rubble and made spaces, so that limited movement was now possible. I then had a go at moving my head and that worked less well, but it needed a little help. My head was bent forward.

After a time I began to hear voices. Up until that moment I had heard nothing. No sound of the explosion or the building crumbling or people screaming.[4]

The tried and tested Civil Defence organisation once again sprang into action as teams from all the various disciplines responded immediately. The tangle of collapsed brick and twisted beams presented a formidable hazard; despite the risk of further collapses, the Civil Defence teams set about the task of searching for and rescuing survivors. One of them was Ben. He lay buried for nearly four hours before he was rescued and the experience deeply affected him. He was taken to hospital and treated for his injuries. To make matters worse his father had also been admitted to the same hospital. He had received a terrible head wound which left him brain-damaged. Ben was taken to see his gravely-ill father who was unconscious, but also very restless as if he were having a nightmare. As he looked at him, Ben noted that his upper body and face had been peppered by flying glass. Some of the cuts had been sown up with two or three stitches, others simply treated with iodine. It was only as he looked that he realised his father's eyes, although shut, were very flat. The doctors had had to remove both of them. It was very hard for Ben to accept the seriousness of his Dad's injuries. He continued:

After a while my mother was brought into the room. She saw me first and put her arms round me and hugged me and kissed me repeatedly, she was overjoyed to see me. Then she turned to my dad. She was devastated by what she saw. This time there were no tears of joy, she was heartbroken. We sat holding hands and then began to talk. Would he live? If so how would he deal with his blindness? After all he was proud of being a craftsman.

His father never regained consciousness and died on 31 March 1945. Ben suffered a deep depression from this traumatic event for at least two years. He found himself thinking murderous thoughts. Had he been equipped with a machine-gun and ammunition he would cheerfully have killed thousands of Germans. Unlike today there was little or no counselling and 'Pull yourself together' was the standard advice. Unusually, in this incident the dead outnumbered the wounded by 134 to forty-three seriously injured.

Whilst the operation to recover the survivors was underway in Stepney the final rocket to hit Greater London inflicted the last civilian casualties in the United Kingdom caused by direct enemy action. The missile struck the ground next to Nos. 61 and 63 Kynaston Road in Orpington, demolishing the houses. Ivy Millichamp, a thirty-four-year-old, was standing in the kitchen in 88, Court Road; she caught the full force of the blast and suffered the cruel fate of being the last civilian killed in Britain during the hostilities. There were no other fatalities. Her husband was asleep in the front room and survived.

A month later, on 26 April, Ivy's sister, Mollie, wrote to their father after a speech by Winston Churchill in which he recorded that the threat from the V2 had finally passed. She said:

> How poignant such a statement comes home to us; yet we are only one family amongst many thousands who have suffered in a worse degree, Ivy's face, as Ernie and I saw it, often recurs to my mind. There is however one consolation. I feel she suffered no pain; death must have been instantaneous.[5]

Ivy was originally laid to rest in an unmarked grave in All Saints Churchyard on 3 April 1945. However, during their research for Volume 3 of *The Blitz Then and Now* the authors discovered an error in her death certificate which they had corrected. They also arranged for a suitable headstone to be erected and a short ceremony was held at the site on Remembrance Sunday in 1989.

If Hitler had succeeded in his dream of launching hundreds of V2 rockets a day, rather than the five of six maximum that was actually achieved, and if this had been supplemented by large numbers of the less technically advanced flying bombs, life in London may have been made intolerable. This would have been particularly so if the missiles were launched in continuous succession with one landing every few minutes.

It was this relentless characteristic of the V-weapon attacks which wore the people down. Churchill expertly summed up the effects of them when he wrote:

> This new form of air attack imposed on the people of London a burden perhaps even heavier than the air raids of 1940 and 1941. Suspense and strain were more prolonged. Dawn brought no relief and clouds no comfort. The man going home in the evening never knew what he might find; his wife, alone all day or with the children, could not be certain of his safe return. The blind impersonal nature of the missile made the individual on the ground feel helpless. There was little that he could do, no enemy that he could see shot down.[6]

The German records show that by 7 April 1945, they had successfully launched 1,190 V2s against London, of which 163 failed during or shortly after launch. Of the successful launches, the fall of 1,115 was detected, and of these 517 fell in Greater London. Appalling though this was for Londoners, it should be remembered that other civilians all over Europe suffered equally badly. Antwerp, a vital port for the Allies, was the target for 1,610 of the rockets and 8,696 flying bombs. Dresden, whose population was swelled with refugees was attacked late in the war by three waves of Allied bombers and had 3,300 tons of bombs dropped on it in less than twenty-four hours.

That said, over five years the British capital had survived the longest and deadliest period in its history. Great chunks of it lay in ruins and all of it was shabby and run-down through lack of maintenance. Many of its famous buildings were destroyed or required substantial repairs. Time and money would resolve these matters. Less tangible was the effects on the lives of the many men, women and children who had suffered serious injuries as a result of the bombs. They would struggle with their wounds for the rest of their lives. Equally painful were the mental scars of those who had lost loved ones, feelings of sorrow and hurt that would only slowly fade with time.

The fact was, though, that every member of the population of London had in some way contributed to the survival of the city and the defeat of the Nazis. All deserve recognition, but in keeping with the introduction there is only space here to mention two groups. That the Metropolitan, City Police and other smaller forces played their part in the victory is indisputable. They had shared the hardships with the people, worked long hours and, more often than not, been amongst the first at the scenes of bombings. Later, police officers helped compile the casualty lists of the dead and wounded and then had the disagreeable job of informing the bereaved of their losses – never an easy task. In the course of carrying out their duties, 226 Metropolitan Police and City Police regular and reserve officers were killed during air raids. Many more were rewarded for acts of bravery. In connection with air raids there were 276 honours, including two OBEs, eighty-two George Medals, four King's Police and Fire Service Medals, seventy-two British Empire Medals, 115 Commendations and one Dutch Cross of Merit.

The men in the Royal Engineer bomb disposal teams clearly also deserve acknowledgment. In general, they were not numerous and were not given to attracting attention. Writing of them, Winston Churchill had remarked that their faces and demeanour seemed somehow grimmer – 'different from those ordinary men, however brave or faithful'. In the early days, and at the time of greatest danger and highest losses, they banded together in close-knit teams. Unlike most soldiers they had a strange existence. They lived in amongst the civilian population they served, playing their part in the very survival of the community. Conversely, when they worked they did so in splendid isolation from all others. Their job was a mixture of hard labour, toiling away to locate deeply buried unexploded bombs, and technical expertise, in knowing how to deal with them once they were uncovered. No matter what precautions were taken, bombs could never be considered completely safe until the fuzes were removed and the explosive steamed out and destroyed. It took cold-blooded courage to tackle one bomb, let alone do it as your everyday occupation.

Cecil Brinton served with a bomb disposal section in London and had seen many of his friends killed, but there was one incident which he has never got over. He was called to a street in London to examine a suspected UXB. On arrival at the scene one woman seemed extremely agitated, but he thought nothing of it. On entering the house, he discovered the bomb had crashed through the building and come to rest on the ground floor. Having removed the fuze he ordered his men to recover the bomb and take it out to the waiting lorry. He then decided to go upstairs to check the damage. It was only now that he discovered the reason the woman was so agitated:

The lady had left her baby in the cot in the bedroom. The bomb had gone through the roof right into the cot. It smashed the cot and the baby to pieces. I got a pillowcase and picked up what I could of the baby. I put it in the pillow case and left it there. I told the ARP and the policemen what I had done and said that I couldn't face the mother. I know what they mean by trauma – it can have a lasting effect.[7]

As for the people, thousands of London's citizens were traumatised by the bombing. In particular, all those involved with Civil Defence were, at times, required to carry out gruesome work and vivid and painful memories were burnt into their subconscious. Often it was a minor detail in a major incident which haunted them for the rest of their lives. Understandably, the death of young children, like that above, seemed to have the most distressing and lasting impact.

A member of the National Fire Service, Mr Phillips of Poplar, had a similar traumatic experience and summed it up when he wrote:

> We had some bad times, we had some good times, some funny experiences and some tragic ones. But a sight that I don't think I will ever forget was that of a rescue squad releasing a small child that had been buried in the collapse of a house. The child had been buried standing up, and was obviously dead. The rescue party were digging away, and they had just uncovered his head and shoulders. It was a terrible morning – rain was pelting down – and I can see that child's head and shoulders, standing above the debris, white faced and clean where the rain had splashed and washed the face of the child.[8]

For Londoners in April 1945, all that mattered was that it was over. One RAF bomb disposal officer, Squadron Leader A.E. Haarer, who was working at the Air Ministry, said: 'We were suddenly all tired and sick to death of war.'

On a more cheerful note, Vera Hodgson,[9] a social worker, wrote simply in her diary: 'No bombs ... ain't it lovely.'

NOTES:
1. Jones, R.V., *op. cit.*
2. Pile, Sir Frederick, *Ack-Ack*, George Harrap and Co., 1929, p.387.
3. Longmate, Norman, *Hitler's Rockets, the Story of the V2*, Hutchinson and Co., London, 1985.
4. Quoted on www.schoolhistory.org.UK/European War/HughesMansions.htm.
5. Ramsey, Winston G, *The Blitz Then and Now* Volume 3, Battle of Britain Prints International Limited, London, 1987.
6. Quoted on London.iwm.org.uk/upload/package/4/dday/pdfs/VWeaponsCampaign.pdf.
7. Jappy, M .J., *Danger UXB*, Channel 4 Books, Macmillan Publishers Ltd, London, 2001.
8. FitzGibbon, Constantine, *op. cit.*
9. Quoted on London.iwm.org.uk/upload/package/4/dday/pdfs/VWeaponsCampaign.pdf.

Chapter 17

A Taste of Terror and Threat of Armageddon

'Terrorism is the price of empire. If you don't wish to pay
the price, give up the empire.'
Pat Buchanon.

After six years of bitter struggle, millions of deaths and enormous destruction, there were great hopes that following the end of the war the world would be a better and more peaceful place. The end of the fighting, however, left new stresses and strains in some parts of the world and these quickly surfaced. In the months that followed the end of the war, the Jewish community in Palestine turned to active resistance and open revolt against British rule. During this period, attacks against the British by Haganah, the Irgun and the Stern Gang escalated, resulting, in some cases, in harsh retribution by the British Army. The conflict became increasingly bitter and spread to London in 1947 as a result of a trial in Haifa.

On 16 April, the British hanged four Irgun members, despite threats of reprisals from the organisation's leaders. They were not empty words and the following day a bomb was found in the Colonial Office in Dover Street, although fortunately it had failed to detonate. The device, wrapped in newspaper, contained a five-pound charge of explosive, four detonators and an improvised firing system using a modified pocket watch.[1] The explosive, Tolamite, and the pocket watch were both made in France. Not surprisingly the construction of the device was, in principle, very similar to designs taught by the Special Operations Executive (SOE) for use by saboteurs during the Second World War. There is no indication of who built the device or how it was delivered. It was dismantled and examined by an unnamed member of HM Inspector of Explosives.

The next attack involved a series of postal bombs, all of which were intercepted by Scotland Yard. Eight arrived in London on 4 June 1947, with a further three being delivered the following day, some of these having being posted in Italy. On 6 June another nine were intercepted. The intended recipients included Ernest Bevan, Anthony Eden, Clement Atlee and Winston Churchill. On 9 June, two Zionists were arrested in Belgian in possession of a further six devices addressed to other prominent people in the UK. The bomb maker was not identified at the time, but later, in an interview with the *Sunday Times* in 1972, Yaacov Elizav, a member of the Stern Gang, confessed to the attacks.

Information on one of the bombs, that addressed to John Freeman, the Financial Secretary to the War Office, has survived. The bomb was built using two envelopes and was designed to function when the inner was withdrawn from the outer. What is fascinating is that the method by which it was rendered safe was recorded. A loop of string was threaded under the outer envelope flaps and another piece of string attached to the corner of the contents of the inner envelope. The strings were then threaded through a hole in an armour-plated shield. By pulling the two strings the envelopes were pulled apart remotely. There was of course a possibility that the bomb might function but the 'bomb disposal expert' was protected by the shield. In the event the device failed to function and was recovered and fingerprinted for evidence. It seems most likely that it was a member of HM Inspector of Explosives that rendered the bomb safe. Other than a sound technical understanding of explosives and their effects, there is no evidence that these men were ever given any formal bomb disposal training. On the arrival at an incident they would use their own initiative and experience to decide how to make an improvised explosive device safe.

The Stern Gang also plotted to bomb London from the air. In Paris, in early September 1947, Rabbi Baruch Korif (the co-chairman of the Political Action Committee for Palestine) and Judith Rosenberger (a Hungarian-born gang member), approached an ex-wartime pilot, Reginald Gilbert of St Louis, with a view to dropping bombs on London. The plan was for a light aircraft to take off from an airfield near Versailles carrying a number of bombs built into fire extinguishers; these would be dropped from the plane as it passed over the centre of the capital. Gilbert accepted the mission on behalf of another pilot and then sensibly went to the French police. They, in conjunction with Scotland Yard, let the plot run until they knew that Korif had the bombs in his possession. He and nine others were arrested and later imprisoned.

Later, in September 1947, another letter bomb, attributed to the Stern Gang, was sent to the War Office in London. It exploded in a Post Office sorting room seriously injuring two of the staff. Over the period a total of twenty-three letter bombs were sent by the Jewish terrorists. In May 1948 a book bomb killed Rex Farran, the brother of an SAS Officer, Roy Farran, who had worked in Palestine in 1947. A second bomb of similar construction, but built into a roll of periodicals, was partially opened by the wife of an unnamed official connected with Palestine. Fortunately, she became suspicious and put the packet down. It was subsequently rendered safe by a member of HM Inspector of Explosives. It was the last bomb linked to Jewish terrorist groups, but not the last from the Middle East.

Many people associate the bombing of aircraft with the rise of terrorism in the 1970s, but this was not the case. Between 1949 and 1967, nineteen civil aircraft are known to have been damaged by the detonation of explosive devices carried on board.[2] In London, at Northolt airport on 13 April 1950, a bomb was smuggled onto a Vickers Viking aircraft named *Vigilant* and was probably hidden in the used towel bin in the toilets. The aircraft took off and set course for France. The bomb exploded whilst it was en route over the English Channel. Initially the pilot, Captain Ian Harvey, thought it was a lightning strike and sent the co-pilot, Frank Miller, back to investigate. He discovered a seriously injured stewardess and, on surveying the damage, it was immediately obvious that an explosion had occurred as there was a massive hole in the rear fuselage. Without any rudder and very limited elevator control, the crew managed to fly the damaged aircraft back to Northolt where it was landed safely. It was only after the landing and inspecting the damage that it became clear how lucky they all were to survive. The bomb had blown a two-by-one-metre hole in the fuselage and it was a real credit to the aircraft's design that the tail did not fall off. For his skill in saving the aircraft, Captain Harvey was awarded a George Medal. There was a major investigation into the incident to try to catch the perpetrator, but the file into the bombing in The National Archives still has many censored sections. One theory suggests that it was an attempted suicide, but this was not proven.

In the post-war years, the legacy of the Blitz continued to plague London's people. Indeed, the end of the fighting did not halt the work of the Royal Engineer bomb disposal teams as unexploded bombs dropped during the conflict were still being regularly found. In addition to these there were many other unexploded munitions – for example, anti-aircraft shells and Home Guard caches, including many dangerous improvised types of grenade. Some of the latter were made under the threat of invasion in 1940, used unstable explosives and had limited safety and arming arrangements. These needed to be treated with great care. Parts of London, particularly some of the most bombed areas of the East End, had also been used prior to the invasion of Normandy to train troops to fight in built-up areas and in these there were a host of other lost or abandoned military munitions.

As in 1918 and 1919, returning servicemen brought back thousands of souvenirs, often munitions, consisting mainly of grenades, mortars and small shells. Most, but by no means all of these were inert. As the years passed and memories faded, many of these souvenirs lost their attraction. In a similar pattern to the post-First World War period, some were handed in to police stations, whilst others were hidden or discarded, put away in attics or, worse still, buried in gardens or on waste land. There they slowly rusted until after many years, often during building work, they were re-discovered. Because of their poor condition it is often impossible to tell if they are explosive-filled or inert and they have to be treated as if they were live. There is no space in this book to recount more than a few of the thousands of conventional munitions disposal tasks which have been necessary to clear up the capital after the Second World War – work which still goes on today.

Initially, as reconstruction started, particularly in the most devastated areas, German bombs (excluding the small incendiaries of which there were hundreds) were discovered on a regular basis. They are still found today, although it is now a much rarer occurrence with, on average, one UXB being discovered in London each year. A document listing all the abandoned unexploded aircraft bombs was produced after the war and continually updated.[3] This provided details of where bombs were thought to have fallen, although there was no guarantee that this information was accurate, and what actions that had been taken to investigate the reports. This often included extensive digging and drilling, as well as the use of magnetometers to try to detect the bombs. Where nothing was found the decision to finally abandon the bomb was made. In most of these cases the conclusion was that the bombs had never been there in the first place.

A review of the Royal Engineers' bomb disposal teams' activities in London in 1959, some fourteen years after the end of the war, gives some idea of the clearance work that was still being undertaken. Reports of unexploded bombs were investigated all over the capital. For example, in John Islip Street Gardens, Westminster, work was started after reports of an abandoned bomb. A shaft eventually revealed that a 500kg bomb had detonated below the surface leaving a camouflet and the matter closed. A second incident in the same area took two months to investigate but was abandoned as negative. At King's College Hospital, Denmark Hill, Twickenham, Chiswick and Hounslow, other lengthy investigations proved negative and searches for bombs were officially abandoned. But at Kennington a 250kg bomb was discovered; at Bow a 50kg bomb; and at Putney another 250kg was found and rendered safe.[4]

The biggest UXB uncovered that year was fopund late on the evening of 6 April 1959. Major Hartley RE, who was on call at the time, received a report of the discovery of a suspect bomb during construction work on the South Bank. At the time the bomb disposal teams were always busy and often the offending items turned out to be old boilers, milk churns or gas cylinders. This time, however, having listened to the police description of the suspect item, it became clear that it was most likely a bomb. It had been uncovered at night by a dragline preparing the foundations for a new building. Six feet long and thirty inches in diameter, it was some twenty-feet down on a steep slope. From the description it was most likely a 1,000kg 'Hermann'.

Hartley, accompanied by Captain Young RE, set off for London, arriving at 03.50 hours in the morning. The duty police inspector took them to the top of the excavation site which was brilliantly illuminated for night work by a bank of floodlights. There he extended his finger and looking along it the two officers could see, perched half way down the slope the unmistakeable shape of a 'Hermann'. A tiny shelf seemed to be all that was holding the bomb in place. Having given advice on the necessary cordon and evacuation measures needed to safeguard the public, which included shutting or, more correctly, preventing the opening of the Bakerloo Line, which ran quite close to the site, they set about the challenge of disposing of the bomb.

They approached it from below and immediately established that 'Sod's Law' was working and that the fuze was in an inaccessible position underneath the body. They had to quickly ascertain what fuze it was, but because clockwork fuzes were rarely fitted to these large bombs, they decided to gently rotate the bomb to locate the fuze pocket. This sounds easy, but great care had to be taken to ensure that it did not break free and roll to the bottom of the excavation. Having swivelled the bomb through ninety degrees to get it nose-to-tail down the slope, they managed to roll it over and locate the fuze. It was a Number 28, a type which they were satisfied presented no immediate danger of direct detonation, even though it still had to be removed before the bomb could be considered safe enough to move. There was, however, the risk that sensitive picrite crystals had formed over the years that the bomb had been in the ground. The normal method of dealing with these crystals was dissolving them in soapy water. To do this two holes had to be drilled in the fuze and, using a pump, a vacuum created. Then a soapy water solution was applied which was sucked into the fuze pocket.

When Hartley and Young tried to do this they discovered that the fuze pocket itself was distorted, leaving small gaps, and that it was impossible to create the necessary vacuum. As a result, they had to resort to dripping the water through the hole to try and get it to any crystals that might have formed. The pair decided to use an extractor to pull the fuze out of its pocket, but, once again because of distortion, this failed. An attempt to carry out the same operation by hand resulted in the fuze itself snapping in two. Now they had a bomb with half the fuze in its pocket, a mass of wires and electrical components, and beneath it the dangerous gaine and flash pellet which could still set it off. They decided to soak the whole of the fuze pocket in penetrating oil to desensitize any explosive there, and once this had been done and given time to work, they chipped out the remainder of the fuze with pliers and callipers. Finally, they reached the flash pellet which they removed. The gaine was soaked in oil and left in place.

Hartley at this stage was still concerned about the possibility of unstable compounds being formed by the reaction of the ammonium nitrate in the filling with the steel case. He decided to remove the base plate of the bomb and extract the filling. This again proved much harder than expected because the bomb had clearly hit something very solid on impact which not only had distorted the fuze pocket but also its body. After much effort they managed to turn the base plate a few times and whilst doing so Hartley noticed that water was dribbling through the screw threads. With water in the bomb the contents were considered to be safe to move and it was loaded onto a truck and taken to Shoeburyness for disposal.

Other than the disposal of conventional munitions and criminal activities using explosives, the 1950s proved to be a period of comparative peace in London. There were a number of incidents involving 'Molotov Cocktails' which were primarily used by protection racketeers. Where these were found complete they were usually recovered by police officers direct to their stations.

There were, however, some peculiar incidents involving explosives which have never been satisfactorily resolved. In the late evening of 8 February 1954, a phone call was made to New Scotland Yard. The caller, who identified himself as a Mr Cox, gave a false telephone number, alleged he had seen two men acting suspiciously at a post box at the junction between Niton Street and Fulham Palace Road. He further stated that when the two men saw him they drove off in a car at high speed. The caller was unable to issue a description of the men and abruptly hung up. It was all very strange.

Police Constable Edward Porter was sent to investigate the call and on arrival at the post box found some wires protruding from the letter slot. He pulled these slowly and gently and after about twenty-feet had come out of the box he discovered a detonator. At this point a fire engine arrived and the senior fireman, Station Officer Morgan, having looked at the detonator, concluded that an infernal machine (surprisingly this term was still being used to describe Improvised Explosive Devices at this time) had been placed in the box. Hastily retiring, Morgan stood his crew ready for action some distance off. Everyone then awaited the arrival of Inspector Arthur Noble, the local duty officer. With assistance from a Post Office employee he opened the box and a stick of gelignite fell out. This and the wire and the detonator were all taken to Fulham Police station.

Whilst this incident was on going, Police Constable Griffiths, who was on communications duty at Fulham Police Station, received another call relating to the incident. This time it was from a police telephone box and an unknown male said in a gruff voice: 'If you want to be in time you'd better hurry as there is something ticking like hell in the letter box by Niton Street up the road.'[5] Then he hung up.

The following morning, on the instructions of HM Inspector of Explosives, the gelignite and detonator were taken to the Royal Arsenal at Woolwich for examination. Later in the afternoon another nine calls were received at various places from a man calling himself 'Jo Jo'. These stated that there was something of interest to the police both at the flower counter in the Woolworths store in North End Road and on a No.14 bus that had just left the area. Police responding to the call duly discovered another stick of gelignite and a detonator in Woolworths. These were placed in a bucket of water and taken back to the police station. Later explosives were also recovered from under a seat of a No.14 bus.

On 11 February there were another eight calls again from the man calling himself 'Jo Jo', but this time, after extensive searches, nothing was found. The following day more calls led to the discovery of explosives on yet another bus. A letter was also received at Scotland Yard from a man claiming to be 'Jo Jo'. Telephone calls and finds continued until 3 March and then stopped for good. Neither the identity of 'Jo Jo' nor his motives have ever been established. Although he was using real gelignite and detonators, HM Inspector of Explosives concluded that these were never intended to be bombs, as there were no power sources or firing switches

Above: One of the most famous images to emerge from the Blitz. Taken at 18.48 hours German time on 7 September 1940, the first day of the Blitz on London, it shows a Heinkel He 111 over Wapping. The area within the characteristic U-bend of the River Thames was designated by the *Luftwaffe* as *Zielräum* (or Target Area) G. (Historic Military Press)

Below: The effects of a concentrated attack on London's dock and industry districts, on 7 September 1940. Factories and storehouses were seriously damaged; the mills at the Victoria Docks (below at left) show damage wrought by fire. (Historic Military Press)

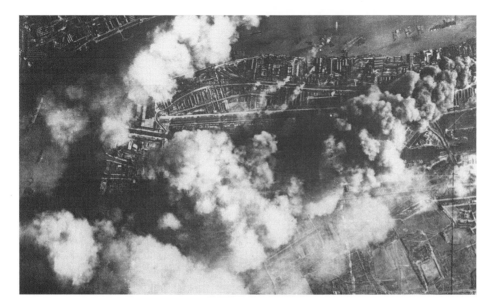

Above: After toiling ceaselessly for over fifteen hours, rescue squads succeeded in extricating alive this casualty who was buried by debris when a bomb dropped by German night raiders wrecked a building in London area, 21 October 1940. (Historic Military Press)

Left: A big killer in all bombing incidents is flying fragments, as this picture graphically illustrates. This is the front of Bishopsgate Police Station after a near miss from a German bomb. (Author)

Above: King George VI and Queen Elizabeth inspect bomb damage at Buckingham Palace during the Blitz, 10 September 1940. (Historic Military Press)

Below: A curious crowd gather at the entrance to Bethnal Green Tube Station following the disaster in which 170 or so people lost their lives during a stampede in an air raid on 3 March 1943. The incident is stated as having been the largest single loss of civilian life in the UK in the Second World War and the largest loss of life in a single incident on the London Underground network. (Historic Military Press)

Above: A photograph showing the damage caused when a German bomb tore a hole in the stonework and clock facing of Big Ben during an attack on London during the night of 10-11 May 1941. (Historic Military Press)

Above left: On Friday, 30 June 1944, a V-1 flying bomb struck the road outside Adastral House in the Aldwych. It was the third worst such attack in terms of casualties, killing forty-eight people and injuring a further 200. (Author)

Above right: An aerial view showing the damage resulting from a German V-2 rocket which exploded at the junction of Wanstead Park Road and Endsleigh Gardens in Cranbrook, Ilford, Essex, on 8 March 1945. As a result of the incident, nine people were killed, fifteen seriously injured and nineteen slightly injured. (Historic Military Press)

Below: A posed picture showing an unknown naval officer dealing with a parachute mine in training. You would not normally be looking at a camera when removing the fuze from a mine! (Author)

Top left: The bomb which failed to explode in the Colonial Office in Dover Street, and which was probably planted by Jewish extremists on 17 April 1947, the day after four Irgun members were hanged in Haifa. (Author).

Top right: Six people were injured when an IRA bomb exploded in a café on the concourse at Euston station on 10 September 1973. Here a plain clothes police officer examines a suitcase left on the concourse floor. Fifty minutes before this device had detonated, an explosion tore through King's Cross station. (Historic Military Press)

Centre left: One man was killed and 212 people were injured when two car bomb explosions shook London on 8 March 1973. One was left outside the Old Bailey, the other went off in Great Scotland Yard. This photograph shows an injured woman being carried to an ambulance. (Historic Military Press)

Left: The statue of Britain's wartime leader, Sir Winston Churchill, views the scene as smoke pours from the roof of the chapel of the House of Commons after it had been set alight following the explosion of an IRA device on 17 June 1974. (Historic Military Press)

Above: On 20 July 1982, the PIRA executed one of its most appalling attacks when it attacked the Blues and Royals on horseback in Hyde Park and, just two hours later, the Band of the Royal Green Jackets in Regents Park. The photograph shows the scene shortly after the Hyde Park bomb detonated. (Historic Military Press)

Below: The four original members of the Metropolitan Police Explosives Office. These men bore the brunt of the early PIRA bombing campaign in London. From left to right can be seen Geoff Biddle, Don Henderson, Ron Wilson and Sandy Hawkins. (Author)

Above: The PIRA bomb at Bishopsgate was the biggest single malicious explosion in London with an estimated charge of 3,000-5,000kg of explosive. (Author)

Below; 'Outright Terror Old and Brilliant', the tag line advertising film *The Descent* on the side of the bus in Tavistock Square. It led to many conspiracy theories but was purely coincidental. (PES)

present and the incidents were regarded as hoaxes. There was some thought that it might have been connected to IRA activity, but sadly some of the documents in the relevant files are still closed to viewing, so 'Jo Jo', as he was known, remains anonymous to this day.

In 1957, the IRA launched their 'border campaign' in Ireland, an offensive which ran in a haphazard manner until 1962. This forced the Metropolitan Police to review its procedures for dealing with possible incidents in London. Special Branch consulted both the Home Office and HM Inspectorate of Explosives to try to establish how incidents involving bombs, mines, booby-traps and incendiaries should be dealt with. The subsequent instructions issued to the police highlight a robust approach to dealing with such matters. As in the 1939-40 campaign, police officers with no formal training were quite clearly expected to take risks examining suspect items. The document stressed that any action would depend entirely on circumstances prevailing at the time and that no hard and fast rules could be applied. Some elementary principles, though, could be laid down. The document then went on to describe how the IRA manufactured homemade explosives like 'Paxo' or 'Lumite' and made use of commercial nitroglycerine-based explosives. They then described the possible systems for initiating such devices and the containers they used. These included suitcases, tyres and inner tubes as well as a variety of different tins and pipes.

The report then described how incidents should be dealt with. The instructions were based on those previously issued in 1939, though with some notable changes, the main one being that putting most modern explosives in water did not render them harmless. Gunpowder, which was less commonly used, was the only explosive which would be rendered inert by such action. Where devices were encountered with slow burning fuses, the advice was to cut the fuse at least three inches (and preferably more) below the last point at which the fuse showed signs of smoke; the reason for being that the flame inside the fuse travelled beyond the point where the signs of burning appeared externally on the outer wrapping. Where chemical igniters were used it was explained that the acid for these was usually contained in waxed balloons and that removing these from a device would render it harmless. Where electrical circuits were used then a device could be rendered safe by cutting the wires in the circuit. It stressed the following: 'It is of the utmost importance, however, that ONLY ONE WIRE AT A TIME SHOULD BE CUT.'[6]

The report explained that if this was not done an electrical circuit could be completed which would cause the device to function. Parcel bombs were to be placed in a cool secure place until the relevant experts could be called to deal with them. What is implied by these instructions is that in the event of an attack the police on the ground would be expected to deal with any device they encountered. Only in the case of parcel bombs would they be left for the experts, who at this time were still officers from the HM Inspector of Explosives.

As far as can be established, no live devices were laid by the IRA during this period, but police officers did deal with a number of hoaxes. In the early 1960s Vic Wilkinson was an Inspector at Cannon Row Police Station. There was a call one evening to a suspect biscuit tin in Trafalgar Square. On arrival at the scene he quickly found it. After prising open the lid a little he saw wires, batteries and an explosive-like substance. Wilkinson directed the duty Sergeant to pick up the tin, take it across to one of the fountains and place it in the water. Unfortunately, it floated and the lid had to be prised open again and held under the water until it filled up and sank. Clearly, in this case, the instructions about not putting devices in water had not permeated through to the police officers on the ground. The area was then cleared whilst a suitable Home Office expert was called in to deal with it. After it had been examined in detail it was declared a hoax.

Wilkinson also recalled how, as a young police constable on one night shift, he was told by the duty sergeant to take some fireworks and ammunition that had been handed in and dump it all in the Thames. He proceeded towards the river on the appointed task but unwisely concluded that it was quite a boring method of disposal so he decided to set off one of the larger fireworks. This he duly placed on a statue in Cheyne Walk. Having lit the fuse he backed off to admire the results of his work. To his horror when it exploded it blew off a chunk of the statue. He quickly gathered up the remainder of the fireworks and ammunition and dumped them in the River Thames as instructed. It makes you wonder what is still in the river now; almost certainly a few unexploded German bombs, dud anti-aircraft shells and other munitions dumped in a similar fashion to those above. Providentially, a combination of the salt water and tide have probably corroded away most of the metal and washed out the explosive by now.

Any account of the bombing of London would not be complete without briefly mentioning the biggest threat to the capital's existence. After a short honeymoon period, the post-Second World War era was dominated by the Cold War and the risk of an East-West confrontation. With it, many of the old worries about bombing re-surfaced. There was a threat from conventional bombs which could now be carried in much larger tonnages in the new generation of multi-engine jet bombers.

Worse than this was the awful prospect of chemical warfare using the new and highly toxic nerve agents, Tabun, Soman and Sarin, developed by the Germans during the war. Equally troubling was the threat from biological weapons, like anthrax, which were developed and manufactured by all the major combatants in the Second World War, but never used. These posed a terrible threat to all.

During the Cold War though, the biggest menace was from atomic bombs. From the 1950s to the end of the 1980s the nuclear arms race produced a succession of bigger and better nuclear weapons and their associated delivery systems. The most critical time came in October 1962 when the Cuban Missile Crisis brought the world to the brink of a nuclear war. Later, policies like Mutually Assured Destruction (MAD) were designed to ensure that neither side could initiate a first strike without risking their own self-destruction from retaliatory missiles.

The whole subject of nuclear attack was the focus of many studies. Most concluded that if nuclear weapons were used, attempts to restrict them to military targets would be most likely to fail. Should this happen, London would be a prime target and, in all but the most benign of scenarios, would be totally destroyed. In simulations of the most severe attacks predicted, the assumption was made that London would be struck by several nuclear warheads of five to ten megatons each. This would kill about eighty-five percent of the population instantaneously or in the immediate aftermath. A nuclear winter would follow which would effectively paralyze any hope of recovery and, other than those in deep shelters with adequate stocks of food, there would be little hope of survival over the next few years.

Even smaller scale attacks using nuclear weapons which only destroyed one third of the capital were thought to precipitate catastrophic consequences for the population. It was expected that post-strike, with high levels of radiation sickness, London would enter a spiral of decline from which it would never recover. It was only if the targets struck were of a military nature that London might survive. The majority of studies concluded that any form of civil defence against the bigger attacks would be futile. Planning was therefore restricted to dealing with the aftermath of a small and limited nuclear exchange. In these circumstances a well-ordered and organized system of civil defence could well help to save many lives and oversee the return to some form of normality.

In the event of an attack, it was established that there would be little more than a four-minute warning from the time of the missile launch being detected by radar until impact. A system was put in place using normal telephone lines which connected the Strike Command Operations

Centre in High Wycombe to up to 250 national Carrier Control Points (CCP) which were mostly in police stations. These police stations were, in turn, linked to 7,000 automated sirens which would be sounded to warn of an impending strike by nuclear weapons. On hearing the sirens most people would probably not have known what they meant and even if they did it is doubtful that they would have had time to do any more than take cover in a building if they were outside. Many police officers serving in the CCPs will recall the relentless 'beep beep' signal broadcast every few minutes which confirmed the warning system was operational.

The disposal of unexploded free-fall nuclear bombs was taken seriously and some training was carried out by the military to determine suitable methods of rendering them safe. Clearly the cost of atomic bombs was such that the fuzing arrangements had to have a high degree of reliability and some built-in redundancy but, even so, it was thought that a few might fail and the working group tasked to examine the problem wrote that:

> Atomic bombs, if they are dropped by the Russians in a war of the near future, are unlikely to fail to explode since every care will be taken and no expense spared to ensure that they operate properly. Nevertheless, experts must be available to deal with any eventuality.[7]

Not surprisingly, all details of the render-safe procedures for nuclear warheads remain highly classified.

Some left-wing councils, not wishing to be involved in any way in preparations for nuclear war, advertised themselves as 'Nuclear Free Zones'. It was never quite clear, to me, how they expected this to work in the event of a nuclear attack.

Although many nuclear weapons still exist, the perceived risk of attack has diminished with the thawing of relations between the East and West and the collapse of the Warsaw Pact. Of all the threats against the capital over the years, an all-out nuclear strike is the only one that has ever had the potential to totally destroy the city and its people. Today the danger has not been completely lifted and, with nuclear proliferation, the possibility of a terrorist group acquiring and using a nuclear device remains a possibility. Although the likelihood is still seen as very low it is a growing risk for the future of the capital.

At the other end of the scale, the criminal use of small quantities of explosive to blow open safes was a common crime right up until the late 1980s. It was made easier by the wide availability of both commercial and military explosive during the period. Sometimes the crimes were perpetrated by ex-National Servicemen who, as they saw it, were putting their training in the armed forces to good use. In those pre-credit card days, when cash was king, large amounts of money would often be held in business premises overnight and were naturally a target for criminals. When using explosive techniques, no safe, vault or strong room is completely secure from attack, but post-war designs were rapidly developed using modern high-grade materials which did provide significant protection in terms of the time spent and amount of explosives needed to open them. The reason for the continued attacks was that many businesses failed to replace their old and vulnerable models of safe.

Most safe blowers directed their efforts against these older safes which were often in relatively small offices and which called for no great skill to open them. At the time, many of these, for example those in post offices and railway stations, were made of wrought or cast iron and dated from the turn of the century. Even when embedded in concrete they were still a gift to an experienced safe blower and, in reality, only provided security against low-level pilfering.

The methods used to break into safes varied but most commonly involved an attack on the lock itself. Explosive could be placed in the keyhole to blow apart the lock, although this did not always result in the 'safe cracker' gaining entry. Alternatively, explosive could be used to blow off combination locks or, after drilling access holes near the lock, filling these with a charge to try and achieve the same result. Sometimes specialist cutting charges were used to shatter the lock itself. Another method was to attack the whole safe by blowing off the door. This involved introducing a charge into the safe and detonating it, of course the disadvantage of this method was that it often damaged the contents. A better way of cracking a safe open was to fill the safe with a liquid. This could be done by drilling a hole in the top of the safe or by forcing water through gaps inside in the doors and then detonating a very small charge. When a high explosive is detonated in water the shock waves are attenuated to a far lesser degree owing to its virtual incompressibility. Using this method, sometimes just a detonator with 0.9 grams of explosive could be enough to blow a safe apart. Attacking the hinges or the walls of the safes themselves was a possibility, but this involved large amounts of explosives, had a high risk of failure and invariably made a lot of noise, all of which made it unpopular with professional safe blowers. Many amateurs though were known get injured trying such methods.

Quite often the explosives used to attack the safes were stolen commercial types which were based on nitroglycerine. When correctly stored and handled these are perfectly safe, but in the wrong hands their condition could rapidly deteriorate and would become very unstable. In such a state it needs to be treated with great care and, in the very worst cases, the only safe method of disposal is to destroy the explosive in situ. As we have seen, up until 1962 the responsibility for providing professional support to the police where crimes involved explosives rested with HM Inspector of Explosives. For various reasons, around this time the department was unable to fulfil the requirement satisfactorily and it was agreed that the Army would undertake this work. This would be done by suitably qualified Ammunition Technical Officers and Ammunition Technicians of the Royal Army Ordnance Corps (RAOC) subject to a number of conditions – which basically amounted to no extra resources or manpower being allocated to the task. In the main, this work involved dealing with explosives at the scene of an attempted robbery. There were some problems, including a lack of suitable specialist equipment and a reluctance of some officers to give evidence in court. By 1963, however, it was clear that the workload being placed on the Army unit responsible for London and the Home Counties was much heavier than was originally anticipated and representations were made to the Metropolitan Police Commissioner to review the situation.

In the interim period Major Don Henderson RAOC was seconded to the Metropolitan Police. As a result of his work, in early in 1964 it was decided that two Explosives Officers should be appointed permanently to the staff of the Metropolitan Police working as part of the Forensic Science Laboratory. Their main duty was to attend safe-blowing incidents to ensure that the scenes were safe for police officers to carry out their investigations and recover evidence. In addition, they were tasked with examining explosives found abandoned, or being held illegally, dealing with parcel bombs, suspicious objects and adolescents' bombs and explosives. The first Explosive Officers did not, at this time, take on the task of dealing with conventional munitions in London which remained the responsibility of the Army.

The posts were taken up by two former RAOC majors. Don Henderson, who had by this point retired, started in August 1964, whilst Geoffrey Biddle followed in November the same year. The pair would have had little idea then of just how much their role would fundamentally change in the early 1970s. Their initial task was to settle in and prove their worth within the Metropolitan Police and its forensic organisation. Previously, when the military had been called to clear scenes involving explosives, in accordance with their training and doctrine they would almost invariably arrange to destroy any residues on site or, if not, very close by. This process, of course, took no account of the destruction of potential forensic evidence. Henderson quickly realised that to make an effective contribution and

318

justify their employment a change of policy was needed. Wherever possible, explosive residues were not destroyed and were recovered as forensic evidence. A system of zoning crime scenes was established and each zone was then methodically searched. This ensured that no evidence was missed and all the items recovered were correctly bagged and labelled. Therefore, within the constraints of safety, the new Explosives Officers would try to ensure that scenes were made safe with the minimum of disruption so that the maximum forensic evidence could be obtained, a policy which still applies today. These methods, learnt during the examination of blown safes, were to pay dividends in the later terrorist bombing campaigns. It enabled components of devices to be identified, allowed bombs to be reconstructed and provided many clues which detectives could use to catch the bombers.

The officers worked in civilian suits and were conveyed to scenes in marked police vehicles during normal working hours. When a task occurred outside these times and at weekends the Explosives Officers drove their own cars to the scenes of crime. In the back they would carry all the tools they needed, including serviceable explosive to be used in extreme cases where they had to destroy unstable nitroglycerine or other dangerous compounds. In the first half year of employment in 1964, the new officers attended seventy-nine safe blowings, dealt with seven bombs, eleven incidents involving the illegal possession of explosives and several other non-explosive related tasks.

At first there was some reluctance to call out the new Explosives Officers. Initially it was felt that they should only go to instances where the safe had been packed with explosive but not actually blown. However, they soon gained a reputation for being able to offer considerable expertise at crime scenes involving explosives and subsequently were called out to more and more incidents. This is supported by the statistics which showed that in 1965 they attended a total of 385 incidents including 319 explosive attacks on safes.

They provided two distinct services. Firstly, they became responsible for ensuring public safety; secondly, they produced comprehensive reports for the investigating officers. Even at scenes where the safes had been blown open, it was often discovered that considerable amounts of explosive, some of it in dangerous condition, were left behind. For example, at one scene, almost a pound of a very unstable explosive was recovered from the door and the internal cavity of a safe.

There were a number of bombings during the mid-1960s, most of them criminal related. In 1964 a parcel bomb was sent to a member of the public, which involved four Jetex solid fuel tablets as the main charge.

The recipient became suspicious of the package and, after partially opening it, took it to the local police station. Here a police officer unwisely continued the opening process and the bomb functioned. He suffered superficial burns to the hands and face. It was noted that this type of accident should not have occurred as the Explosive Officers were now on a twenty-four hour call-out system. Instructions went out that, in the future, it would be mandatory for Explosive Officers to be tasked to examine, and render safe, any suspect packages.

In 1965 a large bomb was placed on the tomb of Karl Marx in Highgate Cemetery. It failed to explode and after being rendered safe was sent for analysis at the Forensic Explosives Laboratory in Woolwich. It consisted of three pounds of dynamite, a clockwork delay, batteries and a detonator, all packed into a canvas bag with clothes on top. It was soon established that all the components were of American origin. Other than the obvious political motive, no reason for the bomb was established and no one was ever caught for planting it.

The majority of other devices being used in this period were all of the pipe-bomb variety, usually containing mixtures of weed killer and sugar. Homemade bomb making was practised by many youths at the time and was considered by some (including the author) to be an amusing and interesting occupation. Just as popular was the construction of model cannon, often in metalwork classes in schools. These, with the aid of some gunpowder from a 'banger' and ball bearings, could be used to shoot holes in planks of wood. The bombs and cannon were rarely used maliciously and, in those days, it was not really regarded as a serious crime. The activity, however, was not risk-free and a number of cannon suffered breach explosions as a result of too much gunpowder. Equally, some of the homemade bombs exploded prematurely, a few seriously injuring the youths who were making them (again including the author).

The Explosive Officers expressed concern about the casual approach that many police officers had when handling and storing homemade explosive or pipe bombs filled with it. Indeed, the largest bomb recovered at the time consisted of twenty-eight pounds of weed killer and sugar contained in a fire extinguisher. It was more than enough to demolish a small house.

An unusual feature of the first year's work undertaken the Explosives Officers was the investigation and clearance of a number of Vietnamese dolls which had been reported in the 'alarmist' press to be booby-trapped. They were not.

In the following year, as a result of the good work inside the Metropolitan Police area, the Explosives Officers were tasked to incidents all over the Home Counties, resulting in the total number of tasks growing to 595, with just over 500 of these involving the explosive attack of safes. Incidentally, 1966 was the centenary of the first recorded use of explosives to blow open a safe.

To meet the unit's steadily growing commitments it was decided to recruit two more Explosives Officers, these being Sandy Hawkins and, a little later, Ron Wilson, both of whom were retired RAOC Ammunition Technical Officers. At the same time, it was recognised that terrorism was a growing threat worldwide and there was a need for further training on bomb disposal duties. One officer attended a 'Counter Bomb' course for two weeks at the Royal Military College of Science at Shrivenham.

During the year, a number of well-constructed hoaxes were dealt with and the report on them concluded that there were 'nerve-wracking times' whilst they were being investigated. The report also outlined the need for the cordon and evacuation of areas whilst render safe procedures were being undertaken. Finally, it was noted that despite the Explosive Officers' best attempts, police officers continued to place bombs in water, a potentially dangerous practice.

In 1967 the pattern of work continued, but one Explosives Officer was injured whilst trying to neutralise an 'infernal machine'. The device had been handled by several police officers before he arrived at the scene and there were strong grounds to support the view that 'foolhardy and quite irregular action' by one of those handling it contributed to the accident. As a result of the incident, Explosive Officers were issued with American-pattern bomb suits to provide a degree of protection against small bombs. They were also issued with 'new transistorised tape recorders' and investigations were made into the use of lightweight X-ray and Polaroid photographic equipment.

Early in the morning of 16 May 1968 there was an explosion on the eighteenth floor of a twenty-two storey block of flats known as Ronan Point which was situated in Butchers Road, Canning Town. As a result, there was a partial collapse of the building in which four people were killed. Initially it was thought to be a gas explosion, but suggestions reached the police that this might not be the case. They therefore decided that their normal procedure for investigating an explosion should be applied and two Explosives Officers, Ron Wilson and Sandy Hawkins went to the scene. They were assisted there by Mr H.J. Yallop from the Explosives Division of the Royal Armament Research and Development Establishment at Fort Halstead – an individual who would later play a pivotal role in the fight against the IRA. There was a major investigation which eventually confirmed that, as first thought, the cause of the disaster was a gas explosion on the eighteenth floor. The gas had leaked into a flat through a substandard connection to a gas cooker and exploded when the tenant struck a match to light the oven. Although the explosion was not of exceptional violence, the pressures induced were sufficient to cause local structural damage. This blew out concrete panels forming part of the load bearing flank wall, and when this collapsed it caused a chain reaction in which the floors beneath collapsed like a pack of cards.

When the first Explosives Officers were recruited their main task was to ensure the safe disposal of explosives or explosive residues where criminals had used them to attack safes. They also dealt with small numbers of bombs made by 'cranks' and criminals, a task for which their training and backgrounds were well suited. Around this time changes in the design of new safes, a reduction in the amounts of cash handled (thanks to credit cards), and better control of explosives, led to the slow demise of the trade of the professional safe blower, although incidents were dealt with right up to the late 1980s.

The steady reduction in these tasks should have eased the Explosives Officers workload, but the world was rapidly changing, and terrorism, using improvised bombs on a scale never experienced before in London, was on the horizon.

NOTES:
1. Seventy-second Annual Report of HM Inspectors of Explosives Reports, for the year 1947, printed October 1948.
2. Board of Trade Accidents Investigation Branch, Report on aircraft damaged or destroyed by deliberate detonation of explosive (sabotage), E.Newton MBE, 1968.
3. Finally Abandoned Unexploded Bombs Region 5 - London.
4. TNA, PRO 305/809: Unit Historical Record Bomb Disposal Unit UK RE.
5. TNA, MEPO 2/9624: Metropolitan Police reports into hoaxes, 1954.
6. Metropolitan Police Special Branch Instruction EXPLOSIVES AND INCENDIARY MATERIALS (used by the IRA) dated 1957.
7. TNA, HO 322/298: Disposal of Unexploded Missiles in a Future War 11 May 1950.

Chapter 18

A Changing World

**'There is no second chance when dealing with explosives –
if in doubt, don't.'**
Conclusion of an Explosives Officer's Lecture Notes, 1968.

The late 1960s saw the arrival of the phenomenon of the urban guerrilla. The earliest groups, including the Tupamoros of Uruguay, The Weathermen of the United States and the Baader Meinhof Group in the old West Germany, all set about committing terrorist acts in their own countries. At the same time, the Americans were engaged in an increasingly bloody and unpopular war in Vietnam. In June 1967, the Six Day War broke out which, once again, saw Arabs and Israelis at each other's throats. The Black September group hijacked and dramatically blew up three aircraft in front of the world's press. Paris erupted in street warfare in 1968 when students clashed with the police. Closer to home, in Londonderry in Northern Ireland there was a massive demonstration of civil unrest. The impact of these events on people all over the world was immense, partly due to the spread of television and the speed at which reports from the international press now appeared on the general public's screens.

Unpredictably, in this period the first serious incidents in London using improvised explosive devices were not directed against Britain itself. They reflected the move towards the globalisation of terrorism and resulted in attacks against Greek, Israeli and Spanish interests.

In February 1968, an elaborate bomb, disguised as a shrub growing in a tub, was deposited on the pavement facing the main entrance to Greek Embassy. It contained a Standard Fireworks three-inch maroon mortar which was aimed in the general direction of the Embassy. The method of initiation for the mortar was a radio-control system which incorporated a clock to provide a delayed arming arrangement. The launcher would have been laid in a safe mode and then armed after a set time by the clock. Once armed, it could be fired remotely, which would enable the maroon to be launched at the Embassy at the terrorist's time of choosing. Trials later indicated that the maroon was capable of passing through a window before exploding. Alternatively, it could also have been used against people who were entering or leaving the premises. Fortunately, it was discovered and rendered safe before it could be fired. It is significant because it was the first radio-controlled device to be deployed in London.

Soon afterwards, a car containing six bombs was intercepted at Dover. This was also significant because the delay for these bombs was based on a device known as a Memopark Timer. These timers became popular with motorists around this period and were produced just after the introduction of parking meters. They could be set for anything up to two hours and then ticked quietly for the allotted time. When this ran out the face of the Memopark would rotate rapidly making a high-speed metallic buzzing sound alerting the motorists to the fact that they needed to move their cars or refill the meter. By attaching a nail to the face of the Memopark, to act as a contact, they could be modified to make cheap and reliable timers. The bombs at Dover utilised these Memoparks – it was the first time they had been seen in the UK. The timers and all their constituent components would become very familiar to both bomb disposal officers and police forensic officers as they later became a standard IRA timer.

In October 1968 terrorists threw a parcel at the Greek Ambassador as he entered his Embassy. He caught it as a reflex action then dropped it instantly, whereupon it exploded on the carpet. This device consisted of a wooden box containing a pyrotechnic composition and an electrical ignition system designed to operate when the lid of the box was opened. When it was dropped by the Ambassador it hit the ground, the lid flew open and it exploded.

Warrant Officer First Class Peter Gurney, of whom we will hear much more later, was involved in another incident at the Greek Embassy in December 1969. He was tasked to deal with two bombs which had been found during a security search of a young man's bag before a reception. For some reason an Explosives Officer was not immediately available and Gurney, who was based at Hounslow, was called to deal with the devices. With his driver he set off for Central London, arriving at the outer cordon a short while later. There he was given a description of the bombs which, by then, had been taken out of the building and placed in a dustbin at the rear of the Embassy.

Gurney set off to inspect the bombs. Having examined them carefully to ensure that there were no anti-handling systems, he cut the wires that led to the detonators and so rendered them safe. It was moments after this had been done that he heard a metallic clicking as one of the Memopark Timers timed out and completed the circuit – which would have initiated the bomb.

In the same year, 1969, there were five attacks on Israeli or Jewish interests. These started in January when a smoke grenade was thrown into the Israeli Tourist Office. In July, simultaneous incendiary time-bomb attacks were made on Marks and Spencer and Selfridges in Oxford Street. The bombs consisted of small bundles of incendiary material initiated by Second World War vintage British military 'L Delays'. These were specialist sabotage switches which were used by the SOE and Special Forces, as well as having been supplied to Resistance movements all over the world during the war. Each device found in London contained a small brass tablet engraved with the worlds P.F.L.P. (Popular Front for the Liberation of Palestine) and an inscription in Arabic.

Next, in August, a time bomb detonated in the reception office of the Israeli-owned Zim Shipping Line in Regent's Street, causing considerable damage. This device consisted of a Russian military hand grenade which was fitted with an electric detonator and a small battery. The requisite time delay was provided by a modified wrist-watch. When the grenade functioned it sprayed the office with fragments but fortunately only one person was injured.

On the home grown-front, on 27 October there was a violent demonstration in Grosvenor Square against American involvement in Vietnam. During this, a number of homemade bombs were thrown at the police. Most used firework compositions or sodium chlorate and sugar and were contained in tins with short firework fuses. One bomb, which fortunately failed to explode, contained over a pound of explosive, more than enough to kill or seriously injury anyone standing close to it had it functioned. (In those days, the police had none of the protective clothing and equipment that they have today.) Several other smaller bombs were thrown and also failed to explode. On the same day, just outside London, the Memorial to John F. Kennedy at Runnymede was attacked and badly damaged by a bomb which used an unknown high explosive as the main charge.

The first group to carry out a sustained terrorist campaign during this period had Spanish origins and could be traced back to the civil war in that country. The organisation called itself the First of May Group after the date of their earliest violent act. They were one of the original international, anti-capitalist, anti-imperialist, revolutionary organisations specifically established to carry out terrorist attacks. The activities of the group were not confined to Spain, and bomb and machine-gun attacks were carried out all over Europe. The first in London was a drive-by shooting at the American Embassy in Grosvenor Square. A group of three men fired a burst of sub-machinegun fire into the plate glass at the front of the building before speeding off, throwing handfuls of leaflets from their car as they fled.

Three months later there were coordinated attacks across Europe with bombs going off in Turin, The Hague and London. The London bombs were at the Spanish Embassy in Belgrave Square and the American Officers' Club at Lancaster Gate.

In February 1969, the Bank of Bilbao and another Spanish-owned Bank were targeted. Both the of these bombs failed to explode and were rendered safe by Explosive Officers and sent to the Explosives Division of the Royal Armament Research and Development Establishment at Fort Halstead, for examination. The communiqué issued by the terrorists at the time has a familiar ring to it today. It was addressed to 'The Pentagon and White House Killers' and proclaimed: 'Every man who does not want to go down on his knees to you can only reply by revolutionary direct action to your world of terrorist planning.'[1]

Around this time the First of May Group was officially disbanded and it was expected that the attacks would cease. Shortly afterwards, however, another bomb went off, this time outside the Bank of Bilbao in King Street, Covent Garden in March 1969. The perpetrators were seen acting suspiciously by two alert police officers in a car who were on routine patrol some thirty metres away. They watched the men advance to the front door of the bank, place a parcel in the doorway and set the fuze, which was an acid delay with a chlorate and sugar mix. Suddenly smoke billowed out into the street and the men began to run, escaping just before the bomb functioned. The police officers were out of their car in an instant and soon had the two men under arrest. The perpetrators were subsequently identified as British citizens – Alan Barlow and Phil Carver – who both claimed to be anarchists. They had in their possession a letter claiming responsibility for the attack on behalf of the First of May Group. Their arrest put a brief halt to the bombings using high explosives, although a number of fire bomb attacks continued against targets throughout the UK. The question for the authorities, which became the focus of the investigation, was how and why had these men got involved with a Spanish terror group?

The First of May Group was not the only faction of young men and women preaching revolution. As already mentioned, in the US there was 'The Weathermen' group, which set out to attack the capitalist system, in Germany the 'Baader Meinhof' gang was committing terrorist acts, whilst there were similar groups, not necessarily as violent, in many other European countries. In London there was a loose collection of left-wing revolutionaries. Amongst the more extreme were John Barker and Jim Greenfield, who had determined that they would follow the First of May's example and start some sort of armed resistance against the state. The logic to justify their actions was that they were the oppressed and it was the class system which kept the working man on the production line and compelled him to live in high rise flats. They saw this as a crime in itself. It forced ordinary people into a mindless cycle of work where they were so 'freaked out', as it was described at the time, by the way that they lived that their only escape was to beat up the people they loved. What the revolutionaries felt needed to be done was to channel that violence towards the people actually creating the situation of oppression in the first place. Oddly, it was clear to them that the bombings would not overthrow or significantly change the status quo, but it would make it that bit harder for those in power to govern. Where petitions were not forcing change, bombs would.

Their campaign took the British establishment and public by surprise. The country, as already recounted, had been attacked in many ways before, but the perpetrators had always had a clear motive, be it Home Rule, independence or self-government. The new group was interested only in the revolutionary process and wanted to change the nature and structure of society itself.

The problem for these new revolutionaries was quite simple; they did not know how to make improvised explosive devices. The solution was to talk to those who could and it was the First of May Group they decided to contact. And so, through left-wing channels, the message was passed: would First of May help supply explosives and weapons, and, more importantly, the training to go with them? The quid pro quo was that the targets the new group would go for would reflect the traditional First of May interests.

In May 1970 an incendiary device was discovered after a telephoned warning stated that a bomb had been left on an Iberian airliner at Heathrow Airport. The bomb was found and rendered safe and sent for forensic analysis. This showed that the initiation system was based on a commercial gas lighter head which was being used in the installation of the new gas appliances designed for use with North Sea gas which then was just coming on stream.

On 22 May 1970, a much more powerful device, using high explosive, was found at the site of the building of the new Paddington Police Station in Harrow Road. At around midday a workman on the site found a newspaper-wrapped package. Assuming it was his mate's sandwiches he picked it up and tossed it across the room to him. His mate unwrapped the newspaper and to his horror discovered the bomb. Peter Gurney was again tasked to the scene and rendered the bomb safe. It contained a commercial detonator and a French-manufactured explosive called Nitramite No.19C which consisted of ammonium nitrate and TNT. Initially no connection was made between the two devices, but the Explosives Division of the Royal Armament Research and Development Establishment at Fort Halstead discovered that the detonator on this bomb was to be initiated by a gas lighter of the same make as the incendiary at Heathrow.

Further work provided more evidence to link the devices. Both had two Ever Ready HP2 high power batteries connected in series which were, incidentally, also used to power the North Sea gas igniters. Both devices had pocket watches which had been modified in a similar manner to provide the delay before firing. Both used the same Sellotape to strap the various components together. Finally, both used a mixture of sodium chlorate and sugar to initiate the detonators. All in all, it was sufficient evidence to suggest that both the devices were, in some way, linked. This puzzled the detectives at Scotland Yard because there was no obvious ideological link between the two targets. The good news was that if this was the start of a new wave of political violence then it had got off to a very poor start.

On 3 July 1970, there were simultaneous attacks in Paris and London against the Spanish state tourist offices and the Spanish and Greek embassies. Next, on 18 August, the office of the Iberian Airlines was attacked in Regent's Street, London. A small bomb exploded which was estimated to have contained about half a pound of high explosive, but it did little damage and received even less press coverage.

Up until this time, the Explosive Officers, when on call outside normal working hours, were using their own personal vehicles to drive to tasks. With the new urgency surrounding the bombings it was decided that this was unacceptable and Austin vans with shelving in the back for equipment and stores were provided. However, outside normal working hours they still had to drive themselves in the vans to incidents wherever they occurred.

A few days later, on 30 August 1970, the unknown bombers struck at a target which they hoped would guarantee press coverage. A bomb exploded outside the residence of the London home of the Commissioner of the Metropolitan Police, Sir John Waldron. He was away at the time and only his daughter was at home, who although not injured, was deeply shocked by the experience.

Following the bombing Sir John was sent a letter stating that he had been sentenced to death. In block lettering it read:

DEAR BOSS

YOU HAVE BEEN SENTENCED TO DEATH BY THE REVOLUTIONARY TRIBUNAL FOR CRIMES OF OPPRESSION AGAINST THE MANY WHO ARE OPPOSED TO THE CAPITALIST REGEIME [*sic*] WHICH YOU KEEP IN POWER.
THE EXECUTIONER HAS BEEN SEVERELY REPRIMANDED FOR FAILING. WE WILL MAKE NO MISTAKES
BUTCH CASSIDY
THE SUNDANCE KID P.P. THE TRIBUNIAL [*sic*]

The bombing and the letter were kept both kept secret and initially neither was reported in the press. The Commissioner himself asked for a Special Branch briefing on why he was the target of such an attack but they were unable to throw any light on the matter.

Just over a week later another bomb detonated, this time it was outside the Chelsea home of the Attorney General, Sir Peter Rawlinson. The communiqué that went with it was in the same block handwriting with a similar message:

YOU CAN DREAM UP ALL THE LAW AND ORDER YOU LIKE. BUT REMEMBER – YOU ARE SUBJECT OF OUR JUSTICE. HE WHO LIVETH OFF THE PEOPLE BY THE PEOPLE HE SHALL DIE.

THE WILD BUNCH.

Once again the press and television networks were asked not to report the incident. It is not clear what effect that this had on the bombers, but it must have been very frustrating. How do you announce the beginning of a revolution to the world if the acts of violence your group commit go unreported and the general public doesn't know that the uprising has started? It was a conspiracy of silence by the authorities to deny the people the chance to support the work of the new urban guerrillas.

The next strike was at Heathrow and this time the bomb exploded in the Iberian Airlines' passenger lounge. Fortunately, there were no injuries, but considerable damage was caused as well as panic at the airport. There were simultaneous attacks in Geneva, Frankfurt and Paris. This time the story could not be suppressed and the news of the attacks were widely reported and attributed to the First of May Group.

Attorney General Rawlinson was attacked again on 8 October and on the following day the Italian Trade Centre in Cork Street, London was bombed. These attacks were claimed on behalf of the Italian anarchist Giuseppe Pinelli. He had been implicated in the bombing of a bank in Italy which killed sixteen people. During his interrogation, according to the Italian Police, he committed suicide by throwing himself out of a fourth floor window. Few people in Italy seemed to believe this explanation.

By now Special Branch had a suspect, Stuart Christie, who was known to have links with Italian anarchism. He had been briefly imprisoned in Spain and had other dubious contacts in France. He was put under full surveillance, and later his flat was raided. Although no incriminating evidence found he was still thought to be responsible for the First of May attacks in England.

The Miss World Contest, held at the Royal Albert Hall on 19 November, was a target far too tempting to miss, particularly for those who saw the event from a women's liberation point of view. Disrupting the live broadcast and then bombing it would guarantee worldwide publicity for the cause. Accordingly, a group of protestors interrupted the proceeding from one of the balconies by throwing flour and intimidating the contestants. They were swiftly removed, but later around 02.00 hours the following morning, a group of four or five men surrounded one of the BBC's outside broadcast vehicles which were lined up outside the venue. One of the men slipped a small device under the vehicle and they immediately fled the scene heading off towards Notting Hill.

A few minutes later there was a small explosion as around four ounces of TNT detonated under the truck. The small size of the charge meant that the damage was slight and the broadcast went on. Once again the group had dismally failed in their aim of gaining maximum publicity.

Remarkably, soon afterwards a drive-by shooting at the Spanish Embassy went completely unnoticed. Only one bullet hit the building and that was not discovered until sometime later by a cleaner. This attack was not only not noticed, but also not reported, and the perpetrators decided that the only way to deal with the lack of news was to report the incidents themselves via communiqués sent direct to the underground press, in their case, the *International Times*. To make sure everyone knew it was from the right group, they devised a stamp from a John Bull printing set and came up with the name of the 'Angry Brigade'. It was used for the first time after the drive-by shooting. The second communiqué sent later in the week stated that: 'Fascism and oppression will be smashed. (Spanish embassy machine gunned Thursday). High pigs, Judges, Embassies, Spectacles, Property.'

This communiqué seemed to link many of the past bombings, the High Pigs being the bomb outside the Waldron residence, 'Judges' referred to the Rawlinson bombs, 'Embassies' was a reference to the attacks there, and 'Property' conveniently covered the other bombings. 'Spectacles' was a less clear reference but was thought to relate to the spectacular and therefore linked to the Miss World bombing.

Politically this was a time of employment unrest, and during the cold damp day of 12 January 1971, the trade unions staged marches against a controversial Industrial Relations Bill which was being debated in the House of Commons. Throughout the day there had been lightning strikes, picketing and clashes with the police. It was, however, at 22.04 hours when a new and much more serious challenge was made to those in charge of the country's security.

At that time, the Right Honourable Robert Carr, Secretary of State for Employment, was at home in his house Monkenholt at Hadley Green. He was in the sitting room with his thirteen-year-old-daughter, working on his papers. His wife was in the kitchen clearing the dishes from the evening meal. Without warning there was the shattering sound of a violent explosion at the back of the house. Carr shouted to his wife and daughter to lie on the floor while he crawled to the door to see what had happened. Smoke was billowing in through the broken glass windows and the kitchen door had been blown in. Carr moved his family to safety in a neighbour's house and from there dialled 999 to report the explosion to the police.

Police Constable Leslie Horslen was driving the local late turn area car (a police term used to describe an response vehicle) at the time with two other officers. They were about to go off duty when the urgent call for police was received. Responding immediately, they sped to the scene arriving within a few minutes. By then a small crowd of people had gathered in front of the house. Horslen was about to speak to Carr about the incident when there was another explosion, this time near the front of the house. One of the policemen described the blast:

> I saw what I can only describe as a lazy sort of flame three or four feet high coming from the ground near the front door. At first I thought it was a gas pipe burning. But after a few seconds the flame burst into a sheet which rose up the front of Monkenholt as high as the first floor window.[2]

Everybody ran from the scene as this second explosion shattered the windows at the front of the house and blew in the hall door. Leslie Horslen had dropped to the road behind the area car and was laying there stunned. He heard one of the other officers say, 'Christ, it's Les. Get an ambulance'. But by then he was recovering his senses and staggered to his feet. The officers immediately began to clear the area.

Although probably not intentional, this was the first case of a secondary device at a terrorist incident in London. The use of a second bomb designed to detonate a short while after the first poses a major threat to police officers and other emergency services responding to the scenes of explosions. In this case, had the second bomb exploded a couple of minutes later there was a good chance that some of the officers may have actually been in the front garden, where they would have been seriously injured if not killed.

The police officers reported the second explosion over the radio, the news of which was quickly passed to Scotland Yard. Chief Superintendent Roy Habershon was assigned to head the subsequent enquiry and immediately made it clear to all that this was, as far as he was concerned, attempted murder and so set things in place on that basis. Explosives Officer Don Henderson also arrived to inspect the damage and give his opinion on the type and size of the devices.

The Angry Brigade, through the press, released a communiqué claiming responsibility for the blast. Worryingly for the authorities, it was clear that they were gaining in confidence and ability. It was impossible to suppress the news of this latest bombing and for the first time the public became aware of the arrival of the Angry Brigade on the political scene. The incident forced the authorities to take the threat of armed revolutionary violence much more seriously than had hitherto been the case.

The explosions at Carr's home also prompted Scotland Yard to reassess the progress of the enquiry into all the previous bombings and it was decided that a specialist squad was needed to track down the Angry Brigade and its supporters. It was initially headed by Chief Superintendent Roy Habershon who had taken charge of the Carr inquiry. It should be made clear that, at this stage, the 'Bomb Squad' was the term used to describe the police officers specifically selected to investigate crimes involving explosives and did not refer to the civilian Explosives Officers attached to the Metropolitan Police who actually rendered bombs safe.

The Angry Brigade, bolstered by news reports of their actions, continued their campaign by detonating further bombs in London. One went off at the trendy Biba Boutique in Kensington High Street, which seemed an odd choice for a target. This was followed by a device left on a windowsill at Tintagel House at midnight on 21 May, this building being used to house the Metropolitan Police's pay computer.

Despite the establishment of the Bomb Squad the police were struggling to make progress with their enquiries, although they were beginning to build up a picture of the left-wing political activists thought to be behind the bombings. Two further bombs caused Sir John Waldron to call another meeting of his senior officers at which he told them that the Angry Brigade must be crushed. To do this the 'Bomb Squad' establishment was expanded to twenty by recruiting seasoned detectives from Special Branch and the Flying Squad. It was led by Commander Ernest Bond, though because of the perceived threat his identify was kept secret and he was known initially only as Commander X.

The Angry Brigade planted two more bombs before a raid on 359, Amherst Road, Stoke Newington netted four of the leading members of the organisation, Anna Mendelson, Hilary Creek, John Barker and Jim Greenfield. At the flat, explosives, detonators, guns and ammunition were recovered. In addition, the incriminating John Bull stamp used in the Brigade's communiqués was also discovered. After a lengthy trial, all were found guilty and sentenced to ten years in prison. The arrest and jailing of the four seemed to break the back of the anarchist struggle and although there were a few more incidents most of these were with fairly primitive firebombs. These, in comparison to the previous attacks, although still criminal were much less serious and they tailed off soon after the end of the trial.

The troubles in the Middle East spilled over into London again in September 1972 when an extensive letter-bomb campaign was launched. It claimed the life of the Cultural Attaché at the Israeli Embassy, Dr Ami Shachori, who died when he opened a letter consisting of a spring-operated improvised explosive device containing just two ounces of explosive. He was sitting at his desk opening his mail when the bomb detonated and blew a jagged hole six inches in diameter in the wooden desktop. A secondary fragment of wood from the desk penetrated the ill-fated doctor's heart and killed him instantly. Had he been holding the letter a little higher up from the desk there is the strong possibility that he would have survived the attack, albeit with serious injuries.

The investigators discovered a further seven letter bombs in pink and blue envelopes of varying sizes with hand-written addresses in the Embassy and these were successfully rendered safe by the on-duty

Explosives Officer, Ron Wilson. He discovered that one partially opened device was in a very sensitive state. The firing lever was being held back by a sliver of paper. To disarm it without touching it, Wilson built a sand bag wall and using two books and a hook and line lowered these very gently on to the lever to press it down and back into the safe position. He then manually cut out the detonator, effectively rendering the bomb safe. The same day a further forty-two letter bombs were delivered to Jewish organisations around the world.

Black September, the Arab terrorist organisation, was behind the attacks and it would send a further 200 postal bombs worldwide over the next four months.[3] Although, historically the use of postal bombs goes back to the 1880s, and the Israelis had used them in 1947, this was the first mass attack using the international postal system. There were many serious security implications, one of the less obvious being that the bombs were delivered by airmail and potentially put at risk all the aircraft that carried them. The attack also set in process changes in post room procedures. Now, all mail sent to government offices and to most other major institutions is screened for suspect devices, normally by X-ray. It was the Black September bombs that initiated the process of screening mail, the result eventually being the establishment of a multi-million-pound industry which is still in place today.

In a bizarre way the attacks by the Angry Brigade and Black September were providential because they reinforced the need for a permanent Bomb Squad and it became an integral part of the investigating arm of the Metropolitan Police. The officers involved became the nucleus of those investigators who would soon face a much more serious threat. Prior to these bombings, incidents involving explosives in London would be investigated at a local level by ad hoc teams of detectives in the various Metropolitan Police divisions. It was obvious that, in the case of terrorist bombings, the lines of enquiry would cross both internal and external boundaries, and to prevent duplication and leads being lost, the Bomb Squad (which had been formed to do this) was put on a permanent footing. At the end of the trial of the Angry Brigade the judge had praised the Bomb Squad's officers for 'Exorcising the evil from within our midst', a sentiment taken from the excommunication curse which ends with the words, 'Close the book, quench the candle and ring the bell'. The officers adopted these words and symbols as the motto for the squad.

Another factor in making the Bomb Squad a permanent department in the Metropolitan Police was that the trouble in Northern Ireland was intensifying and civil disobedience and rioting had given way to shooting and bombing. It was clear to those with a historical perspective that the IRA would most likely decide to take their campaign of violence to the UK mainland. There was, therefore, a need to determine the policies and procedures that would have to be implemented to deter and deal with bombing attacks.

One of these was the use of dogs to find explosives substances. This evolved from the success of drugs detection dogs which had been introduced in the mid-1960s. With the continued use of explosives to attack safes and the increased threat from terrorism, in 1971 it was decided to train two dogs to find nitroglycerine-based explosives. These specialist search dog handlers worked in suits and ties so that, as well as ordinary searches, they could carry out covert work (it seems that in those days many people were very smartly dressed). The unit would grow steadily in size and capability as the terrorist threat in London developed.

As the numbers of attacks by the Angry Brigade and Black September escalated so did the work load of the Explosives Office and, with the troubles flaring in Northern Ireland, still more calls were made on the small number of staff. In 1969, the Explosive Officers dealt with fifty-seven calls to suspect bombs, an average of just one a week. The following year this increased to ninety, and in 1971 to 179, and finally in 1972 to 452. At the time there was not an immediate twenty-four-hour response to incidents unless there was specific intelligence of a pending operation.

The procedure adopted was that, during working hours, if a suspect device was discovered a police traffic car, with an experienced driver, would be despatched to the Explosives Officers office, in Richbell Place, to collect the duty Explosives Officer and drive him to the incident. If it occurred out of hours, then a traffic car would be dispatched to the on-call Explosives Officer's house from where he would be taken to the scene. This system was clearly inadequate and needed to change.

NOTES:
1. Carr, Gordon, *The Angry Brigade*, Victor Gollancz Ltd, London, 1975.
2. ibid.
3. Huntley, Bob, *Bomb Squad*, W.H. Allen, London, 1977.

Chapter 19

Car Bombs and Cutting Wires

'The IRA were to learn that as a means of changing public opinion, bombing was hopelessly inefficient and counter-productive, though this never diminished the appetite for mainland operations.'

Patrick Bishop.

In the early 1970s Northern Ireland descended into chaos and the Republican movement also underwent a fundamental change. The IRA splintered and a new faction, the Provisional IRA or PIRA, was born. It quickly seized and consolidated its hold on power and the seeds were sown for the confrontation that would ultimately last for some thirty years. As the violence in Ireland intensified, the leaders of the new organisation made plans to take the offensive back to the mainland with London the primary target.

The first bomb of the 1970s, however, was not planted by PIRA. In fact, it has never been claimed by a terrorist group or conclusively attributed to one. Most consider it was the work of the Official IRA, although it has been asserted by some that it was the last act of the Angry Brigade. It exploded without warning some 500 feet off the ground at the top of the Post Office Tower at 16.20 hours on Sunday, 31 October 1971. The device, containing an estimated twenty-five pounds of explosive, was hidden above a false ceiling in the toilets on the 31st floor on one of the public observation platforms. The explosion ripped away almost half of the superficial structures on the floor leaving it open and exposed and scattering debris over the ground and rooftops below, although fortunately it did no serious structural damage.

The location of the bomb presented the investigators with unique difficulties. Owing to the considerable magnitude of the work, the task of examining the scene and recovering relevant pieces of evidence from both the Tower and the surrounding scene was, logically, divided into two areas. It was agreed that Don Henderson and Sandy Hawkins would deal with the tower platform and that staff from the forensic branch at Woolwich would search the ground and rooftops of the surrounding area.

The search of the debris on the platform was hindered by flooding from a ruptured water pipe. There was also a tangled pile of razor-sharp shattered metal originating from the structure and fittings of the toilets and from the large metal ducts which were positioned over the site of the explosion. The telecommunications cables carried in these ducts were also shredded, as were the normal domestic electrical cables, which meant that there was a multiplicity of wiring fragments on the platform. There was no official uniform or light protective clothing for the Explosives Officers at this time (and for many years later) and dress was still civilian suits. So clad, Henderson and Hawkins scrambled round the open floor 500 feet up looking for fragments from the bomb with no protection from the weather, water or debris. Despite the difficulties, components from an alarm clock were recovered from the seat of the explosion. In addition, other components from the bomb were discovered on a roof of a house next to the Tower. Despite the recovery of fragments from the bomb, and despite a detailed police investigation, it proved impossible to draw any serious conclusions about the perpetrators of the attack.

In February 1972 the first PIRA car bomb detonated on the British mainland when a vehicle packed with 200 pounds of explosive exploded without warning outside the Parachute Regiment's Officers' Mess in Aldershot. It was allegedly timed to explode at lunch time to cause mass casualties amongst the officers of the regiment but, like many bombs, it exploded prematurely and killed five women cleaners, a gardener and a Roman Catholic priest.

In Northern Ireland, in the early spring of 1973, the PIRA made the decision to plant four car bombs in Central London. About three weeks before the attack they hijacked the necessary cars, a Hillman Hunter, a Vauxhall Viva, a Ford Cortina and a Ford Corsair, at gun point; they were driven south to the border area where they were re-sprayed and fitted with false number plates. Then plastic bags filled with a homemade explosive known as 'Co-op mix' were stuffed into the spaces under the rear seats. Next, sausages of commercial explosive were placed alongside the homemade mix and these were linked with detonating cord to timing and power units under the front seats. The cars were then sent south to Dublin to await shipping to mainland UK. Shortly afterwards, a team of eleven young and inexperienced PIRA volunteers arranged to take the cars in two groups to Liverpool and then on to London. The day before the attack, Dolours Price, who was to run the operation, flew from Dublin to London. In the evening, when others went to reconnoitre the sites for the car bombs, she and her sister, Marian, allegedly went to the Royal Court Theatre to see a play called 'The Freedom of the City' in which a group of Catholics stage a takeover of the Londonderry Guildhall.

The following day, 8 March, the group rose at dawn and positioned their vehicles: one in Dean Stanley Street, the Home of the British Forces' Broadcasting Services offices; the next in Great Scotland Yard, outside the Army's Central Recruiting Office; another outside the Old Bailey; and the final one in the Broadway outside New Scotland Yard. The timers were all set for 15.00 hours (although when using just the hour hand of a clock it is only ever possible to get an approximate time) and the dowel pins were removed from the timing and power units. The teams then headed off to a rendezvous at Trafalgar Square. There they showed the Price sisters their dowel pins to prove the bombs were correctly set and then they left for Heathrow aiming to be back in Dublin before the first of the bombs exploded.

Peter Gurney, who it will be recalled had already dealt with a bomb at the Greek Embassy in 1969, joined the Explosives Office in February 1973 (after a successful career in the Army he was initially unsure of what the future would hold for him). Within a month, intelligence reports had been received that the PIRA were planning major car bomb attacks in London on 8 March. The Explosives Office was, for the first time, put on full-time manning and, at the same time, police officers set about scouring London for any suspect vehicles. The task was huge, but to add to the problem there was industrial action on British Rail and the London Underground and parking restrictions had been lifted to help commuters get to work.

At around 08.30 hours, two officers from the Special Patrol Group, Police Constables Stanely Conley and George Burrows, found what they thought was a suspicious Ford saloon parked outside the post office in the Broadway, almost directly opposite Scotland Yard. It was an outstanding example of first-rate police work; it demonstrated the uncanny ability of well-trained police officers to spot something unusual or out of the ordinary and then follow up their instincts until the matter is satisfactorily resolved. It happens all the time and often the police officers themselves get little public credit for their vigilance and subsequent diligence in following up their suspicions. In this case, the two men not only noticed that the vehicle was heavily laden, but more importantly the number plate NYP 477J was not right for the make and model of the car. Further examination of the plates showed that they had been recently tampered with. Inside the car they noticed an air freshener. This could be used to disguise the smell of the 'Co-op mix' which was made with nitrobenzene and had a very distinctive pungent smell.

The officers reported their findings and the cordon and evacuation of the area began. Moments later, Explosives Officers Geoffrey Biddle and Peter Gurney arrived at the scene in a police car. They, too, disliked the look of the Ford and went forward for a closer inspection. They found the driver's door open and leaned in to open the rear door. Despite the air freshener, the smell of the 'Co-op mix' was unmistakable. Biddle and Gurney quickly located the detonating cord protruding from under the back of the front seat. After examining this they cut it, severing the link between the timing and power unit in the front of the vehicle and the main charge in the back. They then traced the cord to the back seat of the car; on lifting this out they discovered what turned out to be 130 pounds of home-made explosive along with seventeen pounds of commercial explosive to act as a booster charge. The timing and power unit was located under the front seat with the detonator leads running from it and taped to the detonating cord. The lead wires to the detonator were cut and then the timing and power unit removed and examined. It contained a battery, a clothes peg arming device, a test lamp and an alarm clock with the minute hand removed. The car bomb was now safe.

The confirmation that at least one bomb had been planted resulted in a decision being made to 'close England', to try and prevent the bombers escaping. Special Branch officers at all ports and airports were instructed to stop and question all Irish persons leaving for any destination. It paid dividends and the bombers were all arrested at Heathrow, some after actually boarding a British European Airlines flight to Dublin. Despite immediate questioning they refused to reveal the location of any of the other vehicle bombs. According to one detective who was questioning Marion Price, at 14.50 hours she looked at her watch and smiled, thinking that nothing could now stop the bombs exploding. Had the initial bomb not been found by the two Special Patrol Group officers, then the bombers would all have escaped and been back in Ireland before the first explosion.

Back in London every available police officer had been deployed to search for the remaining suspect vehicles, but it was like looking for a needle in a haystack. It was just before 14.00 hours when the first bomb threat was telephoned through to *The Times*, giving the locations of three of the cars and their registrations. Time was short. The bomb in Dean

Stanley Street, packed into the Vauxhall Viva, was located and defused by an Explosives Officer, Sandy Hawkins. It was a replica of the Scotland Yard bomb and contained over 100 pounds of explosive.

The bomb in Great Scotland Yard was tackled by a team of Army bomb disposal experts from the RAOC who had been called into the centre of London to reinforce the Explosives Officers. The immediate area had been cordoned and evacuated, but a lack of experience meant that the distances were insufficient. The Army team decided to try to pull the vehicle away from the buildings and tied a rope around the rear axle, intending to pull it from a safe distance. This was sometimes done in Northern Ireland in case the bomb had an anti-handling system. Just as they were about to start pulling it detonated at 14.44 hours. Sixty-one people were injured and much damage was done.

Another warning gave the location of the fourth car as outside the Old Bailey. The City of London Police was in charge of this incident. It must be remembered that at this time most police officers had absolutely no experience of dealing with bombs, let alone car bombs. They had little, if any, training and no understanding of the power and violence that a bomb of this magnitude could unleash. The suspect vehicle, a Cortina was located shortly after 14.15 hours by Police Constable Christopher Corke and he began the process of evacuating the area. In the Court itself, Police Sergeant Frederick Blease was on duty and he began evacuating the court rooms. Outside, more police officers arrived on scene to help with the evacuation. The understandable lack of experience of such incidents showed and several of the officers were standing around the vehicle at a distance of no more than thirty metres thinking that they would be safe. Another police officer went into The George public house nearby and ordered the drinkers to leave. They looked at him in disbelief, and most carried on drinking, not believing that a bomb was about to go off. A few left but others stayed to finish their drinks.

This highlights a common problem which police officers encounter every time they are called to a suspect item and decide that the area around it must be cordoned and evacuated. Getting people to understand the danger they are in is not easy. Some want to look to see what is going on, rather like 'rubber-neckers' at the scene of a road traffic accident. Many people inside buildings press their noses up against the windows to get a good view of what is occurring, setting themselves up for dreadful injuries from flying glass should a device explode.

As demonstrated by the customers at The George, alcohol makes people brave, self-confident and sometimes arrogant, attitudes that invariably evaporate in the same instant as an explosion. Others, particularly those who like to think they are VIPs, such as some MPs, deem themselves too important or busy to be ordered around by policemen, often making the assumption that the incident is a false alarm. Finally, there are those from the press who are more concerned at getting to the scene to get a picture or a story, oblivious of the danger they are putting themselves in.

The cordon and evacuation of an area in a busy city when a bomb threat has been received can involve the movement of literally thousands of people, and the difficulty of doing this should never be underestimated. Mercifully, though, some people do take warnings seriously. A school bus had just arrived at the Old Bailey and disembarked forty-nine children. Sensibly the teachers heeded the warning given by a police officer and took the children around a corner, out of the line of sight of the bomb and to comparative safety.

At the scene, Explosive Officers Ron Wilson and Don Henderson had just reached the area and were about to approach the suspect car. Other police officers were still far too near the vehicle. The closest was Police Constable Dale Wilkinson of the photographic unit who was called in to take pictures.

At 14.51 hours the hour hand on the clock reached its contact post and the vehicle disintegrated in a massive blast. Wilkinson was hurled across the road and seriously injured; other policemen nearby were blown to the ground. The court buildings were rocked by the explosion and high-velocity fragments scythed through the air, some of them embedding themselves in the doorframe of Hillgate House, over fifty metres away.

As the roar of the explosion died away the uninjured police officers picked themselves up and immediately set about helping the wounded. People were staggering around covered in blood, many of the injuries caused by fragments of flying glass. One man, Frederick Milton, the housekeeper at Hillgate House, was soaked in blood but refused to be evacuated until he had helped rescue and treat two of his injured porters. He collapsed two hours later and died of a heart attack in hospital. (Later the autopsy revealed that the heart attack had actually begun before the explosion. Although the inquest jury decided that he had been murdered, the Director of Public Prosecutions ruled that the medical evidence would not support such a charge.)

One police officer, Malcolm Hine, was hit in the head by part of the car and severely injured. His survival was certainly down to the fact that he was wearing his helmet which protected his skull against the worst of the impact. This is now preserved and is exhibited in the City Police Museum. In total 162 people were injured in the explosion, including many in The George who had, unwisely, refused to be evacuated.

With great foresight, the City of London Police gathered as many photographs of the bombing as they could to help them evaluate the response to the incident. The aim was to identify the key lessons that needed to be learned and what new procedures needed to be adopted when dealing in the future with suspect or confirmed vehicle bombs, and in the worst case, the actions that ought to be taken in the event of an explosion.

The first lesson, of course, was the need for greater cordon and evacuation distances and more urgency when moving people out of the danger zone. In this the police were helped by the sheer terror generated by the PIRA attacks and the subsequent alarmist reporting in the press. The complacency shown by those involved in these first attacks when being told to evacuate was replaced by a level of fear. Subsequently, it was much easier to get most people to comply with instructions to move. London was a frightened city.

Photographs taken immediately after the explosion at the Old Bailey showed bewildered and stunned people just standing in the road. Then office workers and others can be seen spilling out of buildings and onto the street; some went to help the injured, a few just wandered around aimlessly looking at the scene. The clear priority at this stage was the rescue and treatment of casualties. The emergency services put in a full response and soon police cars, ambulances and fire engines had so clogged the streets around the area that it was impossible for some to move, or they were obstructed in carrying out their primary task. It was apparent that there was a need for a rendezvous point, some distance from the site of the incident, from where command and control could be established, and to where emergency service vehicles responding to calls could report for instructions.

Other post explosion photographs showed hundreds of emergency service personnel, senior officers and onlookers swarming all over the site, most doing no good at all. It was established that after the initial firefighting and rescue operations, the area had to be sealed to prevent this mass of people crawling over a crime scene and destroying, or inadvertently removing, evidence on the soles of their shoes or wheels of their vehicles. One issue, the danger of secondary devices at or near the incident, was not addressed.

Today, inside the Old Bailey, there is still evidence of the attack on the heart of British justice. A shard of glass, blown in from one of the windows, has been left where it finished up embedded in the ceiling above the stairway leading to the court rooms.

In political terms, neither side in the affair could claim victory. The bombers had been arrested, but three of their bombs had gone off, producing a satisfying howl from the politicians in Westminster. However, despite this there was absolutely no sign of the hoped for clamour for a withdrawal from Northern Ireland from the British public. The PIRA leaders were going to have to learn that, as a means of changing public opinion, bombing was counter-productive and hardened attitudes all round. Nonetheless, this never diminished their appetite for mainland operations which were seen as central to the overall goal of a united Ireland. The PIRA decided that they were going to bomb mainland Britain like it had never been bombed before and that they were not going to make the same mistakes that led to the arrests at Heathrow.

Thus the PIRA decided that a new team of activists would be put together who would be dedicated volunteers with no criminal records. They would integrate themselves into the London community, but stay away from traditional Irish areas with their wagging tongues. They would operate on their own initiative and minimize contact with their leaders in Ireland. Finally, they would be in for the long haul. It would take the PIRA a while to set up this new team and in the meantime a number of other attacks were carried out.

Bombs were planted firstly in the Midlands and then in London where a series of incendiaries were left in leading shops, including Harrods and Liberty's store in Regent's Street. Most failed to go off, or if they did, only caused minor fires. The next attacks were of a much more serious character and a number of small high explosive devices were left in carrier bags, the first being discovered by a courting couple in Kingswell Parade in Heath Street, Hamstead. The pair was taking a stroll through the covered shopping centre in the late evening when they found a very nondescript shopping bag by a carpet shop's window. They looked inside and saw an alarm clock and a battery with leads leading to another package. They could distinctly hear the clock ticking. Another couple stopped to look at the bag and they decided between them it was a bomb and phoned the police from a call box (there were no mobile phones then). The first officers on scene organised the evacuation of the area, including moving customers from a nearby restaurant. This was just complete when the bomb detonated. The scene was duly examined by Explosive Officers who estimated the bomb contained a charge of some three pounds of explosive.

No warning was given of the attack and it heralded a new phase in the development of the PIRA campaign. It sounds bizarre today when news of various terrorist atrocities is never far from the front page, but back then the concept of bombs being left in innocuous items and exploding without warning was both novel and terrifying. The police were faced with the problem of tracking down a number of faceless, anonymous terrorists. To start with, the task of catching them was to be like chasing shadows. The PIRA campaign, designed to generate sheer terror, was not directed solely against so-called legitimate military or government targets, which at least could be patrolled or guarded. To protect everything in London was simply impossible. The first step was to warn the public to report unattended bags or parcels. Now, as any train or tube traveller knows, it is just a routine warning and something people live with as part of their everyday lives.

The PIRA next posted a wave of parcel bombs to government and military establishments. Each of the hollowed-out books they used contained a concealed charge of four ounces of high explosive – which was more than enough to kill anyone opening them. And open them they did, but a fault in their construction meant that none of them exploded. One of the bombs was unwrapped by a very busy secretary in Downing Street who, on seeing the book, decided it was the equivalent of junk mail and, rather than open it, simply discarded it into a waste paper bin. It was some hours later when the other bombs were reported on the news that she realized what it might be and informed the authorities. It was subsequently located and rendered safe. Instructions were given to ensure that all mail sent to government ministers, and other prominent persons, was intercepted and anything regarded as suspicious was taken to Scotland Yard to be examined in a newly installed X-ray machine. This made the dangerous assumption that a postal bomb would not explode unless it was opened and that it could be safely transported and handled. This is not always the case.

Another public warning about the possibilities of more bombs was issued by the then head of the Bomb Squad, Commander Huntley, who counselled people against the dangers of opening unexpected parcels. The warning, by chance, coincided with an Irish firm sending out hundreds of hand-written envelopes containing sweepstake tickets. These caused countless false alarms, all of which needed careful investigation.

It became clear at this time that it was wholly inappropriate for the Explosive Officers to be driven to suspect bombs relying on ad hoc arrangements made with traffic patrol car drivers. In late August 'Class One' police drivers from traffic branch, suitably qualified in high speed driving techniques, were assigned to the unit. It was recorded at the time that this arrangement provided instant readiness and, by getting to incidents quickly, it had enabled a number of bombs, which would otherwise have exploded, to be rendered safe. The drivers were later withdrawn for a short period, but before the end of 1973 were returned and permanently assigned to the office. These highly-trained police drivers immediately recognised that the Austin vans were completely inappropriate as response vehicles and the first Range Rover was bought to remedy this. The original one was an odd shade of yellow, although subsequent vehicles were white and had the Metropolitan Police markings added.

On 23 August 1973, the capital's transport system was attacked. At the beginning of the evening rush hour, a bomb was discovered in a bag, ironically adorned with a Union Jack, in Baker Street Underground station. It was spotted by a railway porter, Len Mylam, leaning up against a window of a chemist's shop inside the booking hall. He looked inside, saw an alarm clock, wires and battery, and had no doubt about what it was. The police were called and the area evacuated. Ten minutes later the Press Association was warned of a bomb left in the area of the station.

Peter Gurney was tasked to the scene and on his arrival, at 17.00 hours, he immediately organised a further evacuation of people. He then went forward to examine the bag and saw what, to him, was the familiar circuitry of a time bomb, although the explosive charge appeared to be in a separate cardboard box. After thoroughly checking the device without disturbing anything, he cut one of the wires and then lifted the bomb out of the plastic bag. He opened the cardboard box to discover a detonator and commercial explosive; he removed the detonator and so rendered the device safe. After a further examination of the components, he checked the settings on the clock and came to the conclusion that the device was timed to function at 17.37 hours. Everything was then removed to Scotland Yard for photography and detailed forensic examination, during which twelve packets of Eversoft Plastagelatine were identified. Forensic examination of the book bombs had revealed they contained the same explosive and it was therefore possible that the attacks were linked.

Not surprisingly, for a few days afterwards there was a spate of false alarms all over British Rail and the Underground which resulted in considerable disruption to the transport system. Most of the suspect items turned out to be lost or stolen bags or boxes of rubbish which previously were not deemed suspicious, but which were looked at in a different light after the Baker Street bomb. All had to be dealt with as if they were genuine calls; some items were examined by police officers and discounted, but many others had to be treated seriously until an Explosives Officer's examination revealed them to be innocuous. It set a pattern of operation for the police and the Explosives Officers which has been used ever since. There would be periods of comparative quiet followed by spikes of intense activity after each bombing or attempted bombing.

It was inevitable that there would soon be more casualties from the bombing campaign and, despite the warnings about postal bombs, an explosion occurred in the Stock Exchange on 24 August 1973. A package was received there by George Brind, the Secretary General for the Exchange. He was about to open it when his secretary, Miss Joanna Knight, took it from him and began to slit it open with a paper knife. It detonated between them and both were thrown off their feet. Brind escaped serious injury, but Knight suffered multiple cuts to her face and body. They were both lucky to survive.

That night, another telephoned bomb threat preceded the detonation of a bomb in Kilburn. The following day a security guard, Derek Woodward, lost a hand when a book bomb he was examining at the Bank of England exploded.

The same day, a telephone call included the threat that another bomb had been left in the Adams store in Oxford Street. The call illustrated the dangers of vague and sometimes misleading warnings. It was immediately appreciated by local officers that there was no such shop as Adams in Oxford Street. It was also realized that it would be impossible to evacuate the whole of Oxford Street as, in doing so, it was quite possible that people could be moved away from a place of safety and into one of danger, something that has subsequently happened on more than one occasion. All that could be done was to deploy police officers into the area to search outside the shops and get security staff to do the same inside their buildings. Whilst this was in progress a loud pop was heard in the premises of Etams, which led to the discovery of a white plastic bag under a clothes rail. Bomb Squad officers and an Explosives Officer raced to the scene from the Bank of England. When the bag was initially examined, all that was found was some washing powder, firelighters and tea bags, but underneath was the bomb with the by now familiar Eversoft Plastagelatine; there was a total three pounds of the explosive in twelve sticks. In this case the detonator had exploded, but had failed to initiate the main explosive charge. Had it done so, it would, without doubt, have caused death and serious injury to those inside the shop.

That afternoon a hoax call disrupted a cricket match at Lord's, the ground packed with 28,000 spectators. The stands were evacuated with many people being moved onto the pitch itself. A two-hour search revealed nothing and the game continued.

Next, there were a spate of postal bombs in British embassies abroad, as well as more incendiaries in Birmingham. Then, on 30 August 1973, Baker Street Underground Station was attacked again during the evening rush hour. A railwayman found a carrier bag lying on a footbridge and raised the alarm. Explosive Officer Don Henderson attended the scene and descended into the Underground to examine the bag. In his statement he said:

> The base of the carrier bag was on the ground but the top had fallen over, concealing the contents. On hearing a ticking noise coming from the bag I lifted the top and, looking inside, saw what I recognised to be a time-bomb. The clock was lying face downwards and being unable to establish how much time remained before the bomb would explode I decided not to waste time putting on protective clothing. I could see no obvious booby trap mechanisms
>
> I, therefore, placed both hands inside the carrier bag and opening the cardboard box and withdrew the detonator from its position.[1]

Henderson briefly considered leaving the device to fire like this, presumably to find out how long was left on the clock, but decided against this and subsequently disconnected the detonator. At the same time, a train arrived in the station under the footbridge and began disgorging its passengers. Henderson gathered up the bomb and took it to the British Transport Police offices for further examination. There it became apparent that there were only ten minutes or so left on the clock. No warning had been given for this device and the potential for carnage had it exploded was tremendous. In the event the Underground was hardly disrupted at all.

Just after midnight a telephone call stated there was a bomb near Marble Arch. The caller advised that a 600-yard evacuation area was necessary. Just eight minutes later, not sufficient time to even locate the bomb, let alone evacuate the area, it exploded close to Marble Arch at the corner of Oxford Street and Quebec Street damaging cars and shattering windows in the Cumberland Hotel. Fortunately, no one was killed or injured.

It had been a frenetic few days, requiring the police to deal with explosions, bombs and hundreds of false alarms. There was sense of outrage and impotence in face of the continued attacks and the arrogance of the bombers. There was major disruption to the transport network throughout London, but the procedures in place ensured that this time was minimised and, for example, the bomb rendered safe at Baker Street only resulted in the line being shut for half an hour. A similar incident today would result in a considerably longer closure to try and recover every scrap of forensic evidence. Today, quite rightly, there is much greater emphasis on the 'duty of care' to all those concerned in the incident. Even so, sometimes long closures play into the terrorists' hands.

After a short break the attacks started again. At Victoria Station, Police Constable Tony Hoskins, an alert British Transport Police officer, spotted a suspicious bag on a ledge near a ticket office opposite Platform 14. He looked inside and instantly recognised the contents as a bomb. He and two other officers who had just arrived set about the evacuation of the immediate area. As they did so a threat call came into Scotland Yard. It simply stated the bomb was in the station, giving no indication of where it was or when it would go off. Three minutes later it detonated. It takes much more time than that to pass on warnings, locate the suspect device and evacuate people from the area. Tony Hoskins' alertness and immediate action had, once again, protected the public, probably saved many lives and prevented serious injuries. Nevertheless, he and four others were slightly wounded carrying out their duty.

One of the lessons learnt that day was that the area to be searched for forensic evidence needed to be extended. Commander Bob Huntley, the head of the Bomb Squad, went to the scene at Victoria and noted that the area to be searched for forensic evidence had been cordoned off to approximately fifty metres. He decided to walk some distance beyond this and in doing so found a fragment of a screw with a section of wire wrapped around it. He immediately recognised that this could well be a part of the bomb. By now forensic teams were able recover very small blast-damaged components of a device, for example, parts of a watch or an alarm clock, and identify the type and make of the original. This made it possible to link a number of devices which all used the same components, which in turn implied that that they were all made by the same person or team. Due to the discovery of the component well beyond the fifty metre point, Huntley ordered that the area to be searched for forensic evidence should be increased in this and all future incidents.

The PIRA targeted the transport system again and laid two bombs in litter bins which exploded at King's Cross and Euston on 10 September 1973. In the days that followed, there were hundreds of warnings phoned in to the police. They had no choice but to take each one seriously and respond as if a live device might be encountered. At different times all the mainline stations were brought to a standstill and British Rail was forced to shut waiting-rooms, snack bars and left-luggage facilities to try and reduce the areas that needed to be searched in the case of a bomb threat.

Oxford Street seemed to have a compulsive fascination for the bombers. It was considered a key economic target, but more significantly the crowds of people, most of whom carried bags of some sort, meant that it was easy for the bombers to remain anonymous. On 12 September, a secretary taking an old open lift to the fifth floor of the

Prudential building noticed through the mesh that there was an unattended black and white carrier bag on the first floor. By now, thanks to the repeated warnings by Scotland Yard, the pubic were beginning to respond to all such unattended bags and the secretary raised the alarm. The area was cleared and shortly afterwards there was an ear splitting explosion. Outside the building two cars crashed into each other and Oxford Street came to a standstill.

Tragedy struck a few days later when the first RAOC bomb disposal operator to die serving on the mainland UK was killed in Birmingham. Captain Ronald Wilkinson of the RAOC, who dealt with all the bombs outside London, was severely injured when a bomb he was investigating detonated. He was rushed to hospital but died a week later of his wounds. Already ten other RAOC bomb disposal officers had been killed on duty in Northern Ireland. The first death on the mainland was a harsh reminder of the dangers and risks taken by such men.

The next significant incident in London occurred on 28 September 1973, when a bomb was left at the West London Air Terminal in Cromwell Road. A threat call was received at 15.54 hours giving a time of detonation of 16.00 hours, yet again a wholly inadequate time. Fortunately, a police car was close to the terminal and the two police officers in it, Pierre Davidson and Michael Hempston, were on scene almost immediately. Bravely, and with no concern for their own safety, they rushed in and spotted a brown paper parcel on the first landing. At the time the occupants of the building were all being evacuated past the package. The two officers managed to stop this evacuation past the bomb and pushed the frightened people clear of the landing. Moments later the device detonated shattering the building and injuring the two police officers. Once again the fearless and unselfish actions of ordinary police officers prevented members of the public from being killed or very seriously injured.

In October 1973, the fledgling CCTV systems being installed in many premises had the first of many successes. A thin, sharp-faced man with a curly black beard was seen outside the premises of Allen International, in Old Pye Street, Westminster, by a security camera. The man approached the door to the property with two bags in his hands. He put one over the CCTV camera in the entrance, unaware that this was actually a dummy. Higher in the doorway another camera was in operation and upstairs the scene was being monitored by Harold Tracey, the head of Allen International. He guessed what was happening and incensed at what he saw he rushed downstairs and confronted the bomber in the doorway. The latter threw the second bag with the bomb

349

in it at Tracey and fled. Tracey picked up the bomb and threw it back at the fleeing man; it landed in the road. Then, ignoring the bomb, he took off after the perpetrator but unfortunately lost him. He returned to his premises to discover that his staff had raised the alarm and that a police car was standing outside the building. It had parked almost on top of the bomb which was in the gutter. The police asked where it was, and on being told, the driver beat a hasty retreat. The bomb was later defused and four pounds of explosive recovered. Its design was identical to bombs recovered at Baker Street and the Etam shop.

Then there was no recording facility in the fledgling CCTV systems, but Tracey was able to give a good description of the man and a photo-fit picture was soon issued. The response was immediate and the owner of a house in Kilburn stated categorically that the man had rented one of his flats. Further investigations established the man, who had lived with there with his girlfriend, had fled to Ireland. One interesting fact did emerge; the man was reported by several witnesses fleeing into Westminster Underground station. This tied in with a theory that the bombers were using the public transport system to move around. Furthermore, they were using well-lit public toilets to arm their bombs close to the intended targets. This meant that they did not have to travel with the devices 'up and running' with the risk of being caught out if the Underground train they were on was held up in a tunnel. The use of well-lit toilets also reduced the chances of an 'own goal'. It was safer preparing a bomb for firing there than fiddling about trying to arm a device in a dark, badly-lit doorway.

Shortly after this incident, Don Henderson was tasked to another suspect plastic carrier bag lying in the road in Old Pye Street. He immediately went forward to examine it and could clearly hear it ticking. He opened the bag and discovered that inside was a white paper bag. He tore a hole in this to discover an assembly consisting of an alarm clock, which was face down, batteries, two cardboard cartons and associated wiring. Recognising the detonator lead wires he immediately severed these. He then turned the alarm clock over, noting that the time was 21.26 hours and that the minute hand was approaching an electrical contact. By direct observation he realised that the hand touched the contact exactly five minutes later at 21.31 hours. Henderson disassembled the rest of the device, recording that each of the cardboard cartons contained about two-and-a-half pounds of explosive. There had been no warning about the bomb and, had it gone off, Henderson considered that any passers-by would have been killed or seriously injured.

The PIRA next dispatched another series of postal bombs on 16 December, all of which arrived the following day. Brigadier Michael

O'Cock, ex-Irish Guards, was injured when a book bomb he had received exploded in his Kensington home. He was lying on a settee opening his morning mail when, looking into the end of one unexpected brown envelope, he recognised the components of a letter bomb. He immediately reached down to push this under the settee when it exploded and he suffered injuries to his hand.

The following day, on 18 December, a much more serious incident occurred. A telephoned threat was given to the police about a bomb at the junction of Horseferry Road and Marshall Street. The problem with inaccurate warnings was once again illustrated because there is no Marshall Street anywhere near Horseferry Road. The best guess was that the caller had made a mistake and meant Marsham Street which, geographically, did make sense. Police arrived at the scene and began using white tape, commonly seen now but then just being introduced, to cordon off the area. They also used megaphones to warn people to get out of the way. Officers then courageously began the process of checking the cars in the street; no one knew then that they would not find anything suspicious as they were all looking in the wrong place. The location of the device became clear minutes later when a car bomb detonated by Horsferry House in Thorney Street, 100 yards from the location given in the warning. It was a miracle that no one was killed, but there were many serious injuries and some lucky escapes. Fifty-two people were injured; ironically one of them, with terrible wounds from flying glass, was an Irish Catholic, Mrs Rosina Harrington. The imprecise, or deliberately false, location in the threat had meant that some people had been evacuated from a place of safety into the danger area where they were injured. As usual the PIRA tried to place the blame for the injuries at the police's door.

On the same day a car bomb exploded close to the Pentonville Prison Officers' Social Club. A short warning was given but insufficient time was available to locate the car and evacuate people. Considerable damage was done and several individuals injured.

On 19 December 1973, another letter bomb was delivered to Burnaby Drayson MP. He started to open it and found that it contained a calendar. He became suspicious and an Explosives Officer, Jim Greenwood, attended the incident. He stated simply: 'Opening the calendar under precautions I saw what I believed to be the components of a letter bomb and proceeded to disarm it.'[2]

At 16.00 hours on 20 December, Ron Wilson was tasked to a suspect bag lying on the pavement of South Carriage Drive in Hyde Park. On arrival the bag was pointed out and he made a rapid and superficial inspection of it. It was immediately apparent that this was a bomb as

Wilson he could see a clock, batteries, wires and a package all of which were held together with brown tape. He said:

> I noticed that the clock was fitted with only one hand and although part of the face of the clock was obscured by adhesive tape, the hand appeared to be in contact with a screw, which I considered to be acting as an electrode, inserted through the lens of the clock in a position of approximately six o'- clock. Because of the position of the hand of the clock I regarded the device as being in a particularly dangerous condition with the possibility that any slight movement could have completed an electrical circuit with the consequent initiation of a violent explosion.[3]

Wilson cut the wires to the battery and after a careful examination, in which he further separated the components of the bomb, it was packed and labelled for submission to the explosives forensic laboratory. The main charge consisted of two, eight-ounce sticks of explosive, significantly less than the other bombs.

There was a good reason for this. As Christmas was approaching, the PIRA team was running out of explosives. As a result, a series of small bombs containing just a couple of ounces of explosive and encased within cigarette packets was left in locations all over London. Some of these were in cinemas. The first detonated under a seat in Leicester Square, where an audience of a hundred or so were enjoying a film called *Hungry for Sex*. The next interrupted *Mash* at the Swiss Centre, whilst a third went off in the cinema in Panton Street in the middle of *Clockwork Orange*. Luckily there were no serious injuries, although many people suffered from shock. In those days of smoke-filled cinemas what could be more innocent than someone discarding an apparently empty cigarette packet?

On 23 December an ominous warning was received at the Press Association. It simply stated: 'Three Christmas presents for you tonight, for the dead, murdered and interned in Northern Ireland.'[4]

Sure enough three bombs detonated that evening, one outside a police station in Kensington, another outside a shop in Hammersmith and the final one outside the White Lion public house in the Centre Point complex in St Giles Street. Two more bombs exploded outside pubs on Christmas Eve, but Christmas Day itself was quiet. On Boxing Day another device functioned having been left outside the Stage Door pub in Allington Street and two hours later a threat of a device on the District Line halted all services. Finally, a bomb blew up in the telephone kiosk in the booking hall of Sloane Square Underground Station. So ended the bombings of 1973.

It had been a pivotal year for London, which found itself thrown into the forefront of the war against terrorism. It had started with the four car bombs in March, a period of quiet and then from August onwards there had been twenty-eight incendiaries, seventeen postal bombs, twenty-four time bombs and a further two small car bombs.

For the Explosive Office it had been a hectic and, at times, chaotic period. The total number of tasks undertaken by the end of the year was 1,960. There were major changes in operational procedures and the procurement of specialist equipment. It became clear that London needed a permanently manned, immediate response to bomb threats and in the last quarter of the year a twenty-four-hour shift system was introduced and offices allocated on the fifth floor of Cannon Row Police Station. In addition, for the first time the Explosives Officers were provided with their own fully-equipped fast-response vehicles. These were, as already noted, Range Rovers, which were driven by Class One police drivers. The establishment of the unit had now also grown to seven. The new recruits included Roger Goad and Ken Howorth, who had just left the Army. Both were to be killed on duty.

On a broader level, the Metropolitan Police as a whole had also been forced to adapt and change. The political nature of the offence, the general abhorrence of indiscriminate bombing, and the beginning of the era where the media of all kinds were responding to the explosions with pictures and stories within minutes of them happening, placed unprecedented pressure on the police to solve the bombings as soon as possible. It became apparent that there was a need for a much larger establishment of officers in the Bomb Squad and the total was increased seven-fold to over 100. They began to undertake the detailed examination of bomb scenes to recover forensic evidence in a thorough, systematic and logical way. This included sweeping up and sifting all debris in the search for clues and explosive traces used to link cases. The Squad also drew on the support of specialists, including fingerprint experts, forensic scientists, handwriting experts and search dogs. All these elements were welded into place for the one common purpose – the arrest, prosecution and detention of the bombers.

NOTES:
1. Extract from witness statement of Don Henderson, September 1973.
2. Extract from witness statement of James Greenwood, 1974.
3. Extract from witness statement of Ron Wilson, March 1974.
4. Huntley, Bob, *Bomb Squad*, W.H. Allen, London, 1977.

Chapter 20

More Innocent Victims

**'The true terrorist must steel himself against tender
heartedness through a fierce faith in his credo or by a
blessed retreat into a comforting individual madness.'**
H.H.A. Cooper, 1976.

The New Year saw no let-up in the bombing. On 5 January 1974, a
call was made for an Explosives Officer to come and examine a
suspect duffle bag that had been found in the 'Battle of Trafalgar
Exhibition' in Madame Tussaud's. Ron Wilson was on duty and arrived
at the scene at around 15.40 hours. The premises had been evacuated
and, after establishing exactly where the suspect bag was, and the best
route to it, he set off to examine it. He located it in a dark corner of the
exhibition next to a fire extinguisher and a ladder which was leaning
up against a wall. Wilson made a superficial examination of the bag
without opening it and was convinced that it contained a bomb.

Wilson decided to listen to it with an electronic stethoscope to see if
it was ticking and returned to the main entrance where he sent his
driver to collect it from their vehicle. When he came back, Wilson
realised his driver had picked up the wrong instrument case and sent
him back to collect the right one. It was a fortuitous mistake because it
caused a few minutes' delay. After returning to the vehicle to collect the
right case, his driver arrived at the foyer in the front of the building for
the second time. He was about to hand the stethoscope to Wilson when
there was a violent explosion which blew off both doors leading to the
exhibition area. After the dust had settled Wilson went down to examine
the seat of the explosion and concluded that the device had contained
several pounds of explosive. He also realised that had his driver
brought the correct case the first time he may well have been standing
next to the bomb when it exploded. It was an unsettling moment.

As Wilson was dealing with this incident, another bomb threat had been received and Explosives Officer Geoffrey Biddle was sent to deal with it. The caller stated that a device at the Boat Show in Earl's Court was due to explode in forty-five minutes. Earl's Court was partially evacuated and, in accordance with pre-event planning, the exhibitors searched their own stands to try and locate the bomb. Despite scores of people looking, nothing suspicious was found and it seemed to be yet another hoax call. Even so, the wise decision was made to evacuate the whole building until the time the bomb was due to explode, plus a safety margin, had elapsed. Almost on the allotted time, a five-pound bomb detonated inside one of the boats, ripping its hull to shreds. An examination of the scene showed that there were large numbers of tiny porcelain fragments, and it was immediately obvious that the bomb had been placed in the toilet on the boat. When it was searched the exhibitor, understandably, had failed to lift the seat and therefore had not found the bomb.

Work was still going on at the scene of the explosion when the next bomb threat came in, this time to a device in Warwick Way. Police officers quickly located a suspect bag and sealed off the area.

Geoffrey Biddle was tasked direct from Earl's Court to deal with this new threat. After confirming that the necessary cordon and evacuation had been carried out, Biddle approached the suspect device. He recorded:

> An initial examination showed the outer container to be a large plastic carrier bag with carrying handles folded over at the top, inside of which was a thin white coloured plastic bag containing a large corrugated cardboard box and a small cardboard box located to one side, attached to which was an Ever Ready No 126 type dry cell battery with red plastic covered electric wires connected to the terminals, the black plastic screw threaded caps being in position. Tracing the wire circuitry, I noted these wires were joined to white plastic covered leads which I recognised as detonator leads which in turn led through a rough cut-out hole in the side of the larger box and then into what I recognised was the main explosive charge contained in that box. At the time I could hear a distinct ticking of a clock and recognised the contents as being a live electrically operated bomb.
>
> I immediately proceeded to defuse the bomb by cutting one lead close to the positive terminal on the battery and disconnecting the twisted join of the detonator lead connected to the negative terminal thus removing the power source. Then withdrawing the live detonator embedded in one of the explosive cartridges to the main charge.

Biddlee then dismantled the rest of the device and on examining the clock, noted:

> Closer examination showed the clock to be modified by the removal of the minute hand and the insertion of a brass screw interceptor which was positioned above the figure '6'. The clock was still ticking and the hour hand appeared to be touching the interceptor indicating a very narrow margin of time before completing the circuitry and causing the bomb to explode, (believed to be a matter of seconds).[1]

Commander Huntley, the head of the Bomb Squad, met Biddle at Scotland Yard a little later and he noted that the latter was still feeling 'a little wobbly' after the Warwick Road incident. Whilst they were chatting yet another bomb threat was phoned through. This time it was to a device at 8, Harrington Gardens, Kensington. A search of the area began, but in the middle of it the unmistakable sound of a bomb exploding was heard in the direction of Chelsea. Everyone piled into their vehicles and headed off towards the sound of the explosion. A radio call confirmed that a large bomb had detonated in Cadogan Gardens outside the home of Major General Phillip Ward. Fortunately, he and his wife were away in the country. It was established that a device of some fifteen to twenty pounds of commercial explosive had been left at his basement door. There was considerable damage and glass littered the street.

Minutes before midnight came yet another call. This time it was to a device in 'Charrington Gate', Kensington. It was immediately realised that there was no such location and a general search of the Kensington area was set in progress. At 03.00 hours a police officer finally spotted a suspect case in the basement of Kensington Gate House. Biddle, who was by now tired and edgy after his narrow escape in Warwick Road, but still on duty, was tasked to the scene and made the device safe. It was a bomb of significant size; in the suitcase there were twenty-eight pounds of explosive and the normal modified alarm clock initiation system. The five bombs, two of which had been rendered safe, yielded much evidence. Sets of fingerprints were obtained and it became clear that a new team of bombers was operating in London.

On 4 February 1974, Don Henderson was tasked to the scene of an explosion at the *Daily Express* offices, then still in Fleet Street. The incident highlighted the continued lack of awareness of the dangers of comparatively small devices. The bomb, built into a book, was addressed to Sir Max Aitken, but as often happens in the case of VIPs it been opened by his secretary. She was immediately suspicious because the package contained a book which was taped together at one end. She

356

asked for assistance and a Mr James Blair took the book off her and, carrying it by the un-taped end, set off for the office of the head of security, Mr Andrew Meikle. He was examining it when it exploded. In the post-blast investigation, it was concluded that the bomb should have functioned when the secretary withdrew it from the envelope, but for some reason it failed, possibly due to a poor electrical contact. However, the actions taken by Mr Meikle caused it to function, severely injuring him. He was lucky in some respects in that not all the explosive in the bomb detonated, had it done so he may well have been killed. The lesson was, and still is, clear – any package being handled or partially opened which becomes suspect should be gently placed on the nearest hard surface and experts called to deal with it. Despite this, it will be seen that on many subsequent occasions both the police and the public would continue to make irrational decisions when dealing with suspect postal bombs. For those not familiar with explosives and their effects, it is very hard to grasp that a small package which has come through the post and has been partially opened still has the capacity to severely injure or kill.

The PIRA bombers were still at large and although there was plenty of evidence to link the devices together, and to the perpetrators, there were no actual suspects to question and fingerprint. With the numbers of bombs being laid this situation was bound to change and, as more and more leads were followed up, it was inevitable that sooner or later those behind the incidents would be caught. One of the worst outrages committed, this time outside London, was the bombing of a coach on the M62 which left twelve people dead. It resulted in the arrest and subsequent conviction of Judith Ward, although she was later cleared on appeal. The London-based terrorists, however, were still at large, but a lead from an unknown source indicated that John Melia, a twenty-six-year-old Irishman, was involved in the bombing. He and a number of his acquaintances were put under surveillance, but initially nothing subversive was observed.

The surveillance was about to be suspended when a vital link was established. A label from the bomb at Kensington was identified by a taxi driver when it was shown on the *Police Five* television programme. This was similar to one he had seen on a package delivered from a Melton Mowbray firm. Inquiries with the company revealed that they had consigned a box filled with parts of occasional tables to an address in London at which John Melia's associates had been seen. This tentative link was a key breakthrough. The surveillance effort was redoubled and shortly afterwards, on 6 April 1974, four suspects were followed to shopping centres in West London including one in Uxbridge, where the suspects were lost. They were picked up again as they returned to their car and were followed home. It looked like another wasted day until an incendiary device functioned in one of the stores in the Uxbridge shopping centre. It had probably functioned earlier than intended; most were set to go off in the early hours when the fires (in those pre-sprinkler days) would develop unhindered. Police immediately warned the remaining staff in the shops to search their premises and more devices came to light. A few days later the homes of those under surveillance were raided and bomb-making equipment seized. Eventually eight men were arrested and charged with terrorist offences. All of them had been resident in the mainland for a long period and had merged into the local communities. All were Irish born; most had full-time jobs and wives or girlfriends. All were passionate PIRA supporters.

Despite the arrests, the bombs continued. It was the turn of Heathrow on 19 May 1974, when a vehicle-borne device detonated in one of the multi-storey car parks. It was Sunday in the holiday season and thousands of people were jammed into the airport awaiting flights. A vague threat was given relating a bomb in a car park. Police raced to the airport and were desperately trying to clear all four of the parking areas when the bomb, containing some thirty pounds of explosive, detonated. Miraculously no one was seriously injured although an eighteen-inch hole was blown in the floor of the car park and considerable damage was done to surrounding vehicles.

The PIRA succeeded where Guy Fawkes had failed when, on 17 June, they managed to smuggle a bomb into the Houses of Parliament. After it had been placed the terrorists walked out of the building and made another vague telephone bomb threat. This simply stated that a device would detonate somewhere inside the building within five minutes, but no further details were given. The police on duty in the Parliament buildings spread the warning and within minutes an Explosives Officer was on scene. The challenge of searching for the bomb was immense. There were 1,200 rooms, hundreds of staircases and miles of passages to be cleared. Before the task could begin there was a tremendous blast in an annexe off the famous Westminster Hall. It blew off part of the roof and punched a hole in the wall to the canteen kitchens. It also fractured a gas main and soon a fire had taken hold and was threatening to engulf the whole building. Four office workers were trapped in smoke-filled rooms and had to be rescued by firemen. Most seriously injured was a woman cleaner who had a broken leg.

The fire spread through the rafters of the thirteenth century building and threatened the hammer beam roof which was the biggest in the world. Parliament was sealed off and hundreds of firemen called in to fight the blaze. They were aided by a fireboat pumping water from the Thames. It took nearly four hours to get the flames under control and, when the fire was finally out, hundreds of thousands of pounds' worth of damage had been done. The timing of the attack was such that only a few MPs were in the House; nevertheless, Parliament was supposed to be one of the most secure buildings in the land and the comment was made that now nowhere was safe.

The next target was a completely unprotected place, full of innocent civilians, but fortunately for Londoners it was outside the capital. On 21 November 1974, in the worst atrocity on the mainland, two bombs detonated in Birmingham pubs, blasts which killed twenty-one people and injured 162 others, some very seriously. It demonstrated the PIRA's ruthlessness and willingness to use indiscriminate bombings to terrorize the nation and force political change.

As the Bomb Squad expanded to investigate the terrorist attacks it became clear that there was a need to collate all the information about the various incidents in one central location. This task was given to Detective Constable Fred Titchener who set up a small office in Scotland Yard and began the task of indexing and cross referencing all the attacks. In addition, he established a close liaison with the Explosives Officers and attended the scenes of all major incidents in the capital as well as some outside. Titchener also began making technical enquiries about the different types of timers and other components that were being used in devices. Before long many of the individual investigating officers were knocking at his door and asking for assistance with their particular incident. As a result, the UK Bomb Data Centre (UKBDC) was set up to provide technical information about all the attacks. The centre is still running today and, with the international nature of terrorism, maintains close links with other similar Bomb Data Centres all over the world that were set up to emulate the work of the UKBDC.

The Tower of London, a popular IRA target from both the 1880s and the 1930s, was attacked again on 17 July 1974. At 14.05 hours a device exploded in the White Tower killing a young woman, Dorothy Household, and injuring many others. Explosives Officer Jim Greenwood was tasked to investigate the blast. On his arrival he saw a fleet of ambulances parked up and the wounded being removed from the Tower. He entered the building and on the lower ground floor in the Mortar Room found what he thought was the seat of the explosion. It had occurred in the half of the room nearest the crypt; some ventilation pipes had been damaged and part of the floor above had collapsed. A fire hydrant on this floor had been ruptured and water was cascading down on to the debris. The water hampered the initial investigation and it was almost an hour before it was switched off by an engineer. When the water was cleared the forensic screening continued. It was soon established that a bomb of at least ten pounds of high explosive had been hidden under the wooden gun carriage of a naval cannon known as 'Royal George'. The wooden carriage was completely destroyed in the explosion, but the cast iron barrel remained intact. Pieces of zip fastener were recovered at the seat of the blast which pointed to the use of an airline type bag to carry the bomb. This could easily have been placed on the floor and then kicked under the gun carriage where it would have been almost completely out of sight.

In the summer of 1974 a new team of bombers, who were to become notorious for the Balcombe Street siege, entered the country intent on starting another murderous campaign. They moved into individual flats in Fulham and areas of North London where there were Irish communities, but they avoided the pubs and clubs and, in general, maintained a very low profile. The team began striking in late 1974, but stopped in line with the PIRA ceasefire in early 1975. They restarted their bombing campaign in the summer of that year and then continued up until December 1975 when they were caught. The citizens of London suffered a wicked and sustained campaign of violence at the hands of this Active Service Unit (ASU) as they now became known. They attacked a wide range of targets, all considered to be linked to institutions of the British Establishment. They also considered the 'ruling classes' as fair game and consequently set about attacking restaurants in the West End of London. At their peak they averaged one attack a week and during the period murdered eleven people and were responsible for forty-three explosions and a number of shootings.

Prior to the ceasefire, this PIRA active service unit had been responsible for the first deliberate secondary device in London targeting the emergency services. The incident started at approximately 22.05 hours on 27 November 1974, when an explosion occurred inside a pillar box at the junction of Tite Street and Royal Hospital Road, Chelsea. The local police and the on-duty Explosives Officer, Sandy Hawkins, with his driver, Alan Jackson, sped to the area to examine the scene. On arrival, after the initial questioning, Hawkins went forward to examine another suspect device in a bag which had been discovered on a car bonnet. In the event it turned out to be innocuous. The remaining police officers were all standing a short distance from the seat of the first blast when, at 22.26 hours, a second bomb, hidden in a building site some nine feet from the first explosion, detonated. Unlike the second Angry Brigade bomb at Robert Carr's house in 1971, which was probably not deliberate, this was the first true 'secondary device' deployed in London. It was, though, commonplace tactic in Northern Ireland for security forces to be drawn to the scene of an explosion, often to rescue casualties, only to be struck by the blast and fragments from a second bomb, the most notorious example being the double bombing of the Parachute Regiment soldiers at Warrenpoint. In London the investigation revealed that the second bomb contained an estimated three to five pounds of gelignite and had about 200 nails incorporated in the front of the charge to make a claymore type device. This had been aimed at the pillar box and timed to function twenty minutes after the first bomb had detonated. It was a deliberate and vicious attempt to maim or kill the first responders and it was extremely fortunate that there were no fatalities. Sandy Hawkins was slightly injured along with several police officers, one of whom had a nail projected through his helmet. Alan Jackson's Range Rover was peppered by a whole series of nails.

This secondary device resulted in an immediate change in the response to explosions within the capital. It complicated everyone's task and required all police officers attending the scene of an explosion to carry out an immediate search of the incident control point and cordon positions to make sure that they were safe. In theory it is a simple procedure, but is one which is, in reality, hard to implement on the ground. In a built-up area, especially at night, there are hundreds of potential places where the terrorists could conceal a second bomb, including in parked cars.

Three days later there was an attack on the Talbot Public House in Chester Mews. The terrorists attempted to throw two nail bombs with short burning fuses into the bar. The first failed to break the window it was aimed at and bounced back on to the forecourt, where it detonated. The second bomb, of similar construction, smashed through a window of the pub, but fortunately for the patrons failed to detonate. The bomb consisted of four eight-ounce sticks of Frangex, a commercial explosive, surrounded by three pounds of nails, nuts and bolts to act as shrapnel. Had it exploded, this 'Belfast confetti', as it was known, would undoubtedly have inflicted grievous injuries on the customers in the bar. Don Henderson attended the scene and rendered safe the failed device and recovered fragments from the exploded one outside.

An attack on the Military and Naval Club occurred on 11 December 1974 whilst a number of MPs were discussing the return of capital punishment. The terrorists threw a nail-studded bomb into the premises and sped away before it detonated. Passing the Cavalry and Guards Club en route the gang opened fire with a Sten gun and M1 Carbine, spraying the front with bullets; it was a miracle that there were no serious injuries in these two attacks.

On 17 December three bombs were placed in Central London. Police Constable Harry Greig, who was on duty in Tottenham Court Road, was caught up in one of them when a 'no warning' bomb exploded near the telephone exchange between Chenies Street and North Crescent. Minutes before the blast he had stopped to talk to the driver of a panda car who was on patrol in the area. What the two officers did not know was that they were almost on top of the bomb which was hidden behind a wall a few feet away, its timer rapidly running down. After a brief chat they both continued on their separate duties. Less than a minute after they left the spot there was an almighty explosion which sent shudders down Harry Greig's spine. He rushed back to the area which was now a scene of devastation. Having been blown by the force of the explosion, the figure of a young man could be seen lying in the hallway of a house nearby; a quick examination of his body confirmed that he was dead. He was later identified as thirty-five-year-old telephonist George Arthur. The point at which Greig had been standing minutes before was littered with debris and all the houses had had their front windows blown out. Reacting automatically, and aware of the new secondary devices threat, he set about evacuating the people in the immediate area and then helped with the cordon whilst waiting for an Explosives Officer to arrive and check the scene.[2]

Two days later a car bomb detonated outside Selfridges in Oxford Street. A warning had been given and the police managed to clear the area before the bomb exploded. Many Christmas shoppers were huddled in basements when the device went off. An older shopper commented that it was just like the Blitz of 1940-41 all over again.

Harrods made the mistake of claiming that their security was so good that they were 'bomb proof' and people could shop inside without any fear. It was red rag to a bull and the gang picked the shop as their next target. One of the ASU strapped ten pounds of explosive round his waist and went into the store, whilst another carried in the timing mechanism. They met in the toilets, assembled and set a bomb and then left the scene. Fortunately, the bomb was spotted by one of the staff and the immediate area evacuated. Shortly afterwards a call was received stating that three bombs had been left in the store. The bomb in the toilets detonated shortly afterwards starting a small fire. The evacuation of the rest of the building was completed and the fire service fought the fire from outside the building because of the perceived risk from secondary devices. Explosives Officer Jim Greenwood, who attended the incident, decided that a soak time of at least an hour was required before the building could be re-entered and searched for the other bombs. In the event there were none.

No one can dispute that in Northern Ireland the PIRA was a clever and cunning foe. In many of the areas that it operated from it had the support of the local community or, if not, was able to intimidate people to such a degree that there was no fear of their activities being reported to the authorities. In other thinly-populated areas, like parts of the border in South Armagh, PIRA members had ample time to prepare and plan complex attacks against the security forces. To do this they quickly developed a wide range of bombs with an array of different initiation systems. To counter them, the Army's bomb disposal teams, consisting of Ammunition Technical Officers and Ammunition Technicians of the RAOC, by necessity, became the leading experts in rendering devices safe. But it was a steep learning curve and this expertise was paid for at a high price. In the early 1970s the Army personnel suffered serious attrition at the hands of the PIRA bombers and, by the middle of the decade, ten of their number had been killed and others injured on bomb disposal duties. It was clear that in such high-risk circumstances, and with the large numbers of bombs being planted, new methods of disabling them, where possible remotely, had to be devised.

To this end, two key items of equipment were developed and entered service. The first was the small, remote-controlled vehicle which became known as the 'Wheelbarrow'. These were originally developed to attach car tow-ropes to vehicles remotely so that they could be pulled away from target buildings. This could significantly reduce the level of damage from the car bombs of the day which, compared to later examples, contained relatively small quantities of explosive. The Wheelbarrows were, however, developed rapidly and soon were equipped with television systems and remotely controlled booms which could carry shotguns and deliver small explosive charges.

The second piece of equipment was a disrupter known as a 'Pigstick'. This could also be carried and fired from a Wheelbarrow or be deployed manually and fired remotely. It was designed to blow open small devices in a controlled manner without initiating them.

Both these items of equipment were introduced and available for use in London, but there was still tremendous pressure to render safe devices manually in order to preserve the maximum forensic evidence. Moreover, the environment in which the terrorists operated in London was different. The PIRA did not have the advantage of a friendly or easily intimidated population which might turn a blind eye to their activities. Therefore, at the time, they were not able to set up complex attacks.

From a bomb disposal viewpoint, it was also different. Whereas it was acceptable in Northern Ireland to close Belfast City Centre for prolonged periods to deal with suspect devices, this was not the case in London. Part of the Explosives Officers job was, and still is, to be able to make a rapid threat assessment and clear obvious false alarms or hoaxes quickly to enable the people of London to go about their lawful business. A failure to do so would simply play into the terrorists' hands.

The first Explosives Officer, Don Henderson, was a brave and able man and led by example in this respect. On 27 January 1975, five bombs exploded in the capital. In the early hours of the following morning, in the freezing cold, he was tasked to a suspect carrier bag in a shop doorway in Putney Bridge Road. Having arrived at the scene and confirmed that the necessary cordons and evacuation had been implemented he set off to locate the suspect bomb.

Using a powerful torch he soon found a white plastic bag which was on the floor leaning against a wall. He approached the bag and feeling it from the outside came to the conclusion that it was almost certainly a device. He then opened the top to examine the contents. He saw the edge of a battery concealed by a number of sheets of newspaper. Drawing the paper aside he discovered the complete battery, with red and yellow wires leading from each terminal. Without disturbing anything he disconnected one of the wires from the battery and then continued with his examination, being particularly wary of the risk of booby-traps. One of the wires led to a decorative fob watch. It disappeared under a piece of black plastic adhesive tape stuck to the glass face. Another yellow wire from the watch was connected to a white detonator lead wire. The red wire from the battery was connected to the other white detonator lead wire to complete the circuit, all the joints being secured by blue plastic tape. The detonator wires disappeared into the end of a large bundle contained in a polythene bag, again secured with tape. Removing this, Henderson discovered the detonator with a second one taped to it, to boost the initiation of the main explosive charge. This consisted of twenty-four sticks of six-ounce blasting gelatine. He removed the detonators and effectively rendered the device safe. He then replaced all the components, less the detonators, in the original bag and took them to Cannon Row Police Station where he prepared the items as exhibits.

This is a typical example of the bravery displayed by all the Explosives Officers who were serving at the time. There was a historical precedent from the investigation of safe-blowing incidents to gain the best evidence, a perceived lower risk of booby-trap devices, a willingness to take a 'calculated risk' and an admirable sense of duty.

This meant that, despite the availability of Wheelbarrow and disrupters, bombs were often still dealt with manually. It was matter of pride that would ultimately lead to disaster.

A PIRA ceasefire around this time brought a break in the bombing. In the lead up to it, it had become clear that the Explosive Officers' accommodation on the fifth floor of Cannon Row Police Station was becoming unmanageable. There was no lift and rushing down five flights of stairs was not conducive to a quick response. So, in periods of high alert, the Explosive Officers took to sitting in their vehicles outside the building to reduce the time between tasking and responding to incidents. This was recognised as unacceptable in the longer term and to remedy it the Explosive Officers moved a short distance to new accommodation on 23 May 1975.

The new offices, in a single story building off Derby Gate, were formerly opened by the Commissioner, Sir Robert Mark QPM. For obvious reasons, it became known as 'The Bungalow'. It consisted of two large open-plan office sections, a workshop, a small training area, a restroom, a duty bunk and an administrative building. Most importantly, and as proposed by Majendie almost a century before when the new 'telephonic system' was first introduced, there was a hotline direct to the Bomb Squad offices in Scotland Yard. This was a red phone which had a very distinctive ring and it ensured that there was no delay in tasking an Explosives Officer to an incident. When it rang, all other activity in the office stopped and it was answered immediately. The system is exactly the same today. Finally, there was a secure library stacked with information about bombs and bombings from all over the world.

Many of the retired Explosives Officers and their drivers will have fond memories of 'The Bungalow'. A sense of humour, sometimes slightly warped, helped everyone get along. Peter Gurney recalled lightly filling in the answers to Roger Goad's cross-word when he wasn't looking. On another occasion, Gurney and Howorth recorded a message on a small tape recorder and waited for the 'red phone' to ring. When it did the two picked up the phone and immediately set the tape running. A voice on the tape coolly said: 'I'm sorry there's no one here to take your call at the moment. Please leave your message and we'll get back to you as soon as we can. Please speak clearly and slowly after the tone.'[3]

At the other end of the phone a voice was clearly heard to say: 'Christ Almighty! It's an Ansaphone. I've got a f ... Ansaphone. What the hell am I supposed to do now?' Moments later Gurney answered the phone for real, but it took a while for the officer at the other end to appreciate the joke.

The PIRA ceasefire ended in early August 1975. Soon afterwards a bomb exploded in a pub in Caterham. This was followed by another which exploded outside Peter Browns Limited on Oxford Street on 28 August 1975. The scene there was investigated by Explosives Officer Roger Goad and a number of exhibits recovered for further forensic investigation. The bombers would later claim that this bomb was booby-trapped and functioned prematurely, but there is no evidence to support this assertion.

The following day, 29 August 1975, in the late evening, Roger Goad was tasked to a suspect bag outside the K Shoe Shop at 229 Kensington Church Street. When he arrived at the scene Goad decided that some members of the public, despite police warnings, were still in danger and the bag had to be examined immediately. The duty officer, Chief Superintendent James Collie, went forward with Goad to point out the exact location of the suspect bag and, having done so, he stopped some distance back.

Goad went forward alone, calmly and deliberately, to deal with the suspect bomb. He was bending over it when it detonated, killing him instantly. His driver, Police Constable Clary, put out an immediate call on the radio which was picked up by Peter Gurney and Geoffrey Biddle who both sped to the scene. Peter Gurney arrived first at the incident control point, at around 23.30 hours, and stopped for a quick briefing. From there he could see that the front of the K Shoe Shop had been blown out and motionless in front of it was a body. He went forward and satisfied himself that he was unable to do anything for his colleague. After a quick search he returned to the incident control point to try and establish exactly what had happened. He spoke to Police Constable Sloss, who had been the first officer on scene and who had located the suspect bag, but there was nothing out of the ordinary about it. Gurney then returned to the front of the shoe shop to carry out an examination of Goad's body and a thorough search of the area. It was divided into different zones and with the aid of other police officers several bags of exhibits were recovered for forwarding to the Forensic Laboratory. An idea of the workload the Explosives Officers were under at this time can be gauged from the fact that during this time Gurney was tasked away from the scene eight times to deal with other suspect items found in the area.

Gurney later concluded that Roger Goad had been killed by a bomb containing some five pounds of high explosive and that this had detonated whilst he was bent over the device, looking down with both hands in contact with it at the moment that it functioned. The later examination of the forensic evidence was inconclusive, but of key importance was the discovery of two damaged winders for pocket watches. This would indicate that there were two different circuits in

366

the bomb. One might have been an ordinary time switch, but the other may have been used as part of a delay arming system for a booby-trap.

Evidence to support this is recorded in *Time Bomb*, an account of the conviction of the Guildford Four. In it, one of the terrorists later arrested during the Balcombe Street siege, Joseph O'Connell, confessed to setting a booby-trap bomb. He said that they decided to target the 'Bomb Experts' and that on the first attempt, a device laid outside Peter Browns on Oxford Street had detonated prematurely. So they decided to have another go: 'The bomb was boobied [*sic*] with a flick-switch at the bottom. The circuits are false and are concealed in the bomb itself, in the hollowed out explosives. We set it in the car about 100 yards away. It was boobied [*sic*] to catch anyone trying to defuse it.'[4]

Another of the gang, Eddie Butler, boasted of their achievement. He said: 'Our intention was obvious – to get an expert, an explosives expert. We succeeded, didn't we? He didn't take his precautions.'[5]

The fact was that when Goad arrived at the scene he was duty-bound to do something. He went forward, regardless of his own safety, and was, as we have seen, attempting to render the bomb safe when it detonated. Unlike those cowardly people laying the bombs, he was a brave, dedicated man who displayed icy courage dealing with the device that cold night in Kensington. This was recognised after his death with the posthumous award of the George Cross. The Coroner, after confirming a verdict of murder at the inquest, summed up by saying: 'I have the deepest admiration for the almost unbelievable bravery of this man who was acting to protect the public and do his duty.'[6]

On 5 September, the day that Roger Goad was buried, another awful atrocity occurred when a bomb went off in the Hilton Hotel at lunchtime. It was just after midday when a bomb threat was telephoned to the *Evening Standard*, but as was often the case in these early days, the warning was vague and by the time the information had been passed to the police it had become even more inaccurate. The old military anecdote 'Send reinforcements we are going to advance' becoming 'send three and four pence we are going to a dance' being an amusing example of how, under pressure, messages can get corrupted. Police and security staff at the hotel had just begun a search for the bomb when it detonated in the foyer. The effect was devastating. Those members of staff and residents who could, fled from the building whilst others lay screaming in agony; one man had had his leg blown off and was bleeding profusely. As more police and emergency service personnel rushed to the scene another suspect bag was discovered, this causing much anxiety. Bravely the various responders continued the rescue operations and quickly tended to and recovered the wounded.

At the time, because members of the Explosives Office were attending Roger Goad's funeral, a military bomb disposal team had been moved into Cannon Row Police Station. It was commanded by Warrant Officer B.J. Mitchell and he was tasked to the incident to investigate the explosion and deal with the possible secondary device. On arrival at the scene, a Wheelbarrow was deployed and the suspect bag successfully disrupted. It turned out to be a false alarm as it contained personal effects from one of the residents who had abandoned it as they fled the hotel after the first explosion. The final toll was two dead, with sixty-three injured.

Post incident there was much criticism of the police for not responding to the call sooner. There were also claims and counter-claims about the sequence of events leading up to the explosion of the bomb. The police insisted that they had telephoned the duty manager of the hotel and told him of the threat; he denied this. There were also apparent delays in the first police vehicle arriving at the scene. When the police did arrive there was some further confusion because the security staff claimed to have searched the hotel and found nothing.

As often happens in these cases the blame for the casualties was being laid at the police's door and not the perpetrators of the crime. To understand the full picture, it is necessary to look beyond the bomb threat to the hotel. That day, in total, the police had had to respond to no less than 253 hoax bomb calls (although some had been made after the explosion). All of them had to be treated seriously. The number of hoax calls for the week running up to the Hilton explosion ranged from 91 to 162 daily, many of these being made by people with Irish accents. The hotel itself had been mentioned in ten of these calls, all of which proved to be false. The head of the Bomb Squad, Commander Habershon, made the point that the real calls were not necessarily any help:

> They are not really warnings at all. As we are not told the exact position of the device, we could have been evacuating scores of people through the foyer where the bomb was. More people could have been killed by leading them straight on to the bomb.[7]

It was even suggested that the PIRA should provide a codeword in their threat phone calls. This would at least give the police a chance of differentiating the real warnings from the hundreds of other hoax calls they received. They could then set about cordoning and evacuating the area before a bomb went off. In fact, under a cloak of secrecy such a system was in place, it was not in any sense a formal arrangement and had evolved over time with the bombings. However, such was the level of malevolence on the part of the Provisionals that more often than not coded warnings were not given or, conversely, warnings were given with authenticated code words when there were no bombs simply to cause massive disruption. As far as the police was concerned, knowledge of the real codewords was restricted to those who needed to know. There were two reasons for this. Firstly, if the codewords became commonly known then hoax callers could use them to cause further unnecessary disruption. Secondly, there was a general abhorrence on the side of the authorities at the thought of giving credibility to the terrorists by acknowledging the system was in place.

In contrast to the tragic death of Roger Goad and those in the Hilton, Lady Pamela Onslow had a remarkably lucky escape when she opened a book bomb. When it arrived she extracted the book from its envelope. Having partially opened the book, she saw a watch which she assumed had been consigned in this manner as a means of protection. She then pulled the watch from the book and walked away with it thinking that the objects which were attached to it were some form of fancy wrist strap. These were in fact a battery and a detonator; luckily the latter had been pulled out of the main charge, as at this point it exploded causing minor injuries and shock to Lady Onslow.

The PIRA's active service unit now decided to target wealthy areas of London, places where the upper classes and politicians could often be found. It was deemed acceptable by the Provisionals to attack the rich and famous, without scruple, in the heart of the capital. On 9 October 1975, a man was killed when a bomb, which had been left by a bus stop at Green Park close to the Ritz, exploded without warning.

Four days later, the prompt actions of a hall porter who found a bomb and raised the alarm saved the day. Don Henderson, who was on duty, was tasked to the suspect device which was outside Lockets Restaurant in Marsham Street. He arrived on scene at 21.33 hours, at which point he was briefed by the duty officer. Subsequently he went forward and found a black imitation leather bag wedged between ornamental railings on a window just past the entrance to Lockets. He looked inside the top of the bag, which was unzipped, and saw a plastic battery holder containing four batteries wires – and instinctively knew he was dealing with a real device. Without hesitating, he manually severed one of the wires before removing the snap-on connector from the battery holder. He then carefully took apart the rest of the bomb. It consisted of a watch, two detonators and a main explosive charge around which a number of coach bolts had been embedded. After hastily returning to the incident control point to brief the duty officer, Henderson went back to the scene to search for secondary devices, but found none. He subsequently ordered that all cordons remain in position for another thirty minutes and then arranged for explosive search dogs to sweep through the area before it could be declared clear.

Henderson concluded that this was a particularly vicious anti-personnel device which, had it detonated, would have projected glass and coach bolts into the restaurant with everyone inside becoming a casualty, most of them being fatal. He noted that it was only the prompt action of the hall porter who located the device and informed the police that prevented the events actually happening. For his part in this incident Henderson was awarded a George Medal in 1976.

In many ways the authorities seemed impotent in the face of this new and indiscriminate violence. The best that could be done was to give advice on the defensive measures that could be taken to discourage the bombers and reduce the effects of explosions if a bomb went off. This included: improving lighting around buildings; the removal of litter bins and locking away dustbins; re-glazing windows with new laminate glass; fitting flexible transparent sheets of PVC or polycarbonate to outside glass areas; fitting specialist net curtains inside windows; fitting chicken wire outside windows to arrest fragments; employing security guards to patrol outside premises and finally arranging the thorough search of all people's bags when they entered buildings. The use of net curtains, a cheap and simple solution (but with limited effectiveness), was adopted by many government buildings and in particular for the defence of security-related establishments. For many years these sites were clearly identified by the drab, dreary and eventually dirty net curtains which hung inside their windows.

The ASU now decided it was time to target individuals linked to the establishment who had, for whatever reason, upset them. To start with they selected Hugh Fraser, a Conservative MP. Having found out where Fraser lived and after checking his movements they decided to assassinate him with a booby-trapped bomb placed under his car. In theory this attack would be easy to carry out. Firstly, the bomb could be planted covertly in the dark, which meant there was no need for a quick getaway as with the 'throw bombs'. Secondly, there was no risk of innocent civilians getting hurt. Of course, nothing is ever that certain when dealing with explosives and in this instance only the first premise held true.

On the evening of 23 October 1975, the gang went to Fraser's home in Camden Hill Square and set the bomb under the wheel of his Jaguar and before making its escape. It was a large device with some fourteen pounds of explosive. Fraser, however, would not be its victim. Professor Gordon Hamilton-Fairley, an eminent cancer specialist at St

370

Bartholomew's Hospital, was taking his dog for an early morning walk when he spotted the package. He bent down to see what it was, having no reason to suspect that it was a bomb. Most probably he picked it up, at which point it detonated, killing him instantly.

A week later, in a similar attack using a booby-trap bomb, another innocent civilian was seriously injured. Post-blast investigations established that the intended victim was probably another Conservative MP, but the bomb was placed under the wrong car; a Mercedes belonging to solicitor Mr Richard Charnley. It exploded when he started up the vehicle and moved off. Fortunately for him the bomb had been placed well forward, probably under the nearside front wheel, and the strength of the car and the distance from the point of the explosion saved him, although he suffered a broken leg and multiple lacerations from flying debris. Later, much smaller, under-car booby-trap bombs were developed which would be placed directly under the driver's seat using magnets. When these function there is little hope of the victims surviving.

This second case of mistaken identity meant that everyone was at risk and people were warned to check under their cars before getting into them. One paper even advised people not to linger near parked cars – a classic case of scaremongering, as quite how this could be achieved in a city like London was not explained.

On 29 October another bomb detonated without warning, this time outside an Italian restaurant in South Audley Street in Mayfair. Seventeen people were injured; but bombs outside restaurants were not getting the results the terrorists desired and plans were made to throw future bombs in amongst the diners giving them no chance to escape.

On 12 November 1975, in the late evening, there was an attack against Scott's restaurant in Mount Street. The bomb, estimated to contain some two pounds of explosive and studded with ball bearings to provide additional shrapnel, was thrown into the establishment. It landed in the Oyster and Lobster bar, the customers and staff instinctively tried to flee in the seconds before it detonated. When it did, it hurled ball bearings out in all directions. A businessman, John Batey, was killed and fifteen others injured. The front of the restaurant was blown out and the area covered in glass and other debris. The bar caught fire, but the blaze was rapidly extinguished by the fire brigade.

Four days later, as the damage to Scott's was being repaired, another bomb was thrown, again with no warning, into Walton's restaurant in Chelsea. It contained about three pounds of explosive and was also studded with bolts, nuts and ball bearings. Mrs Ivy Brent, who was in the restaurant, recalled sitting at her table with friends when the window shattered as the bomb smashed through it. Mesmerised for a second before she could react and take cover, she recalled looking at it lying between two tables on the floor. She remembered seeing the fuse burning. It was spluttering and looking like the yellow flashes from a sparkler. Moments later it detonated. The front of the restaurant was blown out and there was carnage inside; people staggered out of the smoke filled interior with dreadful wounds where they were comforted by other members of the public who had rushed over to help.

Explosives Officer Ken Howorth made his way directly to the incident and arrived to find a scene of complete chaos. The interior of the restaurant was shattered and, like the bomb the previous week, the improvised shrapnel had, as intended, caused appalling wounds on those innocent victims dining out that evening. Two people were killed and twenty-three injured including a seventy-one-year-old pensioner.

The public was rightly outraged and horrified by these two attacks and the police seemed no closer to catching the gang responsible. In response, Ross McWhirter, the co-editor of the *Guinness Book of Records*, offered a £50,000 reward as part of a 'beat the bombers campaign', for information leading to the capture of the men responsible. In response, the gang ambushed him at his home and shot him dead.

To counter the threat, the police mounted a massive operation called *Op Combo*. Each evening, uniformed and plain-clothes officers, some armed, flooded Central London.

It quickly paid dividends. In Mount Street on 6 December 1975, for example, a Cortina was seen acting suspiciously close to Scott's restaurant. At 21.15 hours the occupants opened fire on the premises with an automatic weapon, but two plain-clothes police officers nearby saw the attack start and one noted the registration of the vehicle and passed it on over the radio. Police officers from all over the area responded and after a car chase in the West End, the terrorists abandoned the Cortina, running into a block of flats in Balcombe Street. There they took an elderly couple hostage. Many Republicans thought the gang would not surrender and go out with guns blazing; others hoped for some sort of deal. Robert Mark, the Commissioner, made it clear there would be no such arrangement, and that the men were 'ordinary vulgar criminals' and that the only place they would be going was prison in Brixton. After six days, rather than going out like lions they walked out like lambs.

What the Balcombe Street Gang, as they became known, did demonstrate was that if the motivation is there, along with the necessary supplies of explosives and a little technical knowledge, the potential to cause chaos is immense. It only takes a small band of ruthless men and women, sufficiently fanatical and enjoying the advantage of surprise, to disrupt the life of a capital city. In a pattern to be repeated over the years, the capture of one set of terrorists only led to a temporary respite as the PIRA began planning to put more bombers in place.

The PIRA's members were not the only bombers at work in London. As the violence in Northern Ireland escalated, stories of Republican fund-raising in pubs, particularly those in the Kilburn area, infuriated Protestant extremists. On 20 December 1975, a bomb was left in a holdall in a doorway outside Biddy Muligans's Irish pub. It was spotted by a customer just moments before it detonated, though most of the patrons had left the bar. When it exploded it shattered the front of the building. Five people were injured. Enquiries revealed that earlier a young man had tried to enter the pub with a holdall, but when challenged by the landlord and asked to open the bag, he had declined and quickly left. It is possible the intention was to leave the bag in the bar where, had it gone off, it would have caused carnage.

At the end of the year, as the PIRA campaign on the mainland was coming up for its third anniversary, Merlyn Rees, the Secretary of State for Northern Ireland, prepared to make a statement about 'The Troubles' to the House of Commons. A quick review of PIRA's activities revealed that they had been responsible for almost 200 explosive devices on mainland Britain. Sixty-one people had been killed (three were shot dead and fifty-nine died in explosions) and over 850 were injured. Unusually, but fortunately for Londoners, the worst of the atrocities had happened outside the capital in Aldershot, Birmingham, Guildford and on the M62 coach.

As the PIRA campaign of violence escalated, the need to gain convictions by gathering and exploiting forensic evidence from the scenes of explosions increased in importance. With each bombing the police procedures and forensic techniques were improving. A simple, but good example of the recovery, reconstruction and investigation of an explosion was demonstrated after the detonation of a bomb in a post box in Golders Green on 16 February 1976. The work was undertaken by scientists from the Forensic Science Laboratory in Woolwich. In this case, the explosion destroyed a pillar box leaving only the circular base plinth in situ after the event. The debris from the explosion, consisting mainly of pillar box fragments, was recovered to Woolwich for detailed examination. There the box was reconstructed and the fragments examined. These showed clearly the spalling effects which are produced when a high explosive is in intimate contact with metal. Chemical examination of these revealed that there were traces of nitroglycerine which was consistent with the use of a commercial explosive typically used by the PIRA.

However, in this explosion no trace of the initiation system could be found which was unusual. From a bomb disposal perspective, one of the most important pieces of information about a bomb is how it is fuzed as this can influence the render safe procedure that is chosen. Normally after an explosion of this magnitude it would be expected that fragments of batteries, the mechanical timer, bits of the detonator and wiring would be recovered. After three exhaustive searches of the debris no piece of any fuzing system was discovered. This flew against the face of experience which would suggest that in all bombings of this type, particularly where the explosion happened in a confined space (the pillar box), there would be some recovery of components. There, therefore, had to be another form of initiation system, one which had been completely destroyed in the explosion. Further chemical examination of the fragments indicated that there were traces of chlorates, chlorides, sulphate and sugar present. In particular, the sulphate exhibited a high level of acidity. Such findings were indicative of a fuzing system based on the spontaneous ignition of sodium chlorate and sugar when it comes in contact with acid. The device, therefore, was most likely set off by a sugar chlorate mixture initiated by an acid which had eaten through some form of rubber membrane. This would be used to set off a plain detonator and hence the main explosive charge. Acid chlorate delay-type devices had proved a popular method of fuzing bombs in the 1939-1940 IRA campaign and with other terrorist groups around the world. However, up to this explosion, they had not been used by the PIRA in operations on the UK mainland. The forensic investigation thus revealed the re-emergence of an old method of initiation – this had important implications for the render-safe procedures used by Explosives Officers in London.

Attacks on the capital's transport system continued and, as already explained, for minimum effort massive disruption could be achieved. This time, however, 13 February 1976, a Friday, proved to be lucky for many people. It was the date of another 'first' in London. At 17.15 hours, at the height of the rush hour, Explosives Officer Jim Greenwood was tasked to give assistance with a suspect case at Oxford Circus Underground Station. On arrival at the scene Greenwood was disturbed to discover that there was almost no cordon and evacuation. After making enquiries with members of the public he made his way down onto the station concourse. There he met two police officers who told him they had found the bag and moved it to a storeroom nearby. One of the officers had forced a lock on the case and on peering inside could see wires and plastic wrappers. Greenwood decided that as the bomb had been moved and partially opened there was clearly no anti-

374

handling systems present and the main threat was from the time delay. He went to the storeroom and opened the case where he discovered sticks of explosive and a wooden plywood box containing batteries and a timer. He rendered the bomb safe and then went back to the police officers. At this point he arranged for the full evacuation of the station, followed by a search for secondary devices. The incident was significant because for the first time a small wooden plywood box type timing and power unit (TPU) was recovered in London; there would be many more.

The following day another device was found, this time in George Street. The device, in a plastic bag, was rendered safe by another Explosives Officer, Neil MacMillan. It also had one of the new TPU's built into a small plywood box. The same night, another bomb exploded without warning in Landward Court. It was a pattern which continued, with further bombs exploding all over Central London without warning. These later bombs reverted to the crude chemical initiation systems already described – and which were prone not only to failure, but also to premature ignition.

On 1 March 1976, in the early evening, police responded to calls to an explosion outside Stanhope Gardens, Kensington. On arrival at the scene the first officers found a badly injured man who was quickly taken to St Stephens's Hospital. He was severely injured and later had a hand and a leg amputated. It was obvious that he might well be the bomber as, after medical treatment, when questioned by the police, he gave a series of false names. Later police issued a photograph of the man and shortly afterwards his sister came forward and identified the bomber. He was Patrick Hackett from County Tipperary, Eire. He had worked briefly as a butcher in Balham. The manager there commented that Hackett had, 'seemed a cheerful sort of chap. Butchers are great jokers and he joined in with Irish jokes – even about bombs.'

The same day, in an internal police re-organisation, the Bomb Squad, as it was still called, was re-named. From this point it became C 13, the Anti-Terrorist Branch.

On 4 March 1976, at 08.48 hours, a bomb on a train detonated as it left Cannon Street station. It was en route to sidings and fortunately there was no one in the carriage where it exploded; however, the blast damaged a passing inbound London train, injuring eight passengers. A few minutes later a second bomb exploded in another empty train, this time whilst it was going over a viaduct near Stoney Street.

The unreliability of the acid delay timers came to the fore again on 15 March when a bomber was nearly killed when a device he was carrying on an Underground train, (but which was travelling over ground) functioned prematurely. The train was near West Ham station when the bomb, in a duffle bag, started smoking. In panic the bomber threw it down on the floor and fled to the end of the carriage. Moments later it detonated, injuring him and nine other people. Luckily there were no fatalities from the blast, but one unfortunate man was injured by part of the train roof which was blown off and hit him whilst he was walking 100 yards away.

The slightly-injured perpetrator leapt off the train and made a run for it. Bravely the driver, thirty-four-year-old Julius Stephen from the West Indies, gave chase. The bomber stopped, turned and shot Stephen in the chest; he died almost instantly. Another man, a twenty-four-year-old Post Office engineer called Peter Chalk who was working nearby, courageously took up the chase. He, too, was shot in the chest and was taken, critically ill, to hospital. The bomber was eventually cornered by a number of unarmed police officers in a nearby yard. Realising he could not escape, he shouted 'You English bastards' and then turned the gun on himself and fired a single shot into his chest. Unlike Julius Stephen, he did not die and was arrested and taken to hospital. Shortly afterwards an appeal was launched to raise money for Stephen who left behind a young wife and family. When it closed, in August 1976, over £17,000 had been raised.

After the explosion, the head of Scotland Yard's Anti-Terrorist Branch, Commander Roy Habershon, warned the public and commuters in particular that they must protect themselves and look out for any unattended bags, suspicious objects or men acting suspiciously. One conservative newspaper columnist was horrified by this approach and said:

> It is not in the British character to go nosing around. Admittedly, we live in a gangster age, but anyone who tried asking me questions would be sharply told to mind his own business. You can't turn us overnight into a race of informers. Nor can the IRA.[8]

With the detention in quick succession of the two injured terrorists it was hoped that there would be a break in the bombing, but the following day another device detonated on a train in Wood Green. It exploded in an empty carriage whilst the train was in the station only minutes before it was due to depart to pick up supporters from an Arsenal-Newcastle match. Luckily, only one man was injured and this was by flying glass as he walked past the train.

In the early hours of 17 March, a device was located on a train at Neasden. It was found by a car examiner, Alfred Evans, who had removed a seat and discovered a suspect bag. He reported the item to his supervisor who unwisely removed it and threw it off the train and on to a sidewalk, a few feet from the track. John Sheldrake, the duty Explosives Officer, rushed to the scene and rendered the device safe. It consisted of five pounds of commercial explosive initiated by an acid delay system. One result of this incident was the decision to seal all the seats on trains with specialist tags to ease the problem of searching them after a warning. It was also clear that in the future, when new rolling stock was built, combating terrorism had to be taken into account in the design and all voids and spaces under seats had to be eliminated. Similar security considerations were also applied to the design of new buildings and many other structures. For example, the elimination of flat window ledges on which a small bomb could be placed.

There was a genuine fear at the time that should a bomb explode on the Underground there would not only be carnage but mass panic resulting in even more casualties. In response, the Metropolitan Police and British Transport Police instigated a massive search operation to check all trains for hidden bombs. They also mounted an operation similar to *Op Combo* where, to discourage further attacks, they flooded the transport system with over 1,000 policemen, including armed and plain-clothes officers.

These tactics forced the bombers to abandon their attacks on the Underground and they switched to an easier target. On 27 March 1976, at the Ideal Home Exhibition in Olympia, a bomb, left in a litter bin, exploded without warning. This time eighty-six people were injured, one of whom, Rachel Hyams, died of her injuries three weeks later. Another victim, Dorothy Yarby, recalled how she and her boyfriend had just passed the bin when there was a massive explosion which bowled them both over: 'People started to run screaming to get away. I had to climb over bodies. There were ten or twelve. One man's leg was in shreds. It was gruesome and I tried not to look at it.'[9]

With so many casualties needing help, and despite an awareness of the possibility of secondary devices, there was a massive response by the emergency services and the area around Olympia soon became completely snarled up with traffic which took hours to sort out. In defiance of the terrorists, the decision was made quickly that the show should go on and, after the forensic examination of the scene and a full search of the premises, the exhibition continued. The baggage checks at the door were carried out more thoroughly and full body frisking was introduced.

The attack was considered more barbaric than any that had gone before; ordinary people, women with small children and the elderly had been targeted. There was no pretence now of targeting military installations or pubs where soldiers went, no cranky concentration on expensive eating places where politicians and the wealthy might be expected to be victims, no pretext of attacking the capital's transport systems; this was just plain murder of the innocent. As happens sometimes, the impact of this devastating attack was overshadowed by the collision of two jumbo jets in Tenerife which killed 650 people; it gave the media something else to concentrate on.

In response to the bombs, the police had appealed to landlords to be 'nosy' and make enquires about all their guests. Inevitably, the outcome was thousands of possible leads – all of which had to be checked. There were results though, and a number of finds and arrests followed this attack and it brought another temporary halt to the bombings.

To keep up the pressure, the PIRA resorted to sending more postal bombs. In May a number were delivered to various people in the capital. Fortunately, most were intercepted. Explosives Officer Ken Howorth was tasked to deal with one of the devices which had been taken to Kensington Police Station. There he was shown the suspect package which had been left isolated in the station yard. After a careful examination he rendered it safe.

By now it should have been clear to all concerned that the proper method of dealing with a suspect bomb was for the area around it to be cordoned and evacuated, and an Explosives Officer tasked to deal with the device it in situ. This did not always happen, especially if the incident was not linked to the IRA. For example, on 29 December, as a result of a domestic incident involving two men and a girl, a suspect bomb, built into a green plastic covered record case, was found in the back of a car. This case was recovered from the vehicle by local police and driven to the Explosives Office in Central London. There it was examined and, after an X-ray, it was established that there was what appeared to be an anti-opening switch under the lid of the case and it was treated as a bomb. It was eventually rendered safe and was discovered to contain the powder from at least 100 shotgun cartridges, batteries, wires and an igniter, all of which were connected to the anti-open switch under the lid of the case. There was also a quantity of nails which were intended to act as shrapnel. All in all, a nasty little device intended for a revenge attack.

On 29 January 1977, a whole series of small blast bombs and incendiaries functioned across the West End and it seemed that there would be another year of bombing. Then, as far as Irish terrorism was concerned, it all went quiet and remained that way for most of the year.

Worldwide terrorist acts were never far from the headlines and a variety of attacks were reported, some were state-sponsored, and many had their roots in the Middle East. London did not escape unscathed. At

21.55 hours on New Year's Eve 1977, a violent and perplexing explosion occurred in a Volvo estate car in Stafford Street, just off Piccadilly. The explosion severely damaged the car which caught fire. This was extinguished by an Army firefighting team in a Green Goddess, which was standing in for striking firemen. Explosives Officer Ken Howorth attended the incident and went to forward to examine the vehicle. The roof had been blown off and inside were the badly charred bodies of two men. To his experienced eye Howorth could see that both had suffered severe injuries from an explosion prior to the fire. It was also established that the seat of the explosion had been inside the car, probably between the driver and the passenger.

Subsequent inquiries revealed that the men were both employees of the Syrian Embassy and a major investigation followed. The key question which needed answering was, were the two Syrians killed by a bomb hidden in their car or where they planning to plant a bomb which for some reason detonated whilst it was being prepared for use? The forensic investigation again provided valuable evidence. Despite the burnt condition of the bodies, it was apparent that both men had had their hands and part of their forearms blown off. This would indicate that at the time of the explosion the pair of them had twisted round and had their hands in very close contact with the bomb. In addition, fragments recovered from the car included pieces of plastic and parts of a watch which were similar to those recovered previously from a white box timing and power unit of a type known to be of Middle East origin. Subsequent international enquiries also linked the device to other attacks, in particular to a bomb which exploded on the same day outside the Egyptian Embassy in Bonn. Although it was impossible to determine conclusively what had happened, all the indications were that the two men had died whilst preparing to plant a bomb probably in or near the Egyptian ambassador's house.

Two aspects of the bombing astonished Ken Howorth. Firstly, under the car he discovered a battered Seiko watch on the tarmac. It had clearly been worn by one of the men who had been killed; to Howorth's surprise it was still working. (He was so impressed that he wrote to the manufacturers commenting on the robust and reliable nature of the design, hoping that he might be sent a free sample, but nothing ever arrived.) Secondly, the roof of the car which had not been found during the initial search of the scene was later discovered some 100 yards away, lying sixty feet up on a flat-roofed building.

Overall 1977 was, as far as bombs were concerned, a relatively quiet year. The 'nutters' (as they were affectionately known) kept the police and Explosives Officers both busy and amused. For example, there was an incident involving a doll stuffed into the railings at the rear of Knightsbridge Barracks. A letter in very poor English attached to the doll talked of starting another world war. The CID assessment was that it was the work of a juvenile with a poor education and lively imagination.

The following year, 1978, was also a quiet year as far as the PIRA was concerned, but there were a number of criminal-related incidents. Looking back at the statistics it is apparent that there were a lot more of these types of bombings than there are today, the reasons for which are not clear. For example, there was an explosion in the Communist Party Headquarters in King Street on 4 April 1978. A victim-operated postal device had been received and a small charge in a glass bottle exploded when it was opened, causing a small fire and minor injuries. Other incidents included a postal bomb sent to the Conservative Party Headquarters on 26 July. Five days later two more letter bombs were sent; one functioned causing minor injuries at the premises of the *Morning Star* newspaper and another was discovered and rendered safe by Explosives Officer John Horne at a bookshop in Charing Cross Road. It seems that in the 1970s, individuals with a grudge or extreme political parties were much more likely to resort to the use of postal or other crude bombs than they are today.

Middle Eastern terrorism erupted again on 20 August 1978. As a group of El Al aircrew alighted from a bus at the Europa Hotel in Duke Street, it was attacked; a number of Soviet style grenades was thrown at them, as well as several bursts of fire from a sub-machinegun. One of the stewardesses was killed in the attack, as was one of the assassins, probably by fragments from a grenade he had thrown. The incident was claimed by the Popular Front for the Liberation of Palestine.

As the year drew to a close information was received that the PIRA was going to mount another Christmas bombing campaign, something that had, by now, become a depressing tradition. A number of devices functioned in provincial towns and cities and it looked like it might culminate with attacks on Central London in the last few shopping days before Christmas. To counter it, the police launched Operation *Santa*. This involved nearly 2,000 officers, many of them armed, being drafted into London's West End to dissuade the bombers. It worked in as much as it forced them to go elsewhere.

On 18 December, in the early morning, a car bomb detonated outside the Oasis swimming baths in Holborn creating a huge fireball. Another car bomb detonated at about the same time in the NCP car park off

Great Russell Street causing a fire. Just after midday another suspect car was located, this time parked outside the Rising Sun public house in Windmill Street. A police officer had noticed a tartan-patterned holdall in the rear of the vehicle behind the passenger seat. Explosives Officer Don Green went to the scene and after gaining access discovered a five-pound device in the holdall which sat on top of a five-gallon drum of petrol. The use of petrol was popular with terrorists in Northern Ireland around this time and the fuel was used to enhance the effects of comparatively small blast bombs which were known as Blast Incendiaries, or BIs for short. With this flurry of activity 1978 drew to a close.

During this period Police Constable Mike Chipperfield was acting as Don Green's Number 2 and driver. Part of the job of working with an Explosives Officer was to explain what was going on to the police duty officer at an incident. There was often a good deal of tension during the initial stages of an investigation into a suspect item and this lasted until the Explosives Officer was able to confirm there was a real device and it had been rendered safe, or it was a hoax or false alarm. Chipperfield remembered that, although broadly similar, each Explosives Officer had a slightly different approach to every task:

My chap, Don, used to get short with people and was nicknamed 'Terse Perce.' There was a campaign going on and we were busy. One day we had dealt with a couple of good calls and had just got back to the office when the hot line went again. There was a suspect dustcart outside Central Hall Westminster.

'Who in God's name would put a bomb in a dustcart!' growled Don.

When we got there it turned out not to be a lorry type, but one of the hand carts. Don Said;

'You wait here Mick, I'll have a look.'

Now Don wore an old parka over his flak jacket and a cloth cap, not the height of sartorial elegance. I kept an eye on proceedings from round a corner. He walked up to the cart and lifted the lid, removed a plastic bag and leaned inside to check. At this point a young PC appeared beside him and tugged his sleeve. Don stunned, shot up and an animated conversation took place, which I couldn't hear. When he got back to our motor Don said, through clenched teeth:

'Do you know what that cheeky bugger said to me?'

'No, what?'

He said, 'Is this your cart sir?'

I said 'I've told you about your casual dress before', and couldn't drive off for a couple of minutes; I was laughing so much. He did have a sense of humour though.[10]

In early 1979 the PIRA decided to sabotage a number of petroleum and gas storage tanks, the aim being to create a spectacular series of explosions. The first indication was the report of an explosion at the Texaco oil storage depot at Canvey Island, Essex. Shortly before midnight a threat from the PIRA was received at the Press Association. It warned of explosive devices at Canvey Island and in the Blackwall Tunnel. Typical of this type of bomb threat at the time, it was too late and misleading directions were given. In fact, the second bomb was at the gas holder station in Blackwall Lane. It detonated just before 02.00 hours on 18 January causing a fire and considerable damage.

In Northern Ireland a new splinter group, the Irish National Liberation Army (INLA), had formed. It decided to assassinate the forthright opposition spokesman on affairs in the Province, the Conservative MP Airey Neave. An INLA reconnaissance team discovered where Neave lived and established that he normally drove a Vauxhall Cavalier. To kill him, the attackers decided to place a booby-trapped bomb beneath his vehicle. It seems most likely that they placed the bomb beneath the car up, against one of the vehicle's structural cross members almost directly under where the foot pedals were, in the early hours of Friday, 30 March 1979. Rather than using a Memopark timer, a modified watch with the minute hand removed was used to arm the device. In it the hour hand would provide a delay between the device being placed under the vehicle and a mercury tilt switch and detonator being brought into the firing circuit. Possibly there was a longer delay than intended or there was a faulty circuit as Neave drove his car to Parliament without incident and left it in the underground car park. There it probably armed. The only thing preventing the bomb detonating now was the small air gap between two electrical contacts inside the mercury tilt switch. In the glass ampoule a bubble of the liquid metal lay motionless, waiting for some movement to cause it to bridge the gap.

It was mid-afternoon when the Neave climbed into his car intent on driving home after his work at the Commons. As he drove his Vauxhall Cavalier up the ramp, at the exit to the car park, the mercury in the tilt switch rolled forward and completed the bomb's electrical circuit. It exploded beneath the vehicle with devastating effect. The Cavalier lurched forward another thirty-five feet before coming to a halt. Rescuers rushed to the mangled wreckage and managed to get Neave out of the car, but he had been fatally injured and died a short while later in hospital. Had he lived, Neave may well have been selected to become the Secretary of State for Northern Ireland in the new Conservative government. After the event, the INLA claimed to have breached the House of Commons' security and actually put the bomb in position there, but this seems unlikely.

As the festive season approached, the possibility of another Christmas bombing campaign was being evaluated, but for various reasons the PIRA did not have the will or the capability to mount an operation. Instead, it resorted to the easy alternative and sent another batch of postal bombs. In an effort to allay the fears of the intended recipients, the devices were all posted in Europe so that there was no apparent Irish connection. Luckily for the victims, one exploded in a sorting office in Dover on 17 December 1979. The forensic examination quickly established that this was most likely linked to Irish terrorism and appropriate warnings were sent out and plans implemented to ensure all suspect mail was properly screened. Two days later a suspect device was discovered at the Paddington sorting office. Contrary to normal procedures, two police officers recovered the device and took it to the Explosives Office in Central London. The wisdom of moving it must be questioned, particularly as it had already been established that the first of the series of devices had initiated prematurely in transit. John Horne, the duty Explosives Officer, quickly established it was a bomb and after careful examination manually rendered it safe. Reports were then received that Lord Croham had received a suspect device at his house in Croydon; this too was investigated and made safe. Over the next few days, further devices were intercepted or identified as suspect by the recipients, and all were disarmed with excellent recovery of forensic evidence.

In May 1980 there were two strange incidents. The first occurred at Catford Police Station. Police Constable Hickling, who was on duty in the early hours of the morning, discovered that an orange, plastic-bodied torch had been left by a Metropolitan Police Orphans' collection box in the front office of the police station. Hickling picked up the torch and, having no reason to consider it suspect, switched it on. There was an explosion as a charge in the torch, linked to the on/off switch, detonated. Although only containing a small quantity of explosive, probably no more than an ounce, the bomb completely shattered the constable's right hand and his forearm almost up to the elbow. The torch itself was blown into many thousands of fragments. Hickling, in considerable shock and pain, was given initial first aid and then rushed to hospital where his injured arm was treated. The explosion was not claimed by anyone, and was not thought to be linked to the PIRA. A possible motive could have been a revenge attack against the police by a local criminal; it will go down in history as one of those odd and unsolved bombings.

The second unusual incident was the detonation of a bomb in the Queen's Gardens Hotel in Central London on 17 May 1980. Explosives Officer Ron Wilson was tasked to the hotel mid-morning after reports of the explosion were received. On arrival at the scene he was informed that the fire brigade had extinguished a small fire in room No.21. Furthermore, firefighters reported that there was dead man in the room, that another had been seriously injured and taken to hospital and another arrested. Wilson proceeded up to the fourth floor to carry out an initial examination and it was immediately apparent to him that some sort of bomb had detonated. The room was in a state of devastation and chaos and whilst looking through the debris he located the body of the dead man. It was clear from his traumatic injuries that he had been close to the bomb when it detonated. Wilson left the scene and organised a doctor to certify the man was dead and then informed the various police branches that this was, indeed, a serious incident. Arrangements were made for the water supply to the building to be switched off because fractured pipes were spewing water all over the room. The electricity was also switched off and for safety reasons the district surveyor called to make arrangements to assess and structural integrity of the building.

Once all these actions had been completed Wilson set about a thorough examination of the scene. Sifting through the wreckage he located two TNT charges, each about half-a-pound in weight, taped together. These he identified as standard American military demolition charges one of which was fitted with a detonator which Wilson immediately removed. Further discoveries included a timer and a battery linked together to make a crude firing circuit. All these items were recovered showing signs of minor blast damage and were clearly in the same room, but some distance from the other bomb when it went off. A further recovery was the remains of a severely damaged soldering iron which had been in close proximity to the first bomb when it detonated. It was concluded that the deceased had been in the process of assembling the second of two bombs when it had functioned prematurely. Enquiries revealed that the men involved were Iranian. Like the Syrians killed in the car three years earlier, the questions that needed answering were who were the men working for and what was the intended target for their bombs? As far as can be established, this question has never been satisfactorily answered.

In June a bomb exploded outside the Kuwait Oil Company in New Bond Street. Although obviously linked to Middle East terrorism, the attack was not attributed to one group in particular.

The year also saw the first potential suicide bomber in a car. On a bleak November evening Explosives Officer Ken Howorth was tasked to a suspect vehicle on Westminster Bridge. The car, a white MGB, was parked on the bridge in an unusual manner. On arrival at the scene, using a powerful telescope, Howorth was able to establish that there was a man sitting at the wheel of the vehicle. Along with the incident commander, Chief Inspector Purnell, Howorth approached the car and asked if they could speak to the driver. It was clear, even under the poor street lighting, that the man was holding black wires and a switch in his hand and that he was quite agitated. The driver informed the two officers that he had a bomb in the petrol tank and another in the boot and that they were controlled by the switch he was holding. Howorth and the Duty Officer then sat down in the road and began to chat to the driver to get a better 'feel' for the incident. He told them about the bomb and that he had another secondary firing system in his sleeve which would be activated if anyone attempted to drag him from the car. After a prolonged conversation with the man, punctuated by him insisting that they go away whilst he changed the alleged firing switch from one hand to another, he agreed that Howorth could inspect the wiring which ran to the boot. As Howorth walked around the back of the car he could see wires running to the boot and more appearing to run into the petrol filler cap which was covered in tape. However, on looking more closely he could see that the wires leading to the petrol tank terminated before the cap itself and were not connected to anything. He also noted that the man was tied into the car by ropes attached round his waist and to the doors. From this inspection Howorth was convinced that this was a hoax and that no explosives were involved.

To be on the safe side, whilst Chief Inspector Purnell distracted the man, Howorth, unobserved by the occupant, quietly cut the cable to the boot, thereby separating it from the firing switch the man was claiming to be holding. After further conversation the man admitted it was a hoax and after cutting the ropes he climbed out of the car. Howorth made him open the boot which was full of personal effects and, as suspected, no explosives were present. Chief Inspector Purnell then had the man arrested and removed to Kennington Police Station. Looking back, it was a very low key, restrained and pragmatic response; the incident would be handled in a very different way today.

The investigations into PIRA activity, both in Northern Ireland and on the mainland, continued at a frenetic pace throughout the period.

Behind the headlines, at the Anti-Terrorist Branch a small team of dedicated detectives was always hard at work making hundreds of enquiries and following up every lead no matter how small. Eventually, all this hard graft paid dividends and on 26 August 1980, as part of their on-going investigations, branch officers raided 144, Trafalgar Road in Greenwich. They found a mass of bomb making material, including explosives, detonators and a selection of TPUs. Many of them incorporated new long-delay electronic timers marked up as one and four days, others were the normal short delay types using the, by now ubiquitous, Memopark. All these timing and power units had one thing in common, their safety and arming mechanisms utilised clothes pegs with electrical contacts in the jaws of the peg. These were held open in the safe position by a dowel pin. Once the dowel pin was removed the contacts would close and the bomb would be armed, the only thing preventing it firing being the Memopark timer or the electronic delay.

Significantly, there was one other TPU which, on initial inspection, looked the same as all the others, but in fact had a very different purpose. It was built into a similar wooden box with batteries and a Memopark timer. In addition, there was a micro switch in the bottom of the box and a small hole through which an extension lever on the micro switch protruded. There could only be one use for such an arrangement and that was as a deliberate anti-handling system designed to kill anyone moving the bomb. It would need to be laid by a cold and calculating killer.

By this time, of the four original Explosives Officers, Sandy Hawkins had retired and the other three were either in, or approaching, their sixties. They had all dealt with many live devices, most manually, taking, as they saw it, calculated risks. In addition, they had all attended countless numbers of hoaxes and false alarms. The shift work, long hours and constant danger had taken their toll on some; Don Henderson had suffered a nervous breakdown and Geoffrey Biddle, who was now sixty-four, had severe arthritis. Ron Wilson in contrast was fit and well and hoped to serve on until sixty-five.

It was acknowledged that Don Henderson could be 'prickly' and difficult to deal with and, not surprisingly, after such a prolonged period of intense operations, relations with some senior police officers had suffered. It was decided to retire him and the other two men under the pretext that, at their age, they were no longer as sharp as they used to be and they might put the public at risk at an incident involving a bomb. Ron Wilson, in particular, was incensed at the decision and appealed through an industrial tribunal to stay on. But the verdict was upheld and so the three retired in 1981.

To their great credit, they had all served with conspicuous bravery through dangerous, hectic and extraordinary times. More importantly, though, they had lived to tell the tale.

It was also around this time that the term EXPO, short for Explosives Officer, came into general use, particularly over police radios. It will be used in the remainder of the book.

NOTES:
1. Extract from witness statement of Geoffrey William Biddle, January 1974.
2. Interview with Harry Greig, 5 June 2006.
3. Gurney, Peter, *Braver Men Walk Away*, HarperCollins, London, 1993.
4. Grant, McKee and Franey, Ros, *Time Bomb*, Bloomsbury Publishing Limited, London, 1988.
5. ibid.
6. *Daily Telegraph*, 4 December 1975.
7. *The Times*, 7 September 1975.
8. Article, *Evening News*, Arran column, 17 March 1976.
9. *Sunday Times*, 28 March 1976.
10.Note from Mick Chipperfield, 2008.

Chapter 21

Terrorism – The Long War.

**'"We claim responsibility" – In these three words are
summed up the evil intent of those who, for whatever
cause, make murder and destruction a way of life.'**
The opening address by the Chaplin General at the dedication of the
memorial for bomb disposal officers.

Early 1981 was pivotal for both sides of the struggle in Northern Ireland and it led to one of the bitterest periods during the long thirty-year conflict. From a Republican point of view, much of the focus was around the prisoners in the Maze, where the dirty protest and the beginning of a hunger strike inflamed Catholic opinion, drawing support away from moderate voices. On the government side, Mrs Thatcher was in power and in no mood to compromise. This entrenching of positions meant that the hardliners held sway and the future looked bleak with little prospect of conciliation. To emphasise the point a suspect device, delivered to Merlyn Rees at the Palace of Westminster on the last day of April 1981, contained a hollowed-out book in which there were batteries, wires and Plastecine. A note inside said, 'IF BOBBY SANDS DIES WATCH OUT FOR THE NEXT ONE'. Sands passed away in May 1981, followed by other hunger strikers. The protest was finally called off in early October, but it left the PIRA resentful, embittered and determined to extract revenge with renewed attacks on mainland Britain, the Thatcher government and London.

The use of command wires to detonate devices in Northern Ireland was a common occurrence but, as previously noted, complex attacks usually occurred in remote border areas or where the local population were generally hostile to the security forces. There, the terrorist's task of laying the command wire and putting the bomb in place was done on ground of his choosing and in comparative safety. Conversely, in

London, this sort of attack was considered unlikely because it was always busy and the population was hostile to the terrorists.

The PIRA thought otherwise and, after a careful reconnaissance, decided to set up a command-wire controlled bomb to ambush a military bus in Chelsea. They assembled two twenty-pound bombs in holdalls and studded these with a collection of over 1,100 six-inch nails and fifty bolts. They then bought a white van and carefully positioned the bombs on the driver's side in the rear compartment; one at the forward end of the cargo carrying area and the other over the rear wheel. Using two bombs increased size of the killing zone produced by the shrapnel packed round the explosive. To further improve the lethality, the bombs were hung on a wire which brought them up to the approximate height of the seats of the military bus which would be their target.

No one noticed the white van parked up by some scaffolding in Ebury Bridge on the morning of 10 October 1981, or the two men dressed in workmen's overalls. Having positioned the van, the pair proceeded to pay out a command wire which ran down the scaffolding to a firing point 100 metres away. Once there, a battery was produced which was connected to the wire. On top of this there was probably a simple firing switch which, when closed, would set off the bomb. Although targeting a military vehicle, callously the ambush took no account of the fact that civilians could well be walking past the van when the device was triggered.

It was just after midday that a white military bus carrying the dismounting guard from the Tower of London approached Chelsea Barracks. The soldiers, from the 1st Battalion Irish Guards, were relaxed as they were about to go off duty. Little did they know that the PIRA had set up a vicious ambush bomb and that they were about to drive into its lethal radius. They were travelling down Ebury Bridge Road when, as they passed a matter of feet from the white van, it erupted in a violent explosion. After initiating the bomb, the perpetrators disconnected the battery and fled the scene.

As planned, when the bomb detonated a mass of nails and bolts was hurled across the road and scythed through the side of the passing bus. Twenty-three of the soldiers suffered from the most savage wounds, many having six-inch nails driven into their bodies. It was remarkable that none were killed. A number of innocent civilians were also close to the white van when the device detonated. Nora Field was struck by a nail which pierced her heart and killed her instantly. Another victim, a young Irish Catholic called John Breslin, was also fatally injured and subsequently died in hospital. A further fifteen civilians suffered injuries, some serious.

In the chaotic aftermath of the attack, two soldiers on the bus, Sergeant Cullen and Guardsman Trafford, set about helping the wounded, the latter saving another soldier's life by carrying out an emergency tracheotomy. They were both decorated for their actions that day.

A week later, the PIRA struck again. This time, it attempted to assassinate Lieutenant General Sir Steuart Pringle. He was specifically targeted because he was the Commandant General of the Royal Marines and, according to the PIRA, a battalion of marines had badly treated the people of West Belfast over the previous four months. Having traced his address to South Croxted Road through *Who's Who*, an under-car booby-trap was placed beneath the wheel arch of his car on the night of 16-17 October. It was late in the morning when the General climbed into his red Volkswagen Passat to set off for work; he had driven approximately twenty feet when there was an explosion. The car was blown off course and came to rest when it hit another parked vehicle. General Pringke, seriously injured, was trapped in the mangled wreckage.

Peter Gurney was tasked to the incident and swiftly arrived on the scene. His immediate concern was for secondary devices and he advised those not directly involved in the rescue or emergency medical treatment of the General to clear the area. He then carried out an immediate search of the locality, including the damaged Passat, but found nothing. The General, still trapped, was conscious and lucid and Gurney spoke to him about the incident. Once he was cut free and removed, the area was completely cleared and the scene examined in more detail. The damage to the car centred on the front offside bulkhead between the engine compartment and the driver's seat area. Some of the bodywork in this area showed that it had been in intimate contact with a high explosive charge at the moment of detonation. Parts of the car had been blown off due to the considerable force of the explosion and the bonnet of the vehicle was found on the roof of a building some sixty feet away. The front wheel and wheel arch had been shattered and parts of them had smashed into a vehicle parked nearby. It was damage typically associated with the use of an under-car booby-trap. General Pringle lost a leg in the explosion and suffered other serious injuries. His rescuers noted that during his rescue he showed considerable fortitude, remaining calm and composed whilst being cut out of the wreckage. He has the dubious distinction of being the most senior serving officer to be injured by the PIRA in the last campaign.

Despite the death of Roger Goad, there was still a precedent to render bombs safe manually whenever possible, and all the EXPOs took a certain pride in this. Disrupters were used, but this was the exception rather than the rule. Manual neutralisation did result in the best forensic evidence and as a senior police officer said at the time: 'It is seldom that the Explosives Officer will decide to "disrupt" an unexploded device. Where the possibility exists, devices are rendered safe manually, the exhibits meticulously packaged and labelled and those exhibits forwarded to RARDE Woolwich for scientific examination.'[1]

It was a procedure that would lead to another catastrophe. In response to a telephone bomb threat received by Reuters, at 14.51 hours on 26 October 1981, two police officers, David Wallace and Damian Manning, went to the Wimpy Bar at 142-144 Oxford Street to search for a reported bomb. Initially nothing was found, but a further warning indicated the device had been left in the toilets. Retrospectively, it was odd for the PIRA to give such detailed information about the location of the bomb. Normally it would just be to the shop or even simply to 'bombs in Oxford Street', the aim being to create massive disruption. In line with this method, more general bomb threats were given for two other devices, one in Debenhams and the other in Bourne and Hollingworth.

Back at the Wimpy Bar, the manager and Wallace set out to search the female toilets, whilst Manning went to the Gents. There, under twin sinks, he discovered what he described as a parcel and a box. The smaller package was similar to a pencil box and was connected by wires to the larger parcel which was covered in sticky tape. Wallace arrived and confirmed the presence of the suspect device, after which the two immediately began the evacuation of the premises. Next, they requested the attendance of an EXPO and Ken Howorth, who was on duty, was ordered to the scene. He arrived at about 15.45 hours and was given a quick briefing. The area had been cordoned and evacuated out to 100 metres and the normally busy street was strangely quiet.

Constable Wallace helped Howorth into some lightweight body armour and went with him to the entrance of the Wimpy Bar, which had been locked. He opened the door and went halfway down the stairs, then pointed out the Gents toilet. Duty done, he turned round and went back to the incident control point. Howorth, carrying a bag full of tools, headed for the basement toilets where the suspect device had been found. In the circumstances he must have known it was likely to be a bomb and, even though he was an experienced and capable operator, and had made similar approaches to suspect items hundreds of times before, he must have been apprehensive. In these circumstances it takes a special kind of courage to go forward to deal with a bomb, particularly when no one is compelling you to do so.

Back at the Bungalow, Peter Gurney had arrived in the office at around 15.40 hours to start the late shift. He was immediately caught up in the action and was being updated about the on-going events prior to his deployment to Debenhams where another, apparently similar, device had just been located.

In Oxford Street, the area in front of the Wimpy Bar was still unusually deserted and the police officers at the incident control point and on the cordons were waiting for Howorth to re-appear with news of the bomb.

Suddenly, the front of the Wimpy Bar disintegrated, hurling wood and glass across the street and, in the same moment, ripping a chunk of concrete from the pavement. The roar of the explosion reached them moments later. It was immediately obvious to those outside that Ken Howorth must have been killed or very seriously injured, and there was a stunned silence. After a few moments, Wallace courageously went back into the building and down the stairs. He saw a scene of total devastation; the thin walls of the toilets had been completely destroyed. He had no doubts that Howorth must have died and he left and went back out into Oxford Street.

Peter Gurney was still being briefed when the first reports of the explosion came through, news which included the probability that Howorth had been killed. He decided to go to the Wimpy Bar first before going on to the second device in Debenhams. Gurney arrived at the outer cordon and after a short update, went forward to examine the scene. He climbed through the shop front and clambered down the stairs, through the wreckage, to look for his colleague. At the bottom of the stairs he scrambled over the rubble towards the seat of the blast. His worst fears were quickly realised. In the wreckage of the gloomy and dusty basement he could see a body and was left in no doubt that it was Howorth. Worse still was the fact that there was nothing that could be done for him. With a second and possibly similar device waiting to be dealt with at Debenhams, Gurney needed to establish, as far as was possible in the prevailing circumstances, what had happened? He recalled:

> I looked at the body again knowing what it had been, but knowing, too, that at this moment all emotion had to be suspended. Body tissue is remarkably resilient; it has to be very close to a bomb blast to destroy it. That was obviously the case here; even though the body was lying about nine yards from the seat of the explosion, the type and the extent of the injury indicated that the deceased had been looking at the bomb, his face close to it, probably touching something when the explosion occurred. But I needed to be sure.
>
> Slowly, carefully, I ran my hands down the sides of the body, sensing rather than seeing its mutilated shape. The action confirmed

what I had half- expected: both arms had been blown off by the explosion. This meant that he had been handling or working on the bomb when it went off. It also meant the device also probably had a particularly nasty booby-trap mechanism.[2]

Gurney left the Wimpy Bar, jumped into his Range Rover and headed for the second suspected device which still needed to be dealt with Gurney. It had been found after the bomb threat by a security guard in the toilets on the third floor of the building. When he had gone into the Gents to search them, the security guard found that three of the cubicles were locked. Classically, he glanced under the door of each one and only saw only two sets of legs. He then opened the door of the vacant toilet using a coin and looked inside. He could see two packages sitting on top of the boxed in, low-level cistern. He closed the door, relocked it, and warned the occupants of the other two cubicles to get out immediately. One man fled instantly, but the other customer, who seemed determined to retain his dignity, insisted on washing his hands first.

When Gurney arrived he was told where the device was and, carrying a loaded 'Pigstick', immediately went forward to deal with it. This was another display of exceptional bravery; going forward to deal with a bomb which, the limited evidence indicated, was very similar to the one that had just killed his friend. On arrival at the toilet, he opened the door using a knife and went in. He could see what he recognised as a timing and power unit linked to an explosives charge which was wrapped in buff plastic tape. It was similar to the description of Howorth's bomb and, acutely aware that there might be an anti-handling system hidden in the charge, he elected to shoot his disrupter into this. Whilst positioning the disrupter he was sure he could hear a Memopark timer clicking away.

Gurney retired to a safe distance and immediately fired the 'Pigstick'. When he returned to the cubicle he found that the device had been successfully disrupted. The next step was to examine the evidence; he was about to do this when he was tasked to yet another suspect item. After arranging for the scene to be secured he left to deal with the new threat, but it turned out to be a false alarm and he quickly cleared it.

In small and tight-knit communities the death of a close friend and colleague has a profound impact. The first question on everyone's mind was, of course, what happened? Howorth was an experienced operator and it was vital that it was established what actions he took in his last few moments in the Wimpy Bar's basement. Had he been unlucky and the timer ran out as he approached the bomb or was there a more sinister reason for his death?

The initial theory was that it had been an anti-handling device, but the key question was what type was it? A thorough examination of the bulk debris, which had been recovered to the Forensic Explosives Laboratories in Woolwich, took over three weeks. There was one feature which helped the scientists; the fact that the timing and power unit was separated, even by such a small distance, from the main charge meant that more of the former survived. After detailed sifting of the recovered debris, fragments of various components were suitable for examination. These included the remains of a micro switch. Up to this time these switches had been used in two roles; firstly, in conjunction with a mercury tilt switch as a booby-trap, and, secondly, as a safety and arming mechanism in long-delay electronic timers. In both these roles the arm of the micro switch was closed by the action of a nail glued to the front of a Memopark timer. In all the cases where this had been done previously, the bomb makers had had to bend the arm on the micro switch down for the system to work effectively. The arm of the micro switch recovered in this instance was still straight which indicated it had been set up for use in another manner. As previously recorded, one of the timing and power units recovered in the cache in Greenwich had a hole cut in the base of the wooden box, sufficiently large for the arm of a micro switch to fit through it. There could only be one purpose for such an arrangement – it was an anti-handling system in which any movement or lifting of the timing and power unit would cause the micro switch to open and, if wired correctly, this would complete an electrical circuit and set off the bomb.

As so often happens, nothing was ever irrefutably proved about the construction of the bomb. What was clear was that the device in the Wimpy Bar consisted of two separate packages linked by the electrical wires. The larger of the two contained a charge of a powerful nitroglycerine-based blasting explosive and an electric detonator. The smaller wooden box, which outwardly looked like a timing and power unit, may have, in fact, contained a delay to arm Memopark timer linked to a battery pack, and the anti-handling micro switch. Once the Memopark had wound round and completed an electrical circuit the only thing preventing the bomb functioning was the weight of the wooden box and its contents. The slightest movement of this could have been enough to cause the bomb to function, which, in this case, it did, killing Ken Howorth instantly.

For his family it was a devastating blow. Ken's son, Steve, was just approaching his twenty-first birthday when his father was killed. Because of the long hours and odd shift pattern his father worked it was quite usual for him not to be at home when the rest of the family was there. In the immediate aftermath he found himself in denial and could not come to grips with the sad fact that his father would never come home. Two or three days after his death, Howorth's car was returned to the family from the London office. Inside it was his old brown briefcase and, when it was opened, a brand new track suit was discovered which was to have been be part of Steve's birthday present. It was only then that he finally accepted his father would never return.

For his devotion to duty, and undoubted bravery, Ken Howorth was awarded a posthumous George Medal which the family accepted in a private audience with the Queen. Peter Gurney's bravery in dealing with the second bomb in Debenhams was also recognised with the award of a Bar to the George Medal he had received during an earlier tour Northern Ireland.

Not long after the incident, Waddingtons produced a board game called *Bomb Blast*. In it, characters including Major Jitters, Tommy Tremble and others went round a board with a ticking clock and a series of bomb disposal tasks. At the end the game the figure with the least bandages won. Howorth's family complained about the insensitive nature of releasing the game at such a time. Despite Waddingtons' claim that it was based on the exploits of Second World War bomb disposal officers, the game was discontinued.

Another 'first' occurred in London on Monday, 23 November 1981, when the PIRA used a booby-trapped toy gun to try and kill a soldier. They left a plastic but realistic looking toy pistol at one of the entrances to Government House at the Artillery Barracks in Woolwich. This particular entrance was only used between 06.00 hours and 18.00 hours, after which the gates were locked. The pistol was pushed under the gates early on the Sunday evening and the terrorists were clearly expecting a soldier to find it and pick it up when the gates were opened for work on the following day. The pistol was, in fact, first discovered by Major Stewart RA who had been working in his office late on the Sunday. On his way home he had driven to the entrance and saw the gun lying on the ground when he got out of his car to close the gates. He went over to have a look at the pistol and bending forward just touched it, but, crucially, without moving it. From this closer inspection he realised that it was made of plastic and logically concluded it was a child's toy, was non-suspicious, and left it there.

The following morning two cleaners, Mrs Hewitson and Mrs Eadsforth, both of whom happened to have dogs, left by this entrance just before 08.00 hours. They both saw the pistol and, like Major Stewart, went to have a look at it. Either Mrs Eadsforth or her dog moved the gun with a foot or paw at which point it detonated, severely injuring both of them and causing minor wounds to Mrs Hewitson. The investigation into the bombing concluded that the toy pistol had been booby-trapped, probably using a mercury tilt switch. It was thought that Major Stewart either did not move it enough to cause it to function, or he had found it moments after it had been laid and there was a delay to arm system which had not yet run its course. In any event, he was a very lucky man. Equally lucky were the soldiers who had been at the entrance first thing on the Monday morning. They did not see the gun because it was still very dark and its position was such that it was in shadow when they had opened the gates. Once laid and armed, this type of booby-trap is completely indiscriminate and, as happened in this case, often catches a totally innocent victim.

Middle East terrorism reared its ugly head again on 13 December 1981. Like previous bombings, it was a disaster for the perpetrators. The first alarm was raised by members of the public who reported that a white Datsun had blown up without warning in Connaught Square. Those responding to the incident found three men of Middle Eastern appearance in the car. The two in the back were dead and the driver severely injured. Examination of the scene suggested that the two men in the back were preparing a powerful pipe bomb for use against an unknown target when it had detonated prematurely.

The New Year of 1982, started with a small PIRA bomb which detonated in the City of London on 2 January. It was then relatively quiet, apart from a few crude criminal devices, some Scottish Nationalist letter bombs and the normal crop of hoax devices and false alarms. It would not last.

The morning of 20 July 1982 heralded a bright, hot and sunny day. Crowds of tourists were soon gathering along the route from Knightsbridge Barracks to Horse Guards for the regular spectacle of the Changing of the Guard. It was men from the Blues and Royals who on duty; they were resplendent as they left their barracks and rode their black mounts, at a walk, down South Carriage Drive. They were a soft military target. At 10.44 hours they were passing a line of parked cars. One of them, a blue Morris Marina, was facing the wrong way. This may well have been done deliberately so that from a distance it was easy to identify.

Somewhere, within line of sight and probably no more than a couple of hundred metres away, a terrorist waited for the main body of the soldiers and their mounts to be alongside the car. With no hesitation, a switch was flicked on a radio control system which sent a firing signal to a receiver, detonating a twenty-pound bomb hidden in the Marina. Like previous attacks, to add to the lethal effect of the explosion, the bomb was studded with thirty pounds of six-inch nails all arranged so that they would spew out across the road.

The quiet of the day was shattered as the bomb detonated. All over the park tourists, dog walkers and others enjoying the sunshine turned towards the sound of the explosion. The nails and the blast scythed through the troop of horses and their riders. It was complete carnage, with men and their mounts cut to the ground. As usual they were not the only casualties and a woman nearby was also severely injured.

It was one of the most appalling scenes with blood from humans and horses mingling and forming huge pools in the road. The blast was heard by officers and soldiers in Knightsbridge Barracks and they rushed to the scene to administer first aid to the injured. The emergency services also rapidly responded and soon the wounded were being whisked away to hospital in a fleet of ambulances.

The duty EXPO, Terry Thompson, had been in post for less than a month. It was his first operational week and only his second day on duty. Although perfectly capable of dealing with any situation that confronted him, the scene that greeted Thompson on his arrival was a brutal reminder of the effects of high explosive. It was clear to Thompson that this must have been a radio control device and that the charge of explosive used was significant. As always, there was the concern that there might be secondary devices and an immediate search of the area and other cars nearby was carried out. Nothing was found – but there was a second bomb. It was in a different park just over a mile away.

When the injured soldiers and civilians had been cleared from the site of the explosion in Hyde Park, there remained the problem of what to do with the maimed horses. It was decided that those most severely injured would be put down. Using their issue .38 revolvers, police officers were instructed to shoot the injured animals. Unfortunately, no one was exactly sure how best to do this and to their dismay they discovered that the pistol rounds often lacked the power to penetrate the horses' skulls. The shots intended to bring mercy only caused more distress. Post-incident instruction was given on the correct way to despatch wounded animals.

One of the wounded horses, Sefton, survived and after twenty-eight pieces of shrapnel had been removed from his body made a full recovery. The story of the injured horse caught the public's imagination and cards and parcels, many containing sugar lumps, were sent to Sefton's stables. Unfortunately, due to the heightened security in place at the time many of these parcels were considered suspect and the on-duty EXPOs were, for a short period, regularly tasked to examine them.

It is perhaps a sad reflection of our times that today many people – excluding the families of the dead and injured, the Blues and Royals themselves and those responding to the explosion – can recall the name of the horse but do not remember the names of Lieutenant Daly, Corporal Major Bright, Lance Corporal Young, and Trooper Tipper, the men who all died that day. There are two reminders though; there is a memorial to the dead and injured in the attack at the point where it happened in South Carriage Drive, and Trooper Tipper's battered helmet has recently been put on display in the Household Cavalry Museum in Horse Guards.

Less than two hours after the explosion in Hyde Park, the Band of the Royal Green Jackets was playing a selection from *Oliver* at the bandstand in Regent's Park. The bandmaster, Warrant Officer David Little, knew about the explosion in Hyde Park and prior to the start of the concert had organised a search of the bandstand and surrounding area but nothing untoward was found. They did not know, and it was not obvious, that there was a small gap between the wooden floor of the bandstand and its concrete base. It was into this gap that PIRA had secreted the second bomb.

It also detonated with devastating effect. Some of the members of the band were sitting right on top of it when it exploded and they stood no chance. Other musicians, slightly further away, suffered horrendous injuries. Forty-seven civilian spectators had been watching the band and four of these were also physically injured when the bomb detonated. Many others were showered with bits of human flesh which traumatised them and left them in deep shock. Some suffered long-lasting psychological scars.

An urgent call for assistance went out, and once again, the emergency services raced to the area. One of the first there was a traffic officer, Police Constable Trevor Heap. Earlier he had gone to the incident at Hyde Park, but on his arrival there were plenty of officers on scene dealing and there was little he could do. He was still in the area when the call to Regent's Park came in and, slipping quickly through the traffic on his motorcycle, he made his way to the incident. The scene as he approached the bandstand was horrific, with the dead and bits of bodies spread around the area. He found Warrant Officer David Little sitting on the ground in a state of deep shock with one of the other surviving musicians. They were trying to go through the band's nominal role to establish who had been killed and injured. Little kept muttering 'but we checked, but we checked' referring to the search of the bandstand before the concert had started. Tragically, but understandably, the well-hidden bomb had not been found.

EXPO Terry Thompson was re-tasked to the incident in Regent's Park and his detailed investigation into the outrage revealed that there was in fact a gap of about three inches between the wooden floor of the bandstand and the concrete base it was built on. The bomb had been hidden in this gap by the PIRA bombers.

The final toll was seven musicians killed. They were: Warrant Officer 2 Graham Barker, Corporal John McKnight, Corporal Robert Livingstone, and Bandsmen Kevin Smith, George Mesure, John Powell and John Heritage. Ten others bandsmen were seriously wounded and fourteen escaped with minor injuries. It brought the total casualties at both incidents to eleven dead and over thirty injured.

In calls from Dublin, responsibility for both attacks was claimed by 'P. O'Niell', a PIRA figure who did not exist but which was used in all their proclamations. The only redeeming feature of the day was that as soon as the news of the explosions spread, hospital workers who had been on strike immediately gave up their protest and returned to work.

The viciousness and malevolence of these two bombings stunned Londoners. The attacks on the soldiers who were, more than anything, one of the capital's tourist attractions had far reaching implications for their future protection. The use of a radio controlled bomb in the first attack meant that all VIPs with close protection and groups of military personnel had to be provided with suitable electronic countermeasures in the future. As often happens after a terrible outrage, when enough blood has been let, and after widespread condemnation from the worlds press, there was a temporary halt in PIRA bombings.

This did not stop attacks by other groups, and the EXPO officers and Scotland Yard were kept busy with a number of letter bombs from animal rights groups, one of which exploded in Downing Street itself. These contained incendiary compositions rather than high explosive; although still capable of causing serious injury and burns, they were of a lower lethality than those sent by the PIRA.

One incident of note occurred at this time. It involved an incendiary device which was received at 'The Reliable Fur Company' in Great Thomas Apostle Street in the City of London. With great aplomb it was collected by a mounted policeman, John Alford, who then cantered with it to Wood Street Police Station and placed it on the desk in the front office. Never had a police station emptied so quickly. The device was subsequently rendered safe by EXPO Don Green.

For a brief period, a group called Makhno's Private Army also sent a number of crude incendiary devices through the post. These targeted Soviet interests but were largely ineffective and the campaign was short lived.

After a period of almost seventeen months, Irish terrorism resurfaced in London. At 15.45 hours on 10 December 1983, a PIRA

ASU struck again. A bomb left outside the rear wall of the Guard Room of the Royal Artillery Barracks at Woolwich detonated without warning. Three civilians and two soldiers were slightly injured. Three days later a further bomb was found hanging from a parking meter in Phillimore Gardens, Kensington. It had apparently been in position for some time before it was spotted. The bomb was rendered safe by EXPO John Horne and it was established that it had never been correctly armed. Investigations indicated that the bomb was most likely abandoned by the terrorists, possibly because of uniformed police patrols in the area.

A week later, on 17 December 1983, one of the busiest shopping days before Christmas, the same ASU parked a car bomb laden with at least thirty pounds of explosive in Hans Crescent, Knightsbridge, which also had a side entrance to Harrods. The first bomb threat was received by the Samaritans and in it the caller, who claimed to be from the PIRA, stated that there was a bomb outside Harrods in a car, two more devices inside the store and a further two bombs in Littlewood's in Oxford Street.

This was the first time a warning had been phoned to the Samaritans, whose staff had to dial 999 to pass the information on to a police control room. Units were then despatched to search for the bombs in deliberately vague locations. As these events progressed, the inadequate warning time given by PIRA was being whittled away. The fact that four of the devices were reported to be inside shops indicated that they were most likely to be small in size and probably in carrier bags or holdalls; the car was a different matter. The police responding to the calls had the impossible task of trying to locate five suspected devices in locations two miles apart

One of the officers that day was Sergeant Chris Stanger, who was in charge of a small traffic enforcement squad whose duties included keeping the traffic moving in the area around Harrods. In carrying these out, Stanger had in fact seen the suspect car a little earlier in Hans Crescent. Retrospectively, he noted it was parked facing the wrong way at a point where the street went from a two-way system to one-way. But this was a common occurrence, and as no bomb threat had been received when he saw it, there was no reason for suspicion.

Before the PIRA warning was received, it happened, by chance, that a suspect package had been reported around the corner from Harrods in a book shop. One of Sergeant Stanger's police constables had gone into the shop and opened the package; it contained nothing but paper. In ninety-nine per cent of cases, once a suspect item has been cleared, there is a logical explanation for its presence and why it became suspicious in the first place. In this case, though, there was no explanation, which put the officers on edge.

It was shortly after this incident had been dealt with that the PIRA warning was broadcast on the police radio, but by then many minutes had passed since the original call. Without hesitation, Sergeant Stanger and his men headed for Harrods to try to locate the bombs. The fact that they had already dealt with an unusual suspect package, and that there were reports of bombs both inside and outside the store, complicated the task of choosing where and how the cordon and evacuation should be implemented. If they evacuated everyone from inside the shop and on to the street it was possible that they would be moved from a place of relative safety (from the smaller bombs) into the danger area from the car, which had still not been located, and potentially contained a much larger bomb.

The difficulties faced by police officers who organise the cordon and evacuation of an incident when there is insufficient or inaccurate information, multiple bombs threats, hundreds of people to be moved, not enough police to direct them, and no guaranteed safe place to move them to, should not be underestimated. The key, as far as Sergeant Stanger was concerned, was to locate the car first and then move people away from it. At this point the Duty Officer, Inspector Stephen Dodd, arrived and Stanger began to brief him on the actions he had taken so far. Neither of them knew that they were only fifteen metres from the bomb. Thirty-seven minutes after the first call the firing mechanism timed out and there was a massive explosion.

The flash blinded Stanger and the blast hurled him to the ground. His immediate reaction was to think, 'So this is what it is like to be dead' and almost immediately afterwards 'Who will look after my wife and children'.[3] Shrapnel from the car entered his stomach, sliced off a finger and the blast badly burnt him. It is possible that he was slightly shielded from the worst of the fragmentation by Inspector Dodd who was standing between him and the car. He suffered multiple wounds and died the following day in hospital.

Shortly after the blast subsided, Stanger's sight began to return and, although still in deep shock, he began to regain his senses. He was lying in the road and somehow part of a car bumper had become wedged between his neck and his raincoat and he was unable to move it or stand up. He ripped his coat to release the bumper and managed to get to his feet and, still dazed, staggered away from the scene.

At the time there were many street-traders in the area which the police would regularly move on, only for them to return a few minutes later. Consequently, both sides got to know each other quite well. It was one of these street traders who saw Stanger as he staggered up the street. He asked him, 'Are you all right?', to which the wounded police officer politely replied, 'Well, I'm afraid I'm not'. It took six weeks in hospital for Stanger to recover from his wounds.

In common with many other people at similar incidents (for example, the bandmaster at Regent's Park), Stanger always wondered if he should have dealt with the incident differently and, if so, would more lives have been saved? The answer is crystal clear; the guilt lies with the bombers and not those police officers bravely responding to the danger and trying to save lives in difficult circumstances with no thought for their own safety.

In addition to Inspector Dodd, two other police officers and three civilians were killed in the blast. A further ninety-six people were injured, including seventeen police officers, all of whom had responded without hesitation to the call to try to protect the public. The two deceased police officers were Noel Lane and Jane Arbuthnot. The civilians were Phillip Geddes, Kenneth Salvesan and Jasmine Cochrane-Patrick. Phillip Geddes was an Oxford graduate and a journalist, and in his honour annual prizes are awarded to aspiring journalists attending Oxford University. In addition, every year there is the Phillip Geddes Memorial Lecture given by a leading journalist. In 2015 it was given by Lyse Doucet, who has been reporting for the BBC for nearly thirty years. Her lecture entitled 'Killing the Messenger, and the Message' described the dangers journalists face reporting in many parts of the world today.

The target was, at the time, totally at variance with the PIRA's declared policy of attacking only 'carefully selected legitimate targets' to which the Provisional leadership had previously agreed. The PIRA Army Council was so taken aback, at least publicly, by the widespread condemnation of the attack that they issued a statement pointing out that the Harrods bomb had not been authorised and the unit involved had exceeded its instructions. It was cold comfort to the injured and bereaved but, after one further attack on Christmas Day, in which a blast bomb detonated in a litter bin in Oxford Street without causing casualties, it did herald another lull in the bombing.

In common with many other European capitals, London continued to attract its fair share of Middle East terrorism. Ominously, in the Middle East itself suicide bombers in the form that we know them now began to make an appearance. It started with attacks on Israeli soldiers, and later against the American and French Marines in the Lebanon. The results were devastating and without doubt contributed to the political decisions to withdraw both sets of troops. From the bombers' perspective the tactic had worked and would inspire others to do the same.

Suicide attacks would eventually spread to London, but for the moment it was blast bombs that were the problem. On 31 August 1983, a small bomb exploded outside the Israeli 'Bank Leumi' in Oxford Circus. Fortunately, no one was injured; no group claimed responsibility for the incident. A year later the Libyan regime brought terror to the streets of London on several occasions. In the first, on 10 March 1984, five bombs were planted by pro-Gadaffi activists in Central London. Four were outside newsagents, the other inside a club frequented by Arabs including Libyan dissidents. Only two of the bombs exploded, including the one in the club, and a total of twenty-seven people were injured.

In many cases, where a bomb fails to detonate, or is rendered safe, particularly at night, there is little publicity attached to the incident and it goes almost unnoticed. On 12 March 1984, EXPO Mick Coldrick was tasked to Regent's Street to the Omar Khayyam night club. There the duty officer, Inspector Craig, briefed him that a cleaner had found a suspect object under a seat in the club. Craig had confirmed this by going forward to check the information and had seen what definitely looked like a bomb. After the briefing Coldrick entered the premises to examine the object:[4]

> I saw a rectangular object with a battery sitting on top of it close to what I deduced was an improvised switch fashioned from a kitchen timer. I could also see the top of an electrical detonator. I noted that a pair of improvised contacts were still about 3/8 of an inch apart. I thought this represented about 8 or 10 minutes time left before the contact was made and a probable explosion. This time device seemed to be stuck in this position. I took an X- ray photograph and left the premises.

Having examined the X-ray, Coldrick went back in to the club and manually disabled the device. He noted that when he cut one of the wires, the timer restarted with a loud tick. He then packaged the separated components for forensic investigation and handed it over to an exhibits officer. He concluded that the device had been in place for some time, probably since the night before, and had failed to detonate. As is often the case with improvised devices it had failed to function. In this instance there was just 3/8th of an inch of air between the electrical contacts which prevented carnage in the nightclub the previous evening.

All the bombs recovered contained about one and a half pounds of Semtex and Smiths kitchen timers. This was the first time this particular explosive was used in London and all were firmly attributed to the Libyans.

A month later, at a demonstration outside the Libyan Peoples Bureau, Woman Police Constable Yvonne Fletcher was shot and later died of her injuries. Under the rules of diplomatic protection all the Libyan staff were sent home and the embassy left empty. Peter Gurney was tasked to search the premises to make sure that no bombs or booby-traps had been left behind by the departing Libyans. This took some time, but nothing was found.

On 12 October 1984, the PIRA almost succeeded in killing Margaret Thatcher, and wiping out the leading members of the Cabinet, when a bomb exploded in the early hours at the Grand Hotel in Brighton. It was soon clear that the bomb itself was not large in size but that it caused a catastrophic collapse when parts of the chimney weighing several tons crashed through the floors below. The use of a very long delay timer raised all sorts of concerns in respect of the measures that would need to be taken to protect VIPs in the future. Following the attack, the Home Secretary addressed the House of Commons and stated that he would involve the Army and the Royal Ulster Constabulary in training police officers in search techniques. The Hoddinot enquiry, following the Brighton bomb, recommended that a Police National Search Centre be established to train and licence police officers to undertake counter-terrorist defensive searches at prominent or specialist public events. In the Metropolitan Police this resulted in the formation of specialist search teams which today still carry out defensive searches before all major public events.

In June 1985 a PIRA campaign to bring terror to British seaside resorts was bought to a halt when twelve people were arrested in the Glasgow area. During the raid detectives found a list of places where bombs on long delay timers were to be found. As a result, a search was instituted and a suspect device was duly discovered in the Rubens Hotel close to Buckingham Palace. EXPO Derek Pickford was tasked to examine it. The bomb had been concealed behind the plinth of a bedside cabinet. After an X-ray had been taken, it was clear that as well as the long delay timer, there were a number of anti-handling circuits. Using the X-ray it was possible to decide on the best place to (selectively) disrupt the bomb and Pickford went back into the hotel and successfully achieved this. Post-disruption it was discovered that there were about five pounds of explosive and a sophisticated booby-trap system. As well as gaining vital evidence from the recovered components it was possible to reconstruct the bomb. When this was done it was clear that even the slightest movement would have been enough to cause it to function.

It was now becoming increasingly clear that, like any other organisation, the Explosives Office needed a more formal structure. Up until this point all the EXPOs were considered equal. As well as bomb disposal duties, each took on an additional responsibility, for example administration or lectures or liaison with other specialist units. However, it was becoming apparent that there was the need for an individual officer to act as the focal point for all enquiries about bombs, bombing and the work of the Explosives Office. Some thought was given to appointing a senior police officer but this notion was rapidly rejected in a rare gesture of unanimity by all the EXPOs. Eventually, it was agreed that Peter Gurney would take up the role as the Senior Explosives Officer. This, of course, made him the SEXPO – a title which had a certain appeal.

In London over the next couple of years there was another lull as far as Irish terrorism and bombing was concerned. In fact, in 1986 there were no PIRA bombs at all in the capital. Other groups, though, emerged to take its place. Around this time the Animal Liberation Front (ALF) began a concerted campaign using incendiaries of various types. The most common employed John Player Special cigarette packets as the outer container. These were hidden amongst goods in shops all along Oxford Street; a few functioned, but most were found and rendered safe. They were primitive in design, but even so were still capable of causing thousands of pounds' worth of damage and disruption in the department stores.

Middle Eastern terrorism resurfaced on several occasions, but there were only two serious episodes. In the first, an Iranian, the son of man well-known for his vehement anti-Khomeini views, was killed in an explosion. The incident occurred on 19 August 1986, in a basement below a video shop in Kensington, which was a centre for propaganda against the Khomeini regime. As well as the death of the son, twelve other people were injured. It was never established whether this was yet another 'own goal' or the result of a bomb planted by someone else.

The other major incident was the attempt to destroy an Israeli Jumbo Jet in flight by a Jordanian national, Nezar Nawaf Mansour Hindawi. Acting with support from the Syrians he hatched a despicable plot in which his pregnant girlfriend, Anne-Marie Murphy, was to be duped into carrying a bomb onto an El Al Boeing 747. The pair were supposed to be travelling together to Israel, but in the lead up to the departure date, Hindawi claimed that, because his employer had already bought him a ticket, he would have to travel separately via Jordan and meet Murphy later.

In an apparent act of kindness, Hindawi gave Murphy a large new holdall with wheels. Unbeknownst to her, though, in the bottom was hidden a thin layer of Semtex which had been wrapped in blue plastic and secured with buff-coloured tape. There was over three pounds of explosive which was more than sufficient to bring down an aircraft. To initiate the device Hindawi and his Syrian associates had disassembled a calculator and built into it a small bomb containing a couple of ounces of Semtex and a detonator. To get the main charge in the bottom of the bag to detonate it was vital that the calculator was placed in very close proximity to it. The day before the flight Hindawi helped Murphy pack her new bag and placed the calculator at the bottom resting millimetres from the main explosive charge. The following day, en route to the airport, Hindawi opened up the bag, removed the calculator, inserted a battery which started a timer running, and then repacked it.

Although he was supposed to be flying that day he had no baggage, but this aroused no suspicion in Murphy. She was deeply in love with the man who had made her pregnant, and had no idea that he planned to murder her, her unborn child and 374 other passengers and crew.

The plan very nearly succeeded and the bag and its contents passed through the normal X-ray screening process. All the items were removed from her bag and the calculator was checked; it worked and gave no cause for concern. However, when an attendant picked up the empty bag to repack her belongings, it seemed remarkably heavy for that particular model. It was taken to another office, stripped down and underneath the bottom cardboard layer the blue plastic package was discovered. When the corner was removed the Semtex was revealed and an alert declared.

Peter Gurney was tasked to deal with the incident and after a short briefing he went to inspect the bag. He immediately recognised the orange-coloured substance as Semtex. He examined the package for signs of an initiation system but found none. He therefore asked to inspect the items that had been carried in the bag. He was shown these and inspected and X-rayed every one of them. When he came to the calculator he examined it closely and noticed the retaining screws on the back seemed remarkably shiny as if they were under a layer of clear glue. Prising open the back of the calculator he could just see some white tape. This was clearly out of place and so he returned to the screws to disassemble the calculator. These were cemented in position with an epoxy resin and so he used some wire cutters to split open the plastic case. Having done so he discovered what he was looking for, a small brown package containing one and a half ounces of Semtex with a detonator embedded in it and linked by wires to the calculator itself. He removed the detonator from the explosive and cut the leads to remove it from the bomb. He then decided to connect a small electrical pyrotechnic igniter to the wires the detonator had been connected to. By watching this it would be possible to establish at what time the bomb was intended to detonate. He then called in the waiting anti-terrorist branch officers and briefed them on what he had found. The pyrotechnic igniter functioned a little while later; a quick calculation showed that had the El Al 747 departed on time it would have been approximately 800 miles away, over southern Europe.

Having kissed his pregnant girlfriend goodbye, Hindawi returned to London to collect his luggage intending to fly to Syria that afternoon. He was planning to travel to Heathrow on the Syrian Arab Airlines crew bus, but when it arrived he was given a letter and asked to visit the Syrian Embassy. There he was met by three men who congratulated him on his work and explained that people in Damascus were 'very pleased with him'. He was then told he would be moved to a safe house where his hair would be cut and dyed. The following day he was met by two more men and told he was going back to the Syrian Embassy. The news of the failed attack was by now out and Hindawi became very nervous and frightened at the idea of going back to the Embassy where he now thought he might be killed, so he ran off. Having roamed the streets for a while he tried to check in to the London Visitors' Hotel. As a result of questioning Anne-Marie Murphy, the police had already circulated Hindawi's description and he was recognised by the staff. They contacted the police and a few minutes later the Jordanian was under arrest.

Within hours Britain broke off diplomatic relations with Syria and all their staff were expelled. Later Hindawi was tried and found guilty and sentenced to forty-five years in prison. In the summing up Mr Justice Mars-Jones said: 'A more callous and cruel deception, and a more horrendous massacre, would be hard to imagine.'

In April 1987, the PIRA sent a number of postal devices to senior civil servants. These devices were built in to Observer Pocket Books. Fortunately, the first device delivered was recognised as suspect by the intended victim's son and he called the police. EXPO Mick Coldrick attended the scene and having confirmed the package contained a book bomb he alerted the anti-terrorist branch to initiate a public warning that there may be more devices in the post. He then rendered the bomb safe and handed the components to an exhibits officer. All the other devices were intercepted and neutralised.

In August 1988 a bomb containing about ten kilograms of high explosive was placed outside an Army barrack block at Mill Hill. This open barracks was an easy target and had clearly been the subject of previous reconnaissance. The device, laid during the night, detonated in the early morning killing one soldier and seriously injuring ten others.

Later in the year, another Christmas campaign was thwarted, though this time with an element of luck. On 21 December, a PIRA terrorist was apparently on guard in a car outside a block of flats in Clapham. He clearly was well-hidden in the car because a youth, not noticing the man, tried to break in to the vehicle. He was promptly shot, although, fortunately, not seriously injured. In the subsequent follow-up operation, a mass of bomb making material was discovered in a flat nearby. Although no terrorists were arrested a great deal of intelligence was gained from the scene.

The success was overshadowed by another ghastly incident and although the bomb did not explode in London, it did transit through Heathrow. The airport was the last stop for Flight 103 the Pan American Jumbo Jet, which took off at 18.25 hours on 21 December and was blown up at 31,000 feet whilst cruising over Lockerbie in Scotland. A small bomb, probably secreted on board in Malta, detonated. It caused a small tear in the aircraft's skin which subsequently caused a catastrophic disintegration of the fuselage, killing all the passengers and crew and many people on the ground in the town below.

On 3 August 1989, Peter Gurney was in the Expo office when reports came in of an explosion at the Beverley Hotel in Sussex Gardens. He left for the scene and on arrival could see that the upper floors of the hotel were on fire, but that this was not yet serious. Firefighting had been temporarily suspended because there had been reports of a second explosion and there were fears that another might occur. Gurney and the Chief Fire Officer made a quick inspection of the room where the initial blast had taken place and, after consultation with the fire-fighters, it was established that the most likely cause of the second explosion was a large aerosol rupturing. Firefighting resumed and the flames were quickly extinguished.

Once the flames were out Gurney made a further search of the room where the initial blast had taken place. He quickly established that the damage was consistent with the detonation of a small quantity of high explosive. He also discovered the badly burnt body of a man. Close examination of the corpse showed that there were injuries, including amputation, which could not be attributed to the fire. After finishing his search of the room he went outside the hotel where another piece of body had been discovered, this showed no signs of fire damage and confirmed the view that the detonation of a high explosive device had occurred and that most likely the victim had been working on the bomb when it detonated prematurely. Yet again it proved impossible to attribute finally the bomb to any known group but Middle Eastern terrorism was once more suspected.

A month later, an under-car booby-trap bomb was discovered lying at the edge of the road in Kelso Place, Kensington, by a member of the public. There was speculation that this had fallen off a car belonging to a very lucky senior Army officer. A week later another similar bomb seriously injured a staff sergeant in Colchester. There was sporadic bombing across the rest of the mainland, the terrorists again going for soft targets like Army education centres and recruiting offices. On 14 May 1990, a bomb hidden in a flower bed outside the Directorate of Army Education at Eltham detonated, injuring seven civilians and causing extensive glass damage. However, the thin nylon film fitted to the insides of the windows successfully retained many of the lethal shards of glass, significantly reducing the numbers of serious casualties.

A week later another under-car booby-trap bomb was placed beneath a minibus belonging to the Army recruiting office in Wembley. At the end of the working day Sergeant James Chapman left for home and climbed into the minibus, reversing it out of its parking slot. As he did so there was a tremendous explosion from right under the centre of the vehicle next to the gear box. Chapman was killed instantly and two other men injured. Later examination of the vehicle indicated that the charge was larger than that in the normal under-car bombs. It was established that Chapman and another Army sergeant had checked under the vehicle, but somehow had missed the bomb. This may have been because the PIRA were now camouflaging them with black paint and the fact that it was hidden next to the gear box.

This was followed by a spate of bombs. At the Honourable Artillery Company in the city, a bomb detonated late in the evening of 9 June 1990. A group of civilians was celebrating a twenty-first birthday party and seventeen of them were injured, most by flying glass. On 21 June a rucksack was found at 08.05 hours outside RAF Stanmore Park in Middlesex. The RAF police were called and they, in turn, summoned the local police. The duty officer went to examine the bag and cut it open to reveal the contents. He saw a PIRA TPU and, after a swift retreat, he put in a request for an EXPO to attend the incident. The bomb detonated shortly afterwards.

Four days later, in the evening, Police Constable Pete Bordini and a colleague were on foot patrol in Central London. They had just walked from Pall Mall into St James's Street and strolled passed the Carlton

Club, seeing nothing suspicious. The two officers continued on their beat; they had turned into Piccadilly and were chatting to a woman when there was a tremendous bang. Although he had never heard an explosion before, Bordini instinctively knew that it was a bomb. The pair ran back to the Carlton Club and arrived at the same moment as another police officer, Paul Humble. The front entrance of the Club was badly damaged; there was a small fire in the reception area and a hole in the floor made by the bomb. They found a couple of fire extinguishers and, leaping across the hole, set about the fires which were soon out. Bordini then got on the radio and reported the explosion and was immediately asked what the premise's number was. He replied he was not sure and when told to look at the door, he explained that there was no longer a door to look at. People at the back of the building were now calling for assistance and Bordini headed off to help, but as he did so the fire brigade began to rescue them. Shortly afterwards a uniformed inspector arrived and, after a short but curt discussion with the firefighters about who was in charge, took over the running of the incident.

Being aware of the possibility of secondary devices, the duty officer ordered that a nearby Japanese restaurant be evacuated. Bordini and another policeman went into the premises which were full of Japanese businessmen along with some high-class prostitutes. They were told to leave but many refused to move. The police officers then spoke to the manager and the staff who immediately agreed to go and, as they left, they grabbed all their personal belongings from the staff changing room. When they had gone it was discovered that there was one bag left. A quick glimpse inside revealed a metal tube and some unusual wiring. The two officers immediately assumed this was a secondary device and shouted further warnings. This time the urgency in their voices was much more evident and everyone fled. They reported the bag to the duty officer who told them to mark it for the EXPO, who was now en route to the scene. The officers grabbed a handful of flour from the kitchen and left a trail to the possible secondary device. In fact, it later turned out to be innocuous.

The EXPO that attended the scene of the explosion was Colin Goodson. He examined the area and carried out all the normal safety checks. His abiding memory of the night is sets of false teeth lying on the floor in one of the club's sitting rooms. Presumably older members of the club were relaxing at the time and were so startled by the blast that their false teeth fell out and were left where they lay as members evacuated the premises.

A month later a series of bomb threats alerted the City of London Police to the possibility of a device in the Stock Exchange. The area was evacuated; an explosion occurred forty minutes later. The bomb had been concealed in a toilet in the visitors' centre on the first floor. A considerable amount of material damage was done, but fortunately, thanks to the police's action in clearing the area, there had been no casualties.

An attempt to assassinate Sir William Waldergrave, a Foreign Office minister, and other senior figures in the counter-terrorism field, including the Commissioner of the Metropolitan Police, Sir Peter Imbert, occurred on 10 January. They were scheduled to address an audience at the Royal Overseas League in Piccadilly, an event that had, unwisely, been subject to some advanced publicity. The responsibility for the security was given to the local police and they decided to arrange a limited sweep of the premises, using search dogs trained to find explosives. This was duly undertaken, but no other search procedures were implemented to prevent a device being subsequently introduced into the venue. The PIRA used this lapse to slip a bomb into the lectern the speakers would be using. Fortunately, because of problems with the sound system an electrician opened the lid of the lectern shortly before the event and discovered the bomb. EXPO Graham Lightfoot was sent to deal with it and, in view of the information provided, went forward and rendered the bomb safe. It was a lucky escape for all concerned. In the subsequent enquiry it was established that better co-ordination of all counter-terrorist searches was required to prevent this type of lapse occurring again.

The attacks by the PIRA in London, as well as others outside the capital, kept the terrorists in the headlines. But the fact was that little political pressure was being generated as a result of their actions. Furthermore, running bombing campaigns on the mainland was notoriously expensive and the terrorists always stood a much higher change of being arrested than they did in Northern Ireland. The PIRA leadership realized another strategy, which had more impact, needed to be found.

NOTES:
1. Proceedings of the Fifth Conference on Terrorist Devices and Methods, May 1981.
2. Gurney, Peter, *op. cit.*
3. Interview with Sergeant Chris Stanger, 6 July 2007.
4. Coldrick, John Michael GM, witness statement, 13 March 1984.

Chapter 22

The Spectaculars

'Every bomb in London is worth many more in Belfast or Londonderry in terms of publicity or destructive effect'.
Sir Hugh Annesley, Chief Constable of the Royal Ulster Constabulary.

Up until this point in the bombing campaign on the mainland, the PIRA leadership had, despite its claims, sanctioned indiscriminate bombing. This resulted in some awful atrocities, including the bombings in Guildford, the M62 coach, Aldershot and Birmingham. In London there was the massacre of the members of the Blues and Royals, the murder of musicians in Regent's Park and the killing of police and civilians at Harrods. The alleged purpose of these attacks was to shock, thereby keeping the Irish issue at the top of the political agenda. Most of the worst atrocities served no purpose other than satisfying a deep-seated desire for revenge. Predictably, the bloodiest attacks created a negative reaction against the PIRA, particularly amongst their more moderate supporters in the United States, where much of their financial support came from. It was apparent to the PIRA leadership that, to be successful, the bombs would have to be more carefully targeted and that mass casualties amongst civilians must be avoided at all costs. Clearly attacks on politicians would have the desired impact and, although strikes on the military were seen as justifiable, it was recognised that they would be unlikely to have a significant impact politically. That said, the death of any service personnel, anywhere, was acceptable and, in the PIRA's eyes, was a worthwhile achievement.

The best method of keeping the Irish question in the forefront of everyone's minds was to target the politicians themselves, as Mrs Thatcher and her government had already found out. In addition to this, pressure could be maintained by disrupting the country's economy, by attacking its financial centre and by making the travelling public's journeys miserable by dislocating the transport system. This could only be done by using massive vehicle bombs or carefully executed attacks with smaller devices or mortars. As far as the former were concerned, the people in Northern Ireland were already learning that really big vehicle bombs built in to trucks or vans, containing up to a ton of explosive, would completely decimate the centres of small provincial towns. The PIRA leadership decided to try and influence government policy by using these methods on the mainland. In the early 1990s they set about planning and putting in place the necessary men and materials in great secrecy.

The first significant attack was one of the most audacious and was an attempt to assassinate the Prime Minister John Major and wipe out members of his Cabinet. They were in session in 10 Downing Street, debating the first Gulf War when, on 7 February 1991, a salvo of mortar bombs was launched at them. They were fired from a white van which was lined up and abandoned next to Spencer Crompton's statue at the junction of Whitehall and Horse Guards Avenue. Three improvised Mark 10 mortar tubes were bolted in the back of the van and arranged so that the bombs would launch through a hole cut in the roof.

This attack, striking at the heart of the government, was professionally planned and executed. A detailed study and reconnaissance must have been undertaken to determine the best place from which to launch the bombs. This took into account the precise direction the van needed to be aimed in for the bombs to strike No.10; how it could be lined up in that direction easily for the attack itself; the range from the firing point to Downing Street; and, finally, a safe route into the firing position, as well as a quick escape for the perpetrators on a motorbike.

The construction of the launching frame and mortars, which were substantial pieces of ordnance, required good engineering skills and they were almost certainly manufactured in Ireland. Trials were probably undertaken to establish the weight of the propellant charge needed to provide the correct range for the attack. The completed launch unit and bombs must then have been smuggled to the mainland, where they were fitted to the carrier vehicle which had had a hole cut in its roof. A firing box was designed to launch the bombs sequentially, with a final setting which initiated a self-destruct system which would set off an incendiary charge to burn out the van. All of this took time, money and patience.

The morning of 7 February 1991, was cold and dreary, and it had just started to snow when, at 10.00 hours, the plan was put into effect. The

413

white van drew up alongside Spencer Crompton's statue in Horse Guards Avenue and was lined up with the pre-arranged aiming point. The mortar sequencing timer was set running and the PIRA bomber jumped out of the vehicle and on to the pillion of an accompanying motorcycle which sped away. The van part-blocked the junction and angry motorists were hooting at it as they tried to get passed. Moments later the mortar bombs were launched in quick succession. They tumbled lazily through the air as their trajectory took them, in an arc, over London District Headquarters and Horse Guards' parade square.

The first mortar bomb landed close to the wall in the garden of No.10, detonating with an ear-splitting crack. It caused a crater one metre across and shattered the windows in Nos. 10 and 11 Downing Street. The second mortar bomb missed the garden and landed just the other side of the wall. During its descent it smashed through the top of the tree planted there, breaking several branches. It did not explode, but deflagrated, the explosive burning rapidly, but not shattering the casing. The third mortar came to rest a little further right, landing on Treasury Green, a small area of grass next to Horse Guards between the wall at the back of Downing Street and Horse Guards Road. Like the second bomb it failed to detonate and ended up buried tail-first in the grass. For those on the receiving end of the mortars all that was known at this point was that there had been an explosion in Downing Street. John Major calmly responded telling the assembled cabinet ministers, 'I think we better start somewhere else'.

Back in Horse Guards Avenue, the transit van burst into flames as the self-destruct charge functioned. Soon the vehicle was completely ablaze destroying any good forensic evidence left by the bombers.

At the time of the attack Peter Gurney was working in his office close by. In a thunder storm there is a clear difference between the noise produced by a nearby lighting strike and one in the distance. The former produces a sharp, vicious crack, whereas the latter results in a much deeper, booming rumbling sound. The same applies to a bomb. When it goes off in the distance you hear more of a rumble as the sound waves echo around off walls or buildings. When a bomb goes off nearby you hear a much sharper, distinct crump. It was more of a crump that Gurney heard and he instinctively knew that there had been a sizable explosion close by.

With his driver he raced down the stairs from his office and jumped into the duty vehicle. They headed out into Whitehall and, on looking right, Gurney could see the white van in flames. At this stage it was still not clear what had happened so he jumped out of his vehicle and ran down the road to have a quick look at the burning van. At the same time police officers were arriving on scene and beginning to usher the public away from the area. Looking through the back of the van Gurney could see burning blankets, and behind them, amongst the smoke and flames, were three large mortar tubes and a hole in the roof. He knew that only one of the bombs had detonated. There were therefore two possibilities; either the bombs had launched and failed to explode or they had failed to launch and were still in their tubes. If the latter was the case, then there were another two possibilities; firstly, they might still launch if the fire ignited the propellant charge built into the base of the bomb, or the bombs themselves might detonate in the fire. This meant that the area around the vehicle had to be cleared and the same applied to the flight path the bombs would take and their most likely impact point.

Gurney ran back down the road and was, at this point, caught on camera waving his arms and encouraging people to move away from the area. He linked up with the duty officer and told him to arrange the complete cordon and evacuation of the area around the burning vehicle and a corridor two hundred metres wide and four hundred metres long from the direction the launch vehicle was pointing in.

At almost the same time another police officer reported that the seat of the first explosion was, in fact, in the garden of No.10 Downing Street. Gurney went straight round to the building and saw a policeman standing at the front door. He went in and instructed everyone to move to the middle of the building until he had examined the seat of the explosion and discovered what had happened to the other two mortar bombs. He then went into the garden where he could see the crater in the lawn next to a small smouldering cherry tree which was much the worse for wear. Yet another police officer now appeared and said that another two bombs appeared to have landed outside the garden wall on Treasury Green, which was no longer green, but covered in a thin layer of snow. According to the police officer it did not look as if they had exploded. The good news at this point was that, if three bombs could be accounted for, the tubes in the van were empty. Gurney went out through the gate to find the bombs.

Mark 10 mortar bombs are not small. Being some 165mm in diameter, and nearly a metre-and-a-half long, they have a filled-weight of sixty kilograms. One bomb was embedded tail-first in the ground and Gurney went to this one first. The fuze was missing and the explosive filling appeared to have ignited and burnt rather than detonating, leaving a white ash in the bomb body.

The other bomb was complete and Gurney went over to examine it. It was still snowing and bitterly cold. When the area around the bomb had been cleared Gurney decided to remove the fuze to render it safe. Unfortunately, he could not raise his driver on the radio to bring his toolkit so he went back into No.10 where, in the boiler room, he found a suitable adjustable spanner and with this he went back out to the bomb.

The fuze in this particular model used a heavy, cylindrical, inertia pellet made from steel which was mounted inside another cylinder. Prior to launch, this was held in place by a safety pin made from a large nail. After firing, the safety pin was pushed out of the fuze by a spring, allowing the inertia pellet to move freely up and down the cylinder. On impact, the inertia pellet would ride forward, strike a percussion cap and initiate the bomb. On the bomb Gurney was examining, he could see the hole in the side of the fuze where the safety pin would have been and clearly he had to insert something into this to stop the inertial pellet moving whilst he removed the complete fuze. He found a suitably-sized twig which he inserted through the hole and then sat astride the bomb and set about undoing the bolts around the top of the fuze. The bomb was extremely hot and Gurney had to keep jumping off it as the heat on his legs became too much to bear. Eventually he successfully removed the bolts and withdrew the fuze. On looking inside he discovered that the body was empty and that the filling had burnt out leaving a white ash.

Having satisfied himself that the bombs were safe, Gurney returned to the launch vehicle which, by now, was completely burnt out. In the shell he could clearly see the three mortar tubes welded into a steel frame. That fact that the vehicle was completely gutted by fire meant that there could be no other hidden devices and he handed the scene over to one of the exhibits officers and went off to another task. John Major and his cabinet had survived a serious attempt to kill them and the PIRA had achieved a notable propaganda coup.

Eleven days later the PIRA struck the transport system targeting the mainline stations. The first bomb exploded, without warning, at 06.20 hours in Paddington. At the time the station was having its roof refurbished and many of the supporting towers were surrounded by scaffolding which was boxed in at the bottom by large hardboard squares. To allow workmen access to the towers there were doors in the hardboard. The PIRA had gained access to one of these doors and had planted a bomb behind it on a sleeper. When it detonated it shattered the wooden cladding. It was later estimated to contain around a kilogram of Semtex. Fortunately, it was too early for there to be many people in the station and there were no casualties.

At 06.42 hours a bomb threat was received stating that there were bombs at all of the mainline stations. In the message a new PIRA codeword was used for the first time and the significance of it was not immediately grasped. It must be remembered that hoaxers rang in bomb threats all the time, often using their own made-up codewords. These were all logged by the Anti-Terrorist Branch, but it was only if they were subsequently linked to real bombs that the significance of them became apparent. On many occasions the same words would be used to cause disruption even when there were no bombs. On others, (and as it later transpired in this case) the codeword would be used for multiple locations when only one bomb had been planted, the aim being, once again, to cause massive disruption for minimal effort.

Whilst the police were investigating the first explosion, a second bomb functioned at Victoria Station. The time now was 07.42 hours and the station was packed with commuters. The bomb detonated inside a steel-lined litter bin as passengers, who had just disembarked from a train, were walking past. One man, David Corner, was a few metres away and a shard of metal from the litter bin penetrated his heart and he was killed. There were two further serious injuries and scores of other minor casualties. The bombs brought the rail services to a halt and thousands of commuters were confined in their trains as frantic searches were put in place at all the mainline stations.

One of the consequences of this attack was the removal of all litter bins from inside stations. Dropping a bomb into a litter bin as you walk past was an easy option for a terrorist; it was unlikely to arouse suspicion. Without the bins, and with a vigilant public, it was much harder to abandon a bomb in a station bar, café or in booking hall where its presence would immediately arouse suspicion. How many people since then, especially the millions of visitors to the capital, have looked at our litter-strewn stations and commented on the state of their cleanliness. Today the litter bins have returned, but for many years, people complained about the lack facilities to dispose of rubbish in stations, not realizing the reason behind the decision to remove them.

The indiscriminate slaughter of an innocent commuter did nothing for the PIRA cause, and once again, they had to reassess their methods. There was a lull in the bombing after the explosions at Victoria and Paddington and the next significant attack was not until June 1991 when a bomb, in a holdall, was left at the Becks Theatre in Hayes and timed to explode during a concert by a military band. Fortunately for all concerned it failed to go off and was found the following morning. EXPO Derek Pickford went to investigate and rendered the bomb safe.

Later in December the PIRA struck at the transport system again, this time detonating a small blast bomb on a single line railway between Clapham Junction and Kensington. There was also a flurry of incendiary devices, with twelve being left in Central London and others on the outskirts during the first two days of the month. The terrorists then moved out of the capital and planted more devices all over the country before returning to London in the middle of the month for the traditional pre-Christmas campaign.

In December 1991 Peter Gurney retired; he had been in post for eighteen years, the last ten of them as the SEXPO. During that time, and in his previous service in the army, he had attended hundreds of bomb calls and had been awarded two George Medals and an MBE for bravery. He was often asked after he retired, sometimes obliquely, how he and other members of the office had continued with their work day after day. He explained that, as well as a detailed technical knowledge of all aspects of explosives, ammunition and bombs, they all had a core inner strength:

> Bomb disposal operators may discuss each other's ideas, problems past mistakes and even near-disasters – the times when we have all thought, oh Christ! This is the end of the line – but they don't debate their innermost feelings. They don't bring to the surface their fears and anxieties because to do so is to tread on dangerous ground; to do so is to bring to light something an individual might not wish (or be strong enough) to confront.[1]

After his departure, Graham Lightfoot took on the mantle of SEXPO and neither he, nor the other members of the office, would have guessed that 1992 would be the busiest on record for the number of tasks undertaken. It started on 10 January at 08.39 hours when the first of a series of bomb threats was received by the police. They were warned that a device had been left in Whitehall Place and that it would explode in thirty minutes. Police officers responded to the call and started searching the vicinity. They soon located a brown briefcase lying on its side in the road and immediately set about cordoning and evacuating the area. The duty EXPO, Colin Goodson, was tasked to attend the incident and arriving just after 09.00 hours he was given a briefing by the duty officer. He then moved forward and was preparing some equipment to deal with the device when it detonated. It was estimated to contain about two kilograms of explosives and caused a limited amount of damage to the surrounding vehicles and buildings.

In the weeks that followed there was a series of bombs and incendiaries. These included explosions at London Bridge Station, which injured thirty people, a device outside the Crown Prosecution Service in Furnival Street, and two bombs which were rendered safe, one in Parliament Street and another in White Hart Lane Railway Station.

Perhaps to make a political statement, as well as cause massive destruction and disruption, on the evening of 10 April 1992, the day after the general election, the first of the really large vehicle bombs was driven into the City of London. The host vehicle, a white Ford Transit, contained a charge later estimated to be the equivalent of between 300-350 kilograms of TNT. Shortly after it was abandoned, the first threat was received at Waterloo Railway Station at 20.55 hours and a recognised codeword given. The caller, who had an Irish accent, was quite clear about its location, stating that there was a bomb outside the Stock Exchange by the Bank of England. This was quite specific as the two buildings stand side by side. The City Police responded immediately, flooding officers into the area and quickly located two unattended vans which fitted the description given in the warning. They began to cordon and evacuate the area which was busier than normal because people were celebrating (or otherwise) the Conservatives' victory at the polls.

At 21.21 hours there was a massive explosion as a bomb detonated. But it was nowhere near the location given in the telephoned threat – it was a quarter of a mile away in St Mary Axe outside the Baltic Exchange. This narrow street channelled the blast laterally along its length and two people walking there were cut down and killed. The explosion caused much disquiet in the City Police control room. As far as they were concerned, there was no guarantee that this was not a second bomb and there was still one somewhere outside the Stock Exchange.

Some of the emergency services were diverted to St Mary Axe and sped the short distance to the area. They were confronted by a level of devastation not seen in the City since the Second World War. There was further confusion when a second coded threat was received, reporting yet another bomb nearby. This had to be taken seriously and the police, already stretched, had to divert resources to try to locate what turned out to be a non-existent device.

As always, the first priority was the rescue and treatment of those trapped and injured. This was made harder because the explosion had blown out many of the lights and hundreds of burglar alarms had been set off, producing a howling racket which masked the sounds of the cries from those needing help. Eventually they were located, extracted, treated and despatched to hospital. The final toll of casualties was three dead, including a fifteen-year-old girl, Danielle Carter, and over 100 injured. It could, though, have easily been much worse.

Just after midnight, another coded bomb threat was received. The caller stated that there was a bomb at Staples Corner. This time it was Metropolitan Police officers who rushed to the area. A well-laden white Bedford van was duly located underneath the northbound elevated section of the A5 Edgware Road. Officers immediately set about closing both this road and the North Circular which crosses the A5 at high level at this point. This had just been completed when the bomb detonated. The strength of reinforced concrete constructions was illustrated because the detonation of another 300-500 kilograms of explosive failed to cause the collapse of the bridge. Because of the good work of the police in cordoning and evacuating the area there were no serious casualties, but the road was closed for over a year whilst repair work was carried out.

Back in the City there was still much to be done. Order had been established, false alarms were being cleared, and the casualties had been removed to hospital. At the Baltic Exchange an incident control point was established in Leadenhall Street.

It was not until the dawn broke that the extent of the damage became clear. Two major financial institutions' buildings were severely damaged; they were the Baltic Exchange, which was the home of the world's leading shipping market, and the Commercial Union, a leading insurance company. Damage to other buildings was significant and glass was blown out to 400 metres, although the worst was confined to an approximate 200-metre radius from the centre of the blast. Around the Baltic Exchange it was estimated that over 500 tons of glass were subsequent swept from the streets.

Putting the Incident Control Point at Leadenhall Street later turned out to a mistake when, two days later, on the Sunday, high winds sprang up and broken glass was blown out of damaged buildings. Falling from a great height some sheets began to spin, and like Frisbees, flew a considerable distance before hitting the streets endangering those on the ground in the control point.

The whole thrust of the response to a bombing of this magnitude must be multi-agency and requires co-ordination at the highest level, with all the components (police, fire-fighters, ambulance, rescue workers, public works officials and structural engineers) working in unison with the ultimate aim of restoring normality to the area. Bomb scenes, even big ones, are of course also scenes of crimes and every effort must be made by forensic officers to recover any evidence in terms of bomb components and vehicle parts to assist with the subsequent police enquiry. Detailed searches can, and often do, provide key forensic evidence for subsequent use in prosecution cases.

After the bombing, tremendous pressure was exerted by business owners who wanted to return to their premises to start the recovery process. This must be planned carefully with safety paramount, but it must be done as quickly as is reasonably possible otherwise the authorities only compound the financial losses already caused by the terrorists.

At the Baltic Exchange, a system of control was quickly established which prevented unapproved access to the area. Before anyone could go back into the less severely damaged buildings it was necessary for them to be checked by qualified engineers to make sure they were structurally safe and free from other hazards. In addition to street level destruction, damage can occur to underground systems, electric and gas lines, sewer and water pipes and telecommunications systems. All have to be checked and made as safe as possible in the prevailing conditions. Starting with the least damaged premises, and working in towards the seat of the explosion where the worst destruction occurred, buildings were made safe and handed back to their owners in a systematic way. This allowed the cordons to shrink progressively as time progressed and ensured rebuilding work could start as soon as possible.

The bill for the repair of the damage was initially estimated at £800 million. The Association of British Insurers, representing Britain's leading underwriters, pointed out that this single bomb had done more damage in London than all of the rest in the twenty-year-long PIRA campaign. It highlighted a significant difference between the treatment of bomb damage in Northern Ireland, where all the repair work was paid for by the tax payer, and on the mainland, where commercial insurance companies carried the risk. It was made clear after this explosion that, in future, this cover might not be sustainable. Premiums would have to rise but, even then, it might prove impossible to provide insurance to cover the damage as a result of terrorist attacks of this magnitude. What was more worrying was the fact that the bomb (and the one at Staples Corner) both used home-made explosive, based on fertiliser, of which PIRA had an unlimited supply.

There was a noticeable effect on Londoners. To all those people who worked in the City, the sight of hundreds of wrecked or damaged buildings was depressing and caused much resentment against the Irish. Buildings in a city are a symbol of an established society and their pointless destruction is no less an attack on civilization than a bomb designed to kill or maim. Furthermore, modern satellite communications broadcast shocking images of the bomb-scene around the world, and many portrayed London as a defenceless target against such forms of attack. From the terrorists' perspective, it was a great success adding to the attractiveness of this type of economic target and the use of very large amounts of explosive.

The primary objective of the police is, of course, to prevent such devices getting into position and being detonated. In the City of London the policing priorities changed overnight. Personnel were stripped from various departments in the force to enable more officers to be deployed on the streets. Restrictions, under the law at the time, meant that it was impossible to set up permanent check points to stop and search vehicles, but arrangements were made for what were known as rolling random roadblocks. These stretched the police powers to the limit, but allowed suspect vehicles to be stopped and searched by armed police. The City also looked at new traffic management plans and a large increase in the CCTV coverage in the area.

On 8 May 1992, M15 announced that the Cold War was over and that they would assume primacy for combatting Irish Republican terrorism on the mainland from the Metropolitan Police. Events would show that this was urgently needed. In a democracy, despite the best efforts of the security forces, it is a sad fact that some bombs will always get through. The enquiry into the explosion at the Baltic Exchange brought home the need to address some of the issues surrounding the deployment of large vehicle bombs. Most pressing was a re-evaluation of the evacuation distances. Until the Baltic Exchange it was considered that a distance of 200 metres was sufficient for a vehicle bomb. Afterwards it was recognised that this was totally inadequate and a minimum distance of 400 metres was specified. Even this was a compromise; an explosion of sufficient magnitude can easily cause injuries beyond this distance and, potentially, fragments can be thrown a kilometre. For all practical purposes, however, having a larger safety distance is counterproductive because, with limited warning times, it is physically impossible to implement them. Even with 400 metres the problem was, and still is, the notification and evacuation of the people at risk. The point was made in a previous chapter that much of London is not built-up and that aircraft bombs dropped at random will often land in areas that are not densely populated. This rule does not apply where terrorists are concerned; their bombs are driven into positions where they will be most destructive. If you select almost any point in the centre of the London where terrorists are likely to leave a large vehicle bomb and then draw a 400 metre radius circle around it, there will most likely be many high-rise buildings. Some of these contain offices for up to 10,000 people. There could therefore be up to 100,000 people that need to be evacuated from the danger zone and this is not a task that can be carried out without considerable pre-planning.

After the Baltic Exchange bomb the police, and particularly the City Police, set about preparing and planning for such an eventuality. The key to success was the rapid dissemination of information about any bomb threats to the occupants of buildings inside the danger zone. They had to be notified and given the opportunity to seek a safer location. The City Police established a dedicated pager system through which bomb warnings could be issued simultaneously. Building managers or company security officers were able to rent the pagers and receive messages about suspect bombs. Another change introduced for a brief period was a step back in time and police officers were re-issued with whistles. Radios had replaced whistles for police communications, but once an officer received a warning by radio he had to shout at people to get them to move. The whistles, with their shrill piercing sound, attracted the attention of people much more than shouted warnings; they seemed to convey a greater sense of urgency and danger.

The other issue addressed in some detail was whether or not people should be evacuated from every building inside the danger area. As previously explained, during the First and Second World Wars being in the open was the most dangerous place to be in an air raid. With large terrorist bombs, evacuating thousands of people into the street potentially put them in much more danger than moving them to safer locations within buildings. Post-blast investigations established that, in many cases, people in buildings not immediately next to the bomb could go to underground floors or the central fire escapes where they would be safe from the blast and flying glass. It will be seen later, in the case of the Bishopsgate bomb, some people in underground floors survived despite being very close to the point where it detonated.

On 15 June 1992 there was another 'first' in the bombing of London when a minicab driver was used to 'ferry' a bomb to its target. It all started at around 23.30 hours when two men called a minicab office in Holloway Road and asked to be picked up. One of the firm's drivers set off with the men, who were carrying rucksacks, and took them, as requested, towards the West End. When they arrived in the Shaftsbury Avenue one of the men produced a hand gun and told the frightened driver that they were members of the PIRA. He drove them around for a while and then was told to stop in St Albans Street. When he did so, the men opened the rucksacks they were carrying and, according to the driver, he heard what he thought was a kitchen timer being set. The men discussed throwing the bombs from the moving vehicle, possibly near St James's Palace. However, they eventually decided against this. The two terrorists then told the driver that a bomb was set to go off in fifteen minutes and he should warn the police. The driver contacted the police, but the device functioned in St Albans Street before any cordon or evacuation could take place. Fortunately, there were no casualties. It was the forerunner of the first proxy bomb in London, but before then, there would be an extraordinary episode which indicates the level of threat that London was facing and the outstanding work of the police and security services in disrupting it. As recorded in the official history of M15: 'The Service's role in preventing a series of City bombings on the scale of that of the Baltic Exchange made an important and perhaps crucial difference to the struggle against the IRA.'[2]

On 8 August, acting on information received, a large articulated trailer was recovered to the Forensic Explosives Laboratory at Fort Halstead for examination. There, the following day, EXPO Phil Yeaman examined the trailer. He gained entry via a hole in the roof and clambered down a ladder into the dark interior. He instantly grasped the enormity of what he saw. Just looking around he could see two large cylindrical objects, a further ten smaller cylindrical containers and two square-shaped items all of which were covered in black polythene and were sat on wooden pallets. Moving round, he also discovered two domestic 'wheelie bins', a Kalashnikov assault rifle, a black polythene bag and a hand pallet transporter. It was immediately obvious to Yeaman that the trailer had been used by the PIRA as a 'mother ship' to store fourteen enormous bombs, each of which, on first estimates, would be around a ton in size. In addition, the two wheelie bins each contained several hundred kilograms of explosive. A further detailed search resulted in the discovery of thirty-three timing and power units and thirty-two detonators. One of the timing and power units was marked as unserviceable. A simple calculation meant that there were enough left for two to be used with each bomb. Finally, and worryingly for the security services, an RPG 7 cleaning kit was discovered. This naturally led to speculation that an RPG 7 rocket launcher and ammunition had been brought on to the mainland UK.

It will never be known how, when or where these bombs were going to be used. Had they all been deployed in one simultaneous attack, then it would have been, without doubt, the most spectacular terrorist attack in history up to that time. In reality the PIRA probably did not have the manpower in London to do this. It seems most likely that they intended to deploy the bombs singly or in pairs to maintain a relentless pressure on the capital and the country's politicians. The discovery and rendering safe of these bombs was probably one of the most successful disruptions of a PIRA operation. It was also a major set-back for them as they had clearly invested a huge amount of time and money in planning, making, transporting and preparing the bombs for use. This success, however, did not stop the attacks.

September and October 1992 saw a continuation of the bombing, mostly using small blast bombs and incendiaries. At Madame Tussuaud's, early one morning an incendiary functioned in the Chamber of Horrors. It triggered the fire alarm and the blaze was quickly extinguished. In the follow-up investigation an explosion was heard, this time in the Planetarium, which is adjacent to Madame Tussuaud's. Examination of the second scene showed that a high explosive charge of Semtex had been built into a PIRA box incendiary case. Like the Germans in the Second World War the aim of these high explosive devices, which could easily kill, was to discourage staff from searching for the normal box incendiaries and carrying them out into the street.

October was particularly busy and fifteen small bombs detonated at a variety of targets all over the capital; these included the transport system, a bridge carrying sewage pipes over the River Lea, and the Comedy Restaurant in Oxenden Street. Most, but not all, were preceded by coded threats and timed to go off in the late evening or early morning. Finding devices under such conditions, and organising the necessary cordon and evacuation, was almost impossible. As always, the warnings were vague and, trying to locate a small bag with a bomb in it, at night, especially if it was hidden under a car or behind a wall, proved enormously difficult.

If something suspicious was found there was no alternative to the established procedures of setting up cordons and organising the evacuation of people at risk. At the time, the majority of uniformed police officers, particularly those in Central London, would have dealt with many calls to suspect devices. Most of these were false alarms (often involving lost or stolen property) but it did not in any way detract from the professional manner that the police on the ground dealt with them. For the individual officers concerned there was always a high degree of menace and moments of high drama once a suspect device was discovered and before and during the initial cordon and evacuation. Where live devices were involved, police officers responding to the calls were naturally at considerable risk.

Next London had its first, and to date, only proxy bomb. Similar tactics had been used in Northern Ireland where innocent people were coerced into delivering vehicle bombs to security force bases. In the evening of 30 October a minicab in North London picked up a couple of 'fares'. Once they were in the vehicle they produced handguns and ordered the driver to head towards Downing Street. Just before they reached Whitehall the gunmen ordered the driver to stop and told him there was a bomb in the back of the vehicle. He was told to drive his cab to Downing Street and abandon it there. To ensure he complied, they said that another vehicle was following them and that if he did not do as he was ordered the bomb in the back would be detonated remotely. Terrified out of his wits, the luckless driver complied with these instructions arriving outside Downing Street at around 20.52 hours. There he jumped out and warned the police officers on duty of the device in the back of his vehicle. He was initially detained by them and the cordon and evacuation process initiated. Fifteen minutes later the bomb detonated, completely destroying the minicab. Fortunately, thanks to the prompt action of the police, there were no casualties.

On the night of 14 November 1992, another massive truck bomb was being driven through London towards an unknown target. Once again, it was two alert police officers who noticed the blue box-bodied Volvo truck and instinctively concluded it was out of place and suspicious. They decided to stop it and question the driver. When the lorry came to a halt in Stoke Newington High Street the driver and passenger decamped and ran off. Police Constable Hall gave chase and cornered one of the men in nearby gardens. As he was about to arrest him, the man produced a Webley revolver and a shot rang out. The bullet grazed the officer's head; naturally he turned to flee and was then shot in the back. Urgent calls for assistance from the officers sparked a massive police response and units, some armed, flooded into the area. Shortly afterwards the revolver was found and a little later two men were arrested.

It was immediately obvious that the Volvo truck potentially contained a bomb of massive proportions and Paul Myring, the duty EXPO, was tasked to the scene. On arrival he went forward to search the lorry which still had its lights on and engine running. In the cab he found two PIRA TPUs connected to two detonators and a length of detonating cord which ran into a length of black hose. This hose went through a hole in the back of the cab and into the box-body of the vehicle. He separated the detonators from the timing and power units and the detonating cord. Making his way to the back of the vehicle he broke into it through a side door and looked inside. The front third of load-carrying area had been compartmentalised using boards and battens and the whole covered in black plastic sheeting. Removing this, Myring discovered what he recognised as home-made explosive. It was later established that there was over three tons of this. In it were embedded three tubes which were to act as boosters and these were, in turn, connected to the detonating cord which ran through the black tubing from the cab. Had the bomb been driven to its intended target, presumably somewhere in the middle of the capital, there is little doubt that, the use of a double initiation system would have ensured the bomb exploded, and it would have caused millions of pounds' worth of damage and potentially many casualties. It was, at the end of the day, another outstanding example of how well-trained and observant police officers prevented a major terrorist outrage. It also demonstrated yet again the dangers faced by unarmed police officers when tackling terrorists, and the exceptional bravery they display in the pursuance of their duty.

The following day, security guards at Canary Wharf noticed two men acting suspiciously near a blue Ford Transit. When challenged, one suspect produced a handgun and threatened the guards before both men fled in a small yellow Escort van. Once again, a major police response followed. A quick look into the blue Ford revealed another huge bomb and EXPO Colin Goodson was tasked to deal with it. At the same time a call went out to search for the missing yellow Ford Escort.

Goodson arrived shortly afterwards and quickly deployed a 'Wheelbarrow' to examine the vehicle remotely. The rear of the van was locked using a metal bar and padlock and it proved impossible to gain more than limited access to the load-carrying area. Next, the front of the vehicle was examined. At this point EXPO Paul Myring, who had dealt with the bomb in Stoke Newington, arrived on scene and both he and Goodson went forward to render the bomb safe. The subsequent forensic examination of the van revealed that it contained 1.6 tonnes of explosive and had two timing and power units, each with a built in anti-handling system.

The same night, Police Constable Paul Challis was on duty at Bethnal Green. At the evening briefing the shift was told that it would almost certainly be deployed down to Limehouse to assist with the surge of calls that would inevitably come in after the news of the Stoke Newington bomb the previous day. After the briefing Challis went on duty in a panda car with Police Constable Mick Darby.

At 23.55 hours, as a result of a member of the public becoming suspicious, they received a call to an abandoned van in Collingwood Street. They drove to the scene where they met the informant who pointed out the suspect vehicle. It was a small yellow Ford Escort van parked underneath the main railway viaduct – oddly it had been dumped with its lights still on. The two officers drove their panda car and parked up next to the vehicle which was bathed in the orange glow of the street lights. They got out went to front of the van and examined the tax disc and at the same time asked for a number plate check on the police national computer. They were relieved to hear that there were no outstanding reports on the vehicle and that it had a registered keeper.

Unknown to the two officers, the van had, in fact, been reported as being linked to the Canary Wharf bomb, but a procedural error had resulted in it not being recorded correctly on the police database. Had they known about the link, the officers would have taken a different course of action. As it was, they continued to investigate the abandoned van.

Darby went to the passenger side of the vehicle and was about to open the door when his colleague called him to the driver's side. He went round to join him and both officers got a strong whiff of petrol fumes coming from the open door. Looking into the vehicle they could just see, in the poor light, a number of unidentified objects covered in a blanket. They decided to investigate these further and went round to the back of the van where they opened both doors. In the semi-darkness they could see the unusual glow of a red light beneath the blanket which Challis then lifted. This revealed a box with a small dial and batteries. Next to the box was a yellowy-looking block which Challis stuck his fingers into. He described it as being wet and sticky.

It was enough for Darby to recognise that it was a bomb and he simply shouted, 'Quick run'. They both turned and ran down the road, shouting to the informant and other passers-by to back off as well. Once they got to a safe distance they radioed in for further assistance.

The duty inspector arrived with more officers and they continued with the cordon and evacuation of the area. At this point the duty inspector noticed that the panda car was still parked next to the suspect vehicle and shouted, 'Who left the panda car down there?' Challis confessed to this and, worried about the effect of the full petrol tank, set off back down the road, jumped in the panda car, and drove it away from the Escort van.

EXPO Paul Myring was tasked to deal with the new threat and arrived shortly afterwards. He was briefed on the incident and, after donning protective clothing, went forward to the vehicle and rendered the bomb safe. Later Constable Challis received a Deputy Assistant Commissioners' commendation for his efforts that night.

Bombs made safe, such as the two just described, provide a wealth of forensic evidence, but it is crucial that this is recorded, photographed and recovered in a safe, logical and approved manner if it is to be admissible in court. This is a long and slow process and necessitates keeping crime scenes sealed for hours – and in the case of major investigations sometimes days. At this time, cordons were manned by police officers. In mid-winter it is a long, cold, boring, unrewarding but essential duty, and one of the calls that is always gratefully received is, 'Tea Pot One is here'. The importance of this vehicle turning up at incidents and providing hot drinks and snacks to the physical well-being and morale of the officers on duty cannot be underestimated.

The success of the police in intercepting one huge vehicle bomb and another being rendering safe did nothing to allay the fears of the insurance industry. The fact was that the PIRA's campaign was now becoming a matter of financial arithmetic and the insurers made it clear that they were seriously considering the withdrawal of cover for damage caused by acts of terrorism. Despite political denials, behind the scenes there had already been some secret negotiations designed to end the violence. These talks continued but progress was slow, with many setbacks as the 'Hawks' and 'Doves' on either side tried to gain ascendancy.

Two weeks later the PIRA struck again; this time a Ford Transit was left in Tottenham Court Road in the early evening of 1 December 1992. Coded threats were also given to a series of bombs which were alleged to be located between Oxford Street and Euston Station. Unclear, or deliberately vague, warnings like this give police officers little chance to carry out their primary duty, which is to save lives. In response to the threat, all available police officers were tasked to the area and the search for the bombs began. As there was no indication of the type of bomb that had been left, it was impossible to give the responding officers any clue as to what they were looking for. Anything, from an abandoned bag to parked vehicles was potentially suspicious.

Whilst this search was being carried out, a police officer trying to evacuate people from nearby buildings heard a sharp crack from a Transit van in Tottenham Court Road. He did not realise it then, but this was in fact the detonator in the device functioning. This was reported over the radio and EXPO Mick Coldrick, who was already en route to the area, went to examine the vehicle. Looking into the back from the driver's seat he could see that there was a large wooden box sitting on two pallets. The box had a lid on it which Coldrick lifted to reveal a pair of timing and power units. He took action to make these safe and then checked the rest of the vehicle. It was later established that one of the timing and power units had actually timed out and that the detonator connected to a booster tube had functioned but failed to set off the main charge. Later examination showed that this bomb had 1.5 tonnes of explosive. The people in and around Tottenham Court Road that night have no idea how lucky they were. It was estimated that at the time the detonator functioned there were still hundreds of people in the immediate area. Had the bomb exploded it is quite certain many of them would have been killed or terribly injured.

The bombing continued when, on 9 December at 17.25 hours, coded threats were received to the effect that a bomb had been left at Woodside Park Underground Station. The caller warned it would detonate after a short fifteen-minute period. Half an hour later an explosion was heard in a car park adjacent to the station. It ripped apart a vehicle, but further investigation by the duty EXPO, Derek Pickford, showed that the device had only partially functioned. Later almost 100 kilograms of explosive was recovered from the remnants of a plastic dustbin inside the shattered remains of the vehicle.

In the by now traditional pre-Christmas campaign against the retail industry, small bombs exploded in a W.H. Smith store and a branch of Argos in Wood Green on 10 December. A week later there were warnings about bombs in John Lewis in Oxford Street. The first of these detonated in the toilets at 10.36 hours. A second device was secreted in a wheelie bin outside the same John Lewis store in a place where people had been evacuated after the first warning. When it functioned, an hour later, several people were injured.

The last PIRA bomb in 1992 exploded in an emergency escape stairwell at Hampstead Underground Station on 22 December. A small device containing about half a kilogram of explosive, it caused no injuries and led to only minor damage. However, calls to suspect items continued up until the end of the year. One of the calls from a rough sleeper at Covent Garden Underground Station resulted in the discovery of a hoax which looked very like a real device and caused much disruption.

So ended 1992 which, to date, has been the busiest year on record for the Explosives Office. In total there were 2,223 calls for assistance, this figure excluded routine daily patrols around the government security zone to check on possible mortar base plate locations. In total ten bombs were rendered safe, forty-one exploded, and there were eight finds of terrorist equipment. The remainder of the incidents consisted of hoaxes, false alarms and the disposal of conventional munitions. Everyone wondered what 1993 would bring.

It was no surprise that it continued in the same vein and started with coded threats to incendiary devices in Oxford Street on 6 January, one of which turned out to be yet another of the lethal high explosive types. Some small high explosive devices were deployed at the end of the month and this pattern continued throughout February. The PIRA then seemed to concentrate on bombing areas outside London. In one attack, in Warrington, two young boys, Jonathon Ball and Tim Parry, were killed and a further fifty-six people injured when a bomb in a litter bin exploded. As usual the warning was inadequate and inaccurate. Some commentators have suggested the focus of the PIRA on areas outside London was because the capital was becoming too dangerous a place for them to operate. Possibly the PIRA wanted a period of calm and a less vigilant police and public because they had, in mind, another devastating strike against the financial heart of the City of London.

Saturday, 24 April 1993, dawned a cold, clear morning and the City, a thriving area during the working week, was quiet. No one noticed a blue Ford Iveco tipper truck being driven into the centre of the financial district and parked in Bishopsgate. In the cab a terrorist set two timing and power units running. Leaving the four-way flashers operating he jumped out of the cab and wearing a 'hoody' and shielding his face he walked away from the vehicle. At 09.15 hours a coded threat was telephoned to Sky News, followed by twelve others to various news organisations and the emergency services. On each occasion almost exactly the same chilling message was read out. The only difference was that in each subsequent call the warning time given decreased. It said:

Get a pen and paper. There is a massive bomb at Bishopsgate between Leadenhall Street and Hounsditch. It's due to go off in 40 minutes, you must evacuate everybody between these streets.[3]

The vehicle was quickly located on the City Police's CCTV cameras and police officers responding to calls for assistance arrived at the scene to begin the cordon and evacuation process. To save lives at bombing incidents it is necessary to evacuate those closest to the device first and then work outwards. To do this the first police officers on scene were required to put themselves at risk inside the danger area. Even at weekends the buildings in the city are staffed by duty managers, security personnel, cleaners and maintenance workers. They all had to be warned and evacuated from the area. Meanwhile, the tipper truck stood motionless in the road, its hazard lights warning of the latent energy of the explosive carried in its steel-sided body. Inside the cab the mechanical timers were remorselessly running down.

As luck would have it the duty EXPO, Dave Williams, was already on a task in North London. He was reassigned to the suspect tipper truck in Bishopsgate and raced to the scene. He arrived at the outer rendezvous point and gave further advice on the cordon and evacuation.

At 10.27 hours the tipper truck disintegrated in the biggest single malicious explosion ever in London (only the accidents at the Regent's Park canal in 1874 and in Silvertown in 1917 being bigger). Post-blast, accurately determining the size of the explosive charge used in a terrorist bomb is a complex problem. Historically much evidence has been collected in the various studies of bombing in the Second World War. In addition, in the nuclear age, much experimental work was carried out using massive charges of TNT to simulate atomic explosions and their effects on various types of structure. Consequently, for TNT there is a great deal of empirical data. This includes the estimation of charge sizes based on the dimensions of craters in different materials. When an estimate of the size of the TNT charge required to cause the observed damage is completed, the next step is to compare the effectiveness of the terrorist explosive, in this case one based on ammonium nitrate, with TNT. From the results it is possible to get an idea of the size of the charge. The post-blast investigation revealed that the weight of home-made explosive in the bomb in Bishopsgate was in the region of 3,000-5,000 kilograms.

A bomb of this size in a densely packed city area affects about fifty buildings severely and a further 200-300 to a lesser degree. From the point of view of blast, the buildings closest to the detonation clearly suffer the worst damage, but in doing so afford a degree of protection to those behind them. Equally the blast from the bomb tends to be channelled between the buildings, causing damage a considerable distance away from the seat of the explosion.

The explosion also demonstrated the different responses of buildings of varying construction. For example, St Ethelburga's Church was an old example of mass construction which relied on the weight of stone to provide its strength. It was overwhelmed by the blast overpressure and collapsed catastrophically. However, the more modern buildings either side of the church, constructed using steel frames and reinforced concrete, survived the blast in terms of their main structure, although, the windows and outer cladding were all smashed and stripped away from the frame, as were many of the internal fixtures and fittings.

The Hong Kong and Shanghai Bank building immediately opposite the tipper truck was a steel-framed reinforced concrete design that had a central core, in the form of fire escapes, which provided it with tremendous strength. In it, one of the security guards on duty that day was responsible for saving many lives. When the first bomb warning was given he shepherded some forty people, less two who initially declined to move, down to the car park which was in the upper basement. Police instructions were then received that the bomb was in Old Broad Street and that the building should be evacuated. The duty manager sheltering with the occupants ignored this instruction and told people to move to the Bishopsgate side of the basement and not to evacuate. Because of the uncertainty created by the contradictory instructions, some people ended up in the upper basement having been moved there by the security guard. He bravely returned to the first floor of the tower block to try to persuade the two members of staff who had declined to seek shelter to take cover in the basement, but they had already gone. He then went on foot via the south staircase of the building to warn a second guard believed to be in the main entrance to take cover. He did not find him as he had already gone to the toilets in the ground floor core, a very safe place.

The first guard, who had taken so much trouble to try and save others, was in the lift lobby on the west side of the core when the explosion occurred. He was injured by falling debris and suffered a broken hand, finger bones and multiple cuts and bruises.

Those who had taken shelter in the basement described hearing the bomb go off as a dull thud of no great violence. This indicates that the ground shock to the basement wall was fairly slight. The blast overpressure from the bomb was also largely kept out of the basement, except in one small area where a lightweight cover slab was dished down by the force of the blast and then fell off its supporting beam. Despite this the people sheltering underneath it were uninjured.

There was, however, significant damage to, and spectacular buckling of, some of the steel beams which supported the ceiling of the basement. These were not far from falling off their supports and had they done so the people sheltering in the basement would have been crushed and killed. It was a close escape, but had they not gone there to shelter they would almost certainly have died. All of the cladding, windows and interior fittings in the building above ground level were totally wrecked.

The Natwest Tower, the tallest building in the city at that time, was struck by the blast as the bomb exploded. It was over 100 metres away from the seat of the explosion and did not suffer serious structural damage. Even so, it is estimated that the side of the building facing the tipper truck was hit by a 135 mph wind which caused it to sway significantly, although not outside its design limits. Most of the windows in the building were shattered and much internal damage caused by the collapse of false ceilings. As happened at the Baltic Exchange, some of this shattered glass, blown from the higher windows, began to spin as it

433

fell and travelled some distance before smashing to smithereens on the ground, or like vertical scythes embedding themselves in the gardens at the back of the building. These glass chards are lethal and reinforce the need for people caught up in such incidents to not only get out of line of sight, but to also get under some form of hard cover.

There was one fatality during the incident – *News of the World* photographer Edward Henry who had gone to the Hong Kong and Shanghai Bank building on hearing the initial reports of a bomb. His body was discovered in the debris some twenty-five metres from where the bomb detonated. Even though he appeared to be hiding behind one of the massive concrete columns he had no chance of surviving and was well within the area of the fireball and lethal blast overpressures. Unlike the generation of people who had lived through the Blitz, people today have little or no idea of the power of explosives. There is a total lack of understanding of the forces involved and how quickly they are unleashed. Unlike the heroes in many films there is no ducking out the way of the blast wave, or outrunning the fire ball. The only safe thing to do when the police issue a bomb warning (if a suitable bomb shelter is not available) is to get out of line of sight of the device as soon as possible, keep away from overhead windows (which is easier said than done) and keep moving away from the suspect device, the further away the better. It is worth reiterating that cordon distances are designed to save lives and where possible prevent serious injury. They do not designate a guaranteed safety zone; they are a compromise between the need to evacuate the people closest to the bomb and recognising that completely safe cordon distances would be impossible to implement because of the practical difficulties of moving the large numbers of people involved.

As intended, the Bishopsgate bomb inflicted heavy damage and disruption on City businesses and put the Northern Ireland question back to the top of the Government's public policy agenda. Initial reports suggested that the damage and loss of business would cost the country over £1,000,000,000. It vindicated the decision of insurers to threaten to withdraw from the market some six months earlier. In fact, the totals were later revised down but it still cost the country between £300-400,000,000 to make good the damage. From a security perspective a 'ring of steel' was placed around the City with road closures, checkpoints and barriers. It worked in as much that it deflected the terrorists to other softer targets.

The problem of how to deal with big vehicle bombs had long been exercising the minds of both bomb disposal officers and scientists in

Northern Ireland and on the UK mainland. For many years the primary attack weapon used to deal with car bombs, usually containing no more than a maximum of around 200 kilograms, was a system known as Paw Paw. This consisted of a black plastic cassette approximately half a metre long and thirty centimetres wide. Inside was a sheet of plastic explosive on top of which was a matrix of shot, very like shotgun pellets. This cassette could be fitted to a fork mounted on the front of a Wheelbarrow and delivered remotely underneath the boot of a vehicle with a suspect bomb in it. When the explosive was detonated, like a shotgun, the shot was blown up through the boot of the vehicle and in doing so would disrupt and often throw out the bombs inside. It proved to be very effective against the early comparatively small bombs contained in beer kegs or milk churns. It was deployed in London, but never used operationally.

As the campaign in Northern Ireland evolved one of the recurring themes was the escalation in the amount of explosive the PIRA used in their vehicle bombs. As they grew in size, they could no longer be hidden and delivered in cars, so vans, and later trucks, were used to carry them. It soon became clear that Paw Paw was no longer capable of successfully disrupting large bombs in such vehicles and a new method of rendering them safe was required. This resulted in the development of the Rapid Access and Disruption Equipment (RADE). This was essentially a disruptive explosive charge which could be quickly and easily positioned inside a vehicle where it could be fired. The effect would be for the vehicle itself to be blown apart and, in the process, any circuitry to the bomb would be disrupted.

In London, EXPO Phil Yeaman developed a modified form of RADE which was known as the Rapid Access Weapon or RAW. Similar in principle to the military system it consisted of a piece of six-foot plastic pipe which had been cut in half lengthwise. To it were attached a number of specialist charges known as Maxi Candles, whilst at the forward end of the pipe there was a separate shaped charge which produced a high-velocity explosive jet, designed to break windows. The whole system could be mounted on a Wheelbarrow and deployed remotely to attack suspect vehicle bombs.

The RAW system was deployed operationally once. In late 1994 urgent reports were received from Diplomatic Protection Officers that a large lorry had been abandoned with its four-way flashers on in Whitehall opposite Downing Street. The scenario exactly matched the pattern of previous PIRA big vehicle bomb attacks. No coded bomb threat was received after the vehicle was abandoned, but this was not uncommon and often happened in Northern Ireland when police or security force bases were attacked. The lorry's location, immediately opposite Downing Street and very close to the Ministry of Defence, put it in the same category. Everyone thought it was another massive bomb. EXPO Colin Goodson was on duty and immediately deployed a RAW on a Wheelbarrow in an attempt to disrupt the suspect device. The charge was positioned inside the cab of the vehicle and fired, destroying the front of the lorry. Moments after this had been done a call was received from one of the police officers on the outer cordon. He said: 'There is a lorry driver here with a can of petrol and he is not looking very happy.'

At a time when London had been attacked by several large vehicle bombs it seemed inconceivable that the driver had abandoned the lorry in such a sensitive area without at least notifying the police officers always on duty around the vicinity.

Another system designed to disrupt large vehicle bombs in vans was known as Shinto. This consisted of a remotely-controlled Landrover which had a small crane mounted on its rear chassis. Four disruptive charges were mounted on the arm of the crane which were capable of defeating large vehicle bombs. The Landrover was sacrificial in this process and was expected to be severely damaged when the charges were fired. All the EXPOs trained continuously on the deployment Shinto. It was not quick to set up and took considerable skill to get it down to the target vehicle and ready for firing. Everyone hoped to be the first to deploy and fire it at a vehicle bomb in London, but Shinto was never deployed operationally and was withdrawn from use in early 2000.

It was replaced with another smaller system known as Furness. This used the same charges as Shinto but they were mounted on a purpose-built remotely-controlled vehicle which was in principle very similar to the Wheelbarrow. The only difference being that Furness was a one-shot system in that it was expected that the robot would be severely damaged when the charges were fired. Like Shinto, it was never deployed operationally and has now been withdrawn from service.

The next significant attack by the PIRA was carried out away from the centre of London, but with a major international destination in mind – Heathrow airport. It was another well-planned and executed operation designed to attract maximum publicity and by a simple knock-on effect, to cause massive disruption to international travellers worldwide.

Just after 17.00 hours on 9 March 1994, a series of bomb threats were received. Using authenticated codewords, this stated that the airport should be cleared and flights stopped because a large number of bombs would explode within the hour. Where, or what these devices were, was not made clear and although pre-planned searches began no-one knew what to look for. Fifty-seven minutes later there were a series of short sharp reports from a red Nissan Micra hatchback left in the Excelsior Hotel car park on the perimeter of Heathrow airport. Moments later the vehicle was seen to burst into flames. The airport police sprang into action and were soon on scene cordoning and evacuating the area. As always in these incidents, no one was initially certain what had happened and the priority was to clear the area in case there were secondary devices. For reasons which will become clear, at this point there was still no indication that it was a mortar attack. The duty EXPO, Dave Williams, had been tasked to Heathrow after the initial warnings and arrived at the car park at 18.22 hours. By then several cars were on fire with the small hatchback, in the centre of them, burning fiercely. About the same time the fire brigade arrived and quickly extinguished the flames. After they had done so, Williams went forward to investigate. In the back of the burnt-out hatchback he saw five tubes welded into a metal frame which he recognised as launchers for PIRA mortar bombs. These were much smaller in size than those used on Downing Street, and were an old design known by the military as the Mark 6. Although the bombs only contained a third of a kilogram of explosive they were capable of producing a lethal shower of fragments. Worse still, the bombs had a range of up to 1,000 metres.

Reports now started filtering in that there had been a series of pops on the airfield itself. The fact that there were only 'pops' and not explosions indicated that the bombs had only partially detonated. The SEXPO, Graham Lightfoot, had gone to the scene and he went airside to try and locate the mortar bombs' impact points. By looking at the position of the Nissan and knowing the range of the Mark 6 mortar it was possible to deduce roughly where the bombs should have landed. In the dark it was not easy, but an initial search went ahead and two bombs were located on the concrete runways. The examination of these showed that although the detonators had functioned the main charge of Semtex had failed to explode. It was decided, on safety grounds, that a detailed search for the other mortar bombs would start in daylight. Just after dawn a full sweep of the area was carried out and the remaining two unexploded bombs were located.

It was noted that there were five mortar tubes in the car, and it was considered most likely that the central tube was used to launch a small projectile to break the rear windscreen of the launching vehicle. The four mortars bombs then had a clear flight path on firing. Lastly an incendiary, self-destruct charge set fire to the car.

Heathrow was fully operational in the morning and amongst the senior managers and police officers there was a feeling of relief that the attack had failed to cause any casualties, damage or disruption on a substantial scale. Had the bombs exploded and fragments hit parked or taxiing aircraft then they would all have had to be grounded until they had been thoroughly inspected and any damage suitably repaired.

The vulnerability of the airport to this type of attack was recognised and a major security operation, involving vehicle check points, was put in place to stop another car being used to launch mortars at the airport. The PIRA, though, was already one, or more correctly two, steps ahead, as it had two more sets of mortars in place, both with long delay sequential timers.

In the evening of 10 March another series of coded threats notified the authorities of an imminent attack on Heathrow. A minute after midnight three small explosions were reported at the southeast corner of the airport. The emergency services responded to the scene together with EXPO Paul Myring. During the search of the area where the explosions were reported, another four Mark 6 mortar bombs were found, all of which had failed to function correctly. The next step was to locate the launch point; this was roughly calculated by taking the average range of the mortars and drawing a line back through the centre of where the bombs landed. A daylight search of the area revealed the mortar base plate located just outside the perimeter in some scrubland, 900 metres from the impact points.

It was an embarrassment for those responsible for security that the PIRA had managed to launch another salvo of mortar bombs at Heathrow. In response, a massive search for other potential mortar baseplate locations was organised. This sounds easy, but if you take the 1,000 metre range of the mortar and add it to the outer perimeter fence of the airport, then an enormous area needs to be covered. Nevertheless, the task was started with the searchers being briefed to look for more mortar launch sites on the surface.

As already alluded to, the PIRA was still one step ahead. A pit had been dug on a small piece of waste land into which a further battery of mortars had been hidden. After setting them in position and starting a long delay timer, the pit was covered with plywood and carefully camouflaged, unless a searcher actually stood on the plywood, there was absolutely no indication of their presence. Early on Sunday, 13 March, a series of coded threats indicated another imminent attack on Heathrow. The airport was closed down and further searches initiated. During these a number of bangs were heard coming from the perimeter at 08.07 hours; almost immediately reports were received that mortar bombs had landed in and around the Terminal 4 building. Thankfully, once again they failed to function. EXPOs Terry Thompson and Mike Coldrick were tasked to the scene. Thompson went to examine the unexploded bombs whilst Coldrick went to Bedfont Road, close to where the mortar base plate was believed to have been.

Coldrick searched the area and found the carefully excavated rectangular trench containing the now-empty launcher with five barrels in a triangular frame. Cables from this ran to a large plastic box. This box contained smaller boxes with wires running to another six large batteries. The smaller boxes were labelled '6D 1H 38m'. It was obvious that this was the delay between switching on the timers and the output to fire the mortars.

Another massive search operation followed as it was feared that there might be yet more buried mortars. It was bad enough for the authorities that there had been three attacks; another one would make the police and security services look utterly incompetent. Fortunately, it was the last.

Another significant development in the bombing campaign around this time was the amount of time and effort that the PIRA was prepared to go to in an effort to disguise their large vehicle bombs. No longer would the explosives be piled into the back of a van or truck. They would be carefully concealed to make it easier for the bombers to get to their targets. On 12 July 1994, a Leyland flatbed truck arrived at Heysham docks from Ireland without a driver and was left in a lorry park awaiting collection. A man arrived to pick up the vehicle, but on being told it was to be checked by customs he made an excuse and quickly disappeared. The subsequent search of the vehicle revealed that it had been modified to carry a huge concealed bomb. The flatbed of the vehicle had been adapted by building a hidden container which was welded and bolted to the inside of the load-carrying frame. This held over 2,000 kilograms of homemade explosive. In addition, two timing and power units and detonators were concealed inside the dashboard. The vehicle may well have been intended for use in another major attack on London. What was disturbing for all those involved in the fight against the bombers was that to the casual observer it looked like an empty flatbed. Had the PIRA managed to get it into position and coded warnings been given, it was quite possible that its appearance might have deceived those on the ground into thinking that it did not contain a substantial device. The result of such a mistake could have had disastrous consequences. Overnight new instructions were issued to all the police forces about how cunningly the new bombs were being concealed.

On 31 August 1994, after a great deal of behind the scenes activity, the PIRA announced a ceasefire and, much to the amazement of many, initially it held. Elsewhere, an ominous new type of terrorism was launched against an unsuspecting public in Tokyo on 21 March 1995. Members of the Aum Shinrikyo Sect released the nerve agent Sarin on several underground trains simultaneously. Fortunately, the amount of gas released was small and it was not a particularly pure form of the agent. Even so, twelve people died, seventeen others were seriously injured and over 3,000 people attended hospital (of whom some 400 were detained). Although perpetrated by a criminal organization and not an international terrorist group, this attack had immediate ramifications for police and security forces all over the world. London was no exception and although some limited measures were in place to deal with chemical attacks, these were mainly based on a military response. In the light of the attack in Tokyo it was clear that these were inadequate and consequently the training of police officers to deal with terrorist incidents involving chemical, biological and radiation hazards was stepped up.

The PIRA ceasefire ended abruptly and unexpectedly with a series of coded bomb threats on 9 February 1996. At approximately 17.40 hours the London Fire Brigade received the first call stating that 'a massive bomb' was in position in Canary Wharf at South Quay Station and that evacuation should start immediately. Other calls followed to the Heathrow and Gatwick switchboards and another was sent to the Mirror Group Newspaper offices at Canary Wharf. Five minutes later, in a further call to an Irish newspaper, a similar bomb threat was made. Finally, the editor of RTE (Ireland's national television and radio broadcaster) was given the warning and a message to the effect that the PIRA ceasefire was now over.

These messages were passed on to the police and the Anti-Terrorist Branch Control Room where the bomb threats were confirmed and orders given for the start of a major evacuation in Canary Wharf. Small numbers of local police officers arrived on scene within minutes of the phone calls and began the difficult and dangerous task of locating the bomb and evacuating the area. One vehicle seemed out of place. It was a Ford Cargo low-loader which was spotted parked on a small road alongside a newsagent's shop at the corner of the South Quay shopping plaza, about ninety metres from the entrance to South Quay Station.

Although suspect, it was not certain that this was the vehicle with the bomb in it and the evacuation of people over a large area continued.

440

The difficulties in doing this have already been explained, but the task was made harder on this occasion for two reasons. Firstly, the general public had no knowledge that the ceasefire had ended and their perception of risk was much lower than it had previously been. Londoners and commuters are accustomed to the constant sight of emergency response vehicles dashing about on 'blues and twos'. Unless the danger is immediate and apparent, which in this case it wasn't, more often than not they ignore them. Secondly, fewer police officers were immediately available to respond to Canary Wharf when compared to incidents in Central London or in the City.

At Canary Wharf trains had to be stopped, but obviously not at South Quay station, roads had to be sealed and people moved out of the way. All these actions sound simple, but in practice it needs close co-ordination and it takes much more time than there is ever available. Cordons have to be manned by police officers, if not the general public simply ignore the striped 'Police do not Cross' plastic tape, and diverted motorists are often able to find minor roads which enable them to avoid the cordons and then drive past the suspect vehicles or packages.

Additional police officers, from various units, were arriving at the scene to assist with the operation, but without a detailed knowledge of the area it was much harder for them to help. At the same time EXPO Nick Nice and his Number 2, Police Constable Tony Ashforth, were on their way to deal with the suspect bomb. They had been tasked to Limehouse Police Station first and from there had gone on to South Quay. When they arrived, there was still considerable confusion, even to the extent that it was still not clear what sort of bomb it might be.

They used their Range Rover to block off a road a couple of hundred meters from the station, but in doing so finished up quite close to the Ford Cargo low loader. They discovered that some police officers were directing people to the station so that they could get on a train to leave the area whilst British Transport Officers at the station were desperately were trying to send them away. This sounds incomprehensible, but was a product of the unclear bomb threat, trouble identifying exactly what and where the bomb was and the arrival of officers who did not know the area well. Even so the police were progressively managing to close roads and clear people from the immediate area. Unfortunately, two men, Ul Haq Bahsir and John Jefferies, were told to leave, but took refuge in the back of their newsagent's shop. They were still sheltering there when the bomb detonated at 19.01 hours, killing them both.

Ashforth was standing close to his Range Rover when the bomb exploded. He remembers a blue flash and instinctively crouching down.

441

After the blast wave had washed over him, fragments from the low loader and debris thrown out from the bomb crater began crashing down all around him and he was hit by a small chunk of stone or concrete. As the noise of the blast faded away he stood up and looked in the direction of the seat of the explosion. It was clear that a major gas pipe had been ruptured as the ground where the low-loader containing the bomb had stood was on fire.

Nice went forward to the crater and was close to the seat of the explosion when a bizarre incident occurred. A man appeared on the roof of a single-storey building quite close by and shouted, 'Can you get me a ladder to help me get down'. Overcoming his surprise, Nice said that he would get the fire brigade to help him in a few minutes. Subsequently, the man disappeared and to this day no one knows who he was or what he was doing on the roof.

What was certain was that the explosion wreaked havoc. Within a fity-metre radius there was severe structural damage and windows were broken up to 500 metres away. The Docklands Light Railway, which ran very close to where the bomb had detonated, suffered significant damage and a number of the reinforced concrete support pillars were stripped of their concrete cladding leaving the reinforcing bars laid bare.

Major components of the vehicle were thrown 300 metres, some of these weighing over a kilogram in weight. During the forensic recovery the retaining plate for a Memopark timer was found and possibly a spring from a two hour Diehl clockwork timer. These components had previously been seen in the PIRA's Mark 17 timing and power units. It was estimated that the device had contained well over one ton of homemade explosive.

The Canary Wharf bomb began a political scramble to find a method of allowing Sinn Fein, the PIRA's political wing, to join the peace talks. The British government changed its hardline stance on a negotiating timetable and arms decommissioning. The *Independent on Sunday* newspaper concluded that 'not since Hiroshima has a single bomb achieved the dramatic political effect of the IRA's strike against London Docklands'. The peace talks re-started in Northern Ireland some four months later but crucially for their success, Sinn Fein was still excluded.

Six days after the Canary Wharf bomb, another series of bomb threats was received, this time to a bomb somewhere in the Charing Cross Road, Shaftsbury Avenue and Leicester Square area. The imprecise location of the device meant that a massive area had to be searched by the police and hundreds of people evacuated. During this an unattended green Jaguar Sports bag was found in a telephone kiosk outside 67, Charing Cross Road. The device was disrupted remotely by the duty EXPO and his Number 2, Police Constable John Botham. This may be significant, because if the peace process is to continue to hold, as it has at the time of writing, this is the last IRA or PIRA bomb to be rendered safe in London – although not the last one to function.

The bomb layer, who was unknown at that point, decided, or was ordered, to carry out another attack, probably to make up for the failure of the first. Three days later on Sunday night, at around 22.30 hours, a No.171 double-decker bus travelling around the Aldwych disintegrated without warning in a blinding flash. Stunned onlookers watched as the injured driver managed to bring the bus to a halt in the middle of the road. A flurry of 999 calls had emergency fire, police and ambulance crews racing to the spot. Very quickly the injured and trapped victims, including the driver, were rescued and treated for their injuries before being taken to hospital. There was, however, one male victim who was clearly dead. He had been blown in half by the explosion and was obviously either next to or carrying the bomb when it detonated. Very early on an observant police officer found a Walther P38 pistol lying on the road. Its discovery suggested that this was an 'own goal' and that a terrorist had been killed by his own bomb, probably as he was descending the steps of the bus. It was most likely that the young bomber was intending to drop his device off somewhere in the Covent Garden area. The following day Anti-Terrorist Branch detectives traced the deceased to an address in Lewisham and he was subsequently identified as Edward O'Brien. A search of the premises revealed a stash of Semtex and other bomb making paraphernalia.

One result of the explosion was that all items of left luggage on buses became immediately suspicious. Although this is clearly understandable, the fact was that the bus was never the intended target of the bomb. Thankfully, the EXPO officers were able to rapidly clear the subsequent spate of calls quickly and with the minimum of fuss.

Hammersmith Bridge, which was the target of an attack in the 1939–40 campaign, was hit again on 24 April 1996. A PIRA team planted two bombs at the southern end of the bridge. Each consisted of a charge of over seven kilograms of Semtex which was more than enough to destroy or at least severely damage the elderly structure. A coded threat was received at 22.22 hours and local officers were despatched to shut the bridge and search for the bombs. The incident again illustrates the bravery of police officers. The bridge was quickly closed to traffic and a police officer went forward in the dark and located the bombs under the roadway. They had just backed off when they heard a sharp crack – followed moments later by another. EXPO Nick Nice had just arrived at

443

the incident and his later examination confirmed that the devices had timed out and the detonators in the bombs had functioned but fortunately these failed to set off the main charge. It was a lucky escape for the police officers and bridge, but not the last attack on it.

The threat of more massive vehicle bombs remained and in London the EXPOs were regularly tasked to deal with numerous suspect vans and lorries, all of which turned out to be false alarms. The expected attack, when it came in mid-June 1996, was another massive vehicle bomb. It exploded in Corporation Street, Manchester, causing millions of pounds' worth of damage.

After this, in July, the police and Security Services had significant successes against the PIRA during two operations called *Airlines* and *Tinnitus*.

The former was to counter a PIRA plot to cripple London's electricity supply by blowing up a number of sub-stations. They had built thirty-seven long delay devices which they intended to place at various sub-stations around the capital.

Taking a leaf out of the old sabotage books, it is probable that they would have attacked exactly the same component at each sub-station. This would have complicated the repair problem because the number of spares held was limited. In the event the plot was foiled and the perpetrators arrested.

Two months later, in September, four pre-prepared bombs averaging about a ton each were discovered at the Abacus Storage Unit in Hornsey during Operation *Tinnitus*, another intelligence-led operation. Other items recovered included Semtex; timing and power units; Kalashnikov assault rifles; pistols and two under-car booby-traps. These two operations resulted in the arrest and conviction of several men and were a significant setback in the PIRA's attempts to attack London.

After the election of New Labour in 1997, the PIRA concluded that, for the time being, more was to be gained from talking than bombing and on 20 July 1997 (the fifteenth anniversary of the attacks in Hyde Park and Regent's Park) the organisation unequivocally restored the ceasefire of 1994.

The end of the year was just short of the twenty-fifth anniversary of the first PIRA bombs in London. A look at the statistics, covering all terrorist and criminal incidents in London, showed that over the period there had been 606 bombings, thirty-six shootings and seventeen kidnaps. These had resulted in the death of eighty-eight people, with a further 1,415, injured.

Over 27,500 pounds of explosive was recovered along with 809 detonators. To these statistics should be added the many hundreds of thousands of hours spent by police officers and others working to protect the public from harm.

NOTES:
1. Gurney, Peter, *Braver Men Walk Away*, Harper Collins, London, 1993.
2. Andrew, Christopher, *The Defence of the Realm, The Authorised History of M15*, Penguin Books, London, 2009.
3. *The City Bombings*, a video produced by the Commissioner of the City of London Police, September 1993.

Chapter 23

Extortion, Racism and a Rocket Propelled Grenade

'Violence is the last refuge of the incompetent.'
Isaac Asimov.

During the lead up to the PIRA ceasefire, and after its implementation, there were a number of other bombings in London which kept the police, and in particular the Anti-Terrorist Branch, busy. Once again Middle Eastern terrorism re-emerged, and a little known Palestinian group claimed responsibility for two car bombs. The first on, 26 July 1994, was left close to the Israeli Embassy. One of its security officers and the on-duty diplomatic protection officers saw the vehicle containing the bomb being parked and were immediately suspicious because of where it was being positioned. They questioned the middle-aged woman who was driving it. Brimming with confidence, she said that she was delivering a package and that she needed five minutes to do some shopping. Unperturbed by the attentions of the officers, she offered to leave the keys of the vehicle behind and then departed towards Kensington. At the time she must have known that there were just minutes left on the clock of the bomb in the boot of the car, but despite this she managed to keep an outwardly calm appearance. Just after midday the vehicle exploded without warning, injuring nineteen people. The time from the vehicle being parked to the explosion was less than six minutes. It was estimated that the bomb contained between ten and twenty kilograms of explosive. Subsequent enquiries indicate that this was probably tri-acetone tri-peroxide (TATP), a very sensitive and dangerous explosive previously only encountered in the Middle East.

In the early hours of the following morning another car bomb exploded without warning; this time outside the premises of Balfour

House in Finchley. This was used by several Jewish organisations to raise money for charity. Luckily the area was quiet and the only casualties were the driver and passenger of a vehicle that had just passed the bomb moments before it exploded. Fortunately, their injuries were only minor.

The next attack linked to the Middle East was made against the *Al Hayat* newspaper office in the Kensington Centre, 66 Hammersmith Road. On Monday, 13 January 1997, at about 09.00 hours, a security officer working for the paper opened a white envelope postmarked Alexandria, Egypt. As he did so it exploded causing serious injuries to his face and stomach. Another person close by was also slightly injured. In the police follow up, a further three devices were identified and these were made safe by EXPO Colin Goodson. Further enquiries revealed that similar devices had been sent to the *Al Hayat* offices in Washington the previous week. This revelation highlighted the importance of the need to coordinate and disseminate information about attacks wherever they may be in the world.

Like so many of the previous Middle Eastern attacks in London, the two vehicle bombs and the spate of postal bombs were isolated events. No one was arrested and the perpetrators remain unknown to this day.

An unusual home-grown criminal extortion conspiracy began on 6 December 1994 when a series of crude postal devices were delivered to six different branches of Barclay's Bank in London. Two of them functioned on opening and one member of staff suffered minor injuries. The devices were immediately linked by their similar construction and the fact that all the envelopes had a conspicuous sticker of a pop group and, underneath it, the words 'Mardi Gra [*sic*] Experience'. These were the first attacks in a sporadic criminal bombing campaign in which there were long periods of inactivity between incidents. None of those involved in the enquiry, including the investigating officers, would have guessed the identity and age of the perpetrator when he was finally arrested.

The attacks spanned four years during which time thirty-six devices were either sent in the post or left outside the targeted premises. Initially the bombs were directed against Barclay's Bank, but later Sainsbury's was also attacked. The motive was extortion, greed and an appetite for notoriety. The attacks were completely indiscriminate, as illustrated by an incident in Forest Hill in March 1998. A device, consisting of a shot gun cartridge fitted into a pipe and initiated by a simple clockwork mechanism, was hidden in a plastic bag and left close to a Sainsbury's supermarket. It functioned without warning as a youth, Dennis Curtis, was walking past and he was hit in the leg by a number of shotgun pellets.

With each subsequent attack the chances of someone being killed, or very seriously injured, mounted and it became imperative that the bomber was caught. By then, a number of ransom demands had been made, and the bomber had arranged to collect money from cash machines using a special card and number. Eventually, after a major surveillance operation he was caught as he tried to collect cash from an ATM. He was heavily disguised and wearing a wig; the officers who arrested him were amazed to discover that, when this was removed he was a man of senior years. He was later identified as sixty-one-year-old Edgar Pearce. After his arrest a search of his home revealed a wealth of evidence, including bomb making material and documentation directly linking him to some of the other attacks. The searchers also discovered a crossbow device which was built into a plastic shopping bag and which was going to be used to shoot a bolt at random at customers at an unknown Sainsbury store. Had the plan come to fruition and a member of the public been hit by a crossbow bolt the consequences could have been fatal as well as severely affecting Sainsbury's commercial activity. Pearce had been caught just in time.

In Northern Ireland the PIRA ceasefire had resulted in yet another split in the republican movement and the 32 County Sovereignty Committee (32 CSC) was formed along with their military wing the Real IRA (RIRA); later another group, the Continuity IRA (CIRA), appeared. These hardliners, dissatisfied with the direction the peace process was taking in Northern Ireland, were intent on undermining it. To gain maximum propaganda for the cause London was, once again, considered a high priority target. In July 1998, a covert operation resulted in the arrest in High Holborn of an Irishman carrying a number of incendiary devices. Subsequently, when his London flat was searched other devices and bomb making equipment were discovered. This included about a kilogram of Semtex. These devices were attributed to the new breakaway Irish terrorist groups which were soon to become synonymous with the worst ever attack in Northern Ireland.

Sometimes a horrific outrage can start a war, and sometimes a similar event can bring all sides to their senses and stop it. The devastating car bomb, which exploded in Omagh on 28 August 1998, and senselessly slaughtered twenty-nine people and injured a further 220, fell into the latter category. It had a huge psychological impact and although disastrous for the people of Omagh it provided much needed impetus to spur on the peace process in Northern Ireland. The revulsion it caused so alienated RIRA, that in the face of overwhelming condemnation, they called a ceasefire on 8 September. It would, though, be a temporary affair.

In the aftermath of the Omagh bomb, as the horror of what happened faded, RIRA regrouped. Still fervently committed to the armed struggle they began preparations for a new campaign. Before this was launched, however, the capital was subject to a short, vicious, no-warning assault by a racist, homophobic bomber.

On 17 April 1999, twenty-two-year-old David Copeland, an angry, insecure and lonely young man, set off for London with the intention of starting a race war on the streets of the capital. The spark needed to start it, in his warped opinion, was the home-made bomb which he was carrying in a holdall. Just walking around with it gave him an unfounded sense of power and purpose. The device was made from instructions he had found on the internet and, to give it added killing power, he had surrounded the explosive with a batch of four-inch nails.

Copeland seemed to hate everything. He felt he was a loser and that he did not fit in with society or his family. He had been weak and powerless at school and since had a desperate need to be part of something. That 'something' eventually resulted in him joining the British National Party (BNP). He became a right-wing racist, dreaming about a white supremacist race and worshiping the Nazi regime with its elite SS. The lack of action in the BNP left him feeling they were more interested in rhetoric than deeds and, acting totally alone, he decided to take matters into his own hands.

With the bomb in a bag, its timer running, he caught a train from his home in Fleet in Hampshire to head to London. Once there he took a taxi to the heart of Brixton with its largely Afro-Caribbean community. There, at the edge of the busy street market, he joined a queue at a bus stop, at which point he placed the bag on the ground. After a short pause he walked away leaving the device behind. A couple of traders saw it and joked that it might be a bomb; one of them picked it up and moved it to the gutter. There a young lad of fourteen had a look inside and could see nails and a large clock. At this point, for the first time, there was real concern that it was a bomb and yet another man picked up the bag and placed it on some pallets outside the Iceland store in Electric Avenue. He too looked inside and what he saw was enough to convince him that this really was an explosive device and it needed to be taken seriously. He started shouting for people to move away and at the same time the first of a number of 999 calls to the police were made.

The manager of the Iceland store was alerted by one of the security guards and began clearing the shop. Bizarrely, at this time, yet another man walked over to the bomb, removed it from its holdall and then fled the scene with the empty bag. At this point the manager of the Iceland store recalled seeing the rectangular body of the bomb surrounded by nails with an alarm clock and wires sitting on top of it. The first police officer had just arrived at the incident and the manager went over to explain what he had seen. He was just about to speak to him when the bomb exploded hurling a shower of nails across the street. People suffered the most horrendous injuries after being struck by the flying nails which embedded themselves in their flesh. One of the seriously injured was a twenty-three-month old baby boy who had a four-inch nail embedded in his head. Fortunately, he survived despite his injuries. Whilst the emergency services were racing to Brixton to help the injured, Copeland made his way home feeling relieved, elated and already planning his next strike.

A major police enquiry was launched by Scotland Yard. The officers assigned to it seizied thousands of hours' worth of CCTV footage from cameras in the area. As usual there was a crop of calls claiming responsibility from other extremist organisations, including groups like Combat 18.

The following Saturday, Copeland set off for London again with another similar bomb, this time intending to attack the mainly Asian people in the markets in the Brick Lane area of the city. Once more the timer was set and running before he left his flat, but half way to the station he realized that he did not have his rail pass and had to go home to collect it. Whilst there, he had the presence of mind to reset the time on the clock of his bomb before departing for the station a second time. In London he got off the train and took a taxi for the final leg of his journey. Arriving at Brick Lane he was desperately disappointed to discover that there were no crowds of people because the market is on a Sunday and not Saturday. With the timer running down he decided to simply abandon the bomb, which he placed between two parked cars and headed for home.

It was found by a passer-by who decided to take it to the police station in Brick Lane, but on arrival he discovered it was closed. He placed the bag in the boot of his car and went back to the police station to find out the opening times. He returned to his car and opened the bag and saw what he described as a brown cardboard box, a plastic lunch box and some screws. He decided to report the matter to the police at Leman Street, and was walking there, when he remembered the explosion in Brixton the previous week. It then occurred to him the bag might contain a bomb and he dialled 999 on his mobile. The police arrived minutes later and as they did so the bomb exploded. The car was wrecked and nails projected in all directions. Fortunately, as the area was quiet, no one was seriously injured.

As the emergency services responded to the scene of the explosion, Copeland once more quietly made his way home. He had decided that his next target would be London's gay community for whom, for some reason, he seemed to hold a special loathing.

By now, after intensive efforts, the police had managed to isolate an image of Copeland from the thousands of hours of CCTV footage that they had seized. They issued a picture of him midweek and Copeland realized that it was only a matter of time before he would be caught. So, gathering the materials to make one final device, he left his flat and set off for London, booking into one of its smaller hotels. Whilst in his room he set about manufacturing another bomb. He changed hotels on the morning of Friday, 30 April, which was also a bank holiday. As a result of the image being released, the police had been inundated with calls and were in the process of responding to the most promising leads, but it was just too late to stop the final atrocity.

That afternoon, with his last bomb in a bag, once again with the timer running but set on a shorter delay, Copeland made his way to Soho where he went into the Admiral Duncan pub. He placed the bag, with the bomb in it, on the floor and ordered a drink from the bar. A couple of people spoke briefly to him and, making the excuse that he needed some money from a cash point, he walked out of the bar leaving the bomb with just minutes left to run on the clock.

It exploded just after he had gone. This time Copeland had included some magnesium in the explosive mixture and this caused some terrible flash burns. The first police officers on scene were confronted by a dreadful scene. It was utter confusion, and shocked and wounded people were spilling out on to the pavement, some with frightful injuries.

Not far away, at Charing Cross Police Station, Police Constable John Sullivan was, with a number of other police officers, having a short break from an assignment to keep an eye on a demonstration outside Downing Street. News of the explosion in Soho quickly spread over the police radio and they arranged to be re-assigned to assist there. Their first task was to go to Trafalgar Square and clear an area for the London air ambulance to land and then escort the doctors and medics up to the scene. They did this, but had to abandon their vehicle a little way off from the pub because of the other emergency service vehicles blocking the route. On arrival at the scene smoke was still billowing out of the Admiral Duncan and injured people were lying all over the road. Sullivan saw a man in the road with badly burnt hair, who was covered with a silver emergency blanket. He went over to help him, as he did so passing a zipped up body bag. The injured man was clearly in deep shock, shaking badly and smelt 'burnt'. Sullivan decided he needed a proper blanket to keep him warm and managed to find one on a nearby ambulance. On returning he lifted the silver blanket and was horrified to see a number of nails protruding from the body of the man. He stayed with him offering reassurance and trying to prevent him from slipping into unconsciousness until it was his turn to be evacuated.

By coincidence that day marked the thirty-fifth anniversary of the establishment of the Explosives Office. To celebrate the occasion a reunion had been organised and past and present members of the office (less the on-duty teams), senior officers and retired members of the Anti-Terrorist Branch were gathering in the atrium at the Imperial War Museum for drinks.

The exception was Phil Yeaman, the duty EXPO, who was en route to the Admiral Duncan. Like many other emergency personnel he had to abandon his vehicle some distance from the scene because of congestion. As always in these types of incident there was still considerable confusion with casualties being treated for their injuries and rescuers going in to the pub to search for missing people. As the reader should now be aware, the key concern for an EXPO in this type of scenario is to check that there are no secondary devices. Yeaman therefore entered the premises:

> I saw members of the London Ambulance Service and London Fire Brigade providing emergency life support to a number of casualties. I saw the seat of an explosion on the floor adjacent to the bar and informed the people in the room that they were to leave as quickly as possible with those undergoing treatment because of the possibility of further devices and possible further injuries caused by the condition of the room. There was what appeared to be an extensively damaged male body on the floor against a wall almost directly opposite the seat of the explosion. I pointed this out to the medical staff and was told by a paramedic that the person was dead.
>
> Once the ground floor was clear of people, I requested three firemen to check that no one was on the upper floors or the cellar area, and that the electricity supply was turned off due to water pouring into the cellar from a burst pipe. When the firemen had left I checked the body on the floor for a pulse, but did not find one. I then conducted a search for secondary devices and any other explosive material in the bar area which contained a variety of abandoned rucksacks, briefcases, handbags and discarded coats and jackets. I saw a number of nails of differing sizes which were twisted and showed signs of them being in close proximity to an explosion.[1]

Yeaman then left the building and arranged for a police officer to prevent others entering as, at that point, it changed from a rescue to the scene of a crime. He then requested arrangements be made for representatives of the gas board and structural surveyors to attend the scene. Finally, he briefed the duty officer on his initial actions and his opinion of the size and nature of the device.

Back in the Imperial War Museum it was obvious that something serious had happened as phones and pagers all started beeping at the same time. The numbers in the atrium rapidly thinned as on-call and senior Anti-Terrorist Branch officers departed. News of the explosion and the likelihood of serious casualties quickly spread around the room. It changed the mood of the occasion to a more sombre tone. All those present had witnessed the carnage caused by bombs and it was saddening to think that, after thirty-five years, nothing much had changed.

Copeland, in the meantime, was resigned to the fact that he would be arrested sooner rather than later and had returned home. He was finally identified from the released CCTV images and at 14.00 hours on the morning of 1 May police raided his flat and he was arrested without a struggle. Bomb making equipment and right wing propaganda were found at the premises. Copeland was subsequently charged with the bombings and later found guilty at his trial. According to the officers that interviewed him he showed no remorse for his actions.

In Ireland, the Good Friday agreement was holding and the peace process between the main political groups was moving forward. However, the minority dissidents groups still refused to join the process and, on 20 January 2000, the RIRA announced to the *Irish News* that their ceasefire was over and called upon all republicans loyal to the cause to take up arms once more. There were a few bombs against military targets in Northern Ireland, but because of the Omagh disaster the leadership was unwilling, or unable, to launch an all-out assault using large vehicle bombs. In an effort to rally support they executed a series of attacks in London. Early in the morning of 1 June 2000, reports were received of an explosion underneath the south side of Hammersmith Bridge. The bridge, a favourite target for republican terrorists, suffered serious damage when a bomb containing around a kilogram of explosive detonated under one of the walkways. The explosion punched a hole in one of the old cast iron support beams. Swabs from the area of the explosion indicated that the explosive used was TNT. In Northern Ireland it had already been established that the RIRA had acquired some Soviet-designed demolition charges, known as the TM

500, each of which contained 500 grammes of TNT. The evidence suggested, therefore, that this was the work of the breakaway dissident republicans.

A month later, after a series of authenticated coded warnings, a device was found by British Transport Police search teams on the railway line near Twyford Avenue, Ealing. This was rendered safe by EXPO Nick Nice. The recovered components included a TM 500 confirming that this device and the one at Hammersmith Bridge were almost certainly the work of a new RIRA bombing team.

As darkness fell on the evening of 20 September 2000, there was another first for London. An unknown terrorist walked across an area of ground known as Spring Gardens, in Vauxhall, and climbed a small grassy knoll. He stood on the top of it and, from some sort of package or rucksack, pulled out a Soviet Rifle Propelled Grenade Model 22 (RPG 22). He would have had to extend the telescoped launching tube, an act which would also cock the firing mechanism. Slipping off the safety catch he placed the weapon on his shoulder and took aim at the building outlined against the skyline over the main railway line running to Waterloo Station. He pressed the trigger; with a loud bang and a flash from the back of the launcher, the rocket-propelled grenade streaked away towards the building in the distance. A couple of seconds later, the rocket struck high up on the eighth floor of the building and the warhead detonated with a sharp crack, typical of a high performance explosive. The building that had been struck was officially called the Government Communications Bureau, but most knew it as the Headquarters of MI6.

The warhead of the RPG 22 is designed to defeat armoured vehicles, including tanks. It works on principles established by Monroe and Neumann, amongst others, and is most commonly known as a hollow charge. The energy from a charge of high explosive is focussed by hollowing out the front face of a conical slab of explosive. When detonated from the rear, the shock wave passes through the explosive and the effect can be likened to light rays going through a lens. The energy from the explosion is directed, forwards and inwards, forming a jet of extremely high temperatures and pressures. If the explosive is formed around a copper cone liner, when the explosive detonates this liner is vaporised, crushed and squeezed like toothpaste out of a tube. The result is the formation of a high velocity jet of molten metal which can cut through armour like butter.

When the rocket hit the building and detonated, this molten slug penetrated the outer wall and carried on into the office space in the building. Fortunately, at this late hour, only the duty personnel and security staff were inside the building and no one was injured. The police and other emergency services were quickly notified of the explosion and a major response put in place. As part of it, EXPO Dick Travers was soon on scene. As always with an unexplained explosion, initially nothing is clear and it takes time to establish exactly what has happened. At the scene, there were only reports of a single explosion as no one had heard the bang as the RPG was launched. This was not surprising as the embankment of the mainline from Waterloo runs between the launch point and the building, some 165 metres away.

At first, there was some suspicion that there might have been an explosion in an office in the building and that this had blown out part of the exterior wall. Because of the sensitive nature of the work undertaken there, initially access was blocked. This, in turn, aroused more suspicion on the part of the first responders. It was many hours later before the empty, discarded, RPG 22 launch tube was discovered and the mystery solved.

Although a spectacular attack, the rocket actually did very little damage, but it did cause much consternation amongst those responsible for protecting VIPs in civilian armoured vehicles, particularly the Prime Minister. A great flurry of questions was asked about the capabilities of the RPG 22 system and a number of trials against lightly armoured vehicles were carried out. The results, as predicted by members of the Explosive Office, was that if the rocket would penetrate the armour on a main battle tank, it would not have much trouble against a much more lightly armoured VIP's car!

The totally indiscriminate nature of leaving booby-trapped devices, built into everyday objects, was once again demonstrated when in February 2001 a fourteen-year-old Army cadet, Stephen Menary, picked up a booby-trapped torch. He found it under a tree near the perimeter fence of a Territorial Army barracks in White City, London. The torch, a right-angle type of military design, had been left by terrorists who were clearly hoping to kill or maim one of the Parachute Regiment soldiers based there. Having picked the torch up Menary took it into a stairwell where he switched it on. Nothing happened so he removed the base and saw a rectangular battery which had become disconnected. He remade the connection screwed the base back on and switched it on again. It detonated causing terrible injuries. He lost his left forearm; the sight in his one good eye (the sight in the other being lost previously due to an illness), was deafened and had serious blast injuries to his chest and abdomen. He spent six weeks in hospital recovering from his wounds. The incident was never claimed by any terrorist group, denial being the obvious answer when an attack goes horribly wrong and an innocent young child severely injured. The evidence though pointed at it being the work of the RIRA.

This was followed in March 2001 by a bomb in a taxi left outside the BBC Television Centre in Wood Lane. A number of coded threats were received and the area cordoned and evacuated. A team led by EXPO Derek Pickford and police officers Tony Ashforth and Tony Popham was quickly on scene. They deployed a 'Wheelbarrow' to try and disrupt the device. It was next to the taxi and positioned ready to shoot out a window when the timer ran out and the device functioned. Along with the taxi the 'Wheelbarrow' was destroyed in the blast, but fortunately no one was seriously injured. The wrecked 'Wheelbarrow' was a reminder of the value of such remote equipment; in the early days of the EXPO office a manual approach to the taxi would have been the order of the day.

Next, a couple of small bombs exploded near the sorting office in Hendon but neither caused much damage and were of little value as far as the terrorist campaign was concerned. Finally, on 3 August 2001, coded bomb threats were received at 23.33 hours warning that a vehicle bomb was due to explode somewhere in Ealing Broadway. Once again police rushed to the scene and began a search for the suspect vehicle but, as with the bomb at Canary Wharf, outside Central London and late at night there are only a few police officers immediately available to respond to such calls. Finding a suspect vehicle, organising suitable cordons and evacuating people are tasks that require large numbers of officers. Reinforcements from Central London were called, along with an EXPO, but the bomb exploded at midnight before any of these had arrived. Eleven people were injured in the blast – most by flying glass – and significant damage was done to the buildings on The Broadway. Parts of the car were blown 200 metres and a water main ruptured where it had detonated. The water caused a considerable amount of flooding and flushed some of the debris half a mile down The Broadway. The key significance of this bomb is that, up to the time of writing, it was the last bomb linked to Irish terrorism to detonate in London. The last Irish bomb on the mainland was at Birmingham on 3 November 2001 when a vehicle containing forty kilograms of homemade explosive partially detonated.

The capabilities of the breakaway dissident republican groups were, at that time, rapidly being whittled away by a combination of a lack of support from within the community in Ireland and by the excellent work of the police and security services. The peace process itself was seen to be succeeding with the main political parties fully engaged in the Northern Ireland Assembly. The talk everywhere was of a peace dividend. In theory, security should have been relaxed and all the counter-terrorist organisations scaled down, but events elsewhere in the world would, once again, have a significant impact on London.

The most dramatic was the suicide attacks on 11 September 2001. All over the world, the images of two passenger jets flying into the Twin Towers in New York, and their subsequent collapse, became ingrained on the minds of a generation. Another airliner crashed into the Pentagon and in the last of the four aircraft hijacked the passengers bravely tried to regain control of the aircraft which caused it to crash short of its target. The final casualty list recorded the deaths of over 3,000 people, more than were killed in the Japanese attack on the American Fleet in Pearl Harbor in 1941. The fact that ten per cent of these individuals were foreign nationals, many of them British, left no doubt about the potential threat from Al-Qaeda and other Islamic extremists right across the world. Any thoughts of scaling back on security were quickly shelved and the police, and other security agencies, refocused their energies on this new threat. It was another attack in America, however, that had a more immediate effect on London.

Nine days after the jets crashed into the Twin Towers and the Pentagon, letters containing a granular substance were delivered to NBC News and the *New York Post*. They contained deadly anthrax spores. On 2 October a sixty-three-year-old man, Bob Stevens, was admitted to hospital with a high fever, vomiting and convulsions. He died of the disease three days later. The Centre for Disease Control and Prevention now became aware of the incident and began an investigation. Two more letters containing the spores were delivered on 9 October and included the warning: '09-11-01. You cannot stop us. We have this anthrax.' A week later twelve more people were being treated for the disease and a nationwide inquiry was underway. The confirmation that a biological warfare agent had been released, which was both invisible and odourless, and which had been dispersed using the letters, spread fear and anxiety amongst an already nervous American population. It would eventually kill five people.

As the news spread, the world became a hoaxer's paradise. A wide range of people, for a variety of motives, began posting envelopes containing powder. Many included letters warning the recipients that the powder they contained was anthrax or other biological agents. London was no exception and soon calls were being received from commercial companies, and worried members of the public, that they had received letters containing white powder. Although, subsequently, they all turned out to be false alarms, the ability of these letters to generate anxiety and fear was undeniable. For example, in one incident, an elderly clerk working at one of the government departments opened an envelope and withdrew a folded letter. As she unfolded the paper she was covered in a dusting of fine-white powder. The text of the letter warned her that she had been contaminated by anthrax and would die in agony in a few days. In accordance with the procedures in place, should such an event occur, she was left alone whilst the rest of the staff were moved to and confined in another office. Just being left alone, while the incident was investigated, caused her considerable distress and even when it was concluded that the incident was a false alarm she was still fearful for her health. In another similar case, at an embassy, a woman collapsed four hours after an incident had been declared a false alarm. After treatment in hospital it was concluded that she had suffered from a delayed psychosomatic reaction.

At the time, no portable biological detectors were available and, where a potentially serious threat existed, samples of powder were sealed in airtight containers and sent to Porton Down for analysis. Although members of the Explosive Office had undertaken training to deal with devices containing chemical, biological or radioactive agents this was of little use against the letters. Common sense and a proportionate response soon became the order of the day, and the EXPOs became expert at identifying common substances. Most of the letters contained sugar, salt or talcum powder; if it had blue flecks it was washing powder, yellow liquids were generally urine and, finally, the most unpleasant to deal with were those containing excrement which, in themselves, harboured thousands of biological hazards. All had to be dealt with in a professional manner, a key factor being the reassurance of the public. This was necessary because, as already explained, even the threat of a chemical or biological agent was enough to generate psychosomatic reactions in some people. Immediate symptoms are of course most unlikely with biological agents because most of them have long incubation times. Some incidents provided an element of humour. A task to deal with a barrel of RICIN (enough to poison whole of the population of the UK) was resolved when the EXPO went forward and discovered a barrel containing RESIN. In another, a letter warned of deadly 'ANFRAX', but this was discounted on the basis that if the sender could not spell it, he or she was unlikely to be able to make it.

Although no one has ever been prosecuted for the American Anthrax attacks which sparked the crisis, it was never, as was originally thought, linked to Islamic extremism and was most likely the actions of an individual American.

In terms of bombings, for London the years from 2002 to 2005 were remarkably peaceful. There were a few criminal incidents, for example in August 2002 an explosion occurred in a flat in Holgate Court, Kings Drive in Edgeware. In it the occupier of the flat, Shanker Venkatesan, was killed whilst preparing home-made explosives. There was no evidence to link him to any terrorist groups and he was probably experimenting on his own. In 2004, a drug addict was killed in Romford when a bomb he was preparing exploded as he was working on it.

In the Explosives Office, everyone was aware of the growing Al-Qaeda threat and the disturbing trend towards the use of suicide bombers. The deployment of British troops in both Iraq and Afghanistan clearly made Britain and British interests overseas prime targets. Elsewhere, the bombs on the trains in Madrid, the destruction of the Paradise hotel in Mombassa, Kenya, the suicide bombings in Casablanca, Morocco and many others were an indication of the international nature of the threat. Reports of British citizens being trained by Al-Qaeda in Afghanistan camps were received and were a real cause for concern.

NOTE:
1. Statement by Philip Yeaman, 2 May 1999.

Chapter 24

Dying to Kill

'Sheer terror bold and brilliant.'
The advertisement on the side of the bus blown up in Tavistock
Square, 7 July 2005.

The reader will recall Lord Tiverton's quote from the introduction
that 'it is bombs not bombers that count' and in keeping with this
philosophy I have avoided describing, in depth, the political motives
of the bombers, be they terrorist or state-sponsored. Equally, I have not
provided detailed technical capabilities of the bomb-delivery systems.
My interest has been the bombs and their effects and, where they fail to
explode, their safe subsequent disposal. It is not possible to take this
course with the suicide bombers of 7 and 21 July 2005. The Zeppelin,
Gotha or Heinkel crews dropping their lethal loads, or IRA terrorists
placing IEDs in position, simply delivered their bombs to the intended
targets. Suicide bombers are not only the delivery system, they are an
intimate and integral part of the device. The suicide bomber may be
involved in its manufacture but, crucially, they deliver it and act as the
fuze choosing the optimum time and place of initiation. They are, quite
literally, a functioning part of the bomb and without their input it will
not work. Undertaking such an extreme action, which requires the
death of the bomber, is not an act easily explained or understood.

In the preceding chapters the conflicts which resulted in attacks on
London have been resolved and the motives for bombing the capital
removed (although a possible exception is Irish Republicanism which
history shows has capacity for resurgence). The 2005 suicide bombs and
failed suicide bombs in the capital are part of a new global conflict. It is
based on religious extremism (which is nothing new) and is truly
international in nature, in that the training and attacks are carried out

worldwide. Disturbingly in London's case, some of the first bombers were British nationals, who had turned against their country.

When examining the London suicide bombers' motives it is clear that their actions are directly linked to events elsewhere the world. American, British and, to a lesser extent, European foreign policies, particularly in Iraq, Afghanistan and more recently in Syria and Libya, are seen in many parts of the Islamic community as imperialist, unjust, and with the hidden agenda of exploiting both the people and their natural resources, particularly oil. The result has been the emergence of religious fundamentalism which is at odds with western societies and much of their current culture. Some young Muslims feel no allegiance to the Crown and their sympathies lie thousands of miles away with the now dead Bin Laden and Al Queda or the recently emerged Islamic State.

More than any other form of terrorist attack, suicide bombers are most likely to cause mass casualties amongst the intended victims. One American study has shown that suicide terrorism only constituted three per cent of attacks, but caused forty-eight per cent of the fatalities. They provide one of the most effective methods of intimidating and spreading fear amongst their enemies. In comparison to the use of conventional weapons, suicide terrorism requires very little means and minimum preparation. In the short term, the suicide bomber can generate a feeling of helplessness, despair and even panic in the attacked population.

A catalyst for the new generation of suicide bombers is the age of digital imagery which has enhanced the so-called 'CNN effect'. Now high-quality digital cameras can record anything that happens anywhere in the world. Cheap computers, smart phones, satellite communications and the internet enable the images to be beamed, streamed and viewed almost anywhere else on the planet. This has had a dramatic impact, which has worked against the West, particularly where images are shown of civilian casualties resulting from munitions malfunctions or targeting errors, for example when unmanned drones are used. At the other end of the spectrum it has enabled videos of attacks against the coalition forces in Iraq and Afghanistan to reach a world-wide audience. A combination of these images has fed the current crisis which has seen the steady rise of the suicide bomber. Censorship, which was once such a powerful tool, is no longer the weapon it used to be.

On the face of it there are political, religious, military, technical and organisational reasons for using suicide bombs. Although the perpetrators may be inspired by some, or all, of these motives, it takes much more than that to turn an individual into a suicide bomber. There are two clear components behind every successful suicide attack; motivated individuals and the organisation that sends them. The bombers' recruitment, training and eventual dispatch is, in most cases, a distinct and well-structured process and the organisations that send them are clearly rationally motivated. It should be clear that suicide bombers are rarely veteran members of the organisation that despatches them. The leaders who inspire others to sacrifice their lives are in search of power; they will not commit such acts themselves as they are too important to die. The senior Al-Qaeda leadership was happy to sponsor the bombers whilst hiding in the hills in Afghanistan and Pakistan. The use of the tactic is seen, by them, as a coercive strategy directed against democratic societies intended to influence their foreign policy.

The process of recruiting is made easier if the potential bomber takes the first step and volunteers for an operation. Generally, the best recruits are those who are young adults or youths, often without their own family commitments, although this is not always the case. Frequently, the selection process starts at a local level with limited indoctrination. It is often inspired by radical Islamic literature, both printed and on the internet, and by sermons from local firebrand clerics.

The volunteer's suitability for the task must then be assessed and involves grooming and brainwashing the candidate. This necessitates a change in a whole set of attitudes and beliefs, and their replacement with a new and sinister purpose. The path to violence is an indoctrination process in which the individual is subject to persuasive thematic material and charismatic images in which the feeling of calling wells up in the bomber and, at the same time, decreases their fear of death. Where groups of suicide bombers are involved a strong sense of comradeship is engendered between them resulting in a bond which will be almost impossible for the individual to break. In fact, the techniques are not far removed from those employed by armed forces around the world in which a group of soldiers are bound together by training, comradeship and actual combat. These soldiers can be persuaded to undertake incredibly dangerous missions where the risk of death or serious injury is very high.

The suicide bombers' training is often undertaken in closed-off and remote camps, where there is no antidote to the psychological indoctrination. There religious and peer pressure are applied in equal measure by a strong, dominant and sometimes brutal organisation. Some argue that suicide bombers are coerced; if they are, it is in such subtle ways that they do not realize it. The promise of martyrdom, as a means to eternal glory, is used to commit the bombers to their missions.

It is recognised that an individual suicide bomber will not win by his or her self, but in combination with others their sacrifice will help show the world the true nature of their commitment and the inhumanity of the enemy. There seems no doubt that after undergoing the indoctrination process the suicide bombers are absolutely committed to their cause and genuinely believe in the promises of an afterlife with God. The time between training and the actual attacks see little dilution in the effects of the indoctrination. If anything the bombers seem to relish the prospect of dying and, in their close circle, bask in the glory of the concept of martyrdom. For example, in the video he made with his daughter, Mohammad Sidique Khan, one of the 7 July bombers, tells his young child that, 'I have to do this thing for our future'. In it he shows affection for her but, this has no influence on his decision to carry out the suicide bombings. More recently, in the USA the parents of a six-month baby handed over the child before setting off on a shooting spree which ended in their death. It is difficult to see how either child will benefit from the attacks, but it does illustrate how thorough the indoctrination process is. In Khan's case he seems to be enjoying the celebrity status which he knows will follow the suicide attacks.

Suggestions that suicide bombers suffer from low social status are not true, but some recent studies indicate that many of them have some borderline personality disorders. Many are plagued by feelings of shame and use defence mechanisms that enable them to cast blame on others. The roots of this disorder are in their childhood experiences, and often result in the individual being attracted to charismatic leaders. They are not leading figures in their communities or organisations, but are often on the fringes of such societies. They are not normally highly educated, but also not illiterate. They are generally not very successful but rarely complete failures. To all outward appearances they are just ordinary people, which is why they are so hard to identify.

Youths with these characteristics are presented with the most exalted myths and fantasies of the society in which they live. They are offered a way of channelling their deep-seated aggression and frustration which will, according to the handlers, change the world and transform them into some sort of mythical hero and secure them a place in history. There are, of course, exceptions to this general rule. Firstly, there are young immature or mentally-ill people who are duped. Another group include those where revenge is the overriding motive, particularly men and women whose families (especially children) have been killed. Dr Bilal Abdulla, who planned and carried out the failed car bomb attacks in London, had developed an intense loathing of the West because of the wars in the Middle East waged by the United States and Britain. The motive for the subsequent attack at Glasgow airport, where he and his accomplice, Mohammed Asha, attempted to blow up the terminal building, combined revenge and the need to make up for the failure of the London bombs. These circumstances, though, do not apply in the case of the London suicide bombers.

A key element in the indoctrination process is the use of portraits and videos made before the bombers set off on their missions. They serve two purposes; firstly, they have become potent symbols of resistance which serve to encourage others and, after an attack, they provide a voice from beyond the grave to allow the suicide bomber to justify his actions and say goodbye to loved ones. Make no mistake, the production is carefully supervised. The suicide is portrayed as a heroic act. There are no signs of helplessness or hopelessness in these videos. They help raise the profile of the bomber to celebrity status. The perpetrators themselves are often seen wearing military uniforms, headbands and brandishing weapons; they look and sound like warriors. They provide the promise that the bomber will not be forgotten and will impress subsequent generations. Listening to their messages once they are dead is, in many ways, chilling. Post-incident, the cold, calm appearance of the bomber who is facing imminent death and is preparing to kill and maim a crowd of innocent victims is shocking. Shehzad Tanweer said: 'What you have witnessed now is only the beginning', and 'We love death the way you love life'. This implies the threat of further attacks and suggests it will get worse before it gets better. The messages help foster a sense of disbelief and powerlessness within the targeted society.

Secondly, the videos play a key role in coercing the bombers to carry out their mission. Once made, it is almost impossible for them to change their minds, there is no way back for the perpetrator; failure to carry out the planned attack will simply result in a further loss of self-esteem and risks condemnation from the community that has actively supported the bomber.

In religiously-motivated attacks there is often a last ceremony before the bomber or bombers set off on their mission. There may also be a religious ritual cleansing before the final attack. In the process the prospective bomber sees his or her picture placed amongst other fallen heroes and the person becomes a living martyr. They are the centre of attention and given an overriding sense of importance. However, like the death of Bobby Sands in the hunger strike in Northern Ireland, it is only the first few martyrs that make history. The same applies to suicide bombers; in later attacks few are remembered, unless the outcome of the bombing is really atrocious.

Although a statement of the obvious, one of the most depressing things about young suicide bombers is that there is no chance of them ever regretting their actions. There is no going back. Many terrorists, as they grow older, reflect on what they have done, and although they still passionately believe in their cause they revert to non-violent means to achieve their aim. The peace being forged in Northern Ireland perhaps best illustrates this point. Those undertaking the fighting at the start of the most recent campaign are now those making the peace. For the young, indoctrinated and highly-motivated suicide bomber there is no chance for such reflection. It helps their handlers maintain the myth of the suicide bomber, once dead there can be no contradictions or questioning of motives.

In my view, the bombers on 7 July 2005, and those whose attacks failed two weeks later, meet most of the criteria described above. The only difference being that those convicted of the failed attacks will have the opportunity to reflect on their actions. It would be interesting to interview them in another twenty years to see if their opinions have changed.

Much has been written about the day of the bombings themselves, and it is not my intention to try to portray each incident in depth. Instead I intend to describe the unfolding events at Aldgate, as this was, by a few moments, the first bomb that exploded. The explosions at Edgware Road and deep underground between King's Cross and Russell Square prompted similar reactions and responses, but I will not cover these in detail.

Up until this point, as far as the EXPO office is concerned, I have, with their consent, named the individuals linked with various incidents, as they have all retired. For obvious security reasons it would be wrong of me to name those EXPOs still serving and I shall not do so. The reader will, by now, understand that bombs that explode present the bomb disposal officer with less of a problem than those that have not. At such scenes there are two priorities. The first is to ensure there are no secondary devices; the other is the need to carry out a preliminary investigation to begin the process of establishing exactly what happened and what type and size of bomb was used.

Attacks against the public transport system in London are not new, but after the killing of 191 people on rush hour trains in Madrid in March 2004, the response to such an attack in the capital was something which was much discussed in the EXPO office. After the Madrid attack it was known that a failed bomb, thought to have been abandoned luggage, was recovered with other property, to a police station. Here it was left until it was opened to try and identify the owner. At that point the device was discovered and later rendered safe. This should never have happened. The public will accept that attacks cannot be stopped, and that the immediate response is bound to be chaotic and confusing. It is not acceptable, however, for a failed bomb to be missed and removed from the scene thus endangering more lives.

As I said in the introduction, words cannot adequately describe the material damage caused by bombs, nor the toll in terms of human suffering, be it physical injury, mental anguish or both. No two incidents could be described as identical, and no single incident looks the same to any two persons involved in it. On the morning of 7 July, hundreds of police officers, firefighters and ambulance crews, responded to the unfolding drama as reports of the explosions flooded in. It is what they are trained to do. They were aided by the staff of the Underground, fellow travellers and other people who always get drawn in and help. They can all be proud of what they did. There were some people, as there always are, who did not get involved, they had important meetings to go to, didn't want to get dirty, or who simply looked the other way. Some of them will regret their decisions. This is certainly true of those caught up in the explosion at Aldgate.

Predictably, people have vivid, but very different recollections of the events which played out that day. Even time, which is constant, seemed to be drawn out or concertinaed depending on the point of view of those involved. For the victims on the trains, many savagely wounded and shocked, it seemed forever before help arrived. For those responding, time was condensed and actions that seemed to take a few seconds often took much longer. Equally, encounters underground were seen from completely different viewpoints, particularly between rescuers and those being rescued.

What follows are a few accounts from the hundreds of emergency service personnel and other people who chose to get involved. They are a snapshot of some of these memories. The common thread for both victims and rescuers is that it was the most harrowing time of their lives.

The mood in London in the early morning of 7 July 2005 was one of jubilation. Those sitting reading their papers on trains, buses or the Underground were digesting the news that the capital had, against the odds, won the competition to hold the Olympics in 2012. It promised the regeneration of much of the East End and great kudos for the capital as a whole. In Scotland, Tony Blair was hosting the opening of the G8 summit. By chance, four days earlier the emergency services had carried out a major exercise based on a terrorist attack using chemical weapons at Bank Station. Although valuable lessons were learned, it would not prepare the responders for the events about to unfold in the centre of London, and may in some small way, have delayed their response.

That morning Mohammad Sidique Khan, Shehzad Tanweer, Germaine Lindsay and Hasib Hussain, all of whom had prepared and planned the attack, met at a car park in Luton. Lindsay travelled alone, arriving in a Fiat Brava; the other three arrived from Leeds in a Nissan Micra. They exchanged greetings, put on four large rucksacks containing their homemade bombs, and caught a train to King's Cross Station. It was there that they were caught on camera at around 08.30 hours before descending into the Underground. It will never be known how they bid each other farewell. Did they shake hands, hug each other or simply exchange a knowing assassins' smile, before they set off to catch four different underground trains?

Shehzad Tanweer boarded a Circle Line train, No.204, and headed out towards Liverpool Street Station. Mohammad Sidique Khan got on the second carriage of a westbound Circle Line train en route to Edgeware Road. Germaine Lindsay caught a southbound Piccadilly Line train. It is not clear what happened to Hasib Hussain. There is a theory that the bombs were going to be detonated underground at the four points of the compass and that Hussain should have got on a Northern Line train. However, he was not familiar with the Underground system and the line had experienced some technical delays that morning. Being the middle of the rush hour, the trains would have been packed and maybe he could not get on one. Alternatively, once alone and in a highly nervous state, and with the awfulness of what he was going to have to do finally dawning on him, he may have decided not to go ahead with the plan. In any event, he failed to catch a train. He then began to walk around outside King's Cross, perhaps hoping that the others had aborted the plan and chosen not to die, but it was already too late.

Police Constable Liz Kenworthy was travelling to work that morning to attend a 'Safer Schools' conference in Westminster. She was on the Circle Line train on which Shehzad Tanweer was travelling. Fortunately for her, she was towards the rear of the train with one full carriage between her and the bomber. She was standing with a rucksack, holding on a rail, just looking out the window of the train doors. We have already encountered Liz's family – her maiden name was Goodwin and it will be recalled that her father had been a conscientious objector during the Second World War. He had joined the Non Combatant Corps and volunteered to work with the Royal Engineer bomb disposal units around London. Liz was about to have her own confrontation with the effects of a bomb.

That same morning, Andrew Brown had flown from Liverpool to London City Airport. He was travelling to Westminster to attend an Airport Operations Association workshop. After a bus journey to Liverpool Street he boarded Circle Line train 204 and took a seat in the rear of the second carriage, just feet from Shehzad Tanweer.

At 08.50 hours Shehzad Tanweer detonated his bomb as the train travelled from Liverpool Street to Aldgate. The blast cut the power to the train and it came to a juddering halt, in the tunnel about 100 metres in from the platform at Aldgate Station. For the passengers in the same carriage there was no hint or warning of what was about to happen. There was no fear or time to be afraid, just a blinding flash. The explosion ripped through the compartment and the scene went from normal to nightmare in a fraction of a second.

Andy Brown recalled nothing more than the flash, followed by a dull thud, and a wave of heat passing through the carriage. He then passed out and was unconscious for an indeterminate time, but probably around ten minutes.

Liz Kenworthy heard a loud crash as the bomb detonated, but initially thought that there had been a collision with another train or that a carriage had come off the rails. The train came to an abrupt halt with all the passengers in her compartment muttering and grumbling about the hold-up. Thinking the accident would cause a delay she drafted a simple text message on her phone stating that there had been an incident and that she would be late for work, but she was ok. She intended to send this as soon she emerged from the tunnel. It was not totally dark, as the train had come to a halt in a triple section of the track, with fluorescent lights, still intact, either side of the tunnel. Moment's later smoke began to filter through the door she was standing next to. It was then that she heard the sounds of people screaming and shouting from the carriages towards the front of the train.

Her police training kicked in and she got out her Warrant Card and made her way towards the commotion at the front end of the train. As she moved into the next carriage she saw a number of lightly wounded people and at this point she grasped that this was not a minor incident. The shouting and screaming was now louder and she pushed on. In the dim light she now saw people cut, bleeding, filthy dirty and walking like zombies down the centre of the train. As she neared the end of the carriage a man said that she should not go any further, but she pushed passed him and reached the doors that led to the bombed compartment.

Around this time Andy Brown slowly regained consciousness, possibly hastened by the fact that he was being electrocuted by some loose wires which were part of the train's low voltage electrical system and which had been blown down in the explosion. He was still sitting, but his upper torso and the seatback had been blown backwards, almost through the shattered window in the carriage. Like many people, his initial thought was that it was an accident; it was dark, very smoky and there was debris, including bent and twisted panelling, spread all around him. He could hear other people groaning and calling for help and as he was not aware of the extent of his own injuries, he automatically attempted to stand up. When he tried to move his legs there was almost no response and, as he regained more of his senses, he realised that he was seriously injured and dropped back into his seat. He looked down at his right leg and could see that it was, as he later described, 'shredded', the left one too was also very badly smashed. Surprisingly, considering his injuries, he does not remember being in any great pain and he recalls being in a clear and calm state. People were still crying for help around him but he knew instinctively that in his parlous condition there was nothing he could do to help them and he resigned himself to waiting for rescuers to arrive.

Liz Kenworthy, still clutching her phone and her Warrant Card, went through the first of the interconnecting doors leading to the carriage where the explosion had occurred. The metal was bent and twisted and she looked through the door to confront a desperate scene. Even though it was dark and smoke-filled she could see that the carriage had been disembowelled. There was a mass of twisted metal, the windows had been blown out and there was a gaping hole in the floor of the train. Like the bombs in the Blitz, the shock wave from the explosion had disturbed decades of ingrained dirt, grime and grit in the tunnel and everything was fifthly and covered in a layer of black soot. Amongst this dreadful scene Liz could see blood spattered around the carriage and a number of people. Some were alive and crying for help, others quiet or unconscious and some, almost certainly, dead.

It was now clear to her what she was dealing with and once more her police training kicked in. She recalled what she had been taught; leave the obviously dead, evacuate the injured and beware of secondary devices. It occurred to her that in this instance it would be impossible to move the injured on her own. Equally, in the dark smoky chaos, she was in no position to search for secondary devices. All she could do was provide some basic first aid and reassurance to the injured.

To her immediate left there was a lady who had been pinioned to the floor of the carriage by some wreckage including a heavy piece of twisted metal on her arm. Liz cleared some of the debris to help her breathe, but left her arm alone as she thought that if she tried to move the metal she might cause more bleeding. At this point the shocked victim was shouting and, as this meant she was breathing, Liz turned her attention to the right of the carriage where there were two more badly injured passengers.

The first, on the right, was another woman who had sustained serious injuries to both of her legs and had further wounds to her lower abdomen. Next to her was Andy Brown who she could clearly see had also suffered severe leg injuries and who was bleeding badly. She spoke to him to reassure him, and he immediately asked if he had lost his leg. She replied that he probably had but that he was going to live. He then asked for her green corduroy jacket which she took off and between them it was wrapped and tied around his leg in an attempt to stem the bleeding.

At this point a man appeared at the doorway of the carriage she had just come through and asked if he could help. Aware of her own mortality she gave him her rucksack, Warrant Card and telephone and then asked him to go and find ties or T-shirts which she could use to stem the bleeding of the three conscious casualties she was talking to. At this time, she noticed another seriously injured man who was moving, but whom she could not reach because of the twisted metal and the hole in the floor. She was acutely aware that, as there was no first aid equipment, she could only give the most basic of help to the injured. She kept talking to all three of the casualties close to her, trying to reassure them that help would soon arrive, and that they would all be ok. Brown was talking quietly, but the two women were crying and shouting.

Soon afterwards the unknown man who had gone to get T-shirts and ties reappeared and handed over what he had managed to find. Liz took a T-shirt and pressed it into the wound on the woman's abdomen and told her to clutch it to her midriff. This she did.

Other than providing constant reassurance there seemed very little that Liz could do and she was aware of a sense of helplessness. She was conscious that some other passengers on the other side of the seat of the explosion were, like her, trying to help the seriously injured. Between them, amongst the jagged metal, were the bodies of those beyond help.

Detective Constable Antonio Silvestro was on duty, in plain-clothes, in the British Transport Police (BTP) offices located immediately above Aldgate Station when he unexpectedly felt the building shake. His first thought was that a vehicle had crashed into the offices, but he quickly realised that something had happened down in the Underground. He immediately went down to the station platform, where some of the staff told him that there had been a power surge, but already black smoke was emerging from the tunnel. Silvestro dashed back upstairs, grabbed a notepad and, within a couple of minutes, was back on the platform. He made the decision to go into the tunnel; he grabbed a torch and florescent jacket, checked that the power to the live rail was off, and, accompanied by some of the Underground staff, headed for the tunnel. As they entered it the first of the passengers emerged from the smoke. They all had black faces and white eyes and, bizarrely, reminded Silvestro of the dark-faced, bright-eyed dancers in Michael Jackson's *Thriller* video. He told them to keep going and set off to find out what had happened to the train. The smoke was still quite thick and had an acrid smell making it hard to breathe. Despite this he went on and, rounding the slight curve in the track, saw the train in the murky darkness for the first time.

As he reached the stranded train he could see people trapped inside the first undamaged carriage and was thinking about how he might get them out as the doors were all firmly shut. He still had no idea that an explosion had occurred but could hear people shouting for help further down the tunnel. Proceeding on he reached the mangled wreckage of the carriage in which the bomb had detonated and at that point realized what had happened.

Above ground, in the Fenchurch Street area, Sergeant Neil Kemp of the City of London Police was running a plain-clothes operation with six other officers targeting pickpockets. The police officers were out on foot and Kemp was sitting in an unmarked back-up vehicle a short distance from Aldgate. The first indication that something was amiss was around 08.55 hours when calls were made for assistance with a power surge and explosion at Liverpool Street. Shortly afterwards another call for assistance was received, this time to smoke issuing from Aldgate Underground Station. As no other police units were available to respond immediately to this second call, Kemp radioed-in that he was close to the area and would investigate. He called off the covert operation and drove to the Aldgate arriving at 09.00 hours. He parked his vehicle and jumped out. As he entered the station he saw a woman, bleeding badly, emerge onto the street. This was his first indication that something serious had happened and, like many others, he assumed that it was most likely that there had been some form of train crash. Kemp, with another officer who had arrived on foot, descended the steps into the station.

Antonio Silvestro had, in the meantime, reached the bombed carriage. He approached it at the point where the doors had been blown off, looked in and made himself known to the people there, explaining who he was. He recalled a young couple who were cradling a woman with serious leg injuries lying across their laps. There was a doctor there too who was holding her up and doing her best to treat her. Silvestro asked what he could do to assist, but like Liz and the other helpers, with no first aid equipment there was little of practical value that he could do. A clear imperative was to start getting more of the lightly wounded people from the bombed carriage out of the tunnel, and help those still stuck on the other carriages to escape from the train.

By now, Sergeant Kemp had arrived on the platform at Aldgate. Some of the station staff, who had stayed on the platform, indicated that they believed that there had been a train crash in the tunnel from which smoke was still issuing. Kemp, like Silvestro, immediately decided that the only course of action was to go to the train and find out what had happened. Leaving one officer to take care of casualties emerging from the tunnel, and after checking that the power had been switched off (a commonly asked question that day), Kemp set off to investigate the incident on the train, encountering more walking wounded, some suffering from burns, blast and glass injuries.

As he approached the train there was still plenty of smoke lingering in the tunnel. His major concern was that a fire might break out and that the uninjured, but trapped, people needed to be evacuated as soon as possible. He passed the carriage where the explosion had occurred; avoiding two obviously dead bodies on the track, and went to check the rear of the train which was still full of passengers, many of who did not know what had happened and seemed unsure of what to do.

Kemp determined that the key action at this point was to inform the City Police control room that a bomb had exploded so they could organise a major response. He headed back to the front of the train, briefly pausing to peer into the bombed carriage. Here he could see what he initially overestimated to be ten to twenty dead and many more wounded. Resisting the urge to provide immediate help, and as his radio would not work underground, he set off for the tunnel entrance to make the all-important radio call. As he walked down the tunnel he came to an overhead storm drain grating and decided to see if his radio worked there. Fortunately, it did, and he called an 'Active Message'. On hearing this broadcast all other users were required to stop transmitting.

Kemp then calmly went through the CHALET mnemonic, providing the best information about, Casualties, Hazards, Access, the Location of the train, the Emergency response required, and the Type of incident – in this case clearly an explosion. For those at the City Police control room this was the first time that they had been given a clear idea of what had happened, and that a bomb was the cause.

At Whitechapel Fire Station, after a hot summer's night, Sub-Officer Sean Clarke was about to go off duty at 09.00 hours when a call came in to a possible explosion in St Botolph Street (which is parallel to Aldgate Street). With two fire appliances he swiftly made his way to the area, the route taking them past the front of Aldgate Station. As they drove by the booking hall they saw smoke and a few people, some of them injured, spilling out on to the pavement. The second fire engine stopped at the front of the station, but Clarke's appliance had already gone too far, so did a quick loop around St Botolph Street and back to the entrance. It gave Clarke a few moments to think. With years of experience of responding to emergency calls (including the fire at King's Cross), he instinctively knew that it was a serious incident. During the loop he told his crew to check that their belt-mounted radiation pagers were switched on.

As they pulled up outside the station more injured people were emerging on to the pavement. The crew immediately grabbed their first aid equipment and began treating the injured. Clarke, as the senior fire officer present, went into the station where he met the duty manager and had a brief discussion about what appeared to have had happened.

He descended the steps and walked along to the end of the platform where he was able to look along the track. By now some of the smoke had cleared and he could see the end of the train and more injured people. He instinctively knew that more resources were needed to deal with the incident. He went back up the stairs and got on to the fire brigade control and declared a major incident. He was later questioned about the speed at which he made this decision. As the events unfolded over London that day no one could have doubted that he made the right call.

By now at least fifteen to twenty minutes had passed since the explosion and Liz kept looking to see if help was coming, but it would be a while longer before full-scale medical assistance arrived. She continued to reassure the three injured passengers closest to her. Outside, on the track, some people were walking past the train towards Aldgate and it seemed to her that they were deliberately avoiding looking towards the shattered carriage. At one point an Asian man came to the window, threw in his tie and then left. By now Andy Brown was finding it hard to breath and asked for some water. Liz reached over to him and tried to clear some of the grime away from his face using a cloth and water she had been given by the man that had taken her rucksack. At this point the doctor on the other side of the seat of the explosion told her not to give him anything to drink. She replied, 'No, I am not I am just cleaning his mouth'.

By now more emergency vehicles were en route to the incident, some from Shadwell and another from Bethnal Green. Tyrone Robinson, the Blue Watch commander, had responded with a single appliance, to a call to 'smoke issuing' from Aldgate Station. En route the call changed from 'smoke issuing' to a possible explosion, but no one was really sure what to expect. On arrival the crew was instructed to dump some cutting equipment on the stairs leading to the platform and lay out a fire hose. Once they had done this they made their way down to the platform itself where they encountered more walking-wounded. Some of these people were clearly very distressed and were escorted up the stairs to the street where, by now, London Ambulance crews were arriving.

In the EXPO office, the CAD (Computer Aided Despatch) system was being monitored and the first ambiguous reports of the incident were being noted. More information about incidents elsewhere on the Underground was also beginning to feed in. The initial information received indicated that there had been a small electrical explosion; possibly in the ticket office in Liverpool Street Station and that there were two fatalities. The cause was thought to be an electrical fault. It was immediately apparent to the duty team that an electrical explosion was unlikely to cause two deaths and they decided to head for Liverpool Street Station. On the way they were re-tasked to Aldgate where, by now, there were reports of many injured people leaving the station. The team arrived to find a confused situation. As always in this type of incident, individual emergency responders set about their own particular tasks whilst in slower time control systems are established. One major concern was raised that this might be a chemical incident. This may have been a result of the exercise four days previously, but the EXPO involved was adamant that this was most unlikely and that rescue of casualties was the main priority.

Back in the tunnel, Sergeant Kemp had returned to the train and was trying, with the officers who had accompanied him, to open the doors in the sides of the rear carriages, using track-side debris, to allow people off. With no power, this was much harder than he anticipated and eventually the people were led off through the rear door. Sergeant Kemp's main concern was still that there was a risk of fire but, as people were now being evacuated, he returned to the severely damaged carriage where the bomb had exploded.

Kemp now encountered Antonio Silvestro who had also returned to the seat of the explosion. It should be remembered that both were in civilian clothes so it was not obvious to either that the other was a police officer. After a short conversation they resolved this and they briefly discussed what had happened and what needed to be done. It was agreed that Kemp would help at the bombed-out carriage and Silvestro would continue to organise the evacuation of the rest of the people on the train.

In the shattered carriage, Andy Brown recalled the face of Neil Kemp appearing over the edge of the devastated compartment. He climbed into the carnage and discovered Liz Kenworthy, the doctor and the other passengers who had been doing their best to give first aid to the most seriously injured. Kemp, along with other officers, began to separate the dead from the severely injured, giving more first aid to the latter. This included helping Brown who by now was in a state of deep shock and, ominously, was beginning to feel very cold.

Liz Kenworthy recalled the relief of seeing Sergeant Kemp and his men, knowing that help was finally on hand. It is very difficult to establish exactly how long this took, but it was probably between twenty to twenty-five minutes after the explosion.

Antonio Sivestro, meantime, was arranging for the final few passengers to be taken off the train and was directing them to Aldgate Station. Most were being evacuated through the rear carriage and then told to walk up to the platform. He recalled an elderly German couple, probably in their late sixties or early seventies, who were walking hand-in-hand along the track. One of them asked politely in heavily accented and broken English, 'Which way out please'. Silvestro pointed the direction to Aldgate Station and the pair, still hand-in-hand, slowly made their way up the tracks. It was a surreal moment and Silvestro momentarily felt like a tour guide. Seconds later he became aware of a woman lying between the tracks who, in the chaos and confusion, seemed to have been overlooked. He crouched down and spoke to her realising that she was badly wounded.

Ian Munro and other firefighters, some wearing breathing apparatus, headed into the tunnel and reached the bombed carriage. There, a badly wounded woman was being lifted from the train. She had serious injuries and was unable to walk and they helped extract her and carried her out to the platform. Retuning once more they came across other emergency service personnel struggling with a badly injured male who was being carried on a ladder. Munro helped carry this casualty up to the surface and then once more returned to the train.

By now a major response was in progress. Firemen and medics had arrived at the destroyed carriage and helped Sergeant Kemp's men extract the most seriously injured casualties. More importantly, the first properly qualified medics appeared and began administering vital, lifesaving aid. Liz introduced them to the three casualties she had taken responsibility for and stressed the need to keep them alive as they had all done so well so far.

For Liz Kenwothy, relinquishing her responsibility for the injured seemed to lift a huge weight off her shoulders and she began to feel the energy draining out of her, but even so she was reluctant to leave. A bond, difficult to define, had developed between the victims and helpers in the carriage. A fireman asked if he could help Liz out of the window, but she refused and said she would climb out on her own. The young unknown man who had been holding her bag, phone and warrant card gave them back to her and then departed; to this day she does not know who he was.

Andy Brown was lifted carefully out of the train onto a stretcher and carried out along the track. At this point Liz Kenworthy, who was later awarded an MBE for her actions, finally started walking out of the tunnel, and as she did so saw yet more first responders heading for the train. Some of them reached Antonio Silvestro who was still with his injured black patient. The medics set about putting in a drip and providing other crucial first aid. Silvestro finished up holding the drip and eventually helped carry the injured woman out to safety.

The duty EXPO, Dick Travers, went down on to the station and into the tunnel and briefly spoke to a BTP inspector who had taken charge of events underground. After a quick discussion he carried on down the track passing seriously injured people being carried out on stretchers going the other way. The priority for him at this stage was to make sure that the rescuers were in a safe working environment and he began methodically checking the luggage and bags which had been abandoned by their owners. Once he had cleared as much as he could in the carriage with the bomb, he did the same in the two carriages either side. He then returned to the seat of the explosion to carry out a quick examination of the scene to see if there was any obvious evidence of the type of device that had caused such havoc. At this stage it was not clear that it was the work of a suicide bomber. In the carnage there were no immediately obvious clues and, other than estimating the size of the explosion, there was nothing else he could do. He returned to the surface to brief the duty officer and provide an immediate assessment to the Reserve at the Anti-Terrorist Branch.

Sergeant Kemp and his men remained in the tunnel assisting where they could. With the arrival of the additional resources, the final few trapped and badly injured people were extracted. It was time to leave and, escorting the last casualty out, he and his men left for the surface where he reported to and briefed the City Police duty officer. The empty train was now a crime scene.

The second bomb exploded, moments after the one in Aldgate, in the second carriage of a westbound Circle Line train. It had just left Platform 4 at Edgware Road and was heading for Paddington. Once again the unsuspecting passengers were faced with the brutal transformation from normality to nightmare in the blink of an eye. At the moment of detonation, the train was passing another going in the opposite direction and both came to an abrupt halt. The explosion once again left an indescribable scene of utter carnage. The emergency services responded to this in a similar manner to that at Aldgate. At first, as always, there was chaos and confusion and it was not clear what had happened. Casualties were emerging from the station as the first responders arrived. The walking wounded were treated and at the same time police officers, firefighters and ambulance crews descended into the station and went to the assistance of those trapped on the train.

In the EXPO office news of a possible second explosion began to filter through. By chance the other duty team had earlier been assigned to examine an old artillery shell found on a building site. They had just cleared this when they were reassigned to Edgware Road.

They arrived outside the station with wounded passengers still being extricated from the Underground. Their key concern was the same as those at Aldgate; were there any secondary devices? They descended to the platform and as they did so they could see smoke still drifting from the tunnel. They detected the acrid smell left after the detonation of a high explosive charge which is familiar to all who have experience working with explosives. They boarded the second train which gave them access to the seat of the explosion in the first which was some sixty metres into the tunnel. Naturally, when approaching an incident where there are known to be dead, wounded and potentially secondary devices, there is some apprehension. A focused approach on the task in hand and a professional interest in trying to work out exactly what had happened and roughly how much explosive had been used, enabled the worst of the horrors to be shut out. In this case the EXPO noted that the dead he saw had such serious and multiple injuries that they would have been killed instantly when the bomb went off, and he took some comfort from the fact that they would not have suffered.

His Number 2, who was with him, commented that the semi-darkness was a bizarre benefit. It blurred the full horror of the scene which would have been much worse in bright light. Equally had it been totally dark there would have been the prospect of the beam from his torch suddenly illuminating one of the deceased. The half-light seemed to dull the worst of the carnage and was enough to prevent sudden or unexpected surprises. After searching the train and clearing all the abandoned property, they returned to the surface to brief the duty officer about what they had done and seen.

Germaine Lindsay triggered the third bomb deep underground on the Piccadilly Line, between King's Cross, St Pancras and Russell Square. He was standing in the rear of the first carriage of the train which was almost 450 metres into the tunnel. The effect of the explosion was bad enough, but at this point the tunnel is very narrow with, on average, only a six-inch gap between the train and the walls. In this confined space the blast was unable to disperse laterally and reflected off the walls funnelling out along the train and tunnel. Those closest to the bomb stood no chance and were killed instantly. Other passengers not close enough to be killed, suffered terrible injuries. Further away still many other people received minor injuries and suffered from shock.

The train came to an abrupt halt and the passengers began to confront the new reality they were in, with the most basic instincts taking over. As always these varied between people with different characters and temperaments. A feature of this incident was that it was very dark – there was much less light than at the other scenes.

One of the most badly injured victims, and probably the closest person to the bomber to survive, gave a vivid account what happened to her. Gill Hicks, a thirty-seven-year-old Australian who had been living in Britain for twelve years, lost both her legs in the explosion. She was the last person to be brought out of the wreckage alive; twenty-six people around her died. She later told the *Daily Telegraph* of her memories of the events subsequent to the explosion in the carriage:

> I remember falling. It felt like slow motion, but in thick gloopy black tar. Everything was black. Voices were slow. Everything was slowed down. Then suddenly you could hear distant screaming. I thought people were screaming at me.

As her eyes adjusted to the darkness she became aware of the awful carnage around her and then, she looked down:

> Both my feet were almost surgically severed. From the knee down I was just looking at bone. It was like looking at an anatomical drawing of the inside of a leg.

Hicks was sufficiently aware of her predicament to realise that if she did not stop herself bleeding she would die, and she removed her scarf, ripped it in two and did her best to tie it round her legs to act as a tourniquet. She decided then that she would not die and quietly waited for help. But it was a long time before the rescuers arrived, and by then she was perilously close to the end. In this incident the additional delays were caused by the depth and distance the train was in the tunnel. Eventually, a policeman or medic came along and bent over her and placed a priority one sticker on her shoulder. She passed out shortly afterwards, having lost so much blood. She later discovered that her heart stopped beating twice and she was not expected to survive her injuries. In addition to the loss of her legs she has scars on her ribs and on her back where a piece of someone else's bone ripped through her body. Fortunately, she was shielded from the worst of this human shrapnel and blast by some of the other victim's bodies, thus just saving her life.

Above ground, at Russell Square Underground Station, a van close to the entrance was deemed suspect and this was manually cleared by the EXPO who attended this scene first before the task of checking for secondary devices in the tunnel went ahead. He went down to the train with a search team and carried out the same actions as those at Aldgate and Edgware Road. He later commented that, as he walked down the track to the train, he was worried about what he knew he was about to see, and was conscious that nothing can prepare you for such an event. Having arrived, he carried out his duties amidst the carnage with a detached professional interest. Later, after the event, he observed that what worries him now is that he was not unduly troubled about what he saw.

This was London's first experience of a simultaneous, multiple bombing causing mass casualties in the age of modern communications. The news spread like wildfire, on the TV, radio and by word of mouth. People with mobiles either phoned, or were phoned by relatives or friends. Tens of thousands of connections were made and quick reassuring conversations and texts sent. Inevitably, however, this surge in the call rate caused most of the mobile networks to be over-loaded and the systems began to crash.

For those in positions of authority it was now clear that a number of bombs had gone off and that there were hundreds of casualties. A massive incident was unfolding but, forty minutes after the first reports, the information being received from various sources was still sketchy and often contradictory. However, fundamental decisions, including the closing of the entire tube network and implementing emergency call out plans, had been taken. A key concern was that in addition to the three bombs that had gone off were there others about to detonate? In the Anti-Terrorist Branch, the staff were keenly aware that in Madrid ten of thirteen bombs laid had exploded. It must be reiterated that at this point there was no indication that this was a suicide attack. One consequence of the closing of the Underground was that people looked for alternative transport, the obvious choice being the buses and soon most of these were travelling at, or near, full capacity.

As the news of the explosions spread, more and more calls began to come in for other suspect devices. From an EXPO office perspective there was one piece of good fortune; as well as the two duty teams, there were three other EXPOs at work, two doing lectures and one training. In addition, the call-out plan implemented after confirmation of the first explosion meant that other off-duty EXPOs were en route to London. All were quickly reassigned to operational duties and tasked to deal with the deluge of calls for assistance that were now beginning to flood in.

After leaving King's Cross station, Hasib Hussain tried to call his accomplices, but with no success. He could have had little doubt that they had carried out their attacks. From all over London police cars, fire appliances and ambulances, all with their two-tones blaring and lights blazing, were converging on the three stations closest to where the bombs had detonated. After wandering around for a while he returned to the King's Cross Station and possibly bought a 9-volt battery in one of the shops there. His movements after this are uncertain, but at some point, probably at Euston Station, he boarded a No.30 bus which was heading for Marble Arch. He went upstairs and sat towards the back of the vehicle. Witnesses on the bus later described him as being very nervous and constantly touching a bag which was on the floor between his feet.

At 09.47 hours, as the bus was moving down Upper Woburn Place, close to the British Medical Association, Hussain finally detonated his bomb. The effect of the explosion highlighted the flimsy construction of the upper body of a bus and the roof peeled off from the back of the vehicle before sheering at the front and landing in the road. The passengers in the back of the bus, both upstairs and downstairs, had no chance and were killed instantly. Further down the car people were severely wounded, including some who had been blown out of the top deck of the bus onto the road. Those fortunate enough to be sitting at the front of the vehicle suffered minor injuries and shock. As they recovered their senses they instinctively got up and clambered down the central steps and away from the scene. Many people were walking passed the bus, at the moment of the explosion, and some of these suffered injuries from flying fragments.

To deal with the unfolding events at Russell Square, the emergency services had set up an incident control point on a road outside the station entrance. It was no more than four hundred metres from Tavistock Square and everyone not underground heard the ominous boom of the explosion on the bus. Some of these emergency personnel raced over to it. One search dog handler recalled that first aid was the priority; he tied his dog to a railing and went over to help the wounded.

One small piece of luck, if it can be classed as such, was that this last bomb exploded outside the British Medical Association and the building became a mini hospital. Fourteen doctors were almost immediately on scene and they were able to carry out basic life-saving actions, with very limited resources, before the first ambulance crews arrived. When the first ambulances turned up with their specialist first aid equipment the doctors were able to carry out other emergency treatment. One of them, who was highly trained in emergency procedures, took overall control and organised the others doctors into proper groups; the wounded were prioritised from the most seriously injured down to the walking wounded. One doctor commented that, 'the treatment that was given to casualties was the sort of thing you see on ER'. There is no doubt that the proximity of these skilled medical practitioners helped save lives. Many of the doctors finished up using skills which they had not used for years.

One police officer recalled a thorny dilemma in the aftermath of the bombing. He had arrived on scene almost immediately and was trying his best to help stem the flow of blood from a man who had had his legs all but blown off. A short distance away a mobile phone was lying on the ground and suddenly it sprang into life. At that time everyone was so busy that no one even considered answering it. However, three quarters of an hour later, long after the area had been cordoned and evacuated, it continued to ring intermittently. The caller was perhaps aware of the terrible events unfolding in London and was trying to contact a friend or loved one, perhaps becoming more and more concerned as time passed that the phone was not being answered. No-one in the immediate aftermath of the bombing wanted to answer an abandoned mobile, because there was no information about the owner of the phone and whether they had survived or not. One officer commented that, 'What would you say if you answered it?'

The EXPO who attended this scene set about his task of ensuring that there were no secondary devices and was concerned by a case left on the bus. At this time there was no evidence that this was the work of suicide bombers; he carried out a controlled explosion to open it, but it turned out to be innocuous.

With the removal of the last casualties, the sites of the explosions were sealed and crime scenes established. Initially they were the focus for the start of a massive police investigation. One priority was to determine what the bombs were; their size, method of initiation, what explosives were used and how they were delivered. On the last point there were two options; the first was an attack very similar to that in Madrid where the rucksacks containing the bombs were abandoned on the trains by the terrorists. These bombs were initiated by mobile phones all set at the same time and it was a possibility that a similar method had been used in London. The other option was that it was the work of suicide bombers. Evidence from the scenes, and later from CCTV footage, confirmed the latter.

By now 999 calls from worried members of the public and concerning suspect bombs all over London were flooding into the Metropolitan Police. These all had to be treated seriously; as far as the police was concerned, no-one knew that the bus bomb was the last. This work continued all day and into the evening. The Underground remained shut and as the working day drew to a close the most common sight in London was of people walking.

In terms of casualties, this was the worst terrorist atrocity ever committed in London; fifty-two dead (excluding the bombers) and 700 wounded, some, as we have seen, with the most terrible injuries. In conventional terms it was the worst bombing in London since a V2 rocket killed 131 people in Stepney on 27 March 1945.

Londoners and those who commute daily to work in the capital displayed a wide variety of reactions as a result of the attack. They ranged from fear, verging on panic and, for some, a real dread of descending into the Underground or climbing on to a bus. At the other end of the scale there was the more stoic attitude of 'I am not prepared to let these people beat me'. On many occasions police officers were asked by members of the public if it was safe to board a particular train on the Underground or a specific bus; questions which were impossible to answer. Most people, regardless of their concerns, had no choice but to use public transport system, but any young Asian males travelling on trains with rucksacks were subject to more than the normal cursory glance.

The intense police investigation into the suicide bombings rapidly identified the bombers, located their abandoned vehicles in Luton (one of which had been towed away because it did not have a ticket) and found the bomb factory in West Yorkshire. An EXPO was tasked to clear the Nissan Micra and in doing so located, and rendered safe, a number of smaller devices. The same officer also attended the search of 18 Alexander Grove, Leeds, where the bombs were manufactured.

Two weeks later, with the memories of the earlier attack still very much in the public's minds, London was struck again but, a miscalculation on the part of the bombers ensured that, apart from shock, there were no casualties. In a copycat assault, another group of four bombers planned to attack three more trains and a bus, the aim, once again, being to cause mass casualties. Unlike the first attack it was not the rush hour, but just after midday.

Like the victims on 7 July, the passengers on the Northern Line train rattling between Stockwell and the Oval were targeted at random. For them it was a normal journey and no one paid any attention to Ramzi Mohammed when he boarded the train and stood facing the central doors with a large rucksack on his back. The carriage was not packed and the passengers included a woman with a young child in a pushchair, Angus Campbell, an off-duty firefighter, and some others. At the pre-arranged time, the three bombers on the Underground trains attempted to initiate their devices.

On the Northern Line train this was recorded exactly as 12.25.44 hours. Ramzi Mohammed connected a battery to the wires which ran to the bomb inside the rucksack on his back. Instead of a devastating explosion, there was a loud crack as the initiating charge detonated. This resulted in the rucksack containing the bomb being ripped apart and the unexploded main explosive charge being dumped on the floor of the train.

The explosion startled the passengers and they all automatically turned to face Mohammed. Most of them immediately realized that this was another attempted suicide attack and for the next two minutes (the time it took to get to Oval Station) they were stuck in the train in fear for their lives.

Ramzi Mohammed was, by all accounts, equally surprised. It would be wrong to say that attempting to commit suicide and murder many innocent people is anything but a cowardly act. However, in the moments leading up to initiating the device, Mohammed's adrenaline would have been pumping and despite the training and indoctrination there must be an intense feeling of anxiety. Having tried to detonate his bomb, presumably with the belief that he would end up in heaven with seventy-two virgins at his feet, the realization that it had failed must have triggered yet further apprehension, fear and, most of all the need to flee.

In the carriage the passengers began moving to either end of the compartment and in, some cases, through the interconnecting doors to get away from the bomber. Mohammed was at this moment screaming and shouting, and flapping at his back with his arms because he was being burned by the hydrogen peroxide from the main charge of the bomb which had come into contact with his skin.

Angus Campbell, the firefighter, recalled that: 'There was smoke issuing from him and from his back and there was also a large amount of smoke issuing from the debris on the floor that had been caused by the attempted detonation.'

The firefighter instantly understood his predicament; he was underground in a tunnel on a moving train and as he later said, 'there was no help coming my way'. He pulled the woman with the pushchair back towards the end of the carriage and at this stage had his first shouted conversation with Ramzi Mohammed.

On the CCTV images Campbell can be seen, but not heard, remonstrating with the bomber, looking at him and the remains of the device on the floor of the carriage, saying 'What's that? What's that?' pointing to the still smoking substance that was on the floor.

Mohammed and laughed and said: 'This is bread.' The one thing it wasn't was bread.

At this point Campbell thought that it might be a failed device or even a 'dirty bomb'. If it was a 'dirty bomb', he wondered, why were the passengers not on the floor choking and dying? There is understandably a little confusion here. A 'dirty bomb' is normally a term used to describe a bomb which has some type of radioactive payload, but no nuclear yield. In this case if the radiation was at such a high dose rate that it caused immediate symptoms to the passengers, it would have been unlikely that the bomber would have survived for any length of time carrying it on his back. Therefore, it seems that Mr Campbell was confusing the term with a chemical dispersion type of device.

When the train stopped at Oval Station and the doors opened, Ramzi Mohammed fled, although several passengers tried to stop him. The train and the station were then fully evacuated and the alarm raised.

In the EXPO office, the first indications that something was amiss were multiple reports of pops or bangs on Underground trains. One report described liquid being sprayed around a carriage and another of a foaming substance. A possible implication of this was that this was a chemical attack. (Chemical devices often use small explosive charges to disseminate their agent.) Moments later the first tasking message came in to Oval Station and the on-call EXPO was dispatched to the incident.

Shortly afterward teams also responded to Warren Street and Shepherds Bush Underground stations.

At Oval Station a rendezvous point had been set up and a duty officer from the British Transport Police was on scene. Other than knowing that the train and station had been evacuated and lines closed, he had little other information. However, Angus Campbell was identified and proved to be a key witness. He explained what had happened on the train and that, after the first pop, a yellow jelly-like substance had been deposited on the floor of the carriage. He was very clear that this was like foam but was not, in his view, foaming. It was also clear that neither he, nor anyone else in the carriage, had had any difficulty breathing and up until this point had suffered no ill effects from exposure to whatever was in the carriage. This, and the fact that the bomber had fled the scene on foot, indicated that if it was a chemical attack it was not a nerve agent as this acts very quickly on the human body. Equally, there were no distinctive smells which are often associated with some of other poisonous gasses.

The mother who had also been very close to the bomber when the initiator functioned was also questioned and, although understandably very shaken, she confirmed she was not feeling any ill-effects from her exposure to whatever had been blown on to the carriage floor. As Mr Campbell had guessed, another possible explanation for what had happened was that a bomb had partially exploded. The next step was to confirm this by approaching and examining the scene. With suitable equipment the EXPO went into the station and descended the stationary escalator to the platform and the vacant northbound train. It was eerily quiet and the first thing he noticed was that the train doors had been shut. This was a good sign because if there was a latent chemical hazard it was partially sealed within the body of train. The fact that the train was also deep underground meant that, from a public protection perspective, if there was any chemical hazard, it was largely contained within the train and the station, and there would be no dispersion caused by the wind.

Walking down the platform looking into the empty train reinforced the EXPO's feeling of isolation. It was odd to be in the Underground with no hustle and bustle and hardly a sound. Looking through the windows opposite the carriage where Ramzi Mohammed had tried to detonate his bomb there was an apparently empty rucksack and, close to it, on the floor the yellow, viscous, gloopy substance. Amongst it, and scattered around the floor of the carriage, were a small number tacks, screws and washers. The gloop looked similar in consistency and colour to pictures of the residual explosive which had been found in Leeds after the 7 July attacks. The tacks, screws and washers were similar to those discovered attached to the bombs which had been rendered safe in the car park in Luton. This further indicated that this was not a chemical attack, but a partially-detonated device.

The final step was to confirm this theory by testing a sample of the suspect substance. All the EXPO vehicles carry a variety of test equipment which provides a limited capability to analyse unknown substances. After a brief consultation with the EXPO's Number 2, who had by now come down to the end of the platform, arrangements were made to bring the most suitable equipment down to the front of the train.

Entering the driver's compartment, the EXPO made his way back through the train down to the area where the yellow gloop was, checking an abandoned rucksack as he passed it. In the carriage where the remains of the device were, he undertook a quick search of the rucksack which had been ripped apart around the seams. This confirmed that, other than the remains of some of the yellow substance, it was empty. Using a pipette, a small sample of the unknown yellow compound was recovered from the mass on the floor. Back at the driver's compartment the field test equipment indicated that the substance contained a high percentage of hydrogen peroxide, by now a well-known component of homemade explosives.

After clearing the rest of the train, including checking a small number of abandoned bags belonging to fleeing passengers, the next priority was to return to the surface, brief the duty officer at the Reserve in the Anti-Terrorist Branch, and the duty officers from the police, fire, and ambulance services at the scene. Equally important was to allow the station CCTV tapes to be recovered.

One of the key duties of an EXPO is to hand over crime scenes to the police forensic retrieval officers who will be responsible, in turn, for gathering all the relevant evidence. To do this the first basic requirement is to be sure the scene is safe or, if not, any potential hazards, and particularly explosive hazards are pointed out. In this case there was a dilemma in that no one knew exactly what the suspect explosive was. Many of the hydrogen peroxide based explosives are very sensitive to external stimuli and, in some circumstances, the only safe method of disposal is to destroy them in situ by demolition.

In these circumstances additional help from other experts is required and assistance was requested from the scientists at the police forensic laboratories to help determine what should be done with the residual explosive on the floor of the train.

Fortunately, the bombers also failed in their attempts to detonate bombs at Warren Street and Shepherds Bush Underground stations and later on a bus in Hackney. At all these scenes broadly similar actions were taken by the EXPOs responding to calls for assistance. As usual, news of the attacks spread like wildfire and once again suspect items started being called in by nervous members of the London public. The police and the on-call EXPOs were, once again, rushing all over the capital to deal with them.

An indication of the activity levels over this period can be gained from the fact between 7 and 31 July, in addition to responding to requests for assistance with hundreds of suspect items, 687 calls were received by the Metropolitan Police Service specifically relating to potential suicide bombers.

The police enquiry into the failed bombings of 21 July had a new and unparalleled urgency. No one was in any doubt that the bombers had intended to cause carnage. With them all on the loose, there was the very real prospect that they might, at any moment, try again, and this time with viable devices. At this stage the main strand of police strategy centred on the overwhelming need to ensure the public's safety. To do so they had to find and arrest at least four very dangerous individuals before they had another chance to commit mass murder. The pressures were immense and ultimately led to the shooting of an innocent man.

The circumstances leading up to the tragic and fatal shooting of Jean Charles de Menezes at Stockwell Underground Station in London on 22 July 2005, are detailed in the Independent Police Complaints Commission (IPCC) investigations referred to as Stockwell 1 and 2. These events are outside the scope of this book. It suffices to say that an EXPO was tasked to Stockwell to deal with any device that might have been present. Once it was established that there was not, the scene was, as normal, handed over to an experienced member of the Forensic Management Team.

It was, in every respect, a disastrous day. Decisions had to be made, at moments of supreme anxiety, on information that was always incomplete, often incorrect or vague and which varied from minute to minute. Post-incident, in the clear light of day, it is easy to critically examine those decisions arrived at in moments of great stress and strain, which had such a heartbreaking impact on events.

Like those who recognized that the Germans should, in the end, be blamed for the casualties at the Café de Paris in the Blitz, the ultimate blame for the death of an innocent man lies squarely at the feet of the four terrorists who failed to kill and maim the day before.

Two years later, on 29 June 2007, terror returned to London, but once again the plans to massacre innocent civilians failed. Two cars with bombs made using gas canisters, petrol, nails and initiated by a remote control were left in Central London. The first was discovered in Haymarket close to the Tiger Tiger nightclub. This failed to function as intended and was rendered safe in the early morning by an EXPO. A second car, which was parked nearby, possibly intended to catch out those responding to the first incident was parked illegally, and was removed from the street to the entrance to the NCP car park in Park Lane. It was there, in the early afternoon, that it was discovered to contain a second bomb. It was also rendered safe.

The perpetrators, dismayed with their dismal failure, later tried to blow up Glasgow airport by driving a fuel-laden jeep into the terminal building. Once again their plan failed and the improvised device in the vehicle did not explode although the terminal building was set on fire.

Since then, until the time of going to print, there have been no terrorist incidents involving bombs in London. Attacks by Islamic extremists though continue worldwide, one of the worst being the shootings and bombings in Paris on 13 November 2015 in which 130 people were killed, and attacks in Brussels in 2016. It is clear that, in London, thanks to the outstanding work of the police and the Security Services, many plots have been foiled. Sadly, though, as this book illustrates, it is impossible to thwart every attack.

At the start of this book, I made that point that it was 'bombs and not bombers that count'. The bombs themselves are physical things and can be measured, weighed and described and, where they explode, the effects estimated and analysed. Looking back at what I have written, it is clear to me that it is not the bombs but the people on the receiving end that count. It is the survivors, emergency services, civil defenders, volunteers, bomb disposal officers and, last but not least, the ordinary people that have, over the last 140 years, made the difference. Because of them the bombs have not succeeded and never will. Whatever happens, London and its people will survive.

Select Bibliography

Published Sources

Allason, Rupert, *The Branch* (Martin Secker and Warburg, London, 1983).

Andrew, Christopher, *The Defence of the Realm – The Authorised History of M15* (Penguin, London, 2009).

Bates, H.E., *Flying Bombs Over England* (Froglet Publications, Kent, 1994).

Bishop, Patrick and Mallie, Eamonn, *The Provisional IRA* (William Heinemann, London, 1987).

Bloom, Mia, *Dying to Kill* (Columbia University Press, New York, 2005).

Brooks, Geoffrey, *Hitler's Nuclear Weapons* (Leo Cooper, London, 1992).

Brown, G.I., *The Big Bang* (Sutton Publishing, Stroud, 1998).

Brown, Norma, *London Police Their Stories* (Merlin Unwin Books, Ludlow, 1998).

Bower Bell, J., *The Secret Army – The History of the IRA 1916-1970* (Anthony Blond, London, 1970).

Burke, Jason, *Al Qaeda* (Penguin, London, 2004).

Byrne, Richard, *Prisons and Punishments of London* (Harper Collins, London, 1989).

Calder, Angus, *The People's War 1939-45* (Johnathon Cape, London, 1969).

Carr, Gordon, *The Angry Brigade* (Victor Gollancz, London, 1975).

Clarke, Robin, *London Under Attack* (Basil Blackwell, Oxford, 1986).

Cole, Christopher and Cheesman E.F., *The Air Defence of Great Britain* (Putnam, London, 1984).

Cooksley, Peter G., *Flying Bomb* (Robert Hale, London, 1979).

Farmery, Peter, *Police Gallantry 1909-1978* (Periter and Associates, New South Wales, Australia, 1995).

FitzGibbon, Constantine, *The Blitz* (Macdonald, London, 1970).

Ffoulkes, Charles, *Arms and the Tower* (John Murray, London, 1939).

Fredette, Raymond, *The First Battle of Britain 1917-18* (Cassell, London, 1966).

Geraghty, Tony, *The Irish War* (Harper Collins, London, 1998).

Grant, McKee and Franey, Ros, *Time Bomb* (Bloomsbury, London, 1988).

Gurney, Peter, MBE, GM and Bar, *Braver Men Walk Away* (Harper Collins, London, 1993).

Haarer, A.E. Squadron Leader, *A Cold-Blooded Business* (Panther Books, London, 1958).

Harris, Clive, *Walking the London Blitz* (Leo Cooper, South Yorkshire, 2003).

Hartley, A.B., MBE, *Unexploded Bomb A Short History of Bomb Disposal* (Cassell, London, 1958).

Hogben, Arthur, *Designed to Kill* (Patrick Stevens, Northamtonshire, 1987).

Hook, John, *The Air Raids on London During the 1914-18 War, Booklet 4 – The Raids on the City of London* (Privately published, 1987).

Hough, Richard and Richards, Denis, *The Battle of Britain, The Jubilee History* (Hodder and Stoughton, London, 1989).

Howgrave-Graham, H.M., CBE, *The Metropolitan Police at War* (HM Stationary Office, London, 1947).

Hunt, Captain J.H., MBE, *Bombs and Booby Traps* (Picton Publishing, Wiltshire, 1986).

Huntley, Bob, *Bomb Squad* (W.H. Allen, London, 1977).

Hyde, Andrew P., *The First Blitz* (Pen and Sword, Yorkshire, 2002).

Ingleton, Roy, *The Gentlemen at War: Policing Britain 1939-1945* (Cranborne Publications, Kent, 1994).

Jackett, Sam, *Heroes of Scotland Yard* (Robert Hale, London, 1965).

Janis, Irvine L., *Air War and Emotional Stress* (The Rand Corporation and McCraw-Hill Book Company, New York, 1951).

Jappy, M.J., *Danger UXB* (Channel 4 Books and Macmillan, London, 2001).

Jeyes, S.H., and How, F.D., *The Life of Howard Vincent* (George Allan, London, 1912).

Jones, H.A., *The War in the Air*, Volume III (Oxford University Press, 1931).

Jones, Neville, *The Beginnings of Strategic Air Power* (Frank Cass, London, 1987).

Jones, R. V., *Most Secret War* (Hamish Hamilton, London, 1978).

Lee Kennett, *A History of Strategic Bombing* (Charles Scribner's Sons, New York, 1956).

Longmate, Norman, *The Doodlebugs* (Hutchinson, London, 1981).

_____, *Hitler's Rockets the Story of the V2* (Hutchinson, London, 1985).

MacDonagh, Michael, *In London During the Great War* (Eyre and Spottiswoode, London, 1935).

MacNaughten, Sir Melville, CB, *Days of My Years* (Edward Arnold, London, 1915).

Marwick, Arthur, *War and Social Change in the Twentieth Century* (Macmillan, London, 1974).

Mason, Francis K., *Battle Over Britain* (McWhirter Twins, London, 1969).

Morris, Captain Joseph, *The German Air Raids on Britain 1914-1918* (H. Pordes, London, 1969).

Nock, O.S., *Britain's Railways at War 1939-1945* (Ian Allen, London, 1971).

O'Brian, Terrence, *Civil Defence* (HMSO, London, 1955).

Owen, James, *Danger UXB* (Little Brown, London, 2010).

Pape, Robert A., *Dying to Win* (Random House, New York, 2005).

Pedahzur, Ami, *Suicide Terrorism* (Polty Press, Cambridge, 2005).

Paris, Michael, *Silvertown 1917* (Ian Henry, Essex, 1986).

Pile, General Sir Frederick, *Ack Ack* (George G. Harrap and Co, London, 1949).

Poland, Rear Admiral E.N., CB CBE, *The Torpedo Men – HMS Vernon's Story 1872-1986* (Privately Published, 1993).

Poolman, Kenneth, *Zeppelins Over England* (Evans Brothers, London, 1960).

Porter, Bernard, *The Origins of the Vigilant State* (Weidenfeld and Nicolson, London, 1987).

Ramsey, Winston G., *The Blitz Then and Now Volumes 1-3* (Battle of Britain Prints International, London, 1987).

Ransted, Chris, *Bomb Disposal and the British Casualties of WW2* (Privately Published, 2004).

Ray, John, *The Night Blitz* (Arms and Armour Press and Cassells Group, London, 1996).

Richards, Denis, *Royal Air Force 1939-45 Volume 1 – The Fight at Odds* (HM Stationery Office, London, 1953).

Roberts, Steve, *A Brief History of Squadron Leader E.L. Moxey GC* (Researched and produced by the Great War Research Services, 2000).

Robinson, Douglas, *The Zeppelin in Combat* (G.T. Foulis, Henely-on Thames, 1971).

Sanson, William, *Westminster in War* (Faber and Faber, London, 1947).

Saunders, Hilary St. G., *Royal Air Force 1939-1945, Volume III, The Fight is Won*, (HM Stationery Office, London, 1954).

Sebald, W.G., *On the Natural History of Destruction* (Carl Hanser Verlag, Germany, 1999).

Short, K.R.M., *The Dynamite War* (Gill and Macmillan, Eden Quay Dublin, 1979).

Smith, Malcolm, *British Air Strategy Between the Wars* (Clarendon Press, Oxford, 1984).

Trench, Richard and Hillman Ellis, *London Under London a Subterranean Guide* (John Murray, London, 1992).

Turner, John Frayn, *Highly Explosive* (George G. Harrap, London, 1961).

_____, *Service Most Silent* (George G. Harrap, London, 1955).

Van Young, Sayre, *London's War* (Ulysses Press, Berkeley USA, 2004).

Wakeling, Eric, *Danger of UXB* (BD Publishing, Bourne End, 1996).

Wallington, Neil, *Firemen at War* (David and Charles, Newton Abbot, 1990).

Wasby, Percival-Prescott, *The Coronation Chair* (Ministry of Works, London, 1957).

White, C.M., *The Gotha Summer* (Robert Hale, London, 1986).

Whitehouse, Arch, *The Zeppelin Fighters* (Robert Hale, London, 1968).

Woodhall, Edwin, *Guardians of the Great* (Blandford Press, London, 1934).

Official Publications

Front Line 1940 – 41 The Official Story of the Civil Defence of Britain, Ministry of Information, HM Stationary Office, London, 1942.

Civil Defence Training Pamphlet No.2 (3rd Edition) – Objects Dropped from the Air, HM Stationary Office, London, 1944.

Air Raids, What you Must Know, What you Must Do! Ministry of Home Security, 1941.

Manual of Bomb Disposal (Provisional) 1941, War Office, 30 October 1941.

Assistance by Troops to the Civil Authorities in Civil Defence – London Area, Security Document No.L.D/10 May 1939.

Dunne, Lawrence MC, *Report on an Inquiry into the Accident at Bethnal Green Tube Station Shelter on the 3 March 1943* (HM Stationary Office, London, 1945).

Royal Armament Research and Development Establishment Reports, Explosives Division, RARDE Memorandums Forensic Explosives Work Annual Surveys, 1961 to 1968.

Police Review – various issues from both world wars.

Unpublished Sources

Air Raid Information Occurrence Book Station Deptford and Rotherhithe 1939-1941.

Harper, John, *The Walsall Bombs*, West Sussex, March 2005.

Huntley, Robert BEM, QPM, *The History of the Bomb Squad*, Metropolitan Police, 1975.

Index

INDEX

494